A Layman's Guide to the Scottish Reformation

Brian J. Orr

HERITAGE BOOKS
2010

HERITAGE BOOKS

AN IMPRINT OF HERITAGE BOOKS, INC.

Books, CDs, and more—Worldwide

For our listing of thousands of titles see our website
at
www.HeritageBooks.com

Published 2010 by
HERITAGE BOOKS, INC.
Publishing Division
100 Railroad Ave. #104
Westminster, Maryland 21157

Other Heritage Books by Brian J. Orr:

As God Is My Witness

Orr-Some: Research into the Orr Family

International Standard Book Numbers
Paperbound: 978-0-7884-3188-3
Clothbound: 978-0-7884-8547-3

For Pamela
Genesis 2:18

The Covenant Banner

Blow softly, ye breezes, by mountain and moor
O'er the graves of Covenant men,
By the muirland and flood that were red with their blood,
Can ye waft the old watchwords again?

"For Scotland and Christ" the breezes of old
O'er the wilds of the Westland bore,
From the Lugar and the Nith to the Lothian Frith,
And the German Ocean's shore.

And where'er they blew, a prayer was breathed
And a holy psalm was sung;
And hands were clasped and the banner grasped
When the Covenant watchword rung.

O for the brave true hearts of old,
That bled when the banner perished!
O for the Faith that was strong in death -
The Faith that our fathers cherished!

The banner might fall, but the spirit lived,
And liveth for evermore;
And Scotland claims as her noblest names,
The Covenant men of yore.[1]

[1] Verses penned by an anonymous elder from Ayrshire, Scotland. John Johnston, *Treasury of the Scottish Covenant* (Edinburgh: Andrew Elliot, 1887), p. 565.

Table of Contents

List of Illustrations

Part I

Part II

Part III

Preface

It is perhaps offering a hostage to fortune to allege that the man in the street probably knows little of Presbyterianism or the Scottish Reformation. Unless a member of the Scottish church or kirk, he might mention John Knox and John Calvin; perhaps he has heard of Martin Luther and his *Theses*. Beyond that I venture that there is nowadays slight knowledge, and even less understanding, of the turbulent years from *ca.* 1525 to 1690 in which the Reformation came to fruition. I therefore offer this modest digest of the period, and dictionary of the main events and issues of the time, in the hope that it enlightens, informs, and encourages an interest in the history of Scotland.

The Scottish Reformation began with two almost contemporaneous events. Firstly, it replaced the Roman Catholic Church by Protestantism. Secondly, the people chose Presbyterianism as their faith long before it and the official Church *of* Scotland was by law established. In a very narrow sense the Reformation was all over by 1560.

Nothing is simple, however, for the Reformation was complicated by the politics of the day; particularly the "Divine Right" policies of the Stuart kings who wanted *their* choice of religion (Episcopacy). There was stubborn dissension on grounds of conscience by some of the congregation, which was followed by the bloody sufferings of the strict Presbyterians, who were known as the Covenanters. It was a further one hundred and thirty years before the Church of Scotland was established by law.

The Reformation therefore spans the very busy and despotic reigns of Mary Queen of Scots, James VI/I[2], Charles I, Oliver Cromwell, Charles II, James VII/II, and ends with the accession of William and Mary. Add to this the rule by Regents during the minority of the sovereign; the Catholic Counter Reformation and fear of wars with France, Spain, and Holland; the Plantation of Ulster and later rebellion in Ireland; the civil wars of the three kingdoms of England, Ireland and Scotland; Cromwell's campaigns in all three kingdoms; the Restoration and revenge of Charles II; the Catholic resurgence under James II; and continued persecution of the Presbyterians in Scotland and Ulster, and you have a very complicated historical cocktail.

The Plantation of Ulster (1610-1630) is an integral part of the story of Presbyterianism as are also the later migrations of the Ulster Scots to the colonies in America. Oppressed and persecuted Scots migrated to Ulster in their thousands during and after the Ulster Plantation and many were killed in the Rebellion of 1641.[3] From Ulster, tens of thousands of Ulster Scots, mainly Presbyterians, migrated to the American colonies from the late seventeenth and through the eighteenth century. These migrants featured prominently in the development of the new lands and the establishment of the Presbyterian Church in the United States of America. Through their experience they contributed directly to the Covenant we know as The Declaration of Independence. President Teddy Roosevelt, himself a great-great-great-grandson on his mother's side of the Rev. Alexander Stobo, a member of the ill-fated Darien Scheme, wrote in his book *Episodes from the Winning of the West*, that the Ulster Scots were

> the kernel of the distinctively and intensely American stock who were the pioneers of our people in their march westward. The vanguard of the army of fighting settlers who with axe and

---

[2] James VI of Scotland succeeded to the English throne in 1603 and became James I of England. He was the first king of Great Britain although political unity with Scotland did not happen until 1707.

[3] In the Plantation of Ulster, the flight of the Irish Earls in 1607 created an opportunity for settlement of a Protestant community on the escheated lands.

> rifle won this way from the Alleghanies to the Rio Grande and the Pacific.[4]

As to the historical records, the establishment of the Church and its system of management encouraged record keeping through the church courts of Kirk Session, Presbytery, Synod and General Assembly. Parish records were first ordered to be kept in 1616. Records were somewhat patchy to begin with, especially during periods of disruption as the official religion varied between Presbyterianism and Episcopacy. On the other hand, the ministers were university graduates and best placed to know about and able to document events at grass roots level. Thus, the majority of the early reference works about the Reformation and the Presbyterian Kirk were written by clerics of all faiths—Catholic, Episcopal, and Presbyterian—and contain frequent biblical quotes and polemic discussion to justify a point of view. With the history thus written, and sometimes from widely divergent theological and theocratic viewpoints, there is also the potential for bias, or at least some colouring of the circumstances surrounding events as they saw them.

Several more books would be required to do justice to the whole period of the Reformation. I have therefore sought to maintain a focus on Scottish and Presbyterian issues although I have included notes on involvement in the English Civil Wars, Cromwell's campaigns, and trigger events in England and Ireland that impacted the Reformation. Included are quotes from original works, some in the old Scots dialect with widely variable spelling, and from sources that are very difficult to find outside the archives and private collections. I have generally used the old spelling for place names, such as Airsmoss instead of Ayr`s Moss. In the appendices are full versions of some of the principal, and rarely quoted, documents of the Reformation.

As I have indicated, *A Layman's Guide to the Scottish Reformation* is a digest of my researches as I delved to understand

---

[4] Roosevelt quoted in Howard Cromie, *Ulster Settlers in America* (Belfast: T. H. Jordan, Ltd., 1976), p. 20. The Darien Scheme was an attempt at building a colony on the Isthmus of Panama 1698-1700. The hope was to access trade in the West Indies and to transport goods from the Pacific overland to the Atlantic seaboard to European markets. It was a disaster and very nearly bankrupted Scotland.

those turbulent times that changed the face of religion in Scotland and Ulster, and led to the political union of Scotland and England in 1707. Within the general text of the *Layman's Guide* short unattributed quotations are from Howie's *Scots Worthies,* a seminal work about the Covenanters. (An index of his characters appears in Appendix 1.)

Above all I seek to inform the interested reader who wants a reasonably simple explanation of the wide variety of events and topics. Should I succeed in capturing your interest, there is a substantial bibliography for possible further reading. I hope I have provided a good read, as well as a modest reference book that is easy to return to.

Acknowledgements

I would add my particular thanks to New Zealand friends Rev. Roy N. McKenzie of Gore, Southland, who has so patiently poured over the drafts and guided my theological interpretation; and Allen Little for the use of the quotation from his family gravestone in Wanlockhead. My thanks also to Sandy Pittendreigh of the Dumfries & Galloway Family History Society; Maurice McIlwrick of the Scottish Genealogy Society, Edinburgh; and Sandy Orr in Scone, all of whom have kindly allowed the use of some of their excellent photographs. Finally, it would be impossible to prepare a book of this kind without the works of other authors, especially the older ones whose almost contemporaneous writings, in some cases, are a primary source for what actually happened. I have endeavoured to give acknowledgment to the sources throughout the book, and I am indebted for the information.

Brian J. Orr

Introduction

If censure was ever appropriate for the misconduct that occurred during the Scottish Reformation (1525-1690), it surely lies upon the puppet politicians of the day and the power seeking individuals, from the King down, who went to extremes to get their way. There were many underlying reasons that might be attributed for the need to have stringent and oppressive laws—excuses if you like—not least of which were fears of war with France, Spain, and Holland. There was also the interminable struggle for religious dominance with the Papists that had roots in the influence that Catholic France had exerted in Scotland for centuries. In later years it was a matter of mutual intolerance and contention with supporters of Protestant Episcopacy. Amongst the nobility, which was still feudal in its outlook, there were struggles for land, position, and power with some, such as the Marquis of Argyll having his own agenda as he sought to consolidate his claim to be the Lord of the Isles.

From the time of James I (reign 1406-1437) the succession of the House of Stuart had gone to the very young—James II was six years old, James III was eight, James IV was fifteen, James V was two, Mary but one week old, and James VI one year old—when they came to the throne. This meant that Scotland had some two hundred years of disjointed rule, a major part of which was by regents who had to fend off the rapacious feudal nobles who often came to Court surrounded by their retainers to influence decisions in their favour. Later, the Queen Regent, Mary of Guise, mother of Mary Queen of Scots, brought French troops to Scotland to assist her attempts to force Catholicism on the country. James VI became the first Stuart king to live through a full reign. The problems in the whole of the Reformation were exacerbated by a succession of queens and kings who sought to impose the religious practices of *their* choice upon a hitherto acquiescent nation.

It is ironic that in 1603 James VI of Scotland succeeded to the English throne and became James I of England—thus a Scotsman ruled two nations which were not united politically until 1707. James had a London power base that facilitated cronyism and the self-seeking interests of an essentially English court which made the problems in Scotland worse. He made some effort to share out posts equitably on a rough ratio of four in ten going to Scots. But there was always an undercurrent of mistrust and jealousy by the English over trade, as well as James' own idealistic views and ambitions. The King's position as head of both State and the Episcopal Church of England impacted his policies against religious non-conformity in England, Scotland, and, to a lesser extent, in Ireland. At the Hampton Court Conference in 1604 James ominously said of the English Puritans, who were quite similar to Presbyterians in those days, "I shall make them conform themselves, or else do worse."[5]

James' boast at the opening of the English Parliament in 1607 grossly underestimated the Scottish people.

> This I may say for Scotland, and may truly vaunt it; here I sit and govern it with my pen; I write and it is done, and by a Clerk of the Council I govern Scotland now, which others could not do with the sword.[6]

By then he had been King of Scotland, infant, boy, and man, for forty years and should have known better. It is true that Scotland had been dragged from its slumber and was enjoying a better economic climate. Trade with England was less restricted, and movement of people between Scotland and London also prompted new ideas and methods for industry and agriculture. But for the Presbyterians it was a transient thing, their hopes and aspirations for a religious settlement were soon trampled under foot. The belief that a remote Privy Council in Scotland was all that was needed for King James and his successors to issue their orders to merely

---

[5] James King Hewison, *The Covenanters. A History of the Church in Scotland from the Reformation to the Revolution*, Vol. 2 (Glasgow: John Smith & Son, 1908; reprinted Edmonton: Still Waters Revival Books, 1996), p. 176; Thomas M'Crie, *Sketches of Church History* (Edinburgh: John Johnstone, 1846), p. 141.

[6] Parliamentary speeches quoted in M. Magnusson, *Scotland: The Story of a Nation* (London: Harper Collins, 2000), p. 399.

created the environment for despotism by compliant appointees in positions of authority.

The Rev. Thomas M'Crie, in *Sketches of Church History*, makes the important point that the Scottish and English Reformations were strikingly different. In Scotland the people were converted to a Protestant faith *before* the civil authorities had even started in that direction. When the time was ripe, all the legislature had to do was ratify the faith that the majority of the nation had adopted. In fact, *there was an approved religion in Scotland before there was an official church.* The consequence of the rule of the Kirk by the people, according to the Scriptures, is that in Scotland there have been various reforms, improvements of standards and changes of testimony that have discarded everything, even by implication, that hinted at the church of Rome. In England the people followed the royal actions and never sought to advance their position beyond the limits that Henry VIII and Queen Elizabeth I had set by law. The nonconformists in England (loosely called Puritans) sought to remove the ceremony and quasi-Catholic practices, such as images, from the church. But, unlike the Presbyterians, they accepted the king as Supreme Governor of the Protestant Episcopal Church of England.[7] From these differences, perhaps, has grown the distorted view of Presbyterianism as a stern and austere religion and its adherents as having a grave demeanour. But that is what it was all about: freedom to worship as the people felt was right with the focus on the Scriptures, Christ as the sole Head of the church, and recognition of God's rights in the civil rule.

It is essential to take a balanced view of what occurred between three hundred and four hundred and fifty years ago, and endeavour to consider issues in the context of those turbulent times. It was not a time of democratic sweetness and light, and we should not judge by the standards and moralities of a twenty-first century strangled with political correctness. It was the age of belief in witchcraft with over a thousand people, mostly women, burnt at the stake in Europe during the seventeenth century. Yet only some twenty-five or so religious heretics met that fate in Scotland during the whole Reformation. The apparent lack of concern for human life is

[7] In Ireland, the official Protestant Church of Ireland was Episcopal and mirrored the English system.

sometimes shocking, but class structures were well defined in a feudal kingdom in which the common man was not much more than a slave. Indeed, white slavery actually existed in Scotland with prisoners sentenced to be house and farm slaves, as well as thousands transported as slaves to America and the sugar plantations in the West Indies.

It should also be remembered that English, Irish, and Welsh nonconformists were subject to persecution, although perhaps not so bloodily as they were in Scotland. Thus, there was religious discontent throughout Great Britain during most of the seventeenth century. From it arose a unity of purpose that culminated in the replacement of James II by the *constitutional monarchy* of William and Mary at the Great Revolution in 1688.

As has been indicated, there was a great deal going on in all three kingdoms. I have endeavoured to deal with events and their consequences elsewhere in a logical fashion, although the main focus is on Scotland. Part I, therefore, outlines the growth of Protestantism and the endorsement of Presbyterianism by the people of Scotland. It then follows through the Regency of the infant Mary, Queen of Scots, to her abdication in favour of her infant son, James IV, on 24 July 1567. The early reign of James VI of Scotland saw the machinations of the regents until his majority and, eventually, his exercise of "kingcraft" that was variously insidious, blatantly biased, clever, cunning, and deceitful. Although his reign was reasonably bloodless, the chicanery left a complicated legacy to unravel. The accession of James to the crown of England in 1603 introduced new factors into the Reformation. The subsequent story through the rest of the reign of James VI/I, the reigns of Charles I, Oliver Cromwell, Charles II, James VII/II, and the struggles against Episcopacy and Erastianism, is adumbrated in Part II. Specific items, topics, and events are further explained in the alphabetical reference section, Part III. The story line is supported by a detailed chronology in Appendix 24.

Three hundred years later there is once again a Scottish Parliament with devolution of many powers to it from Westminster. With this devolution there is scope for Scottish aspirations and a sense of identity to grow. It would be appropriate if the strong traditions of a good education once more included in its syllabus an awareness of the suffering and sacrifices of the Scottish

Reformation and its contribution to democracy. Above all there is the earnest hope that the political partisans, the ecclesiastical schemers and the babblers of political correctness will let the Church alone; and that any attempt to interfere is defended by the people, to whom *their* Church belongs.

Dramatis Personae

A selection of the main players in the drama of the Scottish Reformation.

Beaton, David. Cardinal. Archbishop of St. Andrews. Responsible for martyrdom of George Wishart. Murdered in revenge.

Bothwell, Earl of. See Hepburn.

Cameron, Richard. Minister and martyr. Leader of the strict Covenanters, who were called "The Cameronians."

Campbell. Family name of the House of Argyll. Archibald, 8th Earl and first Marquis of Argyll. Leading Covenanter and martyr.

Campbell, Archibald. 9th Earl. Son of the Marquis. Led a failed rebellion in Scotland against James II. Protestant. Executed.

Cromwell, Oliver. Rose to command the Parliamentary Army in the English Civil Wars. Later Lord Protector of the Commonwealth (Republic) of Great Britain. Also known as "The Usurper." Nonconformist – Independent (Congregationalist, not Puritan).

Dalziel, Thomas, of the Binns. Lt. General. Royalist commander of the armies in Scotland. Also known as "The Beast of Muscovy." Persecutor.

Darnley, Lord. See Stuart, Henry.

Geddes, Janet. Allegedly threw her stool at the Dean of St. Giles cathedral when he preached using the new Order of Service, also known as "Laud's Liturgy."

Graham, David. Brother of John of Claverhouse. Sheriff of Wigtown, involved in the sentence and execution of the Solway Martyrs.

Graham, James. Marquis of Montrose. Covenanter turned royalist supporter; highly successful commander of the royalist army in Scotland during 1644-1645. Executed.

Graham, John of Claverhouse. Later Viscount "Bonny" Dundee. Soldier given the task of enforcing laws against Covenanters. Persecutor. Killed at Killiecrankie.

Guise, Mary of Lorraine, sister of the Duke of Guise. Second wife of James V of Scotland, mother of Mary, Queen of Scots. Regent of Scotland; a staunch French Catholic.

Grierson, Sir Robert, of Lag in Galloway. A magistrate and persecutor. Responsible for several immediate executions without trial.

Hamilton, James. 3rd Marquis and 1st Duke of Hamilton. Of royal lineage, family traditional supporters of the Stuarts. Bankrupt politician, Kings Commissioner in the 1638 General Assembly. Led the Engager army to defeat at Preston. Executed.

Hamilton, Robert, later Sir Robert, of Prestonpans. Commander of the Covenanter army defeated at Bothwell Brig in 1679. Remained a prominent member of the Societies in exile.

Hamilton, Patrick. Nephew of the Earl of Arran and the Duke of Albany. Related to James V of Scotland. Sometimes called the first martyr of the Scottish Reformation. Burnt at the stake.

Henderson, Alexander. Presbyterian minister and martyr. Joint author of the National Covenant (1638) as well as the Solemn League and Covenant (1643).

Hepburn, James. 4th Earl of Bothwell. Courtier to Mary, Queen of Scots, and intrigued with her over Lord Darnley's murder. Allegedly kidnapped, then married, Mary.

Johnston, Archibald. Later Lord Warriston. Advocate. Clerk of the General Assembly; co-author of the National Covenant (1638). Covenanter martyr.

Knox, John. Calvinist evangelical minister and scholar; progenitor of Presbyterianism in Scotland. He was the catalyst that led to the overthrow of Catholicism in Scotland and establishment of Presbyterianism as the official faith.

Lambert, John. General at age twenty-four in Cromwell's army. A brilliant and daring soldier, victor at Inverkeithing. Always a republican and adrift without Cromwell. Attempted a coup in 1659. Imprisoned at the Restoration and died in 1684.

Laud, William. Archbishop of Canterbury, 1633. Persecutor of nonconformists throughout Great Britain, including torture of some Puritans. Episcopalian with very strong Arminian leanings and suspected of Catholic sympathies. Did much to improve the status of the English clergy but alienated the power brokers among the nobility and merchant classes. Reviled by Calvinist—Puritans—Presbyterians, for his changes in church practice which he enforced with orders issued by the Star Chamber and Court of High Commission.

Lennox, Duke of. See Stuart, Esme.

Leslie, Alexander. Later Lord Leven, elderly former Field Marshal in Swedish Army, commander of the Armies of the Covenant for a while.

Leslie, David. Nephew of Alexander Leslie, whom he succeeded as commander of the Covenanter Armies. A colonel in the Swedish Army, Maj. General in 1644 and commanded at Marston Moor. Victor at Philiphaugh, 1645. Withstood Cromwell for a while at Dunbar; captured at Worcester, 1651. Imprisoned in the Tower until 1660, when released, created Viscount Newark and given a pension of £500 a year.

Leslie, John. 1st Duke of Rothes. Kings Commissioner for Charles II at the Restoration. Alleged drunkard, perjurer, and boor. Persecutor.

Maitland, John. Duke of Lauderdale. Secretary of State under Charles I. Virtual ruler of Scotland for over twenty years. Protestant, supported drive for Episcopalian church. As Lord Maitland, he was a Presbyterian Elder at the Westminster Assembly. He understood the Presbyterian arguments but chose to ignore them in favour of implementing the king's will and securing his own aggrandisement.

McColl or **McDonald, Alastair**. Charismatic leader of the Irish troops sent by the Earl of Antrim to join with Montrose against the Covenanters.

McKenzie, Sir George, of Rosehaugh. Lord Advocate of Scotland. Prosecuted many Covenanters. Also known as "Bluidy McKenzie."

McMillan, John. Presbyterian minister at Balmaghie. Left the Revolutionary Church of Scotland to be the first permanent minister of the Societies, and later formed the Reformed Presbytery.

Melville, Andrew. Calvinist minister in Scotland, succeeded John Knox as leader of the Presbyterian movement. Wrote the Second Book of Discipline.

Middleton, John. Soldier, Covenanter to begin with. Apostate, and drunkard. Later Earl of Middleton and Kings Commissioner in Scotland. Responsible for "Middleton's Act" and the outing of ministers.

Mill, Walter. Former catholic priest turned Protestant. Martyred at the age of eighty-two. His martyrdom greatly incensed the people and said to have brought about the downfall of Popery in Scotland.

Monck, George. Supernumary Colonel in 1650, Lt. General in Cromwell's army, September, 1651. Viceroy of Scotland during the Commonwealth. One of few officers with clear grasp of political realities. Took his army to London in 1660 and instrumental in bringing Charles II back to the throne. Created Duke of Albermarle.

Orange, William of. Prince of Orange (Holland). William III, King of England. Husband to Mary Stuart (Mary II). Nephew and son-in-law of James II. Protestant.

Peden, Alexander. An outed Presbyterian minister. Leading conventicler in Scotland and Ireland; also known as "The Prophet" for many accurate forecasts of events to come. Not a "Cameronian" as such.

Pym, John. Leader of the Puritans in the English Parliament under Charles I. Critic of ecclesiastical policies in the 1620s. Feared a popish plot to re-establish Catholicism and absolutism. Forced the issues that led to Parliamentary democracy; very anti-episcopacy.

Renwick, Rev. James. Presbyterian martyr. The last leader of the Covenanters or "Cameronians" before the Revolution Settlement.

Rothes, Duke of. See Leslie.

Sharp, James. Presbyterian minister at Crail, Fife. Later Archbishop of St. Andrews. Turncoat royalist and Episcopalian. Arch persecutor. Assassinated.

Stewart, James. Captain. Son of Lord Ochiltree, took title of Earl of Arran. Favourite of James VI who, with the Duke of Lennox, virtually ruled Scotland. Brother-in-law of John Knox. Denounced Morton. Killed in revenge by James Douglas.

Strafford. See Wentworth.

Stuart, Charles. Charles I, son of James VI/I, King of Great Britain. Protestant, Episcopalian. Executed.

Stuart, Charles. Charles II. Son of Charles I. King of Great Britain. Used military force against the Covenanters. Closet Catholic.

Stuart, Esme. Called D'Aubigny. A cousin once removed of King James VI. Created Duke of Lennox and Lord High Chamberlain. Emissary of the Guise family. Ruled Scotland for a while with the Earl of Arran. Catholic, but Protestant when it suited him.

Stuart, Henry, Lord Darnley. Eldest son of the 4th Earl of Lennox. Second husband of Mary, Queen of Scots. Murdered.

Stuart, James. Name of several kings of Scotland. *James V* married first Madeleine de Valois, second Mary of Guise. Responsible for much French influence at the Scottish Court, including art and architecture. In the Reformation period, *James VI* of Scotland was also James I of England and the first King of Great Britain. Protestant, Episcopalian.

Stuart, James, nominally James VII of Scotland (never crowned), James II of England. Brother of Charles II. King of Great Britain. Responsible for the worst of the persecutions in the Killing Time. Catholic. Father of the "Old Pretender." Deposed.

Stuart, James. Earl of Moray. Natural son of James V, half-brother to Mary, Queen of Scots. Also known as "The Good Regent." Joined the Lords of the Congregation and supported Presbyterianism. Murdered.

Stuart, Mary. Queen of France and Scotland. Wife of Francis II, King of France. Married secondly, Henry Stuart, Lord Darnley; thirdly, James Hepburn, Earl of Bothwell. Catholic. Executed by the English.

Stuart, Mary. Daughter of James II. Queen Mary II of England. Wife of William, Prince of Orange (Holland). Protestant.

Turner, Sir James. Royalist soldier. He and his troops zealously enforced laws against Covenanters; also filled his own pockets with fines and bribes. Arch persecutor.

Tudor, Edward. King Edward VI. Son of Henry VIII and Jane Seymour. Counselled by Archbishop Cranmer, devout and committed Protestant who went to considerable lengths to try and prevent his Catholic half-sister, Mary I, succeeding him.

Tudor, Elizabeth. Queen Elizabeth I of England, daughter of Henry VIII and Anne Boleyn. Succeeded her half-sister, Mary I. Renewed laws for Protestant, Episcopal, Church of England.

Tudor, Mary. Queen of England, daughter of Henry VIII and Katharine of Arragon, half-sister to Elizabeth I. Declared a bastard by Henry. Succeeded her half-brother, Edward VI. Wife of Phillip of Spain. Staunch Catholic and persecutor of the Protestants in England, over three hundred martyrs burnt at the stake in her reign.

Wentworth, Thomas. Later Earl of Strafford. Lord Lieutenant of Ireland. Persecutor of the Irish Presbyterians. With Archbishop Laud, pursued "thorough" policies. Impeached and executed as a political necessity.

Wilson, Margaret. With Margaret McLachlan, one of "The Solway Martyrs." Tied to posts and drowned in the sea.

Part I

Protestantism and Presbyterianism in Scotland: The First Reformation

The Scottish Reformation and the eventual ascendancy of Presbyterianism in Scotland is sometimes portrayed very simplistically as arising from the teachings of John Calvin (1509-1564), who was a French theologian residing in Geneva, and the Scot John Knox (1514-1572), who was an adherent of Calvin's principles. The emergence of evangelism and a Protestant creed in Scotland was not an overnight event, however; nor did it originate solely with the fervour of John Knox fresh from Geneva. It was an evolutionary process with small core groups (such as the Lollards) making contact with one another in Scotland and cross-border contact with English Protestants. John Calvin developed his view of an evangelical church that became Calvinism. John Knox brought form and direction to the Scots' evangelism; he was the catalyst who brought about action to establish a Protestant church and therein Presbytery.

Protestantism was, however, already making progress in England. John Wyckcliffe (1329-1384) produced his manuscript version of the New Testament, written in Old English, in 1380 and he followed with the Old Testament in the next two years. William Tyndale (1492-1536) produced his printed English Bible in 1525. The introduction of printing by William Caxton (1422-1491) made available many more copies of Tyndale's Bible. These were major milestones in the education of the general population who, for the first time, were able to read, interpret, and think for themselves about religion and its moral values.[1]

IOANNES CNOXVS.

From Theod. Bezæ Icones, etc., M.D.LXXX.

John Knox. Originally appearing in *Icones* by Theodore Beza (1580), this illustration is reproduced from John Knox, *Works of John Knox*, Vol. 1, ed. David Laing (Edinburgh: John Thin & Co., 1895).

---

[1] Under the church of Rome the Bible was not freely available, it was in Latin, and it was interpreted by the priests, often accompanied by mysticism and rites.

Another major contributor to the development of Protestantism in England—during the reigns of Henry VIII and Edward VI—was Thomas Cranmer (1489-1556). Cranmer has been variously damned and praised by historians through the ages, but the close relationship he had with the young Edward VI ensured there was both continuity and a firm foundation for the Protestant Church. Edward VI ruled England for only a short time, however, dying young, and his sister, Mary eldest daughter of Henry VIII, ascended the throne. Although "Bloody" Mary, persecutor of the Protestants while queen, sought to return to Catholicism, her sister and her successor to the throne, Elizabeth I, consolidated the Protestant Church of England and thus provided a bulwark for the Scots at a critical time in their own Reformation.

Protestantism in Scotland can be traced even further back, however, to the Romans and some say to the Apostles themselves.

> Scotland's conversion unto the Christian faith was among the first fruits of the Gentiles, of the oldest date, that any standing church holding the head Christ this day can deduce its original from. For it is clear from ancient records, the Christian faith was embraced here a few years after the ascension of our Saviour, being taught by the disciples of John the Apostle; and received afterwards great increment from the Britons flying to Scotland, to escape the persecution of the Emperor Domitian....[2]

In later years sects such as the Celtic Culdees and the fifteenth century Lollards preached a Protestant creed and were pursued as heretics by Rome. The Culdee's testimony

> did more particularly relate to the concerns of Christ's priestly office, which was transmitted from the Culdees to the Lollards, and by them handed down to the instruments of reformation in the following period. Their Testimony indeed was not active, by way of forcible resistance against the sovereign powers; but passive by way of confession and

---

[2] Alexander Shields, *A Hind Let Loose* (Edinburgh [Calton]: John Kirk, 1797; reprint Edmonton: Still Waters Revival Books, 1996), p. 24 *et seq.*

martyrdom, and sufferings and verbal contendings, and witnessing against the prevailing corruptions of the time...errors, idolatries and superstitions of popery; so they did constantly bear witness against the usurpation and tyrannical domination of the antichristian prelates.[3]

That their adversaries did manage their cruel craft, and crafty cruelty, in murdering those servants of God, much after the same methods that ours do.[4]

The Culdees and early Christianity

The persecution by the Emperor Domitian (51-96) took place towards the end of his rule and probably contributed to his assassination. Further persecutions under Emperor Diocletian (245-313) drove many religious minded teachers into Scotland. These refugees may have been the original Culdees and were known as *monachoi*, or monks.[5] However, Calderwood in his *History* is emphatic that they were not monks, since "Monkes by their profession, might not teach."[6]

So, who were the Culdees? They were a religious order and took no part in the civil authority. They appointed their own superintendents to watch over them and to travel about to their various locations—identifiable today by place names with Cell or Kell and Kil such as Kil-marnock, Kil-patrick, Kil-malcolm. The Culdees had their ups and downs but by the early fifth century the Roman legions were largely withdrawn from Britain and they were able to build new churches and pursue their faith. Recorded history during the so called Dark Ages is very sparse, but it is likely that the Culdees joined with St Columba and were among his disciples in Iona from about A.D. 563. The Culdees last monastery was in St Andrews from which they were driven out by the church of Rome in the twelfth century. The remnants of the Culdees joined with the Lollards who came to prominence in the late thirteenth century. The

---

[3] Shields, pp. 30-31.

[4] *Ibid.* This is a reference to the methods used: waiting for an excuse to allege heresy, then quickly invoking church law and burning at the stake.

[5] The word Culdees comes from *Cultores Dei* meaning worshippers of God.

[6] David Calderwood, *The History of the Kirk of Scotland*, Vol. 1, ed. Thos. Thomson (Edinburgh: Wodrow Society, 1842), p. 39.

common thread to all these sects was that they followed the plain and simple evangelism of St. John, rather than St. Peter (through the Pope) being God's representative on earth.

Perhaps the most singular evidence of Christianity in Scotland exists in the southwest in the small village of Ruthwell. The Ruthwell Cross, dating from *ca.* 680, is a magnificent, eighteen-foot-tall preaching cross that has runic text and sculptures with a Christian message carved upon it. This "sermon in stone" tells the story of the Life and Passion of Christ.

There has been much debate about the runes but they are thought to be an ancient North English or Northumbrian dialect. The text correlates closely with "The Holy Rood: A Dream" written by the seventh century monk, Caedmon, which tells the story of the crucifixion from the point of view of the cross itself.

The Holy Rood: A Dream

Then the young hero prepared himself
That was Almighty God
Strong and firm of mood
He mounted the lofty cross
Courageously in the sight of many

I raised the powerful king
The lord of the heavens
I dared not fall down
They reviled us both together
I was all stained with blood
Poured from the man's side

Christ was on the cross yet thither hastening
Men came from afar
Unto the noble one

I beheld that all
with sorrow I was overwhelmed

I was all wounded with shafts
They laid him down limb weary;

They stood at the corpse's head;
They beheld the Lord of Heaven.[7]

The Ruthwell Cross may have been designed to mark the site of a victory by a Christian king of Northumbria over heathen enemies or to commemorate a local event. Regardless of its original purpose, it is clear that the design and general presentation is a work far in advance of the normal cultural expectations of the period. It was probably saved from the Danish and Viking hordes by its relative remoteness inland.

Although instruction was given by the General Assembly in 1642 that the cross should be destroyed as idolatrous, the Rev. Gavin Young, minister at the time, managed to balance his conscience by saving three large portions of the cross which were buried for safe keeping. In near modern times the minister responsible for the re-erection and preservation of the Cross was the Rev. Henry Duncan, founder of the Savings Bank movement in 1810.

The Ruthwell Cross. Above and next page left, the cross standing in its well. Carvings, next page right (left-hand face) Mary Magdalene anointing the feet of Jesus; (right-hand face) Jesus Christ as Righteousness, being recognised as the Saviour by wild beasts. Photos courtesy of A. Pittendreigh.

---

[7] *Official Guide to the Ruthwell Cross* (Edinburgh: Historical Scotland, 1998), p. 5.

The Lollards

The name of "Lollard" was first given in 1300 to a charitable society at Antwerp, who *lulled* the sick by singing to them and probably stems from the German *lollen,* to hum. The radicalism of the Lollards lay in that they denied infant baptism, believed that the main task of a priest was to preach, and that everyone should have access to a Bible in their own language. The denial of infant baptism is no more than the Baptist faith but was seen then as a great heresy.

The Lollards arrived in England before they arrived in Scotland. In England, the Lollards followed John Wyckcliffe (1329-1384), and by 1395 they had their own ministers and were winning popular support. Wyckcliffe and his writings were condemned by Pope John XXIII in 1415 with renewed religious persecutions of Lollards soon following in England.

The Roman Church actively rooted out and prosecuted alleged heresy wherever it could, going after not only Lollards but practitioners of other sects as well. (In fact, "Lollard" was often a catch all name for many types of alleged heresy during this period—including some probable Lutheran views.) By the mid fifteenth century the Lollards' protests became linked with political unrest and they were again severely persecuted. Many fled into hiding in the northern and western regions of England and Wales with some entering Scotland where local pockets of Lollard influence and tradition continued into the sixteenth century.

In Scotland, the Lollards were quite strong in numbers within the districts of Kyle and Carrick, in Ayrshire, where the proprietors of the estates of Carnell, Kinzeancleuch, Ochiltree, Cessnock, Barr, Gadgirth, and Terinzeon were supporters of the sect's beliefs. Howie, in *Biographia Scoticana*, and Calderwood, in *History*, relate that in 1494 Robert Blackatter, first Archbishop of Glasgow, summoned George Campbell of Cessnock, Adam Reide of Barskimminge, John Campbell of Newmiles, Adam Shaw of Pockemmet, Helene Chalmers Ladie Pokellie, N. Chalmers Ladie Stairs, and many others to about thirty in number before King James IV. They were admonished and dismissed. At least two of the men found in Howie's *Scots Worthies*, John Nisbet of Hardhill and William Gordon of Earlstoun, had ancestors who were involved with the Lollards of Kyle. The Campbells of Cessnock were another such family who suffered for their faith.

Lollards were also in Fife, but as an organisation they faltered when the martyrdom of George Wishart in 1546 signified another period of repression. The Lollards' reasons for oppositing Romish practice were similar to the arguments made throughout the Scottish Reformation by John Knox and Andrew Melville (1545-1622). The Lollards condemned the doctrine of transubstantiation (the belief that bread and wine change into the actual body and blood of Jesus Christ during the Communion ceremony), the use of images in churches, pilgrimages, the rite of the mass, the use of holy water, the sacrament of penance, the veneration of relics, and prayers for intercession. Perhaps the most heinous act in Romish eyes was the fact that the Lollards preached in English and proclaimed that the faithful need only the Scriptures to gain salvation.[8] This destroyed the mysticism of the Bible and exposed the priests who had hitherto been the only means of interpreting and delivering the Word of God—in whatever manner, or cost, they felt appropriate.

In addition to the early influences of the Culdees and the Lollards, the Scottish Reformation was also intertwined with the political decision of King Henry VIII of England to reject the Papal control over his kingdom. It was Thomas Cranmer's subtle influence and teaching of Edward VI that gave England a more relaxed, liberal, and evangelical system with a relatively mild administration. Queen Elizabeth I's re-enactment of the acts of Henry VIII finally sealed the end of Catholicism in England, settled Protestantism as the official faith in that country, and provided a bulwark for the Protestant Reformation in Scotland.

In 1556, the year Thomas Cranmer was burned at the stake as a heretic, John Knox visited Scotland and made contact with the Lords of the Congregation. He returned to his flock in Geneva for a while, and to his studies with John Calvin, before returning permanently to Scotland in 1559.

Calvinism

It has been said that Martin Luther (1483-1546) wrote the tune and John Calvin (1509-1564) wrote the words for the Protestant theology. There were differences of opinion and practice between the two and their followers, but it was their influence by word and deed that began to roll back the all-pervading influence of Rome in the Christian church. Calvin and his successor, Theodore Beza (1519-1605), were the principal sources of contact and influence on the continent for John Knox, and his successor Andrew Melville, who took forward the banner of Protestantism in Scotland.

Martin Luther is credited with providing the impetus to the Protestant Reformation in Europe when he nailed his *Ninety-Five Theses*, to the church door in Wittenberg, Germany, in 1517. The *Theses* were a disputation about the practice of Indulgences rampant in the Catholic church at that time.

---

[8] For this reason Patrick Hamilton, great-grandson of King James II of Scotland, was burnt at the stake in 1528. See Appendix 3.

Calvin was born in Noyon, Picardy, France, and a student at Orleans, Bourges and the University of Paris. He was a quiet, studious man who had one strong trait: an indomitable will. Influenced as a student by the work of Martin Luther, Calvin forsook Roman Catholicism and exiled himself in Basle, Switzerland. Here he developed his theology and published his defence of Protestant beliefs in *The Institution of the Christian Religion* (1536). His first attempts at putting his beliefs into practice in 1537 at Geneva failed when the inhabitants rejected his proposal that they should swear loyalty to a Protestant declaration of faith. Disappointed Calvin went to Frankfort where he led a congregation that gave him the pastoral experience he needed. In 1541 he returned to Geneva, where his proposals were now accepted, and began preaching daily to the citizens; writing and publishing an enlarged edition of his *Institution*; and creating his Geneva Academy to which theologians came from all over Europe.

A man who was both methodical and systematic, it was these characteristics that separated Calvin's thinking from the Lutheran doctrines, as he formulated the organisation of the church. A major consideration was that the Church is supreme and should not be controlled by the state in any way. His doctrine of faith equally firmly stated that all knowledge of God is only found in the word of God, and salvation is only possible through the grace of God. He accepted only baptism and communion as church sacraments, warning against having any mystical belief of any physical presence of Jesus from the taking of bread and wine.[9]

Calvin's successor in Geneva and the first rector of the Geneva Academy was Theodore Beza who arrived in 1548 announcing his conversion to Protestantism. Trained as a lawyer, he was also an adviser to the Huguenots in France and a mainstay of the politics of the Reformed Church. His *De jure magistratum* was an important political work. It was under Beza's influence that Geneva became the centre of Reformed Protestantism.

---

[9] Presbyterians believe in the "real presence" of Christ in Communion, but this is a spiritual presence through the promised immanence of the Holy Spirit.

John Knox. Statue at St. Giles Cathedral. Photo courtesy of M. McIlwrick.

John Knox; Mary of Guise, Queen Regent; and the First Reformation

John Knox has been called many things but in the context of the religious reformation then taking place, the comment by Mary, Queen of Scots, sums him up. She considered him "the most dangerous man in all the realm.[10]" Knox was first a priest but having heard George Wishart preach he took up the reformed, Protestant, doctrines in 1543. After some time as a minister in England he went to Frankfort in Germany and to Geneva where he preached to English and Scottish exiles. In Geneva he was influenced by the teachings of John Calvin which he adopted and subsequently brought with him to Scotland. Knox is sometimes unfairly cast as just a zealot and a fanatic when he was simply very earnest in his beliefs. But these were strengths, to which should be added a commanding intellect that could overawe his audience, and a penetrating mind. He was also possessed of very wide experience from his travels and associations with some of the most learned men in Europe. In short he possessed the qualities needed to be a leader, and capable of standing up to the staunchly Catholic Queen Regent, Mary of Guise, mother of Mary Queen of Scots.

In Scotland the death of James V on 14 December 1542 brought the one week old Mary to the throne and with her accession a battle for the Regency. The Earl of Arran was Regent for some years during which there were several incursions into Scotland by the English. Scotland, meanwhile, was under great pressure from the French who supported the Queen Mother, Mary of Guise in her bid to be Queen Regent. On the pretext of keeping order, the Regent Mary was supplied with French troops but this was a tactic to put pressure on England with whom war was looming. With French forces on its borders, the English responded to the threat. The Duke of Somerset defeated the Scots army at Pinkie on "Black Saturday," 9 September 1547. This was followed by the building of a chain of forts along the border and several years of relative peace. However, French influence remained in Scotland and more French troops

---

[10] James King Hewison, *The Covenanters. A History of the Church in Scotland from the Reformation to the Revolution* (Glasgow: John Smith & Son, 1908; reprint Edmonton: Still Waters Revival Books, 1996), Vol. 1, p. 10.

arrived to occupy Edinburgh causing the English to finally withdraw. The young Mary, Queen of Scots, was sent to France where she spent the next thirteen years and married the Dauphin, Francis, later King Francis II.

While the young Scottish queen was in France, there followed a concurrent period of upheaval in Scotland as Mary of Guise sought to impose her authority and that of the Catholic church. Her position and French influence was improved when she became Queen Regent in 1554 but she made enemies through her appointment of Frenchmen to positions of power.

Into this cauldron of intrigue came John Knox in 1555 who had been invited by a growing evangelical movement to preach and plan for the establishment of a reformed faith. Knox preached at Duns House, between Montrose and Berwick—the home of John Erskine; at Calder House, West Lothian, the home of Sir James Sandilands; Finlayston House, Kilmalcolm, the home of Alexander Cunningham, Fifth Earl of Glencairn; at Castle Campbell, home of Archibald Campbell (later Fifth Earl of Argyll); and at other homes in Ayr, Barr, Gadgirth, Kinzeancleuch, and Ochiltree in Ayrshire. Other supporters in the nobility who were strengthened in their faith by Knox's endeavours included Lord Erskine (later, Sixth Earl of Mar) and Lord James Stewart (later Earl of Moray and Regent.) These were men of great influence and power who were able to summon substantial military forces to their aid and had to be regarded with respect. But even so, with French soldiers in support of Mary of Guise, they had to tread carefully. Even the fearless Knox returned to Geneva for a while in July 1556.

The Queen Regent then sought to raise a standing army to bring pressure on England who was close to war with France. However, she encountered the strong resistance of the property owners who would be forced to pay for it. A protest meeting of over three hundred lairds in the Abbey Church of Holyrood in 1556 caused her to yield from the proposal.

In England Mary Tudor, eldest daughter of Henry VIII and now Queen of England, declared war on France in 1557. This spurred the Queen Regent in Scotland to assemble an army near Kelso to attack England. But the assembled Lords of Arran, Huntly, Argyll, and others, declared themselves as assembled only for the defence of Scotland and not for aggression against England.

Meanwhile, in March 1557 the Lords had written to Knox and asked him to return to Scotland. In reply Knox encouraged them to be bold and public, reckoning that their power and influence could help turn the tide against Romanism. This they agreed to do. On 3 December 1557 the first "Band" or Covenant (see Appendix 4 for the full text) was signed by the Lairds of the Mearns to establish the word of God and to labour for the institution and support of "faithful ministers purely and truly to minister Christ's Evangel and Sacraments to His people."[11] Their objectives were very simple and explicit: that the public prayers and administration of the sacraments by ministers should be celebrated in their mother tongue so that all people might understand them, and that the election of ministers according to the custom of the primitive Church, should be made by the people. The signatories to the Band or Covenant were Archibald Campbell, Earl of Argyll; the Earl of Glencairn; the Earl of Morton; Archibald Campbell, Lord of Lorne; and John Erskine of Dun.

Thus came into being "The Congregation of Jesus Christ" or "The Lords of the Covenant" which grew to become a formal opposition to Catholicism. The Congregation then demanded religious freedom to which the Regent responded with the execution for heresy of the eighty-two-year-old Walter Mill on 28 April 1558. He was a former priest who had stopped giving the Mass and joined the evangelical movement. The Congregation immediately demanded that the clergy's power to try for heresy be suspended but the Regent declined to present the matter to the Estates. This prompted the Congregation to make their own direct Protestation to Parliament and to declare that they intended to follow their own consciences.

The death of England's Mary Tudor later that year and the accession of the Protestant Elizabeth I gave hope for the Protestant cause in Scotland. An immediate consequence of Mary's death was the return of many committed Protestants who had been exiled earlier to the Continent. Among them were those from Geneva who had come under the direct influence of Calvin. These people were keen to remove any remaining signs of Popery and became an

---

[11] See Appendix 4.

important element in the subsequent attempts to reform the Church of England.

In Scotland, events came to a head when the Regent Queen Mary of Guise summoned four preachers—Paul Methven, John Christison, William Harlow, and John Willock—to Stirling to answer charges of usurping the ministerial office and preaching sedition. The trial was appointed to take place on 10 May 1559 with the expectation that the ministers would be sentenced to banishment. The Congregation took up the preachers' cause and assembled at Perth to accompany the accused to see the Regent. Meanwhile, in Edinburgh, great consternation arose amongst the Papists when John Knox returned from the continent and preached there before making his way to preach at Crail, St. Andrews, Dundee, and Perth.

In St. John's Church, Perth, there occurred the incident that changed the face of Scotland when, after John Knox had preached, a priest started to say Mass. A boy made some disparaging remarks and was cuffed; in response, he threw a stone at the priest and, although missing, the boy managed to break an image on the altar. Onlookers then threw more stones at the priest and destroyed the ornaments of the church. From this flowed attacks on the monasteries of the Blackfriars, Greyfriars, and Carthusians which were all ransacked and gutted. The scenes were repeated in St. Andrews and Scone.[12]

This "rabelling" was seized upon by Mary of Guise as valid reason to repress the Protestants by fire and sword. This prompted the friends of the Congregation from Angus, Mearns, Fife, and Ayrshire to gather at Perth to defend against the Regent's French army who were in Auchterarder, north of Perth. By June the Congregation was assembled in Edinburgh but French troops caused them to withdraw to Stirling. Negotiations continued with the Regent and she eventually gained agreement for the armed supporters of the Congregation to stand down. At this juncture the Earl of Agyll and Lord James Stewart transferred their allegiance to the Congregation because they were disgusted with the Regent's broken promises to withdraw the French soldiers. A Band, the

[12] Although the ornaments were removed, the fabric of the buildings themselves was not torn down.

Second Covenant, was sworn for mutual defence and the abolition of Popery by the Lords and Barons at Edinburgh on 13 July 1559. On August 1 another Band (the Third Covenant) was sworn in Stirling to work and negotiate together, and to keep one another informed.

In August 1559, French troops landed at Leith and began fortifying it. Here they butchered Scottish women, children, and old men, and dangled their bodies over the walls. The Queen Regent the commented it was "a pleasing tapestry."[13] In October the Congregation declared the Regent Mary deposed in the name of her daughter who, it was alleged, had sold the country to France.

Scottish pleas for help from Elizabeth I of England were finally heard and a large army assembled at Berwick where, on 27 February 1560, an agreement securing Scotland's liberties was signed with the Lords of the Congregation.

Within a month Leith was surrounded and the English fleet lay offshore. There followed another Band (the Fourth Covenant) on the 27 April 1560 to join with the English to remove the French troops.[14] On June 11, the Regent Mary died in Edinburgh Castle probably from dropsy. Her death ended the immediate influence of the Guise family and that of France in Scotland.

The Treaty of Edinburgh, 6 July 1560, settled Scotland's Protestant independence. In August 1560, the Estates assembled to formally sanction the reformed religion, which it did, despite protestations that the assembly was illegal because it had not been called by the Queen of Scotland.

In a short space of just four days Knox and colleagues, collectively referred to as the six Johns—Knox, Spottiswoode, Willock, Row, Douglas and Winram—produced the *First Book of Faith*. This gave a creed to the new Church and, amongst other things, justified the action taken by the Congregation. They also produced the *First Book of Discipline, or the Policie and Discipline of the Church* which addressed the practical issues of managing church matters.[15] Collectively they brought together clear,

---

[13] Hewison, *Covenanters*, Vol. 1, pp. 26-27.

[14] This was the first Covenant to combine religious and political demands.

[15] These were men of scholarship, experience and strong character. Wynram was a doctor of theology, Willock a doctor of medicine, Row an advocate and doctor of Law, and Douglas the Rector of St. Andrews University who was later made the

emphatic, and logical documents that were also scriptural, and gave a firm framework to the Presbyterian Church *in* Scotland.

The *First Book of Faith, or Confession of Faith and Doctrine*, contained a preface, twenty-five articles and a conclusion. It was the doctrinal standard of the Church in Scotland for eighty-six years until the Westminster Confession of Faith was adopted in 1647. The First Book of Discipline contained nine articles, which dealt with the structure of the new church, sacraments, stipends, appointments of elders and deacons, etc., and was presented to the Estates in January 1561. Andrew Melville presented his revision, the *Second Book of Discipline*, to the General Assembly in 1578; it was adopted.[16]

In response to the works produced by Knox and his colleagues, the Estates passed three acts on 24 August 1560:

> The first abolished Papal authority and that of the Catholic prelates.
>
> The second annulled previous legislation that was contrary to the new creed.
>
> The third abolished the Mass and ordered punishments for saying, hearing or being present at a Mass.[17]

The Acts were implemented instantaneously and pastors, teachers, and officials loyal to the old regime were ejected from their positions. Absolutely nothing, save the physical buildings stripped to the bare stone, was taken over by the new Church. So deeply was

---

first Protestant Archbishop of St. Andrews. Spottiswoode was a graduate of Glasgow and had been in England under the patronage of Archbishop Cranmer which ensured he was well grounded in the principles of the Reformation.

[16] The *Book of Discipline* ordered the appointment of ten superintendents in the place of bishops. They were not necessarily ordained, could not ordain others and had no independent jurisdiction; but had a watching and inspection brief more on the lines of a works foreman or school inspector. They were quite specifically temporary appointments through expediency in the early years of the Church. However, the title and role would be an issue in years to follow and was a chink in the armour for the reintroduction of episcopacy by James VI.

[17] The latter act provided that for the first offence it would result in confiscation of property and physical punishment. The second offence would result in banishment. And death for the third offence. It sounds most vindictive but the penalties were drawn up by lay men, not the Church, and death was the same penalty for shooting wild geese and game.

the religion cleansed that for nineteen years bibles had to be imported from England, with the first Scottish version printed by Arbuthnot and Bassandyne in 1576-1579.

The first General Assembly of the Reformed Church *in* Scotland was held in Edinburgh on 20 December 1560 with forty-two members present, only six of them being ministers. Calderwood's *History* records that they appointed the following ministers and superintendents. The ministers were John Knox (Edinburgh), Christopher Goodman (was at Ayr but translated to St. Andrews), Adam Heriot (Aberdeen), John Row (St. Johnston – Perth), Paul Methven (Jedburgh), William Christison (Dundee), David Ferguson (Dumfermline), and David Lindsay (Leith). The superintendents were John Spottiswood (Lothians); John Wynram (Fife); John Willock (Glasgow and the West); John Erskine, Laird of Dun (Angus and the Mearns); and John Carswell (Argyll and the Isles).[18]

The Assembly met in the old Chapel of St. Magdalene in Cowgate, Edinburgh, and did so under its own authority founded on the Word of God. This precedent was carried on for some twenty years without the presence of a commissioner on behalf of the sovereign—despite the intervention of Maitland of Lethington who questioned the absence of the Queen's authority. John Knox responded with the prophetic words "Tack from us the fredome of Assemblies, and tack from us the Evangell[19]"—which is precisely what King James VI did in later years.

Mary Queen of Scots

The First Reformation—the establishment of a Protestant religion—was accomplished but there were tensions to come with the return of the Catholic Mary Stuart, Queen of Scots on 20 August 1561. Having lived in France surrounded by the Guise family, the staunchest of all the Catholic families of France, Mary was also the widow of Francis II, the Catholic King of France, and heiress to the English throne. She had been educated in France under the auspices of her uncle, the Cardinal of Lorraine, and brought up in an

---

[18] Calderwood, *History*, Vol. 2, p. 11.

[19] John Knox, *The Works of John Knox*, ed. David Laing (Edinburgh: James Thin, 1895; reprint Edmonton: Still Waters Revival Books, 1996), Vol. 2, p. 296.

atmosphere of blind commitment to the Church of Rome. It is highly likely that every effort was made to prejudice her against the Reformation before she returned to Scotland, and that she had been convinced that it would be the glory of her reign if she brought back Scotland to the obedience of Rome. From the Catholic point of view there was a double bonus if Mary were to succeed to the throne of England and, in any event, a Catholic Scotland could impose itself on England in pursuit of the greater plan of the Catholic League. Behind this lay the machinations of the House of Guise, Catherine de Medici, and the Duke of Alva, which sought to extirpate heresy in Europe. It can be read into this that Mary was probably prepared to sign the death warrant for very many of her subjects as a result of her own religious intolerance.

Mary might have survived in Scotland had she not so blatantly exposed her Catholicism to the people and wilfully disregarded good advice. She had been counselled by the Earl of Moray not to press religion as an issue and to contain her own practice within the bounds of her home. But the people of Edinburgh were aware of the furnishing of the chapel at Holyrood House and the saying of a Mass on 24 August 1561 that prompted rioting. The next day Mary obtained the Privy Council's agreement to an Edict of Toleration proclaimed at the Mercat Cross that allowed her choice of worship for herself and her Court on pain of death for interfering.

Holyrood Chapel. Thos. Shepherd, *Modern Athens, Edinburgh in the Eighteenth Century* (London: Jones & Co., 1829).

Calderwood's *History* quotes the Edict which had two strands to it. Firstly, the state of religion as it was at the time of Mary's return to Scotland:

> [T]hat they and everie one of them content themselves in quietness, keep silence and civill societie among themselves, and in the meantime, whill the estats of the realme may be assembled, and that her Majestie have takin a finall order by their advice, and publick consent, which her Majestie hopeth sall be to the contentment of the whole: That none of them tak upon hand, privatlie or publicklie, to make anie alteratioun or innovatioun of the estate of religioun, or attempt anie thing against the same, which her Majestie found publicklie and universallie standing at her Majestie's arrival in this her realme under paine of death....[20]

And secondly, as it impacted herself and her household:

> Attour, her Majestie, with advice of her Lords of Secreit Counsell, commands and charges all her lieges, that none of them take upon hand to molest or trouble anie of her domesticall servants, or persons whatsomever, come furth of France in her Grace's companie at this time, in word, deed or countenance, for anie caus whatsomever, either within the palace or without, or make anie derisioun or invasioun upon anie of them, under whatsomever colour or pretence, under the said paine of death....[21]

The tenor of the Edict applied double standards, and the announcement that Parliament and the Queen would consider the state of religion raised the hackles of Knox and the faithful brethren who rightly suspected a Papal plot to restore Catholicism. Under the wing of the Jesuit and papal nuncio Nicolaus Floris of Gouda, the plot was for Mary to marry a powerful Catholic able to coerce the Protestants; appoint Catholic advisers and clergy; establish a

---

[20] Calderwood, *History*, Vol. 2, p. 145.
[21] *Ibid.*

Catholic college, given guidance by papal legates and have the support of Philip of Spain to overthrow the Protestant church. This master plan was by Floris of Gouda who sneered at the ministers of the kirk and preachers claiming them to be illiterate tradesmen without influence and "comfortable in the arms of England."[22] How wrong he was on all counts.

M'Crie, in *Life of Knox*, provides evidence, that Mary was intent on restoring Catholicism in Scotland, which he obtained from the letters of the Cardinal de St. Croix in the Vatican library. This was a report from the Grand Prior of France, Danville, (Mary's uncle), in December 1561, of her doings (including action against a burgh for expelling priests).

> By these means she has acquired greater authority and power, for enabling her to restore the ancient religion.[23]

Intrigue and suspicion at the time caused the Congregation to demand that the government take action under the royal proclamation which forbade interference with the state of religion existing at the time of the arrival of the Queen. They submitted a list of forty-eight Catholics for prosecution. Significant among these was George Gordon, Fourth Earl of Huntly, who had enormous estates in Aberdeen and Inverness which included the lands of the Earl of Moray. Mary was convinced by her courtiers that she ought to intervene to quell a dispute between the Gordons and the Ogilvies against which Huntly rebelled and was killed in the battle of Corrichie, 28 October 1562. A son was also executed and another imprisoned while all the lands were forfeit to the Crown. It is quite probable that Mary was tricked to intervene against the staunch Catholic Huntly and realised this soon after the event, as evidenced in her subsequent strong defiance of Protestant lords. The Protestants, however, remained suspicious and entered into another Band (the Fifth Covenant) at Ayr on 4 September 1562.

The string of events that followed was Mary's undoing. Voices were raised against her with criticism of her headlong dash into

[22] Hewison, *Covenanters,* Vol. 1, p. 50.

[23] Thomas M'Crie, *Life of John Knox* (Edinburgh: William Blackwood & Sons, 1855; reprint Edmonton: Still Waters Revival Books, 1996), p. 381, nUU.

marriage with her cousin Henry Stuart, Lord Darnley, on Sunday, 29 July 1565. Lord Darnley was the eldest son of the Fourth Earl of Lennox and, like Mary, a great-grandchild of Henry VII. As such, he had a claim to the succession of the English throne as well as a claim to the Scottish throne. Mary's marriage to Darnley was not approved of by Queen Elizabeth I or her advisers who had worked hard on the alliance with Scotland. Neither did it help that the Lennox family had many enemies in Scotland.[24]

Also, at the General Assembly that met on 25 December 1565, Mary emphatically stated that she would not ratify the establishment of the Protestant Church nor abjure her own Catholicism. This prompted great fear among the Congregation and a fast was declared. And, finally, a string of almost perverse events fell Mary's way as a result of Darnley's erratic behaviour. Although "King," he failed to turn up at Privy Councils and was seldom available to sign Acts. Given to spending his time carousing and whoring among the low life of Edinburgh, Darnley also intrigued with the Lords of the Congregation. He signed a Band at Newcastle on 2 March 1566 which convinced many of them to return from exile in the expectation that Darnley would replace Mary on the throne. There followed what appeared to be a connected incident with the murder of David Rizzio, Queen Mary's secretary. Rizzio was suspected by many courtiers as being a Papal spy and this may have been the reason for his murder. He was also allegedly a handsome man and something of a musician, so an element of jealousy by Darnley cannot be ruled out. On 9 March a group of nobles led by the Earl of Morton, Lord Ruthven and Lord Lindsay, entered the Queen's private chambers and seized Rizzio; he was stabbed between fifty and sixty times before being thrown down the stairs.[25]

Mary was disgusted with Darnley and his involvement in the murder of Rizzio and she soon fell in with the blandishments of James Hepburn, 4th Earl of Bothwell (1536-1578). Bothwell had

---

[24] Knox was a loud voice and critic of Mary, undoubtedly having some influence on the outcome, but she continued to press Catholicism while her marriage was a personal and political disaster.

[25] John Howie says fifty-three stab wounds. John Howie, *Biographica Scoticana* (Glasgow: John Bryce, 1781; reprint Edmonton: Still Waters Revival Books, 1996), p. 14.

been at Court when Rizzio was murdered but did not intercede; he climbed out of a window and galloped pell mell to safety in his castle at Dunbar.

A new, and fatal, twist in the saga of Darnley then took place. In the early hours of the morning of 10 February 1567 an explosion rent the air of Edinburgh. Darnley was found in his nightclothes in the garden but without any signs of burning or the blast; he appeared to have been strangled. A version of the story goes that Darnley had heard some noise in the apartment below his and had himself lowered from his room in a chair suspended on ropes. On gaining the ground he ran into the conspirators who did their murderous deed.

In the notes to *Biographia Scoticana*, called *The Judgement and Justice of God Exemplified*, Howie refers to Darnley thus:

> [T]he queen decoyed him to Edinburgh; where she and Bothwel laid a plan for his life where in Bothwel was to be the aggressor. In prosecution of which, he with some others entered the king's lodgings in the night, and while he was asleep strangled him and one of his servants, and drew him out of a little gate they had made through the city wall....[26]

He also adds a footnote to his observations on David Rizzio:

> Some historians have been inclined to think, from the intriques this Rizio had with the Queen, that James VI, Charles I, Charles II and James VII had more of the 'nature, qualities, features and complexion of the Italian Fidler, than of the ancient race of the Stuarts, kings of Scotland'[27]

In a subsequent and bizarre event Bothwell carried off Queen Mary to Dunbar Castle on 24 April 1567 where she remained, apparently a not unwilling prisoner. At the General Assembly on 30 December 1567 John Craig responded to an admonishment for declaring the marriage banns of the Queen and Bothwell that

---

[26] Howie, *Biographica Scoticana*, p. 15.
[27] *Ibid*., p. 14.

> the Justice Clerk brought me ane writing subscryved with her hand, bearing in effect that she was neither ravished nor yet retained in captivitie and, therefore, charged me to proclaime.[28]

Mary and Bothwell were suspected of complicity in the murder of Darnley. Bothwell's elevation to Duke of Orkney and Zetland, and their subsequent marriage on 15 May 1567, confirmed this suspicion in the eyes of the people. There quickly followed a change of government and the Protestant noblemen who had taken refuge in England were restored. After a bloodless encounter at Carberry Hill on 15 June 1567, Bothwell fled to Norway and eventual imprisonment in Denmark for the rest of his days. Mary became another Scottish sovereign whose Crown passed to a child, in her case she was forced to abdicate in favour of her one-year-old son, James VI.[29]

The General Assembly must have been conversant with the pending forced abdication. On the previous day, 23 July 1567, they specifically called for the nobility, barons, and others to maintain and defend the Prince. They also notably declared about the commitment of kings and princes to Presbyterianism:

> That all kings, princes and magistrates, whilk hereafter in any tyme to come shall happen to reigne and bear rule over this realme, their first intres before they be crowned and inaugarat, shall make their faithfull league and promise to the trew Kirk of God that they shall maintaine and defend, and be all lawfull means sett forward the trew religion of Jesus Christ, presently professed and established within this realme....[30]

---

[28] *The Booke of the Universal Kirk of Scotland*, ed. Alexander Peterkin (Edinburgh: William Blackwood & Sons, 1839; reprint Edmonton: Still Waters Revival Books, 1996), p. 71.

[29] Mary subsequently made a dash for freedom from her prison at Lochleven and, with a dwindling group of faithful supporters, made a final stand at Langside on 13 May 1568. Here she was again deserted by fortune and forced to make an overnight dash for the Solway Firth and escape into England (and exile).

[30] *The Booke of the Universal Kirk of Scotland*, p. 67.

In the aftermath of Mary's machinations, the Scottish Parliament met and passed an Act on 15 December 1567 that confirmed the so-called national "Establishment" of the Protestant religion *in* Scotland. This recognised Presbyterianism as the official Church in Scotland, but did not create it nor commit the state to supporting it financially. There was, however, a downside as the Parliament altered the provisions of the Book of Discipline by reserving the appointments of ministers through a patron to the "ancient patrons"—the nobles who were jealously guarding their ancient rights and control over church lands. This vexed issue of patronage was an issue that would rear its head again and again.

Throughout her nineteen years in exile, Mary Queen of Scots was a shadow in the background for James who was soon alienated from his mother. She disowned him and he only made a political gesture when it became apparent that she might be executed. The hardest decision was that of Queen Elizabeth I who was petitioned by Parliament 22 November 1586 calling for a "just and speedy execution of the said Queen."[31] Elizabeth replied November 24 asking the Parliament to try to find a different solution but they again insisted on execution. Elizabeth then wrote what must be the classic sitting on the fence reply :

> If I should say unto you that I mean not to grant your petition, by my faith I should say unto you more than perhaps I mean. And if I say unto you I mean to grant your petition, I should then tell you more than is fit for you to know. And thus I must deliver you an answer, answerless.[32]

The exiled Mary, Queen of Scots, gained a few more months of life.

The reign of James VI from 24 July 1567 to 1603—a time of discord and uncertainty for Scotland

With Queen Mary in exile and the Protestant Lords in the ascendancy a period of Regency existed and the institution of the

---

[31] G. W. Prothero, *Select Statutes and other Constitutional Documents* (Oxford: Clarendon Press, 1894), p. 110.
[32] Prothero, *Select Statutes and other Constitutional Documents*, pp. 111, 380-402.

Presbyterian Kirk experienced some stability. But, there was still much scheming and dissent from Catholics both abroad and in Scotland with aspirations of restoring Mary to the throne. Within the Kirk there was ongoing debate concerning issues of Episcopacy and Erastianism, the penury of the ministers, and the degeneracy of the people at large.

The relative peace and quiet ended on 23 January 1570, when James Hamilton of Bothwell Haugh murdered the Regent, the Earl of Moray. This was a major stumbling block because the Kirk—in the form of Knox, Pont, and Row—had drawn up a report on Jurisdiction that they had expected to be approved by the Regent, who was friend of the Kirk, and Parliament. This document set out that the Jurisdiction of the Church covered the ministry, morality, ecclesiastical disputes, patrimony, marriage, and divorce. Notably *patrimony* was included. Had it been enacted a major source of conflict would have been settled. However, disruption ensued and patrimony, the exercise of patronage, and the role of bishops became fermenting issues.

The Earl of Mar convened a meeting of some sixty-two carefully selected ministers and commissioners to a Convocation at Leith on 12 January 1572. Many of those attending had leanings toward episcopacy and favoured a compromise. The consequence of this irregular Assembly was a committee to consider the issues, which produced its Concordat on January 16. The articles suspiciously had the hallmarks of a previously agreed upon form driven by the holders of church lands and accepted by desperate clerics. It opened the door for a century of debate and aggravation for the Kirk.

The Concordat stated

> That archbishops and bishops have charge of the former dioceses; be chosen from qualified preachers; not less than thirty years of age; and 'indewed with the qualities specified in the Epistles of Paule to Timothe and Tytus'; exercise the function of superintendents in the meantime; be subject to the Assembly in spiritual matters, and the king in temporal; be consecrated; be elected and assisted by a chapter of pastors; and resume their benefices and their seats in Parliament.

> That conventual house be maintained; their superiors to be examined before institution by their bishops; their benefices to be first applied to the local pastors.
>
> That benefices, having cure of souls attached, be given to preachers, found to be qualified by bishops or superintendents, after they have subscribed to the Confession, taken the oath of fidelity to the crown, and been ordained.
>
> That other benefices be applied to education.[33]

The heart of the problem lay in the rules for appointing a bishop, which was upon nomination by the King, and, worse, the bishop's oath was a sell out to Erastianism.

> I A.B., now elected Bishop of S. utterlie testifie and declare in my conscience, that your majestie is the onlie lawfull and supreme governour of this realm, als weill in things temporall as in the conservatioun and purgatioun of religioun;.... And further, I acknowledge and confesse to have and hald the said bishoprik and possessiouns of the same, under God, only of your Majestie and Crown Royale of this your realm; and for the saids possessiouns I do my homage presentlie to youre Majestie[34]

For the faithful, the response was another Covenant (the Sixth) at Leith on 2 July 1572.

Further tragedies were the death of John Knox on 24 November 1572 and, on the same day, the election of the Earl of Morton as the Regent; he was no friend to the Presbyterians. An early action by Morton was the Act of Uniformity on 26 January 1573 and the implementation of the "Tulchan Bishops." His policy now became one of seeking to coerce the Kirk and its ministers, taking to the Crown the benefices of the churches and challenging the right to hold Assemblies.

Fortunately a successor to Knox soon appeared in the form of Andrew Melville who returned from abroad in the summer of 1574.

---

[33] Hewison, *Covenanters*, Vol. 1, pp. 73-74.

[34] Calderwood, *History*, Vol. 3, pp. 184-185.

Melville had spent ten years in France and latterly in Geneva studying under Theodore Beza, professor at the Geneva College set up by John Calvin. It was Beza who wrote in a letter to the General Assembly of Scotland: "The greatest token of affection the kirk of Geneva could show Scotland was, that they had suffered themselves to be spoiled of Mr Andrew Melville."[35] On his return to Scotland Melville immediately started into battle with the scheming Regent, the Earl of Morton.

Appointed Principal of the College of Glasgow, Melville revived its standing as a teaching college and took up the automatic seat in the Assembly. Soon he was appointed to several committees to inspect publications, examine bishops, revise the Book of Discipline, and to negotiate with Regent Morton. Resistance began with a debate in the General Assembly of 1575 about bishops not authorised by the Scriptures. From this developed propositions that were strongly resisted by Morton, but Providence may have intervened because, on 12 March 1578, he was replaced as Regent by the twelve-year-old King James VI who then ruled with a Council of twelve.

There was, however, a cloud on the horizon with Rome increasing its pressure against England, Scotland, and Holland, countries that were the mainstays of Protestantism. Catholic France sent Esme Stuart, Monsieur D' Aubigny, and a cousin of King James. He was rightly identified by the Kirk as a Catholic spy in the pay of the Guise family. However, he was also a charismatic thirty-year-old who soon found favour with James VI and was elevated to Duke of Lennox and also made Lord High Chamberlain. He was joined by Captain James Stewart, son of Lord Ochiltree and soon to be the Earl of Arran. Between them the two false courtiers with strong Catholic backgrounds, suborned the young king, filling their own pockets to such an extent that Queen Elizabeth I and the Prince of Orange wrote to warn James what was going on. Supported by rumours and whispers from the people James ordered that the Presbyterian form of worship should be used in all his homes. He appointed James Craig as his chaplain, instructing him

---

[35] John Howie, *The Scots Worthies*, revised, ed. W. H. Carslaw (Edinburgh: Johnson, Hunter & Co., 1870; reprint Edinburgh: Banner of Truth Trust, 1995) p. 91.

to prepare a Confession of Faith. On 28 January 1581 James and the Court signed the first National Covenant, also known as the King's Confession. (See Appendix 5.)

The scheming of Lennox took on another form when James Boyd, Archbishop of Glasgow, died and a replacement had to be appointed. Lennox made a simoniacal purchase of the See by proposing Robert Montgomery, then minister at Stirling, for the post which the King approved in accordance with the Leith Concordat. The Glasgow Presbytery refused to accept him. In April 1582 Lennox interrupted the Presbytery's meeting and imprisoned the Moderator. In response, student riots took place, a protestation was made to the King, and Montgomery was excommunicated. The King's response was typically autocratic and supremacist ordering Montgomery appointed as Bishop and declaring the excommunication void.

The hardening attitude of the young king, already showing his liking for absolute rule, and the influence of his French courtiers, continued to rankle both Kirk and the nobles. Matters came to a head when some eight nobles and forty landed proprietors and burgesses entered into a Bond to kidnap the king and set up a new Council. Ruthven, the new Earl of Gowrie, led the kidnappers. The "Ruthven Raid," as it was called, took place on 22 August 1582. Gowrie was appointed treasurer of the new Council and for ten months was the virtual ruler of Scotland. The church saw the kidnapping as a godsend, and it dealt a deadly blow to the hopes of the Catholic party. Lennox and Arran both left the scene for their own safety. The Kirk made a serious mistake when it entered into politics (when the General Assembly approved of the Ruthven Raid), by ordering ministers to explain it carefully to their congregations. James did not forget or forgive the Kirk for its action. James, now in his eighteenth year and soon to achieve his maturity, escaped from his ten-month imprisonment to St. Andrews Castle on 27 June 1583.

Scotland's troubles were not over. James VI soon banished the Ruthven nobles—including Angus, Mar, Glamis, Hume, Wedderburn and Cesfurd—while Gowrie was consigned to the block. The Earl of Arran returned to Court. The plague fell on Edinburgh. It was a gloomy time that could have been worse if the people had known that their king had written to the Pope on 19

February 1584 promising to be advised by his cousin Guise and "satisfy his Holinesss in all other things."[36] Revenge followed on Andrew Melville who was tried and warded in Blackness Castle. But Melville managed to escape and joined the Ruthven Raiders in England.

James VI convened a Parliament on 19 and 20 May 1584 made up of eight bishops, thirteen abbots, twenty-five lords and twenty-three representatives of the burghs which produced forty-nine acts—the Black Acts. The proceedings of the Parliament, and the legislation proposed by the Lords of the Articles, was held in secret and the General Assembly was thus prevented from learning about the new laws and from making any representations. The Black Acts were followed by an Act of Uniformity that reduced the Church to a state of helplessness with many fleeing to England and Ireland. Protests were met with imprisonment and resulted in a gradual compliance by some ministers.

The opportunity finally came for the Ruthven Raiders to return to Scotland when the Earl of Arran was imprisoned in July 1584 for involvement in a murder. With his influence gone, the Lords seized Stirling Castle on 4 November 1585. Many thought that the King should join his mother in exile; some even favoured the block. In a regard for the king's sacred person, he was allowed to live. Ironically, this allowed the king to continue attacks on the Church with even greater venom; he was determined to assert his supreme authority of all matters temporal and ecclesiastical. Attempts to repeal the Black Acts were opposed and left on the Statute Book while the King tried to bring in full episcopacy at the General Assembly in May 1586. His ruse of holding the meeting at Holyrood was seen through and defeated, however. Parliament, in 1587, ratified the "Liberty of the Kirk," swept out patrimony and made bishops the paid officers of the Crown. More happily, the same Parliament also passed a Franchise Act that extended representation in Parliament to small landowners which was a welcome extension to suffrage.

The execution of Mary Queen of Scots at Fotheringay on 8 February 1587 sent a shock through the Catholic world and caused Pope Sixtus V to encourage Philip of Spain to raise the Armada. Its

---

[36] Hewison, *Covenanters*, Vol. 1, p. 115.

defeat in July 1588 was "game set and match" for Protestantism in Britain. At ground level, however, the thirty years of the Scottish Kirk had not greatly improved the morals and behaviour of the masses who weltered in poverty, drink, and loose morals. Rural areas swarmed with gypsies and beggars, while many parishes had no minister and some still had priests. There was a long way for the Reformation to go, with a dissembling King who was playing games with the Kirk and suspected of Papist tendencies

Within Scotland there remained a strong and very active Catholic party even after the French influence of the Duke of Lennox and Captain James Stuart, Earl of Arran, had been expelled. About a third of the nobility retained their ancient family faith. In the southwest Dumfriesshire and Wigtownshire—later to be strongholds of the Covenanters—retained Catholicism through a large number of families of Irish origin. In the north of Scotland the Earl of Huntly, a long time Catholic sympathiser, was leagued with the Earls of Erroll, Montrose, Morton, Angus, Marr, Bothwell (who was indecisive and vacillated), the Master of Gray, and the Master of Glamis. What is perhaps most surprising is that they were open in their opposition, frequently pushing the king's tolerance to an extreme. Yet James VI at times seemed to be in league with them. He was remarkably lenient, apparently not wishing to provoke a rebellion in the north. When required to take action he usually warded[37] them for a short time before they reappeared at Court. Matters eventually came to a head in 1589 when both William of Orange and Queen Elizabeth I wrote to him, warning of Papist plots.

Letters seized from a manservant, Pringill or Pringle, were sent to James by Queen Elizabeth. These included letters from Morton, Huntly, and Sir Claud Hamilton to the King of Spain as well as letters from Huntly and Erroll to the Duke of Parma. Queen Elizabeth included her own letter (see Appendix 6) which was explicit in her amazement that such a situation could exist and, moreover, that it had not been expeditiously dealt with. In other words, she was telling James to open his eyes and do something about it.

---

[37] To be warded was to be confined to a location pending the king's pleasure; it was a form of open arrest.

Yet with all this evidence, Huntly and Hamilton were simply warded. In April 1589 Huntly, Erroll, Crawford, Montrose, and Bothwell gathered with their forces at Perth, proposing to do battle with the king at Bridge of Dee. However, their support wavered and they yielded to James when he entered Aberdeen on April 20. In May, Huntly, Crawford, and Bothwell were convicted of treason but, yet again, they were only warded. In September they were all released from ward ostensibly to welcome the arrival of James VI and his new Queen (which would not actually happen until the following May). Tellingly, Calderwood, in *History*, notes that a proposal was made by the Synod of the Lothians that the Earls be called to public repentance before the kirk in Edinburgh.

> But in respect of the lenitie that was used, it was thought but an ydle thing, and that it would turne but to plaine mockerie.[38]

A welcome interlude to affairs came with the marriage of King James to the fourteen-year-old Anne, Princess of Denmark, first by proxy in Oslo, Norway, on 24 November 1589 and then personally at Kronenberg Castle in January 1590. Queen Anne, a Lutheran, was enthroned at Holyrood on 17 May 1590 in the presence of members of the Kirk. For a while there almost existed a state of euphoria, with a foolish trust in the king during which the Assembly ordered that ministers subscribe to the Second Book of Discipline. Concern for civil unrest certainly helped the king to collaborate with the Kirk at this time, which in turn encouraged the stalwart Presbyterians to press their case for reform.

Seeing the opportunity, the Assembly of May 1592 sought to repeal the Black Acts, the restoration of patrimony and privileges to the church, the removal of titled ecclesiastics from Parliament, to purge the land of idolatry, and to secure the representation of ministers. On 5 June 1592 Parliament enacted "Ane Act for the abolisheing of the Actis contrair to the trew religion" which soon came to be called the "Great Charter of Presbytery." This Act was ratified in 1690 and again in 1706-1707, remaining an essential element of the Union between England and Scotland.

---

[38] Calderwood, *History*, Vol. 5, p. 60.

However, intrigue remained in the land with the capture of a spy and discovery of documents signed by rebels. Known as the "Spanish Blanks" they revealed a conspiracy for an invasion of Western Scotland by Spain. The nobles included Huntly, Angus, Errol, the Master of Gray, and Gordon of Auchindoune, with many more implicated. James VI's response was to go to Aberdeen and raise another Covenant in 1593 to which some 162 landholders subscribed to the promise that they would not ride with or assist the Earls and Jesuits involved.

This was again a remarkable show of tolerance by the King, feeding the suspicion that he was in league with the conspirators who refused to disarm. The church leaders, led by Andrew Melville, accused the King of causing the national misery and the Synod of Fife excommunicated the conspirators. The king then sought to make the Assembly issue an Act of Oblivion but was rejected. James VI finally came round when the rebels defeated forces under the Earl of Argyll, who had been leading an army to dissipate them and destroy their strongholds. But despite this open rebellion James did not pursue the Earls personally beyond the equivalent of a wagging finger of censure—which they blatantly ignored. The obvious conclusion of the people, and subsequently by history, was that the king was complicit in the manoeuvring by the Catholic Earls. The Kirk remained discontented with its constitutional position and still greatly concerned at the lack of religion and morals among the people. Punishment of crimes was lax and laws went unenforced while parishes were without ministers. Those that were in a manse had minuscule stipends and were mainly living on charity.

In August 1595 arose the celebrated cause of Rev. David Black who was appointed to St. Andrews and sought to take possession of the manse in which was encamped William Balfour of Burley—who refused to quit. Burley reported to the King that Black had slandered the late Queen Mary, and was cited to appear before King and Council. Black entered a plea of no jurisdiction to the civil court when the hearing was interrupted by Andrew Melville who told the king plainly that there were "two kings in Scotland, two kingdoms and two jurisdictions—Christ's and his."[39] In full flow,

---

[39] Hewison, *Covenanters*, Vol. 1, p. 137.

Melville also berated Balfour, who was present, and a discomfited King patched a peace together. The king would, however, remember Melville's intervention and a later occasion at Falkland in September 1596 when Melville famously plucked at his sleeve and called him "God's sillie vassal"—meaning God's weak servant.[40]

Yet again Rev. Black was outspoken, this time being warded beyond the Tay. This led to Walter Balcanqual delivering a critical review of the Black case in St. Giles on 17 December 1596. Subsequently a meeting in the chancel sent a representative group to intercede with the king who was nearby at the Law Courts. Led by Robert Bruce the king erupted in temper demanding explanation why they had met without his permission. As fuel to the flames Lord Lindsay remarked "Meet...We dare do more than that, and will not suffer religion to be overthrown."[41] The king left the room and demanded the doors to the Courthouse be shut. By his panic he exaggerated the meeting into an uprising and fled to Linlithgow Palace where warrants were issued for the Edinburgh ministers—Balcanqual, Bruce, Balfour, and Watson—who escaped. The rumour spread that the Border Reivers were coming at the king's behest to raid the town and the magistrates pleaded with James VI for mercy, undertaking to apprehend and expel any minister at the king's pleasure.

Hardly had the king been soothed when John Welch, a son-in-law of Knox and a Presbyterian zealot, preached in St. Giles and accused the king of being possessed by the Devil. There was no stopping James VI now and he was resolute in stamping out the freedom of the Church. By an Act at Linlithgow on 21 December 1596 he ordered that ministers must take a test and subscribe to a Bond acknowledging the king's superiority in civil and criminal matters on pain of loss of stipend. The Privy Council pronounced the petitioners to be traitors and ordered ministers to acknowledge the king's superiority, also ordering the magistrates to arrest "distasteful" ministers, while forbidding assemblies in Edinburgh. The homes of the four Edinburgh ministers were seized, the city

---

[40] Thomas M'Crie, *Life of Melville* (Edinburgh: Blackwood, 1819; reprint Edmonton: Still Waters Revival Books, 1996), p. 66. Hewison, *Covenanters*, Vol. 1, p. 140.

[41] Hewison, *Covenanters*, Vol. 1, p. 142.

was fined 20,000 merks, and an unpopular Catholic, Alexander Seton, Lord Urqhart, was appointed Provost.

Believing the time ripe, the king pursued his objectives by calling a convention at Perth. The location was far enough away to deter some ministers from attending and was also nearer the royalist (and Catholic), sympathisers in the north. The Assembly met on 29 February 1597 and considered some fifty-five questions that James VI and his secretary had drawn up. After rejecting by vote a claim that the Assembly was not properly convened, events turned to the King's advantage and his demands were met. These included agreement that in General Assembly the king could propose reform of any matter of external government, civil legislation could only be changed by constitutional means, no citizen could be publicly rebuked except of proven crimes, that no General Assembly could meet without the king's approval, and pastors could not be appointed in the cities without his approval. James VI came away satisfied that he now had a platform on which to build his own system of church government that would not interfere in civil matters. A further trump card for the King was the subsequent endorsement of the Perth agreements by the Dundee General Assembly on 10 May 1597, which also agreed the king's proposal for the appointment of nineteen commissioners to consult with him on religious matters. The Church saw this as "the verie needle which drew in the threed of the bishops."[42] How right they were for the Parliament in December 1597 resolved that any bishop, abbot, or prelate appointed by the king should have a voice in Parliament.

James VI then displayed his literary talents, albeit lacking any diplomacy, by publishing a treatise in September 1598 entitled *The Trew Law of Free Monarchies, or the Reciprock and Mutuall duties betwixt a free king and his naturall subjects.* This was a creed of arbitrary power with passive obedience and non resistance of the people, without any exception or reservation whatsoever. Moreover, the king was not bound to obey the law of the land. This he followed with his *Basilicon Doron* in 1599 that was intended as a private print of seven copies only. It showed his real feelings toward Presbytery and the Church advocating the return to

---

[42] Hewison, *Covenanters*, Vol. 1, p. 145.

episcopacy and calling the Church a "conceited partie."[43] Andrew Melville saw a copy and made notes that were passed to the Synod of Fife. The Synod condemned it and in seeming ignorance sent their judgment to the king for his approval. Some of the more offensive parts were amended but James was not pleased at yet another Church intervention with his affairs. However, the king soon demonstrated his Divine Right beliefs by appointing three bishops and sending them as Commissioners to the Parliament.

In August 1600 the Gowrie plot to kidnap the king ended in bloodshed, with the bizarre action of preserving the bodies of the Earl of Gowrie and his brother in salt barrels until they could be tried by Parliament on November 15. The bodies were duly convicted and sentenced to be hung, drawn and quartered. The true purpose of this charade was almost certainly to enable their lands, goods, and gear to be seized for the Crown. The king's venom did not stop there but followed up with five ministers who were sceptical about what happened—Balcanqual, Hall, Watson, Balfour, and the elderly Robert Bruce—who were ordered to be ejected from Edinburgh and replaced by consenting royalists. Bruce was a stubborn man, however, and declined to accept the official version of the plot for which he was banished to France.

In a further exhibition of his absolutist approach James invited the General Assembly due at St. Andrews to sit in the Chapel Royal, Holyrood. Despite protestations at what was obviously a "Privy Council of Religion" the pliable members approved of a further diminution of the Church. Here they approved the appointment of visitors to sixteen districts, which for all practical purposes were diocese who had power to examine pastors presbyteries and the people, that private chaplains (spies) should be billeted on the nobles, while aristocratic young men were to be prevented from leaving the country for their education abroad without having authority.

Queen Elizabeth I died on 24 March 1603 and James VI of Scotland arrived in London for his coronation as King James I of England on May 3. But even so he could not arrive without some controversy due to his having ordered the execution of a thief in Newark without trial. This drew a sarcastic comment from Sir John

---

[43] Hewison, *Covenanters*, Vol. 1 p. 149.

Harrington: "Now if the wind bloweth thus, why not a man be tried before he hath offended?"[44] James soon showed that he came to teach that resisting the royal wish was to oppose Divine will, and that he was as indisputable as God. Foremost now in Scotland was his drive to have a common or uniform church, as he had in England, with himself as supreme head of both church and state.

The legal position of Episcopacy chopped and changed greatly over the remaining 130 years of the Reformation with the Stuart kings imposing it by stealth and ultimately by force, and the people rejecting it.

Presbytery	Episcopacy
17 Aug 1560 - 1 Feb 1572	1 February 1572 - June 1592
June 1592 - October 1612	October 1612 - June 1640
June 1640 - May 1661	May 1661 - June 1690.

[44] Hewison, *Covenanters*, Vol. 1, p 173.

Part II

The Turbulent Seventeenth Century and the Establishment of the Church of Scotland

The seventeenth century was an extraordinarily busy time politically throughout the three kingdoms and not every "jot and tittle" of events (the civil wars, for example) is included here. The resumé that follows outlines the issues that impacted the Kirk through the reigns of the Stuart kings and Cromwell until the Glorious Revolution in 1688. There is a detailed chronology in Appendix 24. Part III is an alphabetical reference section which explains or comments further on particular events and topics.

James VI/I, 1603 - 27 March 1625

Seventeenth-century Scotland began under an autocratic king determined to get his own way. A saving grace was that James threatened but did not use military force to impose his will, using instead the courts and docile organs of government to quiet or remove opponents. James was a determined man and adept at "kingcraft" as he called it, achieving his objectives of episcopacy and supremacy by cunning, deceit, and simple disregard of vociferous but otherwise peaceable churchmen.

His accession to the throne of England in 1603 presented a quite different set of challenges, however. His new realm was larger, more populated, wealthier, and had a presence on the international stage far greater than anything he had encountered in Scotland. He relished the wealth—which he exploited—and this was the basis of English resentment towards him. He discovered there were very severe social and economic problems with a population still largely rural, living in poverty, dependant largely on agriculture, and with vagrancy on the increase. On the religious front he found a strong undercurrent of Puritanism and nonconformity that was suspicious of ceremony and quasi-Catholic practices in the Episcopal Church of England.

The Court was the primary point of contact for the king and his subjects while Parliaments were occasional events, sometimes years apart. The monarch was the government. He was responsible for everything, and operated without any standing army or substantial civil service. Thus, much depended on persuasion and patronage, or reward for services rendered; this provided loyalty and service to the king, and prestige and wealth for the other person. But there was a growing movement for the king to consult with his advisers and with Parliament over legislation. Critically, Parliament was beginning to impose itself on the king through control of finances—itself dependent on the merchants of London. A consequence was that James (and his successors) became far more involved in politics in England than they had in Scotland. This contributed to the Scottish ministers and Privy Council being left to their own devices to implement the king's will.

The Church of England was well established, although there was a Puritan undercurrent that became increasingly focused on the fear of a return to popery. This was a holdover from wars with France and Spain, memories of the Spanish Armada and, in 1605, the Gunpowder Plot. A parallel concern was for the absolutism of the monarchy which people interpreted as going hand-in-hand with Catholicism. In Spain and France it had generated persecution, while in England John Foxe had produced his *Acts and Monuments*—the story of the martyrs during the rule of the Catholic Queen Mary, that fuelled popular concerns. The unease broke into the open in the 1630s with nonconformity and Puritanism to the fore, with moves against the episcopacy and Arminianism of Archbishop Laud and his cohorts

Meanwhile, in 1603, with a relatively splendid Court in London, James was also surrounded with new courtiers, their solicitations, vested interests, and misleading advice. As supreme governor of the Church of England he was attracted by the status, and by the Episcopal system which was consistent with his belief that the claimed equality of Presbyterian ministers could not compare with the monarchy in the State. He saw that bishops could give him a firm establishment in the three Estates of Parliament. Thus "uniformity" of religion in Britain became a word in his vocabulary. Sensing preferment and personal advantage, the Prelates simply flattered him in his desires, seeking to drain the milch cow he offered.

James was not a fool and he pursued his chimerical notion of "No Bishop, no King" by deceit and threat in order to give Scotland the hierarchy of the Church of England. He saw that to get his primary objective of absolute dominion he would have to destroy the infrastructure of Presbyterianism. This he did by removing the relative autonomy of the General Assembly, through breaking the continuity of their meetings. The Constant Moderators in 1606 gave him the opening for establishing bishops who could then establish their authority in Synod and Presbytery. They were his tools to impose absolute rule over the Church. M'Crie in *Life of Melville* records

> The immediate object of the King, by the changes that he made in the government of the Church, was to constitute himself Dictator in all matters of religion; and his ultimate object was, by means of the bishops, to overturn civil liberties of the nation, and to become an absolute master of the conscience, the properties, and lives of all his subjects in the three kingdoms.[1]

In the civil sphere James bragged at the opening of the English Parliament in 1607 that he ruled Scotland by the pen, while his acolytes on the Privy Council obeyed his will. This arrogance was misplaced and sounded a warning about what was to follow; it also sounded an alert to the English nonconformists. In England there had been a Presbyterian Church in Wandsworth since 1572 and a growing nonconformist population. The Puritans were seeking

---

[1] M'Crie, *Life of Melville*, Vol. 2, p. 472.

further reform of the Church of England and removal of Romish practices. In 1606 John Smyth and Thomas Helwys migrated to Amsterdam where, in 1609, the Baptist Church was founded. Helwys published his *Mistery of Iniquity* in 1612, which like the Presbyterians, insisted on the right of religious liberty. In 1620 the Puritan Pilgrim Fathers sailed to religious freedom in the American colonies.

By the end of James' reign the pot was bubbling away in England and Scotland. To this ferment his successors increasingly contributed with coercion of the clergy through the bishops, and the threat and, eventually, excessive use of military force to gain the compliance of the people.

With hindsight, a major event for the Presbyterians in James' reign, was the decision in 1607, to implement a Plantation in Ulster (1610-1630). For James it was an opportunity to secure his borders against possible French intervention through Ireland, to install a reasonably loyal Protestant yeoman militia as a bulwark against the demands of the indigenous Catholic majority, and, coincidentally, to provide a haven for troubled religious dissenters from Scotland.

Ministers of the Kirk followed the movement of the Scots to the Montgomery and Hamilton estates in Down and Antrim from 1607 and subsequently to the Scottish settlements in other counties. Among the earliest permanent ministers was Edward Bryce in 1613 to Broadisland; he was soon joined by Robert Cunningham at Holywood (1615), John Ridge at Antrim (1619), Josias Welch, the grandson of John Knox, at Templepatrick (1626), Robert Blair at Bangor (1623), and John Livingston at Killinchy (1630). These were the mainstays of the early Presbyterian church in Ulster who enjoyed a peaceful coexistence with the Church of Ireland until the resurgence of the Episcopalian bishops in 1632. The atmosphere changed significantly with the arrival of Sir Thomas Wentworth, later Earl of Strafford, as Lord Lieutenant.

Charles I, 1625 - 30 January 1649

There were many undercurrents at work concerning religion and the economic state of the country but Charles exacerbated matters by maintaining a closed court. Access to him personally was strictly limited which increased the isolation of his natural courtiers.

The perception certainly grew that he was greatly influenced by his Catholic wife, Henrietta Maria, whom he had married as part of the Anglo French Treaty of 1624. She kept her Catholic practices, established Catholic chapels, and a house of Capuchin monks in London. Increasingly there seemed to be more Catholic influence at Court, including the Papal agents Gregorio Panzani and George Con. Catholic chapels appeared at the residences of ambassadors which were open to the public. This only exacerbated the fears of people like John Pym, a prominent Member of Parliament, who had long suspected a return to Catholicism and absolutism.

Charles I pursued the same policies as his father but with greater force and venom in all of the three kingdoms. A false start was his revocation of land grants which put the nobility, the main holders of church lands, on alert. Officers of state were required to resign and be reappointed. A new Commission was appointed to hear grievances and a General Revocation ordered the return of all gifts and privileges from the Crown. This enabled annexation of the estates of the Catholic Church (about one-third of Scotland), and was used to rehabilitate the Church. Redistribution of the lands in feu ferme was the means of raising very considerable revenue for the Crown.[2] The aristocracy and other tenants were greatly disturbed by the declaration.

Archbishop William Laud

Archbishop William Laud. James King Hewison, *The Covenanters. A History of the Church in Scotland from the Reformation to the Revolution* (----: John Smith & Son, 1908; reprint Edmonton: Still Waters Revival Books, 1996).

---

[2] In feu ferme meant the sale of hereditary property with a large down payment and an annual rent.

The English Petition of Right in 1628, protesting against Charles' autocratic ways, marked a watershed in his relations with Parliament. With the cessation of war on the continent, he resorted to his "personal rule," treating Parliament with contempt. Aided by Archbishop Laud in England, Thomas Wentworth in Ireland, and a docile Privy Council in Scotland, Charles pursued his attack on the institution of the Presbyterian Church and nonconformity throughout the three kingdoms. This took the form of the Arminian policies of Archbishop Laud and his desire to restore "the beauty of Holiness."[3] The enforced changes included relocation of the altar and enclosing within rails, use of vestments, bowing at the name of Jesus, taking the Communion on the knees, stained glass windows in churches, and compulsory attendance at church with penalties in default. Further changes saw the status of clerics enhanced with their appointment to civil posts such as magistrates. The people, generally, resented the changes and the intervention of bishops in their life style. This gave rise to the "root and branch" petitions of 1640 that sought the abolition of episcopacy in England. There soon followed a "Grand Remonstrance" in 1641 and Charles' attempt to arrest the five members (including the leader of the Puritan opposition, John Pym) in 1642. This farce ended in the raising of the royal standard at Nottingham in August 1643 and civil war.

In Scotland, the appointment of bishops to the Privy Council in 1634 indicated the way things were going as conformity and uniformity were forced on the church and then the people. There soon followed Laud's Liturgy in 1637, Jenny Geddes' stool flying through the air in St. Giles Cathedral, the National Covenant in 1638, and the General Assembly in Glasgow in the same year. Charles was probably ill-advised about the strength of feeling in Scotland and his proclamation in February 1639 to the northern shires of England that the Scots intended to invade was a mistake. The people were aware that Parliament did not approve of, nor had it subsidised, the planned war. As a consequence, the people reluctantly assembled and the war chest had little money in it. In the event the two Bishops Wars ended in stalemate with Charles obliged to negotiate treaties. The wars gained nothing except

---

[3] Psalm 96:8.

acrimony and led to renewal of civil war in England, which in turn spilled over into all the three kingdoms.

In Ulster, the bishops of the Episcopal Church of Ireland shrugged off the accommodation that had existed for two decades under a benevolent Archbishop Ussher and began to insist on compliance with episcopacy. This resulted in several prominent ministers—Blair and Livingston among them—being forced to return to Scotland. The imposition of the Black Oath in 1639 placed a strangle hold on the nonconformist churches and their ministers. The harsh policies of Wentworth, who had sought to relocate the influential Presbyterians to Kilkenny and Tipperary, extended to the land owners who risked forfeiture of their estates if they could not prove ownership. This included the Old English settlers who had difficulty in proving their title from Elizabethan times, which contributed to their joining with the Irish in the later rebellion. The disruption caused by these policies and general unease in Scotland because of the Bishops Wars, encouraged rebellion and the resultant massacres of Protestants in 1641. Wentworth further compounded matters by raising an army ready for use by Charles on the mainland. Sir John Clotworthy, a wealthy Ulster settler, reported to the English Parliament in November1640 that there were two armies in Ireland. The new one was 10,000 strong, well paid, and mainly Catholics, and the old Protestant army that was a year in arrears of pay. Wentworth was impeached within days and charged with treason.

> [H]e had a design to bring over the Irish army into England.... [P]opery had flourished during his rule in Ireland without constraint, he had stirred up enmity between England and Scotland and had incensed the king against parliaments.[4]

The civil wars, mainly in England, were Charles' downfall, although a brilliant campaign by the Marquis of Montrose through 1644 and into 1645 almost had Scotland on its knees. The battle of Naseby on 14 June 1645 settled the military issues and in May 1646

[4] Anthony Fletcher, *The Outbreak of the English Civil War* (London: Edward Arnold, 1981), pp. 13-14.

Charles surrendered to the Scottish army, anticipating that they were more likely to leave his head on his shoulders.

Handed over to the Parliamentarians on payment of the Scottish army's costs, Charles became the guest of the New Model Army. Oliver Cromwell was now leading a "Godly Army" with the troops supplied with a copy of the Soldiers Catechism. Charles eventually escaped to the Isle of Wight where he was approached, in December 1647, by Scottish nobles led by the Duke of Hamilton. The meeting resulted in an agreement called "The Engagement," which was an ill-advised attempt to recover his English Crown by force using Scottish troops.

The Covenanters had been greatly heartened by the outcome of the Westminster Assembly, and the prospects of spreading Presbyterianism as the approved church in the rest of Britain. However, the agreement under the Solemn League and Covenant was, by 1648, starting to crumble because the English people were not prepared to be coerced into a particular religion. The declaration of war by Scotland in April 1648—a consequence of the Engagement—was almost a flag waving exercise for Charles and ended in a crushing defeat at the battle of Preston on 19 August 1648. The Duke of Hamilton was executed while Cromwell entered Edinburgh and imposed martial law. In England, on 4 January 1649, the House of Commons convened a High Court of Justice to try Charles. He was found guilty, despite a valiant defence, and executed on 30 January 1649.

The Second Reformation

A consequence of the Engagement and the defeat at Preston was the short lived but crowning event of the Second Reformation which had begun with the establishment of the Tables in 1637. This was true clerical rule by the Covenanters in Scotland. It was achieved in 1648 following the Whiggamore Raid in September of that year, when the staunch Covenanters ejected the defeated "Engagers" and took control of government. It nominally lasted until 1651 when Charles II was crowned, but the Kirk was again divided between moderates and staunch Covenanters.

This period of civil rule under strict Covenanted principles was both a great success for the Kirk but also a disaster in the making.

One of its first acts was the Act of Classes of 23 Jan 1649 which purged the Scottish army and the civil government of so called "malignants" and Engagers. Among these were many experienced soldiers whose value would later be realised. The next problem for the Covenanters was the execution of Charles I and his succession in Scotland. Perhaps naively, they resented the execution of a Scottish king by the English (although he was their king too) and promptly declared his son the lawful heir to the thrones of Britain, France, and Ireland on 5 Feb 1649. This was in effect a declaration of war.

In support of this declaration, the Scots Parliament passed an Act requiring the king and successors to subscribe to Covenants, and seeking uniformity of religion (Presbytery) in the three kingdoms. This was the substance of the negotiations that then took place with the new king Charles II in Holland, and resulted in the Declaration at Breda of 1 May 1650.

In England, the House of Commons had issued three ground breaking resolutions that established democratic government, and sent a clear message to Charles that the old ways of his father were no more,

> That the Commons of England in Parliament assembled do declare that the people under God are the original of all just power.
>
> They do likewise declare, that the Commons of England assembled in Parliament being chosen by, and representing the people, have the supreme authority of this nation.
>
> They do likewise declare, that whatsoever is enacted and declared law by the Commons of England, assembled in Parliament, hath the force of law; and all the people of this nation are included thereby, although the consent and concurrence of the King and the House of Peers be not had thereunto.

Charles II, 1649-1651

The proclamation of Charles II as king on 5 February 1649 predicated a national war between Scotland and England.

In England, the Parliament was also a purged body, although rather less obedient to the Council of State. As a result, government fell to a series of committees whose recommendations were seldom questioned. Oliver Cromwell, MP, member of the Council of State, sat on many of these committees including the one which decided on war with Scotland. Lord Fairfax did not feel that he could continue as Commander-in-Chief of the Army if Parliament were bent on invading Scotland and offered his resignation. On June 24, Cromwell was appointed Lord General and a new momentum was injected into the Parliamentarian cause. Cromwell crossed the Tweed on July 22 with a force of 10,500 foot and 5,500 horse, and advanced unopposed. The Scottish army withdrew in the face of the Cromwell-led army, while the Church instituted a purge.

Some Scottish officers refused to serve the king unless he clarified his intentions and subordinated himself to God. Caught between "a rock and a hard place" Charles had little option but to accept the harsh terms of a Declaration made at Dumfries on 16 August 1650. This declaration greatly humbled him for the opposition of his father to the Covenants and his mother's idolatry, and acknowledged that he had no ill design in signing the Covenant; annulled an Irish Treaty that he had made with the Duke of Ormond, and promised to promote the Covenant in England and to pass an Act of Oblivion for all except obstructers of the Reformation, traitors and regicides. This public humiliation of Charles and insults to his parents would be remembered and revenged after the Restoration in 1660.

The battle at Dunbar on 3 September 1650 shattered the Scots and Cromwell advanced into Edinburgh on September 7. However, Cromwell still did not control north of the Tay and was not yet master of all Scotland. As a result of this vacuum, Charles saw the opportunity to press his case for support to return to England and claim his crown.

The Western Alliance, a military alliance in the western shires led by Colonels Strachan and Gilbert Ker, objected to the king's duplicity and made *The Humble Remonstrance of the Gentlemen, Commanders, and Ministers, attending the Forces in the West* to the Estates on 17 October 1650. Quoted in Hewison's *Covenanters*, this attributed the Lord's Wrath to:

> The admission of Charles to the Covenant without proof of his professions.
>
> Provoking God by the hasty conclusion of the Treaty and Charles stood disclosed of 'unstraight dealings'
>
> The King's actions in conjunction with Montrose, other malignants and Papists against the work of God and the Covenant.
>
> The unjust proposals to invade England to take booty and force a king on an independent nation.
>
> Backsliding from the Covenants, neglecting to fill public offices with the godly and tolerating malignants.
>
> The sins of covetousness, extortion, self seeking, and trust in the flesh instead of in God.[5]

But their protest was rejected and the forces of the Western Alliance were defeated at Hamilton on 1 December 1650 by the English General John Lambert.

Yet again, internal dissent between factions of the Kirk resulted in schism, this time among the moderate Resolutioners, who sought to ease the restrictions of the Act of Classes of January 1649, and allow some previously banned or "malignants" to return to the army and government. Those against this dilution were the strictest Covenanters who were now labelled Protesters. The Committee of Estates with more royalist supporters, sided with the Resolutioners, making resumption of war with Cromwell inevitable. But first there was the coronation of Charles II.

Prolonged negotiations with Charles had taken place at Breda during which time he was also actively planning revenge for his father's death. By cunning and guile he deceived the Scottish Commissioners, having already commissioned the Marquis of Montrose on 2 February 1650 to be Governor of Scotland. Charles played for time in anticipation that Montrose could continue his earlier glorious run of battles and whip up the kingdom into an acceptance of his cause to regain the English Crown. A failed rising in the Highlands, the defeat and capture of Montrose, and prompt execution exposed the king as duplicitous. He asserted that he had ordered Montrose to withdraw on May 15 but Argyll produced

---

[5] Hewison, *Covenanters*, Vol. 2, p. 22.

evidence that Lord Lothian, the Secretary of State, wrote to him that the king was in no way sorry that Montrose had invaded.

Despite the exposure of the king's duplicity and the warnings given by John Livingston, who had serious reservations about the king's sincerity since Breda, the Covenanters continued to negotiate. King Charles II arrived in Speymouth on 23 June 1650 on board the ship *Skidam* of Amsterdam.

Prevaricating and dissembling to the very end, Charles was forced to subscribe the Covenants before landing on the Scottish shore. He arrived with a retinue of malignants who were compelled to stay on board but he continued to Edinburgh with a select number including Buckingham, Wentworth, Wilmot, Sir Edward Walker, and Chiffinch. Those forbidden to land until they had given satisfaction to the Church and State made a roll call of future persecutors and revenge takers in 1660: Hamilton, Lauderdale, Seaforth, Callendar, Forth, Dumfries, St. Clair, Napier, Sir Robert Dalziel, Thomas Dalziel of the Binns, Lockhart, Charteris of Amisfield, Monro, and Cochrane.

Scone Palace, Scone, Scotland. Photo courtesy of A. C. Orr.

The coronation was held at Scone on 1 January 1651 amid much pomp and ceremony; for the first time laymen proffered the symbols of sovereignty. The Coronation Oath was sworn, the crown was placed on Charles' head by Argyll, and the Earl of Crawford and Lindsay placed the sceptre in his hand. The following day Charles began his secret policy of revenging himself on the murderers of his father. He discounted advice to "treat with Cromwell for one half his cloak before he lost the whole"[6] and levies were raised. At the Parliament at Perth on March 13 he was appointed head of the Army, a patriotic manifesto encouraging the people to rise in arms was issued, and a War Committee was appointed. In June, the Act of Classes was repealed.

Stirling Castle. Photo courtesy of the author.

Cromwell, meanwhile, had been facing the Scottish Army under David Leslie, in his stronghold at Stirling. But fortunes changed when General Lambert defeated the Scots at Inverkeithing on 20 July 1651 where 2,000 Scots died and 1,400 were taken prisoner. This enabled Cromwell to cross the Forth and march on Perth, and left the way open for Leslie to head into England. He did not know that Cromwell and the Council of State had ordered the mobilisation and movement of the English southern armies. On July 31 Charles, General Leslie, and 20,000 men left Stirling for Carlisle. Argyll and

---

[6] Hewison, *Covenanters*, Vol. 2, p. 30.

the Covenanters, who paradoxically favoured conciliation with Cromwell, stood by and watched the new army of penitents march to its unhappy end.

The Scottish royalist army did not get as much help as they had hoped for in England and by August 22 were at Worcester wondering where to go next. Charles seemingly decided to make a stand at Worcester in the hope that he would be joined by supporters from Wales and the southwest. A manifesto declaring for the Covenant was issued with promise of an Act of Oblivion for all except those involved in the regicide. Cromwell meanwhile had marched his army the length of the country and reached Evesham on August 27, thus cutting off the royalists from London. With his other armies in close order they outnumbered the royalist two to one. The annihilation of the Scottish army was complete on September 3. After some six weeks' wandering Charles arrived in France on October 16 where the Pope would not grant him aid unless he converted to Romanism.

While Cromwell had headed south to deal with the Scots at Worcester, General Monck had taken Stirling in August and had turned with seven thousand seasoned troops to take Dundee. A bold dash by eight hundred horsemen under Colonel Matthew Alured seized the Committee of Estates at Alyth on August 28. With virtually the whole government of Scotland heading south under guard, Monck demanded the surrender of Dundee. This was rejected by the Scottish General Robert Lumsden and the city was sacked with much killing and looting on September 1. The other strongholds north of the Tay soon followed, with Blackness Castle blown up and Dunnottar besieged.

In England, Parliament approved the proprietorship (conquest) of the Commonwealth in Scotland and appointed a Committee of twenty-one persons, including Cromwell, to govern the two conquered kingdoms. Scotland was totally subjugated and fortunate to be treated with a rare humanity which allowed a degree of freedom unusual in a defeated nation.

Oliver Cromwell, 1653 - 3 September 1658

Cromwell (Lord Protector 1653-3 September 1658) enforced peace and toleration of most faiths in Scotland, Ireland, and

England. In practice, this was quite lenient towards Catholics and Episcopalians. The Covenanters were unhappy at the toleration of Catholics and other Sectaries but in simple truth they had little choice in the matter. Toleration was confirmed in an Instrument of Government issued in December 1653.

Scotland actually enjoyed a period of relative peace and unparalleled justice when English judges, taking action against malpractices, cleansed the administration of the law. The bickering between Resolutioners and Protesters, and setting up of two church authorities was brought to an end by the dissolution of both of the rival General Assemblies by the military in July 1653. In Ireland the plans to transport leading Presbyterians to Kilkenny and Tipperary were stopped, while land confiscation and reallocation for payment of military service became an issue that continued into the Restoration and beyond. General George Monck (later Duke of Albemarle), was appointed viceroy in Scotland. On 4 May 1654 he proclaimed the establishment of the Protectorate and the integration of Scotland as part of the Commonwealth.

An Ordinance of 8 August 1654 for the settlement of the Church sought to create a Commission of Triers, which was implemented on August 29.[7] Their role was to confirm that preachers were capable and certified by four or more ministers and elders in each of five districts. This was eventually accepted by the Resolutioners (the moderate party) which included Douglas, Dickson, Wood, Hutchison, Smith, and James Sharp. They later gained John Livingston and Patrick Gillespie to the moderate cause. However, the Protesters, including Gillespie, Warriston, and James Guthrie were opposed to the Ordinance on the grounds of Erastianism, offering only further purges as a solution.

In England, Cromwell noted that Presbyterianism had failed to become established there. His secretary, the poet John Milton, tellingly wrote in *On the New forces of Conscience under the Long Parliament* (1646), that "New Presbyter is but Old Priest writ large."[8] This was the English view of Presbyterianism, in a country that was already well-endowed with other nonconformists, and a

---

[7] This commission was made up of people who acted in roles similar to those of examiners or judges.

[8] John C. Johnston, *Treasury of the Scottish Covenant* (Edinburgh: Andrew Elliott, 1887), p. 307.

growing desire for a less rigid organisation and doctrine. The system of classes, as the courts were called, begun in 1646, had not been enforced in the country as a whole, the people preferring a laxer discipline than either Presbytery or the Independents. By 1653 it was clear that the English people were not prepared to be forced into any one denomination.

The second Parliament of Cromwell in 1657 resolved that the Scriptures should be the rule of faith; believers in the Trinity and the Scriptures should not suffer any disability unless they were Popish, prelatic, profligate, or blasphemous persons. This was accepted by Cromwell and the Rump Parliament in 1659. But the next Parliament reverted to the Confession of Faith, enacting that the Solemn League and Covenant should be read annually and hung up in every parish church. The last General Assembly in England met in May 1659. At this time James Sharp became the representative of the Resolutioners in London, beginning his lying, conniving, self aggrandisement such that, in 1659, he was told by the government to stop meddling in public affairs and "to keep within the compass of his own calling."[9] He did not do so because he went as an unauthorised representative to see Charles in Breda.

Cromwell died on 3 September 1658 and was succeeded by his son, Richard, who was forced to resign in 1659. A faction of the army invited the Rump Parliament to return, rejected it in May, and invited it back on 26 December 1659. In Scotland, General Monck watched the growing farce in England and on January 1 he marched south with 6,000 troops arriving in London on 3 February 1660. Parliament, which included the Presbyterians ousted in Pride's Purge, voted for its own dissolution on 16 March 1660. With it went the last serious opportunity to pursue the establishment of Presbyterianism in England. The English elections that followed were in favour of a monarchy and the laxer regimes of the Church of England.

---

[9] Hewison, *Covenanters*, Vol. 2, p. 56.

Restoration of Charles II, 1660 - 6 February 1685

In exile, Charles watched carefully and contacted sympathisers. On 4 April 1660 he signed another Declaration of Breda setting out his terms:

> offering a general pardon except for any not so exempted by Parliament;
> declared a free Parliament;
> a liberty to tender consciences—freedom of religion that did not disturb the peace of the kingdom;
> to allow Parliament to settle disputes over confiscated estates used to pay soldiers;

And, in effect invited Parliament to set its own terms.[10]

On 1 May 1660 the English House of Commons resolved to return to a monarchy, but this time to a limited, constitutional one.

> That this House doth agree with the Lords and do own and declare, that, according to the antient and fundamental laws of this Kingdom, the Government is, and ought to be, by Kings, Lords and Commons.[11]

A vengeful Charles II landed at Dover on 25 May 1660, quickly seeking out and executing former opponents including the Marquis of Argyll; Archibald Johnston, Lord Warriston, and James Guthrie. He pursued the Divine Right principles, and the Episcopal and Erastian policies of his predecessors, resorting to the use of Star Chamber and High Commission Courts to force his will on all three kingdoms. Under his "Personal Rule" Charles bent, if not broke, all the rules to finance his schemes, simply ignoring the will of Parliament until war made him "toe the line" (at least for a while). Hewison, in *Covenanters,* says that:

---

[10] *Ibid.* These terms had been suggested to Charles II by General Monck as the basis for his return.

[11] Charles Grant Robertson, *Select Statutes, Cases, and Documents* (London: Methuen & Co., Ltd., 1904), p. 1.

> time showed him to be a person who concealed his true motives and objectives behind plausible manners and expedient acts of relative kindness. Promises were a convenience to be shamefully broken if and when necessary. He inherited his father's genius for hypocrisy and his grandfathers' inability to understand that his subjects had rights as well as rulers.[12]

Immediate legislation in Scotland was made under the gaze of the Earl of Middleton as the King's Commissioner. On 6 September 1661 a royal proclamation at the Mercat Cross announced the abolition of Presbytery because of "the unsuitableness thereof to his Majesty's monarchical estate."[13] This imposed episcopacy forbade clerical courts, ordered magistrates to gaol nonconformists, and installed the bishops in Parliament. But the cleverest act was a prohibition on making representations which very neatly denied a mechanism for the redress of grievances. If a complaint was made it could be regarded as a criminal offence and result in imprisonment at least. By policies of divide and rule, over three hundred dissenting ministers were ejected from their livings in Scotland by the Act of Collation and Presentation (1662).

It should be remembered, however, that about two-thirds of the ministers in Scotland *accepted* the king's terms so the dissenters were always a minority. It has been calculated that 72 of the 952 ministerial charges were vacant and that 329 were deprived and 551 complied. The result was that, throughout the turbulent years until the Revolutionary Settlement, curates filled the vacancies, becoming a source of severe irritation in many parishes by their domineering and uncouth ways.

The curates were despised for their spying on the congregations, reporting non attendance at the parish church, and seeking enforcement of fines by the military forces. The collection of fines and quartering of troops on non-payers was a brutal and expensive process that ruined many small farmers and heritors.

In England, the early promise of a compromise and a watered down episcopacy that might have enabled some Presbyterians to

---

[12] Hewison, *Covenanters*, Vol. 2, p. 60.

[13] *Ibid.*, p. 134.

comply was lost. The resulting Act of Uniformity was given the Royal Assent on 19 May 1662 and sealed the fate of the nonconformists. About 2,000 nonconformist (mainly Puritan and Independents) ministers were ejected in England on Black St. Bartholomew's Day, 24 October 1662.

In Ulster sixty-four ministers had already been forced from their manses in 1661, and seven were excommunicated and banished to Scotland. Another four were incarcerated in Carlingford Castle for six years simply because they were Presbyterians. The cause of the Presbyterians was not helped by a failed rebellion in 1663 by a Captain Blood, the brother-in-law of Rev. William Lecky, a Presbyterian minister. The plot was betrayed and Blood escaped. Two other alleged conspirators, Rev. John Crookshanks and Rev. Andrew McCormick, fled to Scotland and were killed at the battle of Rullion Green in 1666. William Lecky was tried and executed, and another seventeen ministers were imprisoned on suspicion alone that they may have known about the attempted rebellion. In 1665, the Irish Parliament directed the adoption of the English Liturgy and ordered that ministers must be ordained according to the Episcopalian rite by 29 September 1667 or be disqualified from having an ecclesiastical benefice. Nonconformist ministers were liable to a fine of one hundred pounds if they celebrated the Communion. Despite the ongoing attacks by the Episcopalian bishops, the civil government gradually softened its approach and by 1670 some tolerance of meeting places and kirk attendance had appeared.

In Scotland the first armed resistance was the Pentland Rising in November 1666 which ended in defeat for the Covenanters at Rullion Green. By the 1670s oppression of dissenting ministers and their congregations was grave, with armed resistance becoming the norm for the illegal conventicles. The government became concerned at the apparent lack of support for the church and took measures to enforce attendance, making landlords liable for their tenants.

The apostate James Sharp, now Archbishop of St. Andrews, was the prime persecutor, who blatantly used the revived Court of High Commission to pursue the ministers. His regime deviously obtained evidence of ecclesiastical wrong-doing which was given to the civil justiciary as evidence of a civil crime. The object was to secure a greater penalty for a civil wrong, usually the death penalty.

Alexander Smellie, in *Men of the Covenant*, tells of letters misrepresenting the king's views and of a message to Lauderdale in 1660. The message exposed Sharp's hatred of the Protester or Covenanted party and his overwhelming betrayal of his former colleagues. The message said:

> I fear there can be no remedy against this malady without exercising severity upon the leading impostors, Guthiree, Gillespy, Rutherford which will daunt the rest of the hottheads, who may in time may be beat into sound minds and sobre practices.[14]

Even more damning was a letter to Middleton of 21 May 1661, the King's Commissioner in Scotland, that Sharp was

> holding constant interviews with Lord Clarendon and the English Bishops; that the subject was the establishment of Episcopacy in Scotland; and that the project had his hearty approval.[15]

He was assassinated on Magus Moor on 3 May 1679.

The Battle of Drumclog on 1 June 1679 was the only battle won by the Covenanters; soon after they were destroyed at Bothwell Brig on June 22 when disputes about the Indulgences divided them. Exactly a year later Richard Cameron, in his Declaration at Sanquhar on 22 June 1680, advocated armed resistance. But the "Lion of the Covenant" as he has been called, was killed at Airsmoss on 22 July 1680. Also taken at Airsmoss was David Hackston who had been at Magus Moor when Archbishop Sharp was murdered; he was made to suffer hanging, drawing and quartering.

---

[14] Alexander Smellie, *Men of the Covenant* (London: A. Melrose, 1903), p. 107.
[15] *Ibid.*

Hewison, in *Covenanters*, relates that the position of a Presbyterian in the latter years was not to be envied: "He was liable to be thrown into prison and kept there an indefinite time."[16]

Charged with any offence by any person, who might depart from the accusation, fined, imprisoned, or banished:

> for not attending church,
> for sheltering or speaking to any rebel,
> for refusing to give satisfactory information regarding suspects,
> for listening to field preachers,
> for being one of five (or more) strangers at a prayer meeting,
> for whispering against or criticising the Government,
> for refusing to take the oath of loyalty,
> for refusing to own Episcopacy,
> for crossing the parish boundary to hear the neighbouring incumbent.
> Preacher and layman alike were liable to the death penalty for convening or praying at any outdoor meeting, such as a funeral gathering, unless they had licences.[17]

The 1680s, and especially 1684-1685, became the "Killing Time" when many Presbyterians died for their faith on the gallows at the Grassmarket, Edinburgh. In the countryside, Christians were arbitrarily shot in the fields or hung merely for reading a Bible or holding particular opinions and beliefs.

James II, 1685-1690

The death of Charles II in February 1685 brought his brother James to the throne, although he was never officially crowned king of Scotland. That did not stop him pursuing his own policies of seeking to reinstate popery. The pressures were increased on the Covenanters by the introduction of more Indulgences, stricter enforcement against conventicles, and an increased military

---

[16] Hewison, *Covenanters*, Vol. 2, p. 236.
[17] *Ibid.*

presence which further isolated the faithful remnant. The Covenanters responded with James Renwick's "Admonitory Vindication" which advocated retaliation against informers. The consequent Abjuration Oath was designed specifically to test support for Renwick and was the tool used by the military forces for extending the persecution. Refusal to take the oath rejecting the Admonitory Vindication was cause for instant execution, legally in the presence of two witnesses, but it was not always so.

The Killing Time was at its height between December 1684 and May 1685 when many met an untimely end in the countryside. It is possible that the killings reflected the great concern for a revolt that would join with the impending return of the 9th Earl of Argyll from Holland. But the situation may also have been eased by Renwick's *Protestation and Apologetical Admonitory Declaration* which, tucked away at the end, included a rejection of association with Sectarians, Malignancy, "and any Confederacy therewith."[18] This strong hint that the "faithful remnant" would not join with Argyll may have forestalled further executions.

It is also likely that the long memories of the ministers recalled that, after the Pentland Rising, the young Argyll had been of the government and anti-Covenanter. He had written to Lauderdale that

> The outed ministers that medled in the late Rebellion I think deserve torture, while those who refused submission should be put wher ther needs no troops to suppress them.[19]

Argyll, meanwhile, landed at Campbelltown in Kintyre on May 20 but there was little support. He was captured on June 18 and executed, as his father before him, by beheading with "the Maiden" (the guillotine) in Edinburgh on 30 June 1685.

James II, was an overt Catholic who turned to the exercise of his discretion and toleration as the device that allowed both Catholics and Presbyterians greater freedom of religion. In Ireland, the Catholics had great expectations of King James and were soon receiving appointments in government at all levels and even in the

---

[18] Campbell, *Standing Witnesses* (Edinburgh: Saltire Society, 1996), p. 23. See Appendix 17.

[19] Hewison, *Covenanters*, Vol. 2, p. 202.

English army. This alarmed many and was exacerbated by James' Declaration of Indulgence, which gave religious freedom for all, including the Catholics. A cause celebre at the time was the imprisonment of the seven English bishops who refused to allow the Indulgence to be proclaimed from the pulpit of the churches. They were sent to the Tower but later acquitted.

To an extent James was himself tolerated because the expectation was that the throne would pass to his daughter Mary, a known Protestant. Matters were brought to a head when a son, James Edward (the Old Pretender) was born 10 June 1688. This generated a fear of a Catholic succession that resulted in both England and Scotland inviting William of Orange and his wife Mary (daughter of James II) to take the throne. James hoped for support to emerge but when it did, in the form of John Graham of Claverhouse and 6,000 troops outside London, he created Claverhouse Viscount Dundee, but gave him no orders and then took himself to exile in France.

The interregnum lasted from 11 December 1688 to 13 February 1689.

William and Mary, 1688-1694; William III, 1688-1702

William, Prince of Orange, and Mary accepted the offered throne.[20] William was a very able politician and a soldier who had, for many years, been the mainstay of Protestantism on the continent against the Catholic League bent on extirpation; and the aggrandising policies of Louis XIV of France that threatened Holland. He was careful to make clear his reasons for accepting the thrones in a Declaration of October 1688. William landed at Brixham, in the west of England on 5 November 1688 accompanied by 14,000 troops (referred to by some as his "Butterboxes"). On December 19 he was safely ensconced in St. James' Palace, London.

William summoned a Convention of English legislators that met on 22 January 1689, and concluded that James II had "violated fundamental laws"[21] and abdicated the Government, thus the throne

---

[20] William was known as William III after his accession to the throne.

[21] Hewison, *Covenanters*, Vol. 2, p. 520.

was vacant. The House of Commons and the Lords were united in offering the throne to William and Mary as joint sovereigns. Importantly, the sovereignty issue for the first time became the matter of a vote by Parliament and cast out the principle of divine right.

The Scottish Convention of the Estates was summoned by a letter and assembled in Edinburgh on 14 March 1689. Although a very representative assembly, many of the supporters of James soon departed, including Dundee who marched to Edinburgh Castle to speak to the Duke of Gordon, a Papist and royalist, who still commanded it. Having done so, Dundee and his troops hurried from the city. The castle was surrendered, Dundee declared a rebel, and Catholic supporters were arrested and imprisoned. The country was called to arms. On April 3 a Committee of the Convention made proposals for the settlement of Government on the basis that James had forfeited the throne. The next day the Estates agreed to the proposal. The offer of the crown to William and Mary, and the Claim of Right, were agreed on April 11 and the new joint sovereigns declared at the Mercat Cross. The formal parliament which met on 5 June 1689 ratified the action taken; the bishops did not attend.

William was tolerant of all forms of religion and saw no reason to force beliefs on anyone. This predicated that he would not force Presbyterianism on England and Ireland notwithstanding the Solemn League and Covenant. Moreover, when proffered the Coronation Oath he specifically questioned the persecuting clause "to root out all heresies and enemies to the true worship of God" and said "I will not lay myself under any obligation to be a persecutor."[22] The deputies, Sir James Montgomery and Sir John Dalrymple, reassured him that the formula implied no obligation, to which William replied, "In that sense then, I swear,"[23] and both sovereigns signed the oath.

William's toleration was reflected in his instructions to Melville, the King's Commissioner at the Scottish Parliament which assembled on 15 April 1690. Melville read the king's letter which assured the Estates of his affection and care in relation to the

---

[22] *Ibid.*, p. 525.
[23] *Ibid.*

establishment of Church Government "agreeable to the inclinations of the people."[24] However, William chose to follow a broader, more liberal, approach instructing Melville to adjust the religious settlement according to "that interest is strongest."[25] Significantly, at this time the members of Parliament, as well as its Commissioner, were predominantly moderates.

The concerns and representations of the "faithful remnant," presented by Alexander Shields, were peremptorily and disgracefully rejected by the Committee of the General Assembly and did not even get heard by the body of the House. The result was that the new Charter of Presbyterianism was passed in an "Act ratifying the Confession of Faith and settling Presbyterian Church Government" on 7 June 1690 which had some glaring omissions that were regarded as critical by the Cameronians or Society people.

Parliament ratified the Westminster Confession of Faith, which had been previously ratified in 1649, and Presbyterian government of the Church was established according to the 1592 Great Charter of Presbytery. This was a stumbling block for the Covenanters because it omitted any reference to the work that had been done by the Second Reformation, 1638-1650. Moreover, it made no reference to either the National Covenant of 1638 or the Solemn League and Covenant of 1643. The detestable Act of Supremacy was repealed but the Act Recissory of 1661 (which had annulled the Second Reformation) was left on the statute book, as were the offending slurs that condemned the Covenanted oaths as unlawful and the General Assembly of 1638 as seditious. If that was not enough, the king's *instruction* to Commissioner Melville was Erastianism at work.

The outcome for the Covenanters was another great struggle of conscience. Presbyterianism had been restored but not all the perceived wrongs of the persecutions had been righted: the Covenants had been neglected, prelacy had not been condemned as unscriptural, and the divine right of Presbytery had not been asserted. Worse was to follow as a consequence of expediency. There were only sixty ministers remaining from those ejected in 1662 and almost nine hundred nominal vacancies in the new

---

[24] *Ibid.*, p. 539.
[25] *Ibid.*

Church. The inevitable happened with the acceptance of most of the incumbents: the tolerated and Indulged, and some curates detested by the Covenanters.

The renewal of the Covenants at Borland Hill, Lesmahagow, on 3 March 1689 had re-focused the minds of the Covenanters; it was a "make or break" decision for them, both as individuals and as a dissenting group. There were some who crossed the divide and returned to the established Church. However, the Cameronians and Society people generally chose to remain outside the established church with their non-ecclesiastical organisation until 1743 when the Reformed Presbytery was formed.

James fled to France and aspired to continue his fight for the throne in Ireland where he reappeared in 1690 supported by Irish Catholics and French troops. William recognised the danger of a Catholic driven offensive and was soon on his way there, landing at Carrickfergus with his troops on June 14. James' hopes were crushed at the Battle of the Boyne on 1 July 1690 and he returned to exile in France. The Treaty of Limerick on 3 October 1691 accepted William as King of Ireland.

The Presbyterians in Ulster were disappointed. As a constitutional monarch William could not do all that he wished for them. He was able only to influence existing law while the Episcopalian Irish Bishops, who held a majority in the Irish House of Lords, continued their vindictive actions. Despite this, by 1702 there were nine Presbyteries under three sub synods of Belfast, Monaghan, and Lagan, and an annual Synod that met in June.

A much larger problem was the Test Act in 1704 which required holders of public office to take the Holy Communion according to the Episcopalian rites. Many Presbyterians lost their office, while the majority of alderman and burgesses in Belfast and Londonderry were also forced to step down. Throughout the province, public office holders such as magistrates, postmasters, and town councillors were ejected for their faith. Marriages by Presbyterian ministers were void and many paid lip service to the Episcopal Church of Ireland out of necessity. There was also a positive discrimination by landlords who were encouraged to charge Presbyterians higher rents, they were banned from being school teachers, the leases for church lands prohibited letting to a Presbyterian tenant or building of a Presbyterian church, and, in the towns of Antrim, Downpatrick, and Rathfriland, the doors of the churches were actually nailed shut to prevent services being held.

Not until the reign of King George I (1714-1727) did things begin to improve with a Toleration Act passed in 1719, which exempted ministers from penalties for celebration of their worship. But the Test Act remained in force until 1780 and was a major reason why so many Presbyterians migrated in the eighteenth century. By the eve of the American Revolution more than a quarter of a million Ulster Scots, or Scots-Irish, had chosen to go to the American colonies in search of freedom from discrimination and religious persecution.

Epilogue

The inestimable benefit of hindsight rather begs the questions: Was it all worth it? Was it necessary for the Covenanters to be so obdurate? Could a compromise have been affected? Who was to blame for 130 years of agony and oppression?

There is no easy answer and we have to make up our own minds on this. On the one hand the dedication and commitment unto death of the Covenanters and the Society people draws great admiration, yet their adherence to a “black and white” creed of absolute definitions and, for many, an almost paranoid dislike of popery, was their choice and ultimately their undoing. But that does not mean they were wrong. They had opposed and, through great trials, overcame those who despised God’s Word; they fought and overcame the opponents of the Church and the breakers of its constitution, and they assiduously stated and re-stated their basic principles through the medium of the Covenants. They maintained throughout a purity and clarity of conscience which is difficult to comprehend in our modern society so given to political correctness and compromise. But at the crucial time in 1690 they did not have the leaders of the Knox and Melville mould to take up the cudgels again: to secure the Catechism and Directory, the right to call its own Assemblies, or to loudly protest against the Erastian settlement which stemmed from King Williams *instruction* to his Commissioner, Melville. Moreover, William opened the doors to conforming Episcopalians, which was an act of toleration, and inconsistent with the declaration that prelacy was "an insupportable grievance."[26]

At the Revolution the Covenanters only got part of their desires—with Popery and Prelacy overcome—but were finally frustrated by a king who was latitudinarian and allowed the majority's wishes to rule the day. Today we might glibly say that is the price of democracy, but the Covenanters were shamefully treated by the General Assembly when their representations were rejected out of hand and ultimately deserted by their ministers, Linning, Boyd, and Shields. Thus the "faithful remnant" were still what they had always been, a minority outside the Church of Scotland on points of principle. It leaves a nagging question what would have happened if they had simply been allowed to be a sect outside the established church in the first place? If James VI had had sufficient vision and grace to allow that, Scotland might have been spared so much pain.

It is difficult to find a good word to say about the prelates who were generally self-seeking, self-aggrandising individuals remote from the people. Moreover, their behaviour fuelled the fears that diocesan Episcopacy was but a short step from Popery. There were charitable and reasonably good men among them such as Archbishop Leighton who tried hard, but unsuccessfully, to achieve compromise, becoming so disgusted that he retired from office. The bishops generally were guilty of silence and lacked moral fibre to protest against the doings of their colleagues; but self-preservation, status, and a regular income are strong motivators. History, however, turns the spotlight on the vile, the vindictive, and the dissolute such as Bishop Paterson, the Archbishops Laud and Sharp, and their personal agendas. The misconduct of Sharp, Laud, and the nobility, such as John Leslie, Duke of Rothes, a coarse, illiterate and greedy boor, was gross. While others indulged in excesses of one kind or another, such as Thomas Wentworth, Earl of Strafford in Ireland; men such as John Maitland Duke of Lauderdale, and John, Earl of Middleton, had their "fingers in the till." All this malfeasance was inexcusable; yet even so, it was the standard behaviour of the times.

---

[26] *Ibid.*, p. 523.

The same might be said of the bloody hands of the persecutors: Dalziel of the Binns (the Beast of Muscovy), Sir James Turner (whom Defoe called a butcher), Grierson of Lag (who stands accused on several Covenanter gravestones along with John Graham of Claverhouse), the Highland Host, the informers, and the "flies" (spies) driven by greed. If asked, they would probably have quoted the facile excuse that they were "just following orders." The Crown and its servants condoned chicanery, while kings colluded with ministers to distribute favours and the escheated lands to their favourites. With so many "bad apples in the barrel" it is little wonder that instead of sweet cider it produced an odious and bitter vinegar

The extent to which the Kirk was responsible for making the people Protestant and Presbyterian is debatable. That the people received an education and that their morals were beneficially influenced seems without doubt, and several religious revivals (such as the Six Mile Water revival in Ulster and the Shotts revival) and the Stewarton Sickness provide evidence of this. But the prime agents in making Scotland thoroughly Presbyterian would seem to lie with the arbitrary and tyrannical policies of Charles I and his two sons who, in pursuit of the minority Covenanters, imposed regular church attendance on the majority.

At the root of all the troubles lay the Stuart kings and their singular determination to apply their "Divine will" to which the people, from the highest to the lowest, were expected to simply acquiesce. Having established supremacy in the young Church and aided by the self-seekers with their bad advice, it became inevitable that the royal will would succeed in imposing the king's choice of religion on the people. It is also apparent that James VI deliberately used the bishops, not for their divinity but as compliant tools to help him secure his objective of absolute power and slavery for his subjects.

We only have to look at the chopping and changing between Episcopacy and Presbytery to see the determination of the Stuart line to have their own way. Moreover, the policy was clearly framed in the *Basilicon Doron*: "Episcopacy should be set up and the principal Presbyterian ministers banished from the country."[27]

---

[27] Johnston, *Treasury*, p. 286.

The *True Lawe of Monarchies* was a defence of despotism—all of which were instilled in the psyche of James's son and grandsons. Not content with those tenets Charles I, Charles II, and James II contributed new dimensions of revenge and use of military force. With the Restoration, the policies for the first time took direct action against the common people and instigated twenty-eight years of unnecessary persecution. This was a gross tactical error because the Covenanters could have been suppressed without turning on the mass of the common people. But the desire of each king to have absolute dominion over *all* his people superseded even his dislike of Presbyterianism.

The latent Catholicism of Charles II began to surface with the Indulgences, then the overt Catholicism of James II brought forward a greater resistance from the peoples of England and Scotland who united in the defence of Protestantism. This wider issue relegated the remonstrations of the Covenanters to the second rank at the critical time and resulted in a Protestant, Presbyterian Church *of* Scotland, based on consensus, democratic majority, and political expediency.

There is a lingering thought—a "what if" scenario. What if Henry Hall had not been seized and killed at Queensferry? What if the Queensferry Declaration had made its way to the Presbyterian scholars in Holland? What if the policy had evolved to reject the monarchy and set up a republic? What if the people of Scotland had gone down that route?

What might have been should not prevent us from preparing for what will be. An inscription on a monument in Wanlockhead Churchyard, Dumfriesshire, warns in a reference to Ezekiel 20:37:

We cannot tell
who next may fall
beneath the chastening rod
one must be first
but let us all
prepare to meet our God.

Redrawn by the author from detail in Hyman Shapiro, *Scotland in the Days of James VI* (London: Longman group, Ltd., 1970).

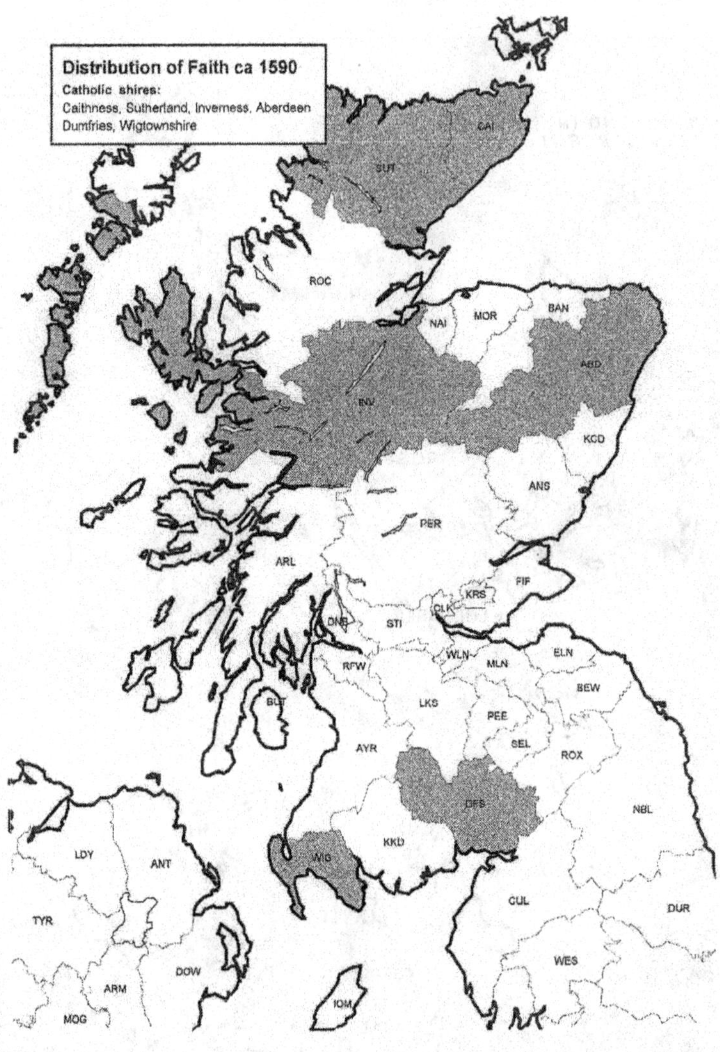

Distribution of faith, *ca*. 1590. Created by the author.

John Maitland, Duke of Lauderdale. Alexander Smellie, *Men of the Covenant* (London: A. Melrose, 1903).

Sir George McKenzie of Rosehaugh, "Bluidy McKenzie." Alexander Smellie, *Men of the Covenant* (London: A. Melrose, 1903).

John Graham of Claverhouse. Viscount "Bonny" Dundee. Alexander Smellie, *Men of the Covenant* (London: A. Melrose, 1903).

Sir James Turner. Alexander Smellie, *Men of the Covenant* (London: A. Melrose, 1903).

James Graham, Marquis of Montrose. James King Hewison, *Covenanters. A History of the Church in Scotland from the Reformation to the Revolution* (Glasgow: John Smith & Son, 1908; reprint Edmonton: Still Waters Revival Books, 1996).

Lt. Gen. Tam Dalziel, the Beast of Muscovy. Alexander Smellie, *Men of the Covenant* (London: A. Melrose, 1903).

Archibald Campbell, Marquis of Argyll. Alexander Smellie, *Men of the Covenant* (London: A. Melrose, 1903).

Archibald Campbell, 9th Earl of Argyll. Alexander Smellie, *Men of the Covenant* (London: A. Melrose, 1903).

Authors of the National Covenant, 1638. *Top*, Archibald Johnston, Lord Warriston. *Bottom*, Rev. Alexander Henderson. Alexander Smellie, *Men of the Covenant* (London: A. Melrose, 1903).

Part III

Events and Topics Concerning the Scottish Reformation, in Alphabetical Order

Aberdeen Assembly, 1605.

This meeting of the General Assembly is important because it did not actually do any church business. It met, was formally convened, arranged the date for another meeting and dissolved. The reason for this was that King James was exerting his claimed prerogative to call Assemblies and appoint the Moderator. The Parliament of 1592 had ratified that the time and place of the next meeting of an Assembly were to be nominated by the preceding Assembly with his Majesty's consent. James, however, prorogued the meeting and altered dates and times. He eventually prorogued indefinitely the meeting that had been rescheduled for July 1605.

The action by the king was recognised by the Presbyterians as a "make or break" occasion of great principle. If they yielded then the continuity of nomination by the preceding assembly was broken and the king's sole authority to call and cancel at will was confirmed. A faithful few gathered at Aberdeen and elected John Forbes, minister of Alford, as Moderator. James sent Stratton of Laurieston as Commissioner, empowering him to dissolve the meeting simply because it did not have the king's permission. At the meeting the assembled ministers resolved to formally constitute the meeting before reading the king's letter. During the reading, a messenger-at-arms commanded the meeting to dissolve on pain of rebellion. They obeyed, but only after the king's commissioner had declined to nominate a day; the moderator therefore appointed the last Tuesday in September in the same place.

The defiance of the ministers at Aberdeen resulted in charges of high treason being preferred against them. Fourteen ministers who defended their conduct were committed to prison. Six of the principal ministers who were judged obnoxious for their fidelity were selected for prosecution. These were John Forbes, the moderator; John Welch of Ayr (the son-in-law of John Knox); Andrew Duncan of Crail; Robert Dury of Anstruther; John Sharp of Kilmany; and Alexander Strachan of Creigh. The packed jury found them guilty of treason and sentenced them to death but then commuted it to banishment. M'Crie, in *Life of Knox*, records that the jury were instructed by the King's Advocate only to consider the declinature because they were already guilty of treason, and the Justice Clerk threatened the king's displeasure if they did not do as advised. The jury finally delivered a guilty verdict at midnight with a majority of three.

Abjuration Act, 1662.

There was more than one Abjuration Act, each usually included an oath to be taken by the people. These were essentially about formally rejecting or disowning another statement. The Abjuration Act of 1662 was a formal rejection of the National Covenant of 1638 and the Solemn League and Covenant of 1643. These were declared to be against the fundamental laws of the kingdom. The Act required all persons taking public office to take an oath of abjuration not to take arms against the king, and rejecting the Covenants. This excluded most Presbyterians from holding official positions of trust.

Abjuration Oath, 25 November 1684. See also: Declarations - Apologetical Declaration, 1684; Appendix 13.

The Abjuration Oath of 25 November 1684 was concerned with rejecting the declaration made by James Renwick in *The Apologetical Declaration and Admonitory Vindication against Intelligencers and Informers*. (See Appendix 16.) Renwick's document, written on behalf of the Society people, stated their sufferings and the principles they held, including their intention to punish oppressors: judges, soldiers, informants, and false witnesses. The oath therefore was offered to suspects. If refused, they could be instantly put to death in the presence of any officer holding a commission from the Privy Council and two witnesses. This was much used in the Killing Time and was the reason for many instant executions of Covenanters in the fields, among the hills, and on their very own doorsteps. The Ordinance of 22 November 1684 prescribing the Oath also specified action that was to be taken against ministers' wives and children:

> You shall turn out all the wives and children of the forfeited estates from their habitations, if it shall appear they have conversed with their parents or husbands, or if they refuse to vindicate themselves by their oath.[1]

The Abjuration ran:

> I A, B. doe hereby abhorr, renunce and disoune, in presence of the Almighty God, the pretendit Declaratione of Warr lately affixed at severall paroch churches in so far as it declares a warr against his sacred Majestie and asserts that it is laufull to kill such as serve his Majestie in church, state, army or countrey, or such as act against the authors of the said pretended declarations now shewne to me. And 1 doe hereby utterly renunce and disoune the villanous authors thereof who did (as they call it) statut and ordaine the same, and what is therein mentioned, and 1 swear 1 shall never assist the authors of the said pretended declarations or ther emissaries or adherents in any poynts of punishing, killing and makeing of warr any manner of way as 1 shall answear to God.[2]

Abuse of Power.

The theme of abuse of power runs throughout the history of the Reformation and particularly after the joining of the Crowns in 1603. Measured against modern standards there would seem to be

---

[1] Johnston, *Treasury*, p. 148.
[2] Hewison, *Covenanters*, Vol. 2, p. 442; Campbell, *Standing Witnesses*, p. 19.

little justification for the use of excessive force and Draconian legislation. Perhaps there is more of a case that the various kings, queens, and their governments were guilty of gross maladministration. They allowed and supported a system of oppression in which individuals such as Archbishop James Sharp; Archbishop William Laud; Bishop Paterson; and Thomas Wentworth, the Earl of Strafford, were able to pursue their own agendas against specific individuals and Presbyterians in general. Others also benefited from the rules; for instance, the Marquis of Argyll was able to follow his own interests in the Western Isles under the guise of lawful authority.

Kings, also, were not above the abuse of power in their roles as monarchs. When James VI of Scotland succeeded to the English throne in 1603 his court removed to London. Here he was surrounded by mainly English courtiers with their own concerns and machinations, and a whole new range of hitherto English problems. James and his successors did not help matters by, first of all, seeking to be absolute monarchs. Secondly, they naively believed that they only had to issue instructions to the Scottish Privy Council in Edinburgh and their will would be done. Thirdly, they were encouraged by the ill advice of others to pursue policies that sought to impose uniformity with England where the King was lawfully the Supreme Governor of the Episcopal Church of England settled by law.

In the early years of his reign, James I of England made a concerted effort to impose his will on Scotland with the particular objective of establishing episcopacy in the church. To this end, deliberate efforts were made to pack the General Assembly that met in Glasgow in 1610. Not only did James direct the Presbyteries whom they were to send, but the Earl of Dunbar came from London with a quantity of gold coins (called "angels," hence the term "Angel Assembly") to bribe representatives as necessary. Episcopacy was ratified by Parliament in 1612. Another instance of a packed Assembly is that at Perth in 1618 when the "Five Articles of Perth" were agreed upon.

Charles I used all and any means to get his way. During his eleven years of personal rule (1629-1640) without a Parliament, he successfully alienated every party, political and religious; he betrayed his closest friends (for instance, his ally Wentworth was a sacrifice he made); and he abandoned Archbishop Laud in the

Tower of London until he also was executed. He deceived the people constantly, and was an outright liar who treated with Catholics while professing to support Protestantism. Above all, he lived and died by one principle: the end justifies the means.

In subsequent years, Charles II made a major error by exercising his discretion to re-establish the Court of High Commission. This court had previously existed under King James VI/I and was meant to deal with discipline in life and religion. It became part of the machinery of oppression. In Scotland, it became the personal fiefdom of Archbishop Sharp where virtually any punishment except the death penalty was permitted. Through this court many of the "outed" ministers were imprisoned or banished without trial before the judiciary, and locked up for years.

Abuse of power to serve personal ends is instanced by the practice of patronage, and simoniacal purchases for appointment to churches and posts in the universities. An example of this is the purchase of the See of Glasgow by the Earl of Lennox in 1582.

A singular area of abuse of power was the way in which legislation was used to impose fines and the monies were diverted to the pockets of the persecutors. Sir James Turner and his troopers were especially active in the southwest where amounts larger than the fine were collected. The soldiers took quarters where they pleased; rioted; and, with hunting dogs, took sheep; raided cattle; ejected wives, widows and children from their homes; beat anyone who complained; violated women; and behaved in a most dissolute and often drunken manner.

In the upper reaches of government, hands were in the till with a vengeance. Lord Chancellor Middleton was caught out and sacked. Yet his successor, Lauderdale, soon began acquiring extra revenues for himself. He had seven salaries, gifts, imposts, mineral rights, shipwreck salvage, gold in Jamaica, and other grants. Hewison, in *Covenanters*, describes Middleton and his associates as "beggars on horseback, living in a Bacchanalian paradise, plundering on all lands."[3] Hewison described Lauderdale as an uncouth tippler, albeit a learned savage.

---

[3] Hewison, *Covenanters*, Vol. 2, p. 117.

Accusations against Prelates. See also: Assassination - Archbishop James Sharp.

Many are the accusations of prejudice and malice but actual formal complaints against individuals are relatively few. The reason seems to be that the lawful authority for ecclesiastical matters was the very system which the Presbyterians were objecting to: what was the point in complaining about a curate, or a bishop, if the ultimate authority was an Archbishop who was himself prejudiced against them? What happened in practice is that the offending individual was publicly excommunicated. To the heathen this may not have mattered but the probability was that a curate or bishop would suffer a modicum of conscience and some social exclusion, as well as a loss of public image and status.

In January 1609 there were a number of pasquills, or anonymous verses, published and distributed that were highly critical of the bishops and their personal peccadilloes. These were in both Latin and English, and were presumably written by an educated person. One example appears in Calderwood's *History*:

Sanct Andrewes loves a cuppe of wine, so Glasgow with a whoore,
Rosse companie, play Galloway, Brechin not to be poore;
Orkney the court, Murray the pot, the Iles aye to deceave,
Dumblane to trick, and Aberdeene a glorious name to have.
By chance Dunkell has lighted so, that Jacob he would be,
But, O Good Cathnesse, when comes thou thy flocke to teach or see ?
For light in doctrine they may all resigne it to Argile,
So faith has left the lowland cleane, gone to the hills awhile[4]

The *Scots Worthies* mentions that Robert Baillie was despatched to London in 1640 to help prepare charges against Archbishop William Laud (1573-1645). The charge was for bringing innovations to the Church of Scotland. A keen supporter of the royal prerogative and opponent of the Puritans, Laud strongly supported ceremony in the church and perceived a need to harmonise the English and Scottish establishments. In 1629, he

[4] Calderwood, *History*, Vol. 7, pp. 2-3.

began to draft a Prayer Book for use in Scotland.[5] In 1633, on a visit to Edinburgh with the king, he preached on the excellence of uniformity. Between 1633 and 1637, Laud gave his full support to those years' intense church-related activities: the type of dress to be worn by ministers and bishops was specified, the English Liturgy was ordered to be used at Holyrood Palace, the Court of High Commission was reconstituted in 1634 to ensure the operation of "novations" (new rules), and, in 1637, the new Service Book (called "Laud's Liturgy"), was published.

It was ironic that, by this time, the Scots considered Laud beneath contempt and that he no longer mattered—there were more important things to be done. But in London public resentment and hostility continued to exist towards Laud.[6] Consequently, Baillie's journey was successful. Laud was impeached by the English Parliament for, amongst other things, tyrannical abuse of power and for his "slit-nose and cropped-ear policy." The Impeachment Articles against Laud read in part:

> VII. That he hath traitorously endeavoured to alter and subvert God's true religion by law established in this realm; and instead thereof, to set up Popish Superstition and Idolatry.... He hath urged popish and superstitious ceremonies, without any warrant of law; and hath cruelly persecuted those who have opposed the same, by corporal punishment and imprisonment; and most unjustly vexed others who refused to conform thereto...contrary to the law of the kingdom.
>
> X. He hath traitorously and wickedly endeavoured to reconcoile the Church of England with the Church of Rome.[7]

Laud's "slit-nose and cropped-ear policy" called for the deliberate disfigurement of nonconformists by slitting noses, clipping ears, and

---

[5] The Prayer Book was first ordered to be used on Sunday, July 23. The Second Reformation may have been sparked by the use of the book in Edinburgh at St. Giles Church and Jennie Geddes' celebrated throwing of a stool at the dean.

[6] To show their dissatisfaction, five hundred city apprentices marched on Lambeth Palace.

[7] Angus Stroud, *Stuart England* (London: Routledge, 1999), p. 68.

branding cheeks. Notable examples were Dr. Leighton and three Puritans: Prynne, Bastwick, and Burton.

Laud lingered in the Tower for some time but was executed at Tower Hill on 10 January 1645.

Several other men also serve as examples of accused prelates. Paterson, Bishop of Galloway was known amongst the diplomats as Mr. Pious or Pope Pious. The Covenanters called him Bishop Bandstrings because of his habit, while preaching, of making sometimes obscene and suggestive hand signals to ladies in the congregation. He was regarded as "one of the most notorious liars of his time, and a vicious, base and loose liver."[8] He was dismissed from the Privy Council in 1684 for obtaining a pension under false pretences, and keeping churches vacant so that he could pocket the stipends. Bishop Fairfull was a teller of disgusting stories and "scarce free of scandal" while Archbishop Alexander Burnet was a serial lover with many indiscrete and illicit affairs.

Act of Classes, 23 January 1649. See also: Engagers – Engagement, 1648; Protesters and Resolutioners.

The Act of Classes for purging the judicatories, and other places of public trust, arose from the ashes of the "Engagement." Although the Act was intended to preserve the nation's safety in the eyes of God, some people saw it as placing Scotland under the tyranny of the Kirk. The Act required that persons in public office be possessed of scriptural qualifications, such as being a Presbyterian church-goer and elder.

There were four categories of malignancy. The first category included military or civil persons who had either promoted the Engagement or had supported the Marquis of Montrose; people falling into this category were banned for life. The second category included persons already censored as malignants; they were banned for ten years. The third category were those who passively accepted or had not used opportunities to publicly condemn the Engagement; they were banned for five years. The fourth category included anyone named as given over to bribery, swearing, drunkenness, profanity, and the like; they were banned for one year. In each

---

[8] Hewison, *Covenanters*, Vol. 2, p. 124.

category, the satisfaction of the Kirk was required in order for an individual to be restored to office.

An immediate effect of this Act was the wholesale change among the government. Treasurer Crawford was replaced by four Commissioners: Argyll, Eglinton, Cassillis, and Burleigh. The Lord Privy Seal Roxburgh was replaced by Sutherland. Secretary Lanark was replaced by Cassillis and Lothian. Clerk Register Gibson of Durie was replaced by Archibald Johnston Lord Warriston. Eight of the Lords of Session were also replaced.

Covenanters' opinions were divided about the Act. The Marquis of Argyll led the hardline but nevertheless saw the need for compromise; he believed that some moderating of the Act had drained the cause of Presbyterianism of some very able people. Hugh Binning was a concerned minister who sought to mend fences. Captain John Paton was a staunch supporter against the Engagers in a military sense. Archibald Johnson, as Clerk to the General Assembly, later opposed the repeal of the Act in a letter to them of 18 July 1651.

Among the people, nobles and commoners alike, there was a resentment from those who had supported the Engagement. Some mitigation was brought about by an Act of 20 July 1649 that enabled Engagers to be accepted back into the fold subject to making a public declaration and acknowledgement of their sin and repentance. (See Appendix 12.) However, forcing the sinner to appear before Kirk Sessions and suffer public humiliation bred resentments that many would settle in the upcoming years.

The Act of Classes would be repealed when Parliament finally met on 30 May 1651 and a new Committee was formed of essentially royalist supporters. The scene was now set for Charles II to return to actual power and make his play for supporters in England to rise and join him.

Act Ratifying the Confession of Faith and Settling Presbyterian Church Government in Scotland, 7 June 1690.

This act began by citing the Claim of Right that Prelacy is "a great and insupportable grievance and trouble to this nation" and ratified all previous acts against Popery. It ratified the Westminster Confession of Faith as containing "the summe and substance of the doctrine of the Reformed Church," established Presbyterian Church government and discipline, annulled all acts and orders contrary to the Protestant and Presbyterian government now established, restored to office ministers ejected since 1661, and appointed the first meeting of the General Assembly to be the third Thursday of October 1690 in Edinburgh. Finally, it authorised the Church "to purge out all insufficient, negligent, scandalous and erroneous ministers from office and benefice."[9]

Curiously and regrettably, no mention was made of the standards of the Catechism or Directory, and a motion to ratify the Scottish Confession with the clause of 1647 that gave the Church the inherent right to call its own Assemblies was lost. These omissions brought criticism from the faithful remnant who had met at Leadhills on 8 April 1690 to subscribe "The Humble Petition of the Persecuted People of the West and Southern Shires" which again sought free Assemblies and a demand for "the vindicating and approving these reproached Covenants."[10] But their petition got no further than a Committee for Church Affairs and was never presented to Parliament. The age of bureaucracy and unelected Committees had arrived.

At the General Assembly on October 16, efforts were made by Alexander Shields, Linning, and Boyd to have the representations heard but they and the petition were rebuffed out of hand. The Committee of the Assembly judged that the petition contained

> peremptory and gross mistakes, unseasonable and impracticable proposals, and uncharitable and injurious reflections, tending rather to kindle contentions than compose divisions.[11]

With such a charge ringing in their ears, members of the General Assembly and, it has to be remembered, the majority, settled for a Presbyterian Church that was tainted with Erastianism. Some held that it was a *fait accomplit*: Parliament had already approved the Confession and disregarded the spiritual independence of the Church. But defensive postures were taken up by the Covenanters when King William indicated that he supported toleration with the

---

[9] Hewison, *Covenanters*, Vol. 2, pp. 537-538.
[10] *Ibid.*, p. 539.
[11] Howie, *Worthies*, p. 588.

Church taking in conforming Episcopalians. This was an "insupportable grievance" in the minds of the Covenanters and was at variance with the Claim of Right.

Act Recissory, 1661.

The Act Recissory of 1661 was the legislation that revoked all the favourable Presbyterian laws enacted since 1638 and opened the door for the return of Episcopacy in Scotland. In a single blow it removed the hard fought for civil and religious liberties of the Scottish people. The Restoration of King Charles II in 1660 marked the end of Presbyterianism as a legal authority and turned them into a dissenting group. Charles II and his minions legislated with a vengeance. The Earl of Middleton acted as the King's Commissioner in Scotland. Middleton supervised over four hundred pieces of legislation. The object of this torrent of laws was to establish and reinforce the king as head of both the civil power and the church. This doctrine of supremacy created in the form of an oath of allegiance caused much suffering in the following years

Articles of Perth, 25 August 1618. See also: Black Saturday.

The declaration and subsequent ratification by Parliament of the Five Articles of Perth was a watershed in the relationship between the Crown and the Presbyterians. The imposition posed by the Articles was the first to directly affect the public who resented interference with their style of worship.

The articles approved at Perth on 25 August 1618 were:

1. The Communion must be received in a kneeling posture. (This was most obnoxious to the Presbyterians).
2. Private Communion was permitted in cases of sickness.
3. Private Baptism was permitted when necessary.
4. Children should be catechised and blessed by bishops (Confirmation).
5. Christmas, Good Friday, Easter, Ascension, and Pentecost were declared as holy days not only of the Catholic Church but also of the whole Kirk.

The Articles were confirmed by the Edinburgh Parliament on 4 August 1621 (called Black Saturday as it was both by deed and fact a dark, stormy day). Following ratification the king wrote to the prelates in a letter of August 12 telling them that

> The sword is now putt into your hands; goe on therefore to use it; and let it roust noe longer till ye have perfited the service trusted to you, or otherwise we must use it both against you and them. If anie or all of you be faint-hearted we are able enough (thanks to God) to put others in your places who both can and will make things possible which ye think so difficult.[12]

The same letter harangued papistrie and urged the prelates to root out all Papists, priests, and traitorous Jesuits, adding

> But as Papistrie is ane disease in the minds, so is Puritaisme in the braine. So the onlie remedie and antidote against it will be a grave, settled, uniforme, and well ordered church, obedient to God and their King....[13]

Ominously, responsibility for enforcing the law was handed to the Court of High Commission. Nonetheless, ministers did express their disagreement with the Articles. Patrick Simpson, a minister at Cramond and then at Stirling, was an ardent opponent of prelacy, having been the nominal Moderator at the Aberdeen Assembly in 1604. It was Simpson who delivered the Protestation to the Earl of Dunbar after Dunbar in the Parliament of 1606. His objections to the Articles were great but he died before they were implemented "blessing the Lord that he had not been perverted by the sinful courses of these times."[14]

John Scrimgeour, minister at Kinghorn in Fife, went as chaplain with James VI to Denmark in 1590 when the king brought back Anne of Denmark as his queen. With others he was summoned before the Court of High Commission for not preaching on holidays and not administering the Communion according to the Articles.

---

[12] Calderwood, *History*, Vol. 7, p. 508.

[13] *Ibid.*

[14] Howie, *Worthies*, p. 109.

After much debate and wrangling he was banished to Bowhill in the parish of Auchterderran.

David Dickson had only recently entered into the ministry at Irvine at the time of the Perth Assembly and was not much concerned about Episcopacy. However, when the rules were forced upon him he took an interest, becoming in time an implacable opponent to the Articles. He was banished to Turriff for a while for his obstinacy but the intervention of influential friends enabled him to return to Irvine.

Ministers were not alone in their protestations. The congregation of the Rev. William M'Annand in Ayr took simple and direct action against ceremony and, in particular kneeling, at the Communion: They walked out and left the minister to it, alone. Paterson, in his *History*, quotes Sir Edward Brereton who noted that

> upon Easter day last, so soon as he went to the commununion table, the people all left the church and departed, and not one of them stayed, only the pastor alone.[15]

When King James I died in 1625, the policy of coercion continued in Scotland and was increased under King Charles I. He continued the enforcement of the laws for non-compliance with the Articles and also tried to introduce other changes in the church.

Assassination - Attempts and Threats. See also: Abjuration Oath; Curates.

Whether called murder or assassination, the intention is to kill someone. In the case of the Presbyterians, it was threats and attempts at assassination for reasons of both politics and religion. Such was the influence exerted by the ministers among the people, and their resistance to the government, that an early or sudden death of an opponent was sometimes an expediency.

Being of noble birth did not exempt one from the threat of assassination. Patrick Hamilton, an early martyr, was a relative of King James V but this did not prevent him from being charged as a heretic and hurriedly burnt at the stake before the king could

---

[15] James Paterson, *History of the Counties of Ayr & Wigton* (Edinburgh: James Stillie, 1863), Vol. 1, Part 1, p. 105.

intercede. Nor did an even closer relationship to the king protect a person.

James Stuart, Earl of Moray, "The Good Regent," was a son of King James V and half-brother to Mary, Queen of Scots, yet he was threatened on several occasions because he was zealous in promoting the Reformation against popery. When in France for Mary's marriage to the Dauphin of France he survived an attempted poisoning in which his Scottish companions died. When visiting his newly widowed sister Mary in 1560, several people were hired to murder him in the street. Though he was warned and escaped, he still had to pass through a stone-throwing crowd shouting "Huguenot." When Mary returned to Scotland, he was sent to the borders with only a small force to deal with some bandits (reivers) probably with the hope that he might be killed. The Earl of Bothwell's plot to kill Moray was foiled when the Earl of Arran informed Moray of it. During the time of Lord Darnley's murder, Moray stayed well out of the way until Mary was deposed, returning as regent for the young King James VI in 1567. He finally fell to an assassin's bullet fired by James Hamilton of Bothwell Haugh, nephew of the Archbishop of St. Andrews, and believed to be working at the behest of the imprisoned Queen Mary.

Many threats were made against the supporters of the Reformation. George Wishart, an apostate priest, was one such supporter. He was soon attacked by jealous Romish clergy for his views and successful preaching in Dundee. In 1539, Cardinal David Beaton succeeded his uncle in the See of St. Andrews and he exerted influence to get Wishart out of Dundee for a while but, on the outbreak of the plague, Wishart returned. This time, Beaton bribed a priest, John Wightman, to kill the minister. The intention was to stab him as he came down from his pulpit. Wightman stood at the foot of the pulpit steps with a dagger in hand but was confronted by a stern-faced Wishart who asked him what he intended and disarmed him. The crowd was aroused but since no harm had come to him, Wishart allowed the priest to go. This did not end the incident, however; Wishart was subsequently burnt at the stake for heresy on 1 March 1546.

The *Scots Worthies* tells us that a group of about a dozen citizens, including Norman and John Leslie of Rothes, William Kirkcaldy of Grange, James Melville of Carnbee, and Peter Carmichael, gathered on 28 May 1546 to assault the castle where

Beaton was in residence. Confronting the vengeful group, Beaton cried mercy saying, "I am a priest –fy, fy – all is gone."[16] He was told to repent since he was to be killed in revenge for Wishart's death. He was duly despatched with two or three stabs. M'Crie, in *Sketches*, says that the people were woken by the commotion and demanded to see the cardinal's body. This was displayed in the tower where, a few months before, he had watched George Wishart's execution.

John Knox was another supporter of the Reformation and a vehement opponent of papacy. Under his influence, great steps had been taken to remove idolatry. Stirred by his success and fearful of what else he might accomplish, an assassin shot at Knox through a window; however, the bullet missed its target and struck a candlestick. It was a further twelve years before age and ill health finally caught up with Knox. At his funeral in 1572, the Regent, the Earl of Morton, said:

> There lies one who in this life never feared the face of man, who hath been often threatened with dag and dagger, but hath ended his days in peace and honour.[17]

A disgraceful attempt was made to murder Archibald Johnston, Lord Warriston, who, with Alexander Henderson, had drafted the National Covenant of 1638. Having gone to Hamburg in 1661 to avoid his enemies, Johnston became ill and was attended by a Dr. Bates who was one of King Charles' physicians. Murder seems intended; Dr. Bates prescribed poison for Johnston's illness instead of a physic and then drew some sixty ounces of blood from him. Johnston survived this excessive draining of blood but his short term memory was destroyed; he remained unable to remember things right up to the day he was executed in 1663.

John Semple was a leading preacher at conventicles and a stern critic who reproved wickedness wherever he encountered it. He was no respecter of persons and on one occasion had apparently upset his host. On his leaving, the host despatched a ruffian of a servant with sword and pistol with instructions to attack him. Semple was not frightened by the armed confrontation and talked

---

[16] M'Crie, *Sketches*, Vol. 1, p. 41.

[17] Calderwood, *History*, Vol. 3, p. 242.

the assailant out of his murder saying that he was not afraid because "I was sure to get the sooner to heaven."[18]

Noblemen and ministers were not the only ones to suffer the threat or attempt of murder. Soldiers Thomas Kennoway and Duncan Stewart were murdered on the night of 19-20 November 1684. Drunken bullies, adulterers, and thieves, they probably deserved to die by the standards of the day. Kennoway, from the Calder district, was well known. He had been engaged in enforcing the law and extorting money from the Whigs for some eighteen years. There was no evidence that the deeds were done by Covenanters but they were blamed nonetheless. The Abjuration Oath was created as a consequence of the declaration of 8 November 1684 (see Appendix 16) and the murders of these soldiers.

Assassination - King James VI/I; King Charles II.

King James VI/I - The death of James VI/I is one of intrigue and alleged double-dealing by George Villiers, Duke of Buckingham. A one-time favourite of the king, Villiers went with Prince Charles, son of James, to Spain in February 1623 to negotiate a marriage with the Infanta.[19] There was animosity between Buckingham and the Marquis of Hamilton, who had protested to King James about allowing his son to go to Spain with one so young and inexperienced as Buckingham. This seems to have festered in the ensuing months until it was reported that the Marquis had died on 6 March 1625 due to poison. Rumours pointed to Buckingham as the perpetrator.

In his *History*, Calderwood draws from an earlier publication in which the story is related that the Duke of Buckingham was responsible for forcing a white powder upon the king shortly before he died. So treated, the king became worse and worse with "violent fluxes of the bellie, so tormented, that his Majestie cryed out aloud, 'O this whyte powder! this whyte powder!'" The Countess of Buckingham (the duke's mother) was said to have "applyed a plaister to the king's heart and breast, whereupon his majestie grew faint, short breathed, and in great agonie." Both these acts were

---

[18] Howie, *Worthies*, p. 379.

[19] The marriage did not transpire.

done in the absence and without the knowledge of the king's physicians. Upon returning, the physicians determined that the king had been poisoned and the Duke of Buckingham ordered them out of the room. He imprisoned one doctor and quarrelled with others to the extent of almost drawing swords. Later, he tried unsuccessfully to get the doctors to certify that the powder he had administered was not harmful, but they refused to do so.[20]

Charles II - The circumstances of the death of King Charles on 6 February 1685 has generated a host of reasons, hypotheses, guesses, and outright fanciful tales. William Veitch was well connected at Court and gives the version that Charles was poisoned on the orders of his brother, James. To achieve this, Charles' mistress, the Duchess of Portsmouth, is alleged to have poisoned the king's claret while a chamber maid poisoned the king's snuff box. When these efforts appeared not to be working, it is alleged that four ruffians were set upon the king and he was strangled with his cravat. Generally, there seemed to be a view that Charles was poisoned by some papists; yet, this is wholly inconsistent with the one certain fact that, on his deathbed, the king declared his Catholic faith, receiving the Last Rites and absolution of his sins from a Father Huddleston. Antonia Fraser, in *King Charles II*, explores several scenarios, including the relationship Charles had with his brother, James, and with whom he seemed to be on good terms.

The official verdict was apoplexy (a stroke) although the king had no paralysis consistent with a stroke. He suffered increasingly severe bouts of convulsions and was treated for malaria which was common in those days, but the type prevalent was not normally fatal. Discounting the more lurid tales of a conspiracy, Charles may well have inadvertently poisoned himself. Charles was an experimenter and spent some time trying to fix (that is, stabilise) mercury which is very toxic. He became very irritable, which is a symptom of mercury poisoning. He may have also suffered from

[20] Calderwood, *History*, Vol. 7, p. 637. Calderwood draws the information from George Eglesheime, *The Forerunner of Revenge upon the Duke of Buckinghame, for the poysoning of the Most Potent King, James, of happie memorie, King of Great Britaine, and the Lord Marqueis of Hammiltoun, and others of the Nobilitie; discovered by Mr George Eglesheme, one of King James his Physicians for his Majestie's persoun above the space of ten yeeres* (n.p.: n.p., 1626). Dr. Eglesheime was a Scottish physician to the king.

kidney disease which would have produced uraemia—a gradual build up of toxic waste in the blood stream. Whatever the actual cause, it is certain that Charles died a long and uncomfortable death.

Assassination - Archbishop James Sharp.

The assassination of James Sharp, Archbishop of St. Andrews, on Magus Moor on 3 May 1679, was one of the main events during the Scottish Reformation. Possibly the most hated man in Scotland, Sharp began his career as a minister of the kirk at Crail in Fife. By dint of being a self-seeking turncoat and traitor to his colleagues, he took his reward by advancement to Archbishop. In that role, Sharp used the Court of High Commission to persecute opponents of episcopacy as well as a vehicle to settle old scores. This he was able to do by ensuring that the quorum for the Court always had his supporters in the majority. The location of the Court would also be moved around so that he was able to call meetings at short notice, not having many, if any, civil representatives attending. There are many instances of his gross abuse of power. A singular description of Sharp is given by Hewison in *Covenanters:*

> Sharp appears in his true colours, verily the base, clattering claw-back of his contemporaries; to the Church, a knave pur sang; to his friends, a spy; to his foes, a persecutor; to his peers a caitiff whom they used but despised; in fine one of the meanest Scots that ever wore a holy robe.[21]

There were at least two serious attempts on Sharp's life and many more threatened. The first involved James Mitchell, a graduate of Edinburgh University who was licensed to preach shortly after the restoration of Charles I in 1660. He felt justified in despatching Archbishop Sharp who, by 1668, was making his mark as chief persecutor of the Presbyterian kirk. On the afternoon of 11 July 1668 Mitchell waited for the Archbishop in Blackfriars Wynd, Edinburgh. When the Archbishop had stepped into his coach, Mitchell fired his pistol with three balls at the door of the coach but succeeded only in hitting the wrist of the Archbishop's companion, Honeyman, Bishop of Orkney. It was a sign of the times that in the

---

[21] Hewison, *Covenanters*, Vol. 2, p. 123.

hue and cry that followed Mitchell escaped, while to the cry that a man had been killed came the response "it was only a Bishop."[22] Mitchell eluded capture for nine years before he was apprehended by Sir William Sharp, the Archbishop's brother. Mitchell was a prisoner on the Bass Rock for a while and was executed in Edinburgh on 18 January 1678.

Archbishop James Sharp. Alexander Smellie, *Men of the Covenant* (London: A. Melrose, 1903).

The second, and successful, attack on Archbishop Sharp happened through serendipity. A group of Presbyterians had gone to the area of Magus Moor intending to capture and chastise a William Carmichael, Sheriff depute of Fife, who had been very zealous in pursuing the Presbyterians.[23] Carmichael did not appear having been warned that some men were asking after him, and probably guessed their purpose. The party was breaking up to return to their homes when information was received from a Mrs. Black, wife of Robert Black of Baldinny, with whom they had stayed the night before. She advised that Sharp was in the locality between Ceres and Blebohole, and would pass by within the hour.

---

[22] Howie, *Worthies*, p. 384.

[23] Depute is a Scottish title. The bearer's duties were comparable to those of a deputy.

The assassination party was: David Hackston of Rathilett, John Balfour of Kinloch, James Russel of Kettle, George Fleming or Fleman Jr. in Balbuthy; Andrew and Alexander Henderson, sons of John Henderson in Kilbrachmont; William Daniel in Caddam; three brothers James, George, and Alexander Balfour in Gilston; Thomas Ness and a local man Andrew Gillan or Guilline, a weaver in Balmerino.

David Hackston was elected to lead the party but declined it saying that he had a private quarrel with Sharp and did not want to detract from the testimony of the action by having it attributed to personal revenge.[24] John Balfour, known as Burley, then took the lead. Intercepting the state coach drawn by six horses, they brought it to a halt by firing their pistols, then slashing the faces of the horses and the postillions, hamstringing the lead horses and cutting the traces. Russel fired his pistol through the window even though the Archbishop's daughter, Isabel, was inside.

Sharp resisted demands to get out of the coach, and Fleming and George Balfour shot at him while others thrust with their swords. Believing him dead the party was starting to move off when, it is said, Isabel Sharp uttered the fateful words, "There's life yet."[25]

The assassins returned to the coach where John Balfour told Sharp he was being killed for shedding the blood of Presbyterians. Further shots and sword attacks finally forced a now wounded Sharp to get out of the coach, pleading to Hackston for help. Hackston's reply was "I shall never lay a hand on you"[26] and, despite the begging of Sharp's daughter to spare his life, he was finally despatched.[27]

So ended twenty years of persecution. Yet a terrible revenge was taken on 18 November 1679 when five prisoners captured at Bothwell Brig, and having nothing whatever to do with Sharp's

---

[24] Three others—James and Alexander Balfour in Gilston, and Thomas Ness—did not join the party in the attack on Sharp, his daughter, and five servants.

[25] James Dodds, *Fifty Year Struggle of the Scottish Covenanters* (London: Houlston & Sons, 1868), p. 227.

[26] *Ibid.*

[27] Smellie, in *Men of the Covenant*, states that nothing was taken from the body except a tobacco box, from which a live humming bee was released (which Balfour termed Sharp's "familiar"), and a Bible. Also in the box were a pair of pistol balls, nail parings thought to be to guard against witches, some silk, and a paper with strange characters on it. "The odour of wizardry hung about the miserable Archbishop to the close." Smellie, p. 270.

death, were hung in chains at Magus Moor as retribution.[28] Of the original party of assassins, only Andrew Guilline and David Hackston were caught and executed for the crime, whereas those physically involved in the murder were not brought to book. The inscription on their memorial stone reads:

> 'Cause we at Bothwel did appear
> Perjurious Oaths refus'd to swear
> 'Cause we Christ's Cause would not condemn
> Were we sentenc'd to Death by Men
> Who Rag'd against us in such fury
> Our dead Bodies they did not bury;
> But upon Poles did hing us high
> Triumphs of Babel's Victory.
> Our lives we fear'd not to the Death
> But constant prov'd to the last breath.

On the reverse:

> Here lies Thos Brown
> James Wood Andrew Sword
> John Weddell & John Clyde
> who suffered martyrdom on Magus Muir
> for their adherence to the Word of God
> and Scotland's Covenanted Work of Reformation
> Nov 25th 1679.[29]

Assertory Act, 16 November 1669. See also: Act of Supremacy.

The Assertory Act legalised the power of the State over the Church in a totally unlimited way providing

> That his Majesty have the supreme authority and supremacy over all persons and in all causes ecclesiastical; and that by virtue thereof the ordering and disposing of the external

---

[28] The five were Thomas Brown of Edinburgh, Andrew Sword of Borgue, John Waddell of New Monkland, John Clide, and James Wood of Newmilns.

[29] Campbell, *Standing Witnesses*, pp. 137-138.

> government and policy of the Church doth properly belong to his majesty; and his successors may settle etc.[30]

The relevance of this all-embracing power was that it laid the path for James II, a Catholic, who could, by a single decree, establish whatever religion he wished. The Act was greatly offensive to the Presbyterians and undoubtedly contributed to the resistance and bloodshed in future years. It was the first Act to be repealed at the Revolution.

Banishment.

Banishment, either within Scotland or outside, was a very common punishment inflicted on ministers who were dissenters or had been "outed." Since banishment could be imposed by the prelates, virtually every minister who was summoned before the Court of High Commission was subjected to varying lengths of imprisonment, sometimes in several different tolbooths or castles, or on the Bass Rock before his case was heard. There was seldom any reason for the delays in dealing with allegations or for moving people around save keeping them from preaching out of malice and spite. It is possible that moving between prisons prevented rescue attempts by sympathisers but it was more likely to disorientate and confuse the prisoner before he was subjected to interrogation and possibly torture.

Ministers might be told to remain in a local place pending the king's pleasure; this was usually pending the consideration of the charges.[31] The place of banishment in Scotland was often to the north, the Highlands, and the Isles, where there was not much Covenanter support; yet sometimes the minister might be allowed to choose his own place of incarceration. Many of those banished out of Scotland went to Holland where there were thriving Scottish communities, especially in Rotterdam.

---

[30] Johnston, *Treasury*, p. 129.

[31] The term "warded" is also a form of banishment—a person might be warded to Dundee, meaning he must remove himself there within a specified period and remain there—a sort of banishment under open arrest. The penalty for breaking a warding, such as slipping off to visit family left behind, could be a financial penalty, or "horning." This meant being declared a rebel with forfeiture of property and titles, with exposure to a more rigid penalty regime, including hanging.

David Black, a colleague of Andrew Melville at St. Andrews, got into trouble by declining the king's supremacy in matters of doctrine. He was first warded to the north side of the Tay at his own expense to await the king's pleasure. He lingered there for nearly a year. Shortly after returning to St. Andrews, he was proceeded against and this time banished to Angus, where he subsequently died.

David Calderwood is a prime example of a minister declining the authority and alleged headship of the church by the king. He first declined authority in 1608 and was confined to his parish where he remained until 1617. He was then called before the Court of High Commission, with the king present, and rebutted all questions and criticisms with great skill. In the end, the king asked if he would obey sentence to which Calderwood replied

> Your sentence is not the sentence of the Kirk, but a sentence null in itself, and therefore I cannot obey it.[32]

He was subsequently held in prison for some time pending the king's pleasure. In August 1619 he escaped to Holland where much of his time was taken up writing his *History of the Kirk of Scotland* until his death in Jedburgh, on 29 October 1650.

Robert McWard and John Brown were stalwarts of the Reformation who after banishment became very influential in Holland. It was to them that other Covenanters often turned; and they were responsible for several ordinations of ministers, including Richard Cameron and later, James Renwick. It was probably because of his advancing years that the very influential Samuel Rutherford was banished to Aberdeen. Other Covenanter greats such as David Dickson, and Robert Blair all suffered banishment within Scotland. A suspicion lingers that this was to keep them within striking distance of the government.

In Ireland, the Dublin Parliament sought to banish the leading Presbyterians from counties Antrim and Down and to re-plant about 260 of them in the Province of Munster. Parliament offered the inducement of cheap land and freedom of conscience. There were two categories of Presbyterians: volunteers under negotiated terms who were assisted and allotted land, and others who did not enter

---

[32] Howie, *Worthies*, p. 203.

into contracts with the government and negotiated their own land purchases. Those with agreements would go to Kilkenny and Tipperary while those who were not contracted would go to Leinster. The Presbyterians were allowed to receive the profits from their existing lands and harvests, to live rent free for two years on the new property, to keep weapons, and to follow their religion.

Cromwell stopped the scheme, however, when he realised that the Presbyterians were essentially law abiding citizens and would not otherwise give much trouble. Moreover, he had seen the opportunity to plant a Protestant population in the provinces of Munster and Leinster by banishing priests and forcing Catholic landowners to move to Connaught and Clare. This banishment resulted in millions of acres becoming available which was used to pay the one thousand or so adventurers who had financed the war and his 35,000 soldiers. Much of the land given to the soldiers was quickly sold. About a quarter of the soldiers actually took up residence and many intermarried with the local Irish.

An important consequence of this movement of people was that land ownership in Ireland changed significantly, placing it in Protestant hands. The land held by Catholics in Ireland fell from about ninety percent in 1603 to fourteen percent after the Treaty of Limerick in 1691. Subsequently, under the Penal Laws in the 1700s, the Catholic land holding was reduced to about five percent. Land ownership and lack of representation in government, both local and national, were the basis for much bitter resentment in future years.

Baptisms.

The authorities demanded that children be baptised by the curates. The result was outright disobedience or nominal compliance followed by a laying on of hands by an outed Presbyterian minister.

It was risky for a Presbyterian minister to baptise children. Donald Cargill's itinerant life was fraught with risk of capture. An instance is quoted where he had preached at Underbank Wood near Lanark in the morning and baptised some children. He was prevailed upon to preach again in the afternoon, with more children being brought forward for baptism. As he was closing the meeting, troopers descended on them and he narrowly avoided capture.

Of all the conventicling ministers the most peripatetic by far was Alexander Peden. He was on his way to Ireland when in the parish of Galston he was asked by one Peter Aird to baptise his child. This being done, Peden then uttered one of his many prophesies telling Aird that "If your friend of the parish (meaning an indulged minister called James Veitch) had baptised your child, you would have been sure to have had your horned beasts in your possession; now you may lose them."[33] A few days later the powers that be came and drove off all his cattle, but Aird himself had fled taking his horses with him else he would have lost them, too.

Battles.

The seventeenth century was a time of great conflict and tension in all three kingdoms of England, Ireland and Scotland. After 1603 there was but one king for all three but, importantly, they were not joined politically. The situation therefore involved successive absolute monarchs trying to impose their will on separate kingdoms, each with their own particular internal issues, and separate legislation. Moreover, all three kingdoms had religious issues that brought conflict with the King. It was also necessary to keep a watchful eye on Europe where war with Spain, France, and Holland was an on-off affair throughout the century. It is difficult to conceive of a more complex century for politics than this. In summary therefore, there was much conflict with the only certainties being that each country successfully meddled in each others affairs to no particular advantage.

In Ireland there was a honeymoon period for nonconformists until about 1630. The resurgence of persecution of the Presbyterians from 1633 was led by Thomas Wentworth, later Earl of Strafford, and the adoption of the uniformity policies that Archbishop Laud was imposing on the Scottish church. Contention also increased between the indigenous peoples and the English and Scottish settlers of the Plantation of Ulster who had taken ownership of seized lands. From this rose the ugly head of religious discrimination and rebellion—the Irish Killing Time of 1641. The response by a Scottish and English army was inevitable. Not much

---

[33] John C. Johnston, *Alexander Peden, The Prophet of the Covenant* (Glasgow: Johnston, 1902; reprint Kilkeel: Mourne Missionary Trust, 1988), p. 119.

later Cromwell imposed peace providing a few years breathing space before persecution of the Presbyterians resumed with the Restoration of Charles II. In the second half of the century the Catholics obtained a degree of tolerance which began to change the tenor of politics. When James II (ruled 1685-1688) came to the throne the Catholic fortunes changed greatly. By 1688 they were dominant in the Army, the law and civil administration with Protestant power greatly weakened. Contention led ultimately to King William being invited to take the English throne and his arriving in Ireland and the battle of the Boyne on 1 July 1690.

In England, a Scottish king, James VI/I, acceded to the throne in 1603. He found that there was religious division with the Puritans and other nonconformists pressing for freedom of worship. In 1629 Charles I started his Personal Rule, appointing in 1633 two arch persecutors: William Laud as Archbishop of Canterbury and Sir Thomas Wentworth as Lord Deputy of Ireland. So the scene was set for the Bishops Wars 1639-1640, Rebellion in Ireland 1641, the Civil War in 1642, and the Commonwealth under Cromwell. After Cromwell came the Restoration of Charles II 1660, the Great Plague of London in 1665, the Fire of London 1666, and ongoing squabbles with France, Spain, and Holland. Finally there arose the "Glorious Revolution" in 1688 when King James II was deposed and William and Mary were asked to take the throne.

In Scotland the Reformation was pressing ahead reaching its purest state in 1649-1650 when the true Covenanters held power. But always present were the machinations of the king and the prelates. In 1643 the Solemn League and Covenant alliance with the English Parliamentarians involved Scotland in the English Civil War. A period of attrition between royalist forces under the Marquis of Montrose (who had changed sides) saw thousands of Covenanters killed and the end of serious armed resistance in set piece battles. Even the Covenanters' battles of Rullion Green and Drumclog were more in the form of skirmishes. When it finally mattered at Bothwell Brig they were racked by internal dispute and faced by a larger, better trained and armed, royalist force which destroyed them. Valiant though they were, the Scottish armies facing Cromwell were divided among themselves and purged of many good soldiers, standing little chance against the professional New Model Army. The later years after the Restoration of Charles II, saw greatly increased persecution, the Killing Time of 1684-

1685, the rejection of James VII/II, and the final success of a free Presbyterian church confirmed in 1690.

The battles that have passed into Covenanter lore are Mauchline Moor (1648), Rullion Green (1666), Drumclog (1679), Bothwell Brig (1679), and Airsmoss (1680). There were, however, many more skirmishes as well as the major events during the Marquis of Montrose's campaign (1644-1645), and, of course, the Civil Wars.

Battles – Airsmoss, 22 July 1680. See also: Declaration at Sanquhar; Queensferry Papers.

Richard Cameron's defiance and declaration of war through the Declaration at Sanquhar, in June 1680, raised the stakes considerably and the search for him intensified. His whereabouts were advised to the military by Sir John Cochran of Ochiltree. On 22 July 1680 about 120 dragoons under the command of Bruce of Earlshall, came across Cameron with about sixty of his followers at Airsmoss, near Muirkirk, Ayrshire at about four o'clock in the afternoon. On seeing that there was no escape Richard Cameron prayed a short while and three times said, "Lord spare the green, and take the ripe." To his brother he said, "Come let us fight it out to the last; for this is the day that I have longed for, to die fighting against our Lord's enemies; and this is the day that we will get the crown."[34]

In the ensuing battle, nine Covenanters were killed including the Cameron brothers, and considerably more dragoons lay on the field such was the ferocity of the Cameronians resistance. Patrick Walker, in his *Life and Death of Richard Cameron: Six Saints of the Covenant*, relates that there were twenty-three horse and forty foot in Cameron's party and that there were twenty-eight troopers killed or died of their wounds within a few days. The Covenanters killed were: Rev. Richard Cameron, Michael Cameron, Robert Dick, Captain John Fowler, John Gemmel, James Gray, John Hamilton, Robert Paterson, and Thomas Watson.[35]

Airsmoss was the turning point for the Cameronians with the death of their charismatic leader. According to Walker, Bruce of

---

[34] Howie, *Worthies*, p. 428; Thomas Cameron, *Peden the Prophet* (Edinburgh: Blue Banner Productions, 1998), p. 428.

[35] Patrick Walker, *Six Saints of the Covenant*, ed. Hay Fleming (London: Hodder & Stoughton, 1901), p. 475.

Earlshall himself, gave a guinea for the privilege of hacking off Richard Cameron's head and hands which he did with a dirk. They were taken as a trophy to Edinburgh. There they were first shown to Cameron's elderly father who was in prison for allowing conventicles on his land and in his house at Falkland. The head and hands were then displayed above the Netherbow Gate.

Also captured was David Hackston of Rathillet, a gallant soldier and the witness to the murder of Archbishop Sharp on Magus Moor. Hackston suffered death by hanging, drawing, and quartering. It is reported by Walker that the hangman

> ripped up his breast with a durk, and taking out his heart alive, going round the scaffold with it fluttering upon the point of the durk; the hangman crying out aloud, "There is the heart of a traitor."[36]

Hackston's hands and head were struck off. One hand was sent to St. Andrews for display while the other was subsequently sent to Cupar where it was interred along with the heads of two other Covenanters who had been executed in Edinburgh 13 July 1681 for being followers of Donald Cargill (the successor to Cameron); they were Laurence Hay, a weaver from Fife, and Andrew Pitulloch, a farm labourer, from Largo. Hackston's head was placed besides his great friend Cameron's above the Netherbow Gate.[37]

The Bond of Mutual Defence is quoted in Thomson's *A Cloud of Witnesses.* This document was found upon Richard Cameron which was signed by him, his brother, and about thirty others. Thomson says it "justly deserveth to be insert here in its proper room, it being most agreeable to the true state of the testimony which these renowned martyrs sealed with their blood."[38]

> We, under subscribers, bind and oblige ourselves to be faithful to God, and true to one another, and to all others

---

[36] Walker, *Six Saints*, p. 233.

[37] Of historical note is that the quartering of Hackston was apparently the first in the "English custom" of actually cutting up the body. The Scots custom hitherto had been only to sever the arms and legs.

[38] *A Cloud of Witnesses for the Royal Prerogative of Jesus Christ*, ed. John H. Thomson (Edinburgh: Hunter & Co., 1871; reprint Harrisonburg: Sprinkle Publications, 1989), p. 500.

who shall join with us, in adhering to Rutherglen Testimony, and disclaiming the Hamilton Declaration, chiefly because it takes in the king's interest, which we are loosed from by reason of his perfidy and Covenant breaking, both to the most high God, and the people over whom he was set, under the terms of his propagating the main ends of the Covenants, to wit, the Reformation of religion ; and instead of that, usurping to himself the royal prerogatives of Jesus Christ, and encroaching upon the liberties of the Church, and so stating himself both in opposition to Jesus Christ the Mediator, and the free government of His house.

And also in disowning and protesting against the reception of the Duke of York, a professed Papist, and whatever else bath been done in this land (given to the Lord) in prejudice to our covenanted and universally sworn-to Reformation. And although, as the Lord who searcheth the heart knows, we be for government and governors, both civil and ecclesiastic, such as the Word of God and our Covenants allow; yet, by this we disown the present magistrates, who openly and avowedly are doing what in them lies for destroying utterly our work of reformation from Popery, Prelacy, Erastianism, and other heresies and errors; and by this we declare also, that we are not any more to own ministers indulged, and such as drive a sinful union with them ; nor are we to join any more in this public cause with ministers or professors of any rank, that are guilty of the defections of this time, until they give satisfaction proportioned to the scandal and offence they have given.[39]

Battles - Bothwell Brig, 22 Jun 1679. See also: Battles Drumclog.

Bothwell Brig will always be remembered as a battle of lost opportunities. Following the modest success at Drumclog three weeks previously the hopes of the Presbyterians ran high. But they lacked decisive leadership and spent a deal of time arguing amongst themselves about doctrinal matters. If they had pursued Claverhouse and his troopers from Drumclog into Glasgow while

[39] *Ibid.*, p. 500.

the iron was hot, there may have been a different outcome. All was not then lost if they had addressed themselves to military issues such as weapons, training and ensuring supplies of munitions. Their divisions this time stemmed from Robert Hamilton, the inexperienced leader of the Covenanter forces, who was against having any of the Indulged in the army. The Indulged were in favour of making representations to the government forces—which they did and received the anticipated rebuff.

James Ure of Shargarton was one of the brave band that with David Hackston and Captain John Paton fought a valiant rearguard action to hold the Brig itself, but were forced to withdraw and watch the troops of Monmouth pass over. He wrote subsequently of the lack of professionalism and supplies, where at one point he had been sent a barrel of raisins instead of gunpowder:

> We were not concerned with an enemy, as if there had not been one within a thousand miles of us. There were none went through the army, to see if we wanted powder and ball. I do really think there were few or none that had both powder and ball, to shoot twice.[40]

Bothwell Brig. Inscription (above) and memorial (right). Photos by the author.

Riven by disagreements, poorly armed with one small brass cannon, short of supplies, and with poor generalship the 4,000 men of the Covenanter army was decisively beaten by a substantial force

[40] Smellie, *Men of the Covenant*, p. 309.

of over 15,000 led by the Duke of Monmouth. The numbers vary with the source but about 400 were killed, many hewn down in flight by Claverhouse and his dragoons, and about 1100 prisoners were taken and penned in the open at Greyfriars Kirk Yard, Edinburgh, some for five months. The last 250 of these prisoners were sentenced to transportation to the colonies and 211 of them drowned on board the *Crown* when the ship sank off Orkney.

Following Bothwell Brig, and as had happened after the earlier Pentland Hills rising in 1666, the government sent in the military to settle the population. In Galloway the land owners were summoned before the Judiciary Court on 18 February 1680 where on very dubious evidence (from paid witnesses and informers) they were declared rebels, sentenced to death in their absence, with their lands forfeit. Among these were MacDougall of Freugh, William Gordon of Earlston and his son Alexander, Gordon of Craighlaw, Gordon of Culvennan, Dunbar of Machermore, and MacKie of Larg. William Gordon of Earlston had in fact been killed on the way to join his son at Bothwell Brig, but his name was included so that his lands could be seized. Into the Galloway region also came John Graham of Claverhouse and his brother Cornet Graham, who had been given a commission by the Privy Council to seize the moveable property of all who had been in the rebellion or had fled.

Battles – Drumclog, 1 June 1679. See also: Battles Bothwell Brig.

Drumclog was the only occasion when the Covenanters gained a military victory over the government forces. Modest though the victory was, it gave great hope to the Covenanters. The battle came about when the Covenanters were assembling near Loudon Hill in Ayrshire, for worship on the Sabbath. Nearby, John Graham of Claverhouse was pursuing the murderers of Archbishop Sharp (3 May 1679) and had taken some prisoners at Hamilton.

Hearing of the conventicle, Claverhouse and his troopers, with about seventeen prisoners, came upon the meeting at Drumclog on the morning of Sunday 1 June 1679. A watchman warned of their approach and the minister, Rev. Douglas, is reputed to have told the young armed men "Ye have got the theory; now for the practice."[41]

---

[41] *Ibid.*, p. 296.

On this occasion, the Covenanters outnumbered Claverhouse and his troopers by about four to one (some claim the Covenanters totalled 1,500, even 7,000 in one account) with the advantage of knowing the ground. Armed with mainly farm implements and the odd fowling gun, they assembled at the bottom of a hill which had marshy ground to the sides; this gave them a secure position from which to mount the attack. Singing a metrical psalm about 250 Covenanters threaded their way through the bogs and took on the troopers at close quarters. The troopers lost thirty-six of their number killed and seven taken prisoner, before they turned and fled towards Glasgow. To the fore in the fighting was a young eighteen-year-old, William Cleland of Douglas, described as a soldier poet, who would later do great service for the Covenanters at Dunkeld.

Inscription on the Drumclog memorial. Photo by the author.

A large number of Covenanters gathered following the victory and marched on Glasgow. However, poor leadership and lack of strategic direction only resulted in skirmishing, so the Covenanters withdrew without taking the city. They gathered in the town of Hamilton where their number grew to about 5,000, but they started arguing amongst themselves and split into two groups: the Indulged or moderates who sought compromise, and the "honest" party led by Robert Hamilton.

Claverhouse famously declared in his report about Drumclog dated 1 June 1679, to his Commander-in-Chief, the Earl of Linlithgow:

> They pursued us so hotly, that we got no time to rally. I saved the standards, but lost on the place about eight or ten men, besides wounded; but the dragoons lost many more.[42]

Battles - Mauchline Moor, 12 June 1648. See also: Engagement - Engagers; Whiggamore Raid.

The Engagement drawn up between the nobles (led by the Duke of Hamilton) and the king, was greatly resented by the smaller land owners and tenants, the rural landless, the poor, and by the ministers. They wanted the full Solemn League and Covenant implemented including the introduction of Presbyterianism in England and Ireland. The Engagement meant a split from the English Parliamentarians, with more civil war which required levies to be raised. Parliament ordered the raising of 30,000 foot and 6,000 horse, and sent envoys, Lord Cochran and the Laird of Garthland, to bring General Munro and his army back from Ireland. There was strong resistance in Glasgow and Sir James Turner was despatched to enforce the order. This he did by the expedient of quartering his troops on the religious and influential—the Magistrates, Council, and Session—who were soon coerced into submission. Many Scots went to Ulster to avoid military service.

A gathering of some 2,000 protesters took place at Mauchline Moor in Ayrshire, on 12 June 1648. Present were some leading figures of the Covenanters including John Nevay and his patron the

---

[42] J. H. Thompson, *The Martyr Graves of Scotland* (Edinburgh: Johnstone, Hunter & Co., 1877), p. 34.

Earl of Loudon, and William Guthrie. The appearance of some 1,600 horse and over 2,000 foot soldier under the command of General Middleton and Colonel Hurry was a cynical attempt to harass the Covenanters for opposing the Engagement. The Covenanters were meanwhile celebrating the Communion and the Earl of Loudon obtained the word of Middleton to allow the gathering to disperse peacefully. His word meant nothing for on the Monday morning the Covenanters were attacked. Some sixty prisoners were taken, including five officers and some clergy. The soldiers and clergy were released and the officers sentenced to death but were pardoned.

The Engagers did not, however, have things all their own way. Also present was Captain John Paton who was less trusting of the Engagers, and had with him his people from Fenwick who were armed. A stout defence was put up with Paton himself credited with killing eighteen of the Engager forces. Middleton and Hurry were both wounded. Metcalf, in his *History of Renfrew*, tells that

> the Lieutenant Generall new maid, callit Middletoun, was evill hurt in the heid and cuitt in thrie partis on his back, and verrie hardlie persewit be ane blacksmyth; and Colonell Hurrie evill hurt alsoe on the heid; as for the common trouperis their was almost as many slain as was of the countrie people.[43]

The implications of Mauchline Moor were great. The preparedness for armed resistance by the Western Association meant they were ready to support the "Whiggamore Raid" in September 1648. This was the march on Edinburgh that displaced the Engagers from power and made way for the two-year rule of the Kirk: the Second Reformation, as it is sometimes called.

Battles - Pentland Rising, Rullion Green, 28 November 1666.

The rising began with the intervention of John Maclellan, laird of Barscob, with three other fugitives, in the bullying of an elderly man by troopers in St. Johns Clachan of Dalry on 13 November 1666.

---

[43] William M. Metcalfe, *A History of the County of Renfrew* (Paisley: Alexander Gardner, 1905), p. 268.

The elderly farmer, named Grier, had not paid fines for non-attendance at church and was being taken by soldiers to harvest some grain. News came to Barscob that the old man was seized, bound and was to be placed on a hot gridiron. Challenged why they were using the old man so the troopers led by Corporal George Deanes drew their swords and Barscob, not having a ball loaded in his pistol, rammed the pipe he was smoking into the barrel and fired at Deanes, who went down. The soldiers were set upon and beaten and the old man released. At Dalry, the local garrison of sixteen soldiers were taken by conventiclers from Balmaclellan, with one soldier killed in the tussle. The enlarged mob then decided to attack Sir James Turner's headquarters at Dumfries where they took him by surprise in his nightclothes. The object was to hold him prisoner and seek a hearing of their grievances by the Privy Council. However, the throng gathered momentum, as did their numbers while they passed through Ayrshire and Lanarkshire, with thoughts of emulating the "Whiggamore Raid" of 1648.

The progress of the rebellion and recruitment of supporters was Dalmellington (18th), Tarbolton (19th), Ayr (20th), Coylton (21st), Ochiltree (22nd), Cumnock (23rd), Muirkirk and Douglas (24th), Lesmahagow and Lanark (Sunday, 25th), Bathgate and Newbridge (26-27th), Colinton (27-28th), and the battle at Rullion Green on the afternoon and evening of Wednesday, 28 November 1666. But information from Edinburgh was that there was little support for the rebellion within the city. Again poorly prepared the Covenanters began to bicker amongst themselves and many left to return to their homes. At Lanark on the 26th the force of about 1,000 men and five officers renewed the Solemn League and Covenant. By the time the group reached the outskirts of Edinburgh and learned of the lack of support, their numbers had fallen to less than a thousand, including thirty two ministers. A decision was taken to go home and they turned to head back towards Galloway. Meanwhile, General Tam Dalziel of the Binns had been shadowing them with a force of about 3000, and fell upon the Covenanters at Rullion Green, about eight miles south of Edinburgh on the slopes of the Pentland Hills. A gallant defence was made but by the evening over fifty Covenanters lay dead, including two Presbyterian ministers from Ireland who had been involved in Captain Bloods Plot, and about a hundred were taken prisoners on the offer of quarter. The rest fled into the hills and headed west; many died of their wounds and were buried where they lay on the moors and bogs.

The significance of the battle of Rullion Green is that it was the first occasion where there had been anything like an organised armed resistance to the government. Despite having been given quarter, many of the prisoners were executed in Edinburgh as traitors on the connivance of Archbishop Sharp and despite the protests of General Tam Dalziel who had given them quarter. Several of the rebels were sent to their home areas for execution as a warning to others. The bloodshed served to shock with its brutality. The armed rising frightened as well as embarrassed the government, and led to a modified policy line which included accommodation of the well behaved.

Rullion Green memorial. Photo by the author.

A Proclamation was issued declaring those persons at Rullion Green to be rebels and traitors, and prohibiting having any contact with them. In a letter dated 18 February 168, the Earl of Tweedale wrote to Lauderdale about the Pentland Rising in which he advises:

> Of the rebels we have comed to this account: 218 have taken the benefit of his Maties gratious pardon; 309 have neglected it; about 80 were kild in the field; 40 execut; 31 dead on the Stewartry and Dumfriseeshyr, we know not what in the rest; 30 are fugitive; and 20 forfawlted; the rest ar fled out of the country, or had noe constant residence, belonging to other shyrs, and ar still vagabonds. Now most conclud, ther wer not 1000 at the fight; and this account is of about 700.[44]

The memorial to the fallen at Rullion Green, a railed enclosure with a single headstone that is now difficult to read, sits on the edge of a copse of trees on the brow of a hill. It is a poignant place to be on a quiet evening with naught but sheep quietly grazing on the slopes. The memorial reads:

Side 1.

Here
and near to
this place lyes the
Reverend Mr John Crookshank
and Mr Andrew M'cormick
ministers of the Gospel and
About fifty other true covenanted
Presbyterians who were
killed in this place in their own
Inocent self defence and
defence of the covenanted
work of Reformation By
Thomas Dalzeel of Bins
upon the 28 of november
1666 Rev 12. 11 Erected
September 28, 1738.

---

[44] Thos. M'Crie, *Memoirs of His Own Life and Times* (Edinburgh: Sir James Turner, 1829), pp. 60-61.

Side 2.

A cloud of witnesses lyes here,
who for Christ's interest did appear
For to restore true Liberty
Overturned then by Tyrrany
And by Proud Prelats who did rage
Against the Lord's own heritage.
They sacrificed were for the Laws
Of Christ their King, his noble cause,
These heroes fought with great renown,
By falling got the Martyr Crown.

A further memorial is to be found in the poem "Rullion Green" by John Stuart Blackie, from his *Songs of Religion and Life*:

Rullion Green

Say not that they were harsh and stern and sour,
Or say they were so but not therefore base;
In iron times God sends with mighty power
Iron apostles to make smooth His ways;
And hearts of rock, close-clamped with many a bar,
He plants where angry billows lash the shore
Thus love by fear, thus peace is pledged by war -
(Stern law!) and gospel paths are paved in gore;
We reap in ease what they did sow in toil
And rate them harsh, and stern, and sour while
Rude warriors rest! God from that ill wrought good
Your strong endurance wrought strong hate of wrong,
Let dark Dunnottar's dungeon solitude,
And the strong Bass, attest your suffering long;
No polished pen, no smooth and courtly verse,
Ye need to prove the virtue of your crime;
Pentland's green slopes, and the bleak moors o' the Merse
Shall be your record to remotest time;
Ourselves your sons, inheriting your stuff,
While we are worthy, shall be praise enough.[45]

---

[45] Johnston, *Treasury*, p. 555.

Other significant battles.

Battles - Boyne, 1 July 1690.

General Schomberg's presence in Ulster from August 1689 brought reassurance to the Presbyterians who returned to their farms and began rebuilding homes. Schomberg and his army soon headed south but there was not much activity through the winter. In February 1690 Wolseley, who was at Belturbet, surprised the Irish at Cavan, captured the town and destroyed a vast amount of supplies before he retreated and took Killeshandra Castle on his return journey. In May Schomberg took possession of Charlemont Fort, a stronghold considered to be one of the most important in Ulster. King William meanwhile found that the English were impatient with the war and he took personal charge, landing at Carrickfergus on June 14. He too moved south quickly and at Loughbrickland he reviewed an army of some 36,000 men: English, Irish, Scots, Dutch, Danish and French Huguenots. On the 25th June he reached Newry and by the 30th was close to the Irish army of some 35,000 at Drogheda on the banks of the river Boyne.

The next day, split into three divisions, William's army forced their way with great difficulty across the river Boyne to do battle with James' forces. Schomberg was killed in the action and William took an active part rallying the troops. A leader from the front, William went forward with a Dutch regiment which captured Richard Hamilton, the Irish commander, and son of Sir George Hamilton of Strabane. The battle was won but the Irish retreated in good order. Watching from Dunore Hill, James soon departed with cavalry escort to Dublin where he arrived in the evening. A defeated James II took ship at Kinsale the following day and fled to France with his hopes for his restoration to the thrones of England, Ireland and Scotland in ruins.

In the Battle of the Boyne, James' army lost about 1,500 men, and William's army lost about five hundred. Ireland was not yet subjugated, however. Limerick was besieged in August 1690 until William decided to lift the siege, put his army in winter quarters and he returned to England. The Earl of Marlborough meanwhile attacked Cork, which surrendered in September 1690, and he went on to take Kinsale in October. There followed a long drawn out siege of Athlone in June 1691, an attack on Aughrim in July 1691, with a return to Limerick in August 1691 to face a force led by the French General St. Ruth. The Treaty of Limerick was signed on October 3. This ended the war and acknowledged William III as king of Ireland.

Battles - Carberry Hill, 15 June 1567. See also: Langside.

Following the murder of Lord Darnley in the explosion on 9 February 1567, there was a strong groundswell of opinion against both Mary, Queen of Scots, and her paramour, the Earl of Bothwell. A trial of Bothwell had come to nothing when his prosecutor the Earl of Lennox failed to appear having turned back with his 3,000 troops when confronted by Bothwell's 4000 Borderers. The elevation of Bothwell to Duke of Orkney and Zetland on 12 May, then marriage three days later, fuelled the flames of opinion. With only the support of the Hamiltons (who hated Lennox) Mary and Bothwell took to the field of battle at Carberry Hill, near Musselburgh, on 15 June to face the lords. They carried a banner that showed Darnley's infant son (the future King James VI) praying for vengeance besides his dead father, beneath a tree, and the legend "Judge and revenge my cause, O Lord." In a bloodless encounter taken up with negotiations, Mary offered to surrender if Bothwell was allowed to escape, which he did riding from out of her life into exile. Mary was brought to Edinburgh and then imprisoned in Lochleven Castle, Kinross, where her keeper was Sir William Douglas, half-brother to the Earl of Moray. Here she remained for some eleven months while public opinion against her gathered strength.

On June 20 one of Bothwell's soldiers was found in possession of a silver casket containing letters from Mary to the Earl of Bothwell. It was soon alleged that the letters proved her complicity in Darnley's death and justified her deposition. John Knox denounced her from the pulpit and the General Assembly similarly raised its voice against her. On 24 July 1567 she was forced to abdicate, despite her protestations, and her son, James VI, was crowned five days later. The Earl of Moray was appointed Regent on 25 August 1567, taking an oath to maintain the Reformation.

Battles – Carbisdale, 27 April 1650.

The battle at Carbisdale was one of forlorn hope, a last desperate attempt by the Marquis of Montrose to come to the aid of his king, now Charles II. Having fled abroad after the battle of Philiphaugh Montrose was devastated by the execution of Charles I, and responded to a personal commission from his son to invade Scotland. With an army of about five hundred German and Danish mercenaries he arrived in Orkney in March 1650. He was able to rally some support but nowhere near what he had hoped for. Learning of his landing the government despatched Colonel Archibald Strachan with about three hundred troops from Inverness. An experienced and allegedly ruthless soldier, Strachan was ordered to harass Montrose while reinforcements were brought up from Brechin. Montrose meanwhile, waited at Carbisdale for royalist supporters from the clans to arrive, but few came. Dug in on a hillside he was tactically well placed to face the impetuous Strachan whom he outnumbered by about four to one. But he fell for a feinted attack and was lured into the open where Strachan's troops broke the inexperienced militia men from Orkney. The mercenaries from Denmark and Germany lasted a while longer but it was soon over with over four hundred royalist soldiers dead and 450 prisoners. Strachan lost one man. Montrose fled and for two days evaded capture disguised as a shepherd. But he was taken prisoner by Neil MacLeod of Assynt, or rather by his wife who gave Montrose shelter and sent runners to fetch her husband and the military. Montrose was taken to Edinburgh arriving there on May 18. On May 21, he was sentenced to be hanged, drawn, and quartered, having already been convicted in his absence for treason. On Tuesday, 22 May 1650, sentence was carried out, his head was displayed at the Tolbooth of Edinburgh while his arms and legs displayed at Aberdeen, Glasgow, Stirling, and Perth.

Battles - Cromdale 1 May 1690.

The battle at Cromdale was the final event in Scotland of James II's attempt to keep to his throne. About eight hundred Highlanders under Major General Thomas Buchan were trapped in a night attack and over three hundred of them were killed. Shortly afterwards,

James was defeated in Ireland at the battle of the Boyne, on 1 June 1690, and he departed into exile.

Battles - Dunaverty, May 1647.

In the aftermath of the hand-over of Charles to the Parliamentarians on February 3, forces were sent north to finalise matters with Huntly, and to the west to exterminate the Macdonalds who were still in rebellion. General David Leslie was again in command, while the brutal and savage executions of prisoners was again the order of the day. At Lismore quarter was given to the defenders but even so some thirty five to forty Irish there were butchered. Leslie with Argyll and 8,000 men then attacked the MacDonalds in Kintyre, driving them into a fort at Southend: Dunaverty. Here, some eight hundred prisoners, men, women, and children were taken and half were massacred. Later at his trial, Argyll defended the action as having been ordered by the Council of War. He had personally allowed a hundred men to leave for service in the French armies. A principal character at the slaughter was John Nivay, an army chaplain and minister at Newmilns, who had incited Leslie to massacre the prisoners. Leslie is alleged to have remarked after the job was done "Now Mr John, have you not once gotten your fill of blood?"[46] Hewison, in *The Covenanters*, tells that some two hundred years later the skulls and bones that littered the area were collected by a Rev. Douglas MacDonald of Sanda, a descendant of the sole male child to survive. They were given a Christian burial in a small walled enclosure in a field near the spot where the garrison was butchered.

Battles – Dunbar, 3 September 1650. See also: Declaration of the English Army; Battle at Hamilton; Protesters; Resolutioners; Whiggamore Raid.

The battle of Dunbar, in September 1650, came at a fateful time for Scotland. The Engagers under the Duke of Hamilton had been routed at Preston in August 1648 and brought the "honest" party, the extreme Covenanters, to power. This had created what has been called the Second Reformation, or the Second Temple, and was a

[46] Hewison, *Covenanters*, Vol. 1, p. 442.

period of true Presbyterianism with both civil and clerical rule. But their ill fated support for Charles II, who had landed in Scotland on 23 June 1650, was their undoing and made war with England unavoidable.

The simple fact was that the last thing England needed was a Covenanted House of Stuart in Scotland. At the very least Charles and the Scots army needed to be confined to north of the Border. Lord Fairfax, commander of the English Parliamentary forces, resigned on grounds of conscience as he felt unable to lead an invasion of Scotland, although he did not object to others doing so. Oliver Cromwell took his place as Lord General, thereby clearing the way for a punitive expedition. At Chillingham Castle in Northumberland, on 19 July 1650, Cromwell held a muster at which there were 16,354 soldiers for his invasion. On July 22, the English army entered Scotland and proceeded at a leisurely pace to Dunbar (26 July) Musselburgh (28 July) and arrived outside a well defended Edinburgh. There followed a period of tactical skirmishes, with Leven sitting fast in Edinburgh and Cromwell seeking to draw him out for an early battle since his own supplies were dangerously low. Eventually the need for supplies by sea meant a retrenchment of Cromwell's forces in Dunbar.

The Scots had made two declarations to levy troops: on July 4 for 5,500 horse and 14,300 foot, and a second Act increased the total to 36,000. This led to an army of about 18,000 foot and 8,000 horse under David Leslie's command. However, the Kirk were unhappy at the defensive policy, which did not require so many men, and on 28 July they set up a subcommittee to oversee the disposition of the Scottish forces. Yet again, there was an orgy of witch hunting and purging of the army between August 2 and August 5, which lost them the services of 3,000 highly experienced men and upwards of eighty experienced officers. It gained for them defeat at Dunbar on 3 September 1650.

Despite his protestations at the expulsion of so many officers and men, Leslie was encouraged to do battle. The decision to do so was finally made by the officers in command: the Earl of Leven, Colonels Montgomery, Strachan, Gilbert Ker, Sir James Lumsden (a veteran of Marston Moor), and Major Generals Sir John Browe of Fordell and James Holborne. They had seen that Cromwell had moved to Dunbar with several thousands sick with dysentery and was re supplying his army. David Leslie meanwhile had his forces in a strong position on Doon Hill but knew that he would have to move from the exposed position within a few days. Leslie then left his position and moved down from the hill to level land next the Brock Burn to do battle. In particular he moved the left wing of the army into a cramped area between a ravine and the slope of Doon Hill. Seeing the movement taking place Cromwell realised that he could bottle up about a third of Leslie's forces by redistributing his own, including the artillery. During the night he manoeuvred his cavalry and cannon into position so that at 4:30 a.m. on September 3 the attack began. In the dawn light, his cannon pounded the Scots cavalry and his three foot regiments swept through the startled Covenanters. By mid morning the battle was resolved with some 4,000 Covenanters dead or wounded and 10,000 taken prisoner. For the able bodied prisoners it was a march to the salt mines in England (Cheshire); recruits for the army in France or slavery in the new colonies in the West Indies and America. Afterwards, Cromwell wrote: "They were made as by the Lord of Hosts as stubble to their swords."[47]

There is some uncertainty to just how many prisoners were taken. About 4,500 were marched south during which some 1,500 died. On 11 September 1650, the residual 3,000 prisoners were counted into Durham Cathedral, which was used as a prison. Dysentery broke out and the prisoners were forced to dig up the stone floor to make a latrine. About 1,600 of them died and were buried in the churchyard of Durham Cathedral in a mass grave. Sir Arthur Haselrigge, who had charge of the prisoners wrote to the Council of War in London, 31 October 1650, that he only had some six hundred healthy prisoners remaining. The majority it seems died and the remainder transported. Augustine Walker, master of the *Unity*, took 150 prisoners and sold sixty of them to the Saugus Iron Works at Lynn for between £20 and £30 each. Fifteen went to Berwick, Maine, and others to nearby York. Overall the best estimates suggest that about one thousand prisoners may have been transported to Virginia, New England, and probably Bermuda.

Hewison, in *The Covenanters*, relates that the "craven generals, the Council of War, the entire cavalry, and the officers of the infantry fled and left the rank and file to their fate."[48] Cromwell

---

[47] Hewison, *Covenanters*, Vol. 2, p. 14.
[48] *Ibid.*

meanwhile asserted that he had only about twenty officers and men wounded. Although blamed for the lost battle, Leslie wrote to Argyll that they might have easily beaten them "if the officers had stayed by their troops and regiments."[49] This was an obvious criticism of the purging by the Kirk which had left Leslie with only the inexperienced and ineffectual officers and inexperienced soldiers. They were, of course, the elect of the Godly and the Kirk was hardly in a position to criticise. Cromwell meanwhile anticipated the next move by Charles writing in a prophetic letter:

> Surely it's probable the Kirk has done their do. I believe the king will set upon his own score now; wherein he will find many friends.[50]

The consequences of Dunbar was the emergence of five ideologically–geographically oriented factions.

The Covenanters at the centre still controlled Parliament, the Committee of the Estates and the Committee of the Kirk. But there was a shudder of horror at the slaughter with realisation that the Second Reformation was in real danger. They controlled the central regions, Stirling, Fife and the northeast.

Argyll and his clansmen still held their ground in the west, although it became clear to him that there was need for compromise and especially for return of some very able soldiers who had been cast out by the Act of Classes, if the monarchy was to be saved.

There were the Covenanters with republican sympathies in the south west. Here there was a minor revolt by Colonels Strachan and Gilbert Ker, who were greatly dissatisfied with Leslie and refused to serve under him. They were bitterly opposed to any weakening of the Act of Classes to admit all and sundry to the royalist ranks and they departed to the west country to recruit their own force. They were soon trounced at Hamilton in December 1650 by General Lambert.

In the Highlands, the presence of powerful support for the royal cause was exposed. The conquered lands under English control were now devastated with many homeless and starving people. There soon developed the schism between the "Resolutioners" and

---

[49] *Ibid.*, p. 15.

[50] *Ibid.*, p. 16.

the "Remonstrants" or "Protesters." And King Charles made a dash for freedom: the Start.

Battles – Dundee, 28 August 1651.

On 14 August 1651, Stirling castle surrendered to General Monck and the Cromwellian forces which left Monck with some 7,000 troops to pacify Dundee. This city was a well fortified and rich from the trading of its many merchants. It was held by Major General Robert Lumsden of Mountquhanie, a seasoned campaigner in Sweden and a brave man who would fight to the death. Monck also learnt of the location of the Committee of Estates who had moved to Alyth, about fifteen miles from Dundee. He sent Colonel Matthew Alured with eight hundred cavalry overnight through torrential rain to surround the town early in the morning of 28 August and captured the Council. In so doing the small force drove off some 4,000 troops who were not therefore available to defend Dundee. This most illustrious body, consisting of most of the Scots government, was shipped to London. They included: Leven, Crawford, Marischal, Ogilvy, Hepburn of Humbie, Fowlis of Colinton, Cockburn of Ormiston, Fotherinham of Powrie, Hamilton of Bargany, Archibald Sydserf, Colonel Andrew Mill, and clerics Douglas (Moderator of the General Assembly) Andrew Ker, Mungo Law, John Smith, James Hamilton, John Rattray of Alyth, George Pittloch the younger, and one James Sharp, minister at Crail.

Although advised by the city ministers to surrender Lumsden and his troops declined to do so leaving Monck no option to batter down the gates and enter by force on 1 September. Carnage ensued with men women and children being slaughtered. The story goes that the defenders left their shirt tails out as a means of identifying one another. Lumsden himself made a last stand in the parish church where it is alleged they were slaughtered after quarter had been given. Lumsden's head was fixed on a pike over the door of the church steeple while in the town the victors entered on a riot of blood, lust and loot. The value of the spoils was said to be £200,000 sterling with some individual soldiers taking £500. Prisoners were everywhere, and a fleet of one hundred and ninety ships captured in the harbour were subject of discussion by English officers seeking prize status. Casualties vary according to which side quotes, but about 1,000 were killed with 140 civilian casualties, and 500 prisoners were taken.

Battles – Dunkeld, 21 August 1689. See also: Killiecrankie.

In the aftermath of Killiecrankie, General MacKay and the remnant of his forces made their way back to Perth. In the victorious but leaderless Dundee's army there were differences of opinion about who should take command, while the Highlanders themselves plundered the baggage train of the defeated Mackay. In the end Colonel Cannon, as a professional soldier, took command much to the annoyance of Cameron of Lochiel who stormed off with his clansmen. Cannon and his army stayed in Perthshire regrouping themselves; in Edinburgh the order was given for the Cameronian Regiment, under the command of a young Colonel William Cleland to march poste haste to Dunkeld. The force of about 800 men arrived in Dunkeld on August 17 where they erected their defences. On August 21, Cannon and about 4,000 troops descended on Dunkeld, engaging in fierce fighting which lasted for about sixteen hours. A last redoubt was at Dunkeld House where William Cleland was shot several times and died. Just when all hope was about to be abandoned, in the late evening, the Highlanders withdrew leaving 300 dead and dying in the town which had been virtually razed to the ground. William Cleland was buried in Dunkeld Cathedral and General MacKay was able to move through the Pass of Killiecrankie to take Blair Atholl. This ended the last serious threat from the supporters of King James in Scotland.

Battles – Hamilton, 1 December 1650. See also: Dunbar.

Following the defeat at Dunbar the Scottish army and its leaders were in disarray and the repeal of the Act of Classes, which had contributed so much to the problem, came too late. Division among the senior officers resulted in several, including Colonels Ker and Strachan, giving up their commissions and taking up arms again with the Western Association.

Cromwell perceived that some action needed to be taken against the threat from the west and despatched his forces to face them. He sent Lambert to Peebles with some 3,000 horse where he joined with Maj. General Walley. Together they were at Lanark by the 28th November. Cromwell with eight regiments of horse rode via Kirk o' Shotts, collected a ninth regiment, and reached Hamilton on the 29th November. Ker, with five regiments and eager for battle, held Bothwell Brig but withdrew during the night in the face of overwhelming odds. Cromwell then retreated leaving the way clear for Lambert's forces to cross the Clyde the next day. Ker underestimated Lambert's strength, thinking he had only 1,200 horse against his 1,600 camped at Rutherglen. When he attacked he found to his cost they were double his own. Thus unwisely tempted into battle on 1 December 1650, the army of the Western Association was cut to pieces at nearby Heiton. Gilbert Ker was wounded and captured along with less than a hundred of his men, about one hundred were killed and the rest scattered and fled. Colonel Strachan attempted to gather survivors together but most melted away into the countryside and went home. Disconsolate and unable to rally resistance, he surrendered to the English and was removed to Edinburgh. In Edinburgh the Castle had held out but eventually Sir Walter Dundas yielded after heavy bombardments. Of a like mind to Strachan both men put their ideology before patriotism. Both were held in high disdain by many who condemned them as a hypocritical traitors, although, ironically, they had merely remained loyal to long held beliefs. For their "sins" they were excommunicated by the Kirk.

Battles – Inverkeithing, 20 July 1651.

Cromwell's subjugation of Scotland had come to a halt before Stirling Castle, where David Leslie and the main Scots Army were securely ensconced and waiting for an opportunity to march with the King into England. They were however, very short of supplies and close to having to come out and face Cromwell, who had meanwhile been busy obtaining flat bottomed boats to carry his army across the Forth. Between July 19 and 20, over 5,000 troops were ferried across and Lt. Gen. John Lambert joined them.

The Scots were forced to take action else Lambert and his small army would overrun Fife and cut off Stirling. Maj. Gen. Holborne with 4,000 troops—a mixture of Highlanders, local militia, archers from Perth, and regular cavalry—reached Inverkeithing before Lambert had finished disembarking his army. With typical daring and tactical flair, Lambert launched into an attack and after some skirmishing a short close quarter fight of no more than quarter of an hour resolved the issue. Holborne fled with some of his cavalry while Sir John Browne and the rest of the horse were overwhelmed. Eight hundred Clan Maclean and seven hundred Clan Buchanan died where they stubbornly stood, refusing to flee. In a ferocious pursuit over a distance of six miles, Lambert's troops brought the total killed to 2,000 and took 1,400 prisoners. Barely a thousand Scots escaped.

The consequence of the short, sharp battle were significant. It meant that Scotland was at Cromwell's mercy, since he could now assault Stirling more easily, and the way was open for him to march on Perth and the north east. David Leslie meanwhile had to decide whether to attack Lambert before any reinforcements reached him, while not risking his army against the full Cromwell led forces south of the Forth. The only other option was to head south into England if opportunity afforded itself. The hiatus was broken when Cromwell saw that Leslie was moving against Lambert and responded by moving more troops across the Forth. But the Scots then withdrew back into Stirling. Cromwell however, continued to move regiments across the Forth using every possible boat he could find and struck out for Perth. In doing so he seems to have deliberately left the way open for the king and the Scots army to escape. Alternatively it might be read that Leslie had also bluffed in order to draw Cromwell across the Forth and thus open his way south. Either way, on July 31 Charles II and the now invading Scottish army headed for England in high hopes of finding royalist support waiting. Doom awaited them at Worcester.

Battles – Killiecrankie, 27 July 1689.

The Irish civil war had gone well for James II and at the time of his arrival in Ireland on 12 March 1689, his hopes must have been reasonably high. Apart from the strongholds of Londonderry and Enniskillen in Ulster the Jacobites held sway, with France in the background seemingly ready to join his cause. In Scotland Claverhouse, Viscount Dundee, was declared a rebel by the Estates on 30 March 1689 and he hurried to raise the standard for James by summoning the clans to a rendezvous at Glenroy on May 18. With about 2,000 clansmen at his command Dundee spent two months engaged in guerrilla warfare until in July he received the support from James in Ireland—but only by about three hundred almost raw recruits. General Mackay of the parliamentary forces was despatched to deal with Dundee and with some 4,000 troops marched towards Blair Atholl where Dundee had his headquarters. On 27 July 1689, Dundee's forces assembled above the pass of Killiecrankie trapping Mackay. From their advantage point the Highlanders charged down and slaughtered the infantry who were unable to fix bayonets before the horde was upon them. Only some 400 survived of Mackay's troops while a thousand or more Highlanders were killed. The battle was won but Dundee himself was struck down and killed by a sniper's bullet. His command was taken over by Colonel Alexander Cannon who had come from Ireland with the single regiment. But the Cameronian Regiment, only founded in Douglas on 14 May 1689, was too strong for him at Dunkeld on 21 August 1689. Without Dundee, the cause of James II floundered and, although he sent Major General Thomas Buchan to revive efforts in the spring of 1690, all was finally lost at Cromdale on 1 May 1690.

Battles – Kilsyth, 15 August 1645.

Kilsyth was one of the string of successes enjoyed by the Marquis of Montrose in his campaign of 1644-1645. It was also an important event politically as the Scottish army under Alexander Leslie (Earl of Leven) was at that time allied with the New Model Army in England, having been successful at the fall of Carlisle in June. In July, Leven had moved even further afield to Hereford. Montrose meanwhile had assembled his forces at Kilsyth, near Stirling, and on August 15 fought the army of the Covenant under Lieutenant General Baillie to gain a decisive victory. The battle ended in a slaughter with most of the Covenanters' foot soldiers killed on the spot, then followed by a chase for some fourteen miles in which most of the remainder of the army was either drowned escaping or hacked down. The *Scots Worthies* tells us that Captain Paton was caught in a bog but, struggling free, went to the aid of Colonels Hacket and Strachan—all three riding off pursued by the enemy. The story continues that they had not gone far when they met fifteen of the enemy of whom they killed thirteen and two escaped. A little further on they were assailed by thirteen more and killed ten. They were then attacked by eleven Highlanders; they killed nine and put the rest to flight. Montrose's victory at Kilsyth therefore effectively destroyed the Scottish home army, placing the country at his mercy. Indeed, it was only the outbreak of a serious bout of plague in the city that prevented Edinburgh being taken. In England David Leslie was despatched with the cavalry to go to Scotland's aid (recalled by the Estates with 4,000 foot and 1,000 dragoons). Leven hurriedly abandoned the siege of Hereford, making for the North of England to be ready to help if needed.

Leven had been very concerned at being so far from Scotland while Montrose was being so successful behind his lines. Coupled with this was a growing disillusionment with the alliance. The army was ill paid, having had one months pay in seven months, and was badly supplied, while the aim of religious uniformity was fading. Moreover, commitment to the alliance was keeping him from the defence of Scotland. The accumulation of these pressures was too much for Leven and he expressed a desire to surrender his commission. The English Parliamentarians on the other hand viewed Leven's turn round and heading North with suspicion, having in mind the possibility of the Scots coming to terms with King Charles I. A change of fortune for the Scots came with David Leslie's defeat of Montrose at Philiphaugh on 13 September 1645. This eased the pressures on Leven who agreed to lay siege to Newark, appearing there in November 1645. The siege was still in progress when King Charles surrendered to the Scots on 5 May 1646. The next day Newark surrendered and Leven and his Army of the Covenant withdrew with its royal prize to the North.

Battles – Langside, 13 May 1568. See also: Carberry Hill.

Following her imprisonment in Lochleven Castle, the fortunes of Mary, Queen of Scots, took a downturn. The revelations of her letters to Bothwell had led to her abdication, under pressure from the dissident nobles, on 24 July 1567. On the continent France was in the throes of civil war, while Spain was at war with Holland. The Pope had withdrawn his favours, so only in England was there a woman's word of comfort from Queen Elizabeth I. Mary first attempted to escape in March but was however, caught. On 2 May 1568, she finally escaped from Lochleven, joining with supporters and the ever faithful Hamiltons. At Hamilton, Mary issued a proclamation revoking her abdication saying it had been obtained under duress (which was probably true). She had a choice of trying to clear her name in Parliament or to do battle. Choosing the option to do battle she and her supporters headed for the west of Scotland where there was evidence of support for her. On May 13, Mary and a considerable force of about 6,500 were making their way to the safety of Dumbarton Castle by way of the southern edge of Glasgow via Rutherglen and Langside. The Earl of Moray heard of the Queen's movement and took his army of about 4,000 out of Glasgow to see which way the Queen would seek to pass. Finding her on the south side of the River Clyde, Moray marched and took possession of a hill near the village of Langside. With Moray were the Earls of Morton, Semple, Hume, Mar, Glencairn, Monteith and a goodly gathering of the citizens of Glasgow. Prominent among the commanders was Sir William Kirkcaldy of Grange who had been involved in the assassination of Cardinal Beaton in 1548 and a sometime supporter of Queen Mary both before and after her exile in England. He was sent forward with cavalry, allegedly each rider taking with him a musketeer, to secure the village of Langside. These musketeers were positioned to be able to pour concentrated fire on the narrow road. This they did when a body of foot soldiers under Lord Claud Hamilton advanced. At this point the royal army faltered then broke and fled with Moray's cavalry wreaking havoc among them. It is said the rout happened because the Commander in Chief of the royal forces, the Earl of Argyll, fell off his horse and panicked his soldiers. Mary turned and rode for the English border where she crossed the Solway into England and exile on 16 May 1568.

Battles - Marston Moor, 2 July 1644.

Following the agreement of the several times amended "Solemn League and Covenant" of 1643, the Scottish Estates furnished an army of 18,000 foot, 2,000 horse, 1,000 dragoons and a train of artillery, while the Parliamentarians agreed to pay £31,000 a month subsidy towards the costs of the army. Alexander Leslie, now the Earl of Leven, was made commander in chief. His first task for the new alliance was to recover the Newcastle coal fields and secure the north eastern ports with their communications to the Continent. On 19 January 1644 the Scottish army crossed the River Tweed and headed for Newcastle. However, firm resistance and the absence of siege facilities caused Leven to bypass the city and join the army of the Eastern Association besieging York. On July 2, the armies met a determined Prince Rupert at Marston Moor. In a battle that swung to and fro for some time the Covenanters did well, especially Lieutenant General David Leslie and three cavalry regiments who supported Cromwell, with Leslie at one point taking command from the wounded Cromwell. In the last phase of the battle Colonel Hugh Fraser's dragoons assaulted the white coated infantry and drove them from the field. The victory for the alliance deprived King Charles of two armies and, when York surrendered two weeks later, the royalist presence in the North of England was broken.

Battles – Newburn, 28 and 30 August 1640. See also: Bishops' Wars.

In 1640, the First Bishops' War had ended with the Treaty of Birks (Berwick), enquiries having been made by the Scots about assistance from the Continent to mediate in their dispute with King Charles I over the enforcement of episcopacy. But the original correspondence fell into the king's hands. He summoned a Parliament to disclose the treason and to get money for an army. Parliament denied him the money and effectively told him the Scottish problem was his, not theirs. In Scotland the Estates assembled in June and made the taking of the Covenant compulsory; passed an act for a triennial Parliament; and appointed a permanent Committee of Estates to act when Parliament was not in session. The Marquis of Argyll was sent to defend the western coast against intrusion from Ireland and the Earl Marischal ordered to take care of royalists in the north around Aberdeen.

Thus, on 20 August 1640 the Scots army took the initiative and marched across the border moving unopposed through Northumberland. Arriving at the River Tyne they forced their way across at Newburn on 28 August 1640. It is fair to say that Lord Conway, commander at Newcastle, had insufficient troops at his disposal and he soon fled the field to Darlington. On Sunday 30 August Newcastle opened its gates and surrendered. Meanwhile petitions were presented to Charles at York and a Council of Peers was summoned to attend at the end of September. To Charles's annoyance, the peers recommended that he come to an accommodation with the Scots. After a long debate a cessation of arms was agreed with the Scots demanding £850 a day for the maintenance of their troops on English soil pending settlement of the question of episcopacy in Scotland. Charles was forced to agree and the Treaty of Ripon was signed, with outstanding matters taken to London for further consideration.

Battles – Philiphaugh, 13 Sept 1645. See also: Irish troops; Kilsyth; No Quarter.

After Kilsyth, Montrose was in virtual command of Scotland. He was recognised as the King's Viceroy, Edinburgh had released prisoners and Glasgow had opened its gates to him. But fate struck hard, because he alienated his Highlanders by forbidding any plundering of Glasgow; Alasdair MacColl (McDonald) was rewarded with a knighthood but preferred to return to the west and continue his war against the Campbells; the Gordons road off in a jealous huff and were seen no more; and there were no replacements coming forward from the Lowlands. Thus denuded, his army was caught by surprise in the early morning mists on 13 September at Philiphaugh near Selkirk. David Leslie's cavalry hacked and butchered their enemy in an orgy of retaliation. Montrose himself fought his way out, first saving the standards, but his cause was at an end. Though he tried to re muster in the Highlands, no support was forthcoming from the Gordons nor the Irish and in May 1646 the king sent word to abandon a hopeless cause. Broken, Montrose went into exile—for a while.

Philiphaugh is remembered also as the scene of the dreadful slaughter of the camp followers, wives, children, wounded, and others, of whom three hundred were butchered like animals, without concern, in the courtyard of Newark Castle, overlooking the river Yarrow. Patrick Gordon of Ruthven wrote in a manuscript history entitled *Britain's Distemper*:

> With the whole baggage and stuff, which was exceeding rich, there remained none but boys, cooks and a rabble of rascals, and women with their children in their arms. All those without commiseration, were cut in pieces; wherof, there were three hundred women, that being natives of Ireland, were the married wives of the Irish. There were

> many big with child, yet none of them were spared, all were cut in pieces, with such savage and inhuman cruelty, as neither Turk nor Scythian was ever heard to have done the like: For they ript up the bellies of the women with their swords; till the fruit of their wombs, some in embryo, some perfectly formed, some crawling for life, and some ready for birth, fell down upon the ground, weltering in the gory blood of their mangled mothers. Oh! impiety; oh horrible cruelty, which Heaven doubtless, will revenge before this bloody, unjust and unlawful war be brought to an end.[51]

Hewison, in *Covenanters*, explains that this must have been done with the cognisance of the Council of War: Argyll, Crawford-Lindsay, Buccleuch, Lauderdale, Lanark, Yester, Barganie, Rutherford, Forrester, and Scot. The massacres did not stop there as some fifty men who had been given quarter were executed. And on the way to Edinburgh about eighty women and children were overtaken, thrown into the river Avon near Linlithgow and drowned.

The captured Irish leaders, O'Cahan and M'Lachlan, were executed in Edinburgh without trial. Hill's *The MacDonnells of Antrim* cites the comment of the Rev. David Dick: "The work goes bonniely on."[52] Sir Philip Nisbet, Sir William Rollo, and Alexander Ogilvy were beheaded in Glasgow. Lord Ogilvy escaped from prison in a dramatic way disguised in his sisters clothes. Lord Johnston of Hartfell, a kinsman of Lord Warriston, was pardoned. Spottiswood, the Lord President was tried and executed at St Andrews on 20 January 1646 along with Nathaniel Gordon and Captain Andrew Guthrie, son of the Bishop of Moray. It is highly likely that the hatred of the Irish stemmed from the 1641 rebellion in which some of the Irish officers had been involved in those atrocities. The Estates ordered all prisoners taken at or after Philiphaugh to be executed "without any assize or process"[53] which included six Irish women who were held in Selkirk gaol.

---

[51] George Hill, *The MacDonnells of Antrim* (Belfast: Archer & Sons, 1873), p. 102-103.
[52] *Ibid.*, p. 104, n174.
[53] *Ibid.*, p. 104-105.

Battles – Preston, 17-19 August 1648. See also: Engagement; Mauchline Moor.

In 1647-1648, the alliance with the English Parliamentarians and the future of the Solemn League and Covenant were crumbling, with the English unable, or unwilling, to fulfil their end of bargain. Not least they were against the extension of Presbyterianism as the true religion in England and very cautious about action against the "Sectaries" which included the Independents or Congregationalists to which Cromwell belonged. In Scotland, "The Engagement" between the Duke of Hamilton and royalist nobles, with King Charles I on 26 December 1647, created great division. The Committee of Estates met in February 1648 and decided that war was inevitable but the ministers were opposed to such action. However, a new Parliament assembled with strong royalist support among the nobles (but excluding Archibald Johnston, Lord Warriston, and the Marquis of Argyll) and a majority agreed on war. On 11 April 1648 an ultimatum was given the English demanding the freedom of King Charles; the army to disband, the establishment of Presbyterianism and discontinuance of the Book of Common Prayer.

The ministers and the Presbyteries, especially from Clydesdale, Carrick, and Cunningham joined with Fife Covenanters to oppose the war and the inevitable levies for men to fight it (see Mauchline Moor). The Engagers with only about 10,000 men who were mostly undisciplined, untrained, and with insufficient arms and support headed south, Hamilton entered Carlisle on 8 July 1648 and was joined by Langdale with some 3,600 better equipped Englishmen. Meanwhile Cromwell had travelled north with 8,000 of the Model Army and came upon the Scots at Preston on August 17. Poor strategy by Hamilton and division of his forces resulted in heavy losses and the Scots broke up while Cromwell's forces harried them and finally crushed them at Uttoxeter on August 25. Hamilton, Langdale and Middleton, as well as 10,000 prisoners fell into the Parliamentarians hands. Pressed men were released subject to an undertaking not to take arms against England; volunteers were transported to the American colonies as slaves and to Venice as conscripts. The adventure finished the royalist support and the "Whiggamore Raid" on Edinburgh saw the Covenanters take the city and power. On 4 October 1648 Cromwell entered Edinburgh and left again on October 7 having concluded his business with the Marquis of Argyll, who was again leader of the Covenanters.

Battles – Worcester, 3 September 1651. See also: Battles - Inverkeithing.

King Charles was crowned at Scone, Perthshire on 1 January 1651 and once again Scotland was supporting its king against the New Model Army of Cromwell. In the June of 1651 the Act of Classes, which had excluded so many from recruitment to the army, was repealed. A new army was levied from new sources but again they were poorly trained and soon paid the price. Cromwell saw the danger that the Scots might unite with royalist supporters in England and sought to make an early attack on the Scots. The Scots army was located at Torwood, north of Falkirk, and able to cover the defence of Stirling. On 15 July Cromwell sent a scouting party of some 5,000 under Lt. Gen. Lambert into Fifeshire with the intention of cutting the supply lines of the Scots. The Scots detached a party of some 4,000 to head off the English. The Scots were attacked and routed on July 20 at Inverkeithing where the Lowland troops fled leaving the foot of clans Buchanan (seven hundred) and MacLean (eight hundred) to be slaughtered. This served to show Cromwell the poor quality of the Scottish forces. Thus encouraged, Cromwell advanced towards Perth which fell on August 2.

There is debate whether Cromwell deliberately left the way open for the Scots army to escape from Stirling or whether there was a double bluff by David Leslie that drew Cromwell into Fife to leave open a route south. One hypothesis is that it would be better to defeat a Scots army in England where they would be seen as foreign invaders more than royalist supporters. This would help to counteract the pockets of royalist support that existed in Lancashire, Cumbria, Wales and the South west of England. On the evening of July 31, David Leslie and the Scots army of 20,000 and the King, was heading for England. By August 6 they had reached Carlisle where the gates to the city remained shut to them and the army itself was reduced by sickness and desertions to no more than 13,000.

Fortune turned against Charles at this juncture as probably less than 2,000 supporters came to his flag when many more had been expected. But it appears that possibly 3,000 Englishmen joined him between Lancashire and arrival at Worcester. It did not help recruitment along the way that the Scots were unpopular, and there was jealousy between the Presbyterians and the royalist "cavaliers." In Lancashire, Charles was very tactless when he sought assistance from Catholic supporters and stayed at Catholic homes. Militarily the Scots swift march south was mirrored by the English armies who had been warned of the possibility this might happen. General Harrison marched from Leith to Newcastle by 5 August and made up two days on the Scots. Lt. General Lambert meanwhile had made up five days in five and was at Penrith, just a day behind, on August 9. Not to be outdone Cromwell and his forces left Leith on August 6, and rested in Ryton, Newcastle on Tyne on August 13, covering over a hundred miles in six days. Harrison and his army moved across to join Lambert in Lancashire and they were joined by Col. Lilburne's regiment. Now a substantial force the English nevertheless continued to shadow the Scots as they headed south. Meanwhile, the English Council of State had called up forces from all over the country to assorted rendezvous. Under the command of General Fleetwood the English southern army congregated at Banbury where they were soon joined by others. On 24 August they were at Warwick ready for battle, and joined by Cromwell. The combined forces were twice those of the Scots'.

At Worcester on 3 September 1651, Cromwell caught up with the Scots army and annihilated it, taking some 10,000 prisoners and killing another 3,000. By September 16 the Council decided that all prisoners below the rank of Captain were to be sent to the plantations, with the intention of getting rid of as many as possible in the shortest time. Those at Chester, Worcester, Liverpool and Shrewsbury were sent to Bristol for onward consignment to Virginia and Bermuda. Three hundred were sent to New England and the Saugus Iron Works where they were sold on as slaves to farmers and mill owners. A thousand others were put to work digging drains in the Fenlands. The great majority of Scots prisoners simply did not return home, the rest dying of wounds, illness, neglect, or overwork.

In Scotland, General Monck's army sacked Dundee on September 1 and butchered eight hundred Scots in the process, having earlier captured the Committee of Estates at Alyth and isolated the nobles. Argyll was forced to submit and became a prisoner in his own lands. The English army marched to Orkney with little resistance and Scotland surrendered to its fate. With victory came the end of the Anglo Scottish War and the exile of Charles. It also brought to Scotland a firm, disciplined, impartial and religiously tolerant government that had not been enjoyed for years.

The singular consequence of the crushing defeats at Dunbar and Worcester was the loss of some 20,000 men—roughly ten per cent of the total adult male population. This loss of the predominantly younger men was a catastrophe for Scotland and took a further generation to recover. This undoubtedly contributed to the peace that fell on Scotland during the Cromwellian rule. There had already been fourteen years of confrontations during the Second Reformation, the Bishops' Wars, and the First English Civil War. Sheer exhaustion had sapped the will of the country to resist further.

Battles - skirmish at Fintry, 8 May 1679.

Fintry lies beyond the Campsie Fells north of Glasgow and about fifteen miles as the crow flies south west of Stirling. It was the location of a conventicle to which Robert Garnock went when he saw that it had been discovered by the military. The meeting on 8 May 1679 was ordered to disperse and were fired upon when they refused to do so. There were said to be forty eight men and sixteen horse in the military party who attacked a group of about eighteen men and some women. The Covenanters were clearly armed as shots were exchanged and "shot one side of the captain's periwig off, at which the foot fled."[54] Robert Garnock was with the Covenanters fighting the troops when they were surrounded by the horsemen; he managed to escape while others were taken prisoner to Stirling. Rather foolishly Garnock returned to Stirling in the evening and was seized by soldiers and imprisoned. Subsequently Garnock was moved to Edinburgh Tolbooth, then Greyfriars Kirk Yard among the prisoners from Bothwell Brig. Here Garnock was instrumental in encouraging the prisoners not to take a Bond to get their release, and received encouragement for this stance from John Blackadder who was in the Bass prison. Garnock was executed at the Gallows Lea between Edinburgh and Leith with four others—D. Farrie, J. Stewart, A. Russell, and P. Forman—on 10 October 1681.

---

[54] Howie, *Worthies*, p. 461.

Battles - skirmish at Lochgoin, *ca.* 1649 and 1679.

Lochgoin was the ancestral home of John Howie, the author of the *Scots Worthies,* and was the scene of a number of raids by the military who knew that it was a regular meeting place of the Covenanters. The particular skirmishes referred to concern Captain John Paton who in 1649 took a party of his militia from Fenwick to deal with some stragglers from the defeated army of the Engagers, who were making a nuisance of themselves. The second event concerning Paton was after Bothwell Brig in 1679 when he and others were taking refuge at Lochgoin. Paton had been declared a rebel and was being pursued when a Sergeant Rae and about five soldiers surprised the company; but Isabel Howie stepped between Rae and James and John Howie, preventing instant bloodshed. Paton, who was resting elsewhere in the house, was woken by the noise and he with others fled to the moors. They were pursued into there and a companion, John Kirkland, shot a Highland sergeant in the thigh. After a long pursuit the Covenanters got away. The military returned to Lochgoin the next day and in revenge plundered the house and took the cattle. Lochgoin features also in a tale that some twenty Covenanters resting there were warned by the elderly resident through his having a vivid dream that soldiers were on the way. He was able to rouse the Covenanters and all escaped safely.

Battles - skirmish at Loudon Hill, 5 May 1681.

Loudon Hill has a place in history as that where Robert the Bruce defeated an English army in May 1307 which caused King Edward I, "Hammer of the Scots" to raise himself from his sick bed to come and deal with him. But Edward died at Burgh on Sands on 7 July 1307. The later skirmish at Loudon Hill on 5 May 1681 was between the Engagers under the Duke of Hamilton and the Covenanters, including John Balfour of Kinloch. Balfour was one of the murderers of Archbishop Sharp and seemingly a fearful enemy who was not afraid to give battle. At Loudon Hill he seized some pistols belonging to the Duke and told the servant to inform his master that he would keep them until they met. When asked by the Duke, the servant gave a description that he was a little man, squint eyed, and of a very fierce aspect. Recognising the description the Duke opined that he prayed he might never see the face as he knew he would not live long if he did.

Battles - skirmish at Midland, November 1683.

John Nisbet of Hardhill was a staunch Covenanter and a wanted man when he met with three friends, Peter Gemmel, George Woodburn and John Ferguson at a house called the Midland in the parish of Fenwick in November 1683. A search party of Colonel Buchan's troopers led by a Lieutenant Nisbet, a cousin of Hardhill, discovered them when the party was forced to return to the house because John Ferguson was aged and unwell. In the course of the encounter there was shooting at close range and fierce hand to hand fighting. Nisbet was wounded six times but not killed as there was a reward of 3,000 merks on his head; the other three were shot dead. Nisbet was taken to Edinburgh and tried, found guilty, and executed on 4 December 1685.

Bible.

There were many versions of the Bible in the early days of the Reformation and credit is given to James VI for what is called the Authorised Version. This arose from the Hampton Court Conference in January 1604 that included the resolution that one uniform translation of the Bible to be made, and only to be used in all churches of England. The request arose from the Puritans who had complained of a number of things that were amiss in the Church, and James remitted it to a committee of fifty-four learned men of whom forty-seven were subsequently employed in the task. It was on the second day at this conference that James uttered his "No Bishop, No King" dictum.

The bishops had banned an English Bible as far back as 1408 because the Lollards had their own translation of the Wycklif Bible translated from the Latin Vulgate. The English language version, translated by Miles Coverdale, was first produced in 1535 but William Tyndale was the first to translate from the Greek and Hebrew. Some ninety per cent of the wording of the Tyndale version was transposed to the later King James version. It is of note that the King James version never received ecclesiastical sanction for use in Scotland. It is known that Alexander Henderson when preaching at the General Assembly in 1639 read from the Geneva Bible. Hugh Binning apparently did use the authorised version. Alexander Peden's Bible, which is in the Museum of Scotland, was a copy of a 1599 translation by the eminent divine, Theodore Beza, who was John Calvin's successor in Geneva.

The English Geneva Bible (sometimes called the Breeches Bible) was in common use after the Reformation and the early days of the Covenant. In 1575 the General Assembly required every parish church to have a copy of the Geneva bible printed by Bassandyne of Edinburgh. In 1579 Parliament enacted that every gentleman worth 300 merks yearly and every substantial seaman and burgess of over fifty pounds in goods or land, should possess a Bible and a Psalm Book for the better instruction of himself and his family. With this sort of grounding in their faith it was little wonder that the common man was able to argue theology with the Bishops who in later years made grand tours of their Diocese.

Bishops - role. See also: Constant Moderators; Tulchan Bishops.

The *Scots Worthies* gives a very interesting reason why King James VI/I was so much in favour of the bishops and reveals the extraordinary cynicism of a king bent on being an absolute monarch.

> The reason why King James VI. was so violent for bishops, was neither their divine institution, which he denied they had, nor yet the profit the Church should reap by them, for he knew well both the men and their communications, but merely because he believed they were useful instruments to turn a limited monarchy into absolute dominion, and subjects into slaves; the design in the world which he had most at heart. Always in the pursuit of his design, he resolved first to destroy General Assemblies, knowing well that so long as assemblies might convene in freedom, bishops could never get their designed authority in Scotland; and the dissolution of assemblies he brought about in this manner...[55]

[55] Howie, *Worthies*, p. 125.

...by interfering with their meeting and proroguing them indefinitely.

In 1572, the Convention of Leith proposed a compromise by which some Episcopal titles could be used subject to control by a General Assembly. These "Tulchan Bishops" were greatly opposed by John Knox and he openly opposed them at the General Assembly, but the title remained. At the General Assembly of 1575 Andrew Melville argued the case for the title of bishop based on the Greek New Testament where it was applied to every minister of the gospel.

The creation of Constant Moderators gave James VI the diocesan Episcopal structure in the Presbyterian Church of Scotland that he desired. His next endeavours were to transfer to his bishops the power and authority to manage the affairs of the Church. In 1609 Parliament had approved the transfer to the bishops of the enforcement of penal laws against Catholics, and also jurisdiction over probate and divorce. The General Assembly in Glasgow in 1610 confirmed the king's supremacy and right to call General Assemblies, directed that Synods under the bishop's moderation should meet twice a year, sentences of excommunication or absolution required the bishops authority, and bishops had the right to make appointments to vacant livings. Notably ministers were forbidden to challenge decisions in public. To enforce the management of the Church two Courts of High Commission were established, one in each See, at Edinburgh and Glasgow, and each had disciplinary powers over offences both in life and religion.

The "spiritual authority" was provided by consecration, of the Scottish bishops by three English bishops in London during 1610. The actions of the General Assembly were confirmed by the 1612 Parliament and full episcopacy was forced on the Church of Scotland. The status of Bishops was a major plank in the policies of Archbishop Laud and a source of discontent among the English Parliamentariens and influential vested interests. Laud sought to get like minded Arminian men to the bishoprics who would pursue his policy of uniformity. He further sought to elevate the status of bishops to emphasise their divinely appointed authority. Laud was also successful in getting many (Episcopalian) ministers appointed as Justices of the Peace to increase their local standing. To improve the Church funding he pursued tenants and holders of church lands for tithes and used the power of the Privy Council to do so where necessary.

At the Restoration of Charles II, James Sharp was appointed Archbishop of St. Andrews on 14 December 1661. The other appointees by the king were Andrew Fairfull to Archbishop of Glasgow (he died in November 1663), James Hamilton of Cambusnethan to Bishop of Galloway (lived to 1674), and Robert Leighton (then aged sixty) to Bishop of Dunblane. They were summoned to London for consecration which was done in Westminster Abbey on 15 December 1661 by the Bishops of London, Worcester, Llandaff and Carlisle. The other bishops were subsequently appointed on the recommendation of Sharp who ensured all the nominees were staunch Resolutioners, and nine of them took their seats in Parliament on 8 May 1662.

Bishops - in Ireland.

The early years of the Plantation of Ulster from 1610 to 1630, and the formation of the Presbyterian kirk there had the good fortune to be under the benign influence of Dr. James Ussher (1581-1656). He was Archbishop of Armagh and Primate of Ireland in which role he produced his Articles of Religion in 1615. These allowed a compromise to be achieved so that Presbyterian ministers could conduct their worship, receive church tithes and coexist with the established Episcopal Church of Ireland. Some ministers accepted Church of Ireland livings although Blair, Welch, and Livingston ministered for many years in the Presbyterian form and without an organised Presbytery.

A significant cloud that descended on Ireland in 1633 was Thomas Wentworth, as Lord Deputy (later the Earl of Strafford) while in England William Laud had become Archbishop of Canterbury and close confidant to Charles I. This unhappy combination saw the same attacks on ministers for non conformity in Ireland as was the case in Scotland and England. Peaceful co existence was shattered by the resurgence of the Bishops seeking control. At the centre of the drama were Robert Blair and John Livingston who were suspended by Bishop Echlin. in 1632. Things came to a head in August 1636 when five of the ministers—Brice, Ridge, Cunningham, Calvert, and Hamilton—were summoned before the Bishop of Down and required to explain their refusal to accept Episcopacy. They were unable in all conscience to accept the Bishop's rule and were sentenced to "perpetual silence within this diocese."[56] Against this background, Rev. Livingston had meanwhile been exploring the possibilities of going to the Massachusetts colony and had begun building the ship, *Eaglewing*. But even here they were thwarted in 1636 by bad weather and the migrants had to return to Ireland and a growing persecution. Orders to arrest Blair and Livingston forced them to make a dash back to Scotland where their talents became available to the Scottish church.

The rebellion of 1641, with thousands of Protestants murdered and subsequently the return of a Scottish army of occupation, curbed the prelates for a while, as did Cromwell's later pacification. But in 1661, sixty one ministers refused to accept prelacy and were ejected from their churches. Another seven ministers were seized and imprisoned in Carlingford Castle and expelled to Scotland; ministers were excommunicated and Bishop Leslie of Raphoe caused four ministers to be incarcerated for six years simply because they were Presbyterians. King Charles was bent upon prelacy in Ireland and filled the diocesan vacancies with his nominees while allowing the surviving bishops to take up their diocese of old. With a majority in the Irish Parliament supporters of episcopacy were in control of affairs and the Bishops maintained a spasmodic program of attacks on non conforming ministers. Leslie of Raphoe was particularly effective and was largely responsible for stirring up his fellow prelates to take action against the Presbyterians.

Until the arrival of King William in 1690 and, despite the privations and persecution which was not as severe as in Scotland, the Presbyterians maintained a presence. There were moments of extreme action by the prelates such as that of Thomas Otway, Bishop of Killala who had a prisoner beheaded without trial. He was also at the centre of controversy when two Presbyterian ministers dared to preach within his diocese, one of whom was held in prison for two years for no more offence than preaching the Gospel. In 1675, John Orr of Letterkenny sought the help of Lord Massarene to intercede with the Prelate of Raphoe, to make him surcease his further persecuting the said John Orr. There was also a variation in tactics by the prelates as they realised that the

[56] Thomas Hamilton, *History of Presbyterianism in Ireland* (Belfast: Ambassador Productions, Ltd., 1992), p. 50.

government was more inclined to take action against Presbyterians for civil and political non conformity. One such case was the allegation by Bishop Ezekiel Hopkins, an ejected Puritan turned apostate, that charitable collections were being used to purchase arms. His successor in the See of Raphoe, William Smith, alleged in 1683 that Presbyterians were at the edge of rebellion and were as desperate and bloody as any the world had.

By the late 1680s, the Presbyterians enjoyed comparative liberty with a gradual building of churches and ordination of ministers. The latter was particularly obnoxious to the Bishops since it meant that there was a continuing supply of clergymen. However, and perhaps surprising for a Catholic king, James II issued a Declaration of Indulgence on 4 April 1687, which suspended the penal laws against non conformists and Catholics and permitted normal worship by both creeds. King James' appointment of Catholics to most positions of power in the army, the justiciary and the corporations set the scene for later troubles and the arrival of a Protestant King William to do battle at the Boyne.

Bishops' Dragnet.

The Bishops' Dragnet was another name for a law passed by Parliament on 10 July 1663, "An Act for Separation and Disobedience to Ecclesiastical Authority." It was a follow up to the ejection of the ministers from their livings (the Act of 11 June 1662). The "outed" ministers continued to preach and conduct services in homes, barns and open fields: conventicles. This was not acceptable to the government, nor the prelates and the curates who had been appointed to the vacancies. The purpose of the Bishops' Dragnet, as it was called, was to force people to attend their own church on pain of fines and, worst of all, required names of delinquents to be sent to the Privy Council who could order corporal punishment. This was the first of the measures intending to force conformity to the Episcopal Church in Scotland. Shortly the collection of fines was passed to the military while the curates kept records of church attendance and reported absentees to the military for follow up action. It was the heavy handed collection of fines by soldiers that was the cause of the Pentland Rising.

Bishops' Wars, 1639-1640.

The Bishops' Wars were so called because of the resistance by the Presbyterians to the rule by bishops (episcopacy) but were the natural consequence of the actions of the Glasgow Assembly of 1638. The king planned for an army of 30,000 which would be reinforced with northern royalists (Huntly in Aberdeen) who would cooperate with Hamilton to descend on Edinburgh. Ten thousand Irish under the Earl of Antrim would overrun Argyll and the West of Scotland while Wentworth with the fleet would sail into the Clyde. The king would advance from the North of England at the head of his troops. By January 1639, Charles had some 7,000 horse and foot soldiers available in the North of England and a further 5,000 were ready to go by ship to Aberdeen to join forces with the Earl of Huntly.

The Covenanters, meanwhile, found willing and experienced recruits from the continent including Alexander Leslie, a Field Marshal in Sweden of great experience and repute. Garrisons were established, defences prepared and 10,000 men mustered in Edinburgh. The first Bishops' War began in March 1639 and lasted for about five weeks during which there was skirmishing by Montrose in Invernesshire, Aberdeen was taken and the Earl of Huntly was tricked into surrendering, seized and sent to Edinburgh. In the south the Covenanters took control of the castles and established garrisons in Edinburgh, Dumbarton, Dalkeith, Strathaven, Douglas, Tantallon, Dumfries, Dairsie and Brodick. By May they had 20,000 men in arms. On May 9, Leslie was commissioned to command the Covenanter Army for defence of the Covenant, under banners proclaiming "For Religioun, the Covenant, and the countrie."[57]

Around Edinburgh, the Covenanters were ready when Hamilton's fleet arrived off Leith on 1 May 1639. On May 30, Charles and his force of about 21,000 arrived at Birks, three miles from Berwick. About twelve miles away, at Duns Law, Leslie and 12,000 men with forty-five pieces of artillery waited. There followed a period of bluff, both sides either ill-informed or ignorant of how poorly the other was in terms of men: inexperienced ploughboys who were poorly armed with obsolete and make-do

---

[57] Hewison, *Covenanters*, Vol. 1, p. 324.

weapons, and badly horsed. The only real action took place in Aberdeen where some eight hundred royalists seized Towie House and on May 14 put the Earl of Erroll and Lord Fraser to flight at Turriff: "the trot of Turriff," as it became known. Montrose and 4,300 troops returned to Aberdeen where they looted and pillaged before leaving again to see off the Earl Marischal at Stonehaven. Military matters were settled when Montrose again secured a victory at the Bridge of Dee in Aberdeen.

On June 6, the Scots presented a supplication for peace and there followed much debate, demands, and counter-demands, before Charles finally conceded the total abolition of Episcopacy, unrestrained meeting of Church courts, and the summoning of biennial or triennial Parliaments. On June 18, Charles admitted defeat and ordered a General Assembly to meet on August 12. The Pacification (Treaty) of Berwick ended a virtually bloodless First Bishops' War. The Covenanters withdrew with Charles's undertaking ringing in their ears to accept civil and ecclesiastical control by the Parliaments and Assemblies respectively. The Treaty of Birks was at best a convenient breathing space but it was rejected by the Scottish General Assembly and The Tables. The Covenanters were wary of the king's intentions and kept their army in training. Charles meanwhile was colluding with Wentworth in the formation of a "New Army" of 8,000 foot and 1,000 horse in Ireland, which was predominantly Catholic. In the Highlands he expected help to contain the Covenanters and link up with the New Army from Ireland. In May Munro occupied Aberdeen and then took revenge on the royalist Gordons. The king meanwhile sought to lure the leading nobles to discussions and probably to seize them, but they were alive to the risk involved. At one stage the Earls of Loudon, Lindsay and Dunfermline were prevented by the people from leaving the city because of the suspected trap. Having made protests one to the other Charles departed to London on July 29.

The General Assembly held on 12 August was another farce of trickery and deceit with an attempt to dupe Henderson to take the Moderators chair, thus opening a door for Constant Moderator allegations. Superficially, the Earl of Traquair, the new Kings Commissioner agreed all the Covenanter claims and promised to ratify them in Parliament. The Parliament met from August 31 until November 14 and Traquair tried to introduce fourteen ministers in place of the bishops. He also tried to initiate the procedure of electing the first eight Lords of the Article, which would have given him control over the preparation of legislation. This was rejected and Argyll, Montrose, and Lauderdale introduced their Church Acts which were duly passed.

On November 14, Traquair prorogued Parliament until 2 June 1640 and declared that the Estates were by their Acts usurping the Kings prerogative and government. This accusation of law breaking promptly resulted in a Remonstrance and a discomforting lambasting for Traquair by the king. In a master stroke of self survival Traquair produced a draft letter seemingly asking the King of France to assist the Covenanters to reach a conciliation, the document was signed by Loudon. Although only a draft that was never sent, Charles saw this as reason enough to gird up his loins for war. The Scots, however, kept to the Treaty of Birks and sought to conciliate the king, who at first refused to see their representatives. When he did see them, Loudon, Dunfermline, Douglas of Cavers, and Provost Barclay of Irvine were seized. Loudon was despatched to the Tower on April 11 whence the king ordered execution without trial and in defiance of a promise of safe conduct. Fortunately for Loudon, the Marquis of Hamilton calmed the king and pointed out the odium if he violated the safe conduct and the execution of a peer of the realm without at least semblance of a trial. Charles angrily tore up the warrant.

In England, Charles sought funds from the House of Commons who declined to help, and the Short Parliament was dissolved. He then sought by artifice, and his royal prerogative, to get an army together. In Scotland the prorogued Parliament met on 11 June 1640 and ratified all the Acts from the Assembly, while Leslie was reinstated as Commander in Chief. By July 31 an army of about 20,000 foot, 4,000 horse, and a large train of wagons with covered tumbrels concealing the cannon inside was assembled. Both Edinburgh and Dumbarton castles were secured and in August 1640 the Covenanting army made a pre-emptive strike and pushed the royalist forces back to the River Tyne. The royalists were defeated at the battle of Newburn on the August 28 and the Covenanters entered the city of Newcastle on the 30th. Charles was beset with lack of supplies and a motley soldiery who were bent on desertion and mutiny. Meanwhile, he had received a deputation of twelve peers and agreed a Council of Peers should meet in York on 24 September. Representatives of the Council were sent to make the

Treaty of Ripon on 26 October 1640. This concluded hostilities, ensuring a military status quo, but the Scots required £850 a day for the quartering of their army which caused Charles to summon the "Long Parliament" to get the necessary funds.

The Bishops' Wars did not bring security to either party. In Scotland there was a move for political change and significantly no representation was given the Covenanters on the newly formed executive. The Marquis of Argyll meanwhile had his own problems with clan warfare in the West. The English Parliamentarians, who were at odds with King Charles, were fearful of the price the Scots might ask for their support whether in terms of money or religion. They saw the presence of the Scots on the borders as a lever in its own struggles for settlement of grievances. John Pym, the Puritan leader in the Commons, demanded the impeachment of Strafford, Laud and others, as well as the abolition of the Star Chamber, the Court of High Commission, and the Council of the North. Unable to do otherwise Charles had to agree to the demands, and in so doing consigned Strafford to the block, 12 May 1641, who famously said "put not your trust in princes."[58] Laud survived a while longer and was executed on 10 January 1645.

Black Acts, 22 May 1584. See also: Presbytery, the Great Charter of 1592.

The Black Acts brought the struggle for and against Episcopacy to a head; it declared all the anti-prelatic acts of the General Assembly to be treason. Parliament confirmed the king's power and supremacy over all states and subjects and declared it unlawful for the General Assembly to meet without the king's permission. The ministers of the church were required to accept the authority of the bishops. The Acts were brought about in great secrecy when the Lords of the Articles (responsible for presenting legislation) were carefully selected for their royalist sympathies and sworn to secrecy when Parliament sat in Edinburgh 22 May 1584. Calderwood's *History* lists them as: Patrick Bishop of St. Andrews, Alexander Bishop of Brechin, Alexander Bishop of Dunkelden, James Bishop of the Isles, Adam Bishop of Orkney, and the Abbotts of Lindores and Pittenweem (alias Colonels Stewart and Blantyre). For the

---

[58] Hewison, *Covenanters*, Vol. 1, p. 352.

Temporality: Huntly, Crawfurd, Montrose, Eglintoun, Rothesse, Lords Livingston and Down, Commissioners of Burrowes, and the Provosts of Edinburgh, Perth, Dundie, and Glasgow.

Inevitably, the ministers opposed the law although some nobles accepted it. Orders were sent to Edinburgh to apprehend two ministers James Lawson and Walter Balcanqual, who fled with about twenty other ministers into England. There then followed a confused period of some eight years with ministers leaving the country rather than submit; while others accepted the change in whole or part. The Act was repealed in 1592 by "Ane Act for Abolishing of the Actis Contrair the Trew Religion" which confirmed the system of the First Book of Discipline (Presbytery) and declared the Black Acts to be "expired, null, and of none avail."[59] The Act of 1592 is also referred to as the Great Charter of Presbytery.

Black Oath – Ireland, 1639.

The Black Oath was the invention of Thomas Wentworth, later Earl of Strafford, who panicked at the strong resistance there was to the 1637 Laud's Liturgy. The Oath had no foundation in law whatsoever and sought to forestall the Ulster Scots from joining the Covenant and supporting their brother Scots in the Bishops' Wars. The oath of loyalty was to be administered to all Ulster Scots over sixteen years of age; it acknowledged the king as supreme in civil and church matters and rejected the Covenants. Commissions were sent to the magistrates to administer the oath in their districts with the oath to be read out publicly, and taken by the people on their knees. The military were sent to see it was done. Enforcement was also monitored by Episcopalian clergy and church wardens who were required to submit lists of Presbyterians who had not taken the oath. It was doubly offensive to the Presbyterians as only Catholics were exempted.

Declining the oath was perilous with very harsh fines imposed. One man, Henry Stewart, was fined £5,000 for himself, the same for his wife and £2000 each for his two daughters and a servant named James Gray. The £16,000 would be over £1 million pounds today. Of course they were unable to pay and were imprisoned. Many of

[59] Acts of Parliament (Edinburgh: Estates of Parliament, 1592), Chapter 8.

the Presbyterians fled to Scotland to avoid the oath. This resistance contributed to Wentworth's plan to banish the Presbyterians from Ulster but came to nothing as he was recalled to London in 1640 where he was arrested. He was executed on Tower Hill 12 May 1641.

The wording of the Oath given in *The Hamilton Manuscripts* is:

> I --- do faithfully swear, profess and promise, that I will honour and obey my sovereign lord King Charles and will bear faith and true allegiance unto him, and defend and maintain his Royal power and authority, and that I will not bear arms, or do any rebellious or hostile act against him, or protest against any of his Royal commands, but submit myself in all due obedience thereunto: and that I will not enter into any covenant, oath or bond of mutual defence and assistance against any persons whatsoever, by force, without his Majesty's sovereign and regal authority. And I do renounce and abjure all covenants, oaths and bands whatsoever, contrary to what I have herein sworn, professed, and promised. So help me God in Christ Jesus.[60]

Dumbarton Rock and Castle. Photo by the author.

[60] *Hamilton Manuscripts*, ed. T. K. Lowry (Belfast: Archer & Sons, 1867), p. 32.

Caerlaverock Castle. Photo courtesy of A. Pittendreigh.

Edinburgh Castle. Thos. Shepherd, *Modern Athens, Edinburgh in the Eighteenth Century* (London: Jones & Co., 1829).

Black Saturday, 4 August 1621.

King James convened a Parliament in Edinburgh on 25 July 1621 with the specific purpose of ratifying the Perth Articles. It was on a particularly clouded and overcast day, Saturday, August 4, that the Acts were actually voted upon and approved by seventy seven votes to fifty. Eleven bishops attended to swell the royalist supporters. Hewison's *The Covenanters*, tells that when the Commissioner, the Marquis of Hamilton, touched the documents with the royal sceptre there were three successive flashes of lightning, each followed by a loud clap of thunder; this was followed by severe hail and rain storms that confined the gathering in the premises for nearly two hours. Some were quick to compare it with the fire storm when the Ten Commandments were handed down. The general opinion seemed to be that "God appeared angrie at the concluding of the Articles."[61] Credibility was given to the belief when floods swept away the bridge in Perth.

Calderwood's *History* details the efforts made to ensure approval was given. This included sending spies to meetings to deliberately oppose the proposal in order to identify who was for and who was against. Notably Sir John Hamilton of Prestoun, who had opposed the Articles in session as a Lord of the Articles, maintained his opposition in open parliament despite being asked to absent himself and threatened with retribution. On the day of the vote extraordinary steps were taken to prevent people from attending and a close watch was kept by one Andrew Hay a servant of the Bishop of St. Andrews, to ensure no unauthorised ministers were admitted.

The Rev. David Barclay of St. Andrews was appointed by the ministers to make a representation and actually gained access. But he was kept waiting and eventually cast out without being heard whereupon he posted copies of the protest on the Parliament House door and at the Mercat Cross. The voting itself was instructed to be by using the words "Agree" or "Disagree." The reason was that the pronunciation, if spoken in a low voice, was easily misheard; coincidentally the clerk recording the votes was instructed that those who did not speak up were to be taken as consenters. The voting was thus rigged.

---

[61] Hewison, *Covenanters*, Vol. 1, p. 202; Calderwood, *History*, Vol. 7, pp. 488-505.

Blood's Plot, 22 May 1663.

A Captain Thomas Blood, an officer in the army who had associated with Cromwellian sympathisers, plotted action against the government. He was the brother-in-law of a Presbyterian minister in Ireland, William Lecky. Two other ministers in the know were Andrew McCormick and John Crookshanks both of whom fled to Scotland when the plot was betrayed by an informer. They were killed at the battle of Rullion Green, 28 November 1666. An informer named Philip Alden made some exaggerated claims but the conspirators "resolved that the King should be put to death and the army governed by a committee, and not by a general."[62] The conspirators were arrested on the morning of 22 May 1663; this was the day when they were supposed to attack Dublin Castle. Blood escaped and the unlucky William Lecky was captured and subsequently executed. Lecky was apparently offered his life if he would accept Episcopacy but declined. It is strange that he should be offered clemency of this sort for an overtly treasonable act and hints at some knowledge on the part of the government that he was not intimately involved with the proposals to kill the king. The suspicion inevitably is that this was an incident manipulated by the prelates to get rid of a Presbyterian minister.

There was, however, a significant knock on for the Presbyterians in the Northern Presbytery as a result of the king ordering that the most seditious of them should be imprisoned. Several ministers had never heard of the plot and the three who had—Rev. Heart, Stewart, and Greg—had refused to have anything to do with it. Ten ministers were confined in Carrickfergus Castle, seven in Carlingford Castle and two in Dublin Castle. They were eventually released and allowed to leave the country with a few having influential friends who obtained permission for them to stay in a private, non preaching, capacity.

At Carrickfergus were Thomas Hall of Larne, William Keyes of Belfast, John Douglas of Broughshane, Robert Hamilton of Killead, James Cunningham of Antrim, John Couthard of Drumal, John Shaw of Ahoghill, James Shaw of Carnmoney, Hugh Wilson of

---

[62] W. T. Latimer, *A History of the Irish Presbyterians* (Belfast: James Cleland, 1902), p. 138.

Castlereagh, Robert Hogsyeard of Ballyshrane, and also Andrew Wike (Baptist), and Timothy Taylor (Independent).

At Carlingford were William Richardson of Killyleagh, John Greg of Newtownards, John Drysdale of Portaferry, Gilbert Ramsay of Bangor, James Gordon of Comber, Alexander Hutcheson of Saintfield, and Andrew Stewart of Donaghadee.

At Dublin were Patrick Adair of Cairncastle and Henry Livingston of Drumbo.

The *Scots Worthies* mentions a Colonel Blood intervening at a meeting at which William Veitch had preached. At the close of the meeting there were cries of "Treason, Treason" to which Colonel Blood cried "Good people, we have nothing but reason, reason"[63] and took the sting out of the situation. This was in 1679 but there is nothing to say that this was the same Blood, now promoted from Captain. However, the *Montgomery Manuscripts* relate that the "Colonel" Blood involved in the Irish plot was also responsible for an attack on the Duke of Ormond whom he seized in St. James Street in London, and was taking to hang at Tyburn when the Duke's servants came to the rescue.[64] Blood also actually managed to steal the Crown and state jewels from the Tower of London and only failed in this because his horse slipped and threw him as he was making his escape. He was described as a daring man with a villainous and unmerciful look, a false countenance, but well spoken and dangerously insinuating. It is thought that Blood may well have been a spy and double agent, who also did errands for the king since Charles II pardoned him and gave him an estate worth £500 a year.

Breda - Treaty with Charles II, 19 March-1 May 1650.

Breda in Holland was the venue for discussions in 1650 between the newly succeeded King Charles II (his father having been executed in January, 1649) and Commissioners from Scotland. There had been an earlier attempt at reconciliation by the Scots in 1649 but this was unsuccessful. The visitation of 1650 sent by the Commission of the Kirk consisted of ministers John Livingston, James Wood, and George Hutcheson and with the Earl of Cassillis and Alexander Brodie as elders. Hopeful that their demands might

---

[63] Howie, *Worthies*, p. 612.

[64] *Montgomery Manuscripts*, ed. George Hill (Belfast: James Cleland, 1869.

be moderate, Charles found them to be very tough. The zealots in power refused to budge on the requirement to swear the Covenants and to settle a Presbyterian system in England and Ireland. He was also required to enforce penal laws against papists. For five weeks he sought to mitigate the worst conditions but in the end gave way and signed a draft agreement on 1 May 1650. On June 2 he and his entourage embarked for Scotland arriving at the Spey on June 23 where he swore to the two Covenants before landing. The *Scots Worthies* gives an interesting view of the affair through the eyes of Livingston who was rightly suspicious of King Charles' motives and honesty. He had seen the king and his chaplains still using the Service Book and perceived that only grief could come of the mission. How right he was; by September 1651 Charles was back in exile where he remained until 1660.

A second Declaration at Breda was made in 1660 which was about the terms submitted to the English Parliament, under which Charles II would be restored to the crown of England, Scotland and Ireland.

Burning at the stake.

Execution by burning at the stake was a punishment from the Inquisition inflicted for heresy and witchcraft. An example of this in Scotland is the burning of James Resby, a follower of John Wickliffe, in 1407. Resby challenged the Pope's claim to rule Christendom as the Vicar of Christ and insisted on personal holiness as a condition of Papal office. M'Crie, in *Sketches*, tells of thirty persons of gentility who were accused of heretical sympathies in 1494 but were let off with an admonishment when they, through having had an education, argued against their accusers. There were others of nobility and education who were not so fortunate, notably Patrick Hamilton (28 February 1527), George Wishart (1 March 1546), and Walter Mill (28 April 1558).

In the seventeenth century there were far more burnings for witchcraft (over one thousand, some eighty per cent of these were women) than for heresy.

But not all died the same way. The common witch was piled about with faggots and bound to the stake, the fire and the heat killing her. The Scottish martyrs were possibly better treated in that their death was aided by tying bags of gunpowder to the body and a cord tied round the neck. Whether the cord was meant to shut off the screams of burning or aid death is uncertain, but drawn tightly by the executioner as the flames gathered force it would have contributed to asphyxiation.

It is illustrative of the times and the malice of the clergy that they would go to extreme lengths to get their way. Patrick Hamilton was related to King James V and came from very distinguished lineage. Aged twenty-three Hamilton had a distinguished stay at Magdeburg University and was the first there to publicly express views against the Church of Rome. He wrote a fulsome work which he called "Patrick's Places" (Appendix 3) in which he defended Protestant views and listed some fifteen "Errors and Absurdities of the Papists." His forthright views made him a target for the priests and to achieve their purpose James V was prevailed upon to make a pilgrimage to the north of Scotland. The young king was thus out of the way and inaccessible should attempts be made to forestall the execution. All did not go well for Patrick Hamilton who was bound to a stake surrounded by coals, timber and other combustibles with a train of powder to light the fire. However, the powder trail simply exploded and burnt Hamilton's side. In some pain therefore he had to wait while further powder was brought from the castle and the execution finally completed in heavy rain. He took six hours to die.

The charges laid against Patrick Hamilton, quoted in Foxe's *Acts and Monuments*, were for holding:

> That man hath no free-will.
> That there is no purgatory.
> That the holy patriachs were in heaven before Christ's passion.
> That the pope hath no power to loose and bind; and that no pope had that power after St. Peter.
> That the pope is Antichrist and that every priest hath the power that the pope hath.
> That Master Patrick Hamelton was a bishop.
> That it is not necessary to obtain any bulls from any bishop.
> That the vow of the pope's religion is a vow of wickedness.
> That the pope's law be of no strength.
> That all Christians worthy to be called Christians, do know that they be in a state of grace.
> That none be saved but they are before predestinated.

Whosoever is in deadly sin, is unfaithful.
That God is the cause of sin, in this sense, that is, he withdraweth his grace from men, whereby they sin.
That it is devilish doctrine, to enjoin any sinner actual penance for sin.
That the said Master Patrick himself doubteth whether all children, departing incontinent after their baptism, are saved or condemned.
That auricular confession is not necessary to salvation.[65]

George Wishart was of a more modest lineage. He was brother to the Laird of Pitarrow in Mearns, who had graduated at Cambridge University. He was first a teacher in Montrose in the summer of 1544 but it was in Dundee that he came to the notice of the priests where he "pulled down the that fabric of superstition and idolatry which they with so much pain had reared."[66] Wishart was the subject of personal spite of Cardinal David Beaton, Archbishop of St. Andrews, who displayed overweening arrogance and disregard for the law that required the approval of the civil authority for an execution. The Governor sensitive to the situation refused authority to which Beaton imperiously replied, "That he had only sent to him out of mere civility without any need for it; for that he, with his clergy had power sufficient to bring Mr Wishart to condign punishment."[67] The execution of George Wishart is very descriptive:

> Soon after, by the appointment of the Cardinal, two executioners came to him, and, arraying him in a black linen coat, they fastened some bags of gunpowder about him, put a rope about his neck, a chain about his waist, and bound his hands behind his back, and in this dress they led him to the stake, near the Cardinal's palace. Opposite to the stake they had placed the great guns of the castle, lest any should attempt to rescue him. The fore-tower, which was immediately opposite to the fire, was hung with tapestry,

[65] John Foxe, *The Acts and Monuments of John Foxe*, ed. George Townsend (London: Seeley, Burnside & Seeley, 1846; reprint Edmonston: Stillwaters Revival Books, 1996.

[66] Howie, *Worthies*, p. 19.

[67] *Ibid.*, p. 26.

> and rich cushions were laid in the windows, for the ease of the Cardinal and prelates, while they beheld the sad spectacle but the merciful Lord vouchsafe to give you all necessaries, both for soul and body.[68]

After his death speech, the fire was kindled and the bags of gunpowder exploded but did not kill him, and the executioner "drew the cord that was about his neck so strait that he spoke no more."[69]

Walter Mill was another martyr who was subject of illegal action by the priests. Having been condemned, the authority to execute was sought from the Provost who refused to give it and promptly left town. In the end a man called Somerville, a domestic employee of the Archbishop acted the part of the temporal judge and Mill was then put to the stake. Walter Mill's execution was much opposed by the populace of St. Andrews who refused to supply ropes and combustible materials for the fire. After the deed was done the people heaped stones on the place of execution as a memorial to the bravery of this eighty-two-year-old martyr; these were later removed by the clergy.

Other sufferers at the stake included Adam Wallace who was burnt on Castlehill, Edinburgh. No less than five alleged heretics were burnt at one stake on 28 February 1538 at Castlehill; they were Robert Forrester, Sir Duncan Simson (a priest), Friar Killore, Friar Beveridge, and Dean Thomas Forrest vicar of Dollar. M'Crie, in *Sketches*, tells of David Stratton, brother to the Laird of Lauriston, who was overcome with religious fervour on hearing Tyndale's translation of the New Testament. He was taken before the Bishop at Holyrood House and refused to recant; he was sentenced to be hung and burnt "to the intent that the inhabitants of Fife, seeing the fire, might be stricken with terror."[70]

Cabal.

This was the acronym for the group of individuals who effectively ruled the three kingdoms for a while under Charles II. The group consisted of Clifford, Arlington, Buckingham, Ashley,

---

[68] *Ibid.*, p. 29.
[69] *Ibid.*, p. 30.
[70] M'Crie, *Sketches*, p. 25.

and Lauderdale. They came to power in the mid-1660's following the downfall of the former Chancellor, Edward Hyde, Earl of Clarendon. With hindsight it is apparent that the Cabal in fact had no common policies to speak of, but were united in carrying through the king's policies in their respective spheres while also ensuring their own pockets were well filled. Both Ashley and Lauderdale knew of the Treaty of Dover and the French connection. They fell from power as a group *ca.* 1673 when Thomas Osborne, Earl of Danby, came to power. Lauderdale managed to avoid impeachment for past misdeeds and negotiated anew his role with Danby and the Prelates in Scotland. He nevertheless continued to hold sway in his fiefdom of Scotland until 1680, although he had to be more tolerant and therefore amenable to the schemes of the likes of Archbishop Sharp.

Cameronians.

The name "Cameronians" was used to describe the followers of Richard Cameron. These followers were also called Covenanters because of their adherence to the National Covenant of 1638 and the Solemn League and Covenant of 1643. The term "Society people" came about when they set up a system of praying societies and a correspondence between groups with regular meetings. "Mountain Men" or "Hill Men" were yet other names arising from their holding prayer meetings (conventicles) in the hills of southwest Scotland. A later name was the "MacMillanites," after their minister, John MacMillan of Balmaghie, who joined them in 1706. Their full title was: *The witnessing remnant of the anti-Popish, anti-Prelatic, anti-Erastian. anti-Sectarian, True Presbyterian Church of Christ in Scotland.*

It should be noted that the title Reformed which was adopted, was not because they considered themselves better than others, but because it reflected their strong attachment to the principles of the Reformation.

At their General Meeting held in Douglas church on 29 April 1689 the Societies had a long debate about malignancy that included the proposal to have a constant armed force ready to resist arbitrary government, popery, and prelacy. The terms of engagement were read to recruits and the Rev. Alexander Shields explained that they would also be seeking to recover and establish the work of the

Reformation against Popery, Prelacy and arbitrary power until the government in both Church and State was brought to its former splendour, meaning the period of the Second Reformation 1638-1640.

The distinctive features of the armed force was that it comprised a separate congregation of armed Presbyterian, Covenanted worshippers, led by regular officers and in spiritual matters led and disciplined by a minister and twenty elders, one for each company. The minister and elders were responsible for promoting piety, moral discipline, worship, and catechising at times which were compatible with military duties. The regiment of about eight hundred men, was soon to prove itself when it marched under Lieutenant Colonel William Cleland, hero of Drumclog and Bothwell Brig, to join battle against Dundee's forces at Dunkeld on 21 August 1689. Having secured their positions the regiment faced the onslaught from the royalist forces, now under the Irishman Colonel Cannon (Dundee was killed at Killiecrankie), and were gradually driven back to the Cathedral. The attackers took houses round the church from where they poured their fire upon the Cameronians. Captain Munro took command when Cleland was shot and led a rally against the houses, setting them on fire to displace the snipers within. The valiant Cameronians fought hard and well driving the Highlanders and Irish troops into the hills. It is reported that during the fray the Cameronians comforted one another by singing psalms while battling odds of six to one. In the aftermath of battle it was found that the regiment had suffered only fifteen men lost while around them lay some three hundred royalists troops. This action contributed greatly to the eventual victory over the demoralised royalists.

Memorial to Col. Cleland. Photo by the author.

Canons.

Canons were the rules or law ordered by church authorities for the management and practice of faith. They were very important in the Middle Ages when church courts administered them. In modern times Canon is a rank for a member of a Cathedral's managing body. The Canonical Hours are the times set apart in the Catholic Church for the offices of prayer and devotion: *matins*, soon after midnight; *Lauds*, daybreak; *Prime*, 6 a.m.; *Terces,* 9 a.m.; *Sext*, noon; *Nones*, 3 p.m.; *Vespers*, 6 p.m.; and *Compline*, bed time.

The Book of Canons of 1636 is important because it was stoutly resisted by the Presbyterian ministers and stirred up public indignation at the popish content. Notably, the Canons did not seek to implement the evangelical episcopacy propounded by Latimer and Cranmer in England, but it sought to enforce the popish prelacy of Archbishop Laud. This resentment set the scene for rejection of the Liturgy which followed in 1637. They are also an example of the absolute rule of the king and the duplicity of the prelates, none of whom bothered to consult the governing body of the kirk or any of its representatives.

The book was drawn up by Scottish Bishops Cowper (Galloway), Forbes (Aberdeen), Maxwell (Ross) and Bellenden

(Dunblane) and sent to Archbishop Laud who made changes and had the book approved for printing under the Great Seal on 23 May 1635. The wordiness of the full title reflected the very unnecessary embellishments that the Presbyterians resented. It was entitled *Canons and Constitutions Ecclesiastical gathered and put in Forme for the Government of the Church of Scotland. Ratified and approved by His Majesties Royall Warrant. and ordained to be observed by the Clergie and others whom they concerne. Published by Authoritie. Aberdene. Imprinted by Edward Roban, dwelling upon the Market Place, at the Armes of the Citie 1636. With Royal Privilege.*

As indicated by the prolix title, the purpose was to introduce the High Church ceremony and quasi-Catholic practices beloved of Archbishop Laud. It also set out that the king was supreme in ecclesiastical matters and had according to Scripture sanctioned the Episcopal Church and its Liturgy. The Rules included:

1. Excommunication for denial of the king's supremacy.
2. Excommunication for any who said the Scottish Book of Common Prayer (1637) was contrary to Scripture.
3. Excommunication for claiming Prelacy was not according to Scripture.
4. Failure to adopt the Liturgy would result in the minister being deposed.
5. The General Assembly could not meet except on the king's order.
6. Ecclesiastical matters must be discussed in ecclesiastical courts presided over by Bishops.
7. Ministers were forbidden to hold private meetings for expounding the Scriptures.
8. Extemporaneous prayer was prohibited.
9. Baptismal fonts to be placed near church doors.
10. Consecrated elements to be handled carefully.
11. Marriage under 21 years to be approved by parents.
12. Half-yearly Synods to meet but presbytery, session, and conventicle suppressed.
13. Conduct in church: removal of hats, kneeling at prayer, standing at the Creed, not leaving during worship.
14. Conformity by teachers, curates, readers.

15. Authorised purchase of a Bible, Book of Common Prayer, pulpit, communion table and vessels, font and alms box.
16. Communion area at upper end of church and decently carpeted with fine white linen for the service.
17. Church and churchyards to be decently maintained.
18. Forbade ecclesiastical intervention in civil matters.
19. Fixed minimum age of officials at not less than thirty years.
20. Bishops were the sole power to punish the breakers of the canons.

Ministers were asked to subscribe to the Book of Canons and thus commit themselves to the Prayer Book which followed in 1637. Alexander Henderson was one of the first ministers to be put to the horn (declared a rebel) because he declined to purchase and use the Service Book and Book of Canons when so ordered by the Archbishop of St. Andrews. With the powers of the High Commission at their disposal, the prelates were now in a position as powerful as their Romish predecessors of the sixteenth century, to enforce compliance.

Causes of the Lords Wrath against Scotland (1651).

The General Assembly at Perth and Dundee in July 1651 was one of disruption, debates, and recrimination between the factions. Samuel Rutherford and twenty-one supporters called the meeting unconstitutional and the king sought to have opponents of the Resolutions to be censored. On July 22, Cromwell descended on Perth and the Assembly hurried to Dundee for safety. There they decided to cite James Guthrie, Patrick Gillespie, James Simson, James Naismith, and John Menzies to appear before the Assembly, but then did not actually do so.

The Protesters held meetings in Glasgow during September and then in October in Edinburgh and agreed ten "General Heads of the Causes why the Lord contends with the land." The pamphlet *The Causes of the Lords Wrath against Scotland manifested in his sad late Dispensations. Whereunto is added a paper, particularly holding forth the Sins of the Ministrey* was published by Christopher Higgins, a printer in Edinburgh, in October 1651 and immediately caused a furore. It is reproduced in full in *The Presbyterian's Armoury*, Vol. 3. The paper was the work of James Guthrie, with possibly some assistance by Hugh Kennedy and Archibald Johnston, and was a manifesto by the Protesting party analysing why they believed their fortunes had been so bad. They had concluded that the problems were the result of sin at every level: personal, ministerial, regal, national, and official. With hindsight, it is possible to agree with them that the worst sin of all, they declared, was the restoration of the monarchy and the crowning of King Charles II at Scone. The remedy then seemed to be further purging of the army, rather than ridding themselves of the king.

So widespread was the influence of the pamphlet that Parliament enjoined the Remonstrators and Protestors with their supporters to remove ten miles from the capital. The document was burned by the common hangman along with Rutherford's *Lex Rex* which also had been proscribed. Owning the paper was one of the charges brought against James Guthrie which led to his execution on 1 June 1661.

Causes of the Lords Wrath against the Land (1679).

This later document, entitled *Causes of the Lords Wrath against the Land*, was the result of a meeting at Shawhead Muir on 18 June 1679 when ministers Cargill, Douglas, King, and Barclay were enjoined to draft it. The document was a recital of all the sins similar to Guthrie's document of 1651. It also appears from the Walter Smith biography in the *Scots Worthies* that Smith had a hand in drafting the document; and that the Hamilton Declaration (a statement of the reasons for being in arms) only five days previous, was the final cause stated for the Lords Wrath.

John Nisbet was a witness against the apostasy in the kingdom and declared his beliefs at length both in writing and in his speech from the scaffold where the drums tried to drown him out. He had some "twenty-six steps of defection" which is said he proved with scriptures thereby demonstrating personal and national backsliding.

Cess tax - objections stated. See also: Abuse of power.

The "cess" was the tax imposed to pay for military occupation but it was not only charged in the post-Restoration period (after

1660). It had been a requirement to pay as a levy for the Engagement in 1648. In this period, the infamous Sir James Turner was sent to Renfrewshire to enforce obedience. In his *Memoirs* Turner wrote:

> I found my work not very difficult, for I shortly learnt to know that the quartering of two or three troopers and half a dozen musketeers was an argument strong enough in two or three night's time to make the hardest-headed Covenanter in the town to forsake the Kirk and to side with the Parliament.[71]

Another method that Turner adopted was to quarter troopers, often in excessive numbers, on none but the Magistrates, Council and Session members, and their supporters. This rigorous pursuit of the religious people (most of whom had some assets and money) brought rapid responses. "In ten days they cost a few honest people...above forty thousand pounds [Scots] besides plundering of those whom necessity forced to flee from their houses."[72]

During Cromwell's occupation the country people had to bear their share of providing "coal and candle" equally with the burghs when the soldiers were acting as garrisons. The elected members of the first joint Parliament made representations to Cromwell about the charges. The garrisons continued for some time because of the Jacobite sympathies that persisted, with the cess charged until the time of Colonel Monck's march on London in 1659.

In September 1678, three regiments of horse were added to the army of King Charles II for service north of the Cheviot Hills and in the Solway region. These regiments were commanded by the Earl of Airlie, the Earl of Home, and John Graham of Claverhouse, later to become Viscount Dundee. The purpose of these regiments was to maintain order and to repress the holding of conventicles. The Convention of Estates ordered in June 1678 that the means to pay for these soldiers was the "cess." It was regarded as particularly obnoxious by the people at large as another burden for them brought about by the activities of the Covenanters. Many of the

---

[71] Metcalfe, *Renfrew*, p 268.
[72] *Ibid.*, n68.

Covenanters themselves paid the tax although the die-hard element reasoned that paying an unjust tax was conniving at the injustice.

To add to the bitterness was the view of Richard Cameron, John Dickson, and others that paying the cess was on par with accepting an Indulgence so that more division occurred amongst the Presbyterians. John MacMillan, the first full-time preacher of the Societies, for example, enquired of parents at baptisms whether they had paid the cess. If they answered "yes" he would refuse to baptise the child. The Society Terms of Communion included the provision that no one could be accepted as a member who had paid the cess, locality, or militia money to the civil authorities. James Renwick was charged, amongst other things, with refusing to pay the cess giving as his reasons:

> For the present cess, enacted for the present usurper, I hold it unlawful to pay it, both in regard it is oppressive to the subject, it is for the maintenance of tyranny, and it is imposed for suppressing the Gospel.[73]

There were several polemical writers about the cess, chief amongst them was Robert McWard of Wamphray who wrote a *Testimony against Paying of Cess to an unjust and unlawful Government or wicked Rulers*.

Loosely grouped under the label of the cess were other needs for money, and not all the taxation was, in fact, used for the suppression of conventicles.

1661 An act to raise £40,000 for the King's use.
1665 A war tax derived from a rate of forty shillings on each pound land.
1665 Act requiring £72,000 monthly for a year in shires and burghs.
1670 An act for £360,000 for the king's use.
1672 A requirement for £864,000 Scots for war against the States General (Holland).
1678 A supply of £1,800,000 Scots for suppression of conventicles.
1681 The supply to continue for five years.

---

[73] Howie, *Worthies*, p. 541.

1685 A supply of £216,000 yearly for life to James II.
1685 An act for Poll monies from parishioners to relieve heritors paying the supply.

Clarendon Code.

This was the name given to the policies of Edward Hyde, Earl of Clarendon, and Lord Chancellor in England from 1661-1665. He was responsible for four particular pieces of English legislation designed to strengthen the Church of England. His laws were subsequently mirrored in Scotland during the persecution of the Presbyterians. The Laws were: (1.) The Corporation Act 1661, by which members of a municipal corporation had to take the Communion in the Church at least once a year. (2.) The Act of Uniformity of 1662 ordered all ministers to be collated by a bishop and to use the Prayer Book. (3.) The Conventicle Act of 1664 which made religious services except the Church of England, illegal. (4.) The Five Mile Act which forbade expelled clergy from living within five miles of a corporate town unless they had taken an oath of loyalty.

Collation and Presentation, Act of, 1662. See also: Bishops' Dragnet; Curates.

When appointed Commissioner to the first Parliament after the Restoration of Charles II, John, Earl of Middleton, was given exact instructions for what was required of him.

To assert the royal prerogative and the king's right to call Parliament.
To disown the Covenanting laws passed in 1643-1649.
To pass an Act of Oblivion, with certain exceptions.
To encourage trade.
To ensure the precedence of the officers of the Crown.
To arrange the proper burial of Montrose.
He was also given private instruction to test the feelings of the people towards episcopacy.

St. Giles Cathedral. Thos. Shepherd, *Modern Athens, Edinburgh in the Eighteenth Century* (London: Jones & Co., 1829).

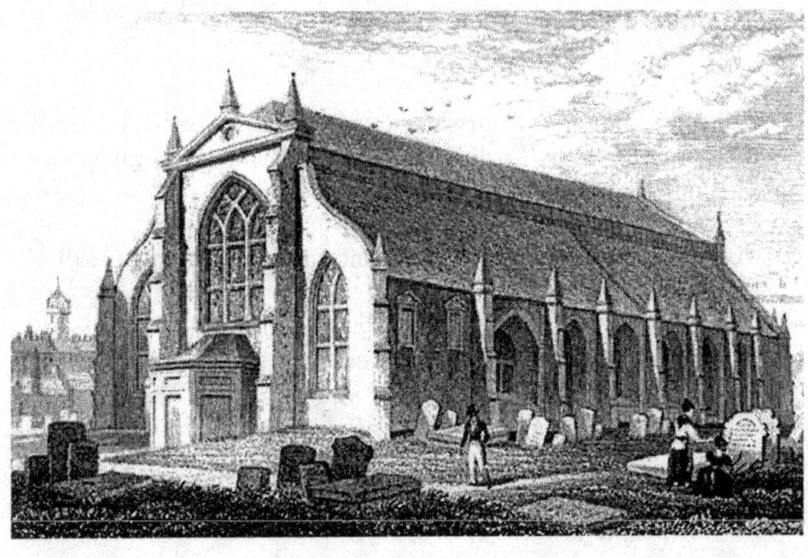

Greyfriars Kirk, Edinburgh. Thos. Shepherd, *Modern Athens, Edinburgh in the Eighteenth Century* (London: Jones & Co., 1829).

Cannongate Church. Thos. Shepherd, *Modern Athens, Edinburgh in the Eighteenth Century* (London: Jones & Co., 1829).

Holyrood House. Thos. Shepherd, *Modern Athens, Edinburgh in the Eighteenth Century* (London: Jones & Co., 1829).

Knox House, Edinburgh. Photo by the author.

Knox House, Edinburgh. Thos. Shepherd, *Modern Athens, Edinburgh in the Eighteenth Century* (London: Jones & Co., 1829).

The parliament met in January 1661 and set to with a will to produce nearly four hundred pieces of legislation, including the restoration of episcopacy and the prelates. The seventh Act was the Act of Collation and Presentation that addressed the issue of benefices. It specifically declared all parishes to be vacant whose ministers had been appointed since 1649 unless they obtained presentation by the former patron and collation from the bishops before September 20. This was followed by the test of loyalty to the king that required celebration of the king's anniversary (May 29), refusal to do so resulted in loss of living and withdrawal of benefice. On September 10, it was agreed that the prelates would meet with their clergy in October, and Middleton and his acolytes would make a visitation to the west country.

When the grand tour arrived in Glasgow, Archbishop Fairfull complained bitterly that the young ministers had not welcomed him or Episcopacy and proposed a peremptory order enjoining all ministers to submit to authority forthwith or quit their manses and move into other Presbyteries. Fairfull believed that the ministers would comply rather than suffer and that probably no more than ten pastors would be obstinate. The Council met in the Fore College Hall, Glasgow on 1 October 1662 and issued an eviction order:

> Ministers who disobeyed recent Acts should forthwith cease their ministry.
> Their pulpits declared vacant.
> Parishioners relieved of paying the stipend and acknowledgement of the ministry on pain of conviction as conventiclers.
> Non compliers to remove outwith of the Presbytery by November 1.
> Ministers neglecting the anniversary thanksgiving to be fined one year's stipend and liable to the full penalty prescribed by the Act.

The Duke of Hamilton later wrote to Bishop Burnet that "they were all so drunk that day, that they were not capable of considering anything that was laid before them, and would hear nothing but the executing of the law, without any relenting or delay."[74]

The consequence of the Act was far greater than Archbishop Fairfull anticipated. Over three hundred ministers lost their livings with the main impact being in the west and southwest of Scotland: Glasgow and Ayr – 63, Dumfries – 30, Galloway – 23, Lothian and

---

[74] Hewison, *Covenanters*, Vol. 2, p. 152.

Tweedale – 23, Merse and Teviotdale – 19, Argyll – 12, Perth and Stirling – 11, and Fife – 10. Not even a second thought proclamation on December 23 extending the deadline to 1 February 1663 was of any avail. As a result of the ejections it was necessary to appoint curates to the vacancies; they became known as the King's Curates.

The ejections were accompanied by civil unrest in which the ministers were often complicit. Major concerns were that stipends were usually by way of grain and were not yet converted into money, and they had to leave their manses in winter. In the southwest the local people physically prevented a successor to John Welch in Irongray from gaining access by congregating in the church yard and stoning the intruders. A military response followed with Commissioners ordering three magistrates who were privy to the disorder and five women to be sent to Edinburgh for trial and fourteen other women gaoled locally. Fines were imposed and bonds required for good behaviour. Resentment was also shown in other ways by locking doors in the face of incumbents; bell tongues were removed so that calls to worship were not heard; incumbents were threatened and abused. Not unexpectedly the attendances at conventicles began to rise while the attendances at the churches dropped. This prompted further legislation and the Bishops' Dragnet.

At Glen Luce Alexander Peden famously closed the pulpit door. He knocked hard upon it three times with his Bible, saying three times over "I arrest thee in my Master's name, and never none enter thee, but such as come in at the door, as I did."[75]

The next to enter was William Kyle in 1693.

Commission of the General Assembly.

The Commission of the General Assembly was made up of nominated members of the Church and had the role of dealing with public business between General Assemblies. In practice this meant that the Commission was a point of consultation with the civil government (the Estates, the Committee of the Estates, and the Privy Council) and kept a finger on the political pulse of the nation. It stood ready to muster support for ministers who were being

[75] Howie, *Worthies*, p. 508.

persecuted. In cases of ministers declining the king's authority in matters of doctrine, it was usually the Commission who would consider the issue and organise national support as appropriate.

A major controversy that came to the Commission was the debate and letter of protest from James Guthrie about the "Public Resolutions." The Resolutions were to allow certain peoples barred under the Act of Classes to be reinstated in the government and the army in the light of the defeat of the Scottish army at Dunbar. The issue divided the Covenanters into two groups with James Guthrie an ardent supporter of the Protesters questioning the legality of the General Assembly at Stirling which had approved the Resolutions. The other group were the Resolutioners.

James Guthrie was a member of the Commission that considered the actions of some nobles under the Earl of Middleton who intended to provide arms for the King. The Commission considered that they should excommunicate Middleton for his deceit and scheming. Guthrie himself did this despite some last minute attempts to stop him. This excommunication, although lifted by the next meeting of the Committee, was at the heart of Middleton's pique when he voted that Guthrie should be executed in 1661.

Committee of Public Affairs.

Set up on 20 July 1676, the Committee was charged with ensuring the implementation of a new inquisition against non-conformity. Many of the earlier acts were re-enacted. (See Appendix 24.) The members were the two archbishops; Argyll, Murray, Mar, Linlithgow, Seaforth, Kinghorn, Dundonald, Elphinstone, Lord Privy Seal, President, Treasurer Depute, Advocate, Justice Clerk, and Lord Collington; any three to form a quorum. Sharp was vice-president with plenary powers "to do all things necessary to his Majestie's service."[76]

Confessions.

In the modern era we are familiar with the concept that a person cannot be forced to give evidence that might incriminate him or herself and it seems strange to read of all the confessions made by

[76] Hewison, *Covenanters*, Vol. 2, p. 257.

the Covenanters. Often they seemed to be their own worst enemy, stating their objections to prelacy and not owning the king's authority in ecclesiastical matters. Yet time and time again their declarations, or testimonies, were produced in evidence against them. Donald Cargill is a clear example of having defended his beliefs stoutly, yet he nevertheless admitted to approving of the use of defensive arms. His confession was produced in evidence and he was found guilty of high treason. This handing over of declarations or defences of faith as evidence was a consequence of the division between civil and ecclesiastical authority.

After the Restoration of Charles II in 1660 the drive against the Covenanters was mainly by the prelates, Archbishop Sharp, in particular, and the use of the Court of High Commission. By pressing charges for not following the orders of the official Episcopal church the Presbyterian dissenters were compromised into making a testimony or explanation of their actions. Indeed the purpose of interview by the prelates was often aimed at eliciting evidence of a civil offence because the penalties were much greater, including execution. Thus torture was used by the prelates and even straight-forward forgery, to get what was desired. The confession of John Nisbet is an example where it was altered and an incriminating reference to connections with Argyll was inserted.

Conscience.

Conscience—the knowledge of right from wrong and the judgment of one's own acts and thoughts—runs throughout the Presbyterian way and the lives of the Covenanters. Bound up with this judgmental approach is the concept of duty to both an earthly and a spiritual king. Taken to its extremes, as the Cameronians and the Societies did, it is difficult to conceive of a state of mind that is more difficult to satisfy. The modern word of angst comes close to describing the torment these Covenanters suffered: remorse about the past, guilt about the present, and anxiety about the future.

There were a host of issues that disturbed the conscience and ultimately caused division among the members of the church. The matter of supremacy in the church, self-governance, and a Christian civil authority were basic issues of doctrine that were relatively easily absorbed and defended. The early arguments against Romanism and prelacy were reasonably well-defined and understood. The problems, however, began with the king's Proclamation at Stirling on 23 February 1638 reinforcing that the imposition of the Service Book and Canons were by his order. It made clear that the king, as well as the prelates, was determined to undermine the constitution and worship of the Church in Scotland. The National Covenant of 1638 raised the fervour of the people and the aspirations of the purists who saw the scope for extending the Presbyterian faith. This was heightened by the Solemn League and Covenant of 1643. In the following year ministers were enjoined to take note of persons who came into their parishes who did not subscribe to the Covenants.

The civil politics of the "Engagement" in 1648 saw King Charles I and the Duke of Hamilton negotiating terms for military assistance against England. The Covenanters regarded this as sinful and perjury by breaking covenanted vows and their alliance with the English Parliamentarians. The failure of the Engagement gave rise to the clerical government of the Second Reformation which was immediately compromised by the Act of Classes. There followed further searching of consciences and schism over the Resolutions. The execution of Charles I in 1649 provided another trial of conscience whether or not to support the succession of Charles II, knowing it must mean war. Then, of course, they chose to oppose Cromwell but were very quickly put in their place and forced to compromise.

To this point, the conscience-stricken Church of all shades of opinion had for over a decade staggered from one crisis to another with zeal often outstripping wisdom. Against this background it is understandable that the people in general were becoming tired of inter-necine squabbles as well as the demands upon them to pay for and serve in civil wars. The enforced peace and compromise under Cromwell was a welcome respite, during which another generation grew up that had not imbibed the fervour of Greyfriars. Perhaps more given to compromise, the mood of the people was reflected in the initial policies of Charles II who determined to isolate the dissenters and turn the populace against them. However, turning upon the common people and using force to gain their compliance was a serious mistake. It brought them directly into the firing line for the first time and opened a defiant second front.

The Restoration of Charles II in 1660 brought a vengeful king determined to crush all opposition to his will. The tactic was to isolate the dissenting minority with policies of divide and rule. Middleton's Act outed over three hundred ministers and it is pertinent that about twice that number stayed in their parishes by accepting the terms. This first division identified the dissenting minority and gave scale to the size of the task. But the interdicting of the curates, the Bishops' Dragnet of 1663, fines, and their enforcement by the military caused the general populace to consider their position about attending church. The penalties for attending conventicles introduced in 1665 were harsher and could mean the death penalty. The Indulgences served to harden the resistance of the purists yet allowed those of lesser conscience religious freedom at a cost. It also served to divide the Church and further isolate the trouble-makers in the eyes of the government. The imposition of the cess and its payment became an issue of conscience, and the injustice of making heritors responsible for the actions of their tenants brought further division to the church and the people.

The Declaration at Rutherglen, in 1679 (see Appendix 13), was an important public declaration of principles condemning laws enacted since the Restoration; the Hamilton Declaration shortly after was an opposing view and supplication to the king. The internal disputes of conscience divided the army at Bothwell Brig in 1679 and effectively put an end to organised armed resistance. Following the Declaration of Sanquhar in 1680, armed defence became a Covenanter tactic. Renwick's "Vindication" gave rise to the Abjuration Oath and the ultimate authority for on the spot executions. And James II, an overtly Catholic king, gave further Indulgences including freedom of religious practice for Catholics. Each and every act by government or the Church was an issue of conscience.

One can only wonder at the strength of convictions held by the likes of the Cameronians and the Societies who held true to their consciences under enormous pressures. They saw the effect that the oppression was having on the populace around them and must have been sorely troubled by it. But such was their total belief that they still stood up to be counted unto the death. That requires a very special kind of person whatever we may think of the rights and wrongs of their cause. It is perhaps fitting that, over three hundred years later, we have to search our own consciences to arrive at an opinion on who was right.

Alexander Shields was a Covenanter who was much troubled with conscience although a strong supporter of Renwick. His particular problem was that in 1685 he felt compromised into signing the Abjuration Oath, albeit under duress and with amendments by him. He managed to escape from prison and joined Renwick, constantly regretting his compliance with the authorities. On 22 December 1686 at a general meeting of the societies he made a full public confession. And, on 3 March 1689 when renewing the Covenants at Borland Hill, Lesmahagow, he again made public confession. Yet despite his protestations he and the other two ministers of the Societies—Linning and Boyd—all joined the Revolution Church, thus leaving the Societies without a minister until John MacMillan joined them sixteen years later.

Consecration of the bishops. See also: Episcopacy.

Although a most subservient and cringing man, Bishop Spottiswood had some concerns that he and his colleagues had not been consecrated as there was a no Apostolic Succession. They were in reality merely Presbyterian pastors and civil servants at the beck and call of the king. James himself suggested that three Scots bishops should come to London and be consecrated; doing so would also answer the allegations from the Presbyterians that he was assuming a Papal role. They could then consecrate the remainder. Spottiswood had quibbles about being consecrated by the Bishop of York and, not unreasonable fears, that it would set a precedent of a Church in Scotland that was subservient to England. Yet, he was content to be consecrated by the Bishops of London, Ely, Rochester, and Worcester. The ceremony took place in London House on 21 October 1610 when Spottiswood (Glasgow), Gavin Hamilton (Galloway), and Andrew Cant (Brechin) were duly anointed.

In May 1611, the established hierarchy of the Church of Scotland consisted of George Gledstanes, Primate and Archbishop of St. Andrews, and John Spottiswood, Archbishop of Glasgow, and bishops Peter Blackburn (Aberdeen), Andrew Lamb (Brechin), Alexander Forbes (Caithness), George Graham (Dunblane), Alexander Lindsay (Dunkeld), Alexander Douglas (Moray), James Law (Orkney), David Lindsay (Ross), Neill Campbell (Argyll), Gavin Hamilton (Galloway), and Andrew Knox (The Isles).

Although glorying in their titles, there was not much else for the bishops because most of the Church lands had been disposed of, and with them the rents. Some did not even enjoy their titles all that long: Hamilton died in 1612, Campbell in 1613, Lindsay in 1613, Gledstanes in 1615, and Blackburn in 1616.

The Parliament of October 1612 ratified the Acts of the Glasgow Assembly, repealed the Act of 1592, and legalised Episcopacy.

Constant or Perpetual Moderators. See also: Bishop's Role; General Assembly Aberdeen 1604, 1605; Tulchan Bishops.

The constant moderator affair began as a change to the manner in which a Moderator was appointed to a General Assembly. It was a thinly disguised device to create a position in the Church to which the king could then substitute bishops.

As part of his continuing endeavour to force episcopacy on the Church of Scotland James VI, persuaded the General Assembly at Dundee in 1599 to agree to commissioners (later termed bishops) who would consult with the king. The king was also responsible for determining how many commissioners there should be. Having obtained this agreement, James next endeavoured to stop the calling of General Assemblies. This was achieved by deferring the Assembly in Aberdeen in 1604 and 1605, and resulted in nineteen ministers who had convened anyway, setting a date for the future meeting themselves. Subsequently, sixteen of them were imprisoned and six more ministers were banished to the outer Isles.

In 1606, a protestation was made by forty-two ministers, including Andrew Melville, to the Estates in Parliament at Perth about the attempt to force prelacy on the Church. At this Parliament two Acts were passed, one confirming the royal prerogative over all estates, persons, and causes whatsoever. The second authorised the restitution of the estates of bishops which would enable the king to make appointments. Despite representations made to a General Assembly at Linlithgow in December 1606, James VI cleverly used the fears of Papacy (the Gunpowder Plot was in November 1605) to introduce persons of standing (bishops) to be Constant Moderator over each Presbytery with a salary of £100 Scots. Hewison, in *The Covenanters*, tells that the agreement was subject to the Church courts supervision but the minutes were falsified or altered to show unambiguous acceptance. Thirteen bishops were made Moderator of the Presbytery in whose bounds they resided and Constant Moderator of his Synod. In this way the king foisted diocesan episcopacy on the Church of Scotland while still maintaining the underlying Presbyterian structure.

Conventicles.

The conventicle or field meeting was a direct consequence of the "outing" of over three hundred ministers from their parishes in 1662. The simple fact was that the people preferred their minister and an evangelical style of worship to the rites and rituals of episcopacy. The curates were greatly resented as usurpers as well as dull preachers dressed up with popish practices. The heartland of the Covenanters was the southwest of Scotland through Ayrshire, Lanarkshire, Dumfries, and Galloway, although there was also strong support in the Borders, Fife and Stirling. The southwest was a region of rolling hills, secluded and heavily wooded river valleys, and expanses of moor and bog where the shepherds were masters of travel. In such a locality gatherings were reasonably safe from intervention by the authorities. The physical features of a location was often utilised to good effect and there are several places linked to Peden by their pulpits. One such is at Ruberslaw near Hawick where a stone is identified as the place he laid his bible. At Coilholme, in the parish of Tarbolton, Ayrshire, Peden utilised a natural amphitheatre where an overhanging rock was a natural sounding board before which his armed guard would assemble, flintlocks at the ready.

For some of the ministers the conventicle became a way of life with the likes of Alexander Peden, John Welch, and John Blackadder, all of whom travelled all over the Lowlands to preach to substantial crowds. Daniel Defoe speaks of having seen a conventicle in Nithsdale with about 7,000 persons in attendance, some of whom had walked fifteen miles to sit on the hillside to listen to the preacher. But there were also house conventicles and meetings held in barns, shepherds' bothies, and houses within the cities of Edinburgh and Glasgow, right under the authorities' noses. At first, the government responded by fining and using the Bishop's Dragnet. Subsequently, there was a Proclamation against conventicles of 7 December 1665, and a further Act against them of

28 July 1670, each ramping up the pressure on both preachers and the congregations.

Smellie, in *Men of the Covenant*, tells of John Blackadder, arriving the evening before a proposed conventicle, who was met by a crowd and he began preaching for an hour and a half at eleven o'clock at night then baptised forty two children before day break. At the Hill of Beath in 1670 Blackadder preached to a great crowd and came to the assistance of a soldier who happened on the conventicle. This conventicle was one of the first to which the congregation came armed. At another conventicle at East Nisbet in the Borders Blackadder held a Communion service in the fields at which sixteen tables were set up and about three thousand two hundred communicated that day. On another occasion with John Welch, a conventicle at Eckford in Teviotdale was attended by over three thousand people. At Girvan on 21 October 1676 Welch and four other ministers held a conventicle for 7,000 and administered the Communion to over 2,000. Welch, Blackadder, Samuel Arnot of Tongland and John Dickson of Rutherglen were involved in a very large gathering at Skeoch Hill in Irongray Parish, in July 1678 when over a period of several days some 14,000 people attended and they dispensed the sacrament of the Lord's Supper to over 3,000 people.

The success of the conventicle was much resented by the authorities, especially the prelates who could foresee the doom of Episcopacy if it was allowed to continue. From about 1670 or so, the meetings frequently had armed members among them which raised a fear of rebellion in the government's mind. As a consequence allowing, even by default, a conventicle to be held on your property, preaching at them and eventually just attending them, was subject of severe penalties. A proclamation of 8 April 1681 imposed the death penalty for preaching at a field conventicle. Finally, in 1687, it became treason, punishable by death, for just attending a conventicle.

Conversion.

The common man and woman in the early seventeenth century were not far removed from the Dark Ages with regard to their worldly knowledge. Witchcraft was still common and pagan rites such as painting doorsteps or thresholds to ward off evil spirits continued until almost modern times. Books were expensive and rare; at best a family might have a Bible that was greatly treasured. Education in village schools was largely confined to the rudiments of reading, writing, and religion through the labours of the minister. Against this background, it is easier to understand why the church and, later, conventicles were so popular as a source of recreation let alone information, learning, and confession of faith.

The Stewarton Sickness was a religious revival that took place in the Parish of Stewarton in Ayrshire from 1625 to 1630 and is credited for bringing many converts to the Kirk. It happened through the influence of David Dickson, the minister in the neighbouring parish of Irvine since 1618. Dickson had spoken out against the Articles of Perth and was ordered to remove to Turriff but, through the influence of the Earl of Eglinton and his countess, he was able to return to Irvine in 1623. M'Crie, in *Sketches*, tells that:

> Crowds, under spiritual concern, came from all the parishes around Irvine and many settled in the neighbourhood, to enjoy his ministrations.[77]

Dickson began giving a weekly lecture on Mondays, which was market day in Irvine, and soon had large crowds attending. These included especially the people of Stewarton who were encouraged by their own minister, Rev. Castlelaw, to attend. Dickson must have had a fairly large manse because there were often crowds of a hundred or more waiting to talk to him and seeking his advice. Such was the desire for Christian counsel that it spread from house to house along the valley of the Stewarton Water. The sacred character of the work was attested

> by the solid, serious, practical religion [that] flourished mightily in the west of Scotland about this time, under the hardships of Prelacy.[78]

Another conversion of the masses that is often quoted is that at a conventicle held at the Kirk o' Shotts on 21 June 1630 by John

---

[77] M'Crie, *Sketches*, p. 190.
[78] Howie, *Worthies*, p. 292.

Livingston. The circumstances in which Livingston came to preach are unusual and he himself said

> I never preached a sermon that I would be in earnest to see again in writing but two: the one was the Monday after the Communion at Shotts and the other after the Communion at Holywood, and both these times I spent the whole night before in conference and prayer with some Christians.[79]

The gathering at Shotts was fostered by the Marchioness of Hamilton who had refurbished the local manse and, by way of payment (the gratitude of the minister, Mr. Home), she asked to have David Dickson and Robert Bruce serve at a Communion service. She attended with several prominent persons including the Lady Culross, the wife of James Colvill, Lord Culross. The Communion service was said to have been accompanied by surprising manifestations of the presence of God. Such was the atmosphere that the people were reluctant to go home, wanting instead to hear more. It was unusual to preach on the Monday following the dispensation of the Lord's Supper but the ministers agreed to do so. The minister due to preach had, however, been taken ill, and Lady Culross suggested that the twenty-seven-year-old John Livingston should fill the gap. Livingston was at the time chaplain to the Countess of Wigton and had preached at Shotts before, but not with such a large congregation. After much persuasion Livingston finally gave in and agreed to preach. He stood before a vast crowd and delivered his sermon based upon Ezekiel 36:25: "Then will I sprinkle clean water upon you, and ye shall be clean." The sermon lasted about an hour and a half. As he was drawing to a close, rain began to fall but, transfixed by the sermon, the people remained listening to him for another hour in which he developed the theme of the despair that fell on the unbelieving when the fire and brimstone of Judgment came upon them. Livingston himself wrote that he got "such liberty and melting of heart"[80] as he never had the like in public before. Howie, in *Scots Worthies*, tells us that "a most discernible change was wrought on about 500 of his hearers, who could date either their

---

[79] *Ibid.*, p. 375-376.

[80] Hewison, *Covenanters*, Vol. 1, p. 205.

conversion or some remarkable confirmation, from that day forward."[81]

Coronation Oath.

At his Restoration in 1660, King Charles II did not, through the duplicity of James Sharp, swear again to uphold the Covenants that he had previously made at his coronation in 1651. His subsequent action against the Presbyterian church showed his disdain for both church and the Scottish people. The Coronation Oath taken at Scone on 1 January 1651 was:

> I, Charles, King of Great Britain, France, and Ireland, do assert and declare, by my Solemn Oath, in the Presence of Almighty God, the Searcher of my Hearts, my Allowance and Approbation of the National Covenant, and of the Solemn League and Covenant, above written, and faithfully oblige myself to prosecute the Ends thereof in my Station and Calling; and that I for Myself and Successors shall consent and agree to all Acts of Parliament enjoining National Covenant and Solemn League and Covenant, and fully establishing Presbyterian Government, the Directory for Worship, Confession of Faith, Catechisms, in the Kingdom of Scotland, as they are approven by the General Assemblies of this Kirk, and Parliaments of this Kingdom; and that I shall give my royal assent to Acts or Ordinances of Parlirament passed, or to be passed, enjoining the same in my other Dominions; and that I shall observe those in my own Practice and Family, and shall never make Opposition to any of these, or endeavour any change thereof.[82]

The Act (No. 58) of the February 1649 Parliament—"Act anent Swearing of Religion and peace of the Kingdome"—was an important milestone. This ordained that the king or any of his successors, before being admitted to regal power should first subscribe, and promise to make all his subjects in the three kingdoms subscribe, the Solemn League and Covenant and consent

[81] Howie, *Worthies*, p. 370.
[82] Hewison, *Covenanters*, Vol. 2, p. 28.

to the statutes enjoining its acceptance and the establishment of Presbyterian Government, the Directory of Worship, the Confession of Faith, and the Catechisms, promising also to observe them in personal practice and in his family. On February 7, the Parliament also ratified and approved the Catechisms and the Confession. Following his Coronation and declaration as the "only Covenanted King with God and His people in the world,"[83] Charles began his secret policy: to revenge his father's death, destroy the regicides, and restore the autocracy beloved of the Stuart kings.

Correspondence Union. See also: Revolution Settlement; Societies.

Following the execution of Donald Cargill on 27 July 1681 the Cameronians or Cargillites—the extreme Covenanters—were left leaderless. In this vacuum they formed themselves into praying societies. At a meeting held at Logan House, near Lesmahagow on 15 December 1681 they decided to maintain their unity by forming a "correspondence union." The prayer meetings were supervised by a district union, who sent a representative to the three monthly General Meeting where disputes, matters of policy and tactics were agreed. The growth of this organisation to eighty societies with seven thousand members was in effect the creation of an underground church and a resistance movement that was ready to accept James Renwick as its new leader in September 1683. The correspondence unions were instrumental in producing and publicising the Lanark Declaration on 12 January 1682. (See Appendix 15.) The Privy Council retaliated with the act that made owning the Declaration or refusing to disown it a treasonable offence punishable by execution on the spot, without trial. James Renwick knew and approved of the Declaration but was unhappy at some of the terms used.

Covenants. See also: Solemn League and Covenant.

Covenants or Bands were a common feature of Scottish society and not just in the Reformation. These were simply agreements to work together for a common purpose, often for defence and can be

[83] *Ibid.*, Vol. 2, p. 29.

traced back to the Lords Hay, Campbell, and Seton who banded together to defend and support Robert the Bruce in 1306. However, banding was illegal for many years and ratified by an Act of 1424. There was a band entered into to protect George Wishart in 1546. A signatory then was the Earl of Bothwell who singularly failed to do anything when Wishart was seized, quickly convicted and burnt at the stake. The Covenants and Bands which appeared first in 1556 by the "gentlemen of Mearns" are distinguished by the fact that they are specifically religious in nature for the promotion and protection of a faith. John Knox was involved in this Band which was entered into at Duns in Forfarshire where John Erskine, a friend of Knox, resided. Later specific religious Bands or Covenants were:

3 December 1557. The first Covenant for renunciation of Popery and defence of the Gospel. (See Appendix 4.)
31 May 1559. The second Covenant, or Band for mutual defence in Perth.
1 August 1559. The third Covenant at Stirling to maintain unity and negotiate as a single body.
27 April 1560. The fourth Covenant for expelling the French.
4 September1562. The fifth Covenant in Ayrshire (Carrick, Cunningham and Kyle).
2 July 1572. The sixth Covenant signed in Leith.
28 January 1581. The National Covenant or Kings Confession, against Popery. Signed by the people 1581; renewed 1590. (See Appendix 5.)
28 February 1638. The National Covenant signed at Greyfriars Kirk, Edinburgh. (See Appendix 8.)
25 September1643. The Solemn League and Covenant sworn in London. (See Appendix 9.)
26 November 1666. Covenant renewed at Lanark.
3 March 1689. Covenant renewed at Lesmahagow.

It is of note that the National Covenant of 1581 was binding only on those who signed it. These are cited in Johnston's *Treasury* as James Rex; Mortoune; Lenox; Argyll; Ruthven; Robert Stewart; Seton; R. Dumfermling, P. Master of Gray; Cathcart; James Halyburtoun; Mr John Crag; John Duncanson; Michael Elphinstoun; P. Young; Robert Erskyne; James Elphinstoun; S. Borthie; Welzame

Crag; John Murdo. James Mr. Ogilvy; Allane Mr. Cathcart; William Schaw; James Steuart; Alexander Seytoun; J. Chisley; James Colvill of East Wemes; George Douglas; Alexander Durem; Walter Steuard, pryore of Blantyre; William Ruthven of Billindane; John Scrymgeour, younger of Glaswall; William Morray; David Murray; James Frasser; Richard Heriot; Maister Thomas Hamilton; Walter Kyer. [84]

It was drawn up by the king's chaplain, John Craig, and consisted of a solemn rejection of the popish system and an engagement to adhere and defend the reformed doctrine of the Church of Scotland.

The National Covenant of 1638 contains a clause that commits future generations: "the present and succeeding generations in this land are bound to keep the foresaid national oath and subscription inviolable."[85] It is clearly intended to bond together future generations, the church, and the Scottish nation. The Marquis of Argyll affirmed this intention at his execution when he said, "But God has laid engagements on Scotland; we are tied by covenants to religion and reformation; those who were then unborn are yet engaged."[86]

It is this belief that lies at the very heart of the Covenanters' tribulations and their protestations about backsliders and the national sin of Scotland. It is the core reason why the United Societies did not join the Revolutionary Church in 1690.

The National Covenant of 1638 was made up of three parts. First, the 1581 King's Confession; second the legal section drawn up by Archibald Johnston, Lord Warriston, that set out the relevant legislation against popery and ratifying the Acts of the General Assembly; third, the grievances and redress sought, which were drawn up by Alexander Henderson. The document itself was described as "a fair parchment above an elne in squair" (a Scottish ell is 37 inches so it was quite large) and was glowingly referred to as "The Constellation upon the back of Aries."[87]

The signing at Greyfriars Kirk was a splendid event but it did not take place on a tombstone outside; the table stones simply were not there at that time. The actual spot is marked within the church next

---

[84] Johnston, *Treasury*, p. 50.
[85] *Ibid.*, p. 81.
[86] Howie, *Worthies*, p. 255.
[87] Hewison, *Covenanters*, Vol. 1, p. 267.

to the central pulpit. The Covenant was subsequently taken round local churches for signature by the people and copies were made and distributed to the major towns of Scotland. The original Covenant is thought to be that in the Huntley House Museum in Edinburgh. Who was first to sign has been a matter of debate, some claiming an elderly Earl of Sutherland to be first; but he was actually twenty-nine at the time and his signature does not appear. In all probability, it was Montrose who signed first, followed by Sir Andro Moray of Balvaird, a former minister at Abdie in Fife who had been knighted in 1633. Other early signatures were those of the nobles, barons, and commissioners of the shires: Rothes, Cassillis, Eglinton, Montgomery, Wemyss, Home, Lindsay, Lothian, Dalhousie, Yester, Burley, Loudon, Melville, Johnston, Carnegie, Fottester, Cranstoun, Boyd, Sinclair, Balmerino, Fleming, Cowpar, Elcho, Drumlanrig, Rowallan, Lyone, Grierson of Lag, and Fergusson of Craigdarroch. Early ministers to sign were Alexander Henderson, George Gillespie, David Dickson. Andrew Ramsay, and Henry Rollock. Archibald Johnston and some sixty representatives from the burghs also signed.

The reaction of the prelates is summed up in the words of the elderly Archbishop Spottiswood who was in hiding waiting for an opportunity to slip across the border into England. He said, "All which we have been attempting to build up during the last thirty years is now at once thrown down."[88]

The king wrote (or someone for him) most undiplomatically what he thought of the crisis and the Presbyterian party in his *Large Declaration*. It began attempting a pun that the Tables were as "stables of unruly horses." It offensively comments:

> Now the first dung which from these stables was throwne on the face of Authoritie and Government was that lewd Covenant and seditious Band annexed unto it.[89]

Not all towns subscribed to the Covenant. Those that did not subscribe were Crail, Inverness, St. Andrews, and Aberdeen to which the stalwarts David Dickson, Alexander Henderson, and Andrew Cant were sent, with Montrose and other nobles, to

---

[88] *Ibid.*, p. 271.

[89] Hewison, *Covenanters*, Vol. 1, p. 279.

persuade the town and country to sign the Covenant. Their journey was not fruitful. Because of non-conformity, Aberdeen was congratulated by the king and £100 pounds was provided to ensure royalist pamphlets could continue in print. Some ministers eventually subscribed in 1639 but the granite city was subsequently embroiled in battles during the campaign of the Marquis of Montrose.

Covenants renewed. Lanark, 26 November 1666. Lesmahagow, 3 March 1689. See also: Revolution Settlement; Societies.

The renewals of the Covenant were in the main a means of stiffening the sinews in times of great troubles. That at Lanark was only days before the battle at Rullion Green in which about fifty Covenanters died and another hundred or so were taken prisoner. There seems to be some doubt about how many people were at Lanark for the renewal of the Covenant. Robert Ker and his party joined "the little handful who renewed the Covenants at Lanark."[90] Hugh McKail and William Veitch tell us that there were about 1,500 people.

The renewal at Borland Hill, near Lesmahagow was driven by a different trouble: that of the United Societies who declined to accept the Revolutionary Settlement because the terms of Covenants had not been adhered to.

***Crown* – ship.**

The *Crown* is one of several ships that appear in Covenanter lore is remembered for the fact that it foundered and sank off of Deerness in Orkney on 10 December 1679 with the loss of 211 Covenanter prisoners. About forty-six survived.

Following the battle at Bothwell Brig on 22 June 1679 some 1,100 prisoners were taken and confined in the make-shift prison in the Greyfriars Kirk Yard, Edinburgh. Many prisoners were released on taking oaths and giving bonds for good behaviour and a residue of 257 prisoners were sentenced to transportation to the American colonies. These were loaded on board the *Crown* which sailed from Leith on November 27 and was later forced into the Orkney port of

---

[90] Howie, *Worthies*, p. 435.

Deerness by bad weather. The captain, Thomas Teddico, however, ignored local advice and set sail only to be wrecked on Scarva Taing rocks. It is reported that the captain was a profane, cruel wretch who refused to allow the prisoners out of the hold as the ship began breaking up.

The number of dead and survivors varies a little, exacerbated by there not being a full list of the 257 said to have been put on board in Leith. The number of survivors vary between forty-six and forty-nine, with between five and nine names not known. Up to ten prisoners may have escaped to Ulster and two families on Orkney claim descent from escaped prisoners. Whatever the numbers, they suffered a cruel fate locked below decks as the ship broke up on the rocks.

Cumbernauld Bond.

The Cumbernauld Bond (or Band) was an agreement in August 1640 between some of the nobles, led by the Marquis of Montrose, that disagreed with the too-radical policies of The Tables, and aimed to constrain the Marquis of Argyll who was tending to follow his own agenda at the expense of others. In between the Bishops' Wars Montrose had begun to have doubts about the National Covenant's requirement to defend both Kirk and King and sought out others of a like conservative mind. It may be that Montrose was seeking safety in numbers before going up against Argyll with whom he was at daggers drawn. However, conscience or not, Montrose was still able to be with the Covenanter army when it struck across the border and captured Newcastle on Tyne on 30 August 1640. Montrose also corresponded privately with King Charles and offered his services but was rebuffed. He was discovered by the Covenanters, through the interception of a courier who was carrying letters, and spent some time a prisoner in Edinburgh Castle for his trouble. He subsequently deserted the Covenanters and conducted a brilliant campaign for the king in the Highlands during 1644-1645.

The signatories to the Cumbernauld Band were the Lords Marschell, Montrose, Wigton, Kinghorn, Home, Atholl, Mar, Perth, Boyd, Stormonth, Seaforth, Erskine, Kilcibright, Anmont, Drummond, Johnston, Lour, D. Carnegy, and Master of Lour. In the following January, twelve of the signatories made an additional declaration that they would do nothing prejudicial to the Covenant.

Curates. See also: Collation.

The Curates were possibly among the most despised men in Scotland beginning in 1662, when the Act of Collation and Presentation was passed. This required ministers who had been appointed since 1649 to accept Episcopalian sanction and to apply to their bishop for permission to continue their ministry. With over three hundred ministers declining to accept the law their parishes were declared vacant and curates were appointed. The west of Scotland was particularly badly hit. *Napthali* quotes the declarations at that time to enforce attendance and acceptance of the curates.

Proclamations emitted at the time of the first planting of the Curates were a direct attack on the people in general:

> That all persons should keep their own Parish Churches, and should not repair to any other except in vacancy, under pain of twenty shillings Scots.
>
> An Edict against unwarrantable Preaching, Praying, or Hearing that made private family prayer, or joining with two three or more domesticks is declared an unlawful conventicle and all who are accessory are punishable accordingly.
>
> Men are required to be assistant to, and concur with the Curate in the exercise of Discipline, as they shall thereto be called.
>
> Discharging all Conventions and meetings whatsoever under the pretence of religion, which are not allowed by Authority, certifying all persons accessory that they shall be looked upon and punished by pecuniary and corporall pains, as seditious persons, at the arbitrenient of the Council, and especially that the Ministers exercising therein, and their resetters and countenancers in any sort shall be liable unto the highest pains due to Seditious persons.
>
> Commanding all Masters of Families, to cause their Servants and all their dependents and all Heritors and Landlords to cause their Tenants and Tax-men to obey all the Acts of Parliament or Council enjoyning Conformity, and particularly to frequent their Parish Churches, and to

> submit and conform to the Curates their Ministry, or else to remove them summarly from their service, and eject them out of their possessions. And also that Heritors take bond and security of their intrant Tennants in time coming, that they and their Cottars and Servants, shall give obedience as said is; and lastly that all Magistrates Burghs cause their Inhabitants; give bond for the like obedience; for which effects, their heritors and Magistrates are warranted to charge them under pain of rebellion: And whomsoever shall contravene this Edict is certified and declared liable to the same pains due to the Non conformists themselves, for whom he hereby is made answerable.[91]

The quality of the curates was variable, with some being no more than callow youths with no experience and little religious training. Some took the job for what they might get from the benefices of the post. The odium attached to being a curate was undoubtedly heightened by the introduction of the Bishop's Dragnet when they were required to keep a record of persons attending church, and to give details of absentees for imposition of fines and collection by the military. It was the heavy-handed collection of fines that sparked the Pentland Rising in 1666.

Deathbed dramatics.

We need to remember when reading of death scenes, especially executions, that the subjects lived in an age where auditories (groups of listeners) were common and speech the principal method of communication. In most instances, according to the *Scots Worthies*, it is a minister or elder of the church declaiming their faith before hanging. For such men a last sermon from the scaffold was their final vindication but was frowned upon by the authorities who were afraid of rousing the rabble. James Renwick's execution was typical of the malice of the authorities who sought to stop him from a public speech on the scaffold, and used the drums to drown

---

[91] J. Stewart and J. Sterling. *Napthali, or the Wrestlings of the Church of Scotland for the Kingdom of Christ.* (Edinburgh: ----, 1693; reprint Edmonton: Still Waters Revival Books, 1996), pp. 213-215. Hereafter called *Napthali.*

him out. For the people it was possibly the only occasion that many would have to see a minister they had only ever heard about before.

The executions were undoubtedly spectacles to watch, preceded by the erection of scaffolds (one for the "turning off the ladder" [hanging] and the second for decapitating the body [and sometimes the hands] for exhibition over the Netherbow Gate). The arrival of the prisoner was surrounded by a degree of ceremony, sometimes with guards preventing attempts to communicate with him. A short speech might be allowed before the drums would roll to drown it out. The prisoner would climb the ladder and sit upon the top rung, the rope put in place; perhaps say a few more words, and the napkin placed over his face so that he might not see the hangman grasp the ladder and flip him off into eternity.

Death by natural means was also scene for rapture in the dying minister. These were, remember, people of intense faith and belief in the hereafter. They had suffered much for their faith and were totally convinced of the glory to come. Robert Rollock was one who said, "I am weary of this life, all my desire is, that I may enjoy the celestial life that is hid with Christ in God."[92] Alexander Henderson was another who, worn out by his great efforts for the Covenant, was almost glad when death came to him, exclaiming, "Never Schoolboy more longed for the breaking up…than I do to have leave of this world."[93] The young James Mitchell seems to have been quite rapturous in his last five or six weeks before dying of a wasting illness. Samuel Rutherford had many visitors in his last days and uttered many savoury speeches, and often broke out in a kind of sacred rapture, exalting and commending the Lord Jesus, especially when his end drew near.[94]

Of a different kind of majesty were the executions of the Marquis of Argyll and the Marquis of Montrose. Argyll was sentenced to beheading which in Scotland was accomplished by "The Maiden," a guillotine. His execution was dignified as would be expected of a man of breeding and his final words a declaration of faith. It was on this occasion that Argyll reminded his auditory that the Covenants were binding on Scotland and on all future

---

[92] Howie, *Worthies*, p. 75.
[93] Smellie, *Men of the Covenant*, p. 21.
[94] Howie, *Worthies*, p. 237.

generations. His son, the 9th Earl of Argyll, was executed for rebellion on 30 June 1685.

James Graham, Marquis of Montrose, however, suffered the ignominy (for a noble) of common hanging. Smellie, in *Men of the Covenant*, gives a splendid picture of Montrose arriving dressed as for his wedding: richly clad in fine scarlet laid over with silver lace, a hat with a golden hat band, and silken stockings. Hewison, in *Covenanters*, goes further, calling him a "Covent Garden coxcomb" after the area near the opera house in London where the dandies of their day would parade. He describes Montrose's execution dress:

> Now he was faultlessly, even gaudily, attired in a black suit trimmed with silver, over which was thrown a scarlet cloak embroidered with silver and lined with crimson. He wore a carnation coloured silk stockings and garters, with shoes having rosettes of the same hue. A fashionable beaver hat with a band of silver lace shaded a fine face and partially covered his lockas of beautiful auburn hair. Seldom had such a handsome galliard adorned a gallows.[95]

For all of Montrose's attire and drama, the body and its trimmings were soon quartered for distribution and exhibition round the country. The head was impaled on the gable end of Edinburgh Tolbooth where the tale is it served for gunnery practice from time to time by soldiers in the castle (an incredible distance for a flintlock). It was finally taken down eleven years later and reunited with the trunk that had been buried in unhallowed ground on the Borough Moor, and the limbs that had been displayed in Aberdeen, Glasgow, Stirling, and Perth.[96]

Declaration.

It was custom and practice to make public declarations at the Market Cross, whether of new laws, condemnations of people and

---

[95] Hewison, *Covenanters*, Vol. 1, p. 467.

[96] A final irony is that Montrose was reburied with great pomp and ceremony by order of the King on 11 May 1661 in St Giles Cathedral. Both he and the Marquis of Argyll lie in splendid mausoleums only yards apart in St. Giles Cathedral, Edinburgh. Montrose is in the Chapman Aisle, Argyll has his memorial on the other side of the cathedral, in St. Eloi's Aisle.

actions, or protests. In Edinburgh, the Mercat Cross has had several locations over the years but it has always been an open-turreted structure with a tall flag pole topped by a unicorn. At the open first floor level the Herald, accompanied perhaps by drum and trumpet, would stand and make his declaration. It was not an easy task for the Herald, and could take time; for instance, in 1662 when the Earl of Middleton's new laws took over seven hours to proclaim. Donald Cargill's sentence of death was proclaimed with the sound of a trumpet. There is some irony in Cargill's statement, on hearing his sentence to be executed preceded by a trumpet blast, "This is a weary sound, but the sound of the last trumpet will be a joyful sound to me."[97]

The Market Cross, in places other than Edinburgh, were favoured by the Covenanters for several important declarations, not least of these being that at Sanquhar, and others at Lanark and Rutherglen.

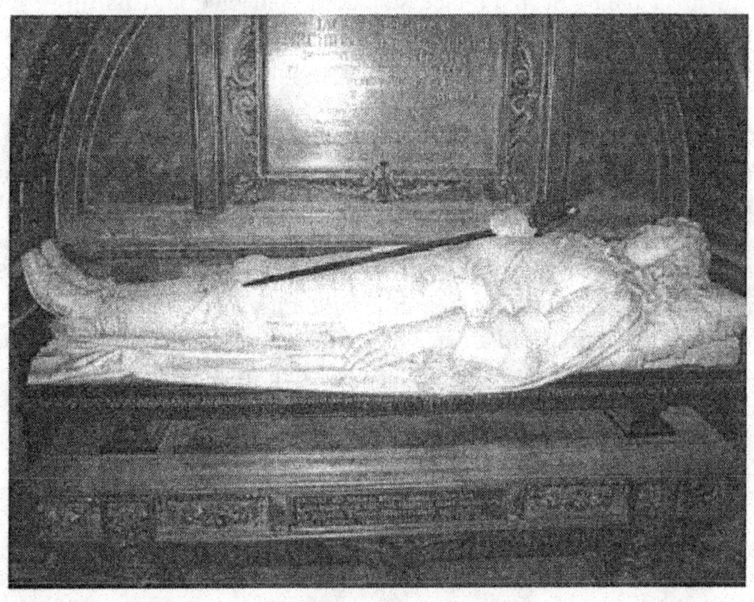

Mausoleum of the Marquis of Montrose, St. Giles Cathedral, Edinburgh. Photo courtesy of M. McIlwrick.

[97] Howie, *Worthies*, p. 451.

Mausoleum of the Marquis of Argyll, St. Giles Cathedral, Edinburgh. Photo courtesy of M. McIlwrick.

Declaration of the Army of England upon their march into Scotland, to all that are Saints, and partakers of the Faith of God's elect in Scotland, 19 July 1650.

This lengthy document of over 4,000 words, and full of rhetoric, was a statement of the reasons for England taking its action. Granger, in *Cromwell against the Scots*, highlights a sentence that compares the earlier Civil War and the current state of affairs:

> We were engaged in a war with...the king for the defence of our religion and liberties. Now, having removed that threat, the Declaration says, here is the same threat recurring, in a new king and a new religion, and so the English must engage in war once more.[98]

---

[98] John D. Grainger, *Cromwell Against the Scots* (London: Tuckwell Press, Ltd., 1997), p. 18.

Declaration - Apologetical Declaration, 8 November 1684. See also: Appendix 16; Vindication.

The Apologetical Declaration and Admonitory Vindication of the True Presbyterians of the Church of Scotland, especially anent Intelligencers and Informers, as it was fully named, was the result of increased persecution of the Covenanters. After the Declaration at Lanark in 1682, the Privy Council had enacted an order which allowed military execution without trial for anybody who owned or would not disown that Declaration. This meant execution on the spot in the presence of two witnesses. There were also more rewards offered for information that turned neighbours against one another.

Renwick's Declaration restated the Covenanter principles and specifically rejected the idea that they would kill all who opposed them. But they asserted that those who persecuted them—judges, soldiers, informers, and bearers of false witness—were God's public enemies and they would be dealt with accordingly. They positively disowned murder, or the killing, because of a different persuasion but maintained that it was both righteous and rational to defend themselves, to rescue their brethren, and prevent their being murdered, and they adopt a martial posture against persecutors:

> [W]hosoever stretched forth their hand against them by shedding their blood either by authorative commanding as the justiciary, or actual doing as the military, or searching out and delivering them up to their enemies as the gentry, or informing against them wickedly and willingly as the viperous and malicious bishops and curates, or raising the hue and cry as the common intelligencers – they should repute them enemies to God and the Covenanted work of Reformation, and punish them according to their powers and the degree of their offence.[99]

---

[99] James Renwick, *The Life and Letters of James Renwick the Last Scottish Martyr*, ed. W. H. Carslaw (Helensburgh: Oliphant, Anderson & Ferrier, 1893), pp. 106-107. Shields, in *A Hind Let Loose*, defends and vindicates the action taken by Renwick.

The manifesto was posted on several church doors and market crosses. The inevitable reaction of the government was to add this Declaration to the list of treasonable activities for which instant death was proscribed. Shortly after the posting of the declaration came the dreadful Abjuration Oath, 22 Nov 1684.

Declaration – Hamilton, 13 June 1679.

The publication of the Hamilton Declaration is alleged to have been an act of betrayal because Robert Hamilton, as the Covenanters' commander at Bothwell Brig, was tricked into signing it. It was afterwards printed and circulated by John Welch and David Hume. This came about through a dispute between David Hume and John Welch, and the hard-line Covenanters who opposed dealings with the Duke of Monmouth and were on the verge of disowning loyalty to King Charles II. A document was presented to Robert Hamilton which was, he thought, the work of Donald Cargill whom he trusted implicitly and, in haste, he signed it. The supplication of Hume and Welch was a reasoned explanation for the use of arms in self defence but on presentation to Monmouth it was rejected out of hand.

The declaration was offensive to the strict Covenanters because it recognised the authority of the king and naively requested the Duke of Monmouth's troops not to fight

> [We] humbly request the King's majesty would restore all things as he found them when God brought him home to his crown and kingdoms.... Finally because we desire no man's hurt nor blood, we request our countrymen, now the standing forces of this kingdom,.... Not to fight against us, lest in so doing they be found fighting against the Lord.[100]

Declaration – Lanark, 12 January 1682. See also: Appendix 15.

The Declaration at Lanark, or *The Act and Apologetic Declaration of the True Presbyterians of the Church of Scotland*, was a consequence of the revolutionary convictions of the strict Covenanters triggered by the Test Act of 1681 that was passed by

---

[100] Johnston, *Treasury*, p. 134.

the Edinburgh Parliament of that year. The Test Act was a singularly ham-fisted shambles of legislation with contradictions throughout; but, most importantly, it barred anybody from public office who would not swear to it. They were required to own the true Protestant religion as defined in the Confession of 1567 and to acknowledge the king as supreme in all things civil and sacred. This further restriction was too much for the Covenanters to bear and some eighty ministers tendered their resignations.

The Lanark Declaration again proposed revolution, acknowledged the Rutherglen and Sanquhar Declarations, and rescinded, annulled and made void (in the Covenanters' view) all legislation whatsoever since 1660. It is of interest that James Renwick knew of the document but did not write it and considered it to have some turns of phrase that were ill-advised.

The Privy Council asked the Court of Session whether the Declaration was treasonable, which they considered it was. Consequently the Privy Council replied with:

> The Lords of his Majesty's Privy Council do hereby ordain any person who owns, or will not disown the late treasonable Declaration upon oath, whether they have arms or not, to be immediately put to death; this being always done in presence of two witnesses, and the person or persons having commission from the Council to that effect.[101]

Declaration – Rutherglen, 29 May 1679. See also: Appendix 13.

The Declaration at Rutherglen was a response to a government proclamation in May 1679 that made field conventicles acts of rebellion. Thomas Douglas and Robert Hamilton (later Sir Robert Hamilton of Preston in 1688), and probably also Donald Cargill and Richard Cameron, drew up and published *The Declaration and Testimony of some of the True Presbyterian Party in Scotland.* This declaration was a statement of principles and condemned laws introduced since the Restoration of King Charles II in 1660. The laws included:

---

[101] Johnston, *Treasury*, p. 147.

the Act Recissory, laws re establishing prelacy;
the requirement that office holders must renounce the Covenant;
the Act that caused ministers to be outed in 1662;
the Assertory Act of 1669 which declared the king as supreme in the church;
and the Act requiring the anniversary of the Restoration (May 29) to be kept as a holiday.

The Declaration was made in dramatic style by a troop of about eighty Covenanters riding into Rutherglen on the May holiday, dousing the celebratory bonfires, burning copies of the acts and fixing their declaration to the market cross.

Declaration – Sanquhar, 22 June 1680. See also: Appendix 14.

There were six or seven Declarations at Sanquhar in all, although those which are most remembered are that by Richard Cameron on 22 June 1680 and that by James Renwick on 25 May 1685. The *Scots Worthies* also refers to Robert Hamilton's Declaration at Sanquhar of 10 August 1692. The others were 6 November 1695, 21 May 1703 and in 1707.

The Declaration of June 1680 was a declaration of war by the strict Covenanters, or Cameronians. *The Declaration and Testimony of the true Presbyterian, anti prelatic, anti Erastian, persecuted party in Scotland* defined three steps in the Reformation of the Church of Scotland attacking popery, prelacy, and the king, whom they believed had forfeited the right to rule through rejection of the Covenants and rule by tyranny. The statement "do declare a war with such a tyrant and usurper" makes clear their intentions and was the first public renunciation of the House of Stuart in Scotland. As such, it was not a declaration of rebellion, but a cry for revolution against tyranny. It was this point that Walter Smith brought out, when asked if he owned the Sanquhar Declaration, when he said, "What the King has done, justifies the people revolting against him. As to these words where the King is called an usurper and a tyrant, he said, Certainly the King is a usurper, and wished he was not a tyrant."[102]

---

102 Howie, *Worthies*, p. 456.

Inscription on the Sanquhar Memorial. Photo courtesy of A. Pittendreigh.

This Declaration deserves notice, both because of the prominence given to it at the time by the persecuted Presbyterians and also because it was used as an excuse for criminal prosecution of those who acknowledged it. "Do you own the Sanquhar Declaration?" was a question to which an answer of "yes" meant they would be subjected to whatever punishment the whim of the judges or the soldiers in the field might see proper to inflict—usually death, and often on the spot.

Declaration – Sanquhar, 28 May 1685. See also: Appendix 17.

King Charles died in February 1685 and his brother, the papist Duke of York, succeeded to the throne. Renwick took this opportunity to witness against the usurpation of a papist and the new King James II's design to overturn the Covenants and the Reformation. The Declaration at Sanquhar, *A Protestation and Apologetical Admonitory Declaration*, arose from a meeting held at Blackgannock, a remote farmhouse in east Nithsdale, and did not have the outright statement of revolution as in Cameron's declaration. It did, however, include a disclaimer against Sectarians, Malignancy, and Confederacy, suggesting that they would not have anything to do with the attempted rebellion of the Earl of Argyll. The posting of the Declaration at Sanquhar was a stirring sight, with some two hundred horsemen attending Renwick in his task.

Declaration by William of Orange, October 1688.

William, Prince of Orange, was in a difficult position as the main Protestant opposition to the Catholic League on the continent and, particularly, the ambitions of King Louis XIV of France. His statesmanship and a series of alliances enabled him to hold off France. By taking the English throne he knew that there could be serious repercussions with Louis supporting James II to recover the throne. He was also James II's son-in-aw, having married his daughter Mary, a Protestant.

In October 1688, following the birth of a son to James in June, William made a Declaration explaining why he was to take up arms in defence of Protestantism and of the liberty of Scotland. He did so because of:

the unconstitutional regimes in England;
the suffering of its downtrodden people;
the violation of anti-Popish statutes;
the despotism of the governors;
the illegal, brutal persecution of the lieges;
the subversion of Protestantism;
the birth of a son to James (which predicated a Catholic dynasty);
and the interests of his wife, Mary.

On 5 November 1688, William and 14,000 troops landed at Brixham and marched on London. On December 18, he was ensconced in St. James' Palace. Three days later, King James II escaped into exile in France, to return to Ireland in 1690 where his aspirations to return to the throne were finally crushed at the battle of the Boyne.

Declarations – Sanquhar, 10 August 1692.

This later Declaration was one of principle and faith after the Revolution. The Church of Scotland was in place but the hard line Cameronians had been deserted by their ministers Shields, Linning, and Boyd. Sir Robert Hamilton became the de facto leader of the remnant societies who declined to join the Church of Scotland because it was not Covenanted. Although questioned about the Declaration, Sir Robert Hamilton was released from prison in May 1693 and remained a devout Reformed Presbyterian until his death on 21 October 1701, at the age of fifty-one years.

It is of note that four Covenanters—John Bell, Thomas McMillan, John Clark, and Herbert Wells—were a few of those who were prosecuted after the Revolution. However, friends interceded for them and they were freed, but not before they issued a formal Protest from the Cannongate Tolbooth on 25 March 1693.

Declinature of Supremacy/Authority.

At the core of the Covenanter beliefs was the supreme headship of Jesus Christ over the Church. They rejected papacy, prelacy, and the claims by the king to be head of the church. "Declinatures" by ministers were often made when refusing to accept the claimed supremacy of the civil authority and the king in matters of doctrine. The structure of the church management and the ready access to the Commission of the General Assembly enabled contentious matters of doctrine to be quickly addressed and support gathered as necessary. Throughout the Reformation this contention as to supremacy resulted in considerable suffering for the ministers as four kings—James I, Charles I, Charles II, and James II—sought to impose their autocratic will.

David Black was summoned to appear before King James VI in 1596 for some remarks he had made in a sermon. However, his colleagues saw the danger of a claim of supremacy over the church being made by the king and Black therefore submitted a declinature. Over three hundred ministers assented and approved of the document. Although subsequently banished to Angus, the clear statement of the issue and the reasoning given for the declinature are a model explanation:

> Before the day of David Black's second citation before the Council, he prepared a still more explicit declinature, especially as it respected the King's supremacy, declaring, that there are two jurisdictions in the realm, the one spiritual, and the other civil: the one respecting the conscience, and the other concerning external things; the one persuading by the spiritual word, the other compelling by the temporal sword; the one spiritually procuring the edification of the Church, the other by justice procuring the peace and quiet of the commonwealth. The latter being grounded in the light of nature, proceeds from God as He is Creator, and is so termed by the Apostle (I Pet. II.), but varies according to the constitution of men ; the former, being above nature, is grounded upon the grace of redemption, proceeding immediately from the grace of Christ, the only King and only Head of His Church (Eph. I., Col. II.). Therefore, in so far as he was one of the spiritual office-bearers, and had discharged his spiritual calling in some measure of grace and sincerity, he should not, and could not lawfully be judged for preaching and applying the Word of God by any civil power, he being an ambassador and messenger of the Lord Jesus, having his commission from the King of kings; and all his commission is set down and limited in the Word of God, that cannot be extended or abridged by any mortal king or emperor, they being sheep, not pastors, who are to be judged by the Word of God, and not to be the judges thereof.[103]

John Welch and others were charged with treason for having convened the General Assembly at Aberdeen in 1605 without the king's authority. In this case they declined because they considered the authority incompetent to judge the nature and constitution of a General Assembly.

Both Calderwood and Rutherford were summoned before the Court of High Commission for non-conformity and each declined the Court's authority to act, which upset the prelates. David Dickson was one among many who rejected the Articles of Perth and he too was banished by the Court of High Commission. In his

---

[103] Howie, *Worthies*, p. 81.

case there was some machinations to try and get him to withdraw his declinature, even to the extent of a friend visiting the archbishop's palace and symbolically lifting up and putting down the offending document. But Dickson saw the entrapment and continued with his banishment in clear conscience.

Then there were the martyrs of the Restoration period where dissent of almost any kind was almost certain to mean execution. James Guthrie made a bold stand in 1651 rejecting the king's authority in respect of a doctrinal thesis which he had used in a sermon. This was made a factor in his trial in 1661 and the excuse for personal pique by the Earl of Middleton, and Guthrie's execution. David Hackston denied the king and called him a usurper, idolater, and perjurer probably in the certain knowledge he was going to be sentenced to death anyway. Robert Garnock's declinature of the king's authority and protest is a classic case where his statements of principal were immediately turned into confession before the justiciary. Before the court had finished with him and his associates they jointly made a further written protest at the tyranny and sin that abounded. Garnock and five colleagues were hung at the Gallows Lea on 10 October 1681 despite their protestations.

Defensive arms.

A familiarity with arms was common among the ministers who served time with the army throughout the campaigns from 1639 to 1652 when Cromwell ended military resistance. It is highly likely that they bore offensive arms too; Rev. John Crookshank and Rev. Andrew McCormick were killed at Rullion Green in 1666. Among the elders of the church were many who had served as professional soldiers abroad and, like Captain John Paton, would defend their faith to the death. It was common to carry arms at most times, whether a short sword or dagger, but from about 1660 it increasingly became the practice when attending conventicles. With the reintroduction of the Court of High Commission in 1664 there was an ever increasing volume of legislation about conventicling and harsher penalties at every turn. With the employment of the military to collect fines and pursue conventicles it was inevitable that clashes would occur. From the Pentland Rising in 1666 onwards armed guards and look outs at remote meetings became routine, as was resistance to soldiers and even the armed rescue of prisoners and jailbreaks. An interesting doggerel poem written about the time of Rullion Green gives a colourful picture of both dress and equipage of the Whigs, armed with just about anything they could put their hands to, and in the absence of a weapon they used their fists. (See Appendix 22.)

Inevitably the carriage of arms was also reason for interrogation by the military and eventually enough to end in summary execution. Renwick's *Admonitory Vindication* was an attack on the forces of the law and made clear why they chose to take up defensive arms against those who attacked them, and to threaten those who informed against them. Similarly, Alexander Shields, in *A Hind Let Loose*, writes about and vindicates such action.

Democracy models.

The Reformation in Europe, from the fifteenth to seventeenth centuries, not only extended the rights of the individual to a free church, but in casting off the shackles and mysticism of religion it was part of an inexorable drive towards a modern democracy. Slowly but surely, through the efforts of travelling scholars and evangelists, the people were provided with information; they learnt to think for themselves and to draw conclusions about acceptable standards of behaviour. Above all, they began to voice their aspirations and band together for a common purpose.

The Scottish peoples have long had the tradition of banding themselves together by solemn oaths for mutual protection and to pursue and promote their common objectives. There was, for example, the early cry for democracy in the Band of 1557 seeking that the election of ministers "should be made by the people" which was subscribed to by the feudal "Lords of the Congregation."[104] The National Covenant of 1581 extended to defending the king and "liberties of our country, ministration of justice and punishment of iniquity."[105] John Buchanan's *De Juri Regni apud Scotos*, in 1590, was a criticism of the divine right of kings and laid down the principles of politics and the maxims of free government.

Archibald Johnston, the advocate, and Alexander Henderson, the theologian, carefully set out the law and the rights of the people for

[104] Johnson, *Treasury*, p. 24.
[105] *Ibid.*, p. 49.

a free religion in the National Covenant of 1638. The Solemn League and Covenant of 1643 extended the scope of Covenants to politics. Later there were the Committees of Correspondence to keep one another informed thus banding together for united action.

Samuel Rutherford in his "Lex Rex" codified the rights of free men and argued strenuously against the arbitrary and tyrannical rule of monarchs. Although he advocated obedience and loyalty he nevertheless considered that a king who perverted justice and oppressed the people should be restrained and in extremis might forfeit the right to be king. This echoing the words of John Knox who had told Mary, Queen of Scots, that princes may be opposed.

These emerging principles worked at the level of the common man through his religion and created a groundswell of opinion that transferred itself to the organisation and structure of government itself. The despotism and then tyranny of the Stuart kings during the Scottish Reformation added greatly to the public feeling for the need to change. It was not just Scotland but England, too, who rejected the autocratic king and declared for democracy and a constitutional monarchy. At the extreme there was the proposal in the Queensferry Papers, to replace the monarchy by a Christian republic.

It took time but the practice of making declarations that set out the aims and objectives of the people with reasoned arguments for change appeared in America during the mid-eighteenth century, particularly in Thomas Paine's *Rights of Man*. Thus, from people of largely Ulster Scot Presbyterian descent came the "Hanover Resolves" of 4 June 1774, the "Mecklenburg Declaration of Independence" of 31 May 1775, and, ultimately the covenant better known as the "Declaration of Independence" of 4 July 1776.

Divine intervention.

Wherever one turns there are examples of Divine intervention in Covenanter lore. The Rev. Robert Simpson's *Traditions of the Covenanters* gives many an example of unexplained happenings and deliverances that oral tradition has passed down through the years. Whatever we might think of the events, the fact that in very many cases a human life was saved must be granted as a worthwhile outcome: a divine deliverance.

Interventions of a physical kind include those of John Welch who certainly enjoyed a charmed existence in France; in the battle for St. Jean d'Angey a cannonball struck the bed in which he was lying and later, when he was helping to fire a cannon, a gun powder ladle was shot from his hand, and he lived through it all. Donald Cargill eluded capture on several occasions by the very narrowest of margins, in one instance passing out of one door while his pursuers entered at the other. Also, on the battlefield at Bothwell Brig, he was struck down and badly wounded yet allowed to go when he admitted to being a minister named Cargill (whose name was on the most wanted list).

With an inevitability all its own Alexander Peden and his fellow prisoners were sentenced to be banished to the American colonies. But, arriving in London the captain of the ship which would transport them there declined to take them when he found that they were God-fearing Christians and not the criminals he expected. They were cast ashore in Gravesend, Kent, and returned in time whence they came as free men. In another shipboard event Peden sought God's assistance to bring a wind to carry them safely from Ireland to Scotland: "Lord, give us a loof-ful of wind…and they got a very swift and safe passage over."[106] A well-known deliverance of Peden concerns his pursuit by soldiers among the hills when he prayed, "Twine them about the hill, Lord, and cast the lap of thy cloak over Old Sandy,"[107] and a thick mist enveloped him and his friends, securing them from capture.

A belief in Providence may well have saved Thomas Hog who, not being a drinking man, left the company of two burgesses he had travelled with. He later learnt that, in a drunken stupor, the two had fallen out and killed one another. Hog was also the vehicle for delivering Providence to others and is credited with several cases of helping sick and dying persons through prayer. Just reward seems to feature in Hog's life as illustrated by the occasion when cast into prison and money nearly gone by which he had procured some comforts, he received a mysterious visitor who on leaving gave him five pounds. Was this a case of virtue having its own reward?

Perhaps the aphorism "fortune favours the brave" applied to William Veitch. From a distinguished family of ministers he had

---

[106] Johnston, *Peden*, p. 130.
[107] *Ibid.*, p. 174.

hopes of becoming a doctor. But, as a minister, he had an eventful and colourful life, much of it in association with persons of influence, and he was an accessory to the escape of the Earl of Argyll to Holland. Early in his ministry he was involved in the Pentland Rising and went on a reconnaissance visit to Edinburgh where, having avoided some dangerous encounters, was finally taken prisoner. He escaped through sheer bravado declaring himself willing to take arms in the front rank against a feared attack by the Covenanters. In the battle of Rullion Green he was surrounded by Dalziel's soldiers and in the gloom was carried along with them for a while before making an escape.

The line between intervention and retribution is thin but a specific instance of the latter concerns a profane trooper who was present at the capture of John King. In response to a question about where he was going, the trooper said, "To carry King to hell."[108] Shortly after his carbine went off and killed him. Psalm 64:7 is appropriately quoted: "But God will shoot his arrow at them; they will be wounded suddenly."

In the Notes to *Biographia Scoticana* entitled *The Judgment and Justice of God Exemplified* (1782), Howie provides a fascinating catalogue of persecutors of all kinds and stations in life. As to be expected, the lists include the major characters of the Reformation from Cardinal Beaton, Archbishop Sharp, Mary of Guise, Mary Queen of Scots, James VI, Charles I; Charles II, and James II. He also includes some of the ministers and commissioners such as Rothes, Middleton, Claverhouse, and Dalziel. A range of apostate ministers and the minions who served the forces of persecution are also mentioned. The thrust of each cameo is of the retribution of the Lord for their misdeeds. Some of the anecdotes are quite scurrilous, such as the allegation that David Rizzio, secretary to Mary Queen of Scots, was in fact the father of James VI (not Lord Darnley). If only a portion of the tales are true, they are a grave condemnation of those named. A veritable seventeenth century, "Name and Shame" listing.

After the death of Richard Cameron at Airsmoss, the *Biographia* tells that Bruce of Earlshall received £500 sterling as a reward and that Ochiltree received 10,000 merks. It tells also that some time after, at break of day, a blood red pillar about two yards long was

[108] Howie, *Worthies*, p. 410.

seen hanging over the house. The same day, at about two in the afternoon, Ochiltree's castle caught fire and burnt to the ground. It was attributed to "the vengeance of Cameron's blood."[109]

Divine Right.

The Divine Right of Kings was the policy and major plank for feudal rulers from about the fifteenth century. For James VI/I, it became a declared policy to which he referred in his speech to the English Parliament on 21 March 1610, which is quoted in Protheroe's *Select Statutes*:

> The state of monarchy is the supremest thing upon earth: for kings are not only God's lieutenants upon earth and sit upon God's throne, but even by God himself they are called gods. There be three principal similtudes that illustrate the state of monarchy: one taken out of the word of God, and the two other out of the grounds of policy and philosophy. In the Scriptures kings are called gods, and so their power after a certain relation compared to Divine power. Kings are also compared to fathers of families: for a king is truly parens patriae, the politic father of his people. And lastly, kings are compared to the head of this microcosm of the body of man....
>
> I conclude then this point touching the power of kings with this axiom of divinity, That as to dispute what God may do is blasphemy,...so it is sedition in subjects to dispute what a king may do in the height of his power.[110]

The same speech sets out James' view on grievances and that Parliament was:

> Not to meddle with the main points of government; that is my craft, "I must not be taught my office."

---

[109] Howie, *Biographica Scoticana*, p. 308.

[110] G. W. Prothero, *Select Statutes and Other Constitutional Documents of the Reign of Elizabeth I and James I* (London: Oxford University Press, 1946), pp. 293-294.

> Not to meddle with his ancient rights "for that were to judge me unworthy of that which my predecessors had and left me."
>
> Do not make a grievance out of settled law. Distinguish between the faults of a person and not the thing itself. (And it mentions as an example: "complain about an abuse by a High Commissioner and not about the Commission itself") "for that were to abridge the power that is in me."[111]

Doctrine of Knox. See also: Lords of the Congregation.

Knox did not mince his words when he denounced the Church of Rome as Antichrist and proposed nothing less than a reconstruction of the doctrines and ecclesiastical system of Scotland. As a student of John Calvin in Geneva he, like the other Protestant Reformers, held to three main principles:

> God had spoken to man through the Scriptures and that God managed man through the Scriptures. The Word of God was a living Word and beliefs and church practices must conform to that essential truth.
>
> Salvation was by the free and undeserved grace of Christ, sometimes called the "justification by faith alone." Man was saved by the action of God alone, in the death and resurrection of Christ, and was called from sin to a new life in Christ.
>
> There was no role for a priest as mediator; there was nothing supporting this in the Scriptures. There was one gospel, one justification by faith, and one status before God common to all men regardless of class.[112]

Knox's dictum about speaking out against false doctrine, cited in *A Hind Let Loose*, casts a light on his often alleged intransigence and his rough words to Mary, Queen of Scots:

---

[111] Prothero, *Select Statutes*, pp. 293-294.

[112] *The History of Christianity*, ed. T. Dowley (Tring: Lion Publishing, Ltd., 1977), p. 373.

> Yea we must speak the truth, whomsoever we offend, there is no realm that hath the like Purity; for all others, how sincere soever the doctrine be, retain in their churches and the ministry thereof, some footsteps of antichrist, and dregs of popery; but we (praise to God alone) have nothing in our churches, that ever flowed from the Man of Sin.[113]

The Calvinist doctrines followed by Knox included rejection of the Pope, the Church of Rome, and all its trappings: the mass, the claim of transubstantiation during the Communion, church music, architecture, images, holy water, candles, etc. Knox also adopted the principle of organising the church both internally and externally, and produced his *Confessions of Faith* (1560), the *Book of Discipline* (1561), and a new liturgy, the *Book of Common Order* (1564).

To achieve his aims, Knox wisely sought and received the support of the most powerful men in Scotland: the Lords of the Congregation. His doctrines were accepted by the Earl of Argyll and the Earl of Moray (Lord Lorne and Lord James, at the time), the Lord Glencairn, and the Earl Marischal (who famously tried to get the Catholic Mary of Guise, the Queen Regent, to hear a sermon, which she scorned). The support of these powerful nobles meant that Knox's voice had to be listened to by the regents who ruled Scotland in this critical time, and thereby enabled a firm foothold to be gained for Presbyterianism.

***Eaglewing* – ship.**

The *Eaglewing* was the first of the ships to become part of Covenanter history and unique for being purposefully built to transport persecuted Presbyterians from Ulster to America. The ship was the consequence of consultations in 1634 with settlers in Massachusetts and letters were sent to John Winthrop, the governor. They must have received encouraging replies because families prepared to emigrate. Unfortunately, the voyage was struck by bad weather and the ship turned back. Some might say it was providential, however, because it meant that ministers of the calibre

[113] Shields, p. 45.

of Robert Blair, John Livingston, and John McClelland were able to contribute more to the Scottish Reformation.

Detail of the ship itself varies a little, in that the tonnage is quoted as 115 tons and also 150 tons. The essential fact is that it was a tiny ship and fully loaded, with 140 passengers, when it sailed from Carrickfergus on 9 September 1636. How far they got before rough seas broke the rudder also varies between three hundred and four hundred leagues from Ireland, and the Newfoundland Banks (about 2,200 miles from Ireland). The reality was that a meeting on board concluded it was not God's will that they should go to America and they returned to Belfast Lough on November 3.

The name was taken from Exodus 14:4: "Ye have seen what I did to the Egyptians, and how I bare you on eagles wings and brought you unto myself."

Engagers – Engagement, 1648. See also: Battles - Mauchline Moor; Whiggamore Raid.

This was the ill-fated treaty between King Charles I and some Scottish nobles, led by the Duke of Hamilton, to raise an army for the king against the English. The army was destroyed by Cromwell at Preston on 17 August 1648. Following the failure of the enterprise the royalist supporters lost power and were replaced by the strict Covenanters who soon began to purge the army and public offices of all "malignants."

There were two events called the "Engagement," one in Scotland and another in Ireland. There was also a "Solemn Engagement" among the English Independent's New Model Army.

The Engagement signed in December 1647 was an agreement by some Scottish nobles to support the king against the English Parliamentarians. The Covenanters led by Argyll held back as they saw the inevitable war if they supported the king against Cromwell and their former allies the English Parliament.

However, the majority of nobles in Scotland, led by the Duke of Hamilton, were sympathetic towards Charles and determined to restore him to his constitutional position. Charles, meanwhile had been faced with new laws in England that took away his command of the forces of the Crown and his veto over Parliament. The options of the Scots were more palatable and, on 26 December 1647, he signed the Engagement under which the Scots would provide an army to invade England. The king undertook to present the Solemn League and Covenant and the National Covenant to Parliament for ratification. He also undertook to accept Presbyterian government for a three-year trial.

In the Scottish Parliament there was much discussion, and objections were raised by the General Assembly who considered the Engagement sinful and perjury by breaking. The nobility held sway and an act was passed requiring all subjects to sign a bond supporting the Engagement. Although condemned by the Covenanters the Engagers, as they became known, raised an army under the Duke of Hamilton and a cess was imposed to pay for it. Although unopposed, the Engagers dealt harshly with the people at large and provoked considerable resentment. The encounter at Mauchline Muir was a consequence of this policy. Lord Eglinton wrote to his son, Colonel James Montgomery, on 21 July 1648, that "they have been most rigorous in plundering this country.... The nobility, gentry and country people are so incensed at their proceedings, it will not fail but will draw to a mischief."[114]

The Engagers under the Duke of Hamilton, Callendar, and Middleton set out to retrieve the royal cause in England and to rescue Charles I from his enemies. They marched to a resounding defeat at the battle of Preston on 17 August 1648 and final surrender at Uttoxeter on 25 August 1648. Hamilton was executed in London 9 March 1649.

Seizing the opportunity, the strict Covenanters (or Whigs, as they were also called) marched on Edinburgh (the Whiggamore Raid) and seized power from the Engagers in September 1648. The Act of Classes in 1649 caused all of government to fall into the hands of the strict Covenanters. For two years, there was true Presbyterian, civil, government before Scotland was exposed to the direct rule of Cromwell.

In Ireland, the Dublin Parliament framed an Oath, called the Engagement which bound the swearer to renounce "the pretended title of Charles Stuart" and to be faithful to the Commonwealth. This came about when Cromwell landed in Ireland on 15 August 1649 and proceeded to bloodily subjugate the country. An attempt was made to force the oath on Presbyterian ministers in Ireland but they declined since they still supported a limited monarchy. Some

---

[114] Metcalfe, *Renfrew*, p. 268.

ministers were imprisoned including Rev. Drysdale of Portaferry, Baty of Ballywalter, Alexander of Grey Abbey, and Main of Island Magee, while others went to Scotland. After King Charles was defeated at Worcester on 3 September 1651, Cromwell was the absolute ruler. The Engagement oath was forced on takers of public offices and heavy penalties imposed on those who would not swear. Slowly over the next ten years the Presbyterians were allowed to continue their ways while Catholics suffered the full rigour of the law.

The Solemn Engagement of 1647 espoused by the New Model Army, which was mainly loyal to Cromwell, was a rejection of the Solemn League and Covenant of 1643. The New Model declaration sought to secure "peace of the kingdom and the liberties of the subject" and included a broad liberty of religion. Specifically, the Covenant was rejected, no one could be forced to take it, and no ecclesiastical authority could coerce the individual. This raised alarms among the Scots and a growing sympathy for King Charles I who had fled London to the Isle of Wight.

Epitaph.

Throughout the southwest of Scotland, in particular, there are several hundred monuments, statues, and plaques to the memory of the Covenanters. Some are just isolated stones by the pathway or a cairn in the wild moorland. Many of the memorials to the Covenanter dead are engraved with the circumstances of their death and quite often the name of the officer(s) commanding the troopers who apprehended him. In many cases these officers would have been responsible for the order to execute, perhaps even pulling the trigger on occasion. Notorious among them are Grierson of Lag, John Graham of Claverhouse, Bannatyne, Major Winram, and Lt. Peter Ingram, to name a few.

As early as 1686 there were considerations by the Societies to collect and publish the testimonies of the martyrs. A Resolution was passed on 21 April 1697 that a true and exact account of the persecutors should be brought to the next meeting. In April 1699 it was minuted that an Index of the Martyrs' Memorials should be prepared and in 1701 details were collected from the various societies. In 1711 the General Assembly instructed ministers to prepare summaries of incidents within their parishes which were used in Wodrow's seminal work published in 1714.

The principle monument to the martyrs is in Greyfriars Kirk Yard, Edinburgh (not far from the Grassmarket where the gibbet often stood), where over one hundred Covenanters were executed between 1660 and 1688. The custom and practice of the day was to hang the prisoner then behead them and place the head on a spike above one of the city gates, often the Netherbow. There is a poignancy in the engraving of the monument at Greyfriars Church Yard that says "the most part of them lies here," because the heads may not have been reunited with the body (some heads, hands, and limbs were sent to the home town of the executed for display).

The original stone for the Martyrs Monument in Greyfriars Church, Edinburgh by James Currie and others, of 1706, is in the Huntly House Museum. The Greyfriars monument dates from 1771. The executed were not allowed to lie in hallowed ground but the gravediggers at the time are thought to have ensured the martyrs were properly buried away from the common thieves and murderers. The inscription reads:

Halt passenger take heed what thou dost see
This tomb doth shew for what some men did die
Here lies interr'd the dust of these who stood
Gainst perjury resisting unto blood
Adhering to the Covenants and Laws
Establishing the same which was the Cause
Then their lives were sacrificed unto the Lust
Or Prelatist's abjur'd though here their dust
Lies mix with murders and other crew
Whom justice did justly to death pursue
But as for this in them no cause was found
Worthy of death but only they were found
Constant and steadfast zealous witnessing
For the prerogatives of CHRIST their king
Which truths were feared by famous Guthrie's head
And all along to Mr. Renwick's blood
They did endure the wrath of enemies
Reproaches torments deaths and injuries
But yet they're these who from such troubles came
And now triumph in glory with the LAMB.

> From May 27th 1661 that the noble Marquess of Argyle suffered to the seventeenth of Febr 1688 that Mr. James Renwick suffr'd were executed at Edinburgh about an hundred of Noblemen Gentlemen Ministers & others noble martyrs for JESUS CHRIST. The most part of them lies here.
>
> This Tomb was erected anno 1706.

Beneath the inscription is sculpted an open Bible with quotations from the Scriptures:

> Rev. 6:9, 10, 11 - And when he had opened the fifth seal, I saw under the altar the souls of them that were slain for the word of God, and for the testimony which they held; And they cried with a loud voice, saying, How long, O Lord holy and true, dost thou not judge and avenge our blood on them that dwell on earth? And white robes were given unto every one of them; and it was said unto them, that they should not rest yet for a little season, until their fellow servants also and their brethren, that should be killed as they were, should be fulfilled.
>
> Rev. 7:14 - These are they which came out of great tribulation, and have washed their robes, and made them white in the blood of the Lamb.
>
> Rev. 2:10 - Be faithful unto death, and I will give thee a crown of life.[115]

Ironically, near the "Covenanter Prison" stands the mausoleum of Sir George MacKenzie who, as King's Advocate, was responsible for the zealous prosecution of the Covenanters and gained for himself the title "Bluidy" MacKenzie. An amusing tale is of the boys from the nearby Heriot's School who would dare one another to challenge Mackenzie's restless spirit by shouting through the keyhole to the mausoleum:

---

[115] Campbell, *Standing Witnesses*, p. 91; Thompson, *Martyr Graves*, p. 65; numerous others.

Bluidy MacKenzie come out if ye daur
Lift the sneck and draw the bar.[116]

Many, if not quite all, known memorials were included in J. H. Thompson's *Martyr Graves of Scotland* (1903). An excellent modern publication is *Standing Witnesses* (1996) by Thorbjorn Campbell which includes map references to assist in finding memorials. Some are now in isolated locations that are difficult to access, as well as on private property. The Scottish Covenanters Memorial Association, a charity, was established in 1966 and does much good work preserving graves and memorials.

The Martyrs Monument, Greyfriars Kirk Yard. Photos by the author.

[116] Johnston, *Treasury*, p. 421; Smellie, p. 280.

The Grassmarket. The gibbet stood approximately where the horse and cart stand. Thos. Shepherd, *Modern Athens, Edinburgh in the Eighteenth Century* (London: Jones & Co., 1829).

McKenzie's Mausoleum, Greyfriar's Kirk Yard. Photo by the author.

Many of the memorials include stones worked and saved by Robert Paterson, "Old Mortality" of Sir Walter Scott's tale. Paterson and Scott met at Dunnottar where Paterson was working on a Covenanter tombstone in the churchyard. Campbell, in *Standing Witnesses*, writes of the style of Paterson, which used ligatures and his own spelling form that enabled the lettering to be densely packed on a memorial. The Dunnottar Churchyard memorial reads:

> HERE. LYES. IOHN. STOT. IAMES. ATCHI
> SON. IAMES. RUSSELL. & WILLIAM BRO
> UN. AND. ONE. WHOSE. NAME. WEE. HAVE
> NOT. GOTTEN. AND. TWO. WOMEN. WHOSE
> NAMES. ALSO. WEE. KNOW. NOT. AND. TWO
> WHO. PERISHED. COMEING. DOUNE. THE. ROCK
> ONE. WHOSE. NAME. WAS. IAMES. WATSON
> THE. OTHER. NOT. KNOWN. WHO. ALL. DIED
> PRISONER. IN. DUNNOTTAR. CASTLE
> ANNO. 1685. FOR. THEIR. ADHERENCE
> TO. THE. WORD. OF. GOD. AND. SCOTLANDS
> COVENANTED. WORK. OF. REFORMA
> TION. REV. 11 CH. 12 VERSE [117]

Paterson was the younger son of Walter Paterson and Margaret Scott born at Burnflatt or Haggiesha, a mile outside Hawick. A stone mason by trade, he became the lessee of Gatelawbridge Quarry at Morton, Dumfriesshire in 1745 and lived with his family at Balmaclellan. He died at Bankend, Caerlaverock on 14 February 1801. In his travels in the southwest of Scotland, Paterson assiduously cut and repaired many Covenanter tombstones and memorials. A very early stone, the Caldon Stone, is in the Newton Stewart Museum, as also are two sculptures of him. A fine sculpture of Paterson and his horse is displayed at the Dumfries Museum and Observatory.

The persecutors of the Reformation also have their epitaphs. Calderwood's *History* provides that to Cardinal Beaton, responsible for the persecution of many and remembered especially for burning George Wishart at the stake in St. Andrews on 1 March 1546.

---

[117] Campbell, *Standing Witnesses*, p. 84.

AN EPITAPH UPON THE INFAMOUS LIFE, AND WRETCHED DEATH OF THAT ENEMY OF ALL RIGHTEOUSNESSE DAVID BEATOUNE, LATE CARDINAL OF SCOTLAND.

Patrone of vice, patterne of treacheric,
Impe of curst malice, wicked chyld of wrath,
Lusts dearest freind, great foe to puritie,
Top-bough of pride, wrack of true Christian faith,
Author of discord, fountaine of mischeefe,
Saints slaughter-slave, truthes enemie the cheefe.

Stranger to God, Pope's prelate, Dagon's priest,
Bashan's fed bull, Sinne's drudge, Rome's favourite,
Scotlands great monster, opposite to Christ,
A false deceitful double hipocrite.
Malignant bramble voyd of all good frute:
Dead dry, worme-eaten, rotten at the rute.

The Dragon's Angell, Satan's cocatrice,
Supplanter of all grace, the Beast's strong rock,
A mappe of errours, register of vice,
The pricking thorne, Heaven's seed which most did chock,
Impenitent, Death's captive, Hell's fyre-brand:
A spectacle of God's revenging hand.[118]

Following page: "Old Mortality," Robert Paterson, shows up in several places. Top: Balmaclellan Church; bottom left: Newton Stewart Museum; bottom right: Grave at Caerlaverock. Photos courtesy of A. Pittendreigh.

---

[118] Calderwood, *History*, Vol. 8, p. 149.

The largely unlamented Archbishop Sharp has an elaborate, highly eulogistic, and grindingly sycophantic, memorial made of Greek and Italian marble at St. Andrews Church of the Holy Trinity.

The inscription refers to the mortal remains within but in 1726 his corpse was removed and never found. His mausoleum is empty.

Of greater honour, however, is the grave of the eminent Samuel Rutherford, located in the Cathedral churchyard, whose epitaph and tombstone reads:

> Here lyes the Reverend Mr Samuell
> Rutherfoord Professor of Divinity in
> the University of St Andreus who Died
> March the 29 1661.
>
> What tongu what Pen or Skill of Men
> Can Famous Rutherfoord Commend
> His Learning justly raised his Fame
> True Godliness Adornd HIS Name
> He did converse with things Above
> Acquainted with Emmanuels Love
> Most orthodox He Was And Sound
> And Many Errors Did Confound
> For Zions King and Zions Cause
> And Scotlands Covenanted LAWS
> Mostly constantly he Did Contend
> Until His Time Was At An End
> Than He Wan TO the Full Fruition
> OF That which He Had Seen in Vision.[119]

David Calderwood had an elegy written on his death:

> The Wood is fallin, the Church not built,
> Nor Reformation endit;
> The Cedar great is now cutt doun,
> Who first that Work intendit.
>
> By toung and pen he did not fear
> T' oppose proud Prelacie;
> His Scriptural arguments did prevail
> Against their Hierarchie.

---

[119] Campbell, *Standing Witnesses*, p. 169.

Both Sectaries and Schismaticks
He did convince with reasoun
His Lyff and Papers weil record
He did abhor their treasoun,

Sing hymnes of joy, sweit soul in peace,
Unto thy great Redeemer;
Untill this persecuted clay
Be joyn'd with Thee for ever. [120]

Escape.

The escapes by Covenanters and the tales relating to escapes are legion, and the basis of many books about them. *Traditions of the Covenanters*, by Rev. Robert Simpson, is a collection of tales from the oral traditions of southwest Scotland. The nature of the escapes in some instances are aided by knowledge of local conditions such as going into boggy land—the moss, to slow down pursuing dragoons. In many cases the sheer desolation of the moss and high moorland and an intimate knowledge of cave locations was all the hunted Covenanters had. Peden was no doubt aware of the local weather conditions in the hills of Dumfries and Galloway that can generate thick mists within minutes. Other escapes were through sheer bravado, the assistance of friends, poor security at some prisons and tollbooths, use of disguises and false names, and extraordinarily good luck, let alone Divine providence.

Captain John Paton had his fair share of escapes, twice while sheltering at Lochgoin. On the first occasion the old man of the house had gone to bed early but he had a recurring dream of soldiers coming. He warned Paton who took heed of it, and narrowly escaped. On the second occasion Paton and others were surprised and almost caught but managed to get away. Later, Paton was riding a horse he had borrowed, but was riding bare back and had bare feet when he encountered some troopers. Paton passed the troopers slowly and got away from them despite (or maybe because of) his lack of dress.

Being a prisoner temporarily held in the castle belonging to a friend certainly helped Henry Hall to escape from Cessford Castle;

---

[120] Howie, *Worthies*, pp. 205-206.

he was a friend of the Earl of Roxburgh, the owner. Presence of mind helped Donald Cargill who was trapped in a house with no means of escape, so he stepped into a window space and others piled up books in front of him, blocking the window. A servant saved Cargill by complaining that a soldier was stealing her master's books when the soldier started to move them.

Beds feature in two tales. Robert Ker was apprehended through an informant who knew that when Ker visited his wife, he would retire into a space behind the bed when visitors called. This unfortunately was his eventual undoing. John Semple on the other hand, one night shared a bed with another minister when the bed collapsed and he fell out of the back of it; at the same time a search party entered the room and seized his companion but Semple escaped.

Donald Cargill had another narrow escape when preaching at a conventicle at Loudon Hill. Here he preached a second time and baptised children in the afternoon when troopers descended on the gathering. In the confusion he ran towards the soldiers but was grabbed by Gavin Wotherspoon who led him into the moss where the horses could not safely follow.

James Renwick was doubly fortunate at a conventicle at Dungavel Hill. Making his way there on foot he was given a horse to ride for a while. While he was still on the horse, the party was attacked by soldiers and his two companions were captured. Because he was on horseback, Renwick made a dash for freedom and, eventually dismounting, hid in a hollow in some stones. Good fortune or Providence saved him from discovery that day.

Disguise and subterfuge were also used by the hunted ministers. Many tales are told of Alexander Peden who used to wear a mask on occasion. Made of leather with human hair and teeth attached, it can be seen in the Museum of Scotland. To the modern eye it looks very crude but in the flickering shadows, moonlight, or in a panicking crowd of a conventicle under attack by soldiers it served its purpose. Alexander Gordon, the son of William Gordon, was saved by a tenant when he was making his escape from Bothwell Brig. The tenant recognised him and pulled him from his horse, dressed him in a woman's clothing and set him to rocking a baby in a cradle. Alexander Shields was sentenced to imprisonment on the Bass Rock but managed to escape, presumably on his way there, by dressing up in women's clothes.

William Veitch was prone to use false names to evade his pursuers. In Newcastle he used his mother's maiden name of Johnstone. On another occasion he was preaching at a house in Beverley in Yorkshire when the house was raided by the mayor and some officers of the town who took down their names. Here he gave the name of William Robertson. But he was in noble company, literally, when he took the Earl of Argyll to London, the Earl using the name Mr. Hope.

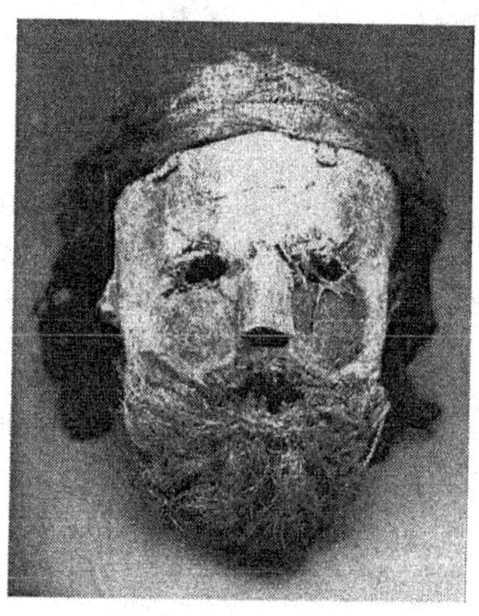

Peden's mask, Museum of Scotland. Photo by the author.

Covenanter lore also relates of some famous escapes from capture through armed attack on the soldiers. The Enterkin Pass escape is probably the best known. The pass is along part of the old drovers road from Galloway to Edinburgh and very narrow at times with the path very close to the gorge. It was at the narrowest and highest point that a party led by Lieutenant Patrick Mulligan found himself, his troopers, and his prisoners surrounded by armed men at Glenvalentine in the Pass. A demand to release the prisoners was made and refused, following which Sergeant Kelt was shot dead by Black James McMichael of Maxwelton.[121] In the melee, some

[121] McMichael later shot the Curate of Carsphairn and was himself killed on 18 December 1684 at Auchencloy in close combat with Claverhouse.

soldiers were killed and some of the prisoners escaped. In Edinburgh the story was told that some prisoners were killed, two fell over the precipices, and two were brought to Edinburgh. A judicial inquiry was ordered and held by the Sheriff depute, James Alexander of Knockhill, in Delgarno on 4 August 1684. The rescue was organised by James "Long Gun" Harkness of Locherben who was later captured but then escaped and lived a long life beyond the Reformation. His collaborators in the plan were James McMichael of the Clachan of Dalry and John Grier from Glencairn. There were about forty others involved, including Adam Harkness of Mitchellslacks, James Corsane of Jedburgh, James Tod, William Herries from Kirkcudbright, and Gilbert Watson, who was described as a spy.

Claverhouse joined the hunt and on August 9 stumbled on six men sleeping in the open in the parish of Closeburn, Dumfriesshire whom he seized and took to the Canongate Tolbooth. Four of the Enterkin rescuers—Thomas "White Hose" Harkness (brother of James); Andrew Clark, a smith aged nineteen years from Leadhills; Samuel McEwen, an orphan lad of seventeen from Glencairn; and Thomas Wood from Kirkmichael—were tried at noon and executed between two and five, all on the same day: 15 August 1684. A fifth person, James Nicol, a merchant from Peebles, was overheard criticising the events and was immediately arrested, charged, and executed on August 27.

Another episode was the attack by about sixty men on the Ducat Tower in Newmilns in 1685. The Tower was holding prisoners taken at a house conventicle on James Paton's farm at Little Blackwood. As a result of their escape, there was hot pursuit by Claverhouse and his dragoons who caught up with John Browning and his uncle John Brown, the "Christian Carrier." Search of the farm at Priesthill revealed documents and arms hidden in a specially built underground room. John Brown refused the Abjuration Oath and was shot on the spot. The younger John Browning, very frightened by his uncle's instant execution, gave names and took the oath. This saved him only temporarily; he was taken before Lieutenant General Drummond, sentenced, and hanged at Mauchline with four other men on 6 May 1685.

Estates – Committee.

The Estates, or Estates of the Realm, are the three classes of persons—the Lords Temporal, the Lords Spiritual, and the Commons—in other words, the nobility, the clergy, and the townsmen (burgesses) who formed the governing body or Parliament.

In the ninth century, under Constantine II, a convention of the Estates started to come to grips with the excesses of the priests ordering them to confine their activities to the church and to set a good example. In Scotland, the first Parliament was probably the meeting called by Robert the Bruce in 1326 at Cambusnethan. He summoned this because he was in need of finances and, for the first time, burgesses of the towns attended. Previously, the attendance on the king was limited to vassals in chief, barons, etc. and freeholders (since 1291). Burgesses started to attend meetings regularly from about 1455.

The Parliament in Scotland was not divided into separate houses of Commons and Lords as in England; instead, all representatives came together in the one place. But, as was the custom and practice, the Parliament met infrequently and much legislation was done through a Committee of the Estates and ratified by Parliament when next it met. There was also a lengthy period when the ruling body in Scotland was merely a Privy Council made up of selected members, and no more than a mouthpiece for absolute monarchs such as James VI/I, Charles I, Charles II, and James VII/II.

With the arrival of Cromwell in Scotland the Committee of the Estates was captured at Alyth in 1651. It reassembled at the Restoration and was once more entrusted with the government of the country, on 1 January 1661. It met under the direction of the Earl of Middleton who, on the directions of his vengeful royal master Charles II, promptly set about rescinding the laws enacted in the interim and enacting new oppressive legislation.

Parliament as such was dominated by the nobility although not all attended every meeting. At the Union in 1707 the make up consisted of ten dukes, three marquisses, seventy-five earls, seventeen viscounts, fifty-two lords, ninety knights of shires, and sixty-seven burgesses, for a total of 314 members.

Execution.

Property, which was sometimes substantial, was usually forfeit to the Crown when a Covenanter was executed, and if they had a coat-of-arms it would be torn and thrown down by the Lyon King of Arms. A consequence was that families would be cast out of their homes to spend their lives in poverty or relying on charity of friends. Such was the case of John Nisbet who was executed on 4 December 1685, and his lands, goods, and gear were forfeited to the king's use.

The method of execution adopted by the authorities were many and often excessively cruel. The main method for execution of the Covenanters was by hanging, usually in the Grassmarket, Edinburgh, which is on the south side of the old city below the castle and just a few yards from the Greyfriars Kirk where the bodies were buried. Here sometimes there were two scaffolds erected. One was to support the ladder which the prisoner climbed and sat upon the top rung, he might say a few words and pray until the napkin was put over his face, and then he would be "turned off" the ladder. The second scaffold was for the "hagging off" of the head, and sometimes the hands and arms, of the prisoner when ordered that they be placed on show as a warning to the populace.

The special or higher class of prisoner, the Marquis of Argyll and David Hackston for example, were executed at the Mercat Cross. Hackstone's hanging, drawing, and quartering was very specifically prescribed by the Privy Council. It is believed that it was the first case where the body (torso) was actually quartered. Hitherto the practice in Scotland had been to sever the limbs at the joints, leaving the torso intact for burial. Thomson, in *The Martyr Graves of Scotland*, quotes the Court's judgment:

> [T]to be drawn backwards on a hurdle to the Mercat Cross and there: at the cross of Edinburgh, and there upon a high scaffold erected a little above the cross have his right hand struck off and after some time to have his left hand struck off, and then to be hanged up and cut down alive, and the bowels taken out, and his heart to be shown to the people by the hand of the hangman, and his heart and bowels to be burnt in the presence of the people, in a fire prepared for that purpose upon the scaffold, and afterwards to have his

> head cut off, and his body divided into four quarters, and his head to be affixed on the Netherbow, and one of his quarters with both of his hands to be affixed at St. Andrews, another quarter at Glasgow, the third at Leith, the fourth at Burntisland, and that none presume to be in mourning for him, nor he to have a coffin, and that none be on the scaffold with him but two baillies, four officers, the executioner and his servants, and this sentence to be put in execution against him this thirtieth day of July instant, betwixt three and five o'clock in the afternoon. And ordained his name, fame, memory; and honours to be extinct, and his arms to be riven and delete furth of the books of arms, so that his posterity may never be able to bruick [hold] or joyse [enjoy] any lands, heritage, titles of dignities within this realm in time comming.[122]

Nobility and Kings were usually executed by having their heads chopped off. In England it was the block and the axe that was used, which could be a quick death if the blow was clean and done with one sweep. But it could also be messy such as with Mary, Queen of Scots, for whom three sweeps of the axe were necessary to decapitate her. When the executioner came to hold her head aloft he dropped it, as it fell out of her luxurious wig to expose her thin grey hair beneath.

In Scotland there was a guillotine, called "the Maiden," which can been seen today in the Museum of Scotland, Edinburgh. It is believed to have been brought from Halifax in Yorkshire by the Earl of Morton, the former Regent, who, ironically, was executed by it on 2 June 1581; it had been determined that he had prior knowledge of Darnley's murder but did nothing about it. The stout wooden frame of the guillotine supports a heavy steel blade which made no mistake when it fell. Thus also suffered the Marquis of Argyll on 27 May 1661. He was later followed on the block by his son, the 9th Earl, who was executed 30 June 1685.

The only other member of the assassins of James Sharp to be caught and executed was Andrew Guilline. He was caught by a suspicious curate when he refused to answer questions about attending church. Apprehended at Cockpen on 11 June 1683, he

---

[122] Thompson, *Martyr Graves*, p. 179-180.

was quickly brought to trial and sentenced to die, first to have his hands struck off, then hanged, beheaded, and his body to be hung in chains at Magus Moor. On 20 July 1683, the sentence was carried out, allegedly by a drunken hangman who took nine blows to sever the hands which were exhibited with the head above the Netherbow Port. His disembowelled body was taken down by friends after a couple of months. They were discovered, however, and sentenced to banishment for "owning" the Archbishop's murder.

In Edinburgh, the gate most used for exhibiting the Covenanter heads was the Netherbow Gate at the end of Cannongate. The location of the original gateway is shown today by brass cobbles set into the street surface at the traffic lights. Another favoured place was the finials on the roof of the old Edinburgh Tolbooth (famed as the "Heart of Midlothian") which was adjacent to St. Giles Cathedral. It was usual for the executioner to cut off the head and hold it aloft with the cry "here is the head of a traitor." Sometimes arms and hands would be sent to the prisoner's home town for nailing to the church door as a warning to others. Ten prisoners executed after the battle of Rullion Green were dealt with in this way despite having been shown quarter. Others, such as William Welsh of Dumfries, were sent for execution and exhibition in their home towns. Ministers of the Covenant usually had their heads affixed over the gate on a spike and their hands pointed mockingly in prayer beneath. The heads would often remain above the gates for many years.

That the executions were spectacles there can be no doubt. For the inhabitants of Edinburgh it was probably the only time they saw people they may have only previously heard of. When Hugh McKail was executed on 22 December 1666 there were five others who were hanged at the same time: Humphrey Colquhoun, Mungo Kaip, Ralph Shiells, John Wodrow, and John Wilson. Donald Cargill, on the other hand, was quite philosophical about his execution, telling a lady visitor while in prison not to worry as they could "knit me up; cut me down and chop off my old head, and then fare well, they have done with me and I with them for ever."[123]

At the executions of John King and John Kid the latter turned to his companion and quipped, "I have often heard and read of a 'kid'

[123] Howie, *Worthies*, p. 451.

sacrificed, but I seldom or never heard of a 'King' made sacrifice."[124]

Below: Grassmarket Memorial, Edinburgh. Top left: Memorial Garden; top right: Site of the gibbet; bottom: The plate bearing the names of those executed on the Grassmarket. Photos by the author.

[124] *Ibid.*, p. 411.

Surprisingly the *Scots Worthies* does not include one of the most celebrated executions of the Covenanter pantheon: the executions by drowning of the Solway Martyrs, Margaret Wilson, aged eighteen, and Margaret (Mc)Lachlan, aged sixty-three. Margaret Wilson, her sister, and brother were the wilful children of Gilbert Wilson. They declined to adhere to the established church with their parents and were followers of James Renwick. Margaret and her thirteen-year-old sister were captured but the younger girl was released after her father gave a £100 bond. Margaret Lachlan was simply a pious widow who was seized while at prayer because she was Presbyterian. Both refused to take the Abjuration Oath and were sentenced to death by drowning. The method of execution by drowning was specifically prescribed for women by order of the Privy Council. Thus the judge sentenced them to be "ty'd to palisados fixed in the sand, within the flood mark, and there to stand till the flood overflowed them and drowned them."[125] The women were tied to stakes below the high water mark and drowned at Wigtown on 11 May 1685.

Martyrs Monument, Wigtown. Photo by the author.

[125] Penninghame Kirk Session, *Extract from the Session Book of the Parish of Penninghame* (Dumfries: J. McDiarmid & Co., 1826; reprint Edmonton: Still Waters Revival Books, 1996), p. 11.

A much earlier execution by drowning was that of Mrs. Robert Lamb of Perth. This followed the feudal principle of "pit and gallows": a pit to drown women in, a gallows to hang men. She was convicted by the priests for refusing to pray to the Virgin Mary while in childbirth, and her husband was convicted of interrupting a friar who was preaching that man could not be saved without praying to the saints. Robert Lamb was executed by hanging, and his wife was tied in a sack and drowned.

Glasgow was the scene of the execution of friends, James Smith and John Wharry. They had the misfortune to be in the vicinity of Inchbelly Bridge when some Covenanters attacked soldiers escorting prisoners to Glasgow. In the attack of a soldier, David Murray was killed and another wounded. Smith and Wharry were discovered in nearby Stevenson Wood, neither armed nor acting furtively. They were seized, taken to Glasgow, and convicted on suspicion alone. They were taken to Glasgow Cross, hanged on a gibbet till half-dead, then cut down and taken by cart to Inchbelly Bridge where they were hung in chains.

The shooting of Covenanters for refusing to take the Abjuration Oath was central to the Killing Time when so many gained the Martyr's Crown. This was the height of the persecution of the strict Covenanters: the Cameronians and the followers of James Renwick. The Killing Time was mainly in 1685 and seemed to coincide with the death of King Charles II in February 1685 through to the accession of his brother as James VII/II. It also coincided with the threats of rebellion in Scotland led by the Earl of Argyll who opposed the Catholic successor, James, and saw the opportunity to restore his fortunes that had been forfeited in 1681. In England, there was fear of rebellion led by Robert Scott, Duke of Monmouth. However, the shootings virtually stopped from 1686 with about two in 1686 and two in 1688. The last Covenanter to be shot was a sixteen-year-old boy, George Wood of Sorn, in June 1688 by a trooper John Reid, who it appears, thought it the thing to do at the time.

Faith - declarations. See also: Declarations; Rapture at Death.

The works of the Rev. Robert Woodrow (the Wodrow Manuscripts *ca.* 1714) are a prime source for researchers and over the years many eminent historians have culled information from them. Rev. Robert Wodrow was minister of Eastwood and married to a granddaughter of William Guthrie of Fenwick. He was commissioned by the General Assembly in 1711 to gather evidence of the sufferings of the Kirk and to whom the respective Presbyteries and Kirk Sessions sent their reports. The *Cloud of Witnesses* originated through the call of the society people at a meeting on 4 April 1699 to record the sufferings of the Martyrs. Many editions have followed its publication in 1714. Thomson's *Cloud* has some sixty-six testimonies, including commentary on the women martyrs Margaret McLachlan and Margaret Wilson (the Solway Martyrs), Isobel Alison, and Marion Harvey.

Napthali, begun *ca.* 1660 and first published in 1667, is one of the few contemporaneous record of the sufferings of the faithful. It predates much of Wodrow, and has many of the original testimonies quoted by writers down the centuries. Named after Jacob's son in Genesis 49:21, Napthali is described as "a hind let loose" (see Alexander Shields' work of that name) and is also interpreted as "one who gives beautiful words." The work was a collaboration between Sir James Stewart of Goodtrees (1635-1713), son of the provost of Edinburgh, and after the Revolution was Lord Advocate. The narrative was written by Rev. James Stirling of Paisley. In 1667 the work was ordered to be surrendered up and burnt, and a penalty of ten thousand pounds Scots imposed for subsequent possession. It fortunately survived to run to several further prints and with some additions made in 1680. It is among the foremost of the collections of declarations of faith.

Declarations of faith and last testaments were frequently made in the hours before execution and in the most trying conditions. Paper, pen, and ink were often denied the prisoner and it would be smuggled into the prison or purchased from the grasping gaoler. What is truly remarkable and indicative of the depth of reading and understanding of the Scriptures is that the fulsome testimonies and declarations were mainly written without access to a Bible. Moreover, it was not just the ministers who had been trained in theology who left these declarations; common men and women also left testimonies of their faith.

Howie's *Scots Worthies*, or *Biographia Scoticana*, is both a declaration of faith by the author and a selected collection of testimonies of faith. It is clear that John Howie was deeply committed to the cause of Presbyterianism and this is reflected in the selection of the Worthies and the way that he has presented his work, often adding a quotation and affirmation of his own. The cameos of the Worthies themselves gives a view of their personal commitment and the struggles of conscience they had which cannot be denied. But the additional comments by the editor of the 1871 publication, W. H. Carslaw, add to the value of the work for the benefit of the reader. Individual declarations of faith are evident in all the biographies but there are also valuable insights into the thinking behind the principal declarations: the National Covenant of 1638, the Solemn League and Covenant of 1643, and the focal Westminster Declaration of Faith. The Westminster Confession was adopted by the General Assembly of 1647 and thus replaced the Scottish Confession of Faith from 1560.

Declarations of Faith otherwise abound in the very many dissertations, sermons, tracts, and letters of the ministers of the time. Many ministers wrote about issues of the day and these were often published as pamphlets for distribution. The substance of sermons by renowned clergy were often taken down and used in subsequent writings and learned discussions. And there is the correspondence of the ministers themselves, which is a continuing declaration of their faith and the support that they gave others. Among the more prominent were James Renwick, who had to almost constantly defend himself against lies and slanders. Johnson, in *Peden*, tells that Donald Cargill was perhaps the first to use the expression "crossing the bar" "as a symbol of the soul's last hours, and of the peaceful decease of the Christian in the articles and accident of death."[126] Cargill wrote, "Fear not, and the God of mercies grant a full gale, and a fair entry into His Kingdom, which may carry sweetly and swiftly over the bar, that you find not the rub of death."[127]

Alfred, Lord Tennyson, wrote his *Crossing the Bar* in 1889:

For though from out our bourne of time and place
The flood may bear me far
I hope to see my pilot face to face
When I have crossed the bar.[128]

---

[126] Johnston, *Peden*, p. 213.
[127] *Ibid.*
[128] *Oxford Book of Quotations*, ed. Angela Partington (London: Oxford University Press, 1941), p. 680.

Samuel Rutherford wrote over two hundred inspirational letters from his exile in Aberdeen which have been reprinted many times. He has been referred to as a "masterly physician of the soul."[129] John Blackadder, when in the Bass prison, wrote to Robert Garnock in the Greyfriars Prison to resist the taking of sinful Bonds. And there was Alexander Peden's letter of July 1685 to the prisoners cast into the Vault of Dunnottar Castle. These were all declarations and encouragement to others to keep their faith.

Fines. See also: Bishops' Dragnet.

The imposition of fines by a court is not of itself a wrong that can be subject of complaint, but under the system imposed by Charles II, in particular, it became an art form for persecution of the poor because statutory fines were collected by threat and military force. From 1662 the crack down on conventicles was accompanied by enforcement of attendance at the parish churches where, in many cases, a curate had been appointed. A requirement made of the curates was to furnish the names of absentees to the local military commander who was responsible for collecting the statutory fines. The worst area for non attendance was in the south west where there were the largest number of outed ministers and thus most of the despised curates employed. The most vacancies in 1662 were in the Synods of Glasgow and Ayr (63), Dumfries (30), Galloway (23), Lothian and Tweeddale (23), Merse and Teviotdale (19), Argyll (12), and Fife (10).

Napthali gives many examples of personal suffering because of this policy and lists "Some Instances of the Sufferings of Galloway and Nithsdale" and the totals of fines paid for the years 1663, 1665, and 1666, in which military force was used. The total came to £51500. 2s.10d (Scots).[130]

> And although these sums (being Scots money) may seem small to strangers, yet considering that they are not levied proportionally from all the people, but some selected

---

[129] Faith Cook, *Samuel Rutherford and His Friends* (Edinburgh: Banner of Truth Trust, 1992), p. 2.

[130] *Napthali*, p. 378.

> persons within the bounds; and that there are some 19 or 20 Parishes of which there is no account at all.[131]

The sums did not include the great expense of free quarters for the soldiers, let alone any bribes paid to them. And it has to be borne in mind that:

> Ordinarily in Quartering, they did not content themselves with sufficiency, but set themselves to consume and waste needlessly; sometimes throwing whole sheep to their dogs, and scattering corn, hay and straw, they and their boyes usually saying, we came to destroy, and we shall destroy you.[132]

Thomson, in *A Cloud of Witnesses*, gives some detail of who were the oppressors and were making money of the poor. Taking the figures from Wodrow, who expended considerable effort collating the information, he lists:

> Fines in the shires of Edinburgh, Selkirk, Berwick Roxburgh, Peebles, Dumfries, Galloway, Ayr, Renfrew, Lanark Fife, Perth £1,743,999.18.08
> Middleton's fines £1,027,353.06.08
> Gentlemen in Renfrew 1684 £ 237,333.06.08
> Gentlemen in Dunbartonshire £ 55,200.00.00
> Gentlemen in Murray (Elgin, Ross, Banff, Sutherland) 1685 £ 120, 933.06.08
> Total (estimated as half of the real total) £3,174,819.18.08 Scots.[133]

The total was therefore in excess of £500,000 sterling or about £30-35 million pounds today. This was roughly £30-35 for every man, woman, and child in Scotland at that time (population at the Union in 1707 was about one million) and about two year's pay for a labourer.

---

[131] *Napthali*, p. 378.
[132] *Ibid.*, p. 379.
[133] Thomson, *Cloud*, p. 554.

First Book of Discipline.

The first General Assembly came together in December 1560, a remarkably speedy achievement, prompted by the fear that Queen Elizabeth I might intervene, and the fact that the sovereign, Mary Queen of Scots, was a Catholic and married to Francis II, King of France. Hardly had the Reformation taken place when the newly widowed Mary left France and set foot in Scotland after thirteen years' absence, intent on restoring Catholicism.

The First Book of Discipline was the work of the Six Johns (see First Book of Faith, below) and drew heavily on the work of Calvin, claiming the specific authority of the Scriptures for the ecclesiastical constitution. It went much further than just the local church and outlined a system of church government for the country, a scheme of national education, provision for the poor and unable, the order of daily life, and the development of the career of ministers. The book was approved by a Convention held on 15 January 1561, and identified the ordinary and permanent office bearers as of four kinds:

The Minister or Pastor, who preached the Gospel.
The Doctor or Teacher, which included those who taught theology in schools and universities.
The Ruling Elder who assisted in the government of the church.
The Deacon who was responsible for the revenues of the church.[134]

In addition, and as a temporary expedient only, because there were so few ministers then in Scotland, there were:

The Readers who publicly read the Scriptures, assisted the minister and when there was no minister, temporarily taking his place.

The Exhorters, were people with some additional grounding in the Scriptures who were able to add to the simple reading.

---

[134] Johnston, *Treasury*, pp. 35-36.

Superintendents to oversee the operation of the church in their appointed locality. They were not possessed of any additional powers or authority and served only as an expedient until the church was on a sound footing. The position was soon abolished but the precedent was often claimed thereafter and contributed to the appointment of the Tulchan Bishops, in 1572.[135]

The growth of the church in the seven years from 1560 was great; from only six ministers at the first General Assembly, it grew to 1080 churches in the charge of 257 ministers, 455 readers, 151 exhorters, and 5 superintendents. The First Book of Discipline was drawn up hastily to meet the emergency caused by the very sudden change from popery and was replaced by Andrew Melville's Second Book in 1578 which was more precise in its definitions.

Among the more contentious issues was the provisions to be made for ministers and sought a liberal standard that included a right to the endowments of its predecessors. This raised the issues of claims on the funds by old ministers and the laymen who had acquired liens of the lands and incomes of the old church. This issue dragged on and was one where Knox did not get his way, the Privy Council deciding on a policy of thirds: one-third to the Crown which included maintaining Presbyterian ministers, and two-thirds to the old clergy (and laymen). This prompted Knox to ask, possibly in a tone of voice edged with sarcasm, what was God's portion. A consequence of this decision was that the schemes for education, of endowed schools attached to every parish church, and more colleges and universities, were nullified by lack of funds.

First Book of Faith.

The turning point in history that saw Scotland turn to a Protestant faith was the death of Mary of Guise, Queen Mother and Regent of Scotland, in Edinburgh Castle on 10 June 1560. With her death the direct French and Catholic influence in Scotland was broken and the Treaty of Edinburgh saw the departure of both French and English soldiers back whence they came. Scotland was at last free to decide things for herself. This was the essential factor in the Scottish

---

[135] *Ibid.*

Reformation, where the drive for change emanated from the people themselves and their wishes were endorsed by the government. This gave far greater freedom than in England where the English Reformation stemmed from the Queen downwards, thus the church was framed around her wishes rather than any corpus of the people.

The Estates met and, despite protests that the assembly was illegal, it determined to carry through a revolution. They asked John Knox to provide a statement of the Protestant doctrine which was done in just four days by the Six Johns. Six ministers, all named John, were responsible for this founding document: John Knox, John Row (the father of William Row), John Spottiswoode, John Winram, John Douglas, and John Willock. These same six were also responsible for The First Book of Discipline (see above). The Confession of Faith professed and believed by the Protestants within the Realm of Scotland itself consisted of twenty-five articles and is similar to the Westminster Confession of Faith that replaced it in 1647.

The Estates then approved the Scottish Confession of Faith declaring it a "wholesome and sound doctrine grounded upon the infallible truth of God's Word."[136] The following week, the Estates produced three Acts, passed on 24 August 1560, that completed the essential work of establishing Protestantism in Scotland. The first Act abolished the pope's authority and the jurisdiction of the Catholic prelates. The second repealed the Acts of previous parliaments that impacted the new doctrine. And the third act forbid the saying, hearing, or being present at Mass under a three-stage penalty that for first offence was confiscation of property; second offence, banishment; and third offence, death.

Five Members

The attempt by King Charles I to arrest one peer and five members of the English Parliament on 4 January 1642 was both a rash and unwise move that cost him dearly. It arose from the passing of the Grand Remonstrance, which had been approved by a small majority of only eleven votes. Charles I's response was to issue an order on 3 January 1642 for the arrest on charge of High Treason, Lord Kimbolton and five MPs from the House of

---

[136] Calderwood, *History*, Vol. 2, p. 37.

Commons: Denzill Holles, Sir Arthur Haselrig, John Pym, John Hampden, and William Strode. Charles I appeared with soldiers in the House of Commons and demanded the arrest of five of the leading members. This petulant behaviour, after he had already indicated his assent to the Grand Remonstrance, cost him the support that he had previously gained. Importantly, the attempted arrests was a direct challenge to the right of free debate by Parliament. The five Members managed to escape but the consequence for Charles I was humiliation and he was cast as an aggressor with no respect for the constitution. Charles left London on January 10 for Hampton Court. Soon there followed the outbreak of Civil War which ended in the Cromwellian regime and Charles I's own execution in 1649.

General Assembly.

The General Assembly is the highest "court" of the Presbyterian Church and has the power to determine all ecclesiastical matters. The underpinning structure is made up of regional Synods, within which there are Presbyteries. Within Presbyteries are the Kirk Sessions for each individual church. Thus, there are layers of authority with representation at all levels and avenues of appeal, if necessary, against localised decisions. The General Assembly's authority was quite awesome as it exercised all the authority of the old Church Courts on morals, and was fearless in its use of the power to excommunicate sinners. It normally met annually but on occasion met more frequently, its date of convening having been decided by the previous meeting. In the interim the interests of the Kirk were met by a Commission or Committee who dealt with day to day business and relationships with the Estates. The right to call assemblies became an issue with James VI and his successors; it remained a bone of contention even at the Revolution Settlement in 1690.

General Assembly, 20 December 1560 (the first).

The first General Assembly of the Church of Scotland came together in Edinburgh on 20 December 1560 when forty-two members gathered in the old chapel in the Cowgate which had been dedicated to St. Magdalene. Surprisingly, perhaps, only six members were actually ministers but there were only twelve at that time in the whole of Scotland. This first Assembly met under its own authority and was based on the Scriptures without there being any civil authority needed or given. Important acts were to adopt the First Book of Discipline, and to accept the nominations of a further forty-three persons considered suitable to act as ministers, readers or teachers bringing the total Presbyterian workers to eighty-five. The persons who attended the Assembly and the locality they represented are cited in Johnston's *Treasury of the Scottish Covenanters* as:

St. Andrews: Christopher Goodman, Minister; David Spence, Robert Kynpont.
Calder: James Douglas, James Moir.
Carnbee: David Weems.
Dunbar: William Lamb. William Boncle,
Dundee: William Christison, Minister, George Lowell, William Carmichael.
Edbh., City: John Knox, Minister; James Baron, Edward Hope.
Edbh. West: William Harlaw, Minister; Robert Fairlie of Braid.
Forfar: Alexander Guthrie of Hackerton, William Durham of Grange.
Kirkliston: John Kincaid.
Kyle: Hugh Wallace of Carnall, John Fullerton of Dreghorn, Charles Campbell of Skeldum.
Leith: David Lindsay, Minister; Andrew Lamb, Patrick Boyman.
Linlithgow: Charles Drummond, Provost; James Witherspoon, Andrew Mill.
Linton: Walter Balfour.
Lothian (East): George Hume of Spott.
Mearns: Laird of Tullyvard, Laird of Fettercairn.
Montrose: John Erskine of Dun, Andrew Mill.
Nithsdale: Laird of Garleis.
Perth: John Row, Minister.
Ratho: Robert Wynram.
Stirling: William Darroch, William Norwell.
Torpichen: John Brown, Thomas Boyd, James Polwart.

It is of note that over forty Assemblies met during the next twenty years or so without any commissioner on behalf of the sovereign.

General Assembly, 25 December 1567.

This General Assembly was responsible for appointing commissioners to meet with six representatives of the Scottish Parliament to determine what were Church matters and to define the Church's authority. The Parliament of that year enacted that the Church was the authority for appointing ministers but the old lay patrons were still allowed to present their nominees. The civil authority recognised the Church of Scotland as the only legal church but importantly had no authority over it.

General Assembly, 1578.

This General Assembly took place with Andrew Melville as Moderator. As John Knox's successor he was a fervent believer in the divine right of Presbytery and a great opponent of prelacy. Melville was responsible for the Second Book of Discipline which is based on the pure Scriptural form of Church government These rules were adopted at this General Assembly. It is noteworthy that these rules were never ratified by the civil authorities yet were regarded as the standard for the Church. They were recognised in civil law in 1592 and after the Revolutionary Settlement in 1690.

General Assembly, 22 May 1592. See also: Black Acts; Presbytery, the Great Charter.

The General Assembly that met on 22 May 1592 in Edinburgh was responsible for The Great Charter of Presbytery of 1592 which was approved by Parliament on 5 June 1592. (See Appendix 7.) First was the repeal of the Black Acts of 1584. A number of pieces of legislation then approved of and ratified General Assemblies, Synods and Presbyteries and also the main elements of the Second Book of Discipline revised and produced by Andrew Melville. The law said that Assemblies were to be held annually, or oftener if necessary, and the time or place of the next meeting was to be set by the King or his Commissioner if in attendance, otherwise by the assembly itself. Lay patronage was retained but ministers could only be approved and ordained by the Presbyteries to whom candidates could be presented by patrons.

General Assembly - Dundee, 7 March 1598. See also: General Assembly – Glasgow, 21 November 1638.

At this Assembly, King James VI of Scotland (later also James I of England) proposed, and it was accepted, that there should be fifty-one representative ministers to form the First Estate. This representation in Parliament was soon exposed as toothless with the members unable to propose business, merely to vote. But importantly this Assembly also passed an Act directing the number of Commissioners to be sent to every Assembly. This was a very great importance at the General Assembly of Glasgow in 1638 and was the major factor in that Assembly's strength and cohesive action. Presbyteries were instructed to send three of their number, a layman representing the barons, and a lay representative for each of the burghs. Every Session was required to send a lay elder to form the elected Presbytery. No scandalous person could be selected nor was the Moderator to be chosen Commissioner without an election and any dispute was to be settled at the Assembly.

General Assembly - Aberdeen, 1604, 1605. See also: Constant Moderators.

The Aberdeen affair, as it might be called, was a significant event in the life of the young Church of Scotland and marked the start of increasing pressure by James VI to impose prelacy. James VI held dear his aim to change the Church of Scotland to the English Episcopal model with himself as Head of the Church. Central to this objective was the need to impose prelacy. To do this he had to break the power of the General Assembly, the way that church meetings were brought together and who acted as Moderator. He aimed to have bishops as the "constant" Moderators of Presbyteries and therefore managing the Church.

His first task, therefore, was to establish his supremacy. The General Assembly was appointed to meet in Aberdeen in July 1604 but then deferred until 2 July 1605. The Privy Council, however, allegedly heard of intentions to oppose some recent laws about episcopacy and therefore prohibited Presbyteries from sending representatives to the General Assembly and did not appoint a date for reconvening. But, on the appointed day, some nineteen ministers convened the Assembly at Aberdeen and then deferred it again to September 1605.

The disobedient ministers were imprisoned then summoned before the Privy Council. Thirteen admitted their fault and were pardoned but warded to the Lewis, the Isles, Kintyre, Ireland, and Caithness. However, the remaining six declined the Crown's authority to judge them on spiritual matters and were tried for treason and banished. Andrew Duncan of Crail was sent to Blackness and then banished to France. The others who were banished were John Forbes of Alford who had been the Moderator, he went to Middleburgh; Robert Dury of Anstruther to Leyden, Holland; John Sharp of Kilmany went to Die in France. John Welch, whom Howie, in *Scots Worthies*, says was not at Aberdeen, nevertheless approved of the meeting and for this was sent to Blackness on 26 July 1605 along with John Forbes; he was then banished to France in November. Andrew Duncan and Alexander Strachan of Creich were allowed to return after about a year.

The Estates met at Perth on 1 July 1606 with the particular objective to set up the Estate of the Bishops. The church was greatly alarmed and Patrick Simpson, a fierce critic of the actions taken over the Aberdeen Assembly, produced a "Protestation" signed by forty-two ministers, including Andrew Melville, that was presented to the Estates. It was to no avail.

General Assembly – Glasgow, 8 June 1610.

This General Assembly is notorious for the intervention by James VI who wrote to some Presbyteries directing who should be sent to the meeting. As a result the Assembly was packed with members who would support the king, but worse was the actions of the Earl of Dunbar who openly went around offering bribes. He had brought with him from London a substantial supply of gold coins called "angels" to distribute, hence the Assembly became known as the "Angelical Assembly." The consequence of this packing was that the king had proposals for prelacy passed. The king got the right to call assemblies, to appoint bishops as moderators of synods, and to approve appointments made by bishops, and the bishops had the power of excommunication and absolution. This was ratified by Parliament in 1612. Parliament then proceeded to make changes even more favourable to the bishops. Full diocesan episcopacy had arrived in Scotland.

General Assembly – Aberdeen, 13 August 1616. See also: Articles of Perth, 25 August 1618.

The General Assembly at Aberdeen in 1616 was called to consider, in particular, issues of popery, but there was the inevitable hidden agenda of the king. The meeting began with the new and vain Archbishop Spottiswood taking the Moderator's chair (without an election) and the Earl of Montrose served as the King's Commissioner. Wholly unrepresentative as usual, it was three days before Montrose unveiled a list of fourteen issues the king desired should be addressed. These were: improvement of benefices, planting peaceable pastors in burghs and the houses of nobility, examine children, a test Confession and catechism that the children learned entitled "God and the King," compiling and enjoining a book of canons, hold communions quarterly (once at Easter and half yearly in rural parishes), encouraging students of theology, ordaining all preachers, baptism to all if asked (with a godfather), and keeping of parish registers. These were duly approved and also recommended confirmation of children by bishops.

Ministers were set to write a new Catechism, to revise the prayer book in use, and a committee considered the canons. A Confession of some fifty-three paragraphs produced four years earlier by John Hall of Edinburgh and John Adamson of Liberton was accepted with one new provision: a test approving of Episcopacy. The extant Confession and King's Confession were not repealed at this time, probably to allow the new Confession to become known. The king now sent to the Committee on the Canons a short list of five items that he wished to be included. Here began the saga of the Five Articles of Perth.

General Assembly – Glasgow, 21 November 1638.

The temperature in Scotland continued to rise with further proclamations met by further protestations from the Kirk and people, at Stirling on February 18 and, in particular, that of 22 September 1638 which was read and proclaimed by Archibald Johnston (later Lord Warriston) at the Mercat Cross, Edinburgh. The breakthrough came with the King allowing inter alia, a free General Assembly to be followed by a free Parliament.

In the run up to the General Assembly, the duplicity of both the King's Commissioner and the king himself is well documented. The King's Commissioner was the Marquis of Hamilton who had received a long list of instructions (twenty-eight) from the king in a letter of 16 May 1638 on how he was to proceed against the dissenters and in his pocket carried a Proclamation to be read in Edinburgh. The king clearly intended a fight to the end regardless of cost as the instructions concluded:

> If you cannot by the means prescribed by us bring back the refractory and seditious to due obedience, we do not only give you authority, but command all hostile acts whatsoever to be used against them...for the doing whereof we will not only save you harmless, but account it as acceptable service done us.[137]

This was followed by another letter on 11 June 1638 where the king said

> And to this end I give you leave to flatter them with what hopes you please so you engage not me against my grounds (and in particular that you consent neither to the calling of Parliament nor General Assembly, untill the Covenant be disavowed and given up): your chief end being now to win time, that they may not commit public follies, until I be ready to suppress them...I will rather die than yield to those impertinent and damnable demands (as you rightly call them) for it is all one, as to yield to be no king in a very short time.[138]

A later letter informed Hamilton that 14,000 foot, 2,000 cavalry and forty guns were being assembled. And, meantime, three war

---

[137] Johnston, *Treasury*, p. 86.
[138] Hewison, *Covenanters*, Vol. 1, p. 287.

ships were being sent "in pretence to defend our fishermen" and six thousand infantry were available to land near Edinburgh.[139]

The General Assembly at Glasgow from November 21 to 20 December 1638 was the focal point of the Second Reformation and followed the swearing of the National Covenant at Greyfriars Church on 28 February. The Assembly itself, with Moderator Alexander Henderson in the chair, was the first free Assembly for thirty-six years and itself did great things. There had been Assemblies in 1606, 1608, 1610, 1616, 1617, and 1618 but these were subject of great interference by the king that they were simply illegal and later declared null and void.

It was a momentous occasion with 140 ministers attending, and ninety-five ruling elders consisting of seventeen noblemen, nine knights, twenty-five landed proprietors or lesser barons, two professors (John Adamson of Edinburgh and John Lundie of Aberdeen) and forty-two burgesses. These representatives also brought with them several advisers each and many had their armed bodyguards; in all, it was a formidable gathering that surprised the King's Commissioner, Hamilton. The size and constitution of the Assembly was, with the proposed trial of the bishops, another reason for his condemnation of the abundance of lay Elders.

After several days of routine work, the Assembly turned to the matter of the prelates and determined to try them. The Bishops and Archbishops declined to attend whereupon the meeting resolved to try them in their absence, which they did. At this the King's Commissioner, the Marquis of Hamilton, ordered the Assembly to stop and formally dissolved it in the king's name on November 29. He made a formal declaration which was promptly met by a formal Protest by Johnston about his early leaving of the Assembly. The same day a Royal Proclamation was issued calling the Assembly a "pretended assembly" and ordered the members to quit the city within twenty-four hours.

Alexander Henderson's subsequent response to the Marquis of Hamilton's demand to dissolve the Assembly was a cordial and tranquil observation:

> All that are heir knows the reasons of the meiting of this Assembly; and albeit we have acknowledged the power of

---

[139] *Ibid.*, p. 287.

> Christain Kings for conveining of Assemblies and their power in Assemblies; yet that may not derogat from Christs right; for he hath given divine warrants to convocat assemblies whether the Magistrats consent or not: therefore, seeing we perceave men to be so zealous of his Master's commands, have not we also good reason to be zealous towards our Lord, and to mentaine the liberties and priviledges of His Kingdom?[140]

It is, however, clear from the minutes of the General Assembly that Henderson took great care to ensure there was a consensus among the attendees; about six did not agree to continue, and to the question whether to proceed against the Bishops, only four declined. With such overwhelming majorities the gathering continued to sit for almost three weeks. The Assembly proceeded to make substantial reforms. Having dealt with the bishops and some prelatic supporters the Assembly turned its attention to re-establishing the Presbyterian system and removing all semblance of Episcopacy.

Act 8 annulled the previous six Assemblies of 1606, 1608, 1610, 1616, 1617, 1618.
Act 9 annulled the oath that had been required of ministers by the bishops.
Act 17 abjured and cancelled the Perth Articles.
Act 18 condemned the Service Book.
Act19 condemned the Book of Canons.
Act 20 condemned the Book of ordination.
Act 21 condemned the Court of High Commission.
Act 22 clarified the meaning of the King's Confession and abjured and removed Episcopacy.
Act 23 deposed and excommunicated the Archbishops of St. Andrews (John Spottiswood) and Glasgow (Patrick Lindsay), and the Bishops of Edinburgh (David Lindsay), Rosse (John Maxwell), Galloway (Thomas Sidserf), Brechin (Walter Whytefoord), Dumblane (James Wedderburn), and Aberdeen (Adam Ballantyne).

---

140 *Records of the Kirk of Scotland*, ed. Alexander Peterkin (Edinburgh: ----, 1838; reprint Edmonton: Still Waters Revival Books, 1996), p. 147.

Act 24 deposed and conditionally excommunicated the Bishops Murray (John Guthry), Lismoir/Argyll (James Fairlie), Orkney (John Graham), Caithness (John Abernethie), Dunkeld (Alexander Lindsay), and the Isles (Neill Campbell).

Act 25 restored the Church Courts.

Act 29 directed the establishment of parochial schools.

Act 41 against those who speak or write against the National Covenant, this General Assembly and its Constitution.

Act 45 condemned chapters, archdeacons, deacons, "and suchlike Popish trash."

Act 53 condemned ministers of the Gospel from holding civil offices such as Justices of the Peace, or sitting in Session, Council, or Parliament.

Act 62 required Presbyteries to publish the explanation for rejecting Episcopacy, the books and the Five Articles as being inconsistent with the Confession of faith.

Act 64 ordered the Covenant of February to be resubscribed with the Assembly's declaration rejecting Episcopacy and associated ceremonies as inconsistent with the Confession of faith.

Act 68 restated the Church's claim to be self-governing and that it had the power to convene its own Assemblies; appointing the next meeting to be in Edinburgh on the third Wednesday in July 1639.

Act 69 required all ruling elders to accept the Covenant and the constitution of the Assembly.[141]

Hewison, in *The Covenanters*, makes the important point regarding the Assemblies' apparent overstepping their authority by setting aside the Acts of Parliament. He points out that the Assembly and its heirs were scrupulous in using the law. In the case of Episcopacy, the laws for ratifying acts of the Church were not legally or morally binding "being neither national nor popular Acts." Archibald Johnston (later Lord Warriston) and Clerk of the Assembly asserted that he knew "certainlie that this office of the

---

[141] Hewison, *Covenanters*, Vol. 1, pp. 312-313.

bishops was never established by any Act of Parliament in Scotland."[142]

When they had finished, on Thursday, 20 December 1638, the freedom and authority of the Church *in* Scotland had been reasserted.

Of the *Scots Worthies*, two noblemen, both Campbells stood up to be counted when the Marquis of Hamilton sought to close the proceedings. John Campbell, the Earl of Loudon, made several intercessions with Hamilton and told him quite plainly that he was wrong. His stance was to cost him dearly later. The other was Archibald Campbell, the 8th Earl (later Marquis) of Argyll who attended as a Privy Councillor but remained as a staunch supporter of the Covenant. Argyll remained at the Assembly and made clear his position as a supporter of the Church. Despite his adopted stance, and at some risk to himself, Argyll stayed at Court in the hope of exerting influence on behalf of the Church.

General Assembly – Edinburgh, 12 August 1639.

David Dickson was Moderator at the Edinburgh General Assembly on 12 August 1639. The event of note was that the king's Commissioner, the Earl of Traquair, first tried to have Alexander Henderson appointed as Moderator. But Henderson had been Moderator the previous year and his proposal was rejected. A second term would have been falling into the trap of appointing a "Constant Moderator" and opening the door to bishops as the constant moderators of the church.

General Assembly – Edinburgh, 1643. See also: Solemn League and Covenant.

The period from 1639 to 1642 was one of great unrest, there having been the two Bishops' Wars (1639-1640), a rebellion in Ireland (1641) that was dragging on with many Protestant and Presbyterian deaths, and Civil War in England beginning in 1642. Out of this disorder came a proposal from the English Parliamentarians to the Estates of Scotland and the General

[142] *Ibid.*, p. 315.

Assembly for a military union. However, the Church of Scotland were more in favour of a religious agreement.

Sir Archibald Johnston, Lord Warriston, was responsible for a motion to the General Assembly declaring the reasons for supporting the request for help:

> The war was for religion.
> The Protestant faith was in danger.
> Honour bound to repay assistance given Scotland in the First Reformation.
> Common cause with the Church of England.
> The prospect of uniformity in religion and worship would strengthen the cause of Protestantism.
> The present English Parliament was friendly to Scotland and may be so in future.
> The king's interference in religious matters was contradictory.

Alexander Henderson drafted the Solemn League and Covenant, which was approved by the General Assembly on 17 August 1643. Later at the same meeting, ministers Henderson, Douglas, Rutherford, Baillie, and Gillespie, and Elders the Earl of Cassillis, Lord Maitland, and Sir Archibald Johnston were appointed to take the Solemn League and Covenant to London for formal swearing and acceptance.

General Assembly – Edinburgh, 12 July 1648.

The Commission of the Assembly met at the same time as the Estates (who approved the Engagement) and remonstrated with the Engagers for their folly. The Assembly met on July 12 and condemned the "unlawful engagement" as sinful because it violated Covenants and proposed the reinstatement of an Episcopal and Erastian King. They then declared the Engagers to be "malignants" and enemies to the righteous cause. Lauderdale and Hamilton were reviled and accused of being Episcopalian supporters. The same assembly, on July 20 and 28, authorised the use of the Larger and Shorter Catechisms that had emerged from the Westminster Assembly.

General Assembly – Edinburgh, 16 October 1690.

This was the first Assembly of the Church *of* Scotland after the Revolution and was a quiet session in terms of legislation as many of the Acts for the settlement of the Church had already been approved. It was the first Assembly for twenty eight years and only about ninety ministers had survived the period, of which sixty were all that was left of the ministers outed in 1662. Among these were Gabriel Semple of Jedburgh, who had been involved with the Pentland Rising; Henry Erskine; and Thomas Hog of Kiltearn. Hugh Kennedy was the Moderator with Lord Carmichael as the King's Commissioner. There was an element of Erastianism in the proceedings as the king had recommended moderation, as a consequence steps were taken to avoid offending anyone.

Yet again the faithful remnant suffered because no reference was made to the Covenant of 1638 or the Solemn League and Covenant of 1643, nor, incredibly, to the Recissory Act. John Hepburn of Urr in Kirkcudbrightshire attempted to bring up these points but was hushed into silence. The Assembly also declined to accept the contendings of the Covenanters while allowing the three ministers of the Societies—Linning, Boyd, and Alexander Shields—to join their communion. This disgraceful bending of the knee and rejection of perfectly valid representations was compounded when General Assemblies were not held in the following three years because of Jacobite plotting.

Gowrie Conspiracy.

The Gowrie Conspiracy is one of the mysteries of the reign of King James VI. The 2nd Earl of Gowrie had been involved in the Ruthven Raid, and had caused the boy King James to burst into tears when he blocked his way from leaving the room they were in. The Earl was executed on 2 May 1584. His son, John Ruthven, 3rd Earl of Gowrie, was a popular provost of Dundee in 1593 who had spent some months abroad in Geneva where he had met the Divine, Theodore Beza. In August 1600, the king and a large retinue came to Gowrie's home in Perth, saying that he had been invited there by the Earl's brother, Alexander. For reasons never disclosed, a scuffle took place in which the brothers were both killed. King James alleged that they had tried to assassinate him and they had been killed in the attempt. The circumstances were widely debated and refuted, much to James' annoyance, and he exhibited extreme spite if anyone questioned the matter.

An alternative twist to the tale is that James had assembled some friends at Falkland Palace to go hunting on 5 August 1600 and had been approached by Alexander Ruthven, the younger brother of the 3rd Earl of Gowrie. Ruthven told the king that he had come across a man, possibly a papal agent or Jesuit spy, burying a pitcher of gold coins in a field outside Perth and invited the king to come and see the man and claim the gold for the Crown. On arriving at the Castle and seeing the stranger, Ruthven allegedly drew a dagger and made to stab the king in revenge for having executed his father. The king's cries for help were heard and a gentleman called John Ramsay stabbed Ruthven in the neck and, when the Earl of Gowrie came into the room, Ramsay also killed him. Ramsay was later knighted and made Earl of Holderness. In a peculiar turn of events some 350 residents of Perth were interrogated and some tortured; and, at the end of August, the bodies of the brothers Ruthven were given a trial before Parliament. The corpses were pronounced guilty of treason then hanged, drawn, and quartered. Bizarre though this was there may have been reason in it as the conviction for treason would formally render the estates of the deceased forfeit to the Crown.

Curiously ministers were required to give thanks for the kings deliverance and they were required to declare their belief of the king's story. On his return to Edinburgh on Monday 11 August 1600 James with some nobles went to the Mercat Cross where his chaplain, Patrick Galloway, preached a sermon whereby he tried to convince the hearers that the Earl and his brother had conspired to kill the king. James, himself, rose and spoke against the brothers and later caused a narrative of the affair to be published. Despite these efforts the public and ministers did not believe James. The public remembered the earlier execution of the Earl's father and they recalled also that the Gowries were staunch Protestants and friends of Elizabeth I. But they were also the undoubted enemies of the popish lords who surrounded the young king at that time.

James remained angry at the comments of disbelief and he summoned ministers before him who were generally cowed into accepting the official version of events. One who did not acquiesce was Robert Bruce who was brought before the king but declined to be a hypocrite and acknowledge the guilt of the Gowries. For his stand Bruce was banned from preaching and banished to France. M'Crie, in *Sketches*, cites the *Life of Melville* and this exchange between the king and Bruce:

> The King acknowledged to Mr Bruce that he ordered Alexander Ruthven to be struck. "I grant" said he, "that I am art and part in Master Alexander's slaughter, but it was in my own defence." "Why brought ye not to justice?" said Bruce: "you should have had God before your eyes." "I had neither God nor the devil before my eyes, man!" said the king, interrupting him, "but my own defence."[143]

The events do, however, tidy up the revenge scenario since the Gowries had been involved in the murder of David Rizzio, had been involved in the death of Lord Darnley, and had been the harsh captors of Mary Queen of Scots, all were now extinguished. It is ironic that James' personal motto was "Beati Pacifici:" Blessed are the Peacemakers.

Graces.

In 1628, Charles I agreed, as an act of grace, not to enforce the oath of supremacy for the Old English Catholics and to allow them security of lands they had held for sixty years. In return, he obtained £120,000 in badly needed funds for the war with Spain. It was expected that the Graces would be ratified by the Irish Parliament. But Parliament was under the control of the New English led by Richard Boyle, Earl of Cork who resented the concession. Subsequently Wentworth pursued the Old English for their lands (because they were not covered by statute) and was the cause for many of them joining with the Irish in the 1641 Rebellion.

Grand Remonstrance. See also: Five Members; Personal Rule.

The Grand Remonstrance was a bill presented by the English Parliamentarians to King Charles I in December 1641 that contained a long list of the king's abuses of power during his "personal

[143] M'Crie, *Sketches*, pp. 138-139.

government" from 1629 to 1640. With Wentworth, the Earl of Strafford, and Archbishop Laud out of the way, Parliament determined to curtail the personal power of the king. At first, the king agreed to meet their grievances but shortly afterwards sought to arrest the Five Members, and precipitated Civil War.

Hampton Court Conference, 1604.

The Hampton Court Conference, convened on 14 January 1604, was the formal opening of James I's campaign for conformity throughout the church in his kingdoms. James is said to have debated well with the Puritans and generally to have been non confrontational. That is until it came to Presbyterianism with whom, he said, he was having no truck. In reply to Dr. Reynolds, he made a angry attack that was no more than a declaration of war. M'Crie in *Sketches* cites thus:

> Presbytery agreeth as well with monarchy as God and the Devil. Then Jack and Tom and Will and Dick shall meet and at their pleasure censure me and my Council and all our proceedings. Then Will shall stand up and say, It must be thus; Then Dick shall reply and say, Nay marry, but we will have it thus. And therefore, here I must once reiterate my former speech, Le Roy s`avisera (the king will look after it). Stay, I pray you, for one seven years before you demand that of me; and if you then find me pursy and fat, and my wind pipes stuffed, I will perhaps hearken to you; for let that government be once up, I am sure I shall be kept in breath; then we shall all of us have work enough, both our hands full. But, Dr Reynolds, till you find that I grow lazy, let that alone.[144]

Then putting his hand to his hat preparatory to leaving the Conference the King continued,

> My Lords the Bishops, I may thank you that these men plead for my supremacy; they think they cant make their party good against you, but by appealing unto it. But if once

[144] M'Crie, *Sketches*, pp. 140-141.

> you are out and they in place I know what would become of my supremacy, for No Bishop, No King as I have said before. If this be all they have to say, I will make them conform, or I will harry them out of this land, or else do worse.[145]

The one substantive thing to emerge from the conference was a decision to produce a new English translation of the Bible; the task was handed to a commission of fifty-four scholars. This was the origin of the King James, or Authorised, version. The work commenced in 1607 and was based largely on William Tyndale's translation printed in Worms in 1525 and contained about ninety per cent of his words. The King James version was published in 1611.

Hampton Court Conference, 1606.

James VI/I now planned to remove some of the leading Presbyterians from the scene before pursuing enactments confirming his universal supremacy and the appointment of bishops. He particularly wanted Andrew Melville out of the way. In a letter dated 21 May 1606, the king invited eight ministers to attend at Hampton Court: Melville, James Balfour Edinburgh, William Scot Cupar, John Carmichael Kilconquhar, Robert Wallace Tranent, Adam Colt Musselburgh, William Watson Burntisland, and James Nicolson of Meigle. Also attending were the archbishops Gledstanes and Spottiswoode, and the bishops of Orkney and Galloway. After much delay the group assembled on 23 September 1606 and discussed the Aberdeen Assembly during which attempts were made to trap Melville. Their undoing was to reply to a question about what would pacify the Church; the reply was "A Free Assembly." That night they were seized and imprisoned. Melville was undone by his writing a Latin epigram that ridiculed a service in the Chapel Royal where the altar had been furnished with two clasped bibles, two unlit candles, and two empty basins. The epigram (translated) ran:

> Why stand there on the royal altar hie
> Two closed books, blind lights, two bassons drie

[145] M'Crie, *Sketches*, p. 141.

Doth England hold God's mind and worship close,
Blind of her sight, and buried in her dross?
Doth she, with Chapel put in Romish dress
The purple whore religiously express?[146]

The epigram reached the king who ordered the Privy Council to interview Melville. At this meeting Hewison, in *The Covenanters*, says Bishop Bancroft endeavoured to take Melville on but was reminded very quickly of his own past, called a traitor to all the Reformed Churches of Europe, and had his dress described as "Romish rags." Howie, in *Scots Worthies*, says this was the Archbishop of Canterbury who was rebuked and Bishop Barlow was reminded of his saying after the Hampton Court that the king had remarked that "he was *in* the Church of Scotland, not *of* it." Melville wanted to know why he had gone "unpunished for making the King of no religion."[147]

Melville was first committed to the custody of Dr. Overwall, the Dean of St. Pauls, but later removed to the Tower by order of the king. He remained in the Tower from May 1607 until April 1611 when he was allowed to go to Sedan in France, where he died in 1622 at the age of seventy-seven. His nephew, James, was warded to Newcastle and died in Berwick on 19 January 1614, aged fifty-nine years. The remaining ministers were allowed to return to Scotland under censure and restriction to certain parishes.

High Commission, Court of.

The Court of High Commission in Scotland originated in 1610 from the exercise of the Royal Prerogative by James I. There were originally two courts, one in each of the archbishoprics of Glasgow and Edinburgh, which were united in 1615. They had no standing in law by way of the parliamentary process and had the role of exercising disciplinary powers over offences in life and religion.

The original Court of High Commission was created by Elizabeth I in 1559. She gave authority to a mixed committee of knights, counsellors, and clerics to enforce "an Act for the uniformity of Common Prayer" and "An Act restoring to the Crown

---

[146] Howie, *Worthies*, p. 98

[147] *Ibid.*, p. 99.

the ancient jurisdiction" [of the Church]. It was specifically enjoined to take action against

> all and singular heretical opinions, seditious books, contempts, conspiracies, false rumours, tales, seditions, misbehaviours, slanderous words or shewings, published, invented or set forth or heerafter to be published invented or set forth by any person or persons against us or contrary or against the laws or statutes of this our realm, or against the quiet governance and rule of our people and subjects in any county, city or borough.[148]

Its all-embracing nature gave enormous power to a quorum of six people, which included the Archbishop of Canterbury and the Bishop of London. Ominously, both of these very posts would later be occupied by William Laud, who became archbishop in 1633.

Under James VI/I, the Court of High Commission was a device for imposing and enforcing episcopacy while the basic structures of Presbytery remained untouched. It was thus initially an irritation but one which hardened in its dealings under King Charles I. The validity and authority of the court was roundly questioned by David Calderwood when summoned before it in 1617 and was deprived of his living for non-conformity. David Dickson was a minister who at first did not object to episcopacy but soon changed his mind. He was summoned before the court on 29 January 1622 and declined its authority. It is indicative of the abuse of power of the court that Archbishop Spottiswoode railed against him and said, "I hanged a Jesuit in Glasgow for a like fault."[149]

The reconstitution of the Court in October 1634 by Charles I was in order to enforce the adoption of "novations" that were to be made, including the Book of Canons (1636) and the Book of Common Prayer (1637). The changes included affirmation of the royal authority in ecclesiastical matters and instructions about the manner of conducting worship. Samuel Rutherford was pursued by the court in 1630 for publishing a critical document, *Exercitationes de Gratia*, and again by the Bishop of Galloway in 1634. In 1638, he was charged with non-conformity when the Marquis of Argyll

---

[148] Prothero, *Select Statutes*, p. 228.
[149] Howie, *Worthies*, p. 290.

intervened on his behalf. In 1637, David Dickson was charged because he had allowed three ministers (Blair, Cunningham, and Livingston) who had been deposed from their livings in Ireland, to participate in the Communion.

The Court became the mechanism for gross abuse by Archbishop Sharp and the persecution of the "outed" ministers following the Restoration of Charles II. Sharp obtained permission to set up the Court following a visit to London in January 1664 with the purpose of execution "of the laws in Church affairs" and was supposed to last until November that year.[150] The constitution of the Court was nine prelates and thirty-five laymen, of whom any five (with at least one prelate) formed a quorum. It quickly followed that there was an inevitable preponderance of bishops and ecclesiastics in the Court who met at short notice in out of the way locations to conduct their oppressive business. At this time the court was able to impose any sentence except the death penalty. It became the vehicle for imposing fines and their collection by the military under Sir James Turner, the pursuit of conventiclers by Claverhouse, and the imprisonment, banishment and selling of prisoners into slavery. There was no appeal against sentence, no one was acquitted by the court and no one escaped without a penalty of some kind.

The court was described as a commission for executing the laws of the Church and the commissioners were authorised to call before them, besides Catholics and "Popish traffickers":

> All obstinate contemners of the discipline of the Church, or for that cause suspended, deprived and excommunicated.
> All keepers of conventicles.
> All ministers who, contrary to the laws and Acts of Parliament or Council, remain or intrude themselves in the function of the ministry in their parishes or bounds inhibited by these Acts.
> All such as preach in private houses or elsewhere without licence of the bishop of the diocese.
> All such people who keep meetings at fasts, and the administration of the sacrament of the Lord's Supper, which are not approven by authority.

---

[150] Hewison, *Covenanters*, Vol. 2, p. 180. It became known as the Crail Court after the parish in Fife where the new Archbishop Sharp was previously the minister.

All who speak, preach, write, or print to the scandal, reproach, or detriment of the estate of government of the Church or Kingdom now established.

All who contemn, molest or injure the ministers who are obedient to the laws.

All who do not orderly attend divine worship, administration of the Word and sacraments performed in their respective parish church by ministers legally settled for taking care of these parishes in which these persons are inhabitants.

All who without any lawful calling. Or as busy-bodies, go about houses and places corrupting and disaffecting people from their allegiance, respect and obedience to the laws.

All who express disaffection to His Majesty's authority, by contravening Acts of Parliament or Council in relation to Church affairs.[151]

When it was found that the application of the powers were not working to the prelates' satisfaction, the device introduced was to arrest and imprison without warrant or reason given, or charge, simply on the strength of a letter signed by one or more of the Commission. A large number of the gentry in the West and South of Scotland were arrested and imprisoned in Edinburgh, Stirling, and Dumbarton. Under Sharp, the Court of High Commission achieved its greatest notoriety where it became the archbishop's tool for venting his great spite upon his former colleagues. Typical was Sharpe's spiteful attempt to slur James Wood's name while the latter lay on his deathbed. Sharp spread slanderous allegations that Wood had recanted which was denied in a notarised statement. It is no surprise that the statement was ordered to be burnt by the Court. The minutes of the proceedings of the Court of High Commission have never been found

Highland Host.

The Highland Host was a term given to the clansmen from the north of Scotland who were recruited for service by the Crown.

---

[151] Metcalfe, *Renfrew*, p. 293.

Fierce fighters they were also adept at pillage and looting, which was their common practice. They were feared for their savagery and uncouth ways. A force of between 8,000 and 9,000 of the Highland Host, which actually contained some Lowlands militia, were billeted upon the people, mainly in Ayrshire and Renfrewshire, for about a month during January and February 1678. Their purpose was to enforce bonds that had been given for good behaviour of bondsmen (landowners and tenants) and their tenants; a secondary purpose was to disarm the populace.

In 1674 the landowners had been bound over to restrain their tenants and servants from attending conventicles and rewards were offered for ministers conducting such services. This highly contentious legislation was greatly resented and exacerbated in 1675 and 1676 when letters of Intercommuning were issued against about an hundred ministers. This meant that anyone having any dealings whatsoever with the named ministers were deemed art and part in their offence. There was considerable unrest especially in the south west of Scotland, and military patrols, and quartering on the luckless populace did not calm the situation. In 1677, the proclamation of 1674 binding landlords was repeated and was the last straw for the hard pressed landlords. Widespread refusal to comply caused the King's Commissioner, Lauderdale, to order that the bonds should be subscribed.

The Highland Host was ordered into the south west of Scotland and Ayrshire in the February of 1678 where they exacted free quarters from the people, and pillaged their homes and lands. They devastated the most prosperous districts of Lanarkshire and Renfrewshire as well as Ayrshire. In districts of Kyle, Carrick, and Cunningham the damage was estimated at £137,000, a huge sum in those days. The excesses were such that some of their own officers and even the government became ashamed and the Host was ordered to return home. This they did retiring with their loot as if from a battlefield assailed by vengeful victims. In Glasgow the students from the university prevented them from crossing the Clyde at one point. The Host were later used in drives against conventicles in 1685 because they were nimble and able to pursue their quarry into the mosses and across rough ground.

Imprisonment. See also: Banishment.

The Covenanter story is very much about imprisonment whether of the many ministers who were cast into prison for their beliefs and resistance to episcopacy; or of the people who took up armed resistance and put their lives in their hands to attend conventicles. There was also the invidious open imprisonment of banishment to remote places within Scotland when often the family of the prisoner was prohibited from joining him. For the Marquis of Argyll there was the unique imprisonment under the Cromwellian regime, of confinement to his estates in Argyllshire for the best part of ten years.

The nature of the prison varied from the local tolbooth to sturdier castles and some particularly remote and stout prisons where visitors would be few. Most towns had a tolbooth in which minor criminals were often held pending appearance before a magistrate. In the countryside there were the fortified homes and castles of the gentry which might be utilised. Larger towns and cities had common prisons for thieves, murderers, rogues and vagabonds. All that remains of the Edinburgh Tolbooth is the "Heart of Midlothian" set in the pavement next to St. Giles Cathedral indicating the site of the fearsome prison, in two parts: one for debtors and one for criminals. Then there were the especially secure, military style, prisons in castles such as Aberdeen, Edinburgh, Stirling, Blackness, Dunnottar, and the Bass Rock. For some there was even the Tower of London.

The Heart of Midlothian, marking the site of the Edinburgh Tolbooth. Photo by the author.

Most of the ministers found themselves confined in assorted tolbooths at some stage and certainly if remitted to Edinburgh to appear before the Court of High Commission on some, often specious, charge. An early resident of Blackness was David Lindsay, minister at Leith, who was incarcerated for objecting to the manipulation of votes in the Parliament that passed the Black Acts in 1584. John Welch, who supported the Aberdeen Assembly of 1605, was sent to the Edinburgh Tolbooth, then to Blackness Castle and ultimately banished to France. John Hamilton, Lord Bargany was thought to be a sympathiser with seditious tendencies whereas he was possibly too free with his opinions. He was imprisoned in Blackness without trial on perjured evidence possibly by persons with eyes upon his estate. He was bailed in June 1680 and later provided a regiment for the public service and King William.

John Dickinson had two visits to the Edinburgh Tolbooth and then spent nearly seven years as a prisoner on the Bass Rock, a bleak and desolate island about three miles off the coast near Dunbar and opposite the ancient Castle of Tantallon. The Bass Rock is itself only about three quarters of a mile in circumference and, at its high point, only 313 feet above sea level. There are sheer cliffs on three sides; on the fourth is a narrow and dangerous landing point. Even on calm days the seas swell and roll round the island with a dangerous tidal flow between it and the mainland: not a place to attempt escape by swimming!

There was also the ill-treatment that stemmed directly from an individual's spite, especially that of Archbishop James Sharp. Such was the case of Thomas Hog who was cast into the Bass Rock prison where he became very ill. The attending doctor, of his own accord, petitioned the Privy Council that Hog should be released before he died. Despite some sympathy from the Lords, Sharp intervened claiming that Hog could "do more hurt to their interests sitting in his elbow chair, than twenty others could do."[152]

With the votes of the prelates to back him, Sharpe had a motion passed that Hog should be carried "to the closest prison in the Bass."[153] Hog was thrown into a deep dungeon but hardly had he got there than his health dramatically improved and he survived. In

---

[152] Howie, *Worthies*, p. 568.
[153] *Ibid.*

later times Hog would say of Sharpe: "commend him to me for a good physician."[154]

Bass Rock. Photo by the author.

Blackness Castle. Photo by the author.

[154] *Ibid.*

Dunnottar Castle. Photo courtesy of A. Pittendreigh.

Covenanter Prison, Greyfriars, Edinburgh. Photo by the author.

Top left: Cannongate Tolbooth. Photo by the author. Top right: Cannongate Tolbooth. Thos. Shepherd, *Modern Athens, Edinburgh in the Eighteenth Century* (London: Jones & Co., 1829). Bottom left: Kirkcudbright Tolbooth. Photo by the author. Bottom right: Sanquhar Tolbooth. Photo courtesy of A. Pittendreigh.

There has been some debate over the years as to who exactly was imprisoned on the Bass. One would expect that the Rev. John Blackadder (who died there) would have a good idea who his companions were. The author of his "Memoirs," Andrew Crichton, gave one list but it is generally accepted that the list of the Rev. James Anderson, contributor to M'Crie's *The Bass Rock: Its Civil and Ecclesiastical History*, is nearest the mark (he rejected twelve of Blackadder's list). The Anderson list, cited in Johnston's *Treasury* is: George Scot of Pitlochie; Robert Bennet of Chesters; Alexander Gordon of Earlston; Sir Hugh Campbell of Cessnock; Sir George Campbell of Cessnock; Rev. James Fraser of Brea; Rev. John Blackadder of Troqueer; Rev. Patrick Anderson, Walston; Rev. John Campbell, Ireland; Rev. John Dickson, Rutherglen; Rev. James Drummond, chaplain to Marchioness of Argyll; Rev. Alex Forrester, St. Mungo; Rev. James Fithie, Chaplain, Trinity Hospital, Edinburgh; Rev. John Grieg, Carstairs; Rev. Thomas Hog, Kiltearn; Rev. Peter Kid, Carluke; Rev. John Law, Campsie; Rev. John McKilligan, Fodderty; Rev. Alexander Peden, New Glenluce; Rev. John Rae, Symington; Rev. Archibald Riddell, Kippen; Rev. Gilbert Rule, Prestonhaugh; Rev. John Stewart, Deer; Rev. Robert Traill, Cranbrook; Rev. Thomas Ross, in the North; Mr. William Bell, preacher; Mr. Alexander Dunbar, preacher; Mr. Robert Gillespie, preacher; Mr. James Macaulay, preacher; Mr. James Mitchell, preacher; Mr. Michael Potter, preacher; Mr. Robert Ross, preacher; Mr. Alexander Shields, preacher; William Spence, schoolmaster, Fife; Major Joseph Learmont, Army; William Lin, writer in Edinburgh; John Spreul, town clerk of Glasgow; John Spreul, apothecary in Glasgow; Robert Dick, saltgrieve to Lord Carington.[155]

Large scale imprisonment was the feature of the Greyfriars Kirkyard where some 1,100 prisoners were held in an open yard for several months after the battle of Bothwell Brig in 1679. The conditions were dreadful with the prisoners having nothing to lie on or to cover themselves from the elements. Their bread allowance was four ounces a day and drinking water obtained from a pipe nearby. They were guarded during the day by an average of eight soldiers, and at night by about twenty four, who were told that if a prisoner(s) escaped they would pay by a life for a life or by throw of

---

[155] Johnston, *Treasury*, pp. 589-590.

the dice. An added terror for the prisoners was that if they rose from the ground during the night they were shot. Communication with the prisoners was only allowed by women who were themselves dreadfully abused and harangued while they often waited for hours to see their man. The final 257 prisoners were sent for transportation to the colonies but their ship, the *Crown*, sank off Deerness and 211 of them drowned. The survivors were nevertheless transported. The area now called the Covenanters' Prison in Greyfriars Kirk Yard is only part of the space that was available in 1679.

The Castle at Dunnottar gained notoriety as a prison for some 167 prisoners cast into "The Whigs Vault," and compared by some to the Black Hole of Calcutta. The vault was in fact two stone store rooms one above the other. The upper vault was probably a granary and measured 54 feet 9 inches long, 15 1/2 feet wide and 12 feet high with two tiny, barred windows. It communicated with the lower vault by a chute into a small wet room that measured 15 feet long, 8 feet wide and 9 feet high. Ventilation was through a small drain at floor level where the prisoners had to lie down by turns to gasp in air. The cell was described as cramped, without room to sit down, the floor was ankle deep in mire, and there was little fresh air to breathe. Here they were allowed no help from friends; it was an offence to communicate with them, as the wife of James Forsyth of Carthat in Annandale found out. She was heavily pregnant when she visited her husband and was arrested and thrown in with the other prisoners where she had her baby and died of neglect. The prisoners suffered greatly from want of food and drink, even having to buy drinking water from the guards who charged exorbitant prices: 20 pence for a pint of ale, and sandy, dusty, meal at 18 shillings a peck.

There was an attempt by twenty-five prisoners to escape but fifteen were recaptured and at least two died in the attempt. The survivors were tortured with burning matches and one, Alexander Dalgleish died from his injuries. The surviving prisoners were released after some months with some taking an Oath of allegiance to gain their release, while about eighty who refused were sent to the American colonies. Among them was Janet Fimerton, an old maid from Edinburgh, who had caught the bible that the martyr John Watt had thrown down from the scaffold on 24 November 1684. Her task in life was to aid in the burial of the executed martyrs. She was held for alleged complicity in trying to bury bodies in Greyfriars that had been seized by students before they could be buried at the gallows foot at the Gallows Lea. She was cast into Dunnottar and later banished for refusing to own King James II. She was on board the *Henry and Francis* that sailed with Dunnottar prisoners as slaves for the colonies and ended up in New Jersey. Janet Fimerton was among the thirty-one passengers on that ship who died at sea.

Andrew Melville was lured to London and was held in The Tower for four years (May 1607 to April 1611), having previously (1583) been sentenced to confinement in Blackness but escaped to England. He was eventually released into the custody of a French nobleman to teach theology at Sedan. Other prisoners in the Tower included the Earl of Loudon in 1639, the Marquis of Argyll in 1660, Archibald Johnston, Lord Warriston in June 1663 before transfer to Edinburgh Tolbooth, and William Carstares in 1674.

An earlier Presbyterian, Andrew Duncan, was one of the ministers who was harried from pillar to post; he attended the Assembly at Aberdeen in 1605 and was imprisoned in Blackness Castle for fourteen months. He also opposed the Five Articles of Perth and was banished to Dundee and separated from his wife and family. He was later imprisoned in Dumbarton Castle, banished to France and then, after some time, allowed to return. John Welch was a prisoner in Blackness for supporting the Aberdeen Assembly. Henry Blythe minister of the Cannongate Church, Edinburgh was sent there because of an injudicious sermon about the commitment of Welch and others to prison. William Rigg of Athernie was imprisoned there in 1624 for failing to kneel at Communion.

There were also the ladies of the Covenant who were held in Edinburgh including Mrs. Janet Hamilton (Lady Gordon of Earlstoun) in 1687. Lady Caldwel and three daughters were detained in Glasgow Tolbooth for three years and her daughter Jean, for six months, in 1683. Lady Campbell of Auchinbreck and Lady Cavers were incarcerated in the Tolbooth of Stirling. Neither were the ladies excluded from the dreadful Dunnottar which included Mrs. Gardiner, widow of the Rev. J. Gardiner; Janet Fimerton, Janet Linton, and the elderly Euphan Thriepland who was tortured with lighted matches between the fingers because she dared to denounce the atrocities that were being committed.

Edinburgh had several places of detention, primarily the castle and the tolbooth and, at the lower end of town (previously a separate parish), was the Cannongate Tolbooth in which many Covenanters resided (and escaped from, as well). Edinburgh Tolbooth is remembered in Scott's "Heart of Midlothian" and its former location is marked today by a heart design incorporated in the pavement outside St. Giles cathedral. The building had several functions as Parliament Hall, a Court of Justice, and City Council Chambers but it is remembered most for its two prisons: a felons prison at the east end and a debtors prison at the west end. An early visitor was the Rev. Nicoll Dalgleish of the West Kirk in 1584 for praying for banished compatriots. David Calderwood was sent there in 1617, as were John Hamilton and John Dickson. William Carstares spent most of 1675-1679 in the tolbooth. The castle was used in 1605 for the nineteen ministers who had been at the Aberdeen Assembly: John Davidson was there in 1599; John Murray, minister of Leith, in 1608; and Robert Bruce in 1621. John Semple, who was arrested with James Guthrie in 1660, spent ten months locked up in Edinburgh Castle where Alexander Moncrieff and Robert Traill joined them for their subscription to the "Paper of 23 August 1660."

Imprisonment could also be very lengthy, and detention pending trial was sometimes prolonged as a means of keeping the prisoner out of circulation and thus from preaching. This happened to some Irish Presbyterian ministers who were incarcerated for six years for simply being Presbyterians. James Mitchell was over two years being prosecuted and made no less than six appearances before the Privy Council, he was subjected to torture, and endured a spell in the Bass before he was finally sentenced and executed. Robert Garnock was held for nearly three years in various prisons before sentencing. But the worst case might be that of Robert Ker of Kersland who was held in Edinburgh Castle for three months, then removed to Dumbarton Castle for a year and a half. He was then transferred to Aberdeen for three months in the depths of winter before being sent to Stirling Castle for some years. and then a second time to Dumbarton. In all, he spent eight years shuttling round the prisons before he was finally banished from Scotland.

Indemnity. See also: Conventicles.

An indemnity arrangement arose from the increasingly tough legislation against conventicles and the preachers attending them. There had already been legislation in December 1665 against holding of conventicles. In the summer of 1670, Parliament passed another act aimed at completely suppressing all religious meetings other than in parish churches. It became law that people should inform on one another, while death and confiscation of property were penalties for preaching at conventicles. Rewards were offered for the conventicle preachers while soldiers and their assistants were indemnified against prosecution if the preacher died in the attempt at capture.

An Act of Indemnity was passed on 9 September 1662 which listed some nine hundred persons liable to fines. The method meant that a military party would arrive in a district and demand not only the outstanding fine but three shillings a day for every trooper to be quartered until the fine, (and the extras) was paid. Seizure of goods was authorised and no escape from the action as the penalty was on whoever the occupier was at the time. No one was too poor to pay with beatings, torture and imprisonment the common methods of collection. For not attending at Church the fine was twenty shillings which was easily enforced by the incumbent having to make a roll call and advising the military of the names. Insult was added to injury when the maltreated were forced into signing a certificate that "the captain had used them civilly and discreetly."[156] A royal proclamation on 17 September 1664 called in all outstanding fines, with further stringent action taken to enforce payment and seizure of property.

Indulgences.

Throughout the Reformation, but especially in the second half of the seventeenth century, there were very many instances of backsliding, retrenchment, and changes of stance and direction brought about both by external circumstances and the individual's conscience. To the staunchest Presbyterians anything that was not Covenanted was sin and reprehensible. At this extreme the simple

---

[156] Hewison, *Covenanters*, Vol. 2, p. 176.

pleasures of children playing on the Sabbath, even cleaning out the fireplace or taking exercise at football or archery, were sinful. The core issues were:

> The obligations on the Church and people of Scotland created by the National Covenant of 1638 and the Solemn League and Covenant of 1643. These were Covenants with God and religious bonds. They could not be broken without the sin of perjury.
>
> Jesus Christ alone was head of the church and his position could not be usurped or compromised in any way. The claim by Charles II to supremacy was regarded as blasphemous and the Indulgences unlawful since they stemmed from the king's exercise of his claim.
>
> The right to have Christian civil government which emphasised free parliaments representing the people.

In reality only the Cameronians or Society People could call themselves Covenanters. Declining the Covenants, accepting Indulgences, or adopting prelatic ways disqualified all others from being true Covenanters. The singular difference for the "faithful remanant" was that they gave a practical testimony to these truths and not merely a theoretical meaning. Thus, in the view of the Covenanters, any and all acceptance of an indulgence was backsliding and a sin.

When persecution did not stop the conventicles or crush the spirit of the people, the indulgence became the device for dividing and seducing the people and their ministers into abandoning fundamental principles for a short term advantage. The offer and acceptance of indulgences more than probably any other issue, was at the very heart of the searching of consciences and actual schism in the Presbyterian Church which had already been rent by the Engagement and the Protester/Resolutioner controversies in earlier years.

The indulgences were offers by the king to allow ejected ministers to resume preaching in their parishes but on certain conditions. On the face of it they were a middle way, a compromise that played around the edges of the demand by the strict Presbyterians for adherence to the Covenants. Ironically the bishops themselves were suspicious because they had not been consulted and saw the Kings independent action to be a warning to them. If he could so easily ignore consultation he could just as easily dispose of them and Episcopacy. Archbishop Burnet said of them: "If an Indulgence be allowed to any person upon any consideration whatsoever, our labour will be lost, and this poor church undone."[157]

But equally the seven Indulgences (three under King Charles II and four under James VI/II) were a gradual racking up of the pressure and further isolation of the die-hard Covenanters.

It should be remembered that there were inordinate pressures on the ministers, not just from issues of conscience and Scripture, but their worldly concerns for house, home, wife and children. The stipend was a mere pittance and ejection made them into wanderers with friends forbidden to give assistance. To give them a cup of water or a piece of bread was illegal; their families were homeless wanderers, shoeless, clad in rags possibly starving and freezing on the cold wet moors. It took a special kind of person, probably supported by his wife, to continue as an outcast turning over and over in their mind: "Is Christ or King Charles Lord of my conscience?"

The First Indulgence was on 15 July 1669 when a small group of ministers were offered the right to return to their original parishes, or another if theirs was not vacant. In order to claim the stipend of the parish the minister had to be presented by the patron and accept collation from the bishop. If unable to accept these conditions they could nevertheless return to their parish and preach and have use of the manse and any glebe lands. They also had to accept attendance at prelatic synods; not permit people from other parishes to attend their services and must not preach against the doctrine that the king was supreme in ecclesiastical matter. This compromise, by *the King's permission*, started the huge rift that was to develop between the Indulged and the Non Indulged ministers. Forty-three ministers returned to the ministry including Robert Douglas of Edinburgh who was indulged in Pencaitland, George Hutcheson of Edinburgh to Irvine, and William Vilant from Ferry Port on Craig to Cambusnethan.

The Second Indulgence on 3 September 1672 allowed those who accepted it to be placed two at a time, or with an existing Indulged minister, as joint pastors sharing the stipend, in a parish where they

[157] Hewison, *Covenanters*, Vol. 2, p. 364.

were could preach in churches, but forbidden to preach outside its bounds. The indulged ministers could not leave his parish without the licence of his bishop; dues should be paid to and discipline accepted from Presbyteries. Ministers outed since 1661 were ordered to attend the parish churches and be certified by magistrates, disorderly ministers were to be reported and apprehended. The vagabond ministry, conventicling and private preaching were declared illegal. The purpose of the Indulgence was to confine as many ministers as possible to the smallest possible locality and thereby limit their influence. It is thought that about ninety ministers accepted this Indulgence.

The Third Indulgence was proclaimed on 29 June 1679 soon after the battle of Bothwell Brig (where division between the Indulged and Non-Indulged was a principal factor in the defeat of the Covenanters). This Indulgence suspended the laws against house conventicles and ordered an exclusion zone of two miles around Edinburgh, one mile around other towns. But there was no Indulgence for the field conventicles or those persons involved in the late rebellion. It maintained the principal of the Kings supremacy in ecclesiastical matters. About fifteen ministers accepted this Indulgence and took up posts as Crown licensees.

The Indulgences of King James VI/II condemned themselves from the outset by the use of what today we call officialese. The phraseology ran along the lines "by our sovereign authority, prerogative, royal and absolute power, which all our subjects are to observe without reserve." Freedom on these terms amounted to a farce and only reinforced the view that there was a hidden agenda: the restoration of Catholicism.

The First Indulgence of James VII/II was on 12 February 1687 which sought to benefit Roman Catholics. It began by tolerating "moderate" Presbyterians and allowing house conventicles and to hear indulged ministers by those accepting or willing to accept the Indulgence. It further indulged Quakers with licensed meeting houses. Field conventicles were still illegal. It then annulled all laws against Roman Catholics, gave freedom of worship, made them eligible for public office and abolished the Test and sought only an oath recognising the king's total authority, his heirs and successors. It satisfied only the Catholic population who were content to accept a new oath of allegiance to the king. James disclaimed any intention to violate consciences and promised to maintain the existing clergy and advance public officials irrespective of religion.

The Second Indulgence was on 31 March 1687 and permitted omission of the oath and allowed Presbyterian ministers to preach in private houses, which they were doing anyway. This was reported to the king by the Privy Council as indicating submission by all Presbyterian ministers.

The Third Indulgence was on 5 July 1687 and suspended all laws against non-conformity and thereby allowed a resumption of free Presbyterian preaching, although the laws against field conventicles remained in force to be prosecuted with all the vigour of the law because, alleged the government, there was now no need for field conventicles. This was further proclaimed on 5 October 1687, reinforcing the pressure on field conventicles. It is said that the proclamation was a response to a request of 21 July 1687 for Toleration given, it was claimed, by all the Presbyterian ministers. (See Appendix 17.)

But the strict Covenanters continued to reject all the Indulgences and maintained that the right to worship God according to his revealed will could not be tolerated or restricted by an earthly ruler. Moreover the Indulgences stemmed from the claim by the king to supremacy in all matters ecclesiastical and were opposed to divine law and headship of Christ over the Church. The third Indulgence was accepted by a majority of Presbyterian ministers in Scotland and led to the attacks by James Renwick on both the granters of the Toleration or Indulgence and the acceptors of the Toleration.

The Fourth Indulgence was on 15 May 1688 and abolished oaths and religious Tests for public office and proclaimed freedom of religion for all. But it still stemmed from the absolute power and supremacy of the king which continued to leave the strict Covenanters outside the pale. In their judgement, James VII/II was doubly at fault not only claiming the supremacy but was himself a Catholic and thus had no right to the Scottish throne.

John Brown of Wamphray wrote a *History of the Indulgence* while in exile. He, tellingly, observed that the Indulgences were contrived to bear down on conventicles as borne out by the closing sentences of the proclamation:

> And seeing we have by these orders taken away all pretence for conventicles, and provided for the want of such as are

> and will be peaceable, if any shall be found hereafter to preach without authority, or keep conventicles, our express pleasure is, that you proceed with all severity against the preachers and hearers as seditious persons and contemners of our authority.[158]

The division between the Indulged and the Non Indulged is illustrated many times over as the hard core Covenanters decried even contact with the Indulged. It is relevant that as the likes of Richard Cameron and Donald Cargill became more isolated there was a groundswell in support of moderatism and compromise which represented the majority of the Presbyterian church. Such was the attempt by a group of indulged ministers who invited Richard Cameron and John Welwood to a meeting with the intention of deposing them, but the Covenanters declined the authority of the meeting.

John Welwood, John Kid, and, later, Richard Cameron were particular opponents of Indulgences and saw it as a duty to be separated from the Indulged. This strong opposition was reflected in three attempts to depose Cameron by Indulged meetings and contributed to his going to Holland in 1678. Here he joined John Blackadder and John Dickson who were also much against the Indulged. The Bothwell Brig dissensions and the actions of John Welch and the Indulged supporters is the prime example of the schism between the opposing views. The obloquy and scorn cast by the Indulged upon James Renwick was further reflected in no less than fifteen separate searches which were specially made in the space of five months, and a reward of £100 sterling offered for his capture.

Instrument of Government, December 1653.

In England the Rump Parliament clung to power as long as it could and finally gave a date of 3 November 1654 for its dissolution. Fed up with the delays, Cromwell dissolved it by military fiat, marching into the Chamber of the House of Commons and after berating the members, ordered them from the premises. Recognising the need for something to replace it as a means of

[158] Howie, *Worthies*, p. 415-416.

checks and balances against a potential dictatorship, the Army circulated congregations round the country and sought nominations of representatives: 129 from England, 5 for Scotland and 6 for Ireland. This assembly was called the Nominated Parliament; it was also called the Barebones Parliament after a member named Praise-God Barebone, a London leather seller and lay preacher. The members were inexperienced and spent some time discussing wild and impractical reforms although it did manage to pass some 30 bills in its five month life. These included relief of creditors and poor prisoners, while civil marriages by Justices of the Peace were legalised. Mechanisms were also created for probate of wills, and the registration of births marriages and deaths. It became divided, however, especially over religion with Millinarian expectations driven by members of the Army and Fifth Monarchy Men.

Perceived as dangerously radical (although not so with hindsight) the Barebones Parliament or Assembly was overtaken in a *coup d'etat* by Cromwellian supporters. Members supportive of the proposal met early one morning, before the vociferous opposition arrived, and resolved to hand over rule to Cromwell. They agreed the Instrument of Government in December 1653, which was the first written constitution in English history. The main ecclesiastical feature was the extension of toleration to all except Catholics, Episcopalians, and sects such as the Ranters and Quakers.

Executive: Executive power to be held by the Lord Protector (that is, Cromwell) with the assistance of a Council of State. On his death, a new Protector would be elected by the Council. Vacancies on the Council to be filled by the Protector, choosing from nominees suggested by the Council and Parliament. Officers of State were to be approved by Parliament. The executive to control the armed forces and a regular revenue to be provided in order to maintain an army of 30,000. In addition, £200,000 was to be provided for the costs of running the government. Any additional funds would depend on Parliament's approval.

Legislative: Parliament was to be called at least once every three years, and could not be dissolved without its consent. Bills of Parliament could be delayed by the Protector for up to twenty days but thereafter would automatically become law. The voting franchise was limited, reducing the size of the electorate, and was to consist of four hundred members, with Scotland and Ireland having thirty seats each. Achieved by abolishing many small boroughs and giving counties more representation. Catholics were not enfranchised. Those who fought against Parliament were disenfranchised for parliaments. Eligibility of country seats: valuation of land holding worth 40 shillings or more per year, revised to those whose total wealth was calculated at £200 or more.

Religion: Freedom of worship for all with the exception of Catholics, Episcopalians, and sects such as the Ranters and Quakers.

Irish troops. See also: No Quarter.

The use of Irish troops by the royalists in Montrose's campaign of 1644-1645 was part of a plan to lure the Scottish army out of England. The Earl of Antrim promised some ten thousand troops to land in the north of Scotland but only about one thousand actually came under the leadership of Alasdair McColl (McDonald) whose father and brother were held prisoner by Argyll. The *Montgomery Manuscripts* tell us that these troops were, in fact, seasoned soldiers who had been fighting in Flanders. Having experience and discipline on their side, good commanders, and a passionate hatred of the Campbells, their success in the field was almost guaranteed against inexperienced farmers summoned to muster for the Covenanters.

The Irish soldiers were not only seasoned in battle but had developed a unique strategy forced upon them by shortages of gunpowder and shot. They would load their muskets with a single shot and fire it at close range to be certain of hitting an enemy, then reverse the gun and use it as a club. By this means their savage charge broke the front ranks of the enemy and they were able to get among them using the short sword with which they were very adept. They were also very disciplined and known for their regrouping when their line was broken, unlike others who would flee. This practice was used to good effect against cavalry who would be allowed through the line; the Irish then closed the gap behind them and the slaughter began.

The Irish troops have been accused of great cruelty and the slaughter of defenceless women and children. But it should be remembered that the Covenanter armies were themselves urged to give no quarter by their accompanying ministers. Certainly the Irish were especially vindictive in their encounters with the Campbells, such as at Inverlochy on 2 February 1645, where they went in hot pursuit for over nine miles in which some 1,700 of the Campbell men were slaughtered. In all some forty ranking Campbells were killed and twenty-two lowland chieftains released on giving their oath not to bear arms again.

The converse became true after the battle of Philiphaugh on 13 September 1645. This time the royalist forces were massacred with over five hundred of the Irishmen cut to ribbons after they had been offered quarter and had surrendered. There followed a slaughter of the camp followers: boys, cooks, and women. Three hundred Irish women, wives of the soldiers and many of them pregnant, were literally cut up: unborn babies were cut from the womb and cast on the ground with their murdered mothers. The horror of this was compounded by Covenanter ministers who incited all and any retribution on the royalists. John Nevay has been identified as the minister who demanded the slaughter of the three hundred defenders at Dunaverty Castle in May 1647, even though the Irishmen had surrendered. Nevay was also involved in armed resistance at Mauchline Moor in 1648.

Justiciary Commissions, Courts.

The Justiciary Commissions or Circuit Courts were brought into existence by a proclamation of 13 April 1683 to be additional to the common courts with specific remits to pursue dissenters, recusants, and enforce the law. The first courts were ordered to sit at Stirling, Glasgow, Ayr, Dumfries, Jedburgh, and Edinburgh. The first circuit of the court began at Stirling on 5 June 1683 where the judges were: Perth - Justice General; Maitland - Justice Clerk; and Lords Foulis, Forret; Lockhart and Balfour and the Sheriffs; Mackenzie, Lord Advocate prosecuted. To this end they used the Porteous (portable) Rolls and Fugitive Rolls that had been set up and used, especially by Claverhouse, as notebooks for persecution. Hundreds appeared to swear to the Test. Persons failing to appear were arrested and caution demanded pending appearance in Edinburgh. Absentees were denounced and placed on the Fugitive Roll (which for 1683-

1684 was huge) with many also sentenced to death, their guilt having been established from testimony of others.

A further Commission was established on 3 January 1684 to continue with full powers until recalled. The appointees include some names writ large in the annals of the Covenanters of the southwest of Scotland. The appointed officers were the Provost of Glasgow and Baillie of Regality; the Sheriff depute of Lanark Sir James Turner; Lieutenant Colonel Winram for the shires of Lanark and Dunbarton; James Alexander, James Johnston of Westerhall, Thomas Loderdale of Isle, David Graham (brother of Claverhouse), Andrew Bruce of Abbotshall, Captain Strachan, and Cornet William Graham for the shires of Dumfries, Kirkcudbright, and Wigtown. Any three were enough to form a bench of judges.

In February 1684 a similar Commission was appointed for Ayrshire and Renfrewshire with Lord Ross being associated with Turner and Winram, and others, of whom five was a quorum. A special Commission was given to Meldrum for Lanarkshire. On 6 September 1684, following a royal command to "extinguish disaffection," there followed four further circuits to which were appointed Hamilton, Mar, Livingston, Queensberry, Drumlanrig, Balcarres, and Claverhouse with any two to act. They received twenty-eight definite instructions about: Disarming and fining non jurors; licensing horses; sending in unlicensed preachers; punishing conventiclers (and husbands for wives); enrolling fugitives (to the Fugitive Rolls); examining indulged ministers; ferreting out inciters to rebellion; apprehending peddlers without passes; searching letter carriers; interviewing penitent rebels; ordering military action; evicting wives and families of forfeited and fugitive persons who do not clear themselves by oath that they have not conversed with their (fugitive) relatives; rendering an account of quartering and fining; hunting down fugitives; suffering only loyal gentlemen to bear arms; no yeoman to travel three miles without a pass; the offering of the oath of allegiance and banishing men and women refusing to take it; examining anyone about their loyalty. Ships captains were ordered to proffer the oath to all passengers and no traveller was permitted to move between jurisdictions without a magistrate's permit. The long list ended with the command:

> You shall put in execution the power of justiciary to be granted unto you by our privy Council, with all rigour, by

> using fire and sword as is usual in such cases; and we do empower our Privy Council to insert an indemnity to you, or any employed by you, for what shall be done in the execution thereof.[159]

Killing Time – Scotland, 1685. See also: Abjuration Oath; Apologetical Vindication (Renwick 1685); Justiciary Courts; Numbers.

Carslaw, in *The Life and Letters of James Renwick*, emotively describes the Killing Time thus:

> Extirpation! that was now the word of the powers of darkness who ruled the country. The execution of the laws was committed wholly and absolutely to the soldiers. They had no limited instructions: they had powers and express orders to go through the whole country and kill; kill in the house, kill in the field, kill one or many, as they should meet them; kill with full indemnity against consequences, kill at their own discretion, and kill instantly and upon the spot. These times are still named with a shudder, 'The killing times of Scotland.'[160]

Covenanter lore in Scotland is very much bound up with the terrible events of what became known as "The Killing Time." This was the period from the summer of 1684 until the autumn of 1685 when persecution of the Covenanters was at its peak.[161] This period also covered the unexpected death of King Charles II; the accession of his brother, the Catholic James VII (II of England), proclaimed on 10 February 1685; and the ill-fated risings of the 9th Earl of Argyll in Scotland in conjunction with that of the Duke of Monmouth in England.

---

[159] Hewison, *Covenanters*, Vol. 2, p. 435.

[160] Renwick, *Life and Letters*, p. 117.

[161] Two contemporary writers place it otherwise: Patrick Walker (Six Saints of the Covenant) begins it from August 15; Rev. Alexander Shields (A Hind Let Loose) begins it at the date of Charles II's death on 6 February 1685. However, the fact remains that this was a period of hyper activity against the Covenanters with most of the executions taking place.

With the hardening of attitudes towards the Covenanters there was also a long backlog of cases yet to be heard by the courts. In 1684 the Justiciary Courts and circuit courts were set up to enforce policy and attempt to speed up justice. A policy evolved of clearing the prisons, which amongst other actions, meant that there was a much quicker process with immediate sentences of death and a requirement to execute within six hours after sentence for those found guilty. The Circuit Courts set up in September 1684 were given the objective of "extinguishing disaffection" and a long list of some twenty eight issues that were to be addressed. It is difficult to conceive how the government thought that enforcement of Draconian legislation was going to help the people like or love the monarch. It was the rule of terror pure and simple.

The gradual and systematic increase in the persecution of the Covenanters began in 1660 with the Restoration of King Charles II. It was soon clear that he had reneged on his former promises and set about imposing episcopacy on Scotland. In 1662 there was the "outing" of over three hundred ministers from their livings. The policy was aided and abetted by the prelates, especially James Sharp, Archbishop of St. Andrews who made great use of the Court of High Commission to pursue his former colleagues. There was a range of Indulgences which gradually isolated the dissidents, while pressure was put on the landowners to conform by taking the Test, and paying substantial sums of money.

The trigger for the "Killing Time" was the Privy Council's reaction to James Renwick's Apologetical Declaration on 24 October 1684. The Privy Council may well have been afraid of the impending arrival and possible rebellion led by the Earl of Argyll and were seeking to round up troublemakers. Whatever the reasons they framed the loyalty oath known as the "Abjuration Oath." This Oath was the vehicle for authorising on the spot execution, in the presence of two witnesses, of any person who refused to take it.

After Renwick's Declaration and the introduction of the Abjuration Oath there was a period of intense activity against the Renwickites and retaliatory actions. These included the murder of the Curate of Carsphairn on 11 December 1684; a raid on Kirkcudbright jail on December 16 and a skirmish at the Bridge of Dee on December 18 in which eight Covenanters were captured or killed. From about January 1685 the government's action was extended to all Presbyterians, not just Renwick and his followers, and even previously indulged ministers came under attack.

Following the death of Charles II and the accession of his brother James in February 1685, events soon took on the ugly hue of the old Roman Church and the Inquisition. James made no bones about his preferences and declared all-out war on any dissenters and anyone whomsoever contested his stated absolute supremacy of all and everything. During his time as viceroy in Scotland he had gathered a group of place men about him and had infiltrated positions of authority with his supporters. His pawn, William, Duke of Queensberry, was responsible for passing the Acts of persecution in the 1685 Parliament that met in Edinburgh between April 23 and August 22. Such was their tenor that the Earl of Melfort accused Queensberry of exceeding his authority, to which James issued a letter of approbation and exoneration: the acts were the decrees of King James. For the rest of his (thankfully) short reign, James merely used his royal prerogative and issued diktats of the royal will.

The politics of the Killing Time were very complex but the stark intensification of action and execution of Covenanters was crystal clear. Thorbjorn Campbell, in *Standing Witnesses*, gives numbers, between December 1684 and November 1685, of forty-three executions with a total of eighty-nine victims. In the whole period of resistance, from 1661 to 1689, Campbell lists ninety-five persons known to have been executed in Edinburgh; a further 172 were killed in the countryside and over 200 were drowned when the *Crown* was wrecked off the coast of Orkney. A summary in the *Scots Worthies* gives a grand total of about 18,000 people transported and killed between 1660 and 1688. (See Number of Sufferers.)

It is probable that we shall never know the exact numbers but suffice it that very many gained the martyrs crown and are known unto God.

Laud's Liturgy - 1637 (Book of Common Prayer for Scotland).
See also: Canons; Tables.

As early as 1556 John Knox had written to a Mrs. Anne Locke about the English Service Book and deplored the "dregs of Papistry which are left in your great book of England (*viz.*, crossing in baptism, kneeling at the Lords' table, mumbling or singing of the litany, etc.) any one jot of which diabolical inventions will I never counsel any man to use."[162]

The Liturgy or "The Book of Common Prayer and Administration of the Sacraments and other parts of Divine Service for the use of the Church of Scotland" was published at Edinburgh in 1637. This was the sister package which, with the Canons published in 1636, aimed at introducing the high church into Scotland: the semi-Catholic episcopacy so favoured by Archbishop Laud. The Liturgy was drafted by Maxwell, Bishop of Ross and Wedderburn, Bishop of Dunblane before submission to Archbishop Laud, whose popish embellishments caused the furore that followed its implementation.

The Canons had decreed that opposition to the Liturgy, because it was contrary to the Scriptures, would be grounds for excommunication, and failure to use the Liturgy would be punished by deponement. There had been strong criticism of the Canons but the issues came to head with the Liturgy which was widely declared to be "popish." Amongst other things, the procedures offended the people by calling the table the "altar" and the minister standing with his back to the congregation when consecrating the communion elements. The calendar of events included commemorative dates of mediaeval saints which had long been cast out by the Presbyterians. Coming on top of the Articles of Perth in 1618, and the Canons in 1636, the resentment of the ministers and people to the Liturgy reached the boiling point.

On 13 June 1637, the Privy Council ordered ministers to obtain two copies of the Liturgy within fifteen days on pain of rebellion, but in their haste to make the order the Council omitted to say that the Liturgy must be used. Thus the scene was set for the historic event in St. Giles Cathedral on 23 July 1637 when a Scotswoman, Jenny Geddes, a booth holder alongside the Kirk and wife of a banished merchant, John Mein, is said to have thrown her small stool at Dean Hannay with the words: "Villain, dost thou say mass at my lug." The stool, or possibly one very similar to that thrown, is in the Museum of Scotland. A brass plate, paid for by Dr. R. H. Gunning of Rio de Janeiro, in the floor of the church indicates from where the stool was thrown:

---

[162] Howie, *Worthies*, p. 52.

Left: The Nithsdale Cross, Dalgarnock, Old Churchyard. Right: Fifty-seven people from Nithsdale suffered for their faith. Photos courtesy of A. Pittendreigh.

> Constant oral tradition affirms that near this spot a brave Scotch woman Janet Geddes on the 23 July 1637 struck the first blow in the great struggle for freedom of conscience which after a conflict of half a century ended in the establishment of civil and religious liberty.[163]

Jenny Geddes' stool, Museum of Scotland. Photo by the author.

[163] Johnston, *Treasury*, pp. 75-76.

Memorial plate, St. Giles Cathedral, Edinburgh. Photo by the author.

A plague on a pillar near the pulpit commemorates Dean Hannay:

> To James Hannay, D.D. Dean of the Cathedral, 1634-39. He was the first and the last who read the Service Book in this church. This memorial is erected in happier times by his descendants.[164]

John Stuart Blackie (1809-1895), the eminent Glaswegian scholar, wrote a short poem of the event:

The Song of Mrs. Jenny Geddes

Twas the 23rd of July in the 1637
On Sabbath morn from high St. Giles.
The solemn peal was given:
King Charles had sworn that Scottish men
Should pray by printed rule.
He had sent a book, but never dreamt
Of danger from a stool.

As when a mountain cat
Springs upon a rabbit small,
So Jenny on the Dean springs
With gush of holy gall:

---

[164] Johnston, *Treasury*, pp. 75-76.

'Wilt thou say the Mass at my lug,
Thou Popish puling fool?
'No! No!' she said, and at his head
She flung the four legged stool.

And thus was done a mighty deed,
By Jenny's valiant hand;
Black Prelacy and Popery,
She drave from Scottish land.
King Charles, he was a shuffling knave,
Priest Laud, a pedant fool,
But Jenny was a woman wise,
Who beat them with a stool.[165]

Alexander Henderson, who had succeeded to Melville's mantle, carefully digested the new Liturgy and made a clear statement to the Privy Council explaining that the Book of Common Prayer had not been authorised by the General Assembly and Parliament, that the church was inherently free, that the ceremonies were divisive and Romish, and the people were unwilling to accept it. The Privy Council, possibly in an act of self preservation, then decided, on 25 August 1637, that it was not compulsory to use the Liturgy. But the king, on September 10, no doubt influenced by Archbishop Laud, angrily directed the Liturgy's use and reprimanded the Privy Council for having suspended it. There then followed a petition to the Privy Council, on September 20, who responded on 17 October 1637 with three proclamations ordering strangers from the city, the Council and Court to remove from Edinburgh, and a condemnation of a publication by George Gillespie called *Dispute against the English Popish Ceremonies*.

The next day, protestations against the Service Book were made to the Lord Chancellor by the "men, women, children and servants of Edinburgh" and also by "the Noblemen, gentrie, ministers, burgesses and commons."[166] Thirty-eight noblemen and hundreds of ministers and gentlemen from all over Scotland (except Aberdeen) subscribed to the petition. At one stage, the ladies of Edinburgh seized Sydserf, Bishop of Galloway, as he was making

---

[165] *Ibid.*, p. 565.
[166] Hewison, *Covenanters*, Vol. 1, p. 256.

his way to the Law Courts and proceeded to disrobe him to see if he was carrying a Romish cross; he was saved the ultimate ignominy of nakedness by arrival of some colleagues who were able to intervene. The protest by the people cleverly used the law whereby their accusation against the prelates was a formal Protest that required a hearing by the courts. They did however, compromise and agree to withdraw from the city leaving behind a committee or commissioners to look after their interests. Next came the setting up of the representative "Tables" and the co-ordinated action by the people.

The scene was now set for a head-on clash with the Privy Council and the King who declared on 19 February 1638 at Stirling, that the Canons and Liturgy were by his Order. He also declared that protests and meetings against them were rebellion and that petitioners were banned from any place where the Privy Council was in session, on penalty of treason. The immediate response was the reading of a formal Protestation at the same Cross of Stirling, probably by Archibald Johnston, and in the presence of Lords Lindsay and Home who had ridden hard some forty miles by night from Edinburgh to be there in time. The King's Proclamation was in effect his acceptance of the allegations of misgovernment and tantamount to a declaration of war. A similar Protestation was read in Edinburgh on February 22 when the Heralds were forced to remain at the Cross and listen; that day, Alexander Henderson and Archibald Johnston were enjoined to draw up a Covenant.

The National Covenant was declared, read, and subscribed on 28 February 1638 at Greyfriars Kirk. The document was partly drafted by Alexander Henderson who had been previously put to the horn by the Archbishop of St. Andrews for refusing to buy and use the Liturgy.

Laudian Policies.

Named after Archbishop William Laud, they reflect his Arminian views and ambitions for the Church of England, which were subjoined by the pursuit of uniformity in the whole of Britain. Laud referred to the "Beauty of Holiness"[167] but the changes were

---

[167] This is a reference to Psalm 96:4. Laud greatly favoured the pomp and ceremony of the church, hence the allegations of popery.

seen both in England as early as 1628, and later in Scotland, as an attempt to reverse the Reformation and to threaten social and political power of the nobility and the gentry. Broadly, his policies were:

Preference for the doctrine of free will, i.e. that God's salvation was open to all and could be won by good works on earth. This was in direct contrast to Calvinism and its belief in predestination.

The emphasis of church services should be towards the sacraments and ceremony, and away from preaching and sermons. It favoured the wearing of elaborate vestments, the use of images and the restoration of stained glass windows in churches.

Altars should be re-sited in a central place in churches at the east end, not in the nave. This meant some re arrangement of family pews which caused great offence.

The clergy to play a greater role in lay affairs and the power for church courts to intervene (interfere) in secular affairs.

Although accused of being a papist, Laud came to prominence with the support of the influential Buckingham family and was a prominent opponent of the increasing Catholic presence at the Court. His opponents especially resented his drive to secure the benefices of the church (much of which were impropriated by the nobility) for the clergy and insistence that ministers be properly funded; this included proper stipends for appointments made under patronage. Other issues such as improving the quality and status of the clergy, ministers and bishops, were resented by the nobility and genteel landowners who regarded them as upstarts.

Legal devices. See also: Abuse of Power.

The range of legal devices used by the government to secure its objectives during the persecution of the Presbyterian dissenters is really quite staggering. It has to be conceded, however, that the sometimes gross actions were usually within the law as it then stood. The reality was that it was bad law that originated in the policies of a despotic king. That said, we need to look at the gradual racking up of pressures on the increasingly divided and isolated Covenanters using a wide range of legal devices.

At the beginning of the Reformation it was a matter of Protestantism against Catholicism. In fact the change to a Protestant and Presbyterian nation came about with remarkable ease because the majority of people wanted it, and with far less bloodshed than the imposition of Episcopacy caused. There is a fine logic to the subsequent policies of the Stuart kings which were aimed at delivering Episcopacy in a Protestant Church of Scotland. It was first necessary to break the structure of the Kirk and the authority and management by the General Assembly. This was achieved by largely bloodless means using "kingcraft" (lying, cheating, packing Parliament and Assemblies with royalist supporters, bribery, threats, and similar actions) which deferred indefinitely the meetings of the General Assembly, such as Aberdeen; implemented the Constant Moderators; and enabled installation of the bishops.

Having broken the structure, the next move was to consolidate procedures within the church. The Canons and Liturgy changes were made in an arbitrary way, which was a big mistake as they were visible, and for the first time impacted the common people. As a consequence resistance to change in the church became pandemic. The Solemn League and Covenant injected a new, wider dimension into the debates when the Presbyterians provided military assistance and aspired to implement their faith in England and Ireland. The politics now became international and a matter of church *and* state, in which the Presbyterians were novices.

After the Restoration and the ejection of over three hundred ministers, the Crown's objectives remained the same. The core resistance was identified and the policies became classic divide and rule: increase the pressures on dissenters and encourage the waverers to cross to the Crown's side. This gave rise to the use of many legal devices including exclusion and deposition from positions of trust; the use of Bonds and Oaths of varying types that enforced the alleged rights of the king, and nibbled away at the dissenters' resolve; fiscal penalties for non-compliance; open arrest and restriction of movement (warding); declaration as a rebel and horning; seizure of property, lands, goods, and gear; prohibition of assisting or having contact with rebels in any way (reset and intercommuning); offering relatively large rewards; the use of the military to enforce collection of fines; using the quartering of troops on the people to enforce payment; and pursuit of rebels, including conventiclers. The exercise of the Royal Prerogative and making Indulgences picked off some waverers among the ministers of the church and also created schism within the Covenanters. Having whittled down the opposition by use of the law, the final tactic was to move in with overwhelming force and crush the remnant.

Inevitably, there were arbitrary actions and those which were simply unjustified and illegal. The use of the Royal Prerogative to set up a Court of High Commission allowed the prelates to harass nonconformists in respect of widely-drawn ecclesiastical laws. Evidence from these interrogations was frequently used to support a civil charge, including treason. The Privy Council and the Secret Committees that were set up sought to extirpate nonconformity under the guise of law. But the commissions issued to the likes of Claverhouse and Drummond sought nothing less than total conformity even if it meant annihilating the people. The Council meanwhile enjoyed the authority to torture prisoners using the boot and the thumbkins. To the minions of the government fell the job of enforcing the law using whatever means was appropriate. This disintegrated into a rule of terror, harassment, extortion, and plain murder.

Long Parliament - and Rump. See also: Pride's Purge.

The Long Parliament in England is so called because it first met 3 November 1640 and was responsible for carrying on the English Civil War. Called by King Charles I to finance the payment of the Scots soldiers at the end of the Second Bishops' War, parliament grasped the opportunity to break Charles I's hold on them. They passed a Triennial Act in February 1641 which ensured that a Parliament would be called every three years, and in May 1641 a revolutionary act which forbade its dismissal without Parliament's own consent. Charles was naturally upset at what he regarded as intrusion on his royal prerogative but that was the price of the huge loans that he needed to buy off the Scots. The Long Parliament was also responsible for the policy that led to the war, the appointment and dismissal of generals, and the execution of King Charles I in 1649.

In 1649, the Presbyterian and remaining royalist Members of the Long Parliament were expelled in Pride's Purge when the dispute between the Independents of the army and the Presbyterian majority in the Parliament came to a head. The remainder of Members, numbering about 154 and called the "Rump," continued to sit and passed an arbitrary Act that set up the High Court of Justice to try King Charles I. The king was tried on January 21, sentenced to death on January 26 and executed in Whitehall on 30 January 1649. Scotland, annoyed that a Scottish King had been executed by the English, declared his son Charles II to be his heir.

The Rump continued until Cromwell turned them out in April 1653 and crossed the line to become a dictator. The Protectorate of Cromwell became the model for a future parliament that recognised the rights of the people, their elected representatives, and the end of absolute monarchy. The Rump was unrepresentative and highly unpopular as it maintained high taxes to pay for the army and navy. It had a Puritan majority and closed the theatres and other entertainment's to the annoyance of the people. It also introduced the Court of High Commission because it felt that normal juries would not convict. The surviving Members of Parliament were recalled in May 1659 and sat until they were finally dissolved on 16 March 1660. The Acts of the Long Parliament after 1642 were unconstitutional and are not on the Statute Book.

Lords of the Articles.

The Committee of the Articles first took form in 1367 under King David when a large number of burgesses assembled at Scone and it was resolved to delegate authority to a Committee of twelve, drawn from the six prominent burghs. Similar circumstances also created the Committee for Causes, which later became the Court of Session or Supreme Court of Justice. The Privy Council retained an interest, especially in matters of public order and riot. The King retained the right to appoint the Judges and was therefore able to exert influence when it suited him.

The Scottish Parliament during the sixteenth century had a majority of nobles who were largely driven by self interest. This posed a potential threat to the Crown and James VI sought to protect his interests by encouraging support from elsewhere. The lawyers and the church he knew were traditionally loyal and the burghers simply wanted peace in order to trade. The latter he encouraged by the Convention of Royal Burghs which met regularly under his patronage. In 1587 the king sought to bring a better balance in Parliament with greater representation of the barons, who were the smaller land owners. The barons were more interested in the security of their tenure of Crown and church lands and had little in common with the nobles. The Privy Council at this time was the focus for policy matters and was at one time representative of the Three Estates: Lords Temporal, Lords Spiritual, and the Commons (nobles, clergy, and townsmen).

When James VI became King of England in 1603 he was determined that the Privy Council was to be his puppet and not a powerful bureaucracy in his absence. Although the Privy Council was filled with the king's nominees he nevertheless developed the Committee or Lords of the Articles. This was an inner circle of loyal supporters with a built in majority for the king, through which were imposed his policies. The Committee consisted of an equal number, normally eight, of each Estate with Officers of State nominated by the king. The bishops chose eight nobles, the nobles chose eight bishops, and they jointly chose another eight from the barons and burgesses. Under Charles I, the Officers of State were eight of his nominees. The Committee of Lords of the Articles had absolute power and were the real rulers of Scotland, their bills had to either be accepted by Parliament or rejected; there was no debate on the content of a bill. The normal Estates or Parliament would adjourn when they were in session and reassemble to ratify its proposals. The system continued until it was abolished in 1689.

Lords of the Congregation. See also: Appendix 4; Covenants.

The Lords of the Congregation took shape as a consequence of the lairds of the Mearns "banding" together to maintain the true preaching of the Evangel during John Knox's visit from September 1555 to July 1556. Converts were found among the nobility including Lord James Stuart (half-brother of Mary Stuart, later the Earl of Moray and Regent); Archibald Campbell, 4th Earl of Argyll; James Douglas, 4th Earl of Morton; the Earl of Glencairn; and Patrick Lindsay, Lord Lindsay of the Byres, Erskine of Dun, and Maitland of Lethington. In December 1557 the first Covenant was signed; it was a "band" pledging to establish and maintain the true word of God and to support His ministers. The "Congregation of Jesus Christ," of which they were the "Lords of the Congregation," stood in open opposition to the Catholic Church and began to press for change with demands to adopt the Prayer Book of Edward VI, the appointment of lay preachers in the absence of sufficient ministers, and the election of a Court of Elders. The first Reformed church was established in Dundee.

Demands for a reform of religion were placed before Mary of Guise, the French Catholic Regent, but she declined to put the petition before the Estates. The Congregation therefore presented a Protestation to Parliament direct and declared an intention to follow their own consciences and to defend themselves if attacked. This open defiance coincided with the death of Mary Tudor and the accession of the Protestant Queen Elizabeth I of England, which raised hopes of English support. But the accession of Elizabeth in England led to Mary of Guise temporarily reversing her earlier toleration of Protestants.

In April 1559, Mary of Guise took a firmer stand and ordered that the preachers were to cease to preach or leave the country. The preachers were then summoned to appear at Stirling on 10 May 1559 but were supported by the Lords of the Congregation who assembled at Perth to accompany the ministers to confront the Regent. Seeing the opposition ranged against her, Mary of Guise agreed to postpone any sentence but on the appointed day she declared the preachers as outlaws in their absence and marched her French troops on Perth. A consequence of this action, and the Queen Regent's broken promise to vacate the city, was the final straw for Lord James Stuart and the Earl of Argyll who openly sided with the Congregation and became prominent members of it.

On June 25, John Knox delivered a strong sermon against popery at Perth and was followed in the church by a priest starting to say Mass at an altar when a boy threw a stone at him. The priest cuffed the boy round the head which prompted the congregation to riot. The monasteries of the Black, Grey, and Cathusian Friars were pillaged and gutted, and a course of confrontation with the sword set in motion. By the end of June the Congregation were in charge in Edinburgh and Mary of Guise had retreated to Dunbar. But French troops overcame the Congregation who, on promises of religious freedom withdrew to Stirling. Mary of Guise, not noted for keeping her promises, then brought in a thousand French troops and fortified Leith, contrary to the truce. The Congregation called out its militia in October but were overcome by the French who had been reinforced in the meantime. Pleas to Queen Elizabeth finally bore fruit and on 27 February 1560 the Duke of Norfolk and the Congregation signed an agreement at Berwick which brought Scotland and its Protestant religion under English protection. A month later an English fleet was in Leith harbour and Mary of Guise was sheltering in Edinburgh Castle, where she died on June 10 after a painful illness.

The Estates met in August and asked Knox and his committee to produce a Declaration of Faith, which was done in four days. On 24 August 1560 the Estates proclaimed three Acts which (1) abolished the Pope's authority; (2) annulled previous Acts contrary to the new Creed; and (3) forbade saying, hearing, or being present at the Mass. Thus in the space of five almost bloodless years the most important event in Scottish history had occurred with the establishment of a Protestant state; and Catholicism and French influence in the country removed. But progress of the Reformation received a check in August 1561 with the return of Mary, Queen of Scots, newly widow of King Francis II of France. Mary brought back her own Catholicism and the Mass which was to remain an issue at least until James VI succeeded her in 1567, when a new issue of episcopacy would replace it.

Malignants.

Malignant was the label variously given to persons who were not Presbyterian and/or true believers and supporters of the Covenants. The term was also used to describe the opposing party (whoever they were) as well as in a very narrow context in some of the internal disputes. In the debate between the Protesters and the Resolutioners the latter were called malignants because they were not adhering to the Covenants. John Nevay is one minister who spoke up about the issue accusing the malignants of "covenant-breaking and land defiling sin."[168] King Charles II is referred to as the "head of malignants."[169] In 1648, the Marquis of Argyll led the Covenanters and the government faction, the malignants were headed by the Duke of Hamilton. Even narrower was the application of the label to anyone who was not a supporter of the

---

[168] Howie, *Worthies*, p. 365.
[169] *Ibid.*

Covenants and Richard Cameron. When Donald Cargill referred to the king as a woeful sight and that his name would stink, we are told that "this did extremely enrage the malignant party against him."[170]

Martial Law, 11 December 1677. See also: Abuse of Power; Highland Host.

The declaration of martial law in December 1677 was "for the protection of the Crown and the established Church."[171] The royal decree authorised a muster of English troops along the border with England and along the northern shores of Ireland (Ulster), a gathering of the Highlanders at Stirling, the call up of the militia, and disarmament of dissenters. All power was transferred to a committee consisting of the Earls of Atholl, Mar, Glencairn, Murray, Linlithgow, Perth, Wigtown, Strathmore, Airlie, Cathness and Ross; any five of whom made a quorum. They were ordered to meet in Glasgow on 26 January 1677.

The decree was the almost inevitable product of Lauderdale's incessant pursuit of law-breakers and his policy of enforcement by rope and gun. There was among the hierarchy of officials hysteria about lawlessness generally with many reports of burglary and assault and resistance, sometimes armed, to enforcement of the Draconian laws. The net was now of the smallest mesh and just about anybody with any inclination to Presbyterianism or other nonconformist practice was ensnared. It is noteworthy that those who could afford it were moving away from the Lowlands and gravitating towards London where they might have some influence in the Court. Lauderdale issued a proclamation on 3 January 1678 that prohibited persons between sixteen and sixty from leaving the kingdom without a licence on pain of treason.

It is highly probable there was also an element of greed in the pursuits since rewards and shares in fines were variously available. Some saw the decree as a charter for planting the Lowlands of Scotland by the Highlanders and for freebooters to rape the land. The prelates also tried to get in on the act by making further recommendations to impose their powers on the populace. The Highlanders saw the golden opportunity for booty and Lauderdale

---

[170] *Ibid.*, p. 441.

[171] Hewison, *Covenanters*, Vol. 2, p. 266.

and his supporters the chance to acquire forfeited lands and estates. Captain John Graham of Claverhouse resigned his commission in the Dutch army in order to hurry home and get his snout in the trough.

Increasing pressure was brought on the nobility to muster when required and to get compliance to the required bond for good behaviour. Rothes, for example, got the heritors of Fife to sign a bond to keep the peace which Lauderdale returned as being insufficient, and included a draft that made them refrain from intercourse with nonconformists and to apprehend them. Lauderdale refused to see a deputation of heritors from Ayrshire because he wanted not less than a fully subscribed bond. Hamilton, Blantyre and Carmichael brought 2,900 heritors to heel in Lanarkshire (coercing the last nineteen by military force). Queensberry similarly had subdued Dumfriesshire save for a handful of minor nonentities. But by May he was reporting that conventicles were never so numerous as the people objected to the Black Bond, as it was called.

Lauderdale's response to the many minor lords and gentlemen who had stood back and done little to help the nobles enforce the law was to make them comply and enter bonds. The ancient writ of lawburrows was also implemented which ordered a person to refrain from violence against another (the state in this case). People who refused the Black Bond were allowed to give a pledge for the good behaviour of themselves and all their dependants (including servants) to comply with the ecclesiastical laws on pain of a fine equal to two years' rent. Many of the great landlords, the nobility, refused to yield and were declared traitors, including Cassillis, Loudon, Crawford, Balmerino, Melville, Newark, Callendar, Kilsyth, Roxburgh, Cochrane, Cathcart, Bargany, Cessnock, Kilbirnie, and Montgomery. When these and other lords sought the ear of the king they declined to put their complaints in writing but Lauderdale, meanwhile, called a hasty meeting of Parliament in their absence, and was given a vote of confidence thus outwitting his critics. In May he issued a royal warrant for the prosecution of murmurers against the persons in authority!

Claverhouse was a hard taskmaster and, if we believe everything said of him, he was a ruthless soldier. One of the breed conditioned by serving abroad and accustomed to doing whatever their superior officer instructed without conscience or concern for the results.

Certainly he soon developed new tactics for pursuing the dissenters of the south west of Scotland from the Mull of Galloway to the Pentland Hills. He victualled his troopers simply by robbing the peasantry, soldiers were to pay for supplies but refusers of demands were to fined and imprisoned; soldiers seizing without lawful authority could be sued in the civil court, a lengthy, expensive and tedious process. Tactics included rapid marches through peaceful vales and sending flying squadrons about keeping the population uncertain and in dread that they might be next on the list. He then developed his rough riders. These were a band of about one hundred riders equipped with horses seized from local people, and paid sixpence a day. These were good horsemen who could pursue rebels into the moss and moors which otherwise prevented pursuit by inexperienced riders. He seized the lairds who said their spouses encouraged the preachers; and ordered the lairds to assemble the parishioners into a specified church so that he could explain the royal clemency and give them a last chance to submit. In one instance, in New Glenluce, several people who had not gone to church regularly were held in Stranraer Castle for twelve weeks before removal to Edinburgh for trial. They were tied in pairs on bareback horses for the journey and on the way the prisoners were constrained to enter into bonds for 1,000 merks and released. These were but a few of the tricks used, let alone the wanton pillage of property and assaults on women and children by his troopers. Claverhouse soon gained rewards; in December 1682 he was made colonel of a new regiment—the Horse in Scotland—which later became His Majesty's Own Regiment. In May 1683, Claverhouse was made a Privy Councillor and soon became an assiduous attendee at meetings where he had a major input to legislation that involved military issues. Hewison, in *The Covenanters*, records that he attended thirty-three times in 1683, fifty-nine times in 1684, and thirty-eight times in 1685. Clearly, he was cognisant of the policy and its prosecution throughout the Killing Times.

Among the other ranks, the troopers doing the enforcement work, brutality was a common trait, even a necessity. They were effectively given free rein and there was no redress unless possessed of clear and supported evidence. There were some successes but generally troopers were given to brutalising and bullying children and women (such as the Nisbet boys who were set up to be shot) who were beaten and kicked to try and make them divulge hiding places. A fifteen-year-old in New Monkland was interviewed by Archibald Inglis and badly beaten and burnt at a fire by his troopers. Another sixteen-year-old, William Hannah of Dumfries, was beaten by soldiers and, although ill with fever, dragged to Edinburgh, subjected to torture with the thumbscrews, robbed, and sold as a slave to Barbados. He returned from the West Indies and became a minister at Scarborough.

Mass attacked.

The celebration of the Mass was an anathema to Knox, Melville, and Protestants in general because it represented papacy in a very open and demonstrative way. The Presbyterians were in favour of simplicity and were greatly opposed to the pomp and ceremony and the worship of graven images. At one level therefore it was the appearance that prompted popular reaction and the sacking of the monasteries and Catholic churches in 1559. But underpinning this was the theological issue of transubstantiation. The Catholic church believed that the elements of the Communion, the bread and wine, were changed into the body and blood of Jesus at Consecration. The Calvin based theology held by Knox believed that the resurrected and glorified Body of Christ is in Heaven. Therefore, the "real presence" in the Lord's Supper is the spiritual presence of Christ by the Holy Spirit, who is now the representative on earth of the Father and the Son.

Mercat Cross.

The Mercat or market cross was a common feature in all towns being the focus for public gatherings and often the site of the market where visiting merchants would display their wares. The Mercat Cross in Edinburgh had a special significance because it was here that the Herald would summon the people by trumpet and beat of the drum to hear the Acts of Parliament and other orders of the Privy Council proclaimed.

The Herald would also sound from the Mercat Cross the summons for miscreants to appear before the Courts and where three blasts of the horn (horning) declared a person a rebel. Archibald Johnston, later Lord Warriston, was involved in several attempts in 1638 to have the Covenanters requests for tolerance proclaimed by the Herald. Perversely Johnston was more successful in 1660 when he was publicly summoned by sound of the trumpet to surrender to the King. When he did not do so he was again declared forfeit in life and property by the Herald at the Edinburgh Cross.

The Mercat Cross in Edinburgh was more than a physical location but a one storey building with a castellated wall on top to add dignity (and possibly provide protection) to the Herald while at work. It would have been a colourful sight no doubt and a popular gathering place for the public. There have been five locations for the Mercat Cross in Edinburgh over the years, but today it adjoins St. Giles Cathedral where it was reconstructed in 1885.

Mercat Cross, Edinburgh. Photo by the author.

Another famous Mercat cross is that at Sanquhar which has been the setting for many famous declarations. In particular it had affixed to it the Declaration of 22 June 1680 by Richard Cameron and his group that openly stated their armed opposition to the government, a declaration of war, in effect. Important public declarations by the Covenanters were also made at Hamilton on 13 June 1679; Rutherglen, 29 May 1679; Lanark, 12 January 1682.

James Renwick's Apologetical Declaration of 8 November 1684 which was widely posted at Mercat crosses in the south west of Scotland.

Military service.

Military service was a popular employment for many young Scots over the centuries and an alternative to which many turned when life was hard either by way of employment or famine. The "galloglass" tended to be the Highlanders who served in Ireland and did much to defend Gaelic Ireland against the Anglo-Norman invasions. Scots served with considerable success in the armies of France and England from about the twelfth century. The Lowlands were also the recruiting grounds for the various armies of Europe where Holland, Spain, Denmark, Poland, Sweden, Germany, and Russia all needed troops during the seventeenth century. During the Thirty Years War it is estimated that about 8,000 Scots were involved at any one time. A total of about 20,000 Scots fought for Sweden and the Protestant cause in that war. Few common soldiers returned to Scotland; survivors either moved on to the next battle where there was pay and pillage or, as in Sweden, settled on land given them by a grateful foreign king and quickly integrated with the local people. However, there were some regular soldiers, especially officers, who returned to Scotland to serve both a royal master and in the Covenanter armies.

The idea of a chaplain accompanying a regiment is not unusual but for the Presbyterian ministers it was a duty they took upon themselves and some were not averse to literally joining the fight. We have only to look at the various battles and skirmishes of Rullion Green, Drumclog, Bothwell Brig; Mauchline Muir, and Ayrs Moss to learn of ministers actively using their swords. At Rullion Green there were thirty-two Irish ministers in the throng. John Crookshank and Andrew McCormick died. Richard Cameron was slain and David Hackston was taken at Airsmoss. Donald Cargill was severely wounded at Bothwell Brig and was miraculously allowed to escape when he admitted he was a minister named Cargill.

Before the Restoration of Charles II in 1660, most ministers served with the army for a period and had the important role of exhorting the troops in support of the Covenant. There were those who served in the army for experience's sake such as George Buchanan who joined with French militia and went on an unsuccessful sortie against the English. James Durham was another who served during the Bishops' Wars, but as a captain, not then being ordained. He was overheard praying with his soldiers by David Dickson who was very taken by the young man and after the prayer Dickson urged Durham to become a minister, which he did. A different volunteer for military experience was the young John Nisbet who went abroad (as many adventurous young Scots did) and was a seasoned campaigner when he swore the Covenants in 1650 and became minister of Hardhill

Alexander Henderson and Robert Baillie went with the Scottish army into England in 1640 and were representatives of the General Assembly at the Treaty of Ripon. Baillie enjoyed the fruits of victory when he was later given the task of drawing up charges against Archbishop Laud for the changes he had forced upon the Scottish Church. The young, newly married, William Guthrie was appointed by the General Assembly to serve with the army and was at Dunbar in September 1650 when the Scottish army was trounced by Cromwell. Robert Blair served with Lord Lindsays regiment against King Charles I and was with the troops that routed 4,000 English soldiers at Newburn, near Newcastle in August 1640. Later, in 1645, Blair was in Perth and happened across his old regiment at Forgandenny where he preached to them, warning that some had become dissolute and profane and would pay the price. Most of the regiment were slain at Kilsyth some three weeks later.

Robert Cunningham served with the Duke of Buccleuchs regiment in Holland before he became minister at Holywood, County Down in 1615. And it was the army chaplains who helped to re-establish the Presbyterian church in Ireland after the 1641 rebellion. The chaplains organised a Session in each regiment and when there were four they constituted the first regular Presbytery in June 1642. But there is always an exception to prove the rule. Robert Garnock, although a blacksmith by trade and presumably physically strong, was so stricken with conscience that he refused to turn out for the local militia in Stirling when the Highland Host were on the march to the south west of Scotland in 1678. He was severely rebuked for his failing to do his duty and for a while was cast out to wander the countryside.

Ministers - settlers in Ireland. See also: Bishops in Ireland; Black Oath; Boyne; Eaglewing; Killing Time in Ireland; Usurper (Cromwell).

The original Irish Presbyterians were essentially Scottish migrants and were not bloodily persecuted in the later years of the seventeenth century as were their Scottish brethren. But they were persecuted by those in authority and suffered their own "Killing Time" during the Rebellion of 1641.

The early years of the Presbyterians, until 1633, were of reasonable peace and tranquillity. In Scotland, King James VI/I, and then Charles I, had been pressing on with episcopacy and supremist policies. In Ireland however, possibly because the King did not want to stir up problems on yet another border, the Scottish ministers mainly took parishes under a benign episcopal Church of Ireland. Some, such as Blair and Livingston, continued to conduct their services in the Presbyterian manner; and lip service was paid to episcopacy by others.

James Ussher, the Archbishop of Armagh and Primate of Ireland, had a Presbyterian background and was tolerant in such things as ordination when acceptable ways round the issues were readily found. Ussher had produced his Articles of Religion in 1615 which was a set of compromises that allowed the Presbyterians to conduct their worship, receive the church tithes and to coexist with the established church. However, all changed in 1633 with the appointment of William Laud as Archbishop of Canterbury. Laud had twice been offered a cardinal's hat by Rome and, although remaining (through naked ambition) in the Church of England, he was strongly in favour of the ceremonies and trappings akin to Romish practice which sat comfortably with the vanity of the Stuart kings, their concepts of Divine Right and their latent Catholicism.

The Montgomery Manuscripts mentions that Sir Hugh Montgomery brought with him from Scotland two or three chaplains. It was these early settlers, mainly from Ayrshire, who came to County Antrim and County Down around 1606 that gave cause for the ministry and would have sought a pastor of their choosing at an early date. The Hamilton Manuscripts record that the Viscount Claneboy settled ministers in all six parishes within his estates. The first full-time minister was Edward Brice who came to Broadisland in 1611 and then its minister from 1613. He had been deposed by Archbishop Spottiswood in December 1613 for alleged adultery and had been forced to flee persecution in Scotland. Soon, Edward Brice was joined by Robert Cunningham at Holywood (1615); John Ridge at Antrim (1619); Josias Welch, the grandson of John Knox, at Templepatrick; a Rev. John Hubbard from Southwark, London, who brought his congregation with him to Carrickfergus (1621); James Glendinning who replaced Hubbard at Carrickfergus (1623); Robert Blair at Bangor (1623); George Dunbar at Larne (1625); James Hamilton at Ballywalter (1625); Andrew Stewart at Donegore (1627); and John Livingston at Kilinchy (1630).

When their peaceful coexistence was shattered by the resurgence of the bishops under the dictate of Laud, Robert Blair and John Livingston were at the centre of the drama. They were suspended by Bishop Echlin in 1632. Things came to a head in August 1636 when five of the ministers—Brice, Ridge, Cunningham, Calvert, and Hamilton—were summoned before the Bishop of Down and required to explain their refusal to accept Episcopacy. They were unable in all conscience to accept the Bishop's rule and were sentenced to "perpetual silence within this diocese."[172] With this sentence upon them the ministers returned to Scotland where they had a major influence in the Kirk's disputes with the king.

Ministers – numbers.

The first General Assembly of the Church of Scotland was constituted at Edinburgh on 20 December 1560. Present were forty-two members of whom only six were ministers, being exactly half of all the Protestant ministers in Scotland at that time. By 1567 there were 252 ministers as well as 467 readers and 154 exhorters. By the time of the Restoration and the Act of Presentation and Collation of 1662 there were some 952 ministers in Scotland. The numbers who declined to accept the superiority of the king over the Church and were thus "outed" is variously quoted as between two hundred and nearly four hundred. The picture is confused because at this time there was the dispute between the Resolutioners and the hard line

---

[172] T. Hamilton, *History of the Irish Prebyterian Church* (Edinburgh: T. & T. Clark, nd), p. 50.

Protesters, yet some of the Resolutioners were unable to accept the gross interference of the state in church matters. The number who were outed, and accepted by historians, seems to have been between 300 and 350, or about one third of the established ministers. The West of Scotland was badly hit with the Synod of Glasgow and Ayr losing about two-thirds of its ministers; over half of the ministers of the Synod of Dumfries were lost.

At the Revolution Settlement in 1690, one Act passed restored the ministers who had been outed in 1662 to their parishes. Only sixty of the original number were then alive. A consequence was that Episcopal ministers or "curates" remained in office for many years as there were simply not enough Presbyterian ministers of the old school. As late as 1710 there were still about 120 curates holding livings although they were not admitted to the Church courts.

Ministers – status.

The status of the Presbyterian ministers was always high even though some historians, and especially critics of the strict Covenanters, the Cameronians and the Society People or Hill Men, may allege the people were uneducated, rude and fanatics. But from their earliest days the ministers were closely associated with people of the highest rank: the Lords of the Congregation; the Marquis of Argyll; and John Gordon, Viscount Kenmuir. The ministers were, of course, among the very best educated persons in the land and their training and calling gave them enormous presence. They were well able to hold their own with courtiers and kings, as Andrew Melville well demonstrated by calling the king "God's sillie vassal" (meaning weak servant). By the very nature of their faith the common people were not illiterate since the church actively sought to provide a rudimentary education, thus they greatly valued reading their Bible, even if they had to struggle to make a living.

Many of the ministers came from landed gentry stock and as supporters of the Covenant against the king, they often stood to lose quite considerable wealth and honours. Being "put to the horn" and forfeited in their lands and property was no empty threat and should be remembered when counting the cost of their sacrifice. The catalogue of these lairds is long and impressive. Hugh Binning and William Guthrie of Fenwick were both sons of landed families.

James Guthrie of Stirling was heir to his father, the Laird of Guthrie in Angus. John Welch, son-in-law to John Knox owned an estate in Collistoun. Gabriel Semple was the son of Sir Bryce Semple of Cathcart. James Hamilton was the son of Sir John Hamilton of Broomhill and brother of Lord Belhaven. Robert Hamilton, later Sir Robert was of the Hamiltons of Preston a very influential family. Robert Melville of Culross was the son of Sir James Melvill of Halhill. Archibald Riddell was the son of Sir Walter Riddell. John Blackadder was heir of the House of Tulliallan and was entitled to the rank and honours of knight-baronet, which he declined. It was not true that all they had to lose was their heads.

There is no doubt that ministers were held in great esteem by all the community, not only because they were church men but also because of their general learning. In some communities the minister might double up as schoolteacher and emergency doctor and was thus a well known figure that people turned to for all sorts of help. It is also as well to remember that there were no daily newspapers and communication was mainly oral. A travelled minister able to illustrate his sermons from his own experiences, or merely able to explain local politics or reported events elsewhere in Scotland, was a focus for the populace in essentially rural communities. The pulpit was a favourite place from which to broadcast declarations and sometimes requirements by government to comply with the law of the land.

All ministers went to one of the colleges, as the universities were then called, obtained their Master of Arts degree and probably stayed on to study for the ministry. Many stayed on as "Regents" or teachers of a subject and also travelled to the Continental colleges. John Knox and Andrew Melville were both learned and esteemed by the colleagues abroad including by John Calvin and Theodore Beza. It was Beza who wrote that "The greatest token of affection the kirk of Geneva could show to Scotland was, that they had suffered themselves to be spoiled of Mr. Andrew Melville."[173]

Some ministers, such as John Livingston, had a remarkable gift for languages; he would study the Scriptures in Hebrew, Chaldee, Arabic, French, German, Italian, Spanish and Latin. This breadth of experience, the contacts they made, and depth of learning made them influential and their opinions worth listening to. The ministers

---

[173] Howie, *Worthies*, p. 91.

who attended the Westminster Assembly, especially George Gillespie, were greatly respected for their knowledge and admired for their extemporary debating abilities.

Thomas Hog was a worker among his parishioners, and especially tackled ignorance with visible and demonstrable energy that won the hearts of the people. Such was the esteem in which he was held that a gentleman came to stay and die at his manse in Kiltearn. John Welch was another "hands on" minister who made it his business to get out into the community, quite literally intervening in fights, reproving dissolute ministers and is credited with saving Ayr from the plague because he turned away two merchants who were later found to be carrying the disease.

Robert Burns was not afraid to declare himself in most things, including his faith. He attended Loreburn Church, of which he said, "I go to hear Mr Inglis, because he preaches what he believes, and practices what he preaches." (See plaque below.)

Inscription on a plate at Loreburn Church. Photo courtesy of A. Pittendreigh.

Monks - proliferation of.

There had been considerable donations of land and money to monasteries and the like in the twelfth, thirteenth, and fourteenth centuries which became a considerable source of income when the land was rented out. King David (1124-53) was a strong promoter of the monasteries and especially favoured the Cistercian, Tironian, and Premonstratensian orders which laid emphasis on hard work and withdrawal from the world. Lincluden Collegiate Church in Nithsdale was a Benedictine nunnery until dissolved in 1389. The particular contribution of these orders was in economic growth; the Border abbeys were engaged in sheep farming; at Newbattle the monks were engaged in coal and lead mining and in Coupar, Fife there was development of arable farming. Much credit has to be given to these monasteries who were the progenitors of an economic revolution in the Lowlands and responsible for many new techniques in agriculture.

Above: Lincluden Collegiate Church. Below: New Abbey, also known as Sweetheart Abbey. Photos courtesy of A. Pittendreigh.

As late as 1596 the monks were still opposing the Reformation, such as Abbott Gilbert Brown of New Abbey who had a public correspondence with John Welch of Ayr and was eventually deported in 1605 after a short stay in Blackness and Edinburgh castles. The monks at New Abbey, also known as Sweetheart Abbey, foresaw the way the Reformation would end and placed their property in the hands of the powerful Maxwell family and appointed them heritable baillies. So long as the monks stayed at the Abbey the Maxwells paid them the revenues and when they were driven away the Maxwells retained the church lands. With the support of such an influential family the departure of the monks was delayed by quite a few years.

The theological issues, along with the conduct and excesses of the Pope and his representatives, were highly visible factors in the Reformation and the issues were expounded by the Reforming leaders such as Martin Luther, John Calvin, and, in Scotland, by John Knox and Andrew Melville. The worldliness and debauchery of the Catholic church in the fifteenth and early sixteenth centuries was deeply offensive to the Protestants but the common man's experience was with priests and monks that proliferated at that time. The once lowly monks had drifted away from their isolated cells, their teaching and helping the poor, and had taken to worldly ways. The income from monastery lands encouraged the monks to take up the role and trappings of wealth. It also rubbed salt into the wounds of the common people who were hard pressed to pay rents and tithes from their meagre production of barley, oats, livestock, eggs, milk, cheese. Even death meant that tribute or payment was taken by the Church who might take the most valuable animal or the best of the deceased's property. The king and nobility were users of the system of patronage such that three sons of James V were appointed abbots when aged five years, a fourth son was a prior at age ten. Other objections were to officers having more than one post such as a Chancellor who was Archdeacon of St Andrews and rector of twenty two churches. The system of buying indulgences was another increasing burden. M'Crie, in *Sketches*, describes the situation thus:

> Swarms of priests and confessors infested every country - penetrating, like the plague of frogs of Egypt, into the recesses of every family, from the chamber of the king

down to the hut of the meanest cottager, and polluting everything they touched.[174]

When the people turned upon the monks and symbols of papacy in the churches at Perth, Stirling, Linlithgow, and Edinburgh during 1559 they did not discriminate between the various orders. There were over a hundred and fifty convents, monasteries and nunneries in Scotland with monks in their cloisters and friars wandering preaching and begging. The variety of orders that the monks represented was many with Templars or Red Monks, Trinity Monks of Aberdeen, Cistercian Monks (White Monks), Carmelite, Dominicans (Black Friars), Franciscans (Grey Friars), Jacobines, and Benedictines. The priests were much employed in making money from the practice of cursing, such as the public denunciation of a thief for his act. The practice encouraged the belief that a wrong might be corrected by imprecation which would be done, at a price, through writing letters or by declaration from the pulpit.

Dundrennan Abbey. Photo courtesy of A. Pittendreigh.

The principal monasteries of Medieval Scotland were to be found mainly in a line that followed the east coast from Berwick on

[174] M'Crie, *Sketches*, p. 12.

Tweed to Inverness, outside the Highland Line. In the far west was Iona, in splendid isolation, and three monasteries in the Dumfries and Galloway region.

Monastery	*Nearby main Burgh*
West: Glenluce)	Kirkcudbright
Dundrennan)	
Sweetheart	Dumfries
Iona	
Paisley	Glasgow
East: Jedburgh)	
Melrose)	Roxburgh
Kelso)	
Dryburgh)	
Coldingham	Berwick on Tweed
Newbattle)	
Holyrood)	Edinburgh
Inchcolm)	
Dunfermline)	Linlithgow
Cambuskenneth	Stirling
St. Andrews)	Perth (St. Johnstone)
Balmerino)	
Scone)	
Coupar	Dundee
Arbroath	Montrose
Deer	Aberdeen
Pluscarden	Elgin
Beauly	Inverness

Melrose Abbey. Photo by the author.

No Quarter in Battles. See also: Battles – Philiphaugh; Irish troops.

"No quarter" was the order of the day in all of the Covenanters battles as it was also in the king's armies. Both sides were equally vindictive and given to extremes of violence. John Nisbet, for example, was considered unkind in seeking the execution of prisoners after the battle of Drumclog and Robert Hamilton was grieved when he learnt some had been spared. This "no quarter" approach is founded on 1 Samuel 15:19 when Saul failed to follow the Lord's word to the letter: to kill all his enemies and lay waste to the land. After the battle of Rullion Green, about a hundred Covenanters surrendered on being given quarter. But that did not hinder the government from hanging ten prisoners on December 7 and another ten in the following two weeks, including Hugh McKail who was not actually in the battle.

The Montrose campaign from June 1644 to September 1645 was very bloody with over 12,000 Covenanters killed and probably as many among the royalists. What was apparent were acts of revenge and "no quarter" given not only to the soldiers, who in some cases had surrendered, but also on their bag and baggage: the wives, children, and camp followers. The sack of Aberdeen was both great and vicious with well-dressed persons stripped naked before their throats were cut (to save the garments from being spoiled), and women were raped then murdered. After the battle of Philiphaugh in September 1645 over five hundred Irishmen were slaughtered after they had been offered quarter and had surrendered. There followed a slaughter of the camp followers: boys, cooks, and women. Three hundred Irish women, wives of the soldiers and many of them pregnant, were cut up and their unborn babies cut from their wombs and cast on the ground with their murdered mothers. The horror of this was compounded by Covenanter ministers who incited all and any retribution on the royalists.

In the period after Philliphaugh and by December 1, many of the Scottish nobility who had taken part were rounded up. Any Irish found or held in prison were summarily executed by order of the Estates, the Scottish Parliament, who directed

> This House ordains the Irish prisoners taken at and after Philliphaugh in all the prisons of the kingdom, especially in the prisons of Selkirk, Jedburgh, Glasgow, Dumbarton and Perth, to be executed without any assize or process.[175]

Amongst the hundreds slaughtered without trial were six women taken out of Selkirk jail.

The later ministers were just as intense in their demands for full implementation of the biblical law. John Nevay was behind the slaughter of three hundred prisoners at Dunaverty, Kintyre, in 1647 and was possibly behind the armed resistance at Mauchline Muir in 1648. It is perhaps surprising therefore that he was allowed to give a bond and enter into voluntary exile in 1662. In 1680, Richard Cameron preached, in his last Sabbath at Clydesdale, that the Lord would lift up a standard against the antichrist and "that 'blood' should be their sign and 'no quarter' their word"[176] and he earnestly wished that it would begin in Scotland. A few weeks later his head adorned the Netherbow Gate in Edinburgh.

Cromwell is reviled by some historians as a bloody murderer for the slaughter of the garrison of Drogheda in Ireland in 1649. Yet it was custom and practice of the age to deal harshly with belligerent defenders who had declined an offer of surrender. The defence of Drogheda by the royalist forces was a major plank in their hope "to draw Cromwell's teeth" before his campaign could overrun Ireland. The defenders knew full well the consequences of rejecting such an offer and would have prepared themselves for bitter hand-to-hand fighting, even to the death. Moreover, taking prisoners was expensive in terms of resources to feed, quarter, and guard them, and meant that soldiers were tied up who could otherwise be fighting. A dead enemy did not return to fight another day.

Number of sufferers.

The Scots Worthies is an often quoted source for the numbers of Presbyterians who died or were subject of 'the utmost hardships and

---

[175] Hewison, *Covenanters*, Vol. 1, p. 430.
[176] Howie, *Worthies*, p. 427.

extremities." The total number given is 18,000 which is for the twenty-eight years of persecution from 1660 to 1688.

Transported to the Colonies West Indies & America	1,700
Banished to the Northern Isles	750
Murdered (drowned on the *Crown*)	200
Imprisoned, confined,	3,600
[includes 800 outlawed; 55 for execution, if caught.]	
Killed in skirmishes	680
Voluntary exile	7,000
Shot and hung without process of law	498
Executed, by law	362
	14,790
Balance to 18,000 who perished on the moors, etc.	3,210

The Martyrs Monument in Greyfriars Kirkyard says that between 27 May 1661 and 17 February 1688 "about an hundred of Noblemen Gentlemen Ministers and other noble martyrs" lie there. The original monument was erected ca 1706.

There are several other sources for numbers, most notable being Robert Wodrow's *The History of the Sufferings of the Church of Scotland* and J. H. Thomson's *A Cloud of Witnesses*, which was based on Wodrow's manuscripts. More recently, Thorbjorn Campbell, in *Standing Witnesses*, provides lists of known and verifiable deaths along with details of surviving memorials:

Executed in Edinburgh	95
Killed, executed, in the countryside	172
Lost on the *Crown*	197 (211)

Over three hundred years later it is impossible to be more accurate than quoted by Howie. But even 18,000 only represents the post-Restoration period as there were between 10,000 and 12,000 more who gave their lives on the battlefield in the cause of the Covenant. The estimates of deaths in battle during Montrose's campaign of 1644-1645 need to be included (below with alternative estimates from other sources in brackets):

Tippermuir	3,000 (1,300 + 800 captured)
Aberdeen	800
Fivy	unknown
Inveraray	900
Inverlochy	1,700 (1,500)
Auldearn	2,000 (3,000)
Alford	700 (1,600)
Kilsyth	3,000 (4,000)
Total	12,100 and probably many more.

To these might be added the losses at:

Preston/Winwick 17-19 August 1648, 1,000 killed, 4,600 captured
Dunbar 3 September 1650, 3,000-4,000 killed and 10,000 captured
Inverkeithing 20 July 1651, 2,000 killed.
Dundee, 1 September 1651, 800 killed.
Worcester,3 September 1651, 2,000 killed and 10,000 captured.

A ball park figure of perhaps 30,000 may have died for their beliefs and Presbytery during the whole of the Scottish Reformation.

Oaths. See also: Abjuration Oath (1684); Black Oath; Coronation Oath.

An oath to bind a person to a particular condition was a commonly used device by the government against the Presbyterians. Whether it was part of a policy of conciliation or a means to further divide the Presbyterians is difficult to judge. The fact is that the oaths that were required of people were not simple statements of loyalty—which the Covenanters could accept—but were tied into the acceptance of the king as supreme in both civil and ecclesiastical matters. This Erastianism was an anathema to the Presbyterians and a fundamental reason why they declined to take such an oath. It is difficult to believe that the government did not know this, and that they therefore cynically used the oath to divide and rule.

The Oath of Allegiance, also called the Oath of Supremacy, produced at the Restoration was a master stroke by the king and Middleton, the King's Commissioner, because it slipped in unnoticed until too late. It provided the king with total supremacy in all things, both civil and ecclesiastical. Too late, Melville and

Cassillis sought to get "civil" inserted, and thus it would remain until the Revolution. The oath runs:

> I for testification of my faithful obedience to my most gracious and redoubted Sovereign Charles, King of Great Britain, France and Ireland, defender of the faith, do affirm, testify, and declare, by this my solemn oath, that I acknowledge my said Sovereign only supreme Governor of the kingdom over all persons and in all causes, civil and ecclesiastical, and shall at my utmost power defend. maintain his majesty's jurisdiction foresaid, against all deadly, and never decline his majesty's power or jurisdiction, as I shall answer to God.[177]

The Test Act of 31 August 1681 was accompanied by another variation on the oath of allegiance. The oath was uncompromising and required all those in public office to swear loyalty and concur in the supremacy of the King in all matters, civil or ecclesiastical. This was used indiscriminately by the likes of Claverhouse and other government agents as another tool of repression, forcing people to take the oath whether they were office holders or not.

There were also oaths which were specific in their wording and purpose. The Abjuration Oath was a specific rejection of James Renwick's Admonitory Vindication published in 1684. It was used as a means of ensnaring the unwary. In Ireland, there was the "Black Oath" which required a declaration of loyalty but also the specific rejection of the Covenants. This was monitored by Episcopalian ministers and church wardens who were required to provide lists of people who had not taken the oath. Refusal was subject to very heavy fines and imprisonment in chains.

There is an irony in the circumstances that King Charles chose not to subscribe to the Covenants when suggested to him by Robert Blair at Newcastle. The king claimed that "he was bound by his great oath to defend Episcopacy in that Church (of England); and ere he wronged his conscience, by violating his coronation oath, he would lose his crown."[178] How duplicitous can a man, or king, get?

---

[177] Hewison, *Covenanters*, Vol. 2, p. 79.
[178] Howie, *Worthies*, p. 349.

The seriousness with which taking an oath was treated was very great among the Covenanters. James Renwick had a problem when declining to take an oath of allegiance at his university graduation ceremony. He was in a state of great conscience and felt so afraid of offending God that he declined public laureation. His graduation was later completed in private. Another to forgo much for his beliefs was Sir Robert Hamilton of Preston, who succeeded to his brother in 1688. He could not in conscience take an oath of allegiance to King William and Queen Mary, or accept the prelactic church government, and did not take up his brother's estate.

Orators.

The very nature of an evangelical church determines that all the ministers were able to preach. Their deep understanding of the Scriptures, training and trials before ordination meant that all were able to extemporise and could hold their own in debate. Moreover, they could, and often did, preach for several hours at a time. In the later days of the conventicles it was not uncommon for perhaps three ministers to rotate with each preaching twice in the day. George Gillespie demonstrated to the Westminster Assembly in 1643 what it was to extemporise by "debating with such perspicuity strength of arguement, and calmness of spirit, that few could equal, none excel him, in that Assembly."[179]

But there were some who had the gift of communication, able to empathise with their congregation and to deliver a sermon in the language of the common man. George Wishart in 1544 was celebrated for his uncommon eloquence. Hugh Binning is rated as one of the best, perhaps unequalled in his day, in England and Scotland. He is described as having easy and fluent diction, void of all affectation and bombast, and an elegance that held the hearers' attention. Robert Bruce was an imposing character with great presence and spoke with a low and deliberate voice. But the power of his expression was such that "the most stout hearted of his hearers were ordinarily made to tremble…they oftentimes went away under deep conviction."[180]

---

[179] Howie, *Worthies*, p. 193.
[180] *Ibid.*, p. 150.

Andrew Gray was one of the prodigies of his day, qualified and ordained to the High Church of Glasgow by the age of twenty. He had a gravity in his conversation that delighted the hearer and he "held forth learning beyond his age, and fixedness of manners beyond his learning."[181] William Veitch, on the other hand, was a stern critic of the government and of his colleagues at times. He must have been a most powerful and awakening preacher from the influence he had upon the manners or morals of those who attended his sermons.

Paper of 23rd August 1660.

Alexander Moncrieff had a very chequered life and for a while seemed to go from one difficulty to another. It is thought that he had some involvement in drawing up the "Western Remonstrance" and the "Causes of Gods Wrath." He was involved in presenting a Protestation and Testimony against Toleration in October 1658 which attacked the Sectaries (Independents and Puritans). He had also been criticised for praying for the absent king, Charles II. But at the Restoration he was then involved in drawing up, with James Guthrie and eight others (including Robert Traill, Senior), a supplication to the newly restored king—the "Paper of 23 August"—for which all but a Mr. Hay of Craignethan were promptly imprisoned in Edinburgh Castle. So much for loyalty, it seemed, since Moncrieff and his colleagues lay in prison for almost a year before brought to trial.

The address was a humble supplication to the king to preserve the Reformed religion and reminded him of the Covenants which he had sworn on his coronation at Scone in 1651. King Charles was in no mood for following the Covenanters dream and was determined on revenge. James Guthrie was never released and was moved between Stirling, Dundee, and Edinburgh before Sharpe's malice, and Middleton's revenge for being excommunicated, saw him to the scaffold.

---

[181] *Ibid.*, p. 215.

Patronage.

Patronage was often abused by the appointment of friends and relatives to positions of influence, power and in earlier times especially for the benefits that might accrue. Even kings were not averse to appointing their natural children to posts to ensure them of an income. It was a particular problem to the Presbyterians since it interfered directly in the congregation's selection or "call" upon a minister of their choice. It was held that there was no warrant in the Scriptures for presentation or imposition of a minister by an external authority, which was founded only in canon law and Romish custom. Patronage was the reason for the division within the Presbyterian Church that led to the creation of the Secession Church in 1733 and the Free Church in 1843.

In rural areas the power of the nobility and to a lesser extent the lairds, made them largely invulnerable to the discipline of the kirk. Some, like the Marquis of Argyll and the Earl of Cassillis were staunch kirk men but many others resented the kirk eroding their control of the social order. In between there were the compromises such as that of William Gordon of Earlstoun, who defended his right to the patronage of Dalry against the appointment of a curate, as he had, with the agreement of the people, already approved a minister for the post.

A minister much against patronage was John McCelland of Kirkcudbright who wrote to his patron on 20 February 1649 expressing his objections and concerns on the debate about patronage that was then going on in Parliament. Shortly after, on 6 March 1649, the Estates of Parliament declared that patronage and presentation of kirks was "an evil bondage" and abolished patronage of the Kirks. The General Assembly subsequently declared that the kirk session had the authority to appoint a minister and if a majority dissented then appeal was allowed to the Presbytery. This became the position until the Restoration of Charles II and the Act Recissory of 1661 that repealed all acts passed after 1633

The infamous Act of 11 June 1662 required a minister to obtain the consent of his patron by 20 September 1662 and submit to collation by the bishop of the diocese. The law also made patrons grant presentations to ministers already in posts. The outing of over three hundred ministers followed. On 19 July 1690, under the Acts ratifying Presbyterian Church Government, patronage was abolished and transferred the right of presenting to heritors and Elders in each parish who recommended to the congregation. There was a right to appeal to Presbytery if the appointment was not acceptable. Patronage remained abolished for twenty one years and was later the cause for another major division within the Church of Scotland.

A Scottish Member of Parliament rose to his feet on 13 March 1712 and proposed the restoration of patronage which was promptly supported and pushed through the House of Commons very quickly so that it was actually under discussion in the House of Lords before a response could be made by the General Assembly. There was much protesting at what might have been a carefully laid plot by High Church Episcopalians and Jacobites. The patronage act was in fact illegal because the Treaty of Union of 1707 had guaranteed the position as to religion and Parliament had no power to change it; however, this protestation also achieved nothing. Patronage remained an issue and for a while was subject of annual protests but the moderation creeping through the Church gradually did away with it. But protest came to a head once again at the Synod of Stirling and Perth on 10 October 1732. Here the outgoing Moderator, Ebenezer Erskine of Stirling preached in an evangelical style that some of the "moderates" disliked and went on to preach that God had never granted to any set of patrons the power to impose servants on His Church. The Moderates, then being a majority, resented his preaching and he was admonished by the next Assembly. However, not a man to be daunted by such things, Erskine protested and was supported by Rev. W. Wilson, Alexander Moncrieff, and James Fisher. They were suspended from office and deprived of their congregations. The four then left the Church of Scotland making a Protestation and Act of Secession on 16 November 1733. On 5 December 1733, at Gairney Bridge, they constituted themselves into the Associate Presbytery. This "Secession" as it became known, asserted the right of the people to elect their own ministers.

Persecution of Knox.

Persecution ran throughout the Reformation but was the result of two different causes. The watershed was the route of Catholicism and French influence and the accession of James VI in 1567. The persecution of heretics by the Catholic priests was on the wane by the mid-1500s and the burning at the stake of Walter Mill on 28 April 1558 was the final straw. John Knox was the catalyst that drove the Reformation through the crucial years of the Regency of Mary of Guise, and the turbulence of Mary, Queen of Scot's short reign before she abdicated in favour of James VI. There was a hiatus as the Reformed religion took root until James VI acceded to the throne of England in 1603 and he became enthused with episcopacy and supreme headship of the church, as it was in England.

John Knox was no stranger to persecution and was adept at reading the signs to enable him to avoid capture and trial. Nearly two years as a French galley slave did not bend him and he was not afraid to face his opponents or call their bluff, such as the Archbishop of St. Andrews who raised a hundred spearmen to prevent him preaching at St Andrews. In the event on 14 June 1559 he preached without interruption and also on three days following. At the end, the provost, baillies, and inhabitants were so taken with his doctrine, the church was stripped of images and pictures, and the monasteries were stripped of all symbols of Romanism.

In the following months the momentum gathered strength and more towns followed suit, outing the symbols of papistry. Communications were established with the English Court and military support obtained. Knox and his colleagues, John Willock, Christopher Goodman, and Alexander Gordon, Bishop of Galloway who had joined the Reformation, were now drawn into the politics and consulted about the suspension of Mary of Guise from the Regency. This inevitably heightened the physical threats to them all. The Queen Regent was most determined to seize Knox and a reward was publicly offered to any one who should apprehend him or kill him. In 1558 Knox published his *First Blast of the Trumpet against the Monstrous Regiment of Women* which did not endear him to Queen Elizabeth, Mary the Queen Regent, or, subsequently, Mary Queen of Scots.

When the young Queen Mary returned to Scotland in 1561, Knox was again in the firing line. She had received reports in France of Knox being a fomenter of discord and had declared that she was determined that he should be punished. When summoned to the palace Knox was accused of treason and the cause of sedition and bloodshed. Famously, he stood up to the young Queen Mary and told her plainly and with respect that "If princes exceed their bounds, no doubt they may be resisted, even by power." [182]

Many times Mary sought to entrap Knox and on several occasions tried womanly wiles and tears. Knox was not, however, overcome by such tactics and resolutely struck to his chosen path. An attempt was made to have him tried by the nobility in December 1563 for calling an allegedly illegal convocation. But, again, Mary was foiled in her endeavours; the nobles acquitted him, despite the attempt by Lethington to take a second vote. In 1565, he again roused anger by preaching at Edinburgh about the wickedness of princes that enraged the queen's consort, Henry, Lord Darnley. Knox was prohibited from preaching while the Court was in residence at Edinburgh but it left before the next Sabbath and the matter was not later pursued. Subsequently the tactics employed against him changed to direct action including an attempt to shoot him and threats against his person causing him to move out of Edinburgh for a while.

Even after Mary had departed into exile in 1568, Knox was pursued by her adherents and in particular the Hamiltons, whose honour was besmirched by the murder of the Regent Moray by James Hamilton of Bothwellhaugh, a nephew of the Archbishop of St. Andrews. Many slanders and malicious accusations were made even after Knox was forced to take things easy following a stroke in October 1570. One was the allegation by Robert Hamilton, minister of Edinburgh, and his brother, Archibald Hamilton, a professor at the university, of Knox being complicit in an attempt to murder Darnley at Perth. Knox responded quickly by threatening to bring the slander before the Church which made Robert Hamilton retract. Archibald Hamilton ended his days on the gibbet when taken prisoner at the siege of Dumbarton Castle 2 April 1571.

M'Crie, in *Life of John Knox*, observed that few men were ever exposed to more dangers or underwent greater hardships than Knox did. From the time he embraced the reformed religion until he breathed his last, he was seldom far from trouble. Yet he rejected offers of protection insisting

> As for the fear of danger that may come to me let no man be solicitous; for my life is in the custody of Him whose glory

---

[182] *Ibid.*, p. 55

> I seek. I desire the hand nor weapon of no man to defend me. I only crave audience; which if it be denied here unto me at this time, I must seek where I may have it.[183]

Persecution - in Europe.

In 1598 the Edict of Nantes had given religious freedom to the Huguenots, the French Protestants, but Louis XIII (1601-1643) subsequently made attacks upon them and Louis XIV (1638-1715) continued their persecution and revoked the Edict in October 1685. The hidden agenda of the Catholic cause in Britain had been taken further in May 1670 when King Charles II's sister, Henrietta of Orleans, negotiated a private Treaty of Dover, under which England and France agreed to partition Holland, and France supplied aid in the establishment of Romanism in Great Britain.

Charles also received an annual pension of £200,000 that meant that he did not have to depend so much on Parliament. With this undercurrent of intrigue and duplicity at the highest levels and a growing opposition among English courtiers to the possibility of an overt Catholic successor to the crown, it is little wonder that the Protestant dissenters had to tread carefully.

Many of the dissenting ministers found their way to Holland and there was a thriving congregation in Rotterdam. But even here the Scottish government sought to pursue them by seeking the intervention of the Dutch. In Rotterdam were the stalwarts and early sufferers of persecution John Brown of Wamphray and Robert McWard who were responsible for ordaining Richard Cameron.

At the instance of Archbishop Sharpe, King Charles II even wrote to the States General asking them to remove James Wallace, Robert McWard, and John Brown, but their hosts took the view that since they had been banished from Scotland they had completed their sentence. As a gesture only, the three ministers were persuaded to take a short respite in Germany.

Personal Rule. See also: Laudian Policies; Petition of Right.

This was the period between March 1629 and November 1640 that King Charles I ruled with his selected advisers and without the

---

[183] M'Crie, *Life of Knox*, p. 131.

support of a Parliament. The end of involvement in wars on the continent—France in 1629 and Spain in 1630—meant that Charles no longer needed Parliament to raise the huge sums of money needed for war. It should be remembered, however, that at the time the assembly of Parliament was an event, it was not yet an institution, and only met when summoned by the king. There had been no parliament between 1614 and 1621, so it was not unusual. However, the king's methods for raising funds outside Parliament impacted a wide selection of the community and with it a long period of alleged abuse of power, some might say tyranny.

With a substantial Crown debt and insufficient funds to meet day to day expenses, Charles resorted to obtuse devices for raising money called prerogative taxation, such as reviving the Distraint of Knighthood. Persons of assets over £40 were required to attend a new king's coronation to be knighted. A fine could be imposed if one failed to attend. The practice had fallen out of use as inflation had risen and the sum encompassed far too many people of the wrong sort to be knights. Charles appointed Commissioners to collect fines from some 9,000 people and raised some £170,000 as a result. He also enforced ancient forestry laws by declaring the boundaries of ancient royal forests to be those of the twelfth century. Many people whose families had lived within the alleged boundaries for generations suddenly found themselves fined. He further extended the authority of the Court of Wards increasing fees from £100 to £1000, and issued authority for monopolies which was contrary to an Act of 1624. Two of his most odious acts were to create the Star Chamber to enforce his will in England and the Court of High Commission in Scotland.

In 1634 he reintroduced a tax, called Ship Money, which was traditionally imposed on the coastal counties to pay for the maintenance of the navy. In 1635 the writ for Ship Money was extended to the inland counties as well. Despite resistance the imposition was very successful and in the first three years raised some £200,000 a year. However, the imposition raised the temperature in the countryside who resented especially the manner in which it was imposed: a sum was ordered to be collected from each county and the sheriff had to collect it as best he could. Charles did not win friends by making the sheriff liable for any uncollected amount. The king's main abettors in this period were Thomas Wentworth who, as Lord Deputy of Ireland, diligently pursued nonconformists there and sought to seize whatever land he could for the Crown, and Archbishop William Laud who pursued the Puritans with a vengeance in England and prompted the resistance of them and the Independents (to whom Cromwell belonged). Laud's activities spilled over into Scotland by the introduction of the revised Service Book (Laud's Liturgy), that prompted the Covenant of 1638 and the Second Reformation.

Petition of Right, 1628 [England]. See also: Personal Rule.

The growing mistrust of people, gentry, nobility, and Parliament with Charles I in the first three years of his reign led to the Petition of Right of 1628. Much distrust focussed on demands for money to wage war and the mismanagement of the war against France and Spain. There were concerns for constitutional and religious principles when Charles pursued ceremony and episcopacy but also began to suspend recusancy laws against Catholics. It was very bad politics for Charles to lend English ships to the French king that were used against the Huguenots. Things came to a head in September 1626 when Charles imposed a "forced loan" amounting to five parliamentary subsidies. This was clearly an attempt to collect taxation without Parliament's approval. The Petition made three demands:

> The king should not levy taxes without Parliament's approval.
>
> No one should be imprisoned without either cause being given or brought to trial.
>
> Soldiers and sailors should not be billeted in private homes by martial law, and declared martial law itself illegal.

There followed the period of Personal Rule by Charles, 1629-1640.

Plantation of Ulster (1610-1630).

The principle of "planting" peoples on escheated land originated with Henry VIII's accession to the throne of Ireland in 1541 and it was under his policy of "surrender and regrant" of lands that the Irish princes received English titles; for instance, O'Neill became

Earl of Tyrone; O'Brien, Earl of Thomond; and Macwilliam Burke of Galway, Earl of Clanrickard. This principle was followed through by later kings and queens. On 4 September 1607, the Earls of Tyrone and Tyrconnel, with some ninety relatives, friends, and followers, fled into exile. These included Maquire, who owned half of County Fermanagh. It was decided that all the lands of Shane O'Neill were forfeit resulting in large portions of counties Tyrone Donegal, Coleraine, Armagh, Cavan, and Fermanagh becoming available for plantation.

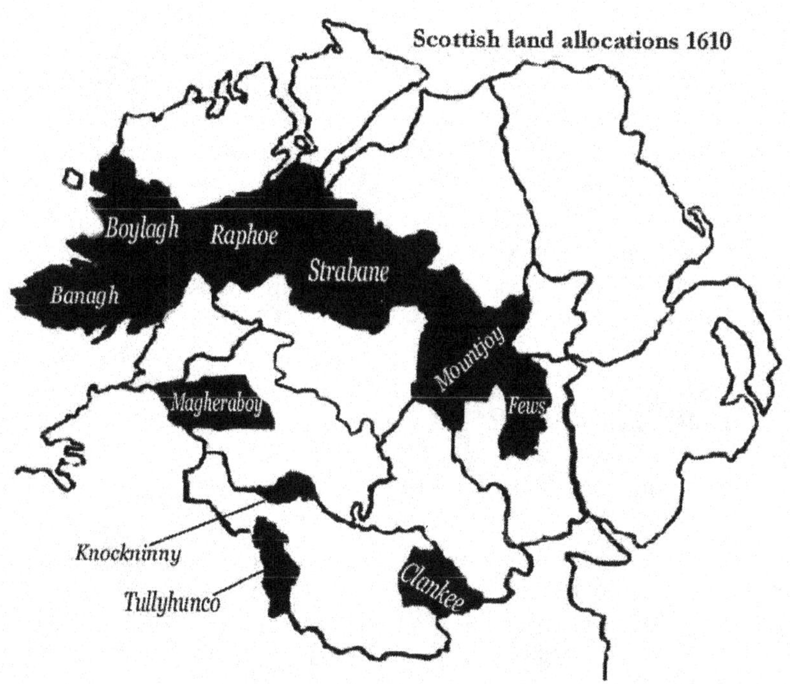

Scottish land allocations, 1610. Drawn by the author.

On 29 September 1607 the Privy Council approved the Plantation scheme. A Proclamation of the Plantation in Ulster was made by the Scottish Council on 8 March 1609. The applicants were generally persons of substance and family ventures with mutual action taken as cautioners or guarantors for one another. These Scottish undertakers were allotted some 81,000 acres. The nine baronies set aside for the Scots were mainly around the periphery of the escheated lands. They were Boylagh, Banagh and Portlough in Donegal; Strabane and Mountjoy in Tyrone; Knockninny and Magheraboy in Fermanagh; Clankee and Tullyhunco in Cavan; and the northern half of The Fews in County Armagh.

Absent from the Plantation allotments were the counties of Antrim and Down, which had already been successfully planted by two Ayrshire Scots entrepreneurs in 1606-1607. These men were Hugh Montgomery, Sixth Earl of Braidstone, and Sir James Hamilton from Dunlop.[184] Both of these landowners brought Scottish settlers to their new estates and each was active in ensuring that their parishes had a minister. The Hamilton and Montgomery estates were the main Scottish locations, until about 1614, with a population of some two hundred to three hundred males. It is estimated that some 10,000 Scots were brought to Ireland by the Montgomery and Hamilton plantations.

The extant Muster Rolls of 1630 show a total of 13,147 adult males, which suggests a total population in excess of 30,000, of which about sixty per cent were Scottish.

Policy of the Church. See also: First Book of Faith; First Book of Discipline; Second Book of Discipline.

The record of the church policy between 1576 and 1596 was drawn up by David Calderwood and presented to the Glasgow Assembly in 1638. At that Assembly, a former clerk, Mr. Sandhills, produced two books that covered from 1592 to Aberdeen in 1618, and Archibald Johnston, Lord Warriston, was able to produce five more books that enabled a register of the church from the beginning of the Reformation to be compiled.

The policy of the Presbyterian church has been basically simple throughout and founded on two great truths. First, Christ's headship in the church despite claims of supremacy and Erastianism. Second, the Covenants. The schisms that came about through Indulgences,

---

[184] Hugh Montgomery was the eldest son of Adam, fifth Earl of Braidstane born *ca.* 1560 and made Viscount Montgomery of the Great Ards in 1622. Sir James Hamilton, later Viscount Clandeboye, was the son of Rev. Hans Hamilton.

Toleration, and the like, merely created shades of the same basic policy.

The Covenanters' claims during the persecution from 1660 to 1688 were only marginally different from central policy because they had their specific difference over the prelatic Church of Scotland, indulged ministers and the Stuart monarchy. But they maintained the obligation upon the Church and nation of the two Covenants; the sole headship of Christ over the Church; and Christian civil government in opposition to an absolute monarchy.

Importantly, the struggle was not about civil and religious liberty nor liberty as a right of man. Their basic principles were theocratic and about the rights of God as revealed in the Scriptures. They were seeking practical recognition of these principles in every sphere of life, including Church and State.

Presbytery - The Great Charter, 1592. See also: Black Acts.

When King James VI went to Denmark to bring back his bride in 1590, he reposed considerable trust in Robert Bruce, then minister in Edinburgh, and effectively left the country in his hands. Whatever the detail of this "watching brief," Scotland was quiet and, on his return, James wrote to Bruce acknowledging his gratitude and debt for his service. For a while, James was most tolerant and even gave the impression of a liking for Presbyterianism. M'Crie tells of the king responding to an English minister who had asked why there was never trouble with heresy in Scotland. The king responded:

> I'll tell you how, man. If it spring up in a parish, there is an eldership to take notice of it; if it be too strong for them, the presbytery is ready to crush it; if the heretic prove too obstinate for them, he shall find more witty heads in the Synod; and if he cannot be convinced there, the General Assembly, I'll warrant you, will not spare him.[185]

Bruce was subsequently the Moderator of the General Assembly that met on 22 May 1592 in Edinburgh which capitalised on the better standing that the church now had with James VI. A list of

---

[185] M'Crie, *Sketches*, p. 121.

requests was considered by Parliament and an "Act for Abolishing of the Actis Contrair the Trew Religion" was passed. This was an improvement on the then existing civil law and ratified the church courts—General Assembly, Synod, and Presbytery—and much of Andrew Melville's Second Book of Discipline. The 'Black Acts' were declared null and void. The Presbyterians did not get everything they wanted, though. General Assemblies still had to be called by the king or his commissioner and only in their absence could the Assembly call itself to meeting. Patronage, a long-time anathema, remained but Presbytery could decide if the patron's nominee was acceptable. The legislation became known as "The Great Charter of Presbytery" and gave legal recognition to the powers of the Church of Scotland which had previously been claimed by the Second Book of Discipline in 1578.

Pride's Purge. See also: Long Parliament - and Rump.

Pride's Purge was the action by Colonel Thomas Pride, on the orders of Henry Ireton (a militant army commander) to arrest certain members of the English Parliament who had voted for negotiations with the king at Newport. There, the king had accepted the Scots' offer of help under the "Engagement." The situation arose after the Presbyterian members and remaining royalist supporters opposed the seizure and proposed trial of Charles I with the likelihood that he would be condemned to death. After a long night's sitting of Parliament a resolution was passed by a majority of forty-six (in a House of over two hundred members attending) that negotiations should be continued with the king. The day after Colonel Thomas Pride with a list in his hand supervised the arrest of forty one members on the first day, and more the following day. Of the 471 Members eligible to sit in the Parliament, 231 were barred. A further forty-five were arrested and the remnant, known as the Rump, continued to sit as if legally constituted. King Charles was arraigned and tried by a High Court of Justice of 135 Commissioners set up by the Rump on January 20. A week later, the judges announced him guilty of treason and the sentenced him to death. Despite very vociferous opposition Charles was beheaded in Whitehall on 30 January 1649. John Milton, who was Cromwell's secretary, observed that God had inspired the English to be the first of mankind who have not hesitated to judge and condemn their king.

There was no doubt that Charles' execution sent a shiver through the crowned heads of Europe in the dread that they, too, might reach such an end.

Privy Council.

Members of the Privy Council of Scotland were the nominees of the king and were responsible for the administration, legislation, and judiciary of Scotland. They were therefore everything to all men and the servile instrument of an autocratic king. In earlier times the Privy Council was representative of the Estates but had become increasingly diluted as James VI flexed his royal muscles.

On succeeding to the English throne in 1603 James VI, now also James I of England, moved his court to London and did not wish to leave any powerful body in Scotland in his absence. He determined therefore that the Privy Counsel would not be any more than a counselling body and he created the Lords of the Articles to be his executive arm. His attitude to the government of Scotland displays his arrogance when he said to the English Parliament in 1607, "Here I sit and governe it with my pen. I write and it is done, and by a Clearke of the Councell I governe Scotland now, which others could not do by the sword."[186]

Proclamation. See also: Protest, Protestation.

The royal proclamation made by the Herald at the Mercat Cross, usually in Edinburgh, was a quick means of declaring and implementing acts by royal authority. In many cases the proclamation was not ratified for lengthy periods until the next Parliament sat. The formal Protest was a legal device to force consideration by the courts of any Proclamations and Acts which were considered unlawful. There were very many Proclamations but one of particular significance was that of 10 October 1666. This made proprietors liable for the good behaviour of all the residents on their lands, with power to evict non conformists. Magistrates were made liable for the burghs, and heads of houses for the conduct of their servants.

---

[186] Magnus Magnusson, *Scotland, the Story of a Nation* (London: Harper Collins, 2000), p. 399.

A Proclamation of 25 March 1667 was another attack on the people and summoned the production and surrender of all personal arms and horses of all non-jurors and non-churchgoers. Not satisfied with that a further Proclamation of 13 June 1667 made heritors and parishioners liable to fines and payment of compensation for affronts and assaults on the "well affected clergy," many of whom were the dissolute curates. This was a new and rich vein to be tapped for fines and revenue which conveniently did not include papists.

Proclamations that a person was declared a traitor (put to the horn) was another device to announce publicly that, in most cases, it was also a crime to aid (reset), these people. And, of course, to let the spies and informers know of another quarry to pursue.

Proclamation against Richard Cameron and Supporters.

The Proclamation against Richard Cameron and his followers on 30 June 1684 followed hard on the heels of the discovery of the Queensferry papers, and the Sanquhar Declaration the previous week. The Proclamation begins erroneously by referring to the Queensferry papers as found on Donald Cargill; they were in fact on the body of Henry Hall. Moreover, Cargill escaped capture on that occasion.

The purpose of the Proclamation is many fold.

First to declare the participants at the Declaration of Sanquhar on 22 June 1680 traitors.

Second to force the land owners to interrogate all their tenants aged sixteen and over about the whereabouts of the alleged traitors, and to give evidence on Oath.

Third to certify the task had been done and to provide names of those who did not appear to the summons or, who declined to give evidence on Oath.

Fourth to give authority for the use of force and an open pardon if the traitors and their associates happened to get killed or mutilated in the arrest.

Fifth to offer rewards DEAD or ALIVE for the named rebels.

Too soon, the hunt was over at Airsmoss on 22 July 1680.

Protest, Protestation.

Throughout the disagreements between the Church and State there was a studied delivery of protests by the Church and people. Not only was this a statement of their desires or demands it was also a legal device. It had long been the custom and practice accepted in the law of Scotland that a formal protest could be lodged and the legality of any new ordinance would be determined in a court of law. A protest therefore protected the people from sudden application of statutes which could be so quickly implemented by a Proclamation at the Mercat Cross. The Covenanters were particularly careful, and successful, in presenting a Protestation at the cross of Stirling on 18 February 1638 and in Edinburgh on 22 February to counter royal proclamations in the run up to the declaration of the National Covenant on 28 February 1638

Subsequently, a royal Proclamation (dated September 9) was read on September 22 which discharged the offensive books (the Canons and the Liturgy), ceremonies, articles, and the Court of High Commission, and ordering all persons to subscribe to the King's Confession, authorising an Assembly and a Parliament, and proclaiming a pardon. The immediate response was a lengthy Protest read by Archibald Johnston and the representatives of the Tables who declared legal instruments with notaries present. The representatives were Montrose for the nobles, Alexander Gibson of Durie for the barons, George Porterfield of Glasgow for the burgesses, Harie Rollock of Edinburgh for the ministers, and Johnston himself for the subscribers to the Covenant. Within the General Assembly at Glasgow in November 1638 a formal protestation was made against the early discharge of the Assembly, again by Johnston, when the King's Commissioner, Hamilton declared the Assembly dissolved.

Protesters and Resolutioners. See also: Act of Classes; Engagers; Engagement; Whiggamore Raid.

Following the defeat of the royalist "Engagers" at Preston by Cromwell, the "honest" party of the Covenanters took control of government under the leadership of the Marquis of Argyll and Lord Warriston. In 1649 the Parliament passed the "Act of Classes" which classified the "malignants," as the Engagers were called, into categories of persons declared unable to be employed in a position of trust for various periods of time. A purge of government and the army rejected very many capable people, but the Covenanters persisted with their action.

The execution of King Charles I in 1649 by the English saw a complete about turn by the Covenanters who now declared for the new King Charles II. Their support was short-lived, however; on 3 September 1650 Cromwell defeated the purged army of the Covenant at Dunbar and occupied Edinburgh. Following the defeat at Dunbar, one of the first considerations was whether to repeal the Act of Classes. The Committee of Estates consulted with the General Assembly who, in July 1651, passed the Resolutions, declaring that:

> In this case of so great and ardent necessity, we cannot be against the raising of all fencible persons in the land and permitting them to fight against this enemy for defence of the kingdom; excepting such as are excommunicated, forfeited; profane, flagitious.[187]

The point at issue was whether the General Assembly could legally ratify the Public Resolutions of Parliament. This was then exacerbated by the propriety, or otherwise, of the repeal of the Act of Classes. The issues exposed the differences between the two factions on the principles of Christian government. The "Protestors" (the strict Covenanters) saw the disasters they had suffered as the consequence of national sin. They saw the remedy to be in spiritual obedience to the will of God, and denied that the end justifies the means. They protested that the principles of the Covenant should be maintained, malignants should not be re admitted, and allegiance to the king should only be on the old constitutional terms of free Parliaments and free Assemblies. The "Resolutioners" saw it as necessary to act in unity for the good of the country, and were not so committed to a spiritual solution. Having obtained the conditional agreement of the General Assembly, Parliament repealed the Act of

[187] Johnston, *Treasury*, p. 120.

Classes in full and disregarded the qualifications the Assembly had made. A new army was levied, along with a highly unpopular cess tax to pay for it, which was commanded and officered by the Resolutioner's supporters. It included many who were strongly opposed to the Covenanters. This division between the "Resolutioners" and the "Protesters" saw many brave soldiers of the Covenant cast out, including Colonels Ker and Strachan who resigned and went west to join the army of the Western Association.

The protesting minority of Covenanters against the action were led by Samuel Rutherford, James and William Guthrie, Henry Hall, and John Livingston; while Thomas Hog was deposed by the Synod of Ross for supporting them. James Guthrie and his colleague Rev. Bennett went so far as to preach against the Resolutioners. For this they were summoned to appear before King Charles and the Committee of the Estates at Perth on 19 February 1651. They appeared on February 22 and declined the king's supremacy in doctrinal matters and, on 28 February 1651, they prepared a strongly worded protestation which was given in. Surprisingly no further action was taken at that time, but James Guthrie would have his declinature of the king's authority given as a charge when he was arrested with John Semple in August 1660 at Edinburgh.

Not everybody in the Protester's ranks were implacably opposed to the Resolutions. Hugh Binning for one saw that nothing but strife would come from the belligerence. John Livingston attended some of the early meetings of the Protesters but was unhappy at the agendas and the increasing division within the Church. Robert Blair and James Durham declined to take sides though they both endeavoured to reunite the factions. Durham observed perceptively that "division was worse by far than either side."[188] Robert Baillie on the other hand eulogised many of the leaders of the Covenant but he attacked them for being "Protesters."

The immediate aims of the Resolutioners cum royalists was to support the king in his bid to regain his father's English throne. But all was lost at Worcester in September 1651.

With the departure of Charles II into exile the issues which divided the two sides became, prima facie, irrelevant and obsolete. But instead of being an opportunity for reconciliation the division

---

[188] Howie, *Worthies*, p. 226.

between the two increased. In practical terms the Resolutioners remained royalist and would accept the king's return on the best terms they could get. They were therefore potential enemies to the Cromwellian Commonwealth. The Protesters were not against the king in an abstract sense, but were inclined to support the existing Commonwealth as being better than any arrangement they could extract from Charles. They each held their own General Assemblies in 1652 wherein each made accusations against the other. In 1653 they held their meetings at the same time in St. Giles, Edinburgh, when the Resolutioner Assembly was broken up by Cromwell's soldiers and the ministers escorted out of the city. The Protester meeting was also suppressed later. The meeting of the General Assembly after 1653 was then prohibited without the permission of Parliament. A beneficial side-effect was that many ministers withdrew from arguing and returned to their pastoral duties. As a consequence, during ten years of the Commonwealth, there was a noticeable improvement among the people.

Puritans - Presbyterian differences.

The label "Puritan" was given to a group of people who wanted a more reformed Church of England along the lines advocated by John Calvin. Confusingly the Presbyterians in Scotland were also called Puritans in the early seventeenth century. The objectives of the two groups were broadly the same. The Marquis of Argyll was a supporter of these early Scottish Puritans. The first Presbyterian church in England was established at Wandsworth in 1572 but English Presbyterianism did not join with Scotland until 1643. After the National Covenant of 1638 the differences were more specific and by the advent of Cromwell the Puritans were a separate identifiable dissident group in England and Holland.

The Puritans in the time of Queen Elizabeth I mostly wanted to abolish ceremonies in the Church of England. In particular they sought to excise ceremonies considered to be remnants of Catholicism—kneeling at Communion; use of the cross in baptism; wearing the surplice—and some questioned whether there was biblical authority for bishops. They also wanted a reformed government of the church with elders and synods, and stricter discipline. This was all consistent with Presbytery. However, neither Queen Elizabeth, who had taken the title "supreme governor" of the Church of England (not "head" of the Church as sometimes erroneously stated) nor her successor, King James I (VI of Scotland), would allow it. King James objected because it was his policy of divine right of kings to be head of the church.

The Puritans remained in the Church of England in the hope of achieving reform. But a separatist group emerged about 1581 led by Robert Browne and they set up a covenanted church which was the beginning of the English Independent Church or Congregationalist movement. The group was pressured by the English government and the bishops and driven abroad to Holland. Browne eventually returned to the Church of England but his place was taken by Henry Barrow, John Greenwood, Francis Johnson, Henry Ainsworth, and John Robinson, who was to lead the "Pilgrim Fathers" to New England.

Oliver Cromwell was not a Puritan but an Independent. The difference being that the Independents believed in toleration of beliefs and creeds although some restrictions were still applied to Catholics taking official jobs. In time these Independents would become the Congregationalist movement. In his relations with Scotland Cromwell was very firm but also tolerant of religion in consequence the Cromwell rule was amongst the most peaceful for many years. An indication of Cromwell's underlying toughness was the debate he witnessed between his own Independent ministers and the Presbyterians represented by Hugh Binning. The Independents were thoroughly defeated and Cromwell asked who the young minister was. With hand on sword he remarked, "He hath bound well indeed [but] this will loose all again."[189]

Queensferry Paper.

The Queensferry Paper was so called because it was discovered in the pocket of a Covenanter, Henry Hall of Haughshead, when he was seized at South Queensferry on 4 June 1680. Hall was in the company of Donald Cargill when they were discovered and an attempt made to arrest them. Cargill made good his escape but Hall subsequently died from his wounds. The document is thought to have been a manifesto intended to be taken by Hall to Holland

---

[189] Howie, *Worthies*, p. 213.

where dissident Scots could consider a new Presbyterian system for Scotland.

Smellie, in *Men of the Covenant*, considers the paper the most advanced of all the Covenanting manifestos. It was a bond strong in its affirmations and denials, and made a solemn confession of faith and frankly disavowed sinful rulers. It further made a declaration in favour of a republic. The document was the first formal statement of the dissident group that became known as the Cameronians, MacMillanites, and Reformed Presbyterians. A document of some 6,000 words it is much longer and definitive than the Declaration at Sanquhar which was made shortly after on 22 June 1680.

The substance of the document given in Hewison's *The Covenanters* was:

1. To covenant with and swear acknowledgement of the Trinity and to own the Old and New Testaments to be the rule of faith.
2. To advance God's kingdom, free the church from Prelacy and Erastianism, and remove those who had forfeited authority.
3. To uphold the Presbyterian Church of Scotland, with her standards, polity, and worship, as an independent government.
4. To overthrow the kingdom of darkness; i.e., popery, prelacy, and Erastianism.
5. To discard the royal family and set up a republic.
6. To decline hearing the indulged clergy.
7. To refuse the ministerial function unless duly called and ordained.
8. To defend their worship and liberties, to view assailants as declarers of war, to destroy those assaulting, and not to injure any "but those that have injured us."[190]

The fifth article recites the reasons for rejecting rule by a single person (the monarchy) and states:

---

[190] Hewison, *Covenanters*, Vol. 2, p. 329. The lengthy, full-text version is in Johnston's *Treasury*.

> We do declare that we shall set up over ourselves, and over what the Lord shall give us power of, government and governors according to the Word of God, and especially that Word, Exodus 18:21: "Moreover, though shalt provide out of all the people, able men, such as fear God, men of truth, hating covetousness, and place such over them; to be rulers of thousands, and rulers of hundred, rulers of fifties, and rulers of tens." That we shall no more commit the government of ourselves, and the making of laws for us, to any one single person, or lineal successor, we not being by God, as the Jews were, bound to one single family; and this kind of government by a single person being most liable to inconveniences, and aptest to degenerate into tyranny, as sad and long experience hath taught us.[191]

Rapture at death.

It is remarkable how often the martyrs of the Reformation went joyfully to their deaths, not only with brave words and declarations of faith to the assembled throng, but in a physical rapture. Modern medicine would probably have some explanation about adrenaline rush or over-active glands of some kind brought on by the circumstances of execution. But pure and simple faith is much preferred as the explanation; these people believed with every breath of their bodies—their commitment was total—that they really did walk with God.

Such was the total dedication to their faith that a similar rapture is to be found in those who were fortunate to live a full life span. David Black was a colleague of Andrew Melville at St. Andrews for a while and much respected for his zeal and fidelity. Banished to Angus, he continued to preach until shortly before his death:

> He found in his own soul also such a sensible taste of eternal joy, that he was seized with the fervent desire to depart and be with the Lord.... "He had a final Communion service and feeling death near he sank to his knees with hands and eyes lifted up to heaven" in the very act of

[191] Johnston, *Treasury*, p. 138.

devotion and adoration, as in a transport of joy, he was taken away.[192]

In a relatively short life of thirty-six years, James Durham was a fearless presenter of the truth which included preaching to Oliver Cromwell and decrying his invasion of Scotland. Cromwell took the public rebuff and dismissed Durham civilly with a warning to refrain from discussing the subject in public. Durham was very pious and like so many just before his death, he had qualms of conscience whether they would gain entry to Heaven. As his end drew nigh he "cried, in a rapture of holy joy,... Is not the Lord good? Is he not infinitely good? See how he smiles! I do say it, and I do proclaim."[193]

The renowned Samuel Rutherford was dying when summoned before the Privy Council and famously declared, "Tell them I have got a summons already before a superior Judge and judiciary, and I behove to answer the first summons."[194] In his latter days he often broke out in a kind of sacred rapture. One morning he fainted and on recovering declared, "I feel, I feel, I believe, I joy and rejoice, I feed on manna. The evening of his death he was heard to say several times Oh! for arms to embrace Him! Oh! for a well tuned harp!"[195]

The martyrs on the scaffold all professed their great faith and without exception went to their deaths with dignity. No one struggled or remonstrated beyond perhaps demanding the right to speak. In many cases their last words were accompanied by the roll of the drums deliberately preventing any last words and testimony from being heard. James Renwick in particular was asked not to speak of the causes for his execution and to the very last was offered a petition to sign that would have saved him. For him the drums rolled to which he said, "Yonder is the welcome warning for my marriage; the bridegroom is coming; I am ready; I am ready."[196] He was told the drums would continue and was asked to pray in private.

---

[192] Howie, *Worthies*, p. 83.
[193] *Ibid.*, p. 230.
[194] *Ibid.*, p. 236.
[195] *Ibid.*
[196] *Ibid.*, p. 545.

But "he went to the scaffold with great cheerfulness, as one in a transport of joy."[197]

Hugh McKail was a devout and staunch supporter of Presbyterianism and suffered great torture with the boot. He counselled fellow prisoners in their last days and hours and is remembered for his last words, sometimes called "The Seraphic Song on the Scaffold":

> And now I leave off to speak any more to creatures, and begin my intercourse with God, which shall never be broken off. Farewell, father and mother, friends and relations! farewell, meat and drink! farewell, sun, moon and stars! Welcome God and father! welcome sweet Jesus Christ, the mediator of the new Covenant! welcome blessed Spirit of Grace, the God of all consolation! Welcome glory! welcome eternal life! and welcome death ! [198]

The two women executed at Edinburgh, Isobel Alison and Marion Harvey, were both young women in their twenties when they were convicted of treason merely because of their opinions. These too went joyfully to their deaths with cries of "Farewell sweet Bible...Farewell sweet Scriptures."[199] On 11 July 1681 the Justiciary Court sentenced three Cargillites to death: Adam Philip, Laurence Hay, and Andrew Pitilloh, a labourer from Largo, Fife. Executed on July 13, they perceived that death was sweeter than life; on the scaffold Pitilloh exclaimed, "O sweet indictment, O sweet sentence for my lovely Lord, O sweet scaffold for contending for the Cause, Covenant, and work of Reformation."[200]

Donald Cargill stunned the Privy Council by his outburst against the apostasy of the Lord Advocate Mackenzie and saying that it was Mackenzie who had lost all fear of God. But on the scaffold Cargill said that "This is the most joyful day that I ever saw in my pilgrimage on earth; my joy is now begun. As he went up the ladder his last words were "The Lord knows I go up this ladder with less

---

[197] *Ibid.*, p. 546.
[198] Ibid., p. 364. Johnston, *Treasury*, p. 331.
[199] Thomson, *Cloud*, pp. 130, 144.
[200] *Ibid.*, p. 166.

fear and perturbation of mind than ever I entered the pulpit to preach."[201]

John Dickson, shortly before his death in 1700, wrote of the inferiority of the Revolutionary Church to that of 1649-1650. He grieved that there had been no building on the foundation created; they had the shell of ordinances and church government but lacked the kernel. He writes of the suffering that had been inflicted and the truths of the Covenants which were in the mouths of the martyrs as they went to their deaths "ascending, as it were, up unto God, in a perfumed cloud of transporting joy."[202]

With ecstasies such as these it was clear that the government had their hands full in any efforts they made to influence the common people.

Rebellion - the 9th Earl of Argyll. See also: Imprisonment; Test Act.

Archibald Campbell, 9th Earl of Argyll, son of the Marquis of Argyll executed in 1661, came to notice of the government through his objection to the "Test Act" of 31 August 1681. This imposed another Oath on the people of Scotland (but excluded the king's brother and sons) and was of itself a contradictory document. In essence it repudiated the Covenants, acknowledged the king's supremacy in civil and ecclesiastical matters and promised passive obedience at all times. In other words acceptance of slavery, a total acceptance of an autocratic king who could do whatever he wished. This outrageous Act and an earlier Act which declared that difference of religion could not forfeit succession (the Duke of York was Catholic) were spoons to stir the pot of discontent.

Argyll protested at the exception of the royal families exclusion from the Test and held the view that they were a potential source of danger. He took the Test but qualified it by declaring a clause "as far as it is consistent with itself and the Protestant religion."[203] He was promptly imprisoned in Edinburgh Castle and charged with treason and perjury. At his trial in December he was sentenced to death. He escaped from Edinburgh Castle in dramatic fashion by

---

[201] Howie, *Worthies*, p. 452.
[202] *Ibid.*, p. 594.
[203] Hewison, *Covenanters*, Vol. 2, p. 354.

exchanging places with a servant accompanying his step daughter Lady Sophia Lindsay who came to visit him. Argyll was then chaperoned to London under the name of "Mr. Hope," by William Veitch.

In England, the Duke of Monmouth, illegitimate son of Charles II, and Lord William Russell, Lord Essex, and Sir Algernon Sydney were conspiring to change the succession: to prevent the Catholic James, Duke of York, from acceding to the throne. They corresponded with Argyll in exile in Holland and had counsel with leading Presbyterians William Carstares and Robert Baillie of Jerviswood. Carstares favoured caution and Baillie was for action forthwith. But the Scots deferred their action while the English spawned the Ryehouse Plot, to murder the King and the Duke of York. This too failed; the king returned to London a day earlier than planned. The plots were discovered and retribution followed.

In April 1685, Argyll and three small ships, the *Anna*, *Sophia*, and *David*, loaded with arms and munitions set sail from Holland. However, they went too far north and touched land in Orkney where two of the party, William Spence and William Blackadder (son of John) were put ashore to gather information. They were quickly seized by royalist troops and the ships sailed on to Campbelltown, in Kintyre. They found only a tepid support and suffered the misfortune of losing their munitions and arms to the English who had seen them being stored at an old fort at Eilean Gheirrig.

In a pre-emptive strike, the Marquis of Atholl marched on the Campbell lands and executed seventeen Campbell chieftains at Inveraray. A monument to them stands in the grounds of Inveraray Castle. Argyll wanted to take decisive action and to march on Glasgow but was overruled and the forces were divided with Sir Patrick Hume and about five hundred soldiers reaching Kilpatrick in June 1685. But Argyll had set out for a friends house the night before and was subsequently captured at Inchannan, near Paisley, by two servants of Sir John Shaw of Greenock and assisted by a local weaver. He was soon in Edinburgh Castle and on 30 June 1685 lost his head to the "Maiden," as had his illustrious father in 1661.

One consequence of Argyll's attempt at rebellion was the incarceration of 167 Presbyterian prisoners in Dunnottar Castle because of the fear that they might have supported him. In the August of 1685 some were released on giving an oath of allegiance and bond for good behaviour; the remainder were sentenced to transportation.

In Ayrshire and the southwest during April 1685, George Barclay sought to preach up support for Argyll with little success. There was no support for Argyll's rebellion from James Renwick and the Society People or Cameronians. Argyll himself had not been a particular friend to them in the past despite his illustrious father. Between 1663 and 1681 the Earl had been a member of the Privy Council including the one which sentenced Donald Cargill. Renwick had some sympathy with the rebellion because it was against Papacy, but it was otherwise inconsistent with the aims of the Covenants, contained no reference to the Covenants and Presbyterian government; and it opened the door to charges of confederation with malignants. An interesting suggestion in Thorbjorn Campbell's *Standing Witnesses* is that there may have been an agreement with the Society People not to assist Argyll's venture because, coincidentally, the Killing Time came to an end quite suddenly at that time.

Religion – Presbyterian uniformity in England and Scotland.
See also: Solemn League and Covenant.

The desire for uniformity of religion in England, Scotland, and Ireland lies behind the troubles suffered by the Presbyterians in Scotland. From the time of the union of the crowns in 1603 the Stuart kings pursued their "Divine Right" policy and sought to enforce uniformity of an Episcopalian religion on Scotland with themselves as the supreme head, as they were already in England and Ireland. But there was also the opposite view for uniformity under Presbyteryianism. The stricter Presbyterians, the Covenanters, saw the opportunity to extend God's realm on earth through the alliance with the English Parliamentary party in the Solemn League and Covenant of 1643. There was already an English Presbyterian movement with its own body of learned ministers that had been founded in Wandsworth in 1572. Moreover, the early Puritan movement was very close to Presbyterianism and had many common objectives. It was the common purpose of an evangelical church devoid of the frippery of Romish practice that united them. The Scots diligently pursued their objective but the intervention of Oliver Cromwell and his toleration of all religion save Catholicism, was to blunt their hopes. Worse was to follow with Civil War and execution of Charles I in 1649 that detracted from this great purpose. However, things were worse under Charles II and James II. Not only was there increasing oppression and eventual slaughter, but there was the overtones of a return to Catholicism and possibly a Catholic king in James II.

A succinct summary is made by P. H. Waddell in his Notes to *Old Mortality* (quoted in Johnson's *Treasury*) :

> These objects, it must be confessed, were too lofty, too severe, and too despotic – founded on ideas of religion itself, and of human nature, too narrow to ever be realised. No king, church, or nation could long be expected to conform to them; but the backsliding, and the covenant breaking, and then the persecution, and the bloodshed; and the atrocious cruelties that followed were first and wholly on the royal side.[204]

Rescue.

Covenanter lore is full of miraculous escapes and valiant rescues which make wonderful reading. *The Traditions of the Covenanters* by Rev. Robert Simpson gives many examples and throws a light on the men and women of the Covenant who went to extraordinary lengths to save their friends who were otherwise likely to be executed. His account of the Enterkin Pass rescue is quite short although he does give a joint testimony of three of the rescuers—Thomas Harkness, Andrew Clark, and Samuel McEwan—which they made shortly before their execution. The testimonies are further quoted in Thomson's *Cloud*. Campbell's *Standing Witnesses* gives more details of the rescue at Enterkin Pass.

This pass was a narrow footpath along the Enterkin Burn under the shadow of the hills, and was the main path from Dumfries to Edinburgh. Passing, as it did, through wild and desolate parts it was a favoured place for rescues and several were effected there. One of the famous rescues was that made in July 1684. Prisoners had been taken after a conventicle held by James Renwick at Blackloch, Slamannan in June and were destined for Edinburgh for trial, and

---

[204] Johnston, *Treasury*, pp. 102-103.

probable execution. Under guard of Claverhouse's troopers the party was ambushed at Glenvalentine in the Pass. In the rescue, a soldier, Sergeant Kelt, and some of the rescuers were killed and wounded, and about fourteen prisoners set free. The rescuers included James "Long Gun" Harkness who is believed to have been the organiser, John or Robert Grierson, and James "Black" McMichael who fired the shot that killed the sergeant.

Claverhouse personally led the search for the perpetrators and ran down some of the ringleaders at Closeburn. James Harkness had previously been captured but, with about twenty-four others, he had escaped on 16 September 1683 from the Cannongate Tolbooth. He also escaped this time round, probably from the Dumfries Tolbooth. His brother Thomas "White Hose" Harkness was not so lucky and he and others were taken to Edinburgh. For the captured "rescuers" there was very peremptory justice; they were charged, convicted, and hanged all in one day: 15 August 1684. Executed were Thomas Harkness of Locherben, Andrew Clark of Leadhills, Samuel McEwen of Glencairn, and Thomas Wood of Kirkmichael. Another man, James Nicol, was seized at the executions for muttering too loudly about them. He was a recusant who had been at Bothwell Brig. He was convicted and hanged on 27 August 1684.

Claverhouse was in command of his troop of about 130 men when they encountered Covenanters who had possibly been at the Declaration at Rutherglen. He took some eighteen prisoners, including John King, to Evandale. On Sunday, June 1, Claverhouse came across the conventicle at Drumclog and was routed by the overwhelming numbers of armed Covenanters. As a result of this the prisoners from Hamilton were released and John King credited with asking Claverhouse as the latter fled, he was "invited by his prisoner of the morning to tarry for the afternoon sermon."[205]

Escapes from custody were quite common, as in the case of James Harkness at the Cannongate Tolbooth. Here, after the 1693 escape of twenty-five prisoners, the magistrates themselves were charged with "passive complicity" but later acquitted. The reality of the prisons was that money spoke. For a consideration a prisoner could buy a private cell, food, and drink, and be in reasonable comfort. If a prisoner had nothing, then he took his chances amongst the general villains and murderers where a religious

---

[205] Smellie, p. 300.

person, man or woman, was likely to be attacked. Robert Garnock was one such person to be abused and assaulted by both jailer and a deranged inmate.

The 9th Earl of Argyll was famously rescued from prison in Edinburgh Castle through the bravery of his step-daughter, Lady Sophia Lindsay, and a page with whom he changed clothes and walked out of prison. In *Men of the Covenant*, Smellie recounts how Argyll changed clothes with the lad and made good his escape: "A servant with a lantern accompanied her and a page bore her train. The latter was a tall awkward country-lad, with a fair wig and his head tied up as if he had been engaged in a fray.[206]

A group of Covenanters were responsible for a daring attack on the Kirkcudbright Tolbooth on 16 December 1684 that released many of their compatriots. Following the rescue Claverhouse once more went in pursuit and caught up with them at Auchencloy where five of them were killed in the skirmish. Two others, Robert Smith and William Hunter, were taken back to Kirkcudbright, tried, and hanged.

The escape from the Ducat Tower at Newmilns arose from loose talk by Peter Ingles whose party of soldiers had brought some Covenanter prisoners there. The prisoners had been seized at a house conventicle at Little Blackwood near Fenwick. Subsequently their captor Ingles spent some time in a tavern and appears to have had too much to drink and in his cups, remarked that most of the troops were away on a raid leaving only a few on guard duty. John Browning and about sixty others raided the blacksmith's shop at Darvel and took sledgehammers to break down the doors of the Ducat Tower. Two soldiers and one of the rescue party, John Law, were killed but the seven prisoners were all released and got away. The aftermath of this escape was that Claverhouse and his troopers took up the search and caught John Browning and with him his uncle John Brown of Priesthill, the "Christian Carrier."

Restoration. See also: Breda.

The Restoration is the name given to the period when King Charles II was restored to the throne of Scotland, England, and Ireland in 1660, until his death in 1685. Charles II had first acceded

---

[206] Smellie, p. 361.

to the throne on the death of his father in January 1649, but then he was only King of Scotland in practice. The negotiations at Breda, in Holland, led to Charles returning to Scotland on 23 June 1650 and his coronation at Scone on 1 January 1651. In England, however, he was opposed by the English Parliamentarians and Cromwell. The Scottish army was routed at Worcester on 3 September 1651 when Charles was forced into a miserable and almost penniless exile. Another Declaration at Breda in 1660, negotiated with the English, gave his terms for returning to the throne of the three kingdoms.

At the Restoration the people of Scotland had been without a king in peace time for over twenty years and a new generation had grown up knowing only of the liberated government of the Kirk and Cromwell. The majority of the people were accepting of change, and keen to regain the country's independence even under another Stuart king. The hopes of the new generation were soon dashed as evidenced by the king's appointments of nobles to positions of state who were against the Presbyterians. The king himself was barely tolerant of the Engagers then in power and expected Scotland to tag along with his policies in England. As Lord Commissioner of Scotland, responsible for calling Parliament and commander in chief of forces to be raised, he appointed the Earl of Middleton. Middleton had private instructions to try the inclinations of Scotland to episcopacy. He was soon to gain notoriety as bringing in, amongst many other acts, the Act of Collation and Presentation that "outed" over three hundred ministers from their livings. The Earl of Glencairn was appointed Chancellor, the Earl of Crawford given the Treasury, and the Earl of Rothes was made President of the Council. Importantly for the Presbyterians, the Earl of Lauderdale was appointed Secretary of State. In this role Lauderdale, who was anti-popery and had Presbyterian leanings, had the ear of the king and was able to exert a moderating influence. He was the virtual ruler of Scotland for twenty years.

Revolution Church. See also: Revolution Settlement; Societies.

The Revolution Church or the Church *of* Scotland, was confirmed by the "Act of Parliament Ratifying the Confession of Faith and Settling Presbyterian Church Government" on 7 June 1690. The Act did not, however, satisfy the staunch Cameronians or

Society people and they did not accept it. They objected to King William and wife Mary (the daughter of King James II) as foreigners because they had been brought up in an Erastian church and lacked scriptural and Covenanted qualifications. They also objected to the Committee of Estates and the Parliament which was made up of former persecutors of the Church; and to the changes which did not go far enough. Prelacy was rejected but not declared unscriptural, Presbytery was not declared to be of divine right and the Westminster Confession of Faith was not declared to have scriptural authority. Perhaps most glaring was the failure to repeal the infamous Act Recissory of 1662, which meant that all that had been achieved between 1638 and 1660, was omitted.

Turning their gaze upon the new settlement, the Societies objected to certain members of the Church polity who had been Indulged or approved of the "Resolutions." A big pill to swallow was the expediency to admit some eight hundred former indulged ministers and even some curates, to ministerial appointments. This was simply because there were only about ninety Covenanted ministers left, of whom sixty-one had been ejected in 1662 and were re-appointed to their old charges. The Societies and Covenanters still objected to the Erastian nature of the Church itself which had been settled on the basis of the Great Charter of Presbytery of 1592, and not on the Second Reformation of 1638.

Perhaps it is easier for the lay person to understand that the objections were founded on policy and politics and the king's wish that the people have whatever religion they wanted. His instruction to Parliament in 1690 was to pass an act establishing that church government which is most agreeable to the inclinations of the people. This was done and understandably was agreed upon by the majority: the moderates of the Church. But for the faithful remnant it was not deemed to have been in accordance with the Scriptures. The dissenters, made up of about twenty Societies and some seven thousand members, remained outside the Established Church for many years without a minister.

For the majority of Presbyterians and the Revolutionary Church it was an end to a century of bloody struggles and they speedily secured legislation—an "Act for Settling the Quiet and Peace of the Church 1693, anent Uniformity of Worship"—that made conformity to the new settlement a condition of becoming a minister. This was followed by the Barrier Act of the General Assembly of 1697, that introduced prior consultation for new rules or constitutions that were binding on the Church. This effectively dealt with any attempts at hasty change and innovations. But there were tribulations and further schism to come in the eighteenth century, albeit without the bloodshed of earlier years.

Revolution Settlement, 1688-1690; also known as the Glorious Revolution. See also: Revolution Church.

The term Revolution Settlement is sometimes applied to the Act that confirmed the establishment of the Church *of* Scotland, but it has a wider context that encompasses the events that led to the deposing of James II, and the invitation to William of Orange and his wife Mary, to take the crown of Britain.

The Catholic King James II came to the throne on his brother's death 6 February 1685 and was largely welcomed by English and Scottish moderates. In Scotland the remnant Covenanters led by James Renwick were fiercely opposed to him but were constrained by the "Killing Time." Rebellions by the Earl of Argyll in Scotland and the Duke of Monmouth in England were unsuccessful. James II position then seemed secure, enough for him to broach his next project: to reinstate Roman Catholics to posts despite the Test Act of 1681. When the English Parliament remonstrated with him he summarily dismissed them and turned to Scotland to obtain their approbation, as an example.

In Scotland some influential nobles, the Earl of Perth who was Chancellor, and Lord Melfort, Secretary of State, announced their conversion to Catholicism. At Holyrood palace ornaments and vestments for the Mass drew an excited response from the people of Edinburgh. An attempt was made at the Parliament in April 1686 to reduce or remove legislation against Catholics but Parliament only agreed to consider a bill for the purpose. In pique Parliament was adjourned and James reverted to royal autocracy and sealed his doom in both kingdoms.

In both England and Scotland James ruthlessly and arbitrarily removed potential opponents from positions of authority, including bishops, privy councillors, and those in public offices. In Scotland he introduced three Indulgences which progressively allowed religious freedom for all, including the Presbyterians (only because he was forced to) and imposed his will on the burghs by appointing his own officials where necessary, including Claverhouse as Provost of Dundee. The imprisoned Presbyterian ministers were released and a majority who accepted the Indulgences, gave thanks to the king.

What led to James II's downfall was his demand that the Declaration of Indulgence should be read out in the churches. This prompted seven bishops, led by Sancroft, Archbishop of Canterbury, to remonstrate with the king, for which they were imprisoned. At their trial they were acquitted. Up to this point James II had been tolerated because there was expectation that his daughter, Mary, a Protestant by his first marriage to Anne Hyde, would succeed him. However, the birth of an heir to James and his second wife, Mary of Modena, on 10 June 1688, fuelled new fears of a Catholic succession which neither country desired. The Whigs and the Tories in the English Parliament then joined together to ask William of Orange and his wife Mary to accept the throne. It is sometimes forgotten that William III was a grandson of King Charles I (his mother was Mary, the eldest daughter of Charles) so the throne was still within the family but with Protestant members.

William of Orange had difficulties of his own in Holland where he was the mainstay of the Protestant cause in Europe, and was fearful of French intervention. However, he came to England landing at Torbay on 5 November 1688 supported by a fleet of nearly six hundred vessels and some 14,000 soldiers as his personal bodyguard. James II meanwhile suffered for his appointment of Catholics in the army where dissension made resistance to William virtually impossible and he was forced to flee. On his first attempt, 11 November 1688, he reached Sheerness in Kent but was recognised and brought back to Rochester. He made a public statement repudiating any help from France but after a few days fled again, this time reaching safety in France. It is thought likely that William allowed James to escape as, had he stayed, he may well have gathered together supporters and there would have been bloodshed, possibly another Civil War.

In Scotland the Privy Council dissolved itself in December, and a Convention of the Estates met on 14 March 1689 which decided to declare William and Mary king and queen of Scotland. The declaration was made at the Mercat Cross on 11 April 1689. Significantly the convention declared that James VII (II of England) was a professed papist and had failed to take the oath at his accession to maintain a Protestant government and had "forfeited the right to the crown, and that the throne had thus become vacant."[207] Commissioners took the Scottish "Claim of Right" and "Articles of Grievance" with them to London. Chief among their demands were:

Repeal of the Act of Supremacy of 1669.
Abolition of bishops.
Abolition of the Lords of the Articles.

After some prevarication, on 11 May 1689 William and Mary accepted the Scottish throne with succession going to Mary's sister, Anne, if there were no heirs of the body. Thus Scotland became a legal limited monarchy.

In England the Parliament took similar steps by passing a Bill of Rights in 1689 on the basis that James had abdicated the throne by leaving the country. They enacted that the crown had no power to suspend laws and no Roman Catholic should be allowed to come to the throne. The consequences of the Revolution in England were:

Limitation on the monarch's powers in England.
A Coronation Oath that they were bound to rule according to Parliament.
The Declaration of Rights was read (although debateable if it was agreed).
It was illegal to:
- suspend statutes created by parliament.
- exempt (dispense) individuals from statutes.
- to maintain a standing army in peacetime.
- to establish commissions for ecclesiastical causes.
Reduced financial settlements, to ensure regular Parliaments were called.
Legal freedom to worship allowed to Protestant dissenters except Unitarians.[208]

There followed the Toleration Act by which all Protestants might worship in their own way. In 1701 the Act of Settlement was passed

---

[207] Metcalfe, *Renfrew*, p. 335.
[208] Robertson, *Select Statutes*, p. 129.

settling that if William and his sister-in-law Anne died without heirs the throne should go to Sophia, Electress of Hanover, the granddaughter of James I of England. Anne was queen from 1702-1714, but this law led to the accession of the House of Hanover by George I in 1714 and thus to the current sovereign.

In Ireland James II made a brief attempt to regain power with the help of the native Catholic population and a French army. William, however, saw the potential for a Jacobite invasion of England and led an English army in a pre emptive strike, winning a decisive victory at the Battle of the Boyne in 1690. France and England were at war almost continuously from 1689-1697 with Louis XIV trying to put James II back on the throne of Britain. The result of the Revolution Settlement or the Glorious Revolution in Ireland was to confirm the ascendancy of a narrow Anglo Irish landed class and an Episcopal church that had little support.

The Revolution Settlement of the Church of Scotland saw the restoration of Presbyterianism but it was not the form or purity of 1648-1649. On 25 April, 1690 the Scottish Parliament repealed the Act of Supremacy of 1669 by an "Act Rescinding the First Act of the Second Parliament of 1669," and passed an "Act Ratifying the Confession of Faith and Settling Presbyterian Church Government," on 7 June 1690. This ratified the Westminster Confession of Faith and established Presbyterian government according to the Great Charter of Presbytery of 1592. Moreover it placed the Church of Scotland into the hands of the ministers who had been ejected since 1661, but even so they were a minority among a generally moderate membership. Notably, for the Covenanters, church government was seen as a matter of expediency and policy, and prelacy was rejected but not declared contrary to the Scriptures.

Notwithstanding the dissatisfaction of the faithful remnant, the essential objectives of religious and parliamentary freedom were achieved. If nothing else, the 130 years of trial and tribulation of the Presbyterian Church finally resolved the supremacy of Christ as Lord of the conscience and this was recognised by the rulers of the nation. Freedom and democracy in Great Britain owes much to their sacrifice.

Root and Branch petitions [England].

The root and branch petitions were representations made by nineteen of the English Counties against the Arminian policies of Archbishop Laud and the increasing and unwarranted intervention of the bishops and the clergy into the daily life of the people. The first petition was made by a group in London who were the supporters of John Pym. It contained some twenty eight articles which were framed in emotive and vitriolic terms alleging that the policies encouraged:

Imposition of a theological monopoly
Attacks on preaching (especially lay preachers)
Encouragement of superstition and ritual
The Book of Canons 1640
The Book of Sports
Use of excommunication for trivial offences
Support for monopolies
Support for impositions (taxation by royal fiat)
Support for Ship Money
Decay of trade and war with Scotland

The petitions argued that Episcopal government was not *jure divino* but of human authority. Notably the petitions emanated from those counties that had seen the firmest application of Arminianism and were also the counties which had some form of Puritan tradition. The counties were: Devon, Somerset, Gloucester, Warwick, Oxford, Buckinghamshire, Bedfordshire, Hertfordshire, Sussex, Surrey, Kent, Essex, Cambridgeshire, Suffolk, Norfolk, Lincolnshire, Nottinghamshire, Cheshire and Lancashire.

The ensuing debates about the petitions led directly to legislation including: abolition of the Court of High Commission and the Star Chamber; abolition of ship money; the end of secular employment of bishops and clergy; and the exclusion of bishops from the House of Lords.

Royal Prerogative.

James VI of Scotland, later James I of England (1603) was a prime exponent of autocratic rule where he, and his successors, firmly believed in the "Divine Right of Kings." The overriding factor in King James VI's make up was his determination to be the supreme authority, king of both State and the Church, after the fashion of Elizabeth I of England. The intensity of his view was expressed in *The Trew Law of Free Monarchies* written in 1598 asserting that "And as ye see it manifest that the King is over-lord of the whole land, so is he master over every person that inhabiteth the same."[209] In the *Basilikon Doron*, addressed to his eldest son, Prince Henry, James told him that he was a little God, and that he was to sit on his throne and rule over other men.[210] In his *Defence of the Right of Kings*, James insisted that kings were the images of God on Earth.

The Kirk in Scotland had grown in strength from 1567 and by 1584 was organised through Kirk Sessions, Presbyteries, Synods and its General Assembly and exercising the jurisdiction of the former Church Courts over moral conduct. King James attacked these institutions with what became known as the "Black Acts" reasserting his personal authority "over all states as well spiritual and temporal within this realm."[211] With this he revived episcopacy and required all ministers receiving a benefice to accept the acts and the rule of the bishops or be deprived of their living. From then until the final fall of Charles II the battle was joined in which there would be changes in direction, compromises and intense persecution all underpinned by the king's desire, nay demand, for absolute authority in all things civil and ecclesiastical. It was not only in Scotland that James I was an autocrat. In a speech to Judges in the Star Chamber 20 June 1616, he emphatically laid down his ground rules which goes some way to explaining why he was so intractable in his dealings with the Kirk:

> Now having spoken of your office in general. I am next to come to the limits wherein you are to bound yourselves, which likewise are three. First encroach not upon the prerogative of the crown; if there falls out a question that concerns my prerogative or mystery of state, deal not with it, till you consult with the king or his council or both; for

---

[209] Prothero, *Select Statutes*, p. 400.
[210] Calderwood, *History*, Vol. 5, pp. 744-745.
[211] Hewison, *Covenanters*, Vol. 1, p. 119.

> they are transcendent matters. That which concerns the mystery of the king's power is not lawful to be disputed; for that is to wade into the weakness of princes, and to take away the mystical reverence that belongs unto them that sit in the throne of God.
>
> Secondly, that you keep within your own benches, not to invade other jurisdictions, which is unfit and an unlawful thing. Keep you therefore all in your own bounds and for my part, I desire you to give me no more right, in my private prerogative, than you give any subject, and therein I will be acquiescent: as for the absolute prerogative of the crown, that is no subject for the tongue of a lawyer, nor is lawful to be disputed.
>
> It is atheism and blasphemy to dispute what God can do: good Christians content themselves with his will revealed in his word, so it is presumption and high contempt in a subject to dispute what a king can do, or say that a king cannot do this or that; but rest in that which is the king's revealed will in his law.[212]

On the Prerogative and Parliament he ominously said:

> [A]and therefore general laws made publicly in parliament may upon known respects to the king by his authority be mitigated and suspended upon causes only known to him. As likewise, although I have said a good king will frame all his actions to be according to the law, yet is he not bound thereto but of his goodwill.[213]

It is little wonder that James' attitude to the government of Scotland as revealed in his address to the English Parliament in 1607, was a vainglorious boast of governing by the pen. The delegation of day to day government to the Scottish Privy Council was conjoined with his appointment of its officials who were certain to follow his will. His other policy managing body was the Lords of the Articles, a committee of selected bishops, nobles and some burgesses with absolute authority. The common man did not stand a

---

[212] Prothero, *Select Statutes*, pp. 399-400.
[213] *Ibid.*, pp. 400-401.

chance in these circumstances and the Kirk simply had to resist at risk of imprisonment or worse, if it was to survive let alone change the king's will.

Ruthven Raid 22 August 1582.

The Ruthven Raid, as it was called, was the result of a rising by the people and reaction by nobles who were thoroughly disgusted with the autocratic and offensive antics of the royal favourites, the Earl of Arran and the Duke of Lennox. A former favourite of the Regent Queen Mary of Guise, the Frenchman, Esme Stuart, became a favourite with the young King James. He was a nephew of the 4th Earl of Lennox and descended in that line from James II of Scotland. Well connected and charismatic so far as the sixteen year old James was concerned, he was also suspected of being a papal agent. Against a background of resentment Esme Stuart sought to bring down the Regent, the Earl of Morton. In this he was aided by a Captain James Stewart of Bothwellmuir, the brother of John Knox's second wife, Margaret Stewart. The Captain interrupted a Privy Council meeting to accuse Morton with complicity in the murder of Lord Darnley. Morton admitted fore knowledge but not direct involvement and was subsequently executed by "the Maiden" in June 1581. For this Esme Stuart was made the first Duke of Lennox; Captain James Stewart was made Earl of Arran, and Lord Ruthven (son of David Rizzio's murderer) made Earl of Gowrie.

When Boyd, the Archbishop of Glasgow, died, the Duke of Lennox offered the vacant See to several ministers on condition that they make over to him a substantial portion of the incomes. This offer was taken up by Robert Montgomery, a minister from Stirling, regarded by many as a vain, feeble and presumptuous person. It was a blatant simoniacal purchase which the General Assembly deplored. In 1582 things came to a head with the king intervening in favour of Montgomery but the General Assembly confirmed a sentence of suspension. The question at issue then being whether the church should obey the state and give up its spiritual independence only recently achieved. Montgomery was summoned before the Assembly but did not appear and was sentenced in his absence to be excommunicated.

Montgomery then entered a meeting of the Presbytery of Glasgow who had assembled for the purpose of his excommunication. Accompanied by magistrates and armed supporters he sought to interrupt the proceedings by force with the Moderator losing one of his teeth in the action. The Presbytery continued and remitted the task to the Presbytery of Edinburgh who instructed John Davidson to proceed. Davidson was threatened by Lennox but despite this, excommunication was pronounced and repeated in churches in Glasgow and Edinburgh the following Sabbath. Shortly after Montgomery was literally chased from Edinburgh by a mob of disgruntled citizens.

Andrew Melville had preached at the General Assembly about the autocratic behaviour towards the church and attempts to reintroduce Popery. Subsequently Melville was with a party making a Remonstrance to the king which was challenged by Arran who asked, "Who dares subscribe these treasonable articles?" Melville responded "We dare."[214] He subscribed the document there and then. Melville was pursued in 1584 by the vindictive Earl of Arran for his alleged treasonable statements and forced to flee to Berwick.

Imprudently perhaps, but with the best of intentions, some nobles seized the boy King James VI while he was on a hunting trip in Atholl, Perthshire. He was met on August 22 by the Earl of Gowrie (who had changed sides), the Earl of Mar, the Master of Glames, the Master of Oliphant, Lochlevin (the younger) the Laird of Cleish, the Laird of Easter Wemes and Sir Lewes Bellendine and others, and invited to visit Ruthven Castle where he found himself a prisoner. He was held in the Huntingtower Castle, Perth (above). On August 23 the abductors tendered a Supplication to the king which explained their reasons for his custody and their great concerns at the behaviour and intent of the Duke of Lennox and the Earl of Arran that threatened the throne and the religion of Scotland. Calderwood's *History* says:

> We have suffered now about the space of two yeeres such false accusations, calumneis, oppressions and persecutions, by the moyen of the Duke of Lennox, and him who is called Erle of Arran, that the like of their insolenceis and enormeteis were never heretofore borne with in Scotland.[215]

---

[214] Howie, *Worthies*, p. 92.

[215] Calderwood, *History*, Vol. 3, p. 638.

The Earl of Arran, who was no coward, rode with his brother William and clashed with forces of the Earl of Mar near Perth; he was refused audience with the king and was taken prisoner. Following his seizure the king was held at Ruthven Castle then at Stirling. During this time he was prevented from escaping by Gowrie and burst into tears to which Gowrie is said to have remarked "better that bairns weep than bearded men."[216] The king was to remember this treatment and would take his revenge.

The king, some say, was forced to sign two proclamations, one that he freely chose to be in Perth, and again when he was moved to Stirling. Meanwhile Lennox moved into Edinburgh from Dalkeith for his own safety then on to Glasgow. The king's letter directing no aid to be given to Lennox pending his removal from the kingdom was proclaimed in Glasgow on 7 September, but it was not until 21 December that Lennox finally departed. In June 1583 James was able to escape on a visit to St. Andrews after being held for ten months. The lords involved in the raid were sentenced to be banished and James did not forgive the church who had condoned the action.

The Earl of Arran now took centre stage as an obnoxious favourite when he was appointed Chancellor in 1584. In April 1584 Stirling Castle was seized by the nobles but surrendered on 24 April when the king and Arran besieged it with an army of twelve thousand troops. The nobles were however, weakened in their resolve when the Earl of Gowrie was seized in Dundee and imprisoned, and they fled to Berwick. Gowrie was executed on 2 May 1584 along with the captain of Ruthven Castle, and three others hanged.

Rye House Plot, 1683.

The Ryehouse Plot was a scheme in 1683 with the object of assassinating King Charles II and his brother James, Duke of York (later James II) in order to secure the succession of the Duke of Monmouth. The plot failed.

In England, during 1682, plans were being made to further a revolution which would leave a constitutional monarchy but exclude the accession of James. The main conspirators were the Duke of

[216] M'Crie, *Sketches*, p. 110.

Monmouth, Lord William Russell, Lord Essex and Sir Algernon Sydney. Monmouth was the illegitimate son of Charles II by a mistress, Lucy Walter, and had commanded the royalist forces at Bothwell Brig. The others were patriots concerned that James, a Catholic, would succeed to the throne. They were in contact with the Earl of Argyll and had thoughts of collaboration with him for simultaneous revolution in Scotland and England.

The king and Duke of York were known by various nicknames. "Slavery" and "Popery" were one label while another was based on their complexions: Charles was dark complexioned and called "Blackbird" while James, Duke of York, was fair and called "Goldfinch." There were several suggestions how they might be killed but eventually the conspirators met at Rye House, near Hoddesdon in Hertforshire to make their final plans. Near to Rye House ran a narrow lane that was regularly used by the king when he went to Newmarket. Along it was a thick hedge on one side and on the other an outhouse that afforded good cover and vantage for the assassins. The house itself was surrounded by a moat and was easily defended by a small party if needs be. But there was no attempt made on the king's life for he returned from Newmarket a day earlier than anticipated. The plot was discovered and Lord William Russell and Algernon Sydney were beheaded.

There was some odium attached to the Scottish churchmen who had been involved in the wider issue of the Earl of Argyll's plans, and William Carstares and Robert Baillie of Jerviswood were obvious targets for inquiries about the doings of Monmouth, Russell, and Sydney. Carstares was cruelly tortured with the thumbkins for over an hour and a half and his testimony was used against Baillie even though a promise had been given that anything he said would not be so used. Baillie, already a very sick man and dying, was executed for his alleged, but unproven, involvement in the Rye House plot on 23 December 1684.

There is suggestion by Howie that James Renwick might have been in the know about the plot as he was returning from Holland about that time. It is possible that Renwick might have encountered the Earl of Argyll in Holland but Howie's inference seems to be because the ship Renwick was travelling on stopped at Rye harbour, the ancient Cinque Port in Sussex, which is nowhere near Rye House in Hertfordshire.

Second Book of Discipline, 1578.

The Second Book of Discipline is important because it replaced and upgraded the First Book by Knox and is the basic standard for the modern Church. M'Crie, in *Sketches*, tells that it traces the essential differences between civil and ecclesiastical power, "declaring that Jesus Christ has appointed a government in his church distinct from civil government, which is to be exercised in his name by such officers as he hath authorised, and not by civil magistrates."[217]

The important distinction, basic to so many arguments, is that the civil power "has for its direct and proper object the promoting of external peace and quietness among subjects; ecclesiastical authority - the directing of men in matters of religion and conscience."[218]

It is further explained that as both powers descend from God and if rightly used tend to a common end, they should complement one another and cooperate without interfering with one another.

The Second Book continues to maintain the right of church courts to convene and settle business independent of the civil authority and confirms the structure of those courts. It condemns the principle of superiority in the church save for teaching presbyter or above minister, and that none is to be put over the minister save with the agreement of the congregation. It also continues to resist lay patronage and maintains that election and assent of the people is requisite for appointments.

Vos, in *The Scottish Covenanters*, makes the very valid point that the Covenanters were *not* opposed to the principle of a church established by the State as a national church and the provision for its financial support from national resources. But the state did not have the right to dictate the policy or review the decisions of the Church.

Secret Committee.

This committee was set up on 26 November 1683 with the objective to coerce more rigorously the people of the Western shires. It sought to accomplish what the Court of High Commission,

---

[217] M'Crie, *Sketches*, p. 102.
[218] *Ibid.*

the Privy Council, and the Justiciary Courts had hitherto failed to do. The members, appointed by the Duke of York, were the Chancellor (Earl of Aberdeen), Lord Treasurer (Queensberry), Lord Privy Seal (Atholl), Earl of Perth, Lord Clerk Register (Sir Thomas Craigie), the Lord Advocate, and Drummond of Lundin, who was later to be the Earl of Melfort.

The main persecutor among these was Melfort who appears to have been devoid of any morals. He was simply an extortionist who sought to extract as much money as he could in order to increase his favour with the king. He was no respecter of the law or legal process and his methodology one of blackmail and extortion. His style is clearly seen in his interpretation of the instructions concerning resetters and absentees from church. An upper limit of three hundred men could be sent to the plantations but no limit was given as to women; he accordingly took this as meaning without limit and sent many hundreds to the plantations in the West Indies.

Sects and Sectaries – opposition.

The Sects and Sectaries, also called malignants, referred to by Presbyterian ministers were really anyone or any group of people holding beliefs different to themselves. The differences might be a shade of theological doctrine, acceptance of an Indulgence, or complete denial of a creed. The existence of such groups was especially relevant when they were subject of Toleration, as under Cromwell, when Quakers, Baptists, Congregationalists, Anabaptists and other Independents were allowed to hold meetings. James II sought to lift the yoke on the Catholics and was obliged to allow freedom of worship to other sects, as well as Presbyterians. All the strict Covenanters spoke against the Sectaries including Samuel Rutherford, and James Guthrie. During his time in the wilderness James Renwick was deliberately slandered and accused of being a sectary by his opponents and even accused of being a Gibbite.

The Gibbites or "Sweet Singers" were a small group of three men and twenty six women who were followers of a former Covenanter, John Gib, a sailor from Borrowstounness (Bo'ness). They rejected just about everything held dear by the Presbyterians including the Covenants, the Westminster Confession of Faith, Acts of the General Assembly, the division of the Bible into chapters and verses, all taxation, and every minister of the Gospel in Scotland.

They lived in the hills around Edinburgh spending time chanting and fasting while waiting for Edinburgh to be destroyed. Donald Cargill made a strenuous effort to convert them but was not successful. John Gib was eventually seized and transported.

Shawhead Muir meeting, 18 June 1679. See also: Causes of the Lords Wrath against the Land (1679).

The meeting of the Cameronians at Shawhead Muir was a council of war just four days before they gave battle at Bothwell Brig. There was much debate about the Indulgences, the Indulgers and their involvement in the battle around that time hence the list of wrongs committed by an apostate Scotland in the "Causes" document. Henry Hall, with Cargill, Douglas, King, and Barclay were given the task of drawing up *The Causes of the Lord's Wrath against the Land* which was a recital of the sins and apostasy of Scotland and what should be done to correct the situation. It followed the lines of the earlier work by James Guthrie in 1651 in the pamphlet, *The Causes of the Lords Wrath against Scotland.*

Slaves. See also: Transportation.

Thousands of offenders, for a wide variety of crimes, were transported to the West Indies to work in the plantations and died from malaria and yellow fever as well as from malnutrition and abuse. As the American colonies developed, prisoners were transported to Virginia, New England, Pennsylvania, New Jersey, the Carolinas, and other colonies, where the market price was in the order of ten pounds for a white slave. A particular group that was ordered to be transported were the prisoners captured by Cromwell at the battles of Dunbar and Worcester.

There were also those who sold themselves as indentured servants for a number of years for the price of their fare to the colonies, usually with the promise of a small sum of money and a few acres when they completed their indenture. But even these servants sometimes ended in slavery.

In Scotland there were still house and farm slaves. These were prisoners who were simply sold as slaves and were provided with engraved collars indicating their owner. Selling criminals as slaves was cheaper than hanging them and much more profitable. One example is Patrick Walker, later author of the *Six Saints of the Covenant,* who was wanted for the shooting of a soldier named Francis Gordon. When captured on 22 July 1684, he was about to be tortured with the boot but Robert Malloch, a slave trader, intervened and craved him for a slave. Walker was so assigned and later escaped from the Leith Tolbooth 18 August 1685, otherwise he would have been transported into slavery. Walker was examined by the Council some eighteen times and imprisoned in Dunnottar; he outlived his persecutors by many years and died in March 1745.

Societies. See also: Battles - Airsmoss; Correspondence Union; Queensferry Papers; Revolution Church; Revolution Settlement; Sanquhar Declaration.

There were two groups or societies in the Covenanters' story. The first was a small private prayer meetings around 1640 which prompted a complaint to the General Assembly by Henry Guthrie, later Bishop of Dunkeld. He was opposed by Samuel Rutherford and the complaint came to naught. Another person in favour of private meetings and prayer was John Welwood but there were clearly variations in beliefs between these basically uncoordinated societies, which gave cause for Robert Garnock to leave one and join another. The absence of co-ordinated policy marks these meetings out from the later United Societies.

The United Societies were the means by which the followers of Cameron and Cargill maintained their fellowship after their leaders deaths in 1680 and 1681, respectively. James Renwick had an early contact with the Societies in October 1681 but he did not become their leader until he was ordained in 1683. The United Societies as they were called, held their meetings throughout the south of Scotland and were organised and supervised by a District Society or Correspondence. Every three months there was a General Meeting to which a representative of the Correspondence was sent. The structure and business conducted was broadly based on the Presbytery. By the end of 1683 there were about eighty societies with about seven thousand men prepared to defend their religion.

The Societies were formed initially after Bothwell Brig (1679) and brought into focus the separation of the Societies from other Presbyterians. They rejected the civil government as stated in the Sanquhar Declaration (1680); the ministers who accepted the

Indulgences, and they also rejected those who had religious fellowship with the Indulged ministers. A supporter of these societies was John Nisbet who became a commissioner attending the quarterly General Meetings.

James Renwick was born in February, 1662, in the village of Moniave in Nithsdale and was influenced in his future path when he witnessed the execution of Donald Cargill. After graduation and ordination he joined them as their preacher and leader in 1683. A very industrious minister he roamed far and wide and soon came to the attention of the government. In September 1684, the Privy Council issued Letters of Intercommuning against Renwick and required all persons to aid in his arrest. None were to offer him help or victuals or have contact with him on pain of death.

> We command and charge all and sundry our lieges and subjects, that they nor none of them presume, nor take upon hand to reset, supply or intercommune with the said Mr James Renwick, rebel aforesaid; nor furnish him with meat, drink, house harbour, victual, nor no other thing useful or comfortable to him; or to have intelligence with him by word, writ or message or any other manner of way whatsoever, under pain of being esteemed art and part with him in the crimes aforesaid.[219]

Renwick's high profile was enhanced further when on 28 May 1685 he and two hundred men rode into Sanquhar to issue his Declaration that was similar in content to that of his predecessor, Richard Cameron, five years before. He subsequently spent some time in the North of England preaching before returning to Scotland in December, 1686, to take part in the General Meeting of the United Societies.

His capture came in December, 1687, when he was overheard praying with friends in Edinburgh and recognised. Thus on February 17, 1688, he was executed in the Grassmarket, Edinburgh, and his head and hands affixed above the Netherbow Gate. With his death the Societies were again without a minister and remained so until John McMillan joined them in 1706. Johnston, in *Alexander*

---

[219] Renwick, *Life and Letters*, pp. 105-106. Art and part meant that they would be liable to the same penalties for the alleged crime, in this case the death penalty.

Peden - The Prophet of the Covenant, relates how the Societies had strict conditions to adhere to. Before any General Meeting they reviewed the societies and membership to ensure they were free from scandal. The "Terms of Communion" as they were called required:

> No one could be recognised as a member who took any of the bonds tendered by the government; who paid cess, locality, or militia money to the civil authorities, or stipend to the curates or indulged clergy; made use of government pass, voluntarily appeared before any court of law, supplied any commodities to the enemy, allowed another to do any of these things in their name, or who in any form recognised the ministry the indulged or silent Presbyterians.[220]

Walter Smith who was executed with Cargill on 27 July 1681, wrote a paper entitled *Rules and Directions Anent private Christian Meetings, for Prayer and Conference to mutual edification, and to the right management of the same*, which gives twenty-four rules for the use of society meetings. These appear in Patrick Walker's *Six Saints of the Covenant* (1732) and also Smith's *22 Steps of Defection or Causes of God's Wrath between 1649 and 1681.*

At the Revolution the United Societies remained outside the settlement; their testimony against Erastianism, the obligations under the Covenants and the concept of Christian government were all ignored. Moreover, they objected to the king and queen—William III and Mary—because they were foreigners, former members of an Erastian church, and had not sworn to the Covenants of Scotland. It is important to note that the Societies, who later became the Reformed Presbyterian Church, never seceded from the Church of Scotland as they had never belonged to it. From 1640 to 1661 the church was the Presbyterian Church of the Second Reformation; from 1661-1688 the Church of Scotland was an Episcopal church. As such the Cameronians or Societies were the only group to maintain the adherence to the Covenants and the beliefs of the Second Reformation of 1638.

An early act by the Societies was to renew the Covenant which they did at Borland Hill, near Lesmahagow on 5 March 1689 at

---

[220] Johnston, *Peden*, p. 158.

which their three ministers, Boyd, Linning and Shields officiated. It was at this meeting that Alexander Shields stood up and declared his "unfeigned sorrow for his former sin of compliance." All three ministers would soon, however, turn again and join the Revolution Church. This leaderless remnant went on to become The Reformed Presbyterian Church of Scotland with its emphatic testimony: *"Anti-popish, anti-prelatic, anti-Erastian, anti-sectarian, true Presbyterian Church of Christ in Scotland.*" There was a further renewal of the Covenants at Auchensaugh, Douglas on 23 July 1712.

An attendant problem for the Societies was the absence of any ordained ministers for a period of nearly seventeen years after the original three ministers deserted them. It was not until 1706 that John MacMillan of Balmaghie broke from the established church and joined the United Societies. A strong and fearless man MacMillan upset some members by his stance but he accepted the call to be their pastor at large with a congregation of some seven thousands spread over the south west of Scotland. He was aided by John MacNeil, a licensed preacher who continued with the Societies until his death in 1732 having served as a licentiate for sixty three years. In 1743, Thomas Nairne, an ordained minister, joined MacMillan which opened the way for the United Societies to set up the Reformed Presbytery on 1 August 1743 at Braehead. From this date the General Meetings of the Societies continued for a while but the Presbytery took over all ecclesiastical functions. It also meant that, at last, the Societies could license new preachers and ordain ministers which included John Cuthbertson, a member of the first American Reformed Presbytery in 1774.

Solemn Engagement. See also: Engagement and Engagers.

This was an agreement drawn up by the New Model Army shortly after King Charles I had been seized at Holdenby. The agreement sought to organise the army to secure the peace of the kingdom and the liberties of the subject. There was a change in the officers, with the quarter or so who were not supportive of Cromwell giving up their commissions; this included Presbyterians who could not accept the inherent religious bias of the "Independents." The New Model Army's proposals for religious settlement was in favour of a broad based tolerance which the Scots could not accept. The Covenant was no longer binding and no one could be forced to take it, or forced to use the Book of Common Prayer. Moreover, no church body whatsoever was allowed to force itself or its views on anyone.

These new rules were clearly unacceptable to the Scots and the Covenanters were disposed to offer King Charles their support on the terms of the 1643 agreement of a Covenanted Church. However, there was a separate and less demanding political move by the Duke of Hamilton and the Earls of Loudon, Lauderdale and Lanark, who negotiated "The Engagement," which the king signed on 26 December 1647. This "Engagement" led to schism in the Church of Scotland.

Solemn League and Covenant, 25 Sept 1643.

At the end of the Bishops' Wars and the return of the English Long Parliament in November 1640 there was a public dissatisfaction with the bishops and episcopacy in the church. This gathered momentum with the attempt to arrest the Five Members. Subsequent to that a bill was passed that removed the bishops from the House of Lords. In 1643 when the Civil War had commenced Parliament passed ordinances that abolished bishops, deans, and chapters. However, the organisation to replace that of episcopacy was much more difficult as the English had to placate both the Scots who sought to extend Presbytery throughout the three kingdoms, and the army who were much more inclined to nonconformity that included religious tolerance. In these circumstances there was little prospect of a full-blown Presbyterian system being accepted right away.

The Solemn League and Covenant of 1643 was a political agreement between the English Parliamentary party and the Scottish Presbyterians. For the Scots it was a religious covenant with the ultimate aim of extending Presbyterianism as the official faith in England and Ireland, and the extirpation of Popery and Prelacy. For the Parliamentarians it was a military treaty whereby the Scottish army would support them against King Charles I in the English civil war that had broken out. But as ever was the case, the different interpretations of the Covenant would lead to division among the parties.

The agreement came about through an approach by the English Parliamentary party to the Estates in Edinburgh and to the General Assembly in August 1643 for a reciprocal military alliance. The English Commission consisted of Sir William Armyn, Sir Harry Vane (the younger), a Mr. Hatcher, Mr. Darley a Member of Parliament, and two ministers Mr. Stephen Marshall who was Presbyterian and Philip Nye an Independent from the Westminster Assembly of Divines. In the discussions the Church of Scotland representatives, which included Robert Blair, made it clear that it preferred a religious bond and set Alexander Henderson, then the Moderator of the General Assembly, to the task of drafting the document.

The English Parliamentarians were unhappy with a clause that would have committed them to reject episcopacy and also to take action against the Independents or Congregationalists for which Oliver Cromwell stood. There was moreover, a strong undercurrent amongst the people of England for a form of episcopacy founded on a tradition of 1,500 years. There was much less objection to abolishing the Laudian changes. This led to amendments that left the door open for the Independents in England: "the reformation of religion in the kingdomes of England and Ireland, in doctrine, worship, and discipline, and Government according to the word of GOD, and the example of the best reformed churches."[221]

The amendments were made and the document presented to and approved by the General Assembly on 17 August 1643. At this juncture the Estates made its price clear requiring £30,000 a month for providing the forces and also three months payment in advance.

The Solemn League and Covenant was sent to London with Alexander Henderson, George Gillespie, Mr. Hatcher and Mr. Nye to be approved and subscribed to by the House of Commons and the Westminster Assembly in a joint meeting on 25 September 1643. After this it was returned to Scotland to be subscribed and sworn to by the Commission of the General Assembly and the Committee of the Estates of the Scottish Parliament. It is pertinent to note that only the Scots actually swore to the document and thus were particularly held to it by their conscience. The document was again sworn to in 1648 and 1649, and was subscribed to by Charles II at

[221] Peterkin, *Records*, Vol. 2, p. 362.

Spey in 1650, and finally on his coronation on New Years Day 1651.

In a separate treaty of 29 November 1643 the details of the arrangement were confirmed. The Scots would provide an army of 18,000 foot, 2,000 horsemen, 1,000 dragoons and a train of artillery. The English Parliament agreed to a subsidy of £30,000 a month which was later increased to £31,000.

The trouble that the Covenanters went to agreeing and publicising the Solemn League and Covenant is quite remarkable, but also very prudent for it left no one in any doubt what it was they intended. The General Assembly followed up the treaty, which was widely sworn to by the people, by requiring ministers to report anybody who disapproved or would not swear to the Covenants. It also became a requirement to subscribe to both covenants for very many public and semi public duties. This for example included students entering universities, even to persons taking the Holy Communion for the first time. A consequence was that the acceptance of the Covenants was debased as the people's self interest sought jobs, preferment and power. This is why James Guthrie wrote, in *The Causes of the Lords Wrath against Scotland*, about the ignorance people had as to the importance of the Covenant, and the lack of sincerity by many who swore to it. J. Vos, in *The Scottish Covenanters*, points out that the requirement to swear to the Covenants was a mistake and should have been a voluntary action. By making it compulsory: "the zeal of the Covenanter leaders exceeded their wisdom because it unintentionally tempted many to accept the Covenants in a dishonest, careless, or least implicit way."[222]

The Independents remained in opposition to the extension of Presbytery throughout 1644 which delayed the creation of classes (courts) and later the adoption of the Directory for public worship. A start was made with the division of the Province of London into 12 classes and foreshadowed the splitting of the counties into Presbyteries. Progress then began to grind to halt as it encountered a groundswell for an Erastian settlement and constraints on the appointment and powers of elders. Moreover, since the victory at Naseby there was no real need for the Scottish Army and thus no

---

[222] Johannes G. Vos, *The Scottish Covenanters* (----: ----, ----; reprint Edinburgh: Blue Banner Productions, 1998), p. 58.

underlying need to agree with their wishes. Thus a half a loaf compromise was adopted by the Scottish Commissioners with an effort to implement Presbytery in London.

When the New Model Army came into being and especially from 1647 onwards, Presbyterians either resigned or were expelled from the English army. In their place were officers the Presbyterians regarded as sectaries who were tolerant of other creeds, except Catholicism. In the face of this major disagreement of principle, The Scottish aspirations gradually crumbled and they were dealt mortal blows by Cromwell's victories at Dunbar and Worcester.

Three centuries later the relevance of the Solemn League and Covenant is sometimes overlooked. Simply put, without it and the troops it provided, the Parliamentarian army might not have overthrown Charles I. Robert Burns spoke in reply to sneering comments about the sufferings of Scotland for conscience and which called the Solemn League and Covenant fanatical and ridiculous. He retorted:

> The Solemn League and Covenant
> Cost Scotland blood - cost Scotland tears:
> But it seal'd Freedoms sacred cause -
> If thou'rt a slave, indulge thy sneers.[223]

Spanish Blanks.

This was another plot in 1592 by the Catholic Earls of Huntly, Erroll and Angus resuming their correspondence and plotting of three years earlier with Spain. Goaded on by fierce persecution, a Catholic intrigue with Philip II of Spain to overthrow the government was bubbling away beneath the surface. With suspicion everywhere the Rev. Andrew Knox, of Paisley, a renowned pursuer of alleged papists, obtained a warrant from the king in 1592 that empowered him, certain nobles, and others of his choosing to seek and apprehend "all excommunicate papists, Jesuits, seminarie priestis and suspect trafficquaris with the King of Spayne and utheris foreynnaris to the subversion of Goddis trew religion."[224]

---

[223] Johnston, *Treasury*, p. 559.
[224] Metcalfe, *Renfrew*, p. 227.

Knox heard from the English secret service that one George Ker, a doctor of Law, brother of the Abbott of Newbattle and an excommunicated person for popery, was in the district. Knox tracked him down to Glasgow and to a vessel in the Clyde which was boarded off the Isle of Cumbrae where Ker was apprehended. Hidden in the sleeves of a sailor were highly incriminating documents that showed the clear link of several nobles to a conspiracy. The papers included some sheets bearing only the signatures of the Scottish lords involved: the "Spanish Blanks" as they became known. This success added greatly to Knox's reputation and he became feared throughout Scotland. The letters are reproduced in Calderwood's *History of the Kirk of Scotland* and certainly look very suspicious. The "Blanks," eight of them, were pieces of paper without a designation or address other than a customary courteous conclusion used with royalty: "your Majesty's very humble and very obedient servant." Two were signed by Angus and Erroll jointly, two by Huntly, one by Angus, another by Erroll, and two in Latin which were signed by all three Earls and Gordon of Auchindoune. None of the other letters provided clear evidence of treason and torture was used to reveal their intention. This revealed that the central plotter was Father William Crichton, a Jesuit, living in Spain who had convinced Philip of Spain to attempt another invasion. Crichton had represented that the Scottish Catholics were amenable to a rising and proposed that an army of 30,000 Spanish troops should invade, restore the faith and march into England and avenge Mary, Queen of Scots. To encourage and confirm Philip's concurrence the Blanks were to be filled in by himself when negotiations were completed, and intended for use as proclamations.

James was aware of the enterprise in June 1592 which was proven by a memorandum from himself to Crichton but this document was withdrawn for safety of his Majesty's honour. It showed plainly that James was playing a dangerous middle course policy, holding off from directly inviting Spain's intervention while he sought to treat with Elizabeth for his title to the English Crown. James was, however, wrong in his estimation of the purpose: it did not seek to place him on the throne of England but that he would be held at Philip of Spain's disposal. Despite prompting from Queen Elizabeth and ministers James again declined to take action against the Earls. A minor player Graham of Fintry was executed on 15

February 1593 but the Earls did not compear to their summonses nor were steps taken to punish them.

The consequence of the affair was a loathing of James and an outcry against his inactivity. The Synod of Fife summarily excommunicated the conspirators who disdainfully "consented" to stand trial in their heartland at Perth. This was regarded with great suspicion by the Kirk and on 17 November 1593 they convened a Committee of Security requiring James to postpone the trial until they were ready to prosecute. In the alternative they proposed to assemble in force at Perth to pursue the defendants to the uttermost. This threat of civil war finally raised James to action. The Estates declared a compromise which proscribed the Catholic religion and required the Earls to conform by 1 February 1594; it also effectively rejected the Blanks as evidence and thus the charges of treason. None of the conspirators complied and neither did they obey orders to go into ward.

Star Chamber. See also: Court of High Commission.

The Star Chamber, so named because it met in a room in which the ceiling was decorated with stars, was an English Court that had its origins in the Middle Ages. King Henry VII adopted it in 1487 as a special court to deal with rebellious nobles because the powers of ordinary courts were of little use. The judges were the Chancellor, and other high ranking officials and was, in effect, a Privy Council with judicial functions. It was used by King James I and Charles I for their own arbitrary actions and unjust procedures. Archbishop Laud and Thomas Wentworth, Earl of Strafford, were regular users of the court in pursuit of their objectives. The Star Chamber was abolished in 1641. The equivalent body in Scotland was the Court of High Commission.

The Start, 4 October 1650.

In the aftermath of the defeat of the Covenanter Army at Dunbar on 3 September 1650 the extremists resolved to make yet more purges which included the king's household. Charles had already made his declaration of repentance on 16 August when, pressed by the Covenanters, he acknowledged his father's sins and his mother's idolatry, which grieved him very much and would be remembered when vengeance was possible. Charles was hardly pleased to be told that twenty four of his household were purged. In a moment of depression perhaps, Charles rode out of Perth on the morning of 4 October 1650 ostensibly to go hawking but intending to reach the Gordons and other royalist supporters in the north. He reached no further than a shepherd's hut at Clova, in South Esk, where he spent a miserable night. The next day he was overtaken by soldiers sent after him and taken back to Perth. This attempt to escape became known as "The Start."

Stipend.

A minister's stipend or salary was fixed by law from an early date. But his income also varied with the benefices that might be available and the teinds (tithes) or tenths of income that might be charged in the parish for support of the established church. In this respect the role of the patron could be an important factor depending on how he supported his nominee, and what services were provided to the patron and his family. For a long time the tithes were paid in kind being one tenth of the produce of the land and livestock from which comes the expression the "parson's pig" or the tithe pig, that is, one in ten of the piglets born. The tithe barn was the place in which the parish tithe corn was stored.

The law carefully set out the expectations of the teinds but it was another thing for the amounts due to be paid on time, or indeed, at all. In 1560 it was agreed that one fourth, or if need be one third, of the benefices available in Scotland should be collected annually for stipends of ministers. In 1567 it was necessary to pass another law requiring payment of the third until the Church had the teinds restored to it, which the lay holders of benefices were to pay. This early system did not work very well and over time new grants, donations etc in the burghs was necessary to fund the stipends. In 1593 there were 107 churches vacant because there was no stipend and in 1596 there were over four hundred churches without an incumbent. These vacancies and the stipend problems were reviewed by a commission appointed in 1592. In 1596, stipends were not payable to ministers who had not acknowledged the king's authority.

In 1617 stipends were raised to five hundred merks or five chalders, and the maximum was set at one thousand merks or ten chalders. In 1627 the quantity was increased to eight chalders; then in 1649 changed to three chalders of victuals (usually corn) and £5 money.

The absence of payment meant that many ministers eked out a precarious living often dependent on the charity of parishioners, or working a few acres of glebe lands that had not been seized by a rapacious laird or noble. It was not unusual for them to take on other activities, such as serving wine and ale or teaching a local laird's children. In many cases the stipend was paid in butter, wool, hemp, lint, cheese, fowl, fish, wildfowl, lambs, other livestock, and cereals. The value of stipends averaged less than £10 sterling a year with some around £16 sterling. Any minister receiving £20 sterling a year was thought to be reasonably well off. Despite the desperate times it is remarkable how some ministers nevertheless were able to endow their parishes with material benefits. One such minister was John Davidson of Prestonpans, who preached for many years without receiving a stipend yet managed to have built at his own expense, a church, a manse, a school, donated a clock and a glebe land.

Straight talking.

Straight talking was in many ways a prerequisite for all ministers since they were led by their convictions to give witness for their beliefs. John Knox and Andrew Melville were two early ministers of the Reformation who were outspoken to an extreme, and often took their lives in their hands when speaking to the queen or king. Both were pursued by the Catholic church as heretics and were fortunate not to be tried for treason. But this was also their strength as they pushed back the boundaries surrounding the Protestant faith at that time. A consequence of their zeal was an element of notoriety that greatly widened the audience for their views while it put opponents on notice that they would not be quieted.

Knox in full flow must have been a dramatic sight. When Mary Queen of Scots returned to Scotland from France she was determined to restore the Catholic faith and immediately started having mass said in her private chapel. The intrepid Knox denounced idolatry from the pulpit of St. Giles Church, Edinburgh and concluded his sermon with "One mass is more fearful to me, than if ten thousand armed enemies were landed in any part of the realm, of purpose to suppress the whole religion."[225]

Subsequently, he was reprimanded by Queen Mary but Knox continued his attacks in his sermons to congregations of three thousand and more. Finally, he had Queen Mary in tears when he protested about her marriage to Lord Darnley and she protested, "Never had prince been handled as she was.... I cannot be quit of you. I vow to God I shall be once revenged."[226]

In the face of such a statement as that by the Queen any ordinary man would fear for his life and probably flee (if he could). But Knox kept up his opposition to idolatry and Rome while Mary went her wilful way to imprisonment and the executioner.

Andrew Melville is famous for his calling King James VI "God's sillie vassal" (meaning weak servant) and for telling him that

> there are two kings and two kingdom's in Scotland; there is King James, the head of the Commonwealth and there is Christ Jesus, the head of the Church, whose subject King James VI is, and of whose kingdom he is not a head, nor lord, but a member.[227]

A fearless critic, Melville ended up in the Tower of London for four years and was eventually allowed to go to Sedan in France where he died in 1622 at the age of seventy-seven years.

David Calderwood was an early sufferer of the prelates and declined the Kings authority in 1608. He was summoned before the Court of High Commission in 1617 and was challenged by King James about his earlier declination and gave rise to the retort from the king:

> I will tell thee what is obedience, man, what the Centurion said to his servant, To this man, Go, and he goeth, and to that man Come, and he cometh; that is obedience.[228]

Calderwood rejected the argument and later rejected the king's sentence saying, "Your sentence is not the sentence of the Kirk, but

---

[225] M'Crie, *Sketches*, p. 82.
[226] *Ibid*., p. 86.
[227] Howie, *Worthies*, p. 96; Calderwood, *History*, Vol. 3, p. 440.
[228] Howie, *Worthies*, p. 202.

a sentence null in itself, and therefore I cannot obey it."[229] Discretion being the better part of valour, Calderwood went to Holland and did not return to Scotland until after James had died in 1625.

Supremacy, Act of. See also: Assertory Act, 1669.

If there is one word that epitomises the Covenanters struggle then "supremacy" should be it. The supremacy of the king in matters of state was never in dispute but the claim to supremacy in the affairs of the Kirk and as its titular head were not for the worldly Kings. This separation of headship of the Kirk, which subsumed the issues of Episcopacy and Erastianism, was the altar on which so many Scottish lives were willingly sacrificed in the seventeenth century.

As early as 1584 King James I began the onslaught upon the Kirk by the enactment of laws, termed the Black Acts, which sought to enforce his supremacy in all things. These Acts ordained that no ecclesiastical assembly (the General Assembly) could meet without the king's consent. It was ordained that no one, either publicly or privately, could speak against the proceedings of the King's Council. It was ordered to be treason to decline the judgement of the King or Privy Council. And, that all ministers had to acknowledge the bishops as their superiors. The declaration of these acts brought much protestation from the ministers and they denounced them from the pulpits. Some twenty ministers were forced to flee across the border into England.

The Kirk now began its century of struggle to retain its independence first recognised by the General Assembly of 1578 when it adopted The Second Book of Discipline. This was sworn to in the National Covenant of 1581 by King James (the King's Confession) but he soon reneged on his sworn commitments.

At the Restoration of Charles II the measure aimed at enforcing supremacy was the Oath of Allegiance introduced in 1661. Labelled as an *Act concerning the president and oath of Parliament*

> I acknowledge my said Sovererane only supream Governor of the kingdom over all persons and in all causes civil and

---

[229] *Ibid.*, p. 203.

> ecclesiastical, renunce and forsake all foreign Power…and shall never decline his Majesties Power and Jurisdiction….[230]

This oath was particularly used against the Covenanters who would be ensnared by questions such as "Do you pray for the king?" and then "Do you own the king?."

The newly ennobled Duke of Lauderdale opened Parliament on 19 October 1669. Its first important enactment was a Supremacy Act on 16 November; the scope of it was breathtaking:

> His Majestie and his successours may settle, enact, and may emit such constitutions, acts, and orders concerning all ecclesiastical meetings and maters to be proposed and determined therein.[231]

The Covenanters feared, perhaps not without reason, that this gave unlimited power to the king and placed him as a pope on Christ's throne. It was also thought that Lauderdale knew of the king's inclination to Popery and was making it easier for making a change in the national faith.

The act was seen by some nobles as constraining the prelates and Sharp tried to get an amendment to add "by law established" but it failed. Ironically, the first to suffer was Archbishop Burnet of Glasgow whom the king ordered to be unfrocked. Sharp tried to intervene but was told by Lauderdale that ministerial office was not a divine right, but depended solely on the supreme magistrate.

Tables – explanation.

The creation of "The Tables" was a consequence of the great uproar that followed the imposition of the Service Book on the Church of Scotland in 1637. There was great opposition to it and many petitions were presented to the Privy Council meeting in Edinburgh on 15 November 1637. Some sixty eight petitions were then presented to the king by the Duke of Lennox. The reply from the king was swift enough, coupled with his anger that the bishops

---

[230] Hewison, *Covenanters*, Vol. 2, p. 79.
[231] *Ibid.*, p. 228.

had not enforced the use of the Liturgy which they had pressed on him. The response was to order all strangers from the city within twenty four hours on penalty of being declared an outlaw; the Court of Session was ordered to move to Linlithgow and then to Dundee where it would be remote from any rabble rousing.

In the tumult the magistrates were coerced into cooperation and a Committee of Public Security was allowed to be set up which included representatives of the supplicants. This allowed the rank and file to disperse while the Committee set itself up as a Convention of the Estates. They occupied the Parliament House and divided themselves into four groups, each meeting in separate rooms—at separate "Tables"—the nobles; country gentlemen, burghs and clergy. Four representatives of each group were selected and authorised to act for their class. A fifth Table was set up as a co-ordinating Table with a representative from each of the other four, with Archibald Johnston, later Lord Warriston, as its Clerk.

The formation of "The Tables" created an efficient organisation which then took the offensive. On 21 December 1637 they demanded that the Privy Council, then sitting at Dalkeith, remove the bishops from among them on the grounds that they could not be both judges and defendants in the matters under dispute. King Charles responded on February 20 with a declaration at Stirling to the effect that the Bishops were unjustly accused as being the authors of the Service Book and Canons, seeing whatever was done by them in that matter was by his Majesty's authority and orders. The declaration prohibited petitions against the Liturgy and insisted that it could not be withdrawn. The king's declaration was rejected and "all who love the cause of God" were called to meet in Edinburgh. Among the ministers Alexander Henderson and David Dickson were to the fore, recalling that in 1580, in similar times of danger to the Church, there had been a National Covenant (1581). From the Edinburgh gathering came the renewal of the National Covenant, drawn up by Henderson and Johnston, which was approved by "The Tables" and signed in Greyfriars Kirk on 28 February 1638.

Test Act, 1681 and 1704.

The Test Act was a declaration intended to remove all Catholics from public office and to cause the stricter operation of the laws against them. A similar Act of March 1673 in England had revealed the Duke of York as a Catholic and caused him to quit the Admiralty. The Test Act of 31 August 1681 included its application to all fanatic and separatists from the national Church, which opened the door for applying the oath of allegiance to Covenanters. It was a long and ambiguous oath that had to be taken by everybody, but specifically excluded the king's lawful brother and sons. The Act also required parish ministers to send in October annually, a list of Papists and other "withdrawers" to their bishop. The oath required to be taken was contradictory as it simultaneously pledged the taker to the Confession of Faith of 1567 and the king's supremacy, which the Confession explicitly denied. It further required absolute and unchallenged acceptance of the king's supremacy in all things civil and ecclesiastical. Described as a medley of popery, prelacy, Erastianism and self contradiction it met with much opposition from the public at large including Sir James Dalrymple, President of the Court of Session, who refused to take it.

Archibald Campbell, 9th Earl of Argyll (son of the Marquis executed in 1661) took the oath but with reservations "so far as is consistent with itself and the Protestant religion."[232] As a result he was accused of treason and sentenced to death in his absence and would pay for it under the blade of "The Maiden" in 1685. It is quite probable that envious eyes had been cast over the extensive Argyll estates and the havering about the Test was just the excuse needed to make inroads on the property. The jury of fifteen was comprised mainly of opponents to Argyll, including Montrose, Airlie, and Claverhouse. Following his flight to France, aided by William Veitch, the Argyll estates were again declared forfeit.

The unpopularity of the Test was, however, wide among the aristocracy as proven by a long list of hereditary jurisdictions and offices which reverted to the Crown because their occupants would not take the Test. These included Buccleuch (Monmouth), Hamilton, Haddington, Nithsdale, Galloway, Cassillis, Kenmure, Rothes (Countess), and Sutherland. Such was the resistance that some of the dissenters joined in a syndicate for which a charter was sought for planting a colony in Carolina.

In May 1682, Sir George Gordon of Haddo, later Earl of Aberdeen, became Chancellor, replacing the Earl of Rothes. The

---

[232] Hewison, *Covenanters*, Vol. 2, p. 354.

new broom sought to ensure that nothing would get in the way of the succession of the Catholic Duke of York to the throne and he began a policy of severe and excessive harassment that used the Test as a weapon against any form of dissent. At this time Claverhouse was appointed Sheriff of Wigtown with powers to fine absentees from church, for conventicling, having baptisms and marriages conducted by outed ministers, and aiding and abetting rebels from Bothwell Brig. In April 1683 the courts at Ayr, Dumfries, and Wigtown were instructed to inquire into harbouring and conversing with rebels but exemption was gained by taking the Test. Over a thousand people in Ayrshire alone were summoned to appear before the Courts to answer petty charges.

In the autumn of 1684 very explicit instructions were given to the enforcing agencies to seize all preachers and chaplains who were unauthorised by a bishop; to search out persons who had fled from their homes; remove the outed ministers who had transgressed (what of is not stated); secure peddlers who had not obtained a pass and to "take caution" for their good behaviour; turn out wives and children convicted of having conversation with offending parents or husbands; assist the curates to bring people to obedience and do away with Kirk Sessions; allow no person except a gentleman of known loyalty who has taken the Test to carry arms; no yeoman was to travel more than three miles from his home without a pass from his minister or a Commissioner of Excise; to put the oath of allegiance to any person and if they refuse banish them to the Plantation (of America and the West Indies). At this time there was not much that the common person might do without the risk of falling foul of the law. The Test Act was not repealed until 1828.

The Test Act in Ireland, 1704, came about through a Bill that sought to prevent the further growth of popery, which was itself in complete defiance of the Treaty of Limerick. The act imposed restrictions on Catholics owning and retaining property to which was added, with Queen Anne's consent, a clause requiring all holders of public offices to take Communion according to the rites of the Episcopal Church of Ireland. The Act passed through Parliament with little opposition and received Royal Assent on 4 March 1704. As a result Presbyterians were excluded from posts as magistrates, postmasters, courts of law, customs and excise, and local government. In Londonderry ten aldermen and fourteen burgesses were forced out. In Belfast the Sovereign (mayor) and twelve burgesses were Presbyterians and were eventually forced from office. Daniel Defoe published a pamphlet entitled *The Parallel; or Persecution of Protestants the Shortest Way to Prevent the Growth of Popery in Ireland* in which he says "the very people who drank deepest of the Popish fury are now linked with those very Papists they fought against."[233]

Thirty-Nine Articles.

The creed of the Church of England adopted by a convocation in 1563 and made law by Act of Parliament in 1571. Articles 1 through 5 refer to universally recognised truths of the Christian religion; 6 through 8, standards of faith; 9 through 18, sin and grace; 19 through 36, Church and Sacraments; 37 through 39, civil order. It is important to note that they were created for a special situation (separation from Rome) and are not interpreted as containing a systematic statement of Christian doctrine. Calvinist objections centred on the lack of an unequivocal endorsement of their views on such as predestination. A Declaration by Charles I in December 1628 affirmed that the 39 Articles were the foundations of the church doctrines and he forbid any further public discussion of controvertible issues. This only fuelled existing concerns about Arminianism and the policies of Laud (then Bishop of London). Underlying this were concerns that Charles I was pursuing a policy of absolutism as exampled by his peremptory tone in this declaration.

Torture.

In the early days of the Reformation the tactics of the Inquisition were inherent in the pursuit of heretics by the Church of Rome although the Inquisition itself never came to Britain. However, cruelty including physical abuse which we might today regard as torture, was endemic and there was a lawful use of physical torture in the presence of the Privy Council. On the other hand there was mass psychological torture, although it was not known as that. The use of threats to do deadly things, such as roasting on a griddle, the process of executing by drowning and telling a prisoner to make his

---

[233] Latimer, p. 273.

peace with God as troopers readied to shoot him, were calculated acts to induce prisoners to confess. Generally the government sought to impose compliance through fear and was the reason for sending Pentland Rising rebels to their home towns for hanging; the fixing of hands and arms to kirk doors; and, the display of heads on public view above especially the Netherbow Gate in Edinburgh.

Displaying the instruments of torture to a prisoner during interrogation was a tactic used by Sir George MacKenzie, the King's Advocate. The use of torture was allowed in the presence of the Privy Council and it became an everyday event in the latter years of the persecution. The device called the 'boot' was a metal case that went round the lower leg into which wedges were driven by hammer gradually breaking and mangling the leg. Hugh McKail suffered torture of the boot which Sir Walter Scott described in "Old Mortality," chapter XXXVI:

"The executioner enclosed the leg and knee within the tight iron case, and then, placing a wedge of the same metal between the knee and the side of the machine, took a mallet in his hand and stood waiting for further orders. A surgeon placed himself by the other side of the prisoner's chair, bared the prisoner's arm, and applied his thumb to the pulse in order to regulate the torture according to the strength of the patient. The President gave a nod to the executioner whose mallet instantly descended on the wedge, and forcing it between the knee and the iron boot occasioned the most exquisite pain, as was evident from the flush on the brow and cheeks of the sufferer." Eleven times the mallet descended until the limb was shattered and shapeless.[234]

Johnston's *Treasury* quotes some lines by Thomas Gibbons:

'Tis not enough felonious caves to fill,
'Tis not enough for cords and steel to kill;
But on the ankle the sharp wedge descends,
The bone reluctant with the iron bends,
Crush'd is its frame, blood spouts from ev'rt pore,
And the white marrow swims in purple gore.[235]

---

[234] Smellie, pp. 176-177.
[235] Gibbons quoted in Johnston, *Treasury*, p. 632.

The Privy Council records of 23 July 1684 referred to a new invention called the "thumbkins," a device that could be screwed down to crush the fingers. They have variously been attributed to Bishop Paterson and, most likely, to Dalziel of the Binns who brought them from Muscovy. The first victim was William Spence, the Earl of Argyll's secretary, who was tortured 7 August 1684. Variants included thumbkins that held the two thumbs close together and, with the prisoner's arms behind his back, were an efficient restraint. William Carstairs was one who was tortured using the thumbkins and forced to give evidence against Robert Baillie of Jerviswood. The use of torture in these times was permitted before the Privy Council, whereas in the field the militia resorted to sheer brutality on occasion, allegedly roasting before a fire, putting a person naked on a hot griddle, letting off guns in prisoner's faces (especially frightening children) and any other inhuman activity they could think of.

James Renwick was one minister who was fearful of torture when laid in irons and held as a close prisoner. It was fear that made him explain the notations in his pocket book when he was taken before the Lord Chancellor. General Dalziel of the Binns threatened David Hackston with roasting for refusing to answer his questions and possibly "the Beast of Muscovy," as he was known, would probably have done it if there had been time. But Hackston was hurried to Edinburgh to be threatened again with torture by the Privy Council which he nowise regarded. Donald Cargill was threatened with torture by the Earl of Rothes, the Chancellor, but Cargill foretold Rothes, "forbear to threaten me, for die what death I will, your eyes shall not see it."[236] Rothes died the morning of Cargills execution. While in prison he was also visited by a gentlewoman who was in tears having heard that he was to be tortured by an iron chair, made red hot to roast him, and a barrel with many spikes to force him into, and roll about the street. Maltreatment of prisoners was common as Robert Garnock found at Stirling, and was seemingly identified early on for execution or transportation for being a ringleader against taking a Bond while in Greyfriars Kirk Yard prison.

The favourite implement used in the presence of the Privy Council was "the boot," a metal case around the limb into which

---

[236] Howie, *Worthies*, p. 450.

were driven wedges that crushed skin and bone and could force the marrow out of the bones. An alternative description, given by Latimer in *A History of the Irish Presbyterians*, is of "four pieces of wood in which a leg of the victim confined. These pieces were then driven together by wedges, which caused them to press so tightly as to make the marrow leave the bone."[237] No doubt use led to design improvements but the end product remained the same. It is thought to have been brought from France where it was called "Le Brodequin." Some historians say that the device, along with the thumbkins, was brought to Scotland by Thomas Dalziel of the Binns.

John Sproull, an apothecary in Glasgow, was twice tortured with the boot and fined £500 sterling. For good measure he was then imprisoned on the Bass Rock for six years. He survived and was long after known as "Bass John Sproull" to distinguish him from another John Sproull, the Provost of Glasgow. Hugh McKail doggedly declined the authority of the Council and suffered ten or eleven strokes spread over a period of time to maximise the pain. His injuries must have been substantial because he was unable to appear before the Council a few days later, and not until a fortnight had passed when he was sentenced to hang at the Edinburgh Cross on 22 December 1666. At a meal with friends two days before his execution he cheerily urged them "Eat to the full, and cherish your bodies, that we may be a fat Christmas-pie to the prelates."[238]

James Mitchell was the man who had attempted to assassinate Archbishop James Sharp in 1668 and he was made to suffer. He was given a severe handling by the authorities and for the best part of a year lay in prison in chains and fetters before his trial commenced. When interrogated by the Privy Council he accepted the inevitable and told them to get on with the torture; he fainted after nine blows had been delivered on the wedges. John Kid was another who suffered the boot and probably more than once, but he too meekly accepted the torture knowing that his execution was inevitable.

Bishop Gilbert Burnet, wrote about the Duke of York, later James II, that he would look on the torture with the boot with an

---

[237] Latimer, p. 149.

[238] Howie, *Worthies*, p. 360.

unmoved indifference "as of a man that had no bowels nor humanity in him."[239]

Transportation. See also: Crown.

The nearest thing to transportation from Scotland before 1603 was banishment outside the kingdom, which usually meant Holland where there was a strong Scots community, and France, Germany and Portugal. Both France and Spain were, of course, Catholic countries so a stay there could be risky. The alternative for the single man was to take up military service on the Continent with the armies of Sweden, Finland, Russia, Germany, and France.

Transportation to the Colonies only became an option after James VI became King of England in 1603. Even then the initial destination was Ireland for troublesome border "reivers;" and many thousands of Presbyterians took refuge there in the Plantation of Ulster. Transportation to the American colonies, including Nova Scotia, were routine destinations from the prisons of both England and Scotland. Transportation for religious dissent in Scotland peaked during the reign of Charles II and James II. Thousands were despatched as slaves to the sugar plantations in the West Indies, and to the eastern sea board of the Americas, especially at that time the Carolinas.

Hewison relates that Cromwell was responsible for disposing of thousands of prisoners captured in his campaigns, not least after the battle of Dunbar, 3 September 1650. Here some five thousand wounded men were released and four thousand prisoners were marched south into England. At Morpeth in Northumberland hundreds died of dysentery and Cromwell gifted one thousand prisoners to the Countess of Winton. The prisoners were also held in Durham Cathedral where some 1,600 men died and were buried in a mass grave in the precincts of the cathedral. The English Council of State ordered that sound prisoners were to be sent to plantations in Virginia and New England; some to French military service, and some were to be kept for the English salt works. Similar treatment was ordered for prisoners taken after the battle of Worcester in September 1651.

---

[239] Hewison, *Covenanters*, Vol. 2, p. 379.

As at 1 July 1679 there were some 1,184 prisoners held in the Greyfriars Kirk Yard. These were gradually whittled down by some taking an oath and giving a bond for good behaviour. However, the hard core of "Ministers, Heritors, and Ringleaders" were candidates for transportation. On June 29, a letter from the king, signed by Lauderdale, granted a warrant for the trial of the prisoners:

> And that you put them to the torture if they refuse to inform you what you have pregnant presumptions to believe they know. When this is done, we do, in the next place, approve the motion made by you of sending three or four hundred of these prisoners to the Plantations, for which we authorise you to grant a warrant to their Transportation.[240]

The principal record for Covenanters that were transported are the Registers of the Privy Council. They record amongst many, that George Scot of Pitlochie (himself a prisoner on the Bass Rock) was given prisoners for transportation from Dunnottar Castle. They were on board the *Henry and Fra*ncis that arrived in Perth Amboy, New Jersey, in December 1685. Others who received gifts include John Ewing; Robert Malloch, a merchant in Edinburgh; Walter Gibson of Glasgow; Robert Barclay of Urie; William Arbuckle, a merchant in Glasgow; Sir Robert Gordon, the younger of Gordonstoun; and his brother, Sir John Gordon.

Alexander Peden was destined for the Virginia colony when he and sixty other Covenanters were ordered to be shipped via London. An occasion for a prophecy, he foretold: "If we were once at London, we will all be set at liberty."[241] This came to pass as the American captain due to take them from London declined to do so when he saw they were good and Godly people.

There were other prisoners from Dunnottar Castle who were transported in 1685, many of them on board the *Henry and Francis* chartered by George Scot of Pitlochie, which landed its human cargo at Perth Amboy in New Jersey after a rough voyage in which some seventy people died, including Scot and his wife. Likewise

---

[240] W. Bryce Moir, *The Flodden Wall. The Covenanters Prison on Greyfriars Yard Edinburgh* (Edinburgh: T. & A. Constable, 1910), pp. 32-33.
[241] Howie, *Worthies*, p. 510.

the forty or so survivors from the *Crown*, in which 211 prisoners drowned, were subsequently sent to the colonies.

Treason charge.

Treason was seemingly a common charge that was bandied about not just by the prelates against the Presbyterian non conformists, but was rife among the nobility during the reign of Mary Queen of Scots. The principal target of the times was the Earl of Moray who was subjected to several murder attempts. One of these was by the Earl of Bothwell whom Moray took to court for "treasonable practices." John Knox was several times charged with treason but he was saved by local magistrates in 1554 at Frankfort, Germany, when he was accused of treason against the Emperors son Philip, and his wife Queen Mary I of England. The magistrates saw through the political accusation and warned Knox, who returned to Geneva and safety. In 1561 he was accused of treason by Mary, Queen of Scots, when she returned from France but Knox was able to defend himself and was acquitted by the Lords of the Council much to the queen's dissatisfaction.

The early reforming ministers such as John Welch seemed to benefit from a lesser punishment for alleged treason as they were banished in the King's pleasure. Later sufferers, mostly in the reign of Charles II, knew such a charge was almost certain to mean death. Welch, like others, declined the king's authority in matters of doctrine and was banished to France where he soon took up a ministry. Samuel Rutherford was of the later school who were quickly charged with treason on the Restoration of Charles II. Rutherford, however, cheated his accusers by answering a call by a superior Judge and judicatory. At about the same time the vengeance of the royalists fell on the Marquis of Argyll who had fourteen articles charged against him, just to make sure a conviction was secured. In the end it was his compliance with Cromwell (which many others also did) that ensured his demise beneath the blade of the "Maiden." James Guthrie was another of the leading Presbyterians to be swept up in the Restoration and subject of the particular vengeance of the Earl of Middleton whom he had excommunicated in 1650. Archibald Johnston, Lord Warriston, was eventually captured, tried and executed for treason although it might be argued that as a lawyer, Clerk of the Tables, co-author of the

National Covenant; Clerk Register etc he had merely recorded the acts of others. It is also likely he had to die because he was too knowledgeable and too powerful an opponent of the new regime; he was also ensnared because of compliance with Cromwell. Hugh McKail was a young minister aged twenty six who was routinely charged with treason for declining the king's authority and who suffered torture with "the boot." Like so many others he went joyfully to his maker commenting after his sentence had been passed: "O how good news; to be within four days' journey to enjoy the sight of Jesus Christ."[242]

Treaties – Birks, 18 Jun 1639; Ripon 1 Oct 1640 and London.
See also: Bishops Wars.

The Treaties of Birks (Berwick) and Ripon brought to a close the short-lived Bishops' Wars between Charles I and the Covenanters. As treaties they were little more than breathing space for the parties to review their positions which would be overtaken by Civil War in England (1642), and the alliance of the Scots with the English Parliamentarians under the Solemn League and Covenant (1643).

In the Bishops' Wars the various regiments had a chaplain from their locality appointed to them and these ministers were on the spot to advise and counsel the terms of the treaties. Alexander Henderson as author of the National Covenant and past Moderator of the General Assembly was an obvious candidate to assist at Birks. John Campbell, Earl of Loudon, was prominent at Birks and subsequently answered the charges that the Scots had breached the treaty, for which he earned the enmity of King Charles. Subsequently he and the Earls of Dunfermline and Rothes, and Alexander Henderson and Archibald Johnston negotiated the Treaty of Ripon. Robert Blair who was with Lord Lindsay's regiment was sent to assist at Ripon and Robert Baillie, who had been with the army in 1639 and 1640, attended the Ripon treaty and the meeting in London where it was finalised.

---

[242] Howie, *Worthies*, p. 359.

Treaty of Limerick, 3 October 1691.

The Treaty of Limerick ended the civil war in Ireland and established William III as king of Ireland. The terms had both military and civil conditions and was not formally concluded until the Lords Justices arrived from Dublin. Militarily all the castles held for King James II were to be surrendered although Irish soldiers had permission to leave the country if they wished. Over 10,000 did so and formed the Irish Brigade in Louis XIV's army. These and their successors became known as the "Wild Geese." The civil articles allowed the Catholics the same rights and privileges they had under Charles II, and permitted them to follow their trades and professions. They were to receive a pardon for all offences committed in the reign of James II and were free from all oaths save the oath of allegiance.

Importantly, although William was fighting for the Protestant cause he did not object to the promises made to the Catholics and declared that he had not come to persecute Papists. The Treaty is generally thought to have been too generous and several important provisions were not subsequently ratified by Parliament, and in time it was disgracefully violated by the government. The English Parliament met late in 1691 and abolished the oath of supremacy in Ireland but in order to exclude Catholics from office required an oath of fidelity and allegiance as in England, this meant the Catholics were required to swear against the doctrine of transubstantiation, which was unacceptable to them. There followed the long period of penal laws against the Catholics and the various land acts that robbed them of ownership.

The cessation of war and the victory of William III at the Boyne did not bring much change for the Presbyterians. Disgracefully treated after the siege of Londonderry they were subject of a continuing attack by the Episcopalian bishops who held a majority in the House of Lords. A curious juxtaposition was the fact that many ministers had gone to Scotland during the troubles and were tempted to stay when they found the persecution there had stopped and Presbytery was established. But several thousands of Scots crossed to Ulster to take advantage of the land that had been vacated. As a result there was for a while fewer ministers for an even larger congregation.

Trouble-makers and rabbling.

There were what may be termed troublemakers on both sides although the Presbyterian ministers were protesting peaceably against the policies of the government and giving witness to their beliefs. It is evident that there were few deliberate and wilful attempts made by the Covenanters to make a nuisance of themselves for the sake of it as there was nothing to be gained by provocative behaviour. In an age when the assembly of five or more persons for prayer was a punishable act, even deemed a riotous assembly, public protest was a dangerous activity. For this reason armed horsemen accompanied various Declarations at Sanquhar, Lanark, Hamilton, and Rutherglen. There were of course, the planned attacks on the military where there was a particular objective such as the ambush at Enterkin Pass to release prisoners being taken to Edinburgh, and the storming of Kirkcudbright Tolbooth to release more prisoners.

There were, however, scuffles brought about by the high handed conduct of the military which was not always confined to the troopers. William Guthrie had occasion to rebuke some English officers who attempted to take Communion without having previously spoken to the minister "or having been found worthy of that privilege."[243] John Semple on the other hand suffered at the hands of troopers who had heard that a Communion service was to be held next day and they destroyed the communion elements and ransacked his house while he was away. Semple next day complained to the commanding officer and was compensated for the lost elements. Angus MacBean was threatened by army officers who proposed to force him from his pulpit. Although he was forewarned of the intended trouble he deliberately preached against the supremacy of King James and Catholicism. When the officers got up to take him MacBean declared "for this I am become the song of drunkards,"[244] which shamed the officers who had hatched the plan while drinking, and they sat down again.

This Scottish word "rabbling" is used to describe especially the actions of the people when they turned upon the churches which were ornate and idolatrous. Predominantly they were Catholic establishments, monasteries, etc but not always so. An episcopalian

---

[243] Howie, *Worthies*, p. 356.

[244] *Ibid.*, p. 556.

church dressed up in the Laudian manner—altar surrounded by rails, icons, and the like—was just as likely to be rabbled if the mood of the people was so minded. Historians frequently describe those involved in rabbling as if a savage uncaring mob bent on destruction. Unquestionably passions ran high but action was usually objective with the furnishings and symbols of popery removed and destroyed. The fabric of the buildings, with a few exceptions, were maintained and reused.

The allegation that John Knox led the rioters in Perth is incorrect. Most certainly he preached against Catholicism and its practices which excited passions but, as such, he did not instruct the people to rabble the catholic churches. Indeed there is evidence that in the last week of June, 1559, Knox and some influential friends hurried to Scone and restrained a mob from Dundee and Perth from attacking the Abbey. It was, however, to no avail because the bishop's servants were offensive and the bishop's son stabbed a man from Dundee. An alarm was raised:

> And so was that Abbey and Palace apointed to Sackage: in doing quhairof they tuk no lang Deliberatioun, bot committed the holle to the Merciment of Fyre.[245]

On 10 December 1688, the advent of William of Orange accepting the throne gave rise to rabbling of Holyrood Abbey, Edinburgh, in which the guard killed some dozen of the crowd. The guard were soon overcome and the rabble wrecked the chapel, looted the Jesuit's quarters and drank the Lord Chancellor's cellar dry. It is of note that the Societies made a special effort to distance themselves from the rabbling by publishing a vindication on 4 January 1689 at the Cross of Douglas.

Rabbling occurred both in Edinburgh and, subsequently, in the countryside, when many of the curates and Episcopalian ministers were chased from the manses. This was usually in revenge by the local people who had suffered twenty years of oppression, fines, and quartering on them by the military, all laid at the curates' door. In many parishes the local people vented their spleen and stored up anger by emptying the manses and violent assaults on the curates.

---

[245] G. Ritchie, *Stones of Destiny* (Scone: Kirk Session of Scone Old Parish Church, 1986), p. 11.

Christmas was considered a good time for such activity as there was food and drink to be taken, as well as the manse plenishings. Many a curate was taken by force to the churchyard, divested of clothing and had them burnt while he, shivering, was forced to beg for his life, give up the kirk keys and swear never to return.

In one instance the minister at Kirkpatrick-Juxta in Annandale, Archibald Fergusson, was driven out by a party of women who literally sliced his clothes from him with knives until he was naked then allowed him to crawl back to his pregnant wife. Robert Bell, minister of Kilmarnock was forced to appear at the market cross and witness the burning of the Prayer Book and of his gown "the garment of the Whore of Babylon" as it was called. Patrick Walker admitted attending some fifteen rabblings and delighted in the terror caused to the curates asking them

> How would they tremble and sweat if they were in the Grassmarket and other places, going up the ladder, with the rope before them, and the lad with the pyoted coat at their tail?[246]

The worst of the disorder was understandably in the southwest of Scotland where so many had suffered so much. There were scores to settled at all levels of society from heritors who had been pushed into bankruptcy to peasantry with a roofless homes and starving family. In context however, it was a paltry retribution on some two hundred curates, for all that the people had suffered.

Twenty-Mile Act, 13 August 1663.

Sometimes also confusingly called the Six Mile Act. This Act is attributed to Sharp's vindictiveness who was jealous of the ejected ministers remaining near to their former manses, and also his fear of having dissident ministers in his locality. He personally was discomforted by the presence of Robert Blair who was forced to remove himself from Kirkcaldy to Meikle Couston in the parish of Aberlour. The Act required that disaffected ministers were to remove themselves and their families at least twenty miles from

---

[246] Hewison, *Covenanters*, Vol. 2, p. 519.

their former churches, six miles outside a cathedral city and three miles outside a royal burgh.

Two Truths.

A later minister in the Reformation, John Dickson, reluctantly accepted the Revolution Church and, in 1698, preached to the Synod at Ayr on the theme of a watchman's role and duty. In this context he regretted the passing of the First and Second Temples, meaning the Church established in 1580 and the Second that which resulted in a clerical government in 1649-1650. In particular, his testimony and regrets were that the Revolutionary Church was not built on the foundations laid in 1649, and was in form rather akin to the earlier church that gave rise to the warning of the "Causes of the Lord's Wrath." Dickson explains why the Covenants were so important and the role they filled and points up his "two truths" which were:

> Christ's Headship in the Church in despite supremacy and bold Erastianism; and our Covenants; which two truths were in the mouths of all our Worthies, when mounting their bloody theatres and scaffolds.[247]

He adds:

> Let us never dream of a reviving spirit among us, till there be a reviving respect to these solemn vows to God.[248]

Tulchan Bishops.

At the time of the First Reformation in 1572, there were very few (less than a dozen) ministers in Scotland. Under the leadership of John Knox the General Assembly approved the temporary positions of "readers" who read the Scriptures to congregations, and "superintendents" who had a role of supervising and reporting to the courts of the Church. However, a private Convention of nobles and some superintendents and moderate ministers met at Leith in 1572. Here it was proposed that the title of "bishop" should be used for the

---

[247] Howie, *Worthies*, p. 594.
[248] *Ibid.*

superintendents who would be members of Presbyteries and equal in rank to them, but not over them.

The nobles were much more driven by greed as they saw the opportunity to obtain the revenues of the Romish offices that had been set aside at the Reformation. As one minister and historian, a Dr. Cunningham, remarked, "There were many among the Lords of the Congregation who hungered and thirsted more after the cornfields of the monks than after righteousness."[249]

These earlier prelates had enjoyed two thirds of the tiends and it now became a question of to what use could these freed up benefices could be put. By law it was only the abbots who could lift the rents of abbey lands; the plan thus was to restore the titles—archbishops, bishops, abbots, and priors—but they remain under the control of the General Assembly. M'Crie, in *Sketches*, tells that the Regent, the Earl of Morton, negotiated that the "bishops" would be nominally in possession of the benefices but would retain only a small sum and pass the balance, to be negotiated, to him and other noblemen who acted with him.

The term "tulchan" referred to the practice of stuffing a calf's skin with straw and placing it in front of a cow to encourage it to give more milk. The new "bishops" were nicknamed the "tulchan bishops" and the remark passed that "the bishop had the title, but my lord has the milk."[250] The first to be appointed was an elderly minister called John Douglas who was presented by the Earl of Moray. A week later Patrick Adamson (also called Patrick Constantine by M'Crie) preached a sermon where he referred to:

> [T]hree sorts of bishops: My Lord Bishop, my Lord's Bishop, and the Lord's Bishop. My Lord Bishop was in the papistry; my Lord's Bishop is now, when my Lord gets the benefice, and the bishop serves for nothing but to make his title sure; and the Lord's Bishop is the true minister of the Gospel.[251]

John Knox was much opposed to the "tulchan bishops" and refused to assist in their ordination and opposed the plan when the

---

[249] Johnston, *Treasury*, p. 43.
[250] M'Crie, *Sketches*, p. 96.
[251] *Ibid.*

General Assembly considered the proposal. For once Knox did not get his way with the consequence that the door was ajar for further moves towards prelacy. At the time of the General Assembly and again as he was on his death bed, Knox rebuked the Earl of Morton for setting up the office of bishop. Later, he warned him that "God would spoil him of all, and his end would be in ignominy and shame"[252] which Morton later acknowledged before his execution.

Act of Uniformity, 19 May 1662 [England].

The full title for this was: An Act for the Uniformity of Public Prayer and Administration of Sacraments, and other Rites and Ceremonies; and for Establishing the Form of Making, Ordaining and Consecrating, Bishops, Priests and Deacons in the Church of England.

In England, throughout 1661, there were consultations and consideration of proposals for the uniformity of public prayers and administration of the sacraments. On the face of it there was a genuine attempt at compromise which at one point produced a watered down episcopacy that may have been acceptable to many non conformists, including some Presbyterians. However, the final Act was severe and the date for implementation was changed first from Michaelmas to Midsummer Day and then to St. Bartholemews Day, August 24. Significantly the date meant that failure to conform resulted in loss of the annual stipend that was due in September.

The Act was explicit in its coverage and directed that "every Parson, Vicar or other Minister whatsoever" was required on or before the Feast of St. Bartholomew, 24 August 1662, to use the new Prayer Book and read Morning and Evening Prayers in his church; and in the presence of his congregation to make a declaration:

> I…do here declare my unfeigned assent and consent to all and everything contained in and prescribed in and by the Book entitled The Book of Common Prayer and Administration of the Sacraments, and other Rites and Ceremonies of the Church, according to the use of the

[252] Howie, *Worthies*, p. 61.

> Church of England, together with the Psalter and Psalms of David, pointed as they are to be sung or said in Churches; and the Form and Manner of Making, Ordaining and Consecrating of Bishops, Priests and Deacons.[253]

Any who failed to conform were to be deprived of their living and all future appointees to the ministry were required to comply within two months.

A further and more stringent oath was required of all persons ecclesiastical, curates, teachers, schoolmasters, professors:

> I…do declare that it is not lawful, upon any pretence whatsoever, to take arms against the King; and that I do abhor that traitorous position of taking arms by his authority against his person, or against those that are commissioned by him; and that I will conform to the liturgy of the Church of England as it is now by law established: and I do declare that I do hold there lies no obligation upon me or on any other person, from the Oath commonly called The Solemn League and Covenant, to endeavour any change or alteration of government either in Church or State; and that the same was in itself an unlawful Oath, and imposed upon the subjects of this realm against the know laws and liberties of this Kingdom.[254]

The problems for the nonconformists were the recognition of the Prayer Book; acceptance and swearing of oaths, including obedience to the Canons; and the need for ordination and the rule of the bishops. Rejection of the Solemn League and Covenant finally ended any Scots aspirations of extending Presbyterianism into England. The numbers vary somewhat but the most accurate count claims 1909 ministers were outed.

---

[253] John T. Wilkinson, *1662 and After, Three Centuries of English Nonconformity* (London: Epworth Press, 1962), p. 47.
[254] *Ibid.*, pp. 47-48.

Uniformity of Worship.

Following the accession of William and Mary, it was deemed necessary to make *An Act for the Settling the Quiet and Peace of the Church, 1693, anent Uniformity of Worship.* It was a ratification of Presbyterianism as the now approved faith of the Church of Scotland and required adherence to the rules of the Church. Simple administration in itself, it was also an Erastian statement being a command about Church procedures by the civil magistrate and another cause for rejection by the "faithful remnant" it read:

> And their Majesties, with advice and consent foresaid, statute and ordain, That uniformity of worship, and of the administration of all publick ordinances within this Church, be observed by all the said ministers and preachers as the same are at present are performed and allowed therein.[255]

Usurper (Oliver Cromwell) opposed.

A usurper is defined as one who takes possession of something unlawfully or by force.

The Presbyterian opinion of Oliver Cromwell has softened over the years although he is still, correctly, called a usurper, as indeed was James II in his claim to the Scottish throne. Under the strict rules of the Kirk, Cromwell was not a ruler by right of lineage, not an anointed king, nor for that matter of the Church of Scotland by law established. Cromwell was not a Puritan save in the broad sense of morality, but he had very strong views about his own faith and was a member of the Congregational Church, one of the Independent "Sectaries" that the Covenanters deplored. It was his toleration of all religions that rubbed salt in the Presbyterian wounds.

In October 1648 Cromwell was in Edinburgh having disposed of the royalists at Preston and Uttoxeter. Uncertain of his intentions, Robert Blair was sent with David Dickson and James Guthrie to ascertain Cromwell's views on monarchical government (which he supported) and toleration (which he was against), and his opinion on government of the Church (which he declined to answer). Coming

---

[255] Johnston, *Treasury*, p. 156.

from the meeting Blair remarked, "If you knew him as well as I, you would not believe one word he says, for he is an egregious dissembler and a great liar."[256]

This seems a curious tale, possibly told with benefit of hindsight, since Cromwell was obviously fighting against the royalists and the king and he was himself an "Independent" in religion. At that time it may just have been political expediency on Cromwell's part because Scotland still had a king (who was executed in 1649) and calling him a dissembler and a liar was appropriate. Rev. John Row (1598-1672) of Aberdeen wrote a famous anagram of Oliver Cromwell—"O vile cruel worm"—which he translated into Latin as *Trux vilis vermis*.

The resentment to the Commonwealth established by Cromwell was general and in 1653 the General Assembly was forbidden to meet without the permission of Parliament. Cromwell meanwhile favoured the Protesters, the stricter Presbyterians and Covenanters, who were in principal opposed to the royalists, and gave them military support to enforce decisions. As a consequence there was a remarkable peace in Scotland. But the Covenanters never accepted the right of Cromwell's authority or that of the Commonwealth, and continued to protest when thought necessary.

Resistance to Cromwell was essentially by gentlemanly discourse and when opportunity afforded itself, remonstrations were made from the pulpit. One such occasion was in Glasgow by James Durham who preached against the invasion of Scotland in Cromwell's presence. Afterwards, Cromwell received Durham very civilly and "desired he forbear insisting on that subject in public."[257] Another occasion was the debate between Hugh Binning and Cromwell's ministers, again in his presence, where Binning totally confounded them. Cromwell asked for the name of the bold young man and commented that "He hath bound well indeed" and clasping the hilt of his sword added ominously, "This will loose all again."[258]

James Guthrie was opposed to the toleration of the "Sectaries" and reluctantly went with the Marquis of Argyll to London where he debated the king's rights with Cromwell's chaplain, Hugh Peters, and asserted the king's title from the pulpit to a congregation which

---

[256] Howie, *Worthies*, p. 350.
[257] *Ibid.*, p. 225.
[258] *Ibid.*, p. 213.

included many army officers. John Livingston also preached before Cromwell and mentioned the king in his prayers which incensed some of the congregation, although Cromwell knowing of Livingston's influence, merely told them to leave him alone "he is a good man, and what are we poor men in comparison of the Kings of England."[259]

Against his own wishes, Archibald Johnston, Lord Warriston, was sent to London by the General Assembly to treat with Cromwell and was talked into accepting the office of Clerk Register. By accepting, Warriston became a prominent ally for Cromwell, but he paid for his complicity with his life at the Restoration of Charles II. Reading between the lines Warriston was in quite severe financial straits and was owed considerable sums by the government; it is likely that necessity and upkeep of a large family drove him to accept the post.

However, the consensus of opinion over time is that Cromwell's rule did more good than harm to the Church of Scotland. Thomas Carlyle wrote, in *Rectorial* (1866), a dual compliment to Cromwell and Knox:

> I don't know in any history of Greece or Rome where you will get so fine a man as Oliver Cromwell…if you examine well you will find that John Knox was the author, as it were, of Oliver Cromwell, that the Puritan revolution would never have taken place in England had it not been for that Scotchman.[260]

Vindication.

The issue of declarations was a common practice and the principal way of recording that communication had taken place. Vindications as such were justifications of particular matters made by way of a declaration. The Rutherglen Declaration of 29 May 1679 (see Appendix 13), was a deliberate statement of principles by the Covenanters as were the several Sanquhar Declarations, especially Richard Cameron's of 22 June 1680. The Queensferry papers, although not published by the Covenanters, was nevertheless

---

[259] *Ibid.*, p. 373.
[260] Johnston, *Treasury*, p. 320.

a statement of principles and justification for those views. James Renwick was to the fore with his "Apologetical Declaration and Admonitory Vindication against Intelligencers and Informers" issued on 8 November 1684 which explained the hardships the Cameronians had suffered, the principles they held true and their justification for dealing with those who persecuted them and bore false witness against them. It drew from the Privy Council the odious order of 22 November 1684 which condemned to instant death in the presence of two witnesses anyone who would not disown the Declaration. His later Declaration at Sanquhar of 28 May 1685 was another vindication of his opposition to King James II/VII.

Of the later ministers, Alexander Shields was responsible for taking Renwick's Vindication to Holland for printing on behalf of the Societies. This document was prepared at Friarminion on 4 March 1687 and entitled *An Informatory Vindication of a Poor wasted Misrepresented Remnant of the Suffering Anti-Popish Anti Prelatic Anti Erastian Anti-Sectarian True Presbyterian Church of Christ in Scotland united together in a General Correspondence. By Way of Reply to Various Accustionas in Letters Informations and Confessions given forth against thme.* It was a defence of the principles of the remnant and gave their reason for resisting the tyranny that fell upon them. They denied they were revolutionaries, nor were they separatists or a new church, but the remnant of the unconquered historic Church of Scotland.

Shields was himself the author of several vindications. He was involved with the Societies when a Vindication was published at Douglas in 1688 which was for action they had taken to turn out some curates and demolished some "Popish monuments of idolatry."[261] Shields also wrote *Mr Renwick's Life, and the Vindication of his Dying Testimony* and *A Vindication of our Solemn Covenants*.

Warning of Retribution and Use of Force. See also: Declaration - Apologetical, at Sanquhar; Defensive arms; Vindication.

John Knox famously took the young Mary, Queen of Scots, to task when she returned to Scotland in August 1561. Knox

---

[261] Howie, *Worthies*, p. 587.

immediately went on the offensive about the return of the mass and idolatry and argued his case before the Court. But he shocked Mary into silence and disbelief when he told her:

> If princes exceed their bounds, they may be resisted even by power, for there is no greater honour and obedience to be paid to princes, than God hath commanded to be given to father and mother. ... To take the sword from them, to bind them, and cast them into prison, till they be brought to a sober mind, is not disobedience, but just obedience because it agreeth with the Word of God.[262]

Giving a warning of the use of force by the Presbyterians was uncommon; and even after the Restoration of Charles II the Covenanters maintained a policy of using arms only in their own defence. Rullion Green, Drumclog and Bothwell Brig were each held out to be defensive actions and not really aimed at removing the king. It was therefore a tremendous shock to the government and a major change of direction when Richard Cameron and supporters rode into Sanquhar on 22 June 1680, rejected the House of Stuart as lawful kings, and declared their intention "to defend ourselves and one another…and if we shall be pursued or trouble… we shall look on it as declaring war… and right ourselves of those that have wronged us.[263]

James Renwick's *Apologetical Declaration and Admonitory Vindication against Intelligencers and Informers* (1684) was the final retaliation by the Covenanters and a *desperate* attempt to defend themselves. It drew from the government the dreadful Abjuration Oath and the law that enabled execution on the spot in the presence of two witnesses.

Western Association and Remonstrance. See also: Engagers; Engagement; Remonstrance; Protesters.

As suggested by its name, the Western Association was a group of local leaders including the Earls of Loudon, Cassillis and Eglinton from the southwest of Scotland, who formed a military

---

[262] Howie, *Worthies*, p. 55.

[263] Johnston, *Treasury*, pp. 141-142.

alliance. These people were supported by Argyll, and represented the radical Covenanters who had been in the "Whiggamore Raid" on Edinburgh that drove the "Engagers" out and established the civil Christian government of the Second Reformation in September 1648. This Covenanted government was responsible for the Act of Classes of 23 January 1649 that purged the army of malignants, including the Engagers. A week later King Charles I was executed and prompted the declaration of his son, Charles II, as king.

This about-turn by the Scots effectively rejected the agreement of the Solemn League and Covenant of 1643, to support the English Parliamentarians, and war broke out. Cromwell attacked and defeated, the Scots at the battle of Dunbar in September 1650 but he still had not conquered north of the Tay. In the hiatus the Committee of Estates and the Commission of the Kirk had removed to Perth where they received a written protest called the "Western Remonstrance" or, more fully, *The Humble Remonstrance of the Gentlemen, Commanders, and Ministers, attending the Forces in the West*, which was presented to the Estates on 17 October 1650. Peterkin's *Records* says the Remonstrance was produced by Sir George Maxwell and read to the Estates at Stirling and that petitions were later presented at Perth on November 19.

The remonstrance arose because, in the west, Colonels Strachan and Gilbert Ker had broken with Leslie's army and had been in contact with Cromwell. They were greatly dissatisfied with the King's behaviour and doubted his intentions. This worried Charles who feared that they would hand him over and prompted him to make contact with supporters in Fife. Charles harboured the fond hope that old supporters of Montrose would come to his side and he made a dash for freedom. On October 4 he appeared to have gone hunting but he rode some forty two miles to the village of Clova where he spent the night in a hovel guarded by a company of Highlanders. He was soon brought back to Perth where he subsequently apologised to the Committee of Estates. This episode became known as "The Start."

The Western Association had met in Dumfries to discuss the position as they were very suspicious of the King and took the view that the defeat at Dunbar was because there had not been sufficient purging of the army. They continued to require full compliance with the Solemn League and Covenant; these and other criticisms were spelt out in their "Remonstrance" précised by Hewison, in *The Covenanters*, as:

1. The admission of Charles to the Covenant without proof of the reality of his professions.
2. Provoking God by the hasty conclusion of the treaty, after the "unstraight dealling" of Charles stood disclosed, this palliating his dissimulation.
3. The kings action in connection with the apostate Montrose and other Malignants and Papists, in opposition to the work of God and the Covenant.
4. The unjust design of some to invade England and to obtain booty and to force a king on an independent nation.
5. Backsliding from the Covenant, neglecting to fill public offices with Covenanters, and tolerating Malignants.
6. The sins of covetousness, extortion, self seeking, and trust in the flesh instead of in God.[264]

The Committee of the Estates were, however, unsympathetic and rejected the document in a Declaration made on 25 November 1650. The Western Alliance were defeated by English troops at an encounter at Hamilton on Sunday 1 December 1650, many were killed, and Colonel Ker was wounded and taken prisoner.

Westminster Assembly.

The Westminster Assembly is properly part of English church history to which the Scots were invited. It was a gathering of Divines who sought to determine the government of the Church of England according to Scripture and clarify the doctrine of the church. The proposal for the Assembly had first appeared as a bill in the English Parliament on 1 June 1642 but it did not get the Royal Assent. Parliament then issued an Ordinance, which did not require the king's consent, and the Assembly first met on 1 July 1643 and transacted its business until 1649. The Assembly consisted of 120 divines and thirty lay assessors of whom ten were lords and twenty were commoners. The ministers (divines) at first included some

---

[264] Hewison, *Covenanters*, Vol. 2, p. 22.

supporters of prelacy but when they saw the tenor of the Assembly they resigned.

Alexander Henderson was Moderator of the General Assembly in 1643 who received the English Parliamentarian representatives and with them drew up the "Solemn League and Covenant" which was sworn to by statesmen and divines in St. Margaret's Church on 25 September 1643. It was a natural consequence of the parliamentary contacts that Henderson, Rutherford, Baillie, and Douglas were sent to the Westminster Assembly, and were soon joined by George Gillespie and three of the ruling elders: Lord Maitland (later the Duke of Lauderdale), Archibald Johnston (Lord Warriston), and the Earl of Cassillis.

Gillespie, in particular, made an impressive speech against Erastianism and Lord Warriston also made an impact upon the meetings with his clear examination and explanation of issues. It was while in London attending the Assembly that Rutherford published his *Lex Rex* and several other papers against Erastianism, and Sectaries. Robert Baillie was held in very high regard and was presented with a silver salver in recognition of his contributions when the Assembly finally broke up.

Interestingly the Scots were naturally "canny" in their dealings with the English. M'Crie, in *Sketches*, cites a letter from Henderson in 1642 that reveals that the Scots were aiming for the moon and expected much less when they sought religious conformity. Henderson wrote:

> We are not to conceive that they will embrace our form. A new form must be set down for us all. And although we should never come to this unity in religion and uniformity of worship, yet my desire is to see what form England shall pitch upon before we publish ours.[265]

The Scots were quite overwhelmed with the outcome which was way beyond their original expectations.

The significance of the Westminster Assembly to Scotland is that it laid down the doctrines of Presbyterianism. It produced a Form of Presbyterian Church government, the Confession of Faith and the Larger and Shorter Catechisms, and a Directory for the Public

---

[265] M'Crie, *Sketches*, p. 284.

Worship of God. The Westminster Confession of Faith was adopted by the General Assembly on 27 August 1647 (Session XXIII) and it and the other standards were confirmed by the Scottish Parliament. They are the basis of today's Presbyterian Church of Scotland.

It is of note that in giving its approbation of the Confession the General Assembly very carefully commented upon the absence of rules about the sorts of ecclesiastical officers and assemblies. It sought to make clear that the rights of Presbyterianism to manage and govern itself, including the calling of Assemblies, was theirs and not the civil authority. These caveats emphasise that the Church of Scotland was an organisation founded on the Scriptures and would have no truck with anything that was Erastian.

Whiggamore Raid. See also: Engagement; Mauchline Moor; Western Association and Remonstrance.

There was strong resistance to the Engagement in the south west of Scotland and the attack on the meeting at Mauchline Moor on Monday 12 June 1648 brought the matter to a head. Shortly after Lord Eglinton wrote to his son, Colonel James Montgomery, about the conduct of the Engagers and concluded his letter with "The nobility and the gentry and country people are so incensed at their proceedings it will not fail but will draw to a mischief."[266] How right he was for the Engagers were roundly defeated by Cromwell at Preston on August 17.

In Edinburgh the Committee of the Estates decided to call up all fencible men to suppress the rising. The troops were placed under the command of the Earl of Lanark who instead of marching west directly, decided to circle through East Lothian and the border region ostensibly to connect with General Munro and his troops from Ireland. This delay in attacking the Covenanters allowed the rising to gather strength. Soon there were supporters from Kyle, Cunningham, Renfrewshire, Clydesdale, Evandale and Lesmahagow. Thus, a band of some 6,000 marched on Edinburgh with the Chancellor, the Earl of Loudon, and the Earl of Eglinton at their head.

Lanark, meanwhile, joined with Munro and stragglers from the battle of Preston who marched to Edinburgh. Here Munro wanted

---

[266] Metcalfe, *Renfrew*, p. 268.

to attack, but Lanark and his Committee refused and eventually the Engagers withdrew to Linlithgow, before deciding to march on Stirling. Another twist in events now took place, as the Earl of Argyll had joined with the Earl of Loudon and had reached Stirling Castle first. But on hearing of Munro's approach Argyll then fled to north Queensferry where he indulged his penchant for taking refuge on a boat offshore. Munro pursued him but was too late, having first to cut a path through the defenders at Stirling Bridge. The Whiggamores at Stirling fell back to Falkirk where the combined forces of Munro and Lanark looked set for an easy victory.

In Edinburgh the arrival of the Covenanters was greeted with joyful celebrations, the magistrates and ministers coming out from the city to greet them and lead them in. In the light of the public approval the Committee of the Estates fell to negotiating with them. On September 26 the Estates yielded up their claim to govern the country and left the Covenanters in control. This was not too soon for the besieged Covenanters at Falkirk where the Engager forces were stood down by order of the Estates. The two armies were disbanded and Munro went abroad. In November Cromwell was received in Edinburgh by Argyll and the Committee of the General Assembly. Shortly after Cromwell's return south, King Charles I was executed on 30 January 1649, and another chapter in Scotland's history was opened.

Peterkin's *Records* quotes a doggerel poem about the Whigs (see Appendix 17), thought by some to have been written around 1679-1680, the time of Drumclog and Bothwell Brig. It gives a vivid description of a motley army of Covenanters that had assembled. Although lacking in discipline and military training, thousands of crudely armed, poorly clad, psalm-singing Scots girt about with total commitment to their cause, must have been an awesome and frightening sight to their opponents. A similar gathering would have marched on Edinburgh in September 1648.

Women, anti.

"To promote a woman to bear rule, superiority, dominion, or empire, above any realm, nation, or city, is repugnant to nature, contumely to God, a thing most contrarious to his revealed will and approved ordinance, and finally it is a subversion of all equity and justice."[267]

THE FIRST
BLAST OF THE
TRUMPET AGAINST
THE MONSTRVOVS
regiment of
women.
*

Veritas temporis
filia.

M· D· LVIII·

Frontis from John Knox, *The Works of John Knox*, ed. David Laing (Edinburgh: Jas. Thin, 1845; reprint Edmonton: Still Waters Revival Books, 1996).

The babblers of political correctness would have had a field day with John Knox's *First Blast of the Trumpet against the Monstrous Regiment of Women* which was a vehement attack on the "practice of admitting females to the government of nations." But it has to be viewed in the light of the times in which the woman's role was in the home and raising children. In the mid-sixteenth century there was philosophical debate about the role of women and Knox had discussed with Swiss Divines the biblical origins for their role. Moreover, there was ample earlier evidence on the issue; Tacitus, for instance, had expressed contempt of those submitting to female rule. In France, women were excluded from the succession (the

[267] M'Crie, *Life of Knox*, p. 107.

misquoted Salic Law which applied to land ownership) and even Edward VI of England had discussed it with the Privy Council.

The *First Blast*, published in 1558, was prompted by the murderous actions of Mary Tudor, a Catholic, who succeeded to the throne of England (reign 1553-1558) and was responsible for the executions of over three hundred Protestants. She died soon after its publication and it came to be regarded as an attack also on Elizabeth I as well as Mary of Guise, the Queen Regent (died 1560) and then Mary Queen of Scots. A sixteenth-century wood cut (below) is an early political comment. It was no more than a statement that the divine law had expressly assigned to man the dominion over women and commanded her to be subject to him; that female government was not allowed under the Jews; that it was contrary to apostolical injunctions; and led to perversion of government. At the time it created considerable resentment from the royal ladies, especially Queen Elizabeth against whom it was not directed. In 1558 Christopher Goodman, a close friend of Knox, joined the fray when he published a pamphlet entitled *How Superior powers ought to be obeyed of their subjects*.

**No Queene in her kingdome can or ought
to syt fast,
If Knokes or Goodmans bookes blowe
any true blast.**

Woodcut from John Knox, *The Works of John Knox*, ed. David Laing (Edinburgh: Jas. Thin, 1845; reprint Edmonton: Still Waters Revival Books, 1996).

M'Crie, in *Life of Knox*, observes that the publication and debate coincidentally took place as the new Queen Elizabeth I took her throne. This prompted a reply by John Aylmer (later Bishop) entitled *An Harborow for Faithful Subjects* that was fulsome in praise of the queen and motivated by ambition. Knox's mistake was to apply the principals generally rather than to confine it to Mary Tudor whose rule was recognised by Aylmer as "Unnatural, unreasonable, unjust and unlawful,"[268] and would not have been out of place.

Thomson's *Cloud* contains notes and declarations of the women martyrs but women do not feature as principals in the *Scots Worthies* except as the wives and friends of the martyrs and are not accorded much credit for the great sufferings that they had forced upon them. Not even the two women, Isobel Alison and Marion Harvey executed in Edinburgh on 26 January 1681 simply for holding opinions contrary to the prelates, are mentioned. The Solway Martyrs, Margaret Wilson and Margaret (Mc)Lachlan, who were executed by drowning on 11 May 1685 at Wigtown are also not mentioned. Another brave and outspoken woman was Christian Fyfe of Fife who was sentenced to be executed on 27 March 1682 but reprieved at the last moment. She was a virago of the Jenny Geddes mould who had visions and thought Sharp's murder a good thing. She bemoaned the death of Cargill and roundly belaboured the judges, bishops, the king and some ministers. The Privy Council concluded that her fanaticism was evidence of madness and reprieved her.

Instances are given of brave defiance to the searching troopers and of inherently brave acts of hiding the hunted husband or friend in Jesus, in the certain knowledge that to be found out would mean at least prison, and possibly death. Particularly in the Killing Time, when the law was that of the military, they were liable to the death penalty for harbouring a outlaw; and were witnesses to the on the spot execution of loved ones. Maternal instinct must have pushed the women to their limits when their children were set upon and bullied in the hope of betraying their father; or simply not knowing what has happened to a husband when the troopers were in the vicinity and hunting people down. Worse, of course, was like Isabel Weir, wife of John Brown, having to stand by helpless as her loved

---

[268] M'Crie, *Life of Knox*, p. 109.

one was executed in front of her and the children, knowing that she must survive in order to take care of the now fatherless bairns.

That women were considered and treated as chattels is but a sign of those times yet, curiously, there is reference to a woman who claimed Alexander Peden was the father of her child. Subsequently the real father owned up and Peden was cleared but it is indicative that celibacy was not a standard expected of the ministers. It is curious, and apparently out of context, that in his last sermon at Collinwood, Water of Ayr, Peden prophesised of things to come—"A bloody sword for thee O Scotland"—and then included "The woman with child shall be ripped up and dashed in pieces."[269] It is probable that this was a reference to images of the Virgin and Child, meaning attacks on idolatry and Catholicism, but was it misogyny in the light of his own experience?

Zeal - defence of Presbyterianism.

Given the trials and tribulations that beset the Reformation and the long battles against Romanism, it required men of courage, vision and great zeal to stand up and be counted for their beliefs. In the vanguard were John Knox and Andrew Melville who created the base on which others could build the Protestant and Presbyterian Church of Scotland. Their zeal and personal bravery tempered with good sense, in the face of fierce opposition, cannot be refuted. They may not have been the creators of the Reformation as such but they were the catalysts who gave direction and structure to the fledgling Presbyterian Church. The later ministers of the Covenant were no less zealous and brave as they gave their lives in the defence of Presbyterianism and the rights of God on earth.

The tactic of pursuit was adopted especially against ministers of standing and public reputation who were seen to be influential. Thus Robert Boyd, after leaving his post as Principal at Glasgow College, was informed against to the king who forced the magistrates to remove him. In Paisley he was dispossessed by the Earl of Abercorn's brother, a staunch papist. Later he found the doors of the church nailed against him and a mob stoned him (this thought to have been at the instigation of the Earl of Abercorn's mother) that he was forced to flee to Glasgow. He died on 5

---

[269] Howie, *Worthies*, p. 518.

January 1627, "his death having been hastened by the successive disappointments and annoyances to which he had been exposed."[270]

The Abercorns (Hamilton) were at the centre of severe persecution in their lands around Paisley in the early days of the Reformation. Paisley was for many years a hotbed of Papistry where the Mass was openly said. It was not until the arrival of the celebrated Andrew Knox, minister at Paisley from 1585, that there was a successful effort to overthrow Romanism in the region. In 1592, Andrew Knox obtained a commission from King James that empowered him, certain nobles, and others of his choosing to seek and apprehend

> all excommunicate papists, Jesuits, seminarie priestis and suspect trafficquaris with the King of Spayne and utheris foreynnaris to the subversion of Goddis trew religion.[271]

It was Andrew Knox who apprehended George Ker; he was the messenger carrying incriminating letters to leading Catholics in Spain (the Spanish Blanks).

The Presbytery pursued the Abercorns, particularly the Dowager Countess of Abercorn, and the Maxwells of Newark for many years. The Dowager Abercorn was excommunicated and the second Earl of Abercorn was excommunicated in 1649 and banished. He sold the lordship of Paisley to the Earl of Angus and removed abroad to escape his tormentors. A feature of the action taken by Presbyteries was their unswerving pursuit. Many instances exist where there were intervals of years between events yet the sick and infirm were pursued, sometimes unreasonably and to excess.

John Craig was a colleague of John Knox and like him, disapproved of the marriage of the Earl of Bothwell and Mary Queen of Scots and declined to declare the banns for their marriage in 1567. Despite Bothwell's bullying he stood his ground. In 1584 he and others declined to accept an Act of Parliament that gave the King power over all estates, temporal and clerical and to submit to the bishops. He was subsequently banned from preaching in Edinburgh but the people had the final say, leaving the Archbishop of St. Andrews to preach to just "a few court parasites." Craig was

---

[270] Howie, *Worthies*, p. 142.
[271] Metcalfe, *Renfrew*, p. 227.

responsible for the drafting of the Covenant of 1581, also known as the King's Confession.

David Black was a colleague of Andrew Melville and was at the centre of a concerted action by the Kirk when he was charged with having made improper remarks about the King and his Council in a sermon. The Kirk saw this as a test of doctrine and with their backing, Black entered a declinature on 18 November 1596, asserting he could answer for all he said but the Council were not competent to judge. Subsequently he and supporters were summoned by trumpet and proclamation at the Mercat Cross and he was eventually sent in ward to the north of the Tay, then to Angus. His was a precedent for future concerted action by ministers especially in defence of Christ's headship of the Church.

George Gillespie was a zealous minister who gave his all for the Kirk and made a particular mark in the debates of the Westminster Assembly. As a measure of their respect for him the Estates voted his widow £1000 on 8 June 1650, but it was not paid because of Cromwell overrunning the country. John Welwood was the son of a minister and a stern critic of the Indulged. He, Richard Cameron and another minister were subject of an attempt by some Indulged ministers in 1677 to depose them but they declined their authority. Welwood was another to prophesy the death of Archbishop Sharp when he preached at Boulterhall, Fife, in 1679 saying, "If that unhappy prelate Sharp die the natural death of men, God never spoke by me."[272]

There are, of course, the well-known workers of the Covenant who did so much to organise and draft the focal Covenants: Alexander Henderson and Archibald Johnston (Lord Warriston) Others, such as Samuel Rutherford, exercised great influence and excelled in teaching the new ministers in their capacity as professor, regent or even Principal of the Colleges. Rutherford was another of great zeal not only in his views on the doctrines of the Kirk but quite indefatigable in his work rate; rising at 3 a.m. he began the day with private prayer before starting on his numerous writings and parochial duties. Such was his learning and reputation he was invited to take the chair of Divinity at Utrecht, which he declined with the words: "I would rather be in Scotland with an angry Jesus,

---

[272] Howie, *Worthies*, p. 400.

knowing He mindeth no evil to us, than in any Eden or garden on earth."[273]

With perhaps the exception of Knox and Melville, James Renwick must have been one of the most zealous of ministers in pursuit of their Covenanted faith, and one who suffered much by way of libel, slander, and malicious tales by opponents. Taking up the mantle of Richard Cameron and Donald Cargill, he first preached to the Society people at Darmeid in September 1683 and laid before the meeting his reasons for criticism of ministers and their defections. He was, therefore, completely open about his position from when "the father of lies began to spue out a flood of reproaches to swallow up and bury his name and work in contempt."[274]

The *Scots Worthies* tells us that the persecution became greater in 1684 but Renwick was still incessant and undaunted in his work. In September he had letters of intercommuning issued against him and this led to the publication of his "Apologetical Declaration and Admonitory Vindication against Intelligencers and Informers," issued on 8 November 1684. On 28 May 1685, he issued his Declaration at Sanquhar protesting at the accession of King James II, a Papist.

The burden of lies and slanders must have been very great indeed such as to turn even Alexander Peden against Renwick for a while, although they were reconciled in a famous meeting as Peden lay on his death bed. The final straw was the issue of the Indulgences in 1687 and an address of July 21 in that year allegedly seeking toleration in the name of all ministers. This led to Renwick criticising not only the granters of Tolerance but also those who accepted it. In 1687 his health deteriorated and despite very great opposition from Indulgers who called him a Jesuit, an outsider, a devil with a white flag and hurtfully, that he had done more to hurt the Church of Scotland than its enemies had in the twenty years past. It was all rather spiteful and the Government made no less than fifteen searches for him in the five months after the Toleration along with a proclamation on 18 October 1687 offering a reward of £100 sterling dead or alive. Renwick continued to hold meetings

---

[273] Howie, *Worthies*, p. 235.
[274] *Ibid.*, p. 531.

when sick and unable to ride, sometimes having to be carried to the place set aside for his meeting.

Appendix 1
The Scots Worthies[275]

Names	*Birth*	*Death*
Baillie, Robert,	30.4.1602	July 1662
Balfour, John, of Kinloch	*ca.* 1640	*ca.* 1689
Binning, Hugh,	1627	1653
Black, David,	1603	
Blackadder, John,	*ca.* 1615	1685
Blair, Robert,	1593	28.8.1666
Boyd, Robert,	1578	5.1.1627
Brown, John,	*ca.* 1610	Sep 1679
Bruce, Robert,	1554 or 9	Aug 1631
Buchanan, George,	1506	28.9.1582
Calderwood, David,	1575	29 Oct 1650
Cameron, Richard,	*ca.* 1650	22.7.1680
Campbell, Archibald, Marquis of Argyle,	1607	7.5.1661
Campbell, John, Earl of Loudon	1598	15.3.1652
Cargill, Donald,	1610	27.7.1681
Craig, John,	1512	1600
Cunningham, Robert,		27.3.1637
Davidson, John,	*ca.* 1605 or 8	
Dickson, David,	1583	Dec 1662
Dickson, John,	*ca.* 1628	1700
Duncan, Andrew,		14.4.1626
Durham, James,	1622	25.6.1658
Fleming, Robert,	1630	25.7.1694
Garnock, Robert,		10.10.1681
Gillespie, George,	21.1.1612	17.12.1648

[275] Howie, *Scots Worthies*. The dates given, especially dates of birth, vary between sources; but the main supporting source is Johnston, *Treasury*.

Gordon, John, Viscount Kenmuir	1599	12.9.1634
Gordon, William, of Earlstoun,		23.6.1679
Gray, Andrew,	1634	Feb 1656
Guthrie, James,	1614	1.6.1661
Guthrie, William,	1620	10.10.1665
Hackston, David, of Rathillet		30.9.1680
Hall, Henry, of Haughhead,		3.6.1680
Hamilton, Patrick,	ca 1503	28.2.1527
Hamilton, Sir Robert of Preston,	1650	21.10.1701
Henderson, Alexander,	1583	19.8.1646
Hog, Thomas,	1628	4.1.1692
Johnston, Archibald,	*ca.* 1611	22.7.1663
Ker, Robert, of Kersland,		14.11.1680
Kidd, John		14.8.1679
King, John		14.8.1679
Knox, John,	1505	24.11.1572
Livingston, John,	1603	9.8.1672
Macbean, Angus,	1656	Feb 1689
M'clelland, John,	1650	
M'kail, Hugh,	1640	22.12.1666
M'ward, Robert,	1628	26.5.1681
Melville, Andrew,	1545	1622
Mill, Walter,	*ca.* 1476	28.4.1558
Mitchell, James,	1621	11.8.1643
Mitchell, James,		18.1.1678
Moncrieff, Alexander,		1688
Nevay, John,		Dec 1669
Nisbet, John, of Hardhill,	1627	4.12.1685
Paton, Captain John,	*ca.* 1602	9.5.1684
Peden, Alexander,	1626	26.1.1686
Renwick, James	15.2.1662	17.2.1688
Rollock, Robert,	1555	8.2.1598
Row, William,	*ca.* 1575	Living 1600
Rutherford, Samuel,	1600	29.3.1661
Scrimgeour, John.	Living *ca.* 1590	
Semple, John,	1607	1677
Shields, Alexander,	1660	14.6.1700
Simpson, Patrick,	1556	30.3.1618
Smith, Walter,	1655	27.7.1681
Stuart, James, Earl of Moray	1531	23.1.1570
Traill, Robert, The Younger	May 1642	May 1716
Veitch, William,	1640	1720
Welch, John,	1569	May 1622
Welch, Josias,		23.6.1634

Welwood, John,	1649	Apr 1679
Wishart, George,	1513	1.3.1546
Wood, James,		15.3.1664

Appendix 2
The Allegations Made Against the Lollards of Kyle in 1494[276]

1. That images are not to be had, nor yitt to be worshipped.
2. That the relicts of sancts are not to be worshipped.
3. That the lawes and ordinances of men varie from time to time, and that by the Pope.
4. That it is not lawfull to fight, or to defend the faith.
5. That Christ gave power to Peter onlie, and not to his successours, to bind and loose within the kirk.
6. That Christ ordeaned no preests to consecrate.
7. That after consecratioun in the masse, there remaines bread.
8. That teinds ought not to be given to ecclesiastiall men, as they were then called.
9. That Christ, at his coming, has taken away power frome kings to judge.
10. That everie faithfull man and woman is a preest.
11. That the Pope is not the successour of Peter, but where Christ said, " Goe behind me, Satan."
12. That the unction of kings ceased at the coming of Christ.
13. That the Pope deceives the people by his bulls, and by his indulgences.
14. That the masses profiteth not the soules that are in purgatorie.
15. That the Pope and the bishops deceave the people by their pardouns.
16. That the indulgences ought not to be graunted to fight against the Saracens.
17. That the Pope exalts himself against God, and above God.
18. That the Pope cannot remitt the paines of purgatorie.
19. That the blessings of the bishops are of none avail.
20. That the excommunication of the kirk is not to be feared.

---

[2] Extracted from the Register of Glasgow and found in Calderwood, *History*, Vol. 1, pp. 49-51. Calderwood notes that many of the articles are almost certainly forged to make them more odious.

21. That in no case it is lawfull to sweare.
22. That the preests might have wives, according to the institution of the law.
23. That true Christians receave the body of Jesus Christ everie day.
24. That after matrimonie be contracted, the kirk may make no divorcement.
25. That excommunication bindeth not.
26. That the Pope forgive not sinnes, but onlie God.
27. That faith should not be givin to miracles.
28. That we sould not pray to the glorious Virgin Marie, but to God onlie.
29. That we are no more bound to pray in the kirk than in other places.
30. That we are not bound to believe all that the doctors of the kirk have writtis.
31. That suche as worshippe the sacrament in the kirk commit idolatrie.
32. That the Pope is the head of Antichrist.
33. That the Pope and his ministers are murtherers.
34. That they who are called principals in the church are theeves and robbers.

Appendix 3
A Brief Treatise of Master Patrick Hamelton, called "Patrick's Places" Errors and Absurdities of the Papists, Touching the Doctrine of the Law and of the Gospel[277]

I. They erroneously conceive opinion of salvation in the law, which is only to be sought in the faith of Christ, and in no other.

II. They erroneously do seek God's favour by works of the law, not knowing that the law, in this our corrupt nature, worketh only the anger of God

III. They err also in this, that whereas the office of the law is diverse from and contrary to the gospel, they, without any difference, confound the one with the other, making the gospel to be a law, and Christ to be a Moses.

IV. They err in dividing the law unskilfully into three parts: into the law natural, the law moral, and the law evangelical.

V. They err again dividing the law Evangelical into precepts and counsels, making the precepts to serve for all men, the counsels only to serve for them that be perfect.

VI. The chief substance of all their teaching and preaching resteth upon the works of the law, as may appear by their religion, which wholly consisteth in men's merits, traditions laws, canons, decrees, and ceremonies.

---

[277] Patrick Hamilton, "Patrick's Places" (1528), *The Acts and Monuments of John Foxe*, Vol. 4, ed. George Townsend (London: Seeley, Burnside & Seeley, 1846; reprint Edmonton: Still Waters Revival Books, 1996), pp. 563, 575-576.

VII. In the doctrines of salvation, remission, and justification, either they admix the law equally with the gospel, or else, clean secluding the gospel. they teach and preach the law, so that little mention is made of the faith of Christ or none at all.

VIII. They err, in thinking that the law of God requireth nothing in us under pain of damnation, but only our obedience in external actions: as for the inward affections and concupiscence, they esteem them but light matters.

IX. They, not knowing the true nature and strength of the law, do erroneously imagine tlaat it is in man's power to fulfil it.

X. They err in thinking it not only to be in man's power to keep the law of God, but also to perform more perfect works than be in God's law commanded; and these they call the works of perfection. And hereof rise the works of supererogation, of satisfaction, of congruity, and condignity, to store up the treasure house of the pope's church, to be sold out to the people for money.

XI. They err in saying, that the state monastical is more perfect for keeping the counsels of the gospel, than other states be in keeping the law of the gospel.

XII. The counsel of the gospel they call the vows ol their religious men, as profound humility, perfect chastity, and wilful poverty.

XIII. They err abominably, in equalling their laws and constitutions with God's law; and in saying that man's law bindeth, under pain of damnation, no less than God's law.

XIV. They err sinfully, in punishing transgressors of their laws more sharply than the transgressors of the law of God; as appeareth by their inquisitions and their canon law etc.

XV. Finally they err most horribly in this, that where the free promise of God ascribeth our salvation only to our faith in Christ, excluding works; they on the contrary, ascribe salvation only, or principally, to works and merits, excluding faith; whereupon ariseth the application of the sacrifice of the mass, "ex opere operato" for the quick and dead, application of the merits of Christ's passion in bulls, application of the merits of all religious orders, and such others above specified more at large in the former part of this history.

Integral to these views was Hamilton's observations on:

Three Cautions to be observed and avoided in the tru understanding of the Law

The first caution; that we through the misunderstanding of the Scriptures do not take the law for the gospel, nor the gospel for the law; but skilfully discern and distinguish the voice of the one, from the voice of the other.

Many there be, who, reading the book of the New Testament, do take and understand whatsoever they see contained in the said book to be only and merely the voice of the gospel: and contrariwise, whatsoever is contained in the compass of the Old Testament (that is, within the law, histories, psalms, and prophets), to be only and merely the word and voice of the law. Wherein many are deceived; for the preaching of the law, and the preaching of the gospel, are mixed together in both the Testaments, as well the old as the New; neither is the order of these two doctrines to be distinguished by books and leaves, but by the diversity of God's spirit speaking unto us. For sometimes in the Old Testament God doth comfort, as he comforted Adam, with the voice of the gospel: Sometimes also in the New Testament he doth threaten and terrify, as when Christ threatened the Pharisees. In some places again, Moses and the prophets play the Evangelists; insomuch thast Jerome doubteth whether he should call Isaiah a prophet or an evangelist. In some places likewise Christ and the apostles supply the part of Moses; and as Christ himself, until his death, was under the law (which law he came not to break, but to fulfil), so his sermons made to the Jews, run all for the most part, upon the perfect doctrine and works of the law, showing and teaching what we ought to do by the right law of justice, and what danger ensued in not performing the same: all which places, though they be contained in the book of the New Testament, yet are they to be referred to the doctrine of the law, ever having them included a privy exception of repentance and faith in Christ Jesus. As for example, when Christ thus preacheth, "Blessed be they that be pure at heart, for they shall see God etc." Again "Except ye be made like these children, ye shall not enter etc." Item, "But he that doth the will of my Father, they shall enter into the kingdom of heaven etc." Item, "the parable of the unkind servant justly cast into prison for not forgiving his fellow etc." The casting of the rich glutton into hell etc. Item 'He that denieth me here before men, I will deny him before my Father etc. with such other places of like condition. All these, I say, pertaining to the doctrine of the law, do ever include in them a secret exception of earnest repentance, and faith in Christ's precious blood. For else, Peter denied, and yet repented. Many publicans and sinners were unkind, unmerciful, and hard hearted to their fellow servants; and yet many of them repented, and by faith were saved, etc. The grace of Christ Jesus work in us earnest repentance, and faith in him unfeigned. Amen !

Briefly, to know when the law speaketh, and when the gospel speaketh, and to discern the voice of the one from the voice of the other, this may serve for a note, that when there is any moral work commanded to be done, either for eschewing of punishment, or upon promise of any reward temporal, or eternal, or else when any promise is made with condition of any work commanded in the law, there is to be understood the voice of the law. Contrary where the promise of life and salvation is offered unto us freely without all our merits, and simply, without any condition annexed of any law, eitber natural, ceremonial, or moral: all those places, whether they be read in the Old Testament or in the New, are to be referred to the voice and doctrine of the gospel. And this, promise of God, freely made to us by the merits of Jesus Christ, so long before prophesied to us in the Old Testament, and afterwards exhibited in the New Testament, and now requiring nothing but our faith in the Son of God, is called properly the voice of this gospel, and differeth from the voice of the law in this, that it hath no condition adjoined of our meriting, but only respecteth the merits of Christ the Son of God; by whose faith only we are promised of God to be saved and justified: according as we read in Rom.iii "The righteousness of God cometh by faith of Jesus Christ in all, and upon all, that do believe," &c.

The second caution or danger to be avoided is, that we now, knowing how to discern rightly between the law and the gospel and having intelligence not to mistake the one for the other, must take heed again that we break not the order between these two, taking and applying the law, where the gospel is to be applied, either to ourselves or towards others. For albeit the law and the gospel many times are to be joined together in order of doctrine, yet the case may fall sometimes, that the law must he utterly sequestered from the gospel: as when any person or persons do feel themselves, with the majesty of the law and judgment of God, so terrified and oppressed, and with the burden of their sins overweighed and thrown down into utter discomfort, and almost even to the pit of hell; as happeneth many times to soft and timorous consciences of God's good servants. When such mortified hearts do hear, either in preaching or in reading, any such example or place of the Scripture which pertaineth to the law, let them think the same nothing to belong to them, no more than a mourning weed belongeth to a marriage feast : and therefore, removing utterly out of their minds all cogitation of the law, of fear, of judgment and condemnation, let them only set before their eyes the gospel, the sweet comforts of God's promise, frewe forgiveness of sins in Christ, grace, redemption, liberty, rejoicing, psalms, thanks, singing and a paradise of spiritual jocundity, and nothing else; thinking thus with themselves, that the law hath done his officein them already, and now must need give place to his better, that is, must needs give room to Christ the Son of God, who is the lord and master, the fulfiller, and also the finisher of the law; for the end of the law is Christ.

The third danger to be avoided is, that we do not use or apply on the contrary side, the gospel instead of the law.

For as the other before, was even as much to put on a mourning gown in the feast of a marriage, so is this but even to cast pearls before swine; wherein is a great abuse among many. For commonly it is seen that these worldly epicures and secure Mammonists, to whom the doctrine doth properly appertain, do receive and apply to themselves most principally the sweet promises of the gospel: and contrairiwise, the other contrite and bruised hearts, to whom belong only the joyful tidings of the gospel and not the law, for the most part receive and retain to themselves the terrible voice and sentence of the law. Hereby it cometli to pass that many do rejoice where they should mourn; and on the other side, many do fear and mourn where they need not: wherefore, to conclude, in private use of life, let every person discreetly discern between the law and the gospel and aptly apply to himself that which seeth convenient.

And again, in public order of doctrine, let every discreet preacher put a difference between the broken heart of the mourning sinner, and the unrepentant worldling, and so conjoin both the law with the gospel, and the gospel with the law, that in throwing down the wicked, ever he spare the weak hearted; and again, so spare the weak, that he do not encourage the ungodly.

And thus much concerning the conjunction and difference between the law and the gospel, upon the occasion of Mr Patrick's Places.

Appendix 4
The First Covenant, 3 December 1557, Edinburgh.

Ane Godlie Band For the maintenance of the Evangel maid be ye Erle of Argill and uyer Noble men.
Subscribed at Edinburgh 3 December 1577.[278]

"We, perceiving how Satan in his members, the Antichrist of our time, cruelly does rage, seeking to overthrow and destroy the gospel of Christ and His congregation, ought, according to our bounden duty, to strive in our master's cause, even unto the death, being certain of the victory in Him; the which, our duty being well considered, we do promise before the majesty of God and His congregation, that we, by his Grace, shall with all diligence continually apply all our power, substance and our very lives, to maintain, set forward, and establish the most blessed Word of God and His congregation, and shall labour according to our powers, to have faithful ministers, truly and purely to minister Christ's sacraments to His people. We shall maintain them, nourish them, and defend them, the whole congregation of Christ, and every member thereof according to our whole powers, and waging of our lives, against Satan, and all wicked power that doth intend tyranny or trouble against the aforesaid congregation. Unto which the Holy Word and congregation we do join us; and so do forsake and renounce the congregation of Satan with all the superstitious abominations and idolatry thereof. And, moreover, shall declare ourselves manifest enemies thereto, by this our faithful promise before God, testified to this congregation by our subscription at these presents."

Subscribed by : A. Erle of Ergyl.
Glencarn.
Mortoun.
A. Lord of Lorne.
Johnne Erskyne of Doun.

[278] Johnston, *Treasury*, pp. 24-25; Hewison, *Covenanters*, Vol. 1, pp. 11-12.

Attached to the Band were two resolutions in which it was resolved to insist on the use of King Edward's Prayer Book in parishes under their control and to promote the reading of the Scriptures privately in houses until the authorities permitted public preaching by true and faithful ministers. These resolutions were important not least because they encouraged the public at large to express their dislike of the ceremonies of the Roman Catholic Church.

Appendix 5
The National Covenant, 28 January 1581
Also known as the "King's Confession"[279]

We all and everie one of us underwritten protest, that after long and dew examination of our owne consciences in matteris of true and false religioun, are now throughly resolved in the trueth by the worde and spirit of God, and therefore we beleve with our heartis, confesse with our mouthes, subscryve with our handis, and constantly affirme before God and the whole world, that this onely is the true Christiane fayth and religion pleasing God and bringing salvation to man, quhilk is now by the mercy of God reveled to the World by the preaching of the blessed evangell, and is receaved, beleved and defended by manie and sindrie notable kyrkis and realmes, but chiefly by the kyrk of Scotland, the kingis majestie, and three estatis of this realme, as Godis eternall trueth and onely ground of our salvation, as more perticulerly is expressed in the confession of our fayth stablished and publictly confirmed by sindrie actis of perlamentis, arid now of a long tymie had bene openly professed by the kingis Majestie and whole body of this realime both in brught and land: To the quhilk confession and formie of religion we willingly aggree in our conscience in all poyntis as unto Godis undoubted trueth and veritie grounded onely upon his written worde. And therefore we abhorre. and detest all contrarie religion and doctrine, but chiefly all kynd of papistrie in generall and pertictiler headis even as they are now damned and confuted by the worde of God and kyrk of Scotland; but in speciale we detest and refuse the usurped authoritie of that Roman Antichrist upon the scripturesof God, upon the kyrk, the civille magistrate and conscience of men: All his tyrannous laes made upon indifferent thingis, agaynst our. christiane libertie; his erroneous doctrine agaynst the sufficiencie of the written worde, the perfection of the lawe, the office of Christ, and his blessed evangell; his corrupted doctrine concernyng origirnall synne, our naturall inabilitie and rebellion to God's Law, our justification by fayth onely, our imperfect sanctification, and obedience to the lawe;the nature, number, and use of the holie sacramentis; his fyve bastard sacramentis,

---

[279] Johnston, *Treasury*, pp. 48-50.

with all his ritis, ceremoneis, and false doctrine added to the ministration of the true sacramentis without the worde of God; his cruell judgement agaynst infantis deperting without the sacrament, his absolute necessitie of baptisme, his blasphemous opinion of transubstantiation or reall presence of Christis body in the elementis, and receaving of the same by the wicked or bodeis of men, his dispensationeis with solemnit othes, perjuries, and degrees of mariage forbidden in the worde, his crueltie agaynst the innocent devorced; his divilish mes, his blasphemous priesthead, his prophane sacrifice for the synnes of the dead and quyck, his canonization of men, calling upon angellis, or sainctis deperted, worshipping of imagrie, relics and croces, dedicating of kyrkis, altaris, dayis, vowes to creatures, his purgatorie, prayeris for the dead, praying or speaking in a strange language, with his processioneis and blasphemous letanie, and multitude of advocattis or mediatoreis; his manyfold ordoures, auricular confession, his despered and uncertayne repentance, his generall and doubtsome fayth, the satisfactioneis of men for their synnes; his justification by workis, his opus operatum, workes of supererogation, meritis, perdones, peregrinationes, and stationeis; his holy water, baptisyng of bellis, cungering of spirits, crocing, saning, anoynting, conjuring, hallowing of Godis good creatures with the superstitious opinion joyned therewith; his worldly monarchy and wicked hierarchie, his three solemnit vowes with all his shavelings of syridrie sortes; his erroneous and bloodie decretes made at Trent, with all the subscyveris and approveris of that cruell and bloodie band conjured agaynst the kyrk of God; and fynally we detetst all his vane allegories, ritis, signes and traditioneis broght in the kyrk without or agaynst the worde of God and doctrine of this true reformed kyrk, to the quhilk we join ourselves willingly in doctrine, faytlh religion, discipline, and use of the holie sacramentis, as lyvely memberis of the same in Christ our head, promising and swearing by the great name of the Lord our God that we shall continue in the obedience of the doctrine and discipline of this kyrk and shal defend the same according to our vocation 'and power all the dayes of our lyves, under the panes conteyned in the law, and danger both of body and saule in the day of God's fearfull judgement. And seing that manie are styrred up by Satan and that Roman Antichrist to promise, swear, subscryve and for a tyme use the holie scaramentis in the kyrk deceatfully agaynst there owne conscience, mynding thereby fyrst, under the externall clok of the religion to corrupt and subvert secretly Godis true religion within the kyrk, and afterward, when tyme may serve, to become open ennemeis and persecutorsis of the same, under vane hope of the papis dispensation, divised agaynst the worde of God to his greater confusion and theyr dowble condemnation in the day of the Lord Jesus, we therefore, willing to tak away all suspition of hypocrisie and of syk dowble dealing with and his kyrk, protest and call the searcher of all heartis for witnes, that our myndis and heartis do fullely aggree with this our confession, promise, othe, and subscription;so that we are not moved for any worldly respect, but are persuaded onely in our conscience through the knowledge and love of Godis true religion prented in heartis by the holie spirit, as we shall answer to him in the day when the secretis of all heartis shal be disclosed. And because we perceave that the quitness and stabilitie of our religion and kyrk doth depend upon the savetie and good behaviour of the kynges majestie as upon ane confortable instrument of Godis mercy graunted to this contrey for the maintaining of this kyrk and ministration of justice amongis us, we protest and promis solemnetly with our heartis under the same othe, hand writ, and panes, that we shall defend his persone and authoritie with our goodis, bodyes, and lyves in the defence of Christis evangell, libertie of our contrey, ministration of justice, and punishment of iniquitie, agaynst all enemeis within this realme or without, as we desyre our God to be a strong and mercyfull defender to us in the day of our death and coming of Lord Jesus Christ, to whome with the Father and Holie Spirit be all honour and glorie. Amen

Appendix 6
Letter of Queen Elizabeth to James VI, February 1589, About the treasonous letters discovered[280]

"MY DEERE BROTHER, - I have ere now assured you, that als long as I found you constant in aimitie towards me, I would be your faithfull watche, to shunne all mishappes or dangers that, by assured intelligence, I might compasse to give you. And according to my good devotioun and affectioun, it hath pleased God to make me, of late, so fortunate as to have intercepted a messinger, (whom I keepe safe for you) that caried letters of high treasoun to your person and kingdome; and can doe no lesse, that with most gladenesse, send you the discovered treasoun, such as you may see, as in a glasse, the true portrature of my late wairning letters; which, if then it had pleased you follow, als weill as read, you might have taikin their persons, receaved their treason, and shunnes their further strenthenin, which hathe growne daylie by your too great neglecting and suffering of so manie practises which, at the beginning, might easilie have been prevented.

Permitt me, I pray you, my deere brother, to use als muche plainnesse as I bear you sinceritie, your supposing to deale moderatlie and indifferentlie to both factions, and not to take or punishe, at the first, so notorious offenders, as such durst send to a forane king for forces to land in your land under what pretense so ever, without your speciall directioun, the same never punished; but rather, hold foote decre and neere, with a parentage of neer allya. Good Lord! me thinke I doe but dreame: no king a weeke would beare this! Their forces assembled, and held neere your persoun, held plotts to take your persoun neere the sea-side; and that all this wrapped up with giving them offices, that they might the better accomplishe their treasoun! These be not the formes of governements that my yeeres have experimented. I would yours had noucht, for I sweare unto you myne sould never in like sort.

I exhort you be not subject to suche weakenesse, to to suffer suche lewdnesse so long to roote, as all your strenth sall not plucke up, (which

---

[280] Calderwood, *History*, Vol. 5, pp. 7-8.

God forbid!) which to shunne, after you have perused this great packet that I sent you, take speedie order least you linger too long; and take counsell of few, but of wise and trustie. For if they suspect your knowledge they will shunne your apprehensioun. Therefore, of a suddantie they must be clapped up in saifer custodie than some others have beene, which hath bred their laughter. You see my follie when I am entered to mater that tuicheth you so neere. I know not how to end, but with my prayers to God to guide you for your best. My agent with you sall tell you the rest.

Your most assured loving sister and consignesse,

(Sic subscribitur) "ELIZABETIHR."

Appendix 7
Ane Act for the Abolisheing of the Actis contrair to the Trew Religion, 5 June 1592
"The Great Charter of Presbytery"[281]

1. It ratifies and approves of all the liberties, privileges and immunities granted to the Church by Acts 1579 c.6,7; 1581 c.1 and others.

2. It sanctions General Assemblies, convened by the Church, once yearly, or as occasion requires, provided the King or his Commissioners be present at the instant of dissolution to nominate the time and place of the next Assembly. In his absence the Assembly can fix the next meeting.

3. It sanctions synodal, provincial, presbyterial, sessional Assemblies, with the whole jurisdiction and discipline of the Church. It does not specify "The Second Book of Discipline" which the Assembly had made into a test in 1590, but this statute quotes the substance of Chapter VII of the Book on the subject of Provincial Assemblies, Presbyteries and the meetings of particular kirks. The statute plainly acknowledges the inherent right of the Church to make ordinances and constitutions for the spiritual sphere, and confines the royal power given in Act 1584 c.2 to temporal affairs.

4. It repeals all Acts favourable to the papistical kirk and prejudicial to the now true Church, notably the statutes of 1443, 1469, 1483, 1551, 1584; and it authorises Presbyteries to take the place of bishops in receiving and collating in benefices all qualified ministers presented by the King and the lay patrons.

---

[281] Summarised in Hewison, *Covenanters,* Vol. 1, pp. 133-134. The Act is quoted in full in *Booke of the Universall Kirk of Scotland*, Appendix II, and in Johnston, *Treasuy*, pp. 54-56.

Other acts were passed which gave presbyteries the right to remove unqualified beneficiaries. Another secured to ministers their manses and glebes of four acres each in extent, together with an assignation of teinds. The ministers emerged well satisfied with their lot but the King and the many who still clung to the mass were not.

Appendix 8
The National Covenant, 28 February 1638, at Greyfriars, Edinburgh[282]

The complete document was in three parts:

1. A recital of the Covenant of 1581, sometimes called the Kings Confession. (See Appendix 5.)

2. A reprise of the legislation that had been enacted since 1581 that sets out the rights of the Reformed Kirk of Scotland. (See below.)

3. The 1638 Covenant. (See below.)

[Item #2.] The Confession of Faith of the Kirk of Scotland, subscribed at first by the King's Majesty and his household in the year of God 1580; thereafter by persons of all ranks in the year 1581, by ordinance of the lords of the secret council and acts of the general assembly; subscribed again by all sorts of persons in the year 1590, by a new ordinance of the council, at the desire of the general assembly; with a general band for the maintenance of the true religion and the king's person, and now subscribed in the year 1638 by us noblemen, barons, gentlemen, burgesses, ministers and commons undersubscribing; together with our resolution and promises for the causes after specified, to maintain the said true religion, and the King's Majesty according to the confession aforesaid and acts of parliament: the tenor whereof here followeth.

[The Covenant of 1581, the King's Confession]

[Item #3.] Like as many Acts of Parliament not only in general do abrogate, annull, and rescind all Lawes, Statutes, Acts, Constitutions, Canons civil or municipall, with all other Ordinances and pratique penalties whatsoever, made in prejudice of the true Religion and

[282] Johnston, *Treasury*, pp. 78-83.

Professours thereof; Or, of the true Kirk-discipline, jurisdiction, and freedome thereof; Or, in favours of Idolatry and Superstition; Or, of the Papisticall Kirk; As Act 3. Act 13. Parl.l. Act 23. Parl.11. Act 114. Parl.12 of King James the sixt, That Papistry and Superstition may be utterly suppressed according to the intention of the Acts of Parliament repeated in the 5 Act Parl.20 K.James 6. And to that end they ordaine all Papists and Priests to be punished by manifold Civill and Ecclesiastical pains, as adversaries to Gods true Religion, preached and by Law established within this Realme, Act 24. Parl.11. K.James 6, as common enemies to all Christian government, Act 18. Parl.16. K.James 6. as rebellers and gainstanders of our Soveraigne Lords Authority, Act 47. Parl.3. K.James 6, and as Idolators. Act 104. Parl.7. K.James 6, but also in particular (by and attour the Confession of Faith) do abolish and condemne the Popes Authority and Jurisdiction out of this Land, and ordaine the maintainers thereof to be punished, Act 2. Parl.1 Act 51. Parl.3. Act 106. Parl.7. Act 114. Parl.12 K.James 6, do condemne the Popes erronious doctrine, or any other erroneous doctrine repugnant to any of the Articles of the true and Christian religion publickly preached, and by law established in this Realme: And ordaines the spreaders and makers of Books or Libels, or Letters, or writs of that nature to be punished, Act 46. Parl.3. Act 106. Parl.7. Act 24. Parl.11. K.James 6, do condemne all Baptisme conforme to the Popes Kirk and the Idolatry of the Masse, and ordaines all sayers, willfull hearers, and concealers of the Masse, the maintainers and resetters of the Priests, Jesuits, traffiquing Papists, to be punished without any exception or restriction, Act 5. Parl.l. Act 120. Parl.12. Act 164. Parl.13. Act 193 Parl.14. Act 1. Parl 19. Act 5. Parl.20. K.James 6. do condemne all erronious bookes and writtes containing erreoneous doctrine against the Religion presently professed, or containing superstitious Rites and Ceremonies Papisticall, whereby the people are greatly abused, and ordaines the home-bringers of them to be punished, Act 25. Parl.1 1. K.James 6. do condemn the monuments and dregs of by-gone Idolatry; as going to the Crosses, observing the Festivall dayes of Saints, and such other superstitious and Papisticall Rites, to the dishonour of God, contempt of true Religion, and fostering of great errour among the people, and ordaines the users of them to be punished for the second fault as Idolators, Act 104. Parl.7. K.James 6. Like as many Acts of Parliament are conceaved for maintenance of God's true and Christian Religion, and the purity thereof in Doctrine and Sacraments of the true Church of God, the liberty and freedom thereof, in her National, Synodal Assemblies, Presbyteries, Sessions, Policy, Discipline and Jurisdiction thereof, as that purity of Religion and liberty of the Church was used, professed, exercised, preached and confessed according to the reformation of Religion in this Realm. As for instance, The 99 Act Parl.1 and 68 Act Parl.6 of King James 6. in the Yeare of God 1579 declares the Ministers of the blessed

Evangel, whom God of his mercy had raised up, or hereafter should raise, agreeing with them that then lived in Doctrin, and Administration of the Sacraments, and the People that professed Christ, as he was then offered in the Evangel, and doth communicate with the Holy Sacraments, (as in the reformed Kirks of this Realm they were publickly administrat) according to the Confession of Faith, to be the true and Holy Kirk of Christ Jesus within this Realm, and decerns and declares all and sundry, who either gainsayes the Word of the Evangel, received and approved, as the heads of the Confession of Faith, professed in Parliament, in the Yeare of God 1560, specified also in the first Parliament of King James 6 and ratified in this present Parliament, more particularly do specify, or that refuses the administration of the Holy Sacraments, as they were then ministrated, to be no members of the said Kirk within this Realm, and true Religion, presently professed, so long as they keep themselves so divided from the society of Christs Body: And the subsequent Act 69 Parl.6. of K.James 6. declares, That there is none other Face of Kirk, nor other Face of Religion, than was presently at that time, by the Favour of God established within this Realm, which therefore is ever stiled, Gods true Religion, Christs true Religion, the true and Christian Religion, and a perfect Religion, Which by manifold Acts of Parliament, all within this Realm are bound to subscribe the articles thereof, the Confession of Faith, to recant all doctrine and errours, repugnant to any of the said Articles, Act 4 & 9 Parl.l. Act 45, 46, 47, Parl.3. Act 71 Parl.6. SAct 106 Parl. 7. Act 24 ri.1 1. Act 123 Parl 12. Act 194 and 197 Parl.14 of K.James 6. And all Magistrats, Sherifs, &c. on the one part are ordained to search, apprehend, and punish all contraveeners; For instance, Act 5. Parl.l. Act 104 Parl.7. Act 25 Parl.11 K.James 6. And that notwithstanding of the Kings Majesty's licences on the contrary, which are discharged & declared to be of no force in so farre as they tend in any wayes, to the prejudice and hinder of the execution of the Acts of Parliament against Papists & adversaries of true Religion, Act 106 Parl.7. K.James 6. On the other part- in the 47 Act Parl.3 K.James 6. It is declared and ordained, seeing the cause of Gods true Religion, and his highnes Authority are so joyned, as the hurt of one is common to both: and that none shal be reputed as loyall and faithfull subjects to our Soveraigne Lord, or his Authority, but be punishable as rebellers and gainstanders of the same who shall not give their Confession, and make their profession of the said true Religion, and that they who after defection shall give the Confession of thir Faith of new, they shall promise to continue therein in time comming, to maintains our Souveraigne Lords Authority, and at the uttermost of their power to fortify, assist, and maintains the true Preachers and Professors of Christ's Evangel, against whatsoever enemies and gainstanders of the same; and namely (against all such of whatsoever nation, estate, or degree they be of) that have joyned, and bound themselves, or have assisted, or assist to set forward, and execute the cruell decrees of Trent, contrary to the Preachers and true Professors of the Word of God, which is repeated word by word in the Article of Pacification at Pertli the 23 of Februar. 1572, and related, the last of Aprile 1573. Ratified in Parliament 1587, and related, Act 123 Pal.12 of K.James 6. with this addition, that they are bound to resist all treasonable uproars and hostilities raised against the true Religion, the Kings Majesty, and the true Professors like as all Lieges are bound to maintain the Kings Majesty's Royal Person, and Authority, the Authority of Parliaments, without the which neither any lawes or lawful judicatories can be established, Act 130, Act 131 Parl.8. K.James 6. and the subjects liberties, who ought onely to live and be governed by the Kings lawes, the common lawes of this Realme allanerly, Act 48 Part-3 K.James the first; Act 79 Parl.6. K.James the 4. repeated in the Act 131 Parl.8. K. James 6. which, if they be innovated or prejudged, the commission anent the union of the two Kingdoms of Scotland and England, which is the sole Act of the 17.Parl. of K.James 6, declares such confusion would ensue, as this Realme could be no more a free Monarchy, because by the fundamentall lawes, ancient priviledges, offices and liberties, of this Kingdome, not onely the Princely Authority of his Majesty's Royal discent hath been these many ages maintained, but also the peoples security of their Lands, livings, rights, offices, liberties, and dignities preserved, and therefore for the preservation of the said true Religion, Lawes, and Liberties of this Kingdome, it is statute by the 8 Act Parl.1, repeated in the 99 Act Parl 7. Ratified in the 23 Act Parl.11 and 114 Act Parl.12 of K.James 6, and 4 Act of K.Charles, That all Kings and Princes at their Coronation and reception of their Princely Authority, shall make their faithfull promise by their solemn oath in the presence of the Eternal God, that, enduring the whole time of their lives, they shall serve the same Eternal God to the uttermost of their power, according as he hath required in his most Holy Word, contained in the old and new Testament. And according to the same Word shall maintain the true religion of Christ Jesus, the preaching of his Holy Word, the due and right ministration of the Sacraments now receaved and preached within this Realm (according to the Confession of Faith immediately preceding) and shall abolish and gainstand all false Religion contrary to the same, and shall rule the people committed to their charge, according to the will and command of God, revealed in his foresaid Word, and according to the laudable Laws and Constitutions received in this Realm. no wayes repugnant to the said Will of the Eternall God; and shall procure, to the uttermost of their power, to the Kirk of God, and whole Christian people, true and perfite peace in all time coming: and that they shall be careful to root out of their Empire all Hereticks, and enemies to the true worship of God, who shall be convicted by the true Kirk of God, of the foresaid crimes, which was also observed by his Majesty, at his Coronation in Edinburgh 1633, as may be seene in the order of the Coronation.

In obedience to the Commandment of God, conform to the practice of the godly in former times, and according to the laudable example of our Worthy and Religious Progenitors, & of many yet living amongst us, which was warranted also by act of Council, commanding a general band to be made and subscribed by his Majesty's subjects, of all ranks, for two causes: One was, For defending the true Religion, as it was then reformed, and is expressed in the Confession of Faith above written, and a former large Confession established by sundry acts of lawful general assemblies, & of Parliament, unto which it hath relation, set down in publick Catechismes, and which had been for many years witli a blessing from heaven preached, and professed in this Kirk and Kingdome, as Gods undoubted truth, grounded only upon his written Word. The other cause was, for maintaining the Kings Majesty, his Person, and Estate: the true worship of God and the Kings authority, being so staidly joined, as that they had the same friends, and common enemies, and did stand and fall together. And finally, being convinced in our minds, and confessing with our mouths, that the present and succeeding generations in this land, are bound to keep the foresaid national Oath and Subscription inviolable, Wee Noblemen, Barons, Gentlemen, Burgesses, Ministers & Commons under subscribing, considering divers times before & especially at this time, the danger of the true reformed Religion, of the Kings honour, and of the publick peace of the Kingdome: By the manifold innovation and evils generally contained, and particularly mentioned in our late supplications, complaints, and protestations, Do hereby profess, and before God, his Angels, and the World solemnly declare, That with our whole hearts we agree and resolve, all the days of our life, constantly to adhere unto, and to defend the foresaid true Religion, and (forswearing the practice of all novations, already introduced in the matters of the worship of God, or approbation of the corruptions of the publick Government of the Kirk, or civil places and power of Kirk-Men, till they be tried and allowed in free assemblies, and in Parliaments) to labour by all means lawful to recover the purity and liberty of the Gospel, as it was established and professed before the foresaid Novations: and because, after due examination, we plainly perceive, and undoubtedly believe, that the Innovations and evils contained in our Supplications, Complaints, and Protestations have no warrant of the Word of God, are contrary to the Articles of the Foresaid Confessions, to the intention and meaning of the blessed reformers of Religion in this Land, to the above written Acts of Parliament, & do sensibly tend to the reestablishing of the Popish Religion and Tyranny, and to the subversion and ruin of the true Reformed Religion, and of our Liberties, Lawes and Estates, We also declare, that the Foresaid Confessions are to be interpreted, and ought to be understood of the Foresaid novations and evils, no less than if every one of them had been expressed in the Foresaid confessions, and that we are obliged to detest and abhorre them amongst other particular heads of Papistry abjured therein. And therefore from the knowledge and consciences of our duty to God, to our King and Country, without any worldly respect or inducement, so farre as humane infirmity will suffer, wishing a further measure of the grace of God for this effect, we promise, and swear by the Great Name of the Lord our God, to continue in the Profession and Obedience of the Foresaid Religion: That we shall defend the same, and resist all these contrary errours and corruptions, according to our vocation, and to the uttermost of that power that God hath put in our hands, all the days of our life: and in like manner with the same heart, we declare before God and Men, that we have no intention nor desire to attempt anything that may turn to the dishonour of God, or to the diminution of the Kings greatness and authority: But on the contrary, we promise and swear, that we shall, to the uttermost of our power, with our means and lives, attend to the defence of our dread Sovereign, the Kings Majesty, his Person, and Authority, in the defence and preservation of the foresaid true Religion, Liberties and Lawes of the Kingdome: As also to the mutual defence and assistance, every one of us of another in the same cause of maintaining the true Religion and his Majesty's Authority, with our best counsel, our bodies, means, and whole power, against all sorts of persons whatsoever. So that whatsoever shall be done to the least of us for that cause, shall be take as done to us all in general, and to every one of us in particular. And that we shall neither directly nor indirectly suffer ourselves to be divided or withdrawn by whatsoever suggestion, allurement, or terrour from this blessed and loyal Conjunction, nor shall cast in any let or impediment, that may stay or hinder any such resolution as by common consent shall be found to conduce for so good ends. But on the contrary, shall by all lawful means labour to further and promote the same, and if any such dangerous & divisive motion be made to us by Word or Writ, We, and every one of us, shall either suppress it, or if need be shall incontinent make the same known, that it may be timeously obviated: neither do we fear the foul aspersions of rebellion, combination, or what else our adversaries from their craft and malice would put upon us, seeing that what we do is so well warranted, and ariseth from an unfeigned desire to maintains the true worship of God, the Majesty of our King, and peace of the Kingdome, for the common happiness of our selves, and the posterity. And because we cannot look for a blessing from God upon our proceedings, except with our Profession and Subscription we join such a life and conversation, as beseemeth Christians who have renewed their Covenant with God; We, therefore, faithfully promise, for ourselves, our followers, and all other under us, both in publick, in our particular families, and personal carriage, to endeavour to keep our selves within the bounds of Christian liberty, and to be good examples to others of all Godliness, Sobernesse, and Righteousness and of every duty we owe to God and Man. And that this our Union and conjunction may be observed without violation we call the living God, the Searcher of our hearts to witness, who knoweth this to be our sincere Desire, and unfained Resolution, as we shall answer to Jesus Christ, in the great day, and under the pain of God's everlasting wrath, and of infamy, and loss of all honour and respect in this World, most humbly beseeching the Lord to strengthen us by his holy Spirit for this end, and to bless our desires and proceedings with a happy success, that Religion and Righteousness may flourish in the Land, to the glory of God, the Honour of our King, and peace and comfort of us all. In witness whereof we have, subscribed with our hands all the premises, &c.

Appendix 9
The Solemn League and Covenant, 25 September 1643[283]

The Solemn League and Covenant for Reformation and Defence of Religion, the Honour and Happiness of the King, and the Peace and Safety of the Three Kingdoms of Scotland, England, and Ireland; Agreed upon by Commissioners from the Parliament and Assembly of Divines in England, with Commissioners of the Convention of Estates, and General Assembly in Scotland; approved by the General Assembly of the Church of Scotland, and by both Houses of Parliament and assembly of Divines in England, and taken and subscribed by them, *Anno* 1643; and thereafter, by the said authority, taken and subscribed by all Ranks in Scotland and England the same year; and ratified by Act of the Parliament of Scotland, *Anno* 1644: And again renewed in Scotland with an Acknowledgement of Sins, and Engagement to Duties, by all Ranks, *Anno* 1648, and by Parliament 1649; and taken and subscribed by *King Charles II. at Spey, June 23, 1650;* and at *Scoon, January 1, 1651.*

We Noblemen, Barrons, Knights, Gentlemen, Citizens, Burgesses, Ministers of the Gospel, and Commons of all sorts, in the Kingdoms of Scotland, England, and Ireland, by the providence of GOD, living under one king, and being one reformed religion, Having before our eyes the glory of GOD, and the advancement of the kingdom of our Lord and Saviour JESUS CHRIST, the honour and Happiness of the King's Majesty and his posterity, and true publick liberty, safety, and peace of the kingdoms, wherein every one's private condition is included: And calling in mind the treacherous and bloody plots, conspiracies, attempts, and practices of the enemies of GOD, against the true religion and professors thereof in all places, especially in these three kingdoms, ever since the reformation of religion; and how much their rage, power, and presumption are of late, and at this time, increased and exercised, whereof the deplorable state of the church and kingdom of Ireland, the distressed estate of the church and kingdom of England, and the dangerous estate of the church and kingdom of Scotland, are present and public testimonies; we

---

[283] Johnston, *Treasury*, pp. 98-100.

have now at last,(after other means of supplication, remonstrance, protestation, and sufferings,) for the preservation of ourselves and our religion from utter ruin and destruction, according to the commendable practice of these kingdoms in former times, and the example of GOD'S people in other nations, after mature deliberation, resolved and determined to enter into a mutual and solemn League and Covenant, wherein we all subscribe, and each one of us for himself, with our hands lifted up to the most High GOD, do swear,

1. That we shall sincerely, really, and constantly, through the grace of GOD, endevour, in our several places and callings, the preservation of reformed religion in the Church of Scotland, in doctrine, worship, discipline, and government, against our common enemies; the reformation of religion in the kingdoms of England and Ireland, in doctrine, worship, discipline, and government, according to the word of GOD, and example of the best reformed Churches; and shall endevour to bring the Churches of God in the three kingdoms to the nearest conjunction and uniformity in religion, confession of faith, form of church-government, directory for worship and catechising: that we and our posterity after us, may, as brethren, live in faith and love, and the Lord may delight to dwell in the midst of us.

2. That we shall in like manner, without respect of persons, endeavour the extirpatation of Popery, Prelacy, (that is, Church-government by Archbishops, Bishops, their Chancellors, and Commissaries, Deans, Deans and Chapters, Archdeacons, and all other ecclesiastical Officers depending on that hierarchy,) superstition, heresy, schism, profaneness, and whatsoever shall be found contrary to sound doctrine and the power of godliness, lest we partake in other men's sins, and thereby be in danger to receive of their plagues; and that the Lord may be one, and his name one, in three kingdoms.

3. We shall, with the same sincerity, reality, and constancy, in our several avocations, endeavour, with our estates and lives, mutually to preserve the rights and privileges of the Parliaments, and the liberties of the kingdoms; and to preserve and defend the King's Majesty's person and authority, in the preservation and defence of the true religion, and liberties of the kingdoms; that the world may bear witness with our consciences of our loyalty, and that we have no thoughts or intentions to diminish his Majesty's just power and greatness.

4. We shall also, with all faithfulness, endeavour the discovery of all such as have been or shall be incendiaries, malignants, or evil instruments, by hindering the reformation of religion, dividing the king and his people, or one of the kingdoms from another, or making any faction or parties amongst the people, contrary to this League and Covenant; that they may be brought to publick trial, and receive condign punishment as the degree of their offences shall require or deserve, or the supreme judicatories of

both kingdoms respectively, or others having power from them for that effect, shall judge convenient.

5. And whereas the happiness of a blessed peace between these kingdoms, denied in former times to our progenitors, is, by the good providence of GOD, granted unto us, hath been lately concluded and settled by both parliaments; we shall each one of us, according to our place and interest, endevour that they may remain conjoined in a firm peace and union to all posterity; and that justice may be done upon the willful opposers thereof, in manner expressed in the precedent article.

6. We shall also, according to our places and callings, in this common cause of religion, liberty, and peace of the kingdoms, assist and defend all those who enter into this League and Covenant, in the maintaining and pursuing thereof; and shall not suffer ourselves, directly or indirectly, by whatsoever combination, persuasion, or terror, to be divided and withdrawn from this blessed union and conjunction, whether to make defection to the contrary part, or to give ourselves to a detestable indifference or neutrality in this cause which so much concerneth the glory of GOD, the good of the kingdom, and honor of the King; but shall, all the days of our lives, zealously and constantly continue therein against all opposition, and promote the same, according to our power, against all opposition, and promote the same, according to our power, against all lets and impediments whatsoever; and, what we are not able ourselves to suppress or overcome, we shall reveal and make known, that it may be timely prevented or removed: And all which we shall do in the sight of GOD.

And, because these kingdoms are guilty of many sins and provocations against GOD, and his Son JESUS CHRIST, as is to manifest by our present distresses and dangers, the fruits thereof; we profess and declare, before GOD and the world, our unfeigned desire to be humbled for our own sins, and for the sins of these kingdoms: especially, that we have not as we ought valued the inestimable benefit of the gospel; that we have not labored for the purity and power thereof; and that we have not endeavoured to receive CHRIST in our hearts, nor to walk worthy of him in our lives; which are the causes of other sins and transgressions so much abounding amongst us: and our true and unfeigned purpose, desire, and endeavour for ourselves, and all others under our power and charge, both in publick and in private, in all duties we owe to GOD and man, to amend our lives, and each one to go before another in the example of a real reformation; that the Lord may turn away his wrath and heavy indignation, and establish these churches and kingdoms in truth and peace. And this Covenant we make in the presence of ALMIGHTY GOD, the Searcher of all hearts, with a true intention to perform the same, as we shall answer at that great day, when the secrets of all hearts shall be disclosed; most humbly beseeching the Lord to strengthen us by his HOLY SPIRIT for this end, and to bless our desire and proceedings with such success, as may be deliverance and safety to his people, and encouragement to other Christian churches, groaning under, or in danger of, the yoke of antichristian tyranny, to join in same or like association and covenant, to the glory of GOD, the enlargement of the Kingdom of JESUS CHRIST, and the peace and tranquility of Christian kingdoms and commonwealths.

Appendix 10
The Westminster Confession of Faith[284]

The Confession of Faith was agreed by the Assembly of Divines at Westminster: Examined and approved 27 August 1647, by the General Assembly of the Church of Scotland; and subsequently ratified by Acts of Parliament 1649 and 1690.

CHAP I. - *Of the Holy Scripture.*

I. Although the light of nature, and the works of creation and providence, do so far manifest the goodness, wisdom, and power of God, as to leave men inexcusable; yet they are not sufficient to give that knowledge of God, and of his will, which is necessary unto salvation. Therefore it pleased the Lord, at sundry times, and in divers manners, to reveal himself, and to declare that his will unto his church; and afterwards, for the better preserving and propagating of the truth, and for the more sure establishment and comfort of the church against the corruption of the flesh, and the malice of Satan and of the world, to commit the same wholly unto writing: which maketh the holy Scripture to be most necessary; those former ways of God's revealing his will unto his people being now ceased.

II. Under the name of Holy Scripture, or the Word of God written, are now contained all the books of the Old and New Testaments, which are these:

Old Testament

Genesis Exodus Leviticus Numbers Deuteronomy Joshua Judges Ruth 1 Samuel 2 Samuel 1 Kings 2 Kings 1 Chronicles 2 Chronicles Ezra Nehemiah Esther Job Psalms Proverbs Ecclesiastes Song of Songs Isaiah Jeremiah Lamentations Ezekiel Daniel Hosea Joel Amos

[284] Westminster Assembly (1643-1652), *The Westminster Confession of Faith,* (Edinburgh: Andrew Anderson, 1679).

Obadiah Jonah Micah Nahum Habakkuk Zephaniah Haggai Zechariah Malachi

New Testament

Matthew Mark Luke John Acts Romans 1 Corinthians 2 Corinthians Galatians Ephesians Philippians Colossians 1 Thessalonians 2 Thessalonians 1 Timothy 2 Timothy Titus Philemon Hebrews James 1 Peter 2 Peter 1 John 2 John 3 John Jude Revelation

All which are given by inspiration of God to be the rule of faith and life.

III. The books commonly called Apocrypha, not being of divine inspiration, are no part of the canon of the Scripture, and therefore are of no authority in the church of God, nor to be any otherwise approved, or made use of, than other human writings.

IV. The authority of the holy Scripture, for which it ought to be believed, and obeyed, dependeth not upon the testimony of any man, or church; but wholly upon God (who is truth itself) the author thereof: and therefore it is to be received, because it is the Word of God.

V. We may be moved and induced by the testimony of the church to a high and reverent esteem of the Holy Scripture. And the heavenliness of the matter, the efficacy of the doctrine, the majesty of the style, the consent of all the parts, the scope of the whole (which is, to give all glory to God), the full discovery it makes of the only way of man's salvation, the many other incomparable excellencies, and the entire perfection thereof, are arguments whereby it doth abundantly evidence itself to be the Word of God: yet notwithstanding, our full persuasion and assurance of the infallible truth and divine authority thereof, is from the inward work of the Holy Spirit bearing witness by and with the Word in our hearts.

VI. The whole counsel of God concerning all things necessary for his own glory, man's salvation, faith and life, is either expressly set down in Scripture, or by good and necessary consequence may be deduced from Scripture: unto which nothing at any time is to be added, whether by new revelations of the Spirit, or traditions of men. Nevertheless, we acknowledge the inward illumination of the Spirit of God to be necessary for the saving understanding of such things as are revealed in the Word: and that there are some circumstances concerning the worship of God, and government of the church, common to human actions and societies, which are to be ordered by the light of nature, and Christian prudence, according to the general rules of the Word, which are always to be observed.

VII. All things in Scripture are not alike plain in themselves, nor alike clear unto all: yet those things which are necessary to be known, believed, and observed for salvation, are so clearly propounded, and opened in some place of Scripture or other, that not only the learned, but the unlearned, in a due use of the ordinary means, may attain unto a sufficient understanding of them.

VIII. The Old Testament in Hebrew (which was the native language of the people of God of old), and the New Testament in Greek (which, at the time of the writing of it, was most generally known to the nations), being immediately inspired by God, and, by his singular care and providence, kept pure in all ages, are therefore authentical; so as, in all controversies of religion, the church is finally to appeal unto them. But, because these original tongues are not known to all the people of God, who have right unto, and interest in the Scriptures, and are commanded, in the fear of God, to read and search them, therefore they are to be translated into the vulgar language of every nation unto which they come, that, the Word of God dwelling plentifully in all, they may worship him in an acceptable manner; and, through patience and comfort of the Scriptures, may have hope.

IX. The infallible rule of interpretation of Scripture is the Scripture itself: and therefore, when there is a question about the true and full sense of any Scripture (which is not manifold, but one), it must be searched and known by other places that speak more clearly.

X. The supreme judge by which all controversies of religion are to be determined, and all decrees of councils, opinions of ancient writers, doctrines of men, and private spirits, are to be examined, and in whose sentence we are to rest, can be no other but the Holy Spirit speaking in the Scripture.

CHAP II. - *Of God, and the Holy Trinity.*

I. There is but one only, living, and true God, who is infinite in being and perfection, a most pure spirit, invisible, without body, parts, or passions; immutable, immense, eternal, incomprehensible, almighty, most wise, most holy, most free, most absolute; working all things according to the counsel of his own immutable and most righteous will, for his own glory; most loving, gracious, merciful, long-suffering, abundant in goodness and truth, forgiving iniquity, transgression, and sin; the rewarder of them that diligently seek him; and withal, most just, and terrible in his judgments, hating all sin, and who will by no means clear the guilty.

II. God hath all life, glory, goodness, blessedness, in and of himself; and is alone in and unto himself all-sufficient, not standing in need of any creatures which he hath made, nor deriving any glory from them, but only manifesting his own glory in, by, unto, and upon them. He is the alone fountain of all being, of whom, through whom, and to whom are all things; and hath most sovereign dominion over them, to do by them, for them, or upon them whatsoever himself pleaseth. In his sight all things are open and manifest, his knowledge is infinite, infallible, and independent upon the creature, so as nothing is to him contingent, or uncertain. He is most holy in all his counsels, in all his works, and in all his commands. To him is due from angels and men, and every other creature, whatsoever worship, service, or obedience he is pleased to require of them.

III. In the unity of the Godhead there be three persons, of one substance, power, and eternity: God the Father, God the Son, and God the Holy Ghost: the Father is of none, neither begotten, nor proceeding; the Son is eternally begotten of the Father; the Holy Ghost eternally proceeding from the Father and the Son.

CHAP III. - *Of God's Eternal Decree.*

I. God, from all eternity, did, by the most wise and holy counsel of His own will, freely, and unchangeably ordain whatsoever comes to pass: yet so, as thereby neither is God the author of sin, nor is violence offered to the will of the creatures; nor is the liberty or contingency of second causes taken away, but rather established.

II. Although God knows whatsoever may or can come to pass upon all supposed conditions, yet hath he not decreed anything because he foresaw it as future, or as that which would come to pass upon such conditions.

III. By the decree of God, for the manifestation of His glory, some men and angels are predestinated unto everlasting life; and others foreordained to everlasting death.

IV. These angels and men, thus predestinated, and foreordained, are particularly and unchangeably designed, and their number so certain and definite, that it cannot be either increased or diminished.

V. Those of mankind that are predestinated unto life, God, before the foundation of the world was laid, according to his eternal and immutable purpose, and the secret counsel and good pleasure of his will, hath chosen, in Christ, unto everlasting glory, out of his mere free grace and love, without any foresight of faith, or good works, or perseverance in either of them, or any other thing in the creature, as conditions, or causes moving him thereunto; and all to the praise of his glorious grace.

VI. As God hath appointed the elect unto glory, so hath he, by the eternal and most free purpose of his will, foreordained all the means thereunto. Wherefore, they who are elected, being fallen in Adam, are redeemed by Christ, are effectually called unto faith in Christ by his Spirit working in due season, are justified, adopted, sanctified, and kept by his power, through faith, unto salvation. Neither is any other redeemed by Christ, effectually called, justified, adopted, sanctified, and saved, but the elect only.

VII. The rest of mankind God was pleased, according to the unsearchable counsel of his own will, whereby he extendeth or withholdeth mercy, as he pleaseth, for the glory of his sovereign power over his creatures, to pass by; and to ordain them to dishonor and wrath for their sin, to the praise of his glorious justice.

VIII. The doctrine of this high mystery of predestination is to be handled with special prudence and care, that men, attending the will of God revealed in his Word, and yielding obedience thereunto, may, from the certainty of their effectual vocation, be assured of their eternal election. So shall this doctrine afford matter of praise, reverence, and admiration of God; and of humility, diligence, and abundant consolation to all that sincerely obey the gospel.

CHAP IV. - *Of Creation.*

I. It pleased God the Father, Son, and Holy Ghost, for the manifestation of the glory of his eternal power, wisdom, and goodness, in the beginning, to create, or make of nothing, the world, and all things therein whether visible or invisible, in the space of six days; and all very good.

II. After God had made all other creatures, he created man, male and female, with reasonable and immortal souls, endued with knowledge, righteousness, and true holiness, after his own image; having the law of God written in their hearts, and power to fulfill it: and yet under a possibility of transgressing, being left to the liberty of their own will, which was subject unto change. Beside this law written in their hearts, they received a command, not to eat of the tree of the knowledge of good and evil; which while they kept, they were happy in their communion with God, and had dominion over the creatures.

CHAP V. - *Of Providence.*

I. God the great Creator of all things doth uphold, direct, dispose, and govern all creatures, actions, and things, from the greatest even to the least, by his most wise and holy providence, according to his infallible foreknowledge, and the free and immutable counsel of his own will, to the praise of the glory of his wisdom, power, justice, goodness, and mercy.

II. Although, in relation to the foreknowledge and decree of God, the first Cause, all things come to pass immutably, and infallibly; yet, by the same providence, he ordereth them to fall out, according to the nature of second causes, either necessarily, freely, or contingently.

III. God, in his ordinary providence, maketh use of means, yet is free to work without, above, and against them, at his pleasure.

IV. The almighty power, unsearchable wisdom, and infinite goodness of God so far manifest themselves in his providence, that it extendeth itself even to the first fall, and all other sins of angels and men; and that not by a bare permission, but such as hath joined with it a most wise and powerful bounding, and otherwise ordering, and governing of them, in a manifold dispensation, to his own holy ends; yet so, as the sinfulness thereof proceedeth only from the creature, and not from God, who, being most holy and righteous, neither is nor can be the author or approver of sin.

V. The most wise, righteous, and gracious God doth oftentimes leave, for a season, his own children to manifold temptations, and the corruption of their own hearts, to chastise them for their former sins, or to discover unto them the hidden strength of corruption and deceitfulness of their hearts, that they may be humbled; and, to raise them to a more close and constant dependence for their support upon himself, and to make them more watchful against all future occasions of sin, and for sundry other just and holy ends.

VI. As for those wicked and ungodly men whom God, as a righteous Judge, for former sins, doth blind and harden, from them he not only withholdeth his grace whereby they might have been enlightened in their understandings, and wrought upon in their hearts; but sometimes also withdraweth the gifts which they had, and exposeth them to such objects as their corruption makes occasions of sin; and, withal, gives them over to their own lusts, the temptations of the world, and the power of Satan, whereby it comes to pass that they harden themselves, even under those means which God useth for the softening of others.

VII. As the providence of God doth, in general, reach to all creatures; so, after a most special manner, it taketh care of his church, and disposeth all things to the good thereof.

CHAP VI. - *Of the Fall of Man, of Sin, and of the Punishment thereof.*

I. Our first parents, being seduced by the subtlety and temptation of Satan, sinned, in eating the forbidden fruit. This their sin, God was pleased, according to his wise and holy counsel, to permit, having purposed to order it to his own glory.

II. By this sin they fell from their original righteousness and communion with God, and so became dead in sin, and wholly defiled in all the parts and faculties of soul and body.

III. They being the root of all mankind, the guilt of this sin was imputed; and the same death in sin, and corrupted nature, conveyed to all their posterity descending from them by ordinary generation.

IV. From this original corruption, whereby we are utterly indisposed, disabled, and made opposite to all good, and wholly inclined to all evil, do proceed all actual transgressions.

V. This corruption of nature, during this life, doth remain in those that are regenerated; and although it be, through Christ, pardoned, and mortified; yet both itself, and all the motions thereof, are truly and properly sin.

VI. Every sin, both original and actual, being a transgression of the righteous law of God, and contrary thereunto, doth, in its own nature, bring guilt upon the sinner, whereby he is bound over to the wrath of God, and curse of the law, and so made subject to death, with all miseries spiritual, temporal, and eternal.

CHAP VII. - *Of God's Covenant with Man*

I. The distance between God and the creature is so great, that although reasonable creatures do owe obedience unto him as their Creator, yet they could never have any fruition of him as their blessedness and reward, but by some voluntary condescension on God's part, which he hath been pleased to express by way of covenant.

II. The first covenant made with man was a covenant of works, wherein life was promised to Adam; and in him to his posterity, upon condition of perfect and personal obedience.

III. Man, by his fall, having made himself incapable of life by that covenant, the Lord was pleased to make a second, commonly called the covenant of grace; wherein he freely offereth unto sinners life and salvation by Jesus Christ; requiring of them faith in him, that they may be saved, and promising to give unto all those that are ordained unto eternal life his Holy Spirit, to make them willing, and able to believe.

IV. This covenant of grace is frequently set forth in Scripture by the name of a testament, in reference to the death of Jesus Christ the Testator, and to the everlasting inheritance, with all things belonging to it, therein bequeathed.

V. This covenant was differently administered in the time of the law, and in the time of the gospel: under the law, it was administered by promises, prophecies, sacrifices, circumcision, the paschal lamb, and other types and ordinances delivered to the people of the Jews, all fore signifying Christ to come; which were, for that time, sufficient and efficacious, through the operation of the Spirit, to instruct and build up the elect in faith in the promised Messiah, by whom they had full remission of sins, and eternal salvation; and is called the Old Testament.

VI. Under the gospel, when Christ, the substance, was exhibited, the ordinances in which this covenant is dispensed are the preaching of the Word, and the administration of the sacraments of Baptism and the Lord's Supper: which, though fewer in number, and administered with more simplicity, and less outward glory, yet, in them, it is held forth in more fullness, evidence and spiritual efficacy, to all nations, both Jews and Gentiles; and is called the New Testament. There are not therefore two covenants of grace, differing in substance, but one and the same, under various dispensations.

CHAP VIII. - *Of Christ the Mediator.*

I. It pleased God, in his eternal purpose, to choose and ordain the Lord Jesus, his only begotten Son, to be the Mediator between God and man, the Prophet, Priest, and King, the Head and Savior of his church, the Heir of all things, and Judge of the world: unto whom he did from all eternity give a people, to be his seed, and to be by him in time redeemed, called, justified, sanctified, and glorified.

II. The Son of God, the second person in the Trinity, being very and eternal God, of one substance and equal with the Father, did, when the fullness of time was come, take upon him man's nature, with all the essential properties, and common infirmities thereof, yet without sin; being conceived by the power of the Holy Ghost, in the womb of the virgin Mary, of her substance. So that two whole, perfect, and distinct natures, the Godhead and the manhood, were inseparably joined together in one person, without conversion, composition, or confusion. Which person is very God, and very man, yet one Christ, the only Mediator between God and man.

III. The Lord Jesus, in his human nature thus united to the divine, was sanctified, and anointed with the Holy Spirit, above measure, having in him all the treasures of wisdom and knowledge; in whom it pleased the Father that all fullness should dwell; to the end that, being holy, harmless, undefiled, and full of grace and truth, he might be thoroughly furnished to execute the office of a mediator, and surety. Which office he took not unto himself, but was thereunto called by his Father, who put all power and judgment into his hand, and gave him commandment to execute the same.

IV. This office the Lord Jesus did most willingly undertake; which that he might discharge, he was made under the law, and did perfectly fulfill it; endured most grievous torments immediately in his soul, and most painful sufferings in his body; was crucified, and died, was buried, and remained under the power of death, yet saw no corruption. On the third day he arose from the dead, with the same body in which he suffered, with which also he ascended into heaven, and there sitteth at the right hand of his Father, making intercession, and shall return, to judge men and angels, at the end of the world.

V. The Lord Jesus, by his perfect obedience, and sacrifice of himself, which he, through the eternal Spirit, once offered up unto God, hath fully satisfied the justice of his Father; and purchased, not only reconciliation, but an everlasting inheritance in the kingdom of heaven, for all those whom the Father hath given unto him.

VI. Although the work of redemption was not actually wrought by Christ till after his incarnation, yet the virtue, efficacy, and benefits thereof were communicated unto the elect, in all ages successively from the beginning of the world, in and by those promises, types, and sacrifices, wherein he was revealed, and signified to be the seed of the woman which should bruise the serpent's head; and the Lamb slain from the beginning of the world; being yesterday and today the same, and forever.

VII. Christ, in the work of mediation, acts according to both natures, by each nature doing that, which is proper to itself; yet, by reason of the unity of the person, that which is proper to one nature is sometimes in Scripture attributed to the person denominated by the other nature.

VIII. To all those for whom Christ hath purchased redemption, he doth certainly and effectually apply and communicate the same; making intercession for them, and revealing unto them, in and by the Word, the mysteries of salvation; effectually persuading them by his Spirit to believe and obey, and governing their hearts by his Word and Spirit; overcoming all their enemies by his almighty power and wisdom, in such manner, and ways, as are most consonant to his wonderful and unsearchable dispensation.

CHAP IX. - *Of Free Will.*

I. God hath endued the will of man with that natural liberty, that it is neither forced, nor, by any absolute necessity of nature, determined to good, or evil.

II. Man, in his state of innocence, had freedom, and power to will and to do that which was good and well pleasing to God; but yet, mutably, so that he might fall from it.

III. Man, by his fall into a state of sin, hath wholly lost all ability of will to any spiritual good accompanying salvation: so as, a natural man, being altogether averse from that good, and dead in sin, is not able, by his own strength, to convert himself, or to prepare himself thereunto.

IV. When God converts a sinner, and translates him into the state of grace, he freeth him from his natural bondage under sin; and, by his grace alone, enables him freely to will and to do that which is spiritually good; yet so, as that by reason of his remaining corruption, he doth not perfectly, nor only, will that which is good, but doth also will that which is evil.

V. The will of man is made perfectly and immutably free to good alone, in the state of glory only.

CHAP X. - *Of Effectual Calling.*

I. All those whom God hath predestinated unto life, and those only, he is pleased, in his appointed and accepted time, effectually to call, by his Word and Spirit, out of that state of sin and death, in which they are by nature, to grace and salvation, by Jesus Christ; enlightening their minds spiritually and savingly to understand the things of God, taking away their heart of stone, and giving unto them a heart of flesh; renewing their wills, and, by his almighty power, determining them to that which is good, and effectually drawing them to Jesus Christ: yet so, as they come most freely, being made willing by his grace.

II. This effectual call is of God's free and special grace alone, not from anything at all foreseen in man, who is altogether passive therein, until, being quickened and renewed by the Holy Spirit, he is thereby enabled to answer this call, and to embrace the grace offered and conveyed in it.

III. Elect infants, dying in infancy, are regenerated, and saved by Christ, through the Spirit, who worketh when, and where, and how he pleaseth: so also are all other elect persons who are incapable of being outwardly called by the ministry of the Word.

IV. Others, not elected, although they may be called by the ministry of the Word, and may have some common operations of the Spirit, yet they never truly come unto Christ, and therefore cannot be saved: much less can men, not professing the Christian religion, be saved in any other way whatsoever, be they never so diligent to frame their lives according to the light of nature, and the laws of that religion they do profess. And, to assert and maintain that they may, is very pernicious, and to be detested.

CHAP XI. - *Of Justification.*

I. Those whom God effectually calleth, he also freely justifieth: not by infusing righteousness into them, but by pardoning their sins, and by accounting and accepting their persons as righteous; not for anything wrought in them, or done by them, but for Christ's sake alone; nor by imputing faith itself, the act of believing, or any other evangelical obedience to them, as their righteousness; but by imputing the obedience and satisfaction of Christ unto them, they receiving and resting on him and his righteousness, by faith; which faith they have not of themselves, it is the gift of God.

II. Faith, thus receiving and resting on Christ and his righteousness, is the alone instrument of justification: yet is it not alone in the person justified, but is ever accompanied with all other saving graces, and is no dead faith, but worketh by love.

III. Christ, by his obedience and death, did fully discharge the debt of all those that are thus justified, and did make a proper, real, and full satisfaction to his Father's justice in their behalf. Yet, inasmuch as he was given by the Father for them; and his obedience and satisfaction accepted in their stead; and both, freely, not for anything in them; their justification is only of free grace; that both the exact justice and rich grace of God might be glorified in the justification of sinners.

IV. God did, from all eternity, decree to justify all the elect, and Christ did, in the fullness of time, die for their sins, and rise again for their justification: nevertheless, they are not justified, until the Holy Spirit doth, in due time, actually apply Christ unto them.

V. God doth continue to forgive the sins of those that are justified; and, although they can never fall from the state of justification, yet they may, by their sins, fall under God's fatherly displeasure, and not have the light of his countenance restored unto them, until they humble themselves, confess their sins, beg pardon, and renew their faith and repentance.

VI. The justification of believers under the Old Testament was, in all these respects, one and the same with the justification of believers under the New Testament.

CHAP XII. - *Of Adoption.*

I. All those that are justified, God vouchsafeth, in and for his only Son Jesus Christ, to make partakers of the grace of adoption, by which they are taken into the number, and enjoy the liberties and privileges of the children of God, have his name put upon them, receive the spirit of adoption, have access to the throne of grace with boldness, are enabled to cry, Abba, Father, are pitied, protected, provided for, and chastened by him, as by a Father: yet never cast off, but sealed to the day of redemption; and inherit the promises, as heirs of everlasting salvation.

CHAP XIII. - *Of Sanctification.*

I. They, who are once effectually called, and regenerated, having a new heart, and a new spirit created in them, are further sanctified, really and personally, through the virtue of Christ's death and resurrection, by his Word and Spirit dwelling in them: the dominion of the whole body of sin is destroyed, and the several lusts thereof are more and more weakened and mortified; and they more and more quickened and strengthened in all saving graces, to the practice of true holiness, without which no man shall see the Lord.

II. This sanctification is throughout, in the whole man; yet imperfect in this life, there abiding still some remnants of corruption in every part; whence a riseth a continual and irreconcilable war, the flesh lusting against the Spirit, and the Spirit against the flesh.

III. In which war, although the remaining corruption, for a time, may much prevail; yet, through the continual supply of strength from the sanctifying Spirit of Christ, the regenerate part doth overcome; and so, the saints grow in grace, perfecting holiness in the fear of God.

CHAP XIV. - *Of Saving Faith.*

I. The grace of faith, whereby the elect are enabled to believe to the saving of their souls, is the work of the Spirit of Christ in their hearts, and is ordinarily wrought by the ministry of the Word, by which also, and by the administration of the sacraments, and prayer, it is increased and strengthened.

II. By this faith, a Christian believeth to be true whatsoever is revealed in the Word, for the authority of God himself speaking therein; and acteth differently upon that which each particular passage thereof containeth; yielding obedience to the commands, trembling at the threatenings, and embracing the promises of God for this life, and that which is to come. But the principal acts of saving faith are accepting, receiving, and resting upon Christ alone for justification, sanctification, and eternal life, by virtue of the covenant of grace.

III. This faith is different in degrees, weak or strong; may be often and many ways assailed, and weakened, but gets the victory: growing up in many to the attainment of a full assurance, through Christ, who is both the author and finisher of our faith.

CHAP XV. - *Of Repentance unto Life.*

I. Repentance unto life is an evangelical grace, the doctrine whereof is to be preached by every minister of the gospel, as well as that of faith in Christ.

II. By it, a sinner, out of the sight and sense not only of the danger, but also of the filthiness and odiousness of his sins, as contrary to the holy nature, and righteous law of God; and upon the apprehension of his mercy in Christ to such as are penitent, so grieves for, and hates his sins, as to turn from them all unto God, purposing and endeavoring to walk with him in all the ways of his commandments.

III. Although repentance be not to be rested in, as any satisfaction for sin, or any cause of the pardon thereof, which is the act of God's free grace in Christ; yet it is of such necessity to all sinners, that none may expect pardon without it.

IV. As there is no sin so small, but it deserves damnation; so there is no sin so great, that it can bring damnation upon those who truly repent.

V. Men ought not to content themselves with a general repentance, but it is every man's duty to endeavor to repent of his particular sins, particularly.

VI. As every man is bound to make private confession of his sins to God, praying for the pardon thereof; upon which, and the forsaking of them, he shall find mercy; so, he that scandalizeth his brother, or the church of Christ, ought to be willing, by a private or public confession, and sorrow for his sin, to declare his repentance to those that are offended, who are thereupon to be reconciled to him, and in love to receive him.

CHAP XVI. - *Of Good Works.*

I. Good works are only such as God hath commanded in his holy Word, and not such as, without the warrant thereof, are devised by men, out of blind zeal, or upon any pretense of good intention.

II. These good works, done in obedience to God's commandments, are the fruits and evidences of a true and lively faith: and by them believers manifest their thankfulness, strengthen their assurance, edify their brethren, adorn the profession of the gospel, stop the mouths of the adversaries, and glorify God, whose workmanship they are, created in Christ Jesus thereunto, that, having their fruit unto holiness, they may have the end, eternal life.

III. Their ability to do good works is not at all of themselves, but wholly from the Spirit of Christ. And that they may be enabled thereunto, beside the graces they have already received, there is required an actual influence of the same Holy Spirit, to work in them to will, and to do, of his good pleasure: yet are they not hereupon to grow negligent, as if they were not bound to perform any duty unless upon a special motion of the Spirit; but they ought to be diligent in stirring up the grace of God that is in them.

IV. They who, in their obedience, attain to the greatest height which is possible in this life, are so far from being able to supererogate, and to do more than God requires, as that they fall short of much which in duty they are bound to do.

V. We cannot by our best works merit pardon of sin, or eternal life at the hand of God, by reason of the great disproportion that is between them and the glory to come; and the infinite distance that is between us and God, whom, by them, we can neither profit, nor satisfy for the debt of our former sins, but when we have done all we can, we have done but our duty, and are unprofitable servants: and because, as they are good, they proceed from his Spirit; and as they are wrought by us, they are defiled, and mixed with so much weakness and imperfection, that they cannot endure the severity of God's judgment.

VI. Notwithstanding, the persons of believers being accepted through Christ, their good works also are accepted in him; not as though they were in this life wholly unblamable and unreprovable in God's sight; but that he, looking upon them in his Son, is pleased to accept and reward that which is sincere, although accompanied with many weaknesses and imperfections.

VII. Works done by unregenerate men, although for the matter of them they may be things which God commands; and of good use both to themselves and others: yet, because they proceed not from an heart purified by faith; nor are done in a right manner, according to the Word; nor to aright end, the glory of God, they are therefore sinful, and cannot please God, or make a man meet to receive grace from God: and yet, their neglect of them is more sinful, and displeasing unto God.

CHAP XVII. - *Of the Perseverance of the Saints.*

I. They, whom God hath accepted in his Beloved, effectually called, and sanctified by his Spirit, can neither totally nor finally fall away from the state of grace, but shall certainly persevere therein to the end, and be eternally saved.

II. This perseverance of the saints depends not upon their own free will, but upon the immutability of the decree of election, flowing from the free and unchangeable love of God the Father; upon the efficacy of the merit and intercession of Jesus Christ, the abiding of the Spirit, and of the seed of God within them, and the nature of the covenant of grace: from all which ariseth also the certainty and infallibility thereof.

III. Nevertheless, they may, through the temptations of Satan and of the world, the prevalency of corruption remaining in them, and the neglect of the means of their preservation, fall into grievous sins; and, for a time, continue therein: whereby they incur God's displeasure, and grieve his Holy Spirit, come to be deprived of some measure of their graces and comforts, have their hearts hardened, and their consciences wounded; hurt and scandalize others, and bring temporal judgments upon themselves.

CHAP XVIII. - *Of Assurance of Grace and Salvation.*

I. Although hypocrites and other unregenerate men may vainly deceive themselves with false hopes and carnal presumptions of being in the favor of God, and estate of salvation (which hope of theirs shall perish): yet such as truly believe in the Lord Jesus, and love him in sincerity, endeavoring to walk in all good conscience before him, may, in this life, be certainly assured that they are in the state of grace, and may rejoice in the hope of the glory of God, which hope shall never make them ashamed.

II. This certainty is not a bare conjectural and probable persuasion grounded upon a fallible hope; but an infallible assurance of faith founded upon the divine truth of the promises of salvation, the inward evidence of those graces unto which these promises are made, the testimony of the Spirit of adoption witnessing with our spirits that we are the children of God, which Spirit is the earnest of our inheritance, whereby we are sealed to the day of redemption.

III. This infallible assurance doth not so belong to the essence of faith, but that a true believer may wait long, and conflict with many difficulties before he be partaker of it: yet, being enabled by the Spirit to know the things which are freely given him of God, he may, without extraordinary revelation, in the right use of ordinary means, attain thereunto. And therefore it is the duty of everyone to give all diligence to make his calling and election sure, that thereby his heart may be enlarged in peace and joy in the Holy Ghost, in love and thankfulness to God, and in strength and cheerfulness in the duties of obedience, the proper fruits of this assurance; so far is it from inclining men to looseness.

IV. True believers may have the assurance of their salvation divers ways shaken, diminished, and intermitted; as, by negligence in preserving of it, by falling into some special sin which woundeth the conscience, and grieveth the Spirit; by some sudden or vehement temptation, by God's withdrawing the light of his countenance, and suffering even such as fear him to walk in darkness, and to have no light: yet are they never utterly destitute of that seed of God, and life of faith, that love of Christ and the brethren, that sincerity of heart, and conscience of duty, out of which, by the operation of the Spirit, this assurance may, in due time, be revived; and by the which, in the meantime, they are supported from utter despair.

CHAP XIX. - *Of the Law of God.*

I. God gave to Adam a law, as a covenant of works, by which he bound him and all his posterity to personal, entire, exact, and perpetual obedience, promised life upon the fulfilling, and threatened death upon the breach of it, and endued him with power and ability to keep it.

II. This law, after his fall, continued to be a perfect rule of righteousness; and, as such, was delivered by God upon Mount Sinai, in ten commandments, and written in two tables: the four first commandments containing our duty towards God; and the other six, our duty to man.

III. Beside this law, commonly called moral, God was pleased to give to the people of Israel, as a church under age, ceremonial laws, containing several typical ordinances, partly of worship, prefiguring Christ, his graces, actions, sufferings, and benefits; and partly, holding forth divers instructions of moral duties. All which ceremonial laws are now abrogated, under the New Testament.

IV. To them also, as a body politic, he gave sundry judicial laws, which expired together with the state of that people; not obliging any other now, further than the general equity thereof may require.

V. The moral law doth forever bind all, as well justified persons as others, to the obedience thereof; and that, not only in regard of the matter contained in it, but also in respect of the authority of God the Creator, who gave it. Neither doth Christ, in the gospel, any way dissolve, but much strengthen this obligation.

VI. Although true believers be not under the law, as a covenant of works, to be thereby justified, or condemned; yet is it of great use to them, as well as to others; in that, as a rule of life informing them of the will of God, and their duty, it directs and binds them to walk accordingly; discovering also the sinful pollutions of their nature, hearts, and lives; so as, examining themselves thereby, they may come to further conviction of, humiliation for, and hatred against sin, together with a clearer sight of the need they have of Christ, and the perfection of his obedience. It is likewise of use to the regenerate, to restrain their corruptions, in that it forbids sin: and the threatenings of it serve to show what even their sins deserve; and what afflictions, in this life, they may expect for them, although freed from the curse thereof threatened in the law. The promises of it, in like manner, show them God's approbation of obedience, and what blessings they may expect upon the performance thereof: although not as due to them by the law as a covenant of works. So as, a man's doing good, and refraining from evil, because the law encourageth to the one, and deterreth from the other, is no evidence of his being under the law; and, not under grace.

VII. Neither are the aforementioned uses of the law contrary to the grace of the gospel, but do sweetly comply with it; the Spirit of Christ subduing and enabling the will of man to do that freely, and cheerfully, which the will of God, revealed in the law, requireth to be done.

CHAP XX. - *Of Christian Liberty, and Liberty of Conscience.*

I. The liberty which Christ hath purchased for believers under the gospel consists in their freedom from the guilt of sin, the condemning wrath of God, the curse of the moral law; and, in their being delivered from this present evil world, bondage to Satan, and dominion of sin; from the evil of afflictions, the sting of death, the victory of the grave, and everlasting damnation; as also, in their free access to God, and their yielding obedience unto him, not out of slavish fear, but a childlike love and willing mind. All which were common also to believers under the law. But, under the New Testament, the liberty of Christians is further enlarged, in their freedom from the yoke of the ceremonial law, to which the Jewish church was subjected; and in greater boldness of access to the throne of grace, and in fuller communications of the free Spirit of God, than believers under the law did ordinarily partake of.

II. God alone is Lord of the conscience, and hath left it free from the doctrines and commandments of men, which are, in anything, contrary to his Word; or beside it, if matters of faith, or worship. So that, to believe such doctrines, or to obey such commands, out of conscience, is to betray true liberty of conscience: and the requiring of an implicit faith, and an absolute and blind obedience, is to destroy liberty of conscience, and reason also.

III. They who, upon pretense of Christian liberty, do practice any sin, or cherish any lust, do thereby destroy the end of Christian liberty, which is, that being delivered out of the hands of our enemies, we might serve the Lord without fear, in holiness and righteousness before him, all the days of our life.

IV. And because the powers which God hath ordained, and the liberty which Christ hath purchased, are not intended by God to destroy, but mutually to uphold and preserve one another; they who, upon pretense of Christian liberty, shall oppose any lawful power, or the lawful exercise of it, whether it be civil or ecclesiastical, resist the ordinance of God. And, for their publishing of such opinions, or maintaining of such practices, as are contrary to the light of nature, or to the known principles of Christianity (whether concerning faith, worship, or conversation), or to the power of godliness; or, such erroneous opinions or practices, as either in their own nature, or in the manner of publishing or maintaining them, are destructive to he external peace and order which Christ hath established in the church, they may lawfully be called to account, and proceeded against, by the censures of the church, and by the power of the civil magistrate.

CHAP XXI. - *Of Religious Worship, and the Sabbath-day.*

I. The light of nature shows that there is a God, who has lordship and sovereignty over all, is good, and does good unto all, and is therefore to be feared, loved, praised, called upon, trusted in, and served, with all the heart, and with all the soul, and with all the might. (Rom. 1:20, Acts 17:24, Psalm 69:68, Jer. 10:7, Psalm 31:23, Psalm 18:3, Rom. 10:12, Psalm 62:8, Josh. 24:14, Mark 12:33) But the acceptable way of worshiping the true God is instituted by himself, and so limited by his own revealed will, that he may not be worshiped according to the imaginations and devices of men, or the suggestions of Satan, under any visible representation, or any other way not prescribed in the Holy Scripture. (Deut. 12:32, Matt. 15:9, Act 17:25, Matt. 4:9-10, Deut. 15:1-20, Exod. 20:4-6, Col. 2:23)

II. Religious worship is to be given to God, the Father, Son, and Holy Ghost; and to him alone; (Matt. 4:10, John 5:23, 2 Cor. 13:14) not to angels, saints, or any other creature: (Col. 2:18, Rev. 19:10, Rom. 1:25) and, since the fall, not without a Mediator; nor in the mediation of any other but of Christ alone. (John 14:6, 1 Tim. 2:5, Col.3:17)

III. Prayer, with thanksgiving, being one special part of religious worship, (Phil. 4:6) is by God required of all men: (Psalm 65:2) and, that it may be accepted, it is to be made in the name of the Son, (John 14:13-14, 1 Pet. 2:5) by the help of his Spirit, (Rom. 8:26) according to his will, (1 John 5:14) with understanding, reverence, humility, fervency, faith, love, and perseverance; (Psalm 47:7, Eccl. 5:1-2, Heb. 12:28, Gen. 18:27, James 5:16, James 1:6-7, Mark 11:24, Matt. 6:12-15, Col. 4:2, Eph 6:18) and, if vocal, in a known tongue. (1 Cor. 14:14)

IV. Prayer is to be made for things lawful; (1John 5:14) and for all sorts of men living, or that shall live hereafter: (1Tim. 2:1-2, John 17:20, 2 Sam. 7:29, Ruth 4:12) but not for the dead, (2 Sam. 12:21-23, Luke 16:25-26, Rev. 14:13) nor for those of whom it may be known that they have sinned the sin unto death. (1 John 5:16)

V. The reading of the Scriptures with godly fear, the sound preaching and conscionable hearing of the Word, in obedience unto God, with understanding, faith, and reverence, singing of psalms with grace in the heart; as also, the due administration and worthy receiving of the sacraments instituted by Christ, are all parts of the ordinary religious worship of God: beside religious oaths, vows, solemn fastings, and thanksgivings upon special occasions, which are, in their several times and seasons, to be used in an holy and religious manner.

VI. Neither prayer, nor any other part of religious worship, is now, under the gospel, either tied unto, or made more acceptable by any place in which it is performed, or towards which it is directed: but God is to be worshiped everywhere, in spirit and truth; as, in private families daily, and in secret, each one by himself; so, more solemnly in the public assemblies, which are not carelessly or willfully to be neglected, or forsaken, when God, by his Word or providence, calleth thereunto.

VII. As it is the law of nature, that, in general, a due proportion of time be set apart for the worship of God; so, in his Word, by a positive, moral, and perpetual commandment binding all men in all ages, he hath particularly appointed one day in seven, for a Sabbath, to be kept holy unto him: which, from the beginning of the world to the resurrection of Christ, was the last day of the week; and, from the resurrection of Christ, was changed into the first day of the week, which, in Scripture, is called the Lord's day, and is to be continued to the end of the world, as the Christian Sabbath.

VIII. This Sabbath is then kept holy unto the Lord, when men, after a due preparing of their hearts, and ordering of their common affairs beforehand, do not only observe an holy rest, all the day, from their own works, words, and thoughts about their worldly employments and recreations, but also are taken up, the whole time, in the public and private exercises of his worship, and in the duties of necessity and mercy.

CHAP XXII. - *Of lawful Oaths and Vows.*

I. A lawful oath is a part of religious worship, wherein, upon just occasion, the person swearing solemnly calleth God to witness what he asserteth, or promiseth, and to judge him according to the truth or falsehood of what he sweareth.

II. The name of God only is that by which men ought to swear, and therein it is to be used with all holy fear and reverence. Therefore, to swear vainly, or rashly, by that glorious and dreadful Name; or, to swear at all by any other thing, is sinful, and to be abhorred. Yet, as in matters of weight and moment, an oath is warranted by the Word of God, under the New Testament as well as under the Old; so a lawful oath, being imposed by lawful authority, in such matters, ought to be taken.

III. Whosoever taketh an oath ought duly to consider the weightiness of so solemn an act, and therein to avouch nothing but what he is fully persuaded is the truth: neither may any man bind himself by oath to anything but what is good and just, and what he believeth so to be, and what he is able and resolved to perform.

IV. An oath is to be taken in the plain and common sense of the words, without equivocation, or mental reservation. It cannot oblige to sin; but in anything not sinful, being taken, it binds to performance, although to a man's own hurt. Nor is it to be violated, although made to heretics, or infidels.

V. A vow is of the like nature with a promissory oath, and ought to be made with the like religious care, and to be performed with the like faithfulness.

VI. It is not to be made to any creature, but to God alone: and, that it may be accepted, it is to be made voluntarily, out of faith, and conscience of duty, in way of thankfulness for mercy received, or for the obtaining of what we want, whereby we more strictly bind ourselves to necessary duties; or, to other things, so far and so long as they may fitly conduce thereunto.

VII. No man may vow to do anything forbidden in the Word of God, or what would hinder any duty therein commanded, or which is not in his own power, and for the performance whereof he hath no promise of ability from God. In which respects, popish monastical vows of perpetual single life, professed poverty, and regular obedience, are so far from being degrees of higher perfection, that they are superstitious and sinful snares, in which no Christian may entangle himself.

CHAP XXIII. - *Of the Civil Magistrate.*

I. God, the supreme Lord and King of all the world, hath ordained civil magistrates, to be, under him, over the people, for his own glory, and the public good: and, to this end, hath armed them with the power of the sword, for the defense and encouragement of them that are good, and for the punishment of evil doers.

II. It is lawful for Christians to accept and execute the office of a magistrate, when called thereunto: in the managing whereof, as they ought especially to maintain piety, justice, and peace, according to the wholesome laws of each commonwealth; so, for that end, they may lawfully, now under the New Testament, wage war, upon just and necessary occasion.

III. The civil magistrate may not assume to himself the administration of the word and sacraments, or the power of the keys of the kingdom of heaven; yet he hath authority, and it is his duty, to take order, that unity and peace be preserved in the church, that the truth of God be kept pure and entire, that all blasphemies and heresies be suppressed, all corruptions and abuses in worship and discipline prevented or reformed, and all the ordinances of God duly settled, administered and observed. For the better effecting whereof, he hath power to call synods, to be present at them, and to provide that whatsoever is transacted in them be according to the mind of God.

IV. It is the duty of people to pray for magistrates, to honor their persons, to pay them tribute or other dues, to obey their lawful commands, and to be subject to their authority, for conscience' sake. Infidelity, or difference in religion, doth not make void the magistrates' just and legal authority, nor free the people from their due obedience to them: from which ecclesiastical persons are not exempted, much less hath the pope any power and jurisdiction over them in their dominions, or over any of their people; and, least of all, to deprive them of their dominions, or lives, if he shall judge them to be heretics, or upon any other pretense whatsoever.

CHAP XXIV. - *Of Marriage and Divorce.*

I. Marriage is to be between one man and one woman: neither is it lawful for any man to have more than one wife, nor for any woman to have more than one husband, at the same time.

II. Marriage was ordained for the mutual help of husband and wife, for the increase of mankind with legitimate issue, and of the church with an holy seed; and for preventing of uncleanness.

III. It is lawful for all sorts of people to marry, who are able with judgment to give their consent. Yet it is the duty of Christians to marry only in the Lord. And therefore such as profess the true reformed religion should not marry with infidels, Papists, or other idolaters: neither should such as are godly be unequally yoked, by marrying with such as are notoriously wicked in their life, or maintain damnable heresies.

IV. Marriage ought not to be within the degrees of consanguinity or affinity forbidden by the Word. Nor can such incestuous marriages ever be made lawful by any law of man or consent of parties, so as those persons may live together as man and wife. The man may not marry any of his wife's kindred nearer in blood than he may in his own, nor the woman of her husband's kindred nearer in blood than of her own.

V. Adultery or fornication committed after a contract, being detected before marriage, giveth just occasion to the innocent party to dissolve that contract. In the case of adultery after marriage, it is lawful for the innocent party to sue out a divorce: and, after the divorce, to marry another, as if the offending party were dead.

VI. Although the corruption of man be such as is apt to study arguments unduly to put asunder those whom God hath joined together in marriage: yet, nothing but adultery, or such willful desertion as can no way be remedied by the church, or civil magistrate, is cause sufficient of dissolving the bond of marriage: wherein, a public and orderly course of proceeding is to be observed; and the persons concerned in it not left to their own wills, and discretion, in their own case.

CHAP XXV. - *Of the Church.*

I. The catholic or universal church, which is invisible, consists of the whole number of the elect, that have been, are, or shall be gathered into one, under Christ the head thereof; and is the spouse, the body, and the fullness of him that filleth all in all.

II. The visible church, which is also catholic or universal under the gospel (not confined to one nation, as before under the law), consists of all those throughout the world that profess the true religion; and of their children: and is the kingdom of the Lord Jesus Christ, the house and family of God, out of which there is no ordinary possibility of salvation.

III. Unto this catholic visible church Christ hath given the ministry, oracles, and ordinances of God, for the gathering and perfecting of the saints, in this life, to the end of the world: and doth, by his own presence and Spirit, according to his promise, make them effectual thereunto.

IV. This Catholic Church hath been sometimes more, sometimes less visible. And particular churches, which are members thereof, are more or less pure, according as the doctrine of the gospel is taught and embraced, ordinances administered, and public worship performed more or less purely in them.

V. The purest churches under heaven are subject both to mixture and error; and some have so degenerated, as to become no churches of Christ, but synagogues of Satan. Nevertheless, there shall be always a church on earth, to worship God according to his will.

VI. There is no other head of the church but the Lord Jesus Christ. Nor can the pope of Rome, in any sense, be head thereof; but is that antichrist, that man of sin, and son of perdition, that exalteth himself in the church against Christ, and all that is called God.

CHAP XXVI. - *Of Communion of Saints.*

I. All saints, that are united to Jesus Christ their head, by his Spirit, and by faith, have fellowship with him in his graces, sufferings, death, resurrection, and glory. And being united to one another in love, they have communion in each other's gifts and graces; and are obliged to the performance of such duties, public and private, as do conduce to their mutual good, both in the inward and outward man.

II. Saints by profession are bound to maintain a holy fellowship and communion in the worship of God, and in performing such other spiritual services as tend to their mutual edification; as also in relieving each other in outward things, according to their several abilities and necessities. Which communion, as God offereth opportunity, is to be extended unto all those who in every place call upon the name of the Lord Jesus.

III. This communion which the saints have with Christ, doth not make them in any wise partakers of the substance of his Godhead; or to be equal with Christ in any respect: either of which to affirm is impious and blasphemous. Nor doth their communion one with another, as saints, take away, or infringe the title or propriety which each man hath in his goods and possessions.

CHAP XXVII. - *Of the Sacraments.*

I. Sacraments are holy signs and seals of the covenant of grace, immediately instituted by God, to represent Christ, and his benefits; and to confirm our interest in him; as also, to put a visible difference between those that belong unto the church, and the rest of the world; and solemnly to engage them to the service of God in Christ, according to his Word.

II. There is, in every sacrament, a spiritual relation, or sacramental union, between the sign and the thing signified: whence it comes to pass, that the names and effects of the one are attributed to the other.

III. The grace which is exhibited in or by the sacraments rightly used, is not conferred by any power in them; neither doth the efficacy of a sacrament depend upon the piety or intention of him that doth administer it: but upon the work of the Spirit, and the word of institution, which contains, together with a precept authorizing the use thereof, a promise of benefit to worthy receivers.

IV. There be only two sacraments ordained by Christ our Lord in the gospel; that is to say, Baptism, and the Supper of the Lord: neither of which may be dispensed by any, but by a minister of the Word lawfully ordained.

V. The sacraments of the Old Testament, in regard of the spiritual things thereby signified and exhibited, were, for substance, the same with those of the New.

CHAP XXVIII. - *Of Baptism.*

I. Baptism is a sacrament of the New Testament, ordained by Jesus Christ, (Matt. 28:19) not only for the solemn admission of the party baptized into the visible church; (1 Cor. 12:13) but also, to be unto him a sign and seal of the covenant of grace, (Rom. 4:11, Col. 2:11, 12) of his ingrafting into Christ, (Gal. 3:27, Rom. 6:5) of regeneration, (Tit. 3:5) of remission of sins, (Mark 1:4) and of his giving up unto God, through Jesus Christ, to walk in newness of life: (Rom. 6:3,4) which sacrament is, by Christ's own appointment, to be continued in his church until the end of the world Matt. 28:19, 20).

II. The outward element to be used in this sacrament is water, wherewith the party is to be baptized, in the name of the Father, and of the Son, and of the Holy Ghost, by a minister of the gospel, lawfully called thereunto (Matt. 3:11, John 1:33, Matt. 28:19, 20).

III. Dipping of the person into the water is not necessary; but Baptism is rightly administered by pouring, or sprinkling water upon the person (Heb. 9:10, 19, 20, 21, 22, Acts 16:33, Mark 7:4).

IV. Not only those that do actually profess faith in and obedience unto Christ, (Mark 26:15, 16, Acts 8:37, 38) but also the infants of one, or both, believing parents, are to be baptized (Gen 17:7, 9, Gal. 3:9, 14, Col. 2:11, 12, Acts 2:38, 39, Rom. 4:11,12, 1 Cor. 7:14, Matt. 28:19, Mark 10:13, 14, 15, 16, Luke 18:15).

V. Although it be a great sin to contemn or neglect this ordinance (Luke 7:30, Exod. 4:24, 25, 26), yet grace and salvation are not so inseparably annexed unto it, as that no person can be regenerated, or saved, without it; (Rom. 4:11, Acts 10:2, 4, 22, 31, 45, 47) or, that all that are baptized are undoubtedly regenerated (Acts 7:13, 23).

VI. The efficacy of Baptism is not tied to that moment of time wherein it is administered; (John 3:5, 8) yet, notwithstanding, by the right use of this ordinance, the grace promised is not only offered, but really exhibited, and conferred, by the Holy Ghost, to such (whether of age or infants) as that grace belongeth unto, according to the counsel of God's own will, in his appointed time (Gal. 3:27, Tit. 3:5, Eph. 5:26, Acts 2:38, 41).

VII. The sacrament of Baptism is but once to be administered unto any person (Tit. 3:5).

CHAP XXIX. - *Of the Lord's Supper.*

I. Our Lord Jesus, in the night wherein he was betrayed, instituted the sacrament of his body and blood, called the Lord's Supper, to be observed in his church, unto the end of the world, for the perpetual remembrance of the sacrifice of himself in his death; the sealing all benefits thereof unto true believers, their spiritual nourishment and growth in him, their further engagement in and to all duties which they owe unto him; and, to be a bond and pledge of their communion with him, and with each other, as members of his mystical body.

II. In this sacrament, Christ is not offered up to his Father; nor any real sacrifice made at all, for remission of sins of the quick or dead; but only a commemoration of that one offering up of himself, by himself, upon the cross, once for all: and a spiritual oblation of all possible praise unto God, for the same: so that the popish sacrifice of the mass (as they call it) is most abominably injurious to Christ's one, only sacrifice, the alone propitiation for all the sins of his elect.

III. The Lord Jesus hath, in this ordinance, appointed his ministers to declare his word of institution to the people; to pray, and bless the elements of bread and wine, and thereby to set them apart from a common to an holy use; and to take and break the bread, to take the cup, and (they communicating also themselves) to give both to the communicants; but to none who are not then present in the congregation.

IV. Private masses, or receiving this sacrament by a priest, or any other, alone; as likewise, the denial of the cup to the people, worshiping the elements, the lifting them up, or carrying them about, for adoration, and the reserving them for any pretended religious use; are all contrary to the nature of this sacrament, and to the institution of Christ.

V. The outward elements in this sacrament, duly set apart to the uses ordained by Christ, have such relation to him crucified, as that, truly, yet sacramentally only, they are sometimes called by the name of the things they represent, to wit, the body and blood of Christ; albeit, in substance and nature, they still remain truly and only bread and wine, as they were before.

VI. That doctrine which maintains a change of the substance of bread and wine, into the substance of Christ's body and blood (commonly called transubstantiation) by consecration of a priest, or by any other way, is repugnant, not to Scripture alone, but even to common sense, and reason; overthroweth the nature of the sacrament, and hath been, and is, the cause of manifold superstitions; yea, of gross idolatries.

VII. Worthy receivers, outwardly partaking of the visible elements, in this sacrament, do then also, inwardly by faith, really and indeed, yet not carnally and corporally but spiritually, receive, and feed upon, Christ crucified, and all benefits of his death: the body and blood of Christ being then, not corporally or carnally, in, with, or under the bread and wine; yet, as really, but spiritually, present to the faith of believers in that ordinance, as the elements themselves are to their outward senses.

VIII. Although ignorant and wicked men receive the outward elements in this sacrament; yet, they receive not the thing signified thereby; but, by their unworthy coming thereunto, are guilty of the body and blood of the Lord, to their own damnation. Wherefore, all ignorant and ungodly persons, as they are unfit to enjoy communion with him, so are they unworthy of the Lord's table; and cannot, without great sin against Christ, while they remain such, partake of these holy mysteries, or be admitted thereunto.

CHAP XXX. - *Of Church Censures.*

I. The Lord Jesus, as king and head of his church, hath therein appointed a government, in the hand of church officers, distinct from the civil magistrate.

II. To these officers the keys of the kingdom of heaven are committed; by virtue whereof, they have power, respectively, to retain, and remit sins; to shut that kingdom against the impenitent, both by the Word, and censures; and to open it unto penitent sinners, by the ministry of the gospel; and by absolution from censures, as occasion shall require.

III. Church censures are necessary, for the reclaiming and gaining of offending brethren, for deterring of others from the like offenses, for purging out of that leaven which might infect the whole lump, for vindicating the honor of Christ, and the holy profession of the gospel, and for preventing the wrath of God, which might justly fall upon the church, if they should suffer his covenant, and the seals thereof, to be profaned by notorious and obstinate offenders.

IV. For the better attaining of these ends, the officers of the church are to proceed by admonition; suspension from the sacrament of the Lord's Supper for a season; and by excommunication from the church; according to the nature of the crime, and demerit of the person.

CHAP XXXI. - *Of Synods and Councils.*

I. For the better government, and further edification of the church, there ought to be such assemblies as are commonly called synods or councils:

II. As magistrates may lawfully call a synod of ministers, and other fit persons, to consult and advise with about matters of religion; so if Magistrates were open enemies to the church, the ministers of Christ, of themselves, by virtue of their office, or they, with other fit persons upon delegation from their churches, may meet together in such assemblies.

III. It belongeth to synods and councils, ministerially to determine controversies of faith, and cases of conscience; to set down rules and directions for the better ordering of the public worship of God, and government of his church; to receive complaints in cases of maladministration, and authoritatively to determine the same: which decrees and determinations, if consonant to the Word of God, are to be received with reverence and submission; not only for their agreement with the Word, but also for the power whereby they are made, as being an ordinance of God appointed thereunto in his Word.

IV. All synods or councils, since the apostles' times, whether general or particular, may err; and many have erred. Therefore they are not to be made the rule of faith, or practice; but to be used as a help in both.

V. Synods and councils are to handle, or conclude nothing, but that which is ecclesiastical: and are not to intermeddle with civil affairs which concern the commonwealth, unless by way of humble petition in cases extraordinary; or, by way of advice, for satisfaction of conscience, if they be thereunto required by the civil magistrate.

CHAP XXXII. - *Of the State of Men after Death, an of the Resurrection of the Dead.*

I. The bodies of men, after death, return to dust, and see corruption: but their souls, which neither die nor sleep, having an immortal subsistence, immediately return to God who gave them: the souls of the righteous, being then made perfect in holiness, are received into the highest heavens, where they behold the face of God, in light and glory, waiting for the full redemption of their bodies. And the souls of the wicked are cast into hell, where they remain in torments and utter darkness, reserved to the judgment of the great day. Beside these two places, for souls separated from their bodies, the Scripture acknowledgeth none.

II. At the last day, such as are found alive shall not die, but be changed: and all the dead shall be raised up, with the selfsame bodies, and none other although with different qualities, which shall be united again to their souls forever.

III. The bodies of the unjust shall, by the power of Christ, be raised to dishonor: the bodies of the just, by his Spirit, unto honor; and be made conformable to his own glorious body.

CHAP XXXIII. - *Of the Last Judgment.*

I. God hath appointed a day, wherein he will judge the world, in righteousness, by Jesus Christ, to whom all power and judgment is given of the Father. In which day, not only the apostate angels shall be judged, but likewise all persons that have lived upon earth shall appear before the tribunal of Christ, to give an account of their thoughts, words, and deeds; and to receive according to what they have done in the body, whether good or evil.

II. The end of God's appointing this day is for the manifestation of the glory of his mercy, in the eternal salvation of the elect; and of his justice, in the damnation of the reprobate, who are wicked and disobedient. For then shall the righteous go into everlasting life, and receive that fullness of joy and refreshing, which shall come from the presence of the Lord; but the wicked who know not God, and obey not the gospel of Jesus Christ, shall be cast into eternal torments, and be punished with everlasting destruction from the presence of the Lord, and from the glory of his power.

III. As Christ would have us to be certainly persuaded that there shall be a day of judgment, both to deter all men from sin; and for the greater consolation of the godly in their adversity: so will he have that day unknown to men, that they may shake off all carnal security, and be always watchful, because they know not at what hour the Lord will come; and may be ever prepared to say, Come Lord Jesus, come quickly, *Amen.*

Appendix 11
The Execution Warrant for King Charles I, 29 Jan. 1649[285]

At the High Court of Justice for the trying and Judging of Charles Stuart, King of England, 29 January 1649

Whereas Charles Stuart, King of England, is and stands convicted, attainted and condemned of High Treason, and other high Crimes; and Sentence upon Saturday last was pronounced against him by this Court, to be put to death by the severing of his Head from his Body; of which Sentence, Execution yet remaineth to be done: These are therefore to will and require you to see the said Sentence executed in the open Street before Whitehall, upon the morrow. Being the 30th day of this instant Month of January between the hours of 10 in the Morning, and 5 in the afternoon of the same day with full effect. And for so doing, this shall be your sufficient Warrant. And these are to require all Officers, Soldiers, and others, the good People of this Nation of England, to be assisting unto you in this Service.

Given under our Hands and Seals

John Bradshaw, Tho. Gray, Oliver Cromwell, Edward Whaley, Michael Livesey, John Okey, John Danvers, John Bourcher, Henry Ireton, Thos. Maleverer, John Blackiston, John Hutchinson, William Goffe, Tho. Pride, Peter Temple,, Tho. Harrison, John Huson, Henry Smith, Peregrine Pelham, Simon Meyne, Tho. Horton, John Jones, John More, Hardress Waller, Gilbert Millington, George Fleetwood, John Alured, Robert Lilburn, William Say, Anthony Stapeley, Richard Deans, Robert Tichburne, Humphrey Edwards, Daniel Blagrave, Owen Roe, William Purefoy, Adrian Scroope, James Temple, Augustine Garland, Edmond

---

[285] *Records of the Kirk of Scotland*, p. 584.

Ludlow, Henry Martin, Vincent Potter, William Constable, Richard Ingoldsby, William Cawley, John Barkstead, Isaac Ewers, John Dixwell, Valentine Walton, Gregory Norton, Tho. Chaloner, Tho. Wogan, John Ven, Gregory Clement, John Downs, Tho. Wayte, Tho. Scot, John Carew, Miles Corbet.

To Col. Francis Hacker, Col. Huncks,
And Lieut. Col. Phray; and to every one of them.

Appendix 12
Declaration and Acknowledgement of Sin, and Repentance for having joined with the Engagers, Prescribed in an Act of 20 July 1649[286]

I...After due consideration of the late Engagement in War against the Kingdom of England; And having also considered the course pursued and promoted by the Earl of Lanark, George Monro, and their Adherents in and about Stirling, and by others in the late Rebellion in the North, against all which not only eminent Testimonies of Gods Wrath have been given in defeating of them, but they were in themselves sinfull breaches of Covenant, and preferring the interest of man unto God; I do herefore in God sight profess, that I am convinced of the unlawfulness of all these ways, as contrary to the Word of God, and to the Solemn League and Covenant, not only in regard of the miscarriages of these that were imployed therein, but also in respect of the nature of these courses themselves; And therefore professing my unfained sorrow for my guiltiness by my accession to the same, do renounce and disclaim the foresaid Engagement and all the courses that were used for carrying on the same, either before or after the defeat of the Engagers, as contrary to the Word of G O D and Solemn League and Covenant, and destructive to Religion and the work of Reformation; And I do promise in the power of the Lords strength, never again to own any of these or like courses; And if hereafter at any time I shall be found to promote any Malignant Designe or course, that I shall justly be accompted a perfidious Covenant- breaker and despiser of the Oath of God, and be proceeded against with the highest Censures of the Kirk; Likeas, I do hereby promise to adhere to the National Covenant of this Kingdom, and to the Solemn League and Covenant

---

[286] Acts of the General Assembly, 1648, Session XIX, quoted in *Records of the Kirk of Scotland*, pp. 543-544. This declaration had to be made publicly by all who sought to return to the Covenanted fold after the disaster of the Engagement. (For the sake of clarity, the "f" used in some spelling has been changed to "s.")

betwixt the Kingdoms, and to be honest & zealous for Promoving all the ends thereof, as I shall be called thereunto of God, and to flee all occasions and temptations that may lead me into any the like snares against the same. Subscribed at the day of.

Appendix 13
Declaration at Rutherglen, 29 May 1679[287]

AS the Lord hath been pleased to keep & preserve His interest in this Land, by the Testimonies of some faithful witnesses from the beginning: So in our day, some have not been wanting, who through greatest hazards have added their Testimonies to these who have gone before them, by suffering death, banishment, torturings, forfaultries, Imprisonments, & what not, from a perfidious & cruel Adversary to the Church & Kingdome of our Lord Jesus Christ in the Land. Therefore, we owning the same Interest of Christ, according to the word of the Lord, & the National & solemn League & Covenant, Desire to add our Testimony to the Testimonies of the worthies that have gone before us (though we be unworthy, yet hoping as true members of the Church of Christ in Scotland) And that against all things done prejudicial to this Interest, from the beginning of the work of Reformation, Especially from the year 1648 to 1660. And more Particularly from the said year 1660 & downwards, against the Acts following: As, Against the Act of *Supremacy*; The *Declaration*, whereby our Covenants were condemned; The *Act* for eversion of the established Government of the Church & for establishing of Abjured *Prelacy*; The *Act Rescissory* of all Acts of Parliaments & Assemblies, for establishing the Government of the Church according to the word; The *Act of Glasgow*, putting the same in execution, whereby at one time were violently cast out above three hundred Ministers, without any Legal Procedure; Likewise The *Act* for appointing an holy *Anniversary day*, to be kept every 29th of *May*, for giving thanks for the setting up an usurped power, destroying the Interest of Christ in the Land: whereby the Creature is set up to be worshipped in the room of our great Redeemer, And a power is assumed which is proper to the Lord only; For the appointing of ordinances in his Church, as particularly the Government thereof & the keeping of holy days, belongeth to no Prince, Prelate, nor person on earth, but only to our Lord Redeemer. And further, we give our Testimony against all sinful & unlawful *Acts*, emitted & executed,

---

[287] Johnston, *Treasury*, p 131-132.

published & prosecuted by them, against our Covenanted Reformation. And for Confirmation of this our Testimony, We do here this day, being the 29 of *May* 1679 publickly & most justly burn the foresaid Acts, at this Cross of *Rutherglen*, being the Chief Burgh of the Nether ward of *Clidsdale*; As they perfidiously & blasphemously have burnt our holy Covenants, through several Cities of these Covenanted Kingdoms. We hope none will take exceptions at our not subscribing this our Testimony, being so solemnly given: for we are ready to do it if necessary, And to enlarge it with all our faithful suffering brethren in the Land.

Appendix 14
The Declaration and Testimony of the True Presbyterian, Anti-Prelatic, Anti-Erastian, persecuted party in Scotland. Published at Sanquhar, 22 June 1680.[288]

It is not amongst the smallest of the Lord's mercies to this poor land, that there have been always some who have given their testimony against every cause of defection that many are guilty of; which is a token for good, that he doth not, as yet, intend to cast us off altogether, but that he will leave a remnant in whom lie will be glorious, if they. through his grace, keep themselves clean still, and walk in his way and method as it has been walked in, and owned by him in our predecessors of truly worthy memory; in their carrying on of our noble work of reformation, in the several steps thereof, from Popery, Prelacy, and likewise Erastian supremacy-so much usurped by him who, it is true, so far as we know, is descended from the race of our kings; yet he hath so far debased from what he ought to have been, by his perjury and usurpation in Church matters, and tyranny in matters civil, as is known by the whole land, that we have just reason to account it one of the Lord's great controversies against us, that we have not disowned him, and the men of his practices, whether inferior magistrates or any other, as enemies to our Lord and his crown, and the true Protestant and Presbyterian interest in this land-our Lord's espoused bride and Church. Therefore, although we be for government and governors, such as the Word of God and our covenant allows; yet we, for ourselves, and all that will adhere to us as the representative of the true Presbyterian Kirk and covenanted nation of Scotland, considering the great hazard of lying under such a sin any longer, do, by these presents, disown Charles Stuart, that has been reigning, or rather tyrannizing, as we may say, on the throne of Britain these years bygone, as having any right, title to, or interest in, the said crown of Scotland for government, as forfeited, several years since, by his perjury and breach of covenant both to God and his Kirk, and

---

[288] Quoted in Robert Simpson, *Traditions of the Covenanters* (Edinburgh: Gall & Inglis, 1867), pp. 26-28; Johnson, *Treasury*, p 141-142.

usurpation of his crown and royal prerogative therein, and many other breaches in matters ecclesiastic and by his tyranny and breach of the very reges regnandi in matters civil. For which reason we declare, that several years since he should have been denuded of being king, ruler, or magistrate, or of having any power to act or to be obeyed as such. As also we' being under the standard of our Lord Jesus Christ, Captain of Salvation, do declare a war with such a tyrant and usurper, and all the men of his practices, as enemies to our Lord Jesus Christ, and his cause and covenants; and against all such as have strengthened him, sided with, or anywise acknowledged him in his tyranny, civil or ecclesiastic; yea, against all such as shall strengthen, side with, or anywise acknowledge any other in like usurpation and tyranny-far more against such as would betray or deliver up our free reformed mother Kirk unto the bondage of Antichrist, the Pope of Rome. And, by this, we homologate that testimony given at Rutherglen, the 29th of May 1679, and all the faithful testimonies of those who have gone before, as also of those who have suffered of late. and we do disclaim that Declaration published at Hamilton, June 1679, chiefly because it takes in the king's interest, which we are several years since loosed from, because of the aforesaid reasons, and others which may, after this, if the Lord will, be published. As also, we disown and by this resent the reception of the Duke of York, that professed Papist, as repugnant to our principles and vows to the Most High God, and as that which is the great, though not alone, just reproach of our Kirk and nation. We also, by this, protest against his succeeding to the crown, and whatever has been done, or any are essaying to do in this land, given to the Lord, in prejudice to our work of reformation. And to conclude, we hope. after this, none will blame us for, or offend at, our rewarding those that are against as they have done to us, as the Lord gives opportunity. This is not to exclude any that have declined, if they be willing to give satisfaction according to the degree of their offence.

Appendix 15
The Act and Apologetic Declaration of the True Presbyterians of the Church of Scotland. Published at Lanark, 12 January 1682.[289]

Although we ought to take in good part, whatever God in His infinite wisdom hath, for the punishment of our sin, Carved out unto us, and Eye and acknowledge him alone In it; - and though we always ought to acknowledge government and governors as ordained by him, in so far as they rule and govern according to the rules set down by him in his word, and constitutive laws of the nation, and ought to cast the mantle of love on the lesser errors of governors, and give the best countenance to their administration that the nature of their actions will bear; - yet when all these laws, both of God and the kingdom, conditional and constitutive of the government, are cassed and annulled, by pretended laws, and the highest o f usurpation, and an inexplicable prerogative in matters ecclesiastic, and arbitrary government in matters civil, is arrogate; - when a banner of impiety, profaneness, and atheism is avowedly displayed against the heavens; a door open of all sorts and sizes, and the remedy thereof still denied by him who should be as a sun and shield to the people, when the parliaments, who ought to be the grand trustees of the kingdom, to whom it belongs in such a case to secure the civil and spiritual interests, are so prelimited by law, as that no true son of the state or church hath liberty to sit and vote there, so that the parliaments, and all places of public trust, and offices of the kingdom from the highest to the lowest, are made up of none but those who are corrupted, overawed, overruled, and bribed: What shall the people do in such an extremity? Should they give their reason as men, their consciences as christians, and resign their liberties, fortunes, religion, and their all to the inexorable obstinacy, incurable wilfulness, and

---

[289] Johnston, *Treasury*, p. 144.

malice of these, who in spite of God and man (and notwithstanding of their many oaths and vows both to God and his people) are resolved to make their own will the absolute and sovereign rule of their actions, and their strained indulgences, and the measure of the subjects hope and happiness? Shall the end of government be lost, through weakness, wickedness, and tyranny of governors? Must the people by an implicit submission and deplorable stupidity, destroy themselves, and betray their posterity, and become objects of reproach to the present generation, and pity and contempt to the future? Have they not in such an extremity, good ground to make use of that natural and radical power they have, to shake off that yoke, which neither we nor our forefathers were able to bear; which accordingly the Lord honoured us (in a general and unprelimited meeting *of the estates and shires of* Scotland) to do; *a convention of unprelimited members, a convention of men who had only the glory of God and the good of the commonwealth before their eyes,* - the like whereof the present reigning tyrant could never since his home-coming pretend to? At which *convention*, he was most legally, and by general consent cast off, by the Declaration afterwards published at Sanquhar by especial warrant from the said *convention.* But that we may not seem to have done that, or yet to do the like, upon no grounds, or yet upon few and small grounds, we shall hint at some of the many thousands of the misdemeanours of the now cast off tyrant in his overturning of our church and state.

And *First*, at his very entry, as if he had attained to *Nero's* desire, at one blow, in his first parliament, he cut off the neck of that noble constitution of church and state, which our noble and worthy ancestors had made; and not thinking it enough treacherously and falsely to perjure himself, he made such constitutions and laws (if it be not an abuse of language to call them so) as that none but fools of his own feather, and such as would run with himself to the same excess of riot, should have access to the very nearest place or office in the kingdom. And though that in itself is enough, yet not the thousand part of what he hath done.

2. Did he not take to himself a licentious privilege, the exalting of himself unto a sphere exceeding all measures divine and human, tyrannically obtruding his will for a law, both in matters civil and ecclesiastic, making us a laughingstock to the neighbouring nations, who imagined that what he was doing (however tyrannous in itself) to be consonant to our law, blaming the badness of the law instead of the badness of the governors, whereas nothing could be less consonant to the tenor and end of our, and all other laws, divine and human. For we have reason to praise the Lord, who eminently assisted our ancestors in framing of our laws, so that we may (upon good ground) say, that there is no nation *in civilibus* hath better, and *in ecclesiasticis* so good laws as we; having (by God's providence) attained unto a more excellent and strict reformation than any nation. The observing of which laws, was the very

constitutive and absolute condition whereupon he was admitted to the Royal office, and without which he was not to have the exercise of his power, and to which he was most solemnly and deeply sworn oftener than once, with his hands lifted up to the most High God; *He himself declaring the subjects tye no longer to remain or continue, than the ends and constitutions of these convenants were pursued and preserved by him.* All which are (contrary to his engagement foresaid) by his pretended (and as aforesaid constitute) parliaments cassed and annulled, and the laws no more made the rule, but his own will in his letters: So that we are made the reproach of the nations, who say we have only the law of letters, instead of the letter of the law.

3. Hath it not been his constant method to adjourn and dissolve parliaments at his pleasure, when they (though his own creatures) were so sensible of his misdemeanours, that they began to question, and when questioned by them, ye may easily conjecture what they were.

4. Hath he not seated himself as supreme head over all persons, in all causes civil and ecclesiastic? and by virtue of that arrogantly arrogated power, fabricate a chimeric government, or rather pageantry in the church, with such ludibrious eminences, pompous power and pride, through the vanity of men's depraved imaginations, the grievous and mysterious abuse, from whence have issued all the calamities, all the languishing sorrows, and confounding shames and reproaches, which in this day of blackness and darkness, have invaded, involved, polluted and pestered the church and kingdom. And thus hath he approven himself to be the *Defender of the Faith!* under which the godly party, true sons of the church and nation, have been groaning these twenty years bygone, and in great numbers murthered and slain in the fields, led as lambs to the slaughter upon scaffolds, imprisoned and kept in irons, and with exquisite tortures tormented, exiled, banished, and sold as slaves amongst savages: all which they endured most patiently a long time, or ever they offered to appear in public in arms against him. And all this they have met with as a reward (just upon the Lord's part, though unjust and ungrate as to his part) for their too great and inordinate love wherewith they prevented him in the day of his distress; being the first and only beginning of his unhappy restorations.

5. Time will fail us to narrate, what taxings, cessings, and every way impoverishing of the subjects, and grinding of the faces of the poor, dilapidating the pendicles, rights, and revenues of the crown, for no other end, but to employ them for keeping up a brothel, rather than a court, since there is no court in the world hath attained unto such a height of debauchery and depravedness, as that court by his example hath done. For

Regis ad exemplum totus componitur orbis.

6. And lastly, as if it had not been enough to exercise such a tyrannical and arbitrary power himself, he, by a late parliament such as the former,

intends that his cruelty and tyranny should not die with himself, but that he shall in his time install such an one (if not worse) as himself, contrary to all law, reason and religion, and in that parliament to unhinge very protestantism itself, by framing a *test*, such as no protestant (how corrupt soever) can take, and so ridiculous that it is made the laughing stock even of enemies themselves.

Is it then any wonder, considering such dealings and many thousands more, that true *Scotsmen* (though we have been always and even to extremity sometimes loyal to our kings) should after twenty years tyranny break out at last, as we have done, and put in practice that power, which God and nature hath given us, and we have reserved to ourselves, as our engagements with our princes having been always conditional, as other kingdoms are implicitly, but ours explicitly?

Let none therefore object against the legality of what we have done, or are doing: for we offer as (how inconsiderable we are said to be) to prove ourselves to have done nothing against our ancient laws civil or ecclesiastic, against any lawyers or divines whatsoever, our ancient laws being judges; and we having safety to pass and repass (if the public faith after so many breaches can be trusted) for that effect. So then let no foreign kingdoms or churches through misinformation or false copies (as they are many) of what we act or do, because we have no access to the press as they; we say let them not take up a wrong opinion of us or our proceedings: for we are only endeavouring to extricate ourselves from under a tyrannous yoke, and to reduce our church and state to what they were in the years 1648 and 1649.

We therefore, have conveened, *in our name and authority*, ratify and approve what hath been done by the Rutherglen and Sanquhar declarations. And do by these present *rescind, annul, and make void,* whatsoever hath been done by *Charles Stuart* or his accomplices in prejudice to our ancient laws and liberties, in all the several pretended and prelimited parliaments and conventions, since the year 1660. And particularly, the late parliament holden at *Edinburgh* the 28th *July* 1681, by a commissioner professedly popish, and for villany exiled his native land, with all the acts and laws there statue and enacted: as that abominable, ridiculous, unparalleled, and soul perjuring *test* and the rest.

We therefore command and charge you, to pass to the Mercat cross of *Lanerk, and in our name and authority, publish this our act and declaration, as ye will be answerable.*

Given at--------the 15th December, 1681.

Appendix 16
The Apologetic Declaration, and Admonitory Vindication of the True Presbyterians of the Church of Scotland: Especially anent intelligencers and informers, 8 November 1684.[290]

Albeit we know that the people of God in all ages have been cruelly persecuted and maliciously reviled, by apostates from, and enemies to, the truths of our Lord Jesus Christ; yet such hard usage and virulent reproachings, hath not (at least ought not) to have abated the zeal of tender hearted Christians, in the prosecution of holy and commanded duties. Therefore as hitherto (through grace assisting) we have not been driven to lay aside necessary obliging duties, because of the viperous threatenings of men, who are given up of a holy and wise God to lay out all their might, and power, for promoting a course of wicked profanity, by virulent persecution and ignominious calumnies (to all of whom nevertheless that are reconcilable unto God we heartily wish eternal salvation) So we declare our firm resolution of constant adherence to our covenants and engagements; whereby we are bound to have common friends and foes with our covenanted reformation, and to look upon what is done to one as done to all of us; and also our unanimous adherence to our faithful declarations, wherein, we have disowned the authority of Charles Stewart (not authority of God's institutions, either among Christians or Heathens) and all authority depending upon him, for reasons given elsewhere; (disclaiming all such things as infer a magistratical relation betwixt him and us) and wherein also we have declared war against him and his accomplices, such as lay out themselves to promote his wicked and hellish designs. Therefore, that therein our mind may be the more clearly

---

[290] Robert Wodrow, *History of the Sufferings of the Church of Scotland* (Glasgow: Blackie & Son, 1836), Vol. 4, p. 148. Partial quote available in Shields, p. 177.

understood, and for preventing further mistakes anent our purposes, we do hereby jointly and unanimously testify and declare, that as we utterly detest and abhor that hellish principle of killing all who differ in judgement or persuasion from us, it having no bottom upon the word of God, or right reason; so we look upon it as a duty binding upon us, to publish openly unto the world, that forasmuch as we are firmly and really purposed not to injure or offend any whomsoever, but to pursue the ends of our covenants, in standing to the defence of our glorious work of reformation, and of our own lives: yet (we say) we do hereby declare unto all, that whosoever stretch forth their hands against us, while we are maintaining the cause and interest of Christ against his enemies, in defence of the covenanted reformation; by shedding our blood actually, either by authoritative commanding, such as bloody counsellors (bloody we say, insinuating clearly by this and other adjective epithets, an open distinction, betwixt the cruel and blood-thirsty, and the more sober and moderate) especially that (so called) justiciary, general of forces, adjutants, captains, lieutenants, and all in civil and military power, who make it their work to embrue their hands in our blood, or by obeying such commands, such as bloody militia men, malicious troopers, soldiers, and dragoons; likewise such gentlemen and commons, who through wickedness and ill will, ride and run with the foresaid persons to lay search for us; or who deliver up any of us into their hands to the spilling of our blood; by enticing morally, or stirring up enemies to the taking away of our lives, such as designedly and purposedly advise, counsel, and encourage them to proceed against us to our utter extirpation; by informing against us wickedly, wittingly, and willingly, such as viperous and malicious bishops and curates, and all such sort of intelligencers, who lay out themselves to the effusion of our blood, together with all such, as in obedience to the enemies commands, at the sight of us, raise the hue and cry after us; yea, and against all such, as compearing before the adversaries courts upon their demand, delate us and any who befriend us, to their and our extreme hazard and suffering; we say, all and every one of such shall be reputed by us enemies to God and the covenanted work of reformation, and punished as such, according to our power and the degree of their offence; chiefly if they shall continue after the publication of this our declaration, obstinately and habitually, with malice to proceed against us any of the foresaid ways; not at all exeeming from present punishment, such as formerly have been chief ringleaders and obstinate offenders; and withal leaving room for civil and ecclesiastic satisfaction before lawful and settled judicatories, for the offence of such persons as our power at this time cannot reach, or the degree of their punishment according to their offences is hard for us to be determined. Finally, we do hereby declare, that we abhor, condemn, and discharge any personal attempts, upon any pretext whatsomever, without previous deliberation, common or competent consent, without certain probation by sufficient witnesses, the guilty person's confession, or the notoriousness of the deeds themselves. Inhibiting also and discharging any of our emissaries whomsoever, to stretch forth their hands beyond the certainly known degrees of any of the foresaid persons offences. Now let not any think (our God assisting us) we will be so slack handed in time coming, to put matters in execution, as heretofore we have been, seeing we are bound faithfully and valiantly to maintain our covenants and the cause of Christ: Therefore let all these foresaid persons be admonished of their hazard. And particularly all ye intelligencers, who by your voluntary informations endeavour to render us up to the enemies bonds, that our blood may be shed: for by such courses ye both endanger your immortal souls, if repentance prevent not, seeing God will make inquisition for shedding the precious blood of his saints, whatever be the thoughts of men, and also your bodies, seeing ye render yourselves actually and maliciously guilty of our blood, whose innocency the Lord knoweth: however, we are sorry at our very hearts, that any of you should chuse such courses, either with bloody Doeg to shed our blood, or with the flattering Ziphites to inform persecutors where we are to be found. So we say again, we desire you to take warning of the hazard that ye incur, by following such courses: for the sinless necessity of self-preservation, accompanied with holy zeal for Christ's reigning in our land, and suppressing of profanity, will move us not to let you pass unpunished. Call to your rememberance, all that is in peril is not lost, and all that is delayed is not forgiven. Therefore expect to be dealt with as ye deal with us, so far as our power can reach; not because we are acted by a sinful spirit of revenge for private and personal injuries; but mainly because, by our fall, reformation suffers damage, yea, the power of godliness, through ensnaring flatteries, and terrible threatening, will thereby be brought to a very low ebb, the consciences of many more dreadfully surrendered, and profanity more established and propagated. And as upon the one hand we have here declared our purposes anent malicious injurers of us, so upon the other hand, we do hereby beseech and obtest, all you who wish well to Zion, to shew your good-will towards us, by acting with us, and in your places and stations, according to your ability, counselling, encouraging and strengthening our hands, for this great work of holding up the standard of our Lord Jesus Christ. Think not that in any ways you are called to lie by neutral and indifferent, especially in such a day; for we are a people by holy covenants dedicated unto the Lord, in our persons, lives, liberties, and fortunes, for defending and promoting this glorious work of reformation, notwithstanding all opposition that is or may be made thereunto, yea, and sworn against all neutrality and indifferency in the Lord's matters: and moreover we are fully persuaded, that the Lord who now hideth his face from the house of Jacob will suddenly appear, and bring light out of darkness, and perfect strength out of weakness, and cause judgement return again to righteousness.

Thus having declared our deliberated, lawful, and necessary purposes, concerning this matter, in order to the publication of the same, we do hereby statute and ordain, that upon the eighth day of November copies of this our declaration be affixed upon a sufficient and competent number of the public market crosses of the respective burghs, and of the patent doors of the respective kirks within this kingdom.

Given upon the 28th October 1684.

Appendix 17
The Protestation and Apologetic Admonitory Declaration of the Contending & Suffering Remnant of the true Presbyterians of the Church of Scotland, against the proclaiming James Duke of York, King of Scotland, England, France, and Ireland, the lawfulness of the present pretended parliament, and the apparent inlet of popery, &c.
Published at Sanquhar, 28 May 1685.[291]

It hath pleased the holy and wise God, to exercise the church of Scotland now of a long time, with wrestling and warfaring, under the yoke of cruel oppressors, who have made it their whole work to extirpate the true worship and worshippers of God out of the land, they make it highly criminal to own Christ as sole supreme over his own house, to mention any adherence to Scotland's reformation and covenants, and to take the written word of God to be the only rule of faith and manners, discerning any to forfeit right to estate, life, and liberty who are of Presbyterian principles, who will not make a full surrender of conscience unto them, to be carried about as they please, complying with all contradictions, and contradictory impositions which their diabolic spirits may invent, who are clearly seen to be void of all religion, reason, and humanity; so that they proceed against all recusants with the height of barbarity and hellish cruelty, refusing to hear them profess subjection to rulers only in the Lord, and according to his word, yea, cutting them off in the fields without giving them any time to deliberate upon death, yea oftentimes without so much as to commit their spirits unto the Lord, but butcherously slaying them, without taking notice what they are, or what (according to their own

---

[291] *Testimony Bearing Exemplified: A Collection* (Paisley: Neilson, 1791), pp. 267 *ff*. A partial quote is available in Shields, pp. 181-184.

law) is to be led against them: Moreover, these arbitrarians have so raged, that they have now brought the land to that (Oh! poor miserable and lamentable slavery) that the freest subject and best gentleman in the kingdom, is by their acts, laws, and proceedings holden obliged to give an oath *super inquirendis* before any single soldier or dragoon meeting them upon the way. Lo all this and much more, we have met with, as just upon the Lord's part, though most unjust upon man's for our manifold sins and iniquities; and in a special manner for our not purging our judicatories and armies, when the power was in our hands, of men disaffected to the cause and interest of Christ; for our bringing in known malignants to places of power and trust among us; and for inordinate affection unto, and lusting after the deceast tyrant, Charles the Second, and advancing him to the regal throne, even while known by many palpable discoveries (as are to be seen in the causes of God's wrath with the church of Scotland) to retain his heart enmity at the covenanted work of reformation, which sins we desire to confess and mourn for, before God, angels and men; as also our sin in not timeously rejecting the foresaid Charles, when he brake covenant and all parts of his coronation oath: howbeit fearing the lying under such a sin any longer, when we were brought to a very small remnant, we did by open declarations, disclaim his pretended authority, upon many important grounds and reasons, as is to be seen elsewhere, particularly in our declaration published at Lanark, January 12, 1682 years. All which declarations we do hereby ratify and approve.

So now, the Lord in his goodness and wisdom having removed the foresaid Charles from his tyranny by death: and a few wicked and unprincipled men of this kingdom, having by open proclamation proclaimed James duke of York, though a profest Papist and excommunicate person, and not yet received into the church again, to be king of Scotland, England, France, and Ireland: we the contending and suffering remnant of the true Presbyterians of the church of Scotland, calling to mind the many bonds and obligations that lie upon us from the Lord; and being desirous to be found faithful in this day of temptation, to avoid accession to the guilt in which many have involved themselves, to exoner our consciences as in his sight, to testify our resentment of the deed, and to make it appear unto the world that we are free thereof, whether by concurrence or connivance; do here deliberately, jointly, and unanimously protest against the foresaid proclamation of James duke of York, to be king, as said is, in regard that it is the choosing a murderer to be a governor, who hath shed the blood of the saints of God; in regard that it is the height of confederacy with an idolater, which is forbidden by the law of God: in regard that it is contrary to the declaration of the general assembly of the church of Scotland, of the date 27th July 1649 years; in regard that it is contrary to many wholesome and laudable acts of parliament, as act 8, parliament first, repeated in the 99th act, parliament 7, ratified in the 23d act, parliament 11. 114th act, parliament 12 of King James VI. For there is a continual obligation & stipulation between a king & people, as both of them are tied to God, so each of them are tied to other, for the performance of mutual & reciprocal Duties; And as contrare to 24th act, parliament 11, King James VI. where papists are discerned to be punished by manifold civil and ecclesiastic pains, as adversaries to God's true religion: yea, they are ordained to be punished as common enemies to all Christian government; act 8, parliament 16, King James VI. And in regard that it is inconsistent with the safety of the faith, conscience, and Christian liberty of Christian people, to choose a subject of Antichrist to be their (especially supreme) magistrate. And so it is, that we understand that part of the 4th sect. chap. 23, of our Confession of Faith, and in a general and abstract sense, where it is said (in opposition to sectarians, who assert that such are not lawful kings, who either know not Christ, or believe not in him) that *infidelity or difference in religion, doth not make void the magistrate's just and legal authority, nor free the people from their due obedience to him*: We acknowledge it to be true indeed, that infidels and these of a different religion are not (chiefly because such) presently to be declared no magistrates, for *magistratus non est magistratus qua Christianus, sed qua homo*: so it is that the magistratical power considered *generaliter*, given for the good of human societies, may be in the person of an infidel, or one of a different religion, but considered *specialter*, given for the good of the church, it is only in the person of a professor of the true religion. Hence, in travelling or trafficking in foreign lands, be the persons in whom is the power, infidels or of a different religion, we cannot refuse subjection to their laws, so far as they are consistent with the written word of God, and our true Christian liberty. Howbeit, our covenants and acts of parliament have put a bar upon the admission of any person, if either infidels or of a different religion, while such, to govern in Scotland: and the practice of our church confirms it, in refusing the crown to the late deceast tyrant Charles II until he subscribed such demands as were sent unto him; and especially upon the admission of a known enemy to the true religion, to govern: for it could not but be both highly sinful and irrational for us, to entrust an enemy to the work and people of God, with the interest of both.

Also conceiving that this pretended parliament is not a lawful parliament, in regard that the election of commissioners is limited and prejudged, in the due liberty thereof, by their acts and laws: in regard that the members are convicted of avowed perjury, which, according to the Scottish law, maketh a man incapable of being so much as a witness, in regard they are men of blood, the chief being convicted of avowed murder, whereby they are under the lash of the law; and in regard of their carrying on apostacy, and making way for the man of sin: we do in the like manner, upon these and many other important grounds and reasons, protest against the validity and constitution of this present parliament, as not being free and lawful against their assuming to themselves any authority, or exercising any power or jurisdiction, for making of acts or laws for judging of causes, determining of controversies, or proceeding in any parliamentary way. And in particular, we protest against their proceeding to any approbation or ratification of the foresaid proclamation of James duke of York, to be king, as said is: and that they may not go on further, to set the crown upon his head, they being incapable to give it, & he to receive it.

And further seeing, bloody Papists, the subjects of Antichrist, become so hopeful, bold, and confident, under the perfidy of the said James duke of York, and popery itself so eminent, and (oh lamentable!) like to be intruded again (if God's mercy and power meeting together in a wonderful way prevent it not) upon these covenanted lands, an open door being made thereunto, by its accursed and abjured harbinger Prelacy, which these three kingdoms are equally sworn against. We do in the like manner, protest against all kind of popery in general and particular heads, the jurisdiction of the pope, all the heretical and erroneous doctrine of the church of Rome, their tyrannous laws made against Christian liberty, their erroneous and bloody decrees, their vain ceremonies and superstitions, their allegories, rites, signs, and traditions, their laws, statues, acts, constitutions, canons, civil or municipal, with all other ordinances and practique penalties whatsoever, made in prejudice of the true religion and the professors thereof, or of the true church discipline, and jurisdiction or freedom thereof, and every other thing contrary to sound doctrine and the power of godliness, abjured most explicitly by our national covenant, abrogated, annulled, and rescinded by our acts of parliament, as act 3. Act 31, parl. 1. Act 23, parl. 11. Act 114. parl. 12. Act 5, parl. 20, King James VI. We say, we do protest against all kind of Popery whatsoever, against its entering against into this land, and against every thing that doth, or may directly or indirectly, make way for the same, disclaiming likewise all sectarianism, malignancy, and any confederacy therewith.

Moreover, taking to our serious consideration, the low, deplorable and obscured state of the churches of England and Ireland, and that we are all bound in one covenant and solemn league together, we (in the bowels of Christ) do in like manner hereby admonish you our brethren in these our neighbouring and covenanted lands, that ye remember how far ye have sadly failed in pursuing the ends of our covenants (as we ourselves also have done, which we desire to confess, imploring God's forgiveness to you and us both) how ye have suffered your Lord's enemies to rob you of all your privileges and pleasant things: how ye have given up yourselves to be seduced by complying lukewarm and court flattering brethren; and how ye have passed by, lightly looking upon our bleeding wounds, denying us help, though we have been like to give up the ghost; and what great accession ye have to the giving Popery such an open door to enter upon our land again. Remember these things, and consider what the Lord is now calling for at our hand: break off your sinful ways by repentance; and abandon all lukewarmness and indifferency in the Lord's matters, give up with your own things; be tender of God's declarative glory, which is lying at the stake: quit yourselves like Christians and men; and stretch your hands to the helping, strengthening, encouraging, and comforting a poor wasted, wronged, wounded, reproached, despised, and bleeding remnant (with whom you are in covenant) setting yourselves against all the injuries and affronts done to our blessed Lord Jesus Christ, against the man of sin, the kingdom of Antichrist, and all the limbs and parts thereof. And here, with all sincerity of mind, and unfeignedness of resolution, we promise to act unto you the part of covenanted brethren in the Lord, to the utmost of our power. Likewise, we do hereby in like manner, call unto you, all protestant reformed churches, kingdoms, and commonwealths, that you would take to your serious consideration the low and dangerous state of the gospel interest, and advert to the growth and increase of popery in all places, bestirring yourselves timeously against it, lest ye be too late, and lose what much blood and contending may not recover again; considering the distressed case, whereinto we are brought, as a share of the true protestant interest; and refreshing us with your help: and withal, as ye tender the advantage of Christ's cause, which to own is the Christian's glory, that ye engage not yourselves in any quarrel, or with any person whatsomever, till you know that the quarrel be rightly stated, and that the persons in the judgment of charity are seeking the advancement of the kingdom of Christ, lest that ye join yourselves to these who may lead you back to Egypt, and so you provoke the Lord to destroy you in the wilderness.

Finally, we being misrepresented to many, by the wicked malice of our avowed enemies, and the sinful prejudice of others, who misrepresenting our late declaration, affixed at several parish church doors (which we do hereby ratify and approve) perverting the true and obvious sense thereof. And through blind malice and prejudice mistaking our designs therein (else their consciences give their tongue the lie) hold us forth as persons of murdering and assassinating principles: all which principles and practices, we do hereby declare before God, angels and men, that we abhor, renounce, and detest, as also all manner of robbing of any, whether open enemies, or others, which we are most falsely aspersed with, either in their gold, their silver, their gear, or any household stuff. Their money perish with themselves; the Lord knows that our eyes are not after these things. And in like manner, we do hereby disclaim all unwarrantable practices committed by any few persons reputed to be of us, whereby the Lord hath been offended, his cause wronged, and we all made to endure the scourge of tongues; for which things we have desired to make conscience of mourning before the Lord, both in public and private. As the unwarrantable manner of killing that curate of Carspharin (though he was a man of death, both by the law of God and man, and the fact not materially murder) it being gone about contrary to our declaration, without deliberation, common or competent consent, (the conclusion and deed being known only to three or four person) in a rash, and not in a Christian manner. And also other offences being committed at the time, which miscarriages have proven a mean to stop and retard lawful, laudable, and warrantable proceedings, both as to matter and manner. But let not guilty persons think themselves indemnified. Howbeit, we require and hope, that all whosoever in this our land, our neighbour or foreign lands, who have not a wilful prejudice at the cause and way of God, will not give ear unto reports, which stated enemies, or prejudiced pretended friends give of us, that they will not impute the miscarriages of one or more persons, to us or all of us; who desire that nothing may be looked on hereafter, as our deed, which wanteth common consent or approbation, and that they will not receive a wrong impression of us and our proceedings: for we call the living God, the Searcher of hearts, to witness, that this only is our sincere desire, and unfeigned resolution, to continue in the profession and obedience of the true religion of Jesus Christ, according to his word, our covenants, national and solemn league, to defend the same, and to resist all contrary errors, corruptions, and innovations, according to our vocation, and the utmost of the power that God doth, or may put in our hands.

Now, we hope none who have not made a full surrender of conscience, and are not bent to welcome popery into the land, will be offended at what we have here done: For, in the Lord's sight, we durst do no less, whatever occasion of persecution our God's enemies may take from the same: For we could not see at the time any other way to discharge our duty before the Lord, to exoner our consciences, and to free ourselves of the connivance at popery, which we pray the Lord may stop, and not lay the guilt of its increase to the charge of us and our posterity.

Therefore, we appoint and ordain, that incontinently ye our emissaries pass upon the twenty-eighth day of May 1685 years, unto the market cross of Sanquhar; and there, by open proclamation, make intimation of this our declaration, leaving copies of the same affixed upon the foresaid market cross, and other patent places of the foresaid burgh.

Given at ------upon the 28th day of May 1685.

Appendix 18
The Toleration Letter to James II, 21 July 1687[292]

To the King's most excellent majesty. The humble address of the Presbyterian ministers of his majesty's kingdom of Scotland.
We your majesties most loyal subjects, the ministers of the Presbyterian persuasion in your ancient kingdom of Scotland, from the due sense we have of your majesty's gracious and surprising favour, in not only putting a stop to our long sad sufferings for non-conformity, but granting us the liberty of the public and peaceable exercise of our ministerial function without any hazard: as we bless the great God, who hath put this in your royal heart, do withal find ourselves bound in duty to offer our most humble and hearty thanks to your sacred majesty, the favour bestowed being to us, and all the people of our persuasion on valuable above all our earthly comforts, especially since we have ground from your majesty to believe that our loyalty is not to be questioned upon the account of our being Presbyterians who as we have, amidst all former temptations, endeavoured, so we are firmly resolved still to preserve an entire loyalty in our doctrine and practice (consonant to our known principles, which according to the holy scriptures, are contained in the confession of faith, generally owned by Presbyterians in all your majesty's dominion) and by the help of God so to demean ourselves, as your majesty may find cause rather to enlarge than to diminish your favours towards us: thoroughly persuading ourselves from your majesty's justice and goodness, that if we shall, at any time, be ratherwise represented, your majesty will not give credit to such information, until you have due cognition thereof: and humbly beseeching, that those who promote any disloyal principles and practices (as we disown them) maybe looked upon as none of ours, whatsoever name they may assume to themselves. May it please your most excellent majesty, graciously to accept of this our most humble address, as proceeding from the plainness and sincerity of loyal and thankful hearts, much engaged by your royal favour, to continue our fervent prayers to the King of Kings for divine illumination and conduct, with all other blessings

---

[292] Shields, p. 208.

spiritual and temporal, ever to attend your royal person and government, which is the greatest duty can be rendered to your majesty, by
Your majesty's most humble, most faithful, and most obedient subjects.
Subscribed in our names, and in the name of the rest of our brethren of our persuasion at their desire.

Which received this gracious return.

The king's letter to the Presbyterians in his ancient kingdom of Scotland.
"We love you well; and we heartily thank you for your address: we resolve to protect you in your liberty, religion, and properties all our life; and we shall lay down such methods, as shall not be in the power of any to alter hereafter. And, in the mean time, we desire you to pray for our person and government."

To which may be added that kind compliment of the Chancellor's:
"Gentlemen, my master hath commanded me to tell you, that I am to serve you in all things within the compass of my power."

Appendix 19
Act of Parliament Ratifying the Confession of Faith and Settling Presbyterian Church Government, 7 June 1690[293]

Our Sovereign Lord and Lady, the King and Queen's Majesties, and three Estates of Parliament, conceiving it to be their bound duty, after the great deliverance that God hath lately wrought for this Church and Kingdom, in the first place, to settle and secure therein the true Protestant religion, according to the truth of God's Word, as it hath of a long time been professed within this land As also the government of Christ's Church within this nation, agreeable to the Word of God, and most conducive to the advancement of true piety and godliness, and the establishing of peace and tranquility within this realm: And that, by an article of the Claim of Right; it is declared that Prelacy, and the superiority of any office in the Church above Presbyters in, and hath been, a great and unsupportable grievance and trouble to this nation, and contrary to the inclinations of the generality of the people ever since the Reformation - they having reformed from Popery by Presbyters - and therefore ought to be abolished: Likeas, by art Act Of the last Session of this Parliament Prelacy is abolished: Therefore their Majesties, with advice and consent of the said Three Estates, do hereby revive, ratifie, and perpetually confirm, all Laws, Statutes, and Acts of Parliament made against Popery and Papists, and for the maintenance and preservation of the true reformed Protestant religion, and for the true Church of Christ within this kingdom, in so far an they confirm the same, or are made in favours thereof. Likeas, they, by these presents, ratifie and establisib the Confession of Faith, now read in their presence; and voted and approved by them, as the publick and avowed Confession of this Church, containing the sum and substence of the doctrine of the Reformed Churches (which Confession of Faith is subjoined to this present Act). As also they do establish, ratifie, and confirm the Presbyterian. Church government and discipline; that is to say, the government of the Church by Kirk-Sessions, Presbyteries, Provincial

[293] Johnston, *Treasury*, pp. 152-153.

Synods, and General Assemblies, ratified and established by the 114 Act, Ja. 6. Par. 12, anno 1592, entituled, Ratification of the Liberty of the true Kirk, etc., and thereafter received by the general consent of this Nation, to be the only Government of Christ's Church within this Kingdom: reviving renewing, and confirming the foresaid Act of Parliament, in the whole heads thereof, except that part of it relating to Patronages which is hereafter to he taken into consideration: and rescinding, annulling, and making void the Acts of Parliament following, viz, Act anent Restitution of Bishops, Ja. 6, Par. 18. Cap. 2. Act Ratifying the Acts of the Assembly, 1610, Ja. 6. Par. 21. Cap. 1. Act anent the Election of Archbishops and Bishops, Ja. 6, Par 22. Cap. 1. Act entitled, Ratification of the five articles of the General Assembly at Perth, Js. 6. Par. 23. Cap. 1. Act entitled, For the Restitution and Re-establishment of the Antient Government of the Church, by Archbishops and Bishops, Cha. 2. Par. 1. Sess. 2. Act 1st. Act anent the constitution of a National Synod. Ch. 2. Par. 1, Sess. 3. Act 5. Act against such as refuse to Depone against delinquents Cha. 2, Par. 2. Sess. 2. Act 2. Act entituled, Act acknowledging. and asserting the Right of Succession to the Imperial Crown of Scotland, Ch. 2. Par. 3. Act 2. Act entituled, Act anent Religion and the Test, Ch. 2. Par. 3. Act 6, with all other Acts, Laws, Statutes, Ordinances and Proclamations, and that in so far allenarly as the said Acts and others generally and particularly above mentioned are contrary, or prejudicial to inconsistent with or derogatory from, the Protestant Religion, and Presbyterian Government now Established; and allowing and declaring that the Church Government be established in the hands of, and exercised by, these Presbyterian Ministers, who were Outed since the first of January, 1661, for non-conformity to Prelacy, or not complying with the courses of the times, anit are now restored by the late Act of Parliament, and such Ministers and Elders only as they have admitted, or received, or shall hereafter admit, or receive : And also, that all the said Presbyterian ministers have, and shall have right to the maintenance, rights, and other privilages, by law provided, to the Ministers of Christ's Church within this Kingdom, as they are, or shall be, legally admitted to particular Churches. Likeas in pursuance of the premises, their Majesties do hereby appoint the first meeting of the General Assembly of this Church, an above established, to be at Edinburgh, the third Thursday of October next to come, in this instant year, 1690. And because many conform Ministers either have deserted, or were removed from preaching in their Churches, preceding, the thirteenth day of April, 1689, and others were deprived for not giving obedience to the Act of the Estates, made the said 13 of April,1689, entituled Proclamation against the owning of the late King James, and appointing public prayer for King William and Queen Mary: Therefore their Majesties, with advice and consent foreseid, do hereby declare all the Churches, either deserted, or from which the conform Ministers were removed, or deprived, as said is, to be vacant, and that the Presbyterian Ministers exercising their ministry within any of these Paroches (or where the last incumbent in dead), by the desire or consent of the Paroch, shall continue their possession, and have right to the benefices and stipends, according to their entry in the year, 1689, and in time coming, ay and while the Church, as now Established, take further course therewith. And to the effect, the disorders that have happened in this Church may be redressed, their Majesties, with advice and consent foresaid, do hereby allow the general meeting, and representatives of the foresaid Presbyterian Ministers and Elders, in whose hands the exercise of the Church Government is established, either by themselves, or by such Ministers and Elders as shall be appointed and authorized visitors by them, according to the custom and practice of Presbyterian Government throughout the whole Kingdom, and several parts thereof, to try and purge out all insufficient, negligent, scandalous, and erroneous Ministers, by due course of ecclesiastical process and censures; and likewise for redressing all other Church disorders. And further, it is hereby provided, that whatsoever Minister, being convened before the said general meeting, and Representatives of the Presbyterian Ministers and Elders, or the visitors to be appointed by them, shall either prove contumacious in not appearing, or be found guilty, and shall be therefore censured, whether by suspension, or deposition, they shall ipso facto be suspended from, or deprived of, their stipends and benefices.

Appendix 20
The Cameronian's Dream[294]

In a dream of the night I was wafted away
To the moorlands of mist, where the martyrs lay;
Where Cameron's sword and his Bible are seen
Engraved on the stone where the heather grows green.

'Twas a dream of those ages of darkness and blood,
When the ministers' home was the mountain and wood;
When in Wellwood's dark moorlands the standard of Zion,
All bloody and torn, 'mong the heather was lying.

'Twas morning, and summer's young sun, from the east,
Lay in loving repose on the green mountain's breast;
On Wardlaw and Cairntable the clear shining dew
Glistened sheen 'mong the heath-bells and mountain flowers blue.

And far up in heaven, in the white sunny cloud,
The song of the lark was melodious and loud;
And in Glenmuir's wild solitudes, lengthened and deep,
Was the whistling of plovers, and the bleating of sheep.

And Wellwood's sweet valley breathed music and gladness;
The fresh meadow-blooms hung in beauty and redness;
Its daughters were happy to hail the returning,
And drink the delights of green July's sweet morning.

---

[294] Johnston, *Treasury*, p. 547. Called by historian R. Wodrow "The Vision: A Poem on the Slaughter of Mr Richard Cameron and Others at Airsmoss, written by an Ayrshire Shepherd Lad." It first appeared in the *Edinburgh Magazine* in 1821 when the author, James Hyslop, had charge of a school in Greenock. He was a school master on board the war ship *Tweed* and died of fever on one of the Cape Verde Islands in 1827, aged twenty-nine.

But, ah! there were hearts cherished far other feelings,
Illum'd by the light of prophetic revealings,
Who drank from this scenery of beauty but sorrow,
For they knew that their blood would bedew it to-morrow.

'Twas the few faithful ones who, with Cameron, were lying
Concealed 'mong the mist, where the heath-fowl was crying;
For the horsemen of Earlshall around them were hovering,
And their bridle-reins rang through the thin misty covering.

Tho their faces grew pale and their swords were unsheathed,
Yet the vengeance that darkened their brows was unbreathed;
With eyes raised to heaven, in meek resignation,
They sung their last song to the God of Salvation.

The hills with the deep mournful music were ringing,
The curlew and plover in concert were singing;
But the melody died 'midst derision and laughter,
As the hosts of ungodly rushed on to the slaughter.

Though in mist and in darkness and fire they were shrouded,
Yet the souls of the righteous stood calm and unclouded;
Their dark eyes flashed lightning, as, proud and unbending,
They stood like the rock which the thunder is rending.

The muskets were flashing, the blue swords were gleaming,
The helmets were cleft, and the red blood was streaming,
The heavens grew dark, and the thunder was rolling,
When in Wellwood's dark moorlands the mighty were falling.

When the righteous had fallen, and the combat had ended,
A chariot of fire through the dark cloud descended;
Its drivers were angels, on horses of whiteness,
And its burning wheels turned upon axles of brightness;

A seraph unfolded its doors bright and shining,
All dazzling like gold of the seventh refining,
And the souls that came forth out of great tribulation,
Have mounted the chariots and steeds of salvation.

On the arch of the rainbow the chariot is gliding,
Through the paths of the thunder the horsemen are riding.
Glide swiftly, bright spirits, the prize is before ye,
A crown never-fading, - a kingdom of glory!

Appendix 21
A Children's Covenant[295]

A Covenant Transaction with the Lord, by a society of Young Children, who met together in a meeting in Pentland Town, in the time of persecution, when there was no faithful minister in Scotland, anno 1683, etc that great burning and shining light, Mr. James Renwick, came an ordained minister from Holland.

This is a covenant made between the Lord and us, with our whole hearts, and to give up ourselves freely to him, without reserve, body and soul, to be his children, and him to be our God and Father; if it please the holy Lord to send the Gospel to the land again. That we stand to this covenant which we have written between the Lord and us, as we shall answer at the great day, that we shall never break this covenant, which we have made between the Lord and us. That we shall stand to this covenant which we have made; and if not, it shall be a witness against us in the great day, when we shall stand between the Lord and his holy angels. O Lord give us real grace in our hearts to mind Zion's breaches, that is in such a low case this day; and make us to mourn with her; for thou hast said, " them that mourn with her in the time of her trouble, shall rejoice when she rejoiceth ; when the Lord will come and bring back the captivity of Zion." When He shall deliver her out of her enemies' hands. When she King shall come and raise her from the dust, in spite of all her enemies that will oppose her, either devils or men. That thus they have banished her king Christ out of the land, yet He will arise and avenge his children's blood, at her enemies' hands, which cruel murderers have shed.'

Upon the back of this covenant was written as follows:-

'Them that will not stand to every article of this covenanh which we have rnade betwixt the Lord and us, that they shall not go to the kirk to hear any of these soul-murdering curates, we will neither speak nor converse with

---

[295] Hewison, *Covenanters*, Vol. 2, pp. 396-397.

them. Any that breaks this covenant they shall never come into our society. We shall declare before the Lord, that we have bound ourselves in covenant, to be covenanted to him all the days of our life, to be his children and Him our covenanted Father.

We subscribe with our hands these presents.

Beterick Uurnperston,	*Agnes Aitkin,*
Janet Brown,	*Margaret Galloway,*
Helen Moutray,	*Helen Straiton,*
Marion Swan,	*Helen Clark,*
Janet Swan,	*Margaret Brown,*
Isobel Craig,	*Janet Brown,*
Martha Logan,	*Marion M'Moren.*
Christian Laurie	

Psalm, viii. 2 "Out of the mouths of babes and sucklings hast thou ordained wisdom."

Appendix 22

A Doggerel Poem, *ca.* 1680, about the Whigs[296]

It was in Januar or December,
[Or else the end of cauld November]
When I did see the outlaw Whigs
Lye scattered up and down the riggs,
Some had hoggers, some straw boots,
Some uncovered leggs and coots,
Some had halbards, some had durks,
Some had crooked swords, like Turks;
Some had slings, some had flails,
Knit with eel and oxen tails;
Some had spears, some had pikes,
Some had spades which delvit dykes;
Some had guns with roustie ratches,
Some had peat for firie matches;
Some had bows, but wanted arrows,
Some had pistols without marrows;
Some the coulter of a plough,
Some syths had, men and horse to hough;
And some with a Lochaber axe
Resolved to give Dalziell his paiks;
Some had cross-bows, some were slingers,
Some had only knives and whingers;
But most of all, (believe who lists,)
Had nought to fight with but their fists:
They had no colours to display;

---

[296] *Records of the Kirk of Scotland*, p. 533; Hewison, *Covenanters,* Vol. 2, pp. 198-199. This quotes the first nineteen lines with an additional, second, line—'Or else the end of cauld November'—and refers to a contemporary manuscript about the time of Rullion Green, 29 November 1666. William Mackenzie cites almost these same words as "The Whigs Supplication" by Samuel Colvil, Edinburgh 1711. William Mackenzie, *The History of Galloway From the Earliest Period to the Present Time* (Kirkcudbright: John Nicholson, 1841; reprint Bowie: Heritage Books Inc., 2002), p. 164.

They wanted order and array;
Their officers and motion- teachers
Were verie few beside their preachers;
Without horse, or artilzerie pieces,
They thought to imitate the Sweeses,
When from Novarr they sallied out,
Tremoville and brave Trivulee to rout.
For martial musique everie day
They used oft to sing and pray,
Which chears them more, when danger comes,
Than others' trumpets and their drums,
With such provision as they had,
They were so stout, or else so madd,
As to petition once again;
And, if the issue proved vain,
They were with resolved, with one accord,
To fight the battells of the Lord.

Appendix 23

Psalm 23, version of 1565[297]

The Lord is onely my supporte, and
he that doeth me fede;
How can I then lack any thing
Where-of I stand in need ?

He doeth me folde in cottes most safe,
The tender grasse fast by:
And after driueth me to the streames,
Which runne most pleasantly.

And when I fele my self nere loste,
The doeth he me home take,
Conducting me in his right paths,
Euen for his owne names sake.

And thogh I were euen at deaths doe,
Yet wolde I feare none il:
For why they rodde and shepherds croke
I am conforted still.

Thou haste my table richely dekt,
In despite of my foe;
Thou haste mine head with baume refresht,
My cuppe doeth ouerfloe.
And finally while breth doeth last,
They grace shal me defende:
And in the house of God will I
My life for ever spende.

---

[297] Knox, Vol. 6, p. 335. From English Church of Geneva. *Forme of Prayers and Ministration of the Sacraments, Psalmes of David in English Meter.* Psalm XXIII. Attributed to W. Whittingham, version printed in Edinburgh, Robert Lekprevik (1564).

Appendix 24
A Chronology of the Reformation

+ indicates a battle or skirmish

1494

The Lollards of Kyle summoned to appear before King James IV and admonished.

1525

Importation of Martin Luther's works into Scotland prohibited.

1527

28 February. Partick Hamilton, martyr, burnt at the stake. Scotland almost totally Catholic, except for the Lollards in the southwest and Fife. Hamilton's *Mr. Patrick's Places* sets out his views on the errors of the Roman Church. (See Appendix 3).

1530

John Knox took Priest's Orders (renounced *ca.* 1535-1540).

1538

Scottish King James V marries Mary of Guise, a French Catholic.

1542

13 December - James V dies; the baby Mary Stuart becomes Queen of Scots when she is one week old. The Reformation takes shape with preaching by George Wishart.

1546

George Wishart is condemned and burnt at the stake 1 March 1546. *29 May* - Cardinal Beaton murdered in revenge.

1547

English victorious at Pinkie; garrisons are set up and used as rallying points for the Scottish Protestants. Knox and pupils take refuge in the

Castle of St. Andrews on April 10, but he is captured by the French and made a galley slave when the castle surrenders on July 30.

1548

10,000 French troops land in Scotland and occupy Edinburgh. Mary, Queen of Scots, engaged to French Dauphin, goes to France.

1549

February - Knox freed, appointed to Berwick. Preaches in England for seven years. Declines offer of Bishop of Rochester in 1552.

1551

Henry II of France issues Edict of Chateaubriand (forty-six articles condemning Lutherans); persecution starts and spills over to Protestantism generally. Knox appointed a chaplain to King Edward VI of England.

1553

6 July - Edward VI died; Mary Tudor becomes Queen of England. She is a fervent Catholic, persecution of Protestants begins.

1554

Regency passes to the Catholic French Queen Mother, Mary of Guise. Catholic alliance strengthened by marriage of Mary Tudor to Philip of Spain.

1555-1556

John Knox visits Scotland in September 1555 went to Geneva 5 July 1556 for his own safety (returns in 1559). Lairds of the Mearns band to maintain the preaching of the evangel.

1557

3 December - Protestant nobility draw up the First Covenant and become known as the "Lords of the Congregation."

1558

24 April - Mary, Queen of Scots, marries Francis II, King of France. *17 November* - Mary I of England dies. Elizabeth I becomes Queen of England. Knox publishes his *First Blast of the Trumpet against the Monstrous Regiment of Women.*

1559

16 January - Coronation of Elizabeth I of England. *25 January to 8 May* - English Parliament meets. The acts of Henry VIII establishing the Church of England re-enacted; episcopacy confirmed and Edward VI's version of the *Book of Common Prayer* approved for use. Papal jurisdiction in England is abolished; it is a watershed event for the Protestants in both Europe and Scotland. *2 May* - Knox returns to Edinburgh from Geneva. *10 May* - Regent Mary of Guise orders Protestant ministers to Stirling, then declares them outlaws. *31 May* - Second Covenant renounces popery and joined for mutual defence. *11 June* - Knox preaches in St. Andrews. Provost, bailies, and townspeople agree to set up a Reformed Church. *25 June* - Knox preaches against papacy in Perth; sacking of churches and monasteries begins. Regent Mary made a fire and sword response to the sacking, deploying French troops to march on Perth, burn the homes and put to the sword any rebels.[298] The Earls of Argyll and Moray join the Lords of the Congregation. *10 July* - Henry II of France dies; Francis becomes king and Mary, Queen of Scots, is also Queen of France. *1 August* - Third Covenant for mutual defence at Stirling.

1560

Alliance with the Protestant English government of Queen Elizabeth I in 1560; treaty signed February 27. English fleet blockades Leith. *27 April* - Fourth Covenant at Edinburgh (Leith) to expel the French. *10 June* - Mary of Guise dies. *6 July* - Treaty of Edinburgh establishes Scotland's Protestant independence. *August* - Knox urges Scottish Parliament to declare the Reformed Faith (Presbyterianism) the national religion. Popery is condemned. *17 August* - Confession of Faith ratified and the Presbyterian religion formally established in Scotland *20 December* - The first General Assembly met. *First Book of Discipline*, including the Confession of Faith, produced by John Knox and others. *5 December* - Francis II of France died.

1561

19 August - Mary Queen of Scots returns to Scotland at the request of the Protestant nobility; campaigns to revert Scotland to Catholicism

1562

4 September - Fifth Covenant signed by the Barons and Gentlemen of Kyle, Carrick, and Cunningham at Ayr. *28 October* - Catholic Earl of Huntly killed at + Corrichie.

1563

In the Queen's absence, her servants are interfered with while at prayer in Holyrood Chapel,. Knox convenes Church Court to try those responsible. *24 October* - Knox accused of treason for calling meeting; Privy Council clears him of the charge.

---

[298] "Made a fire and sword" meaning "to burn down homes and put to the sword, to kill, ones opponents."

1565

29 July - Mary marries her cousin Henry Stuart, Lord Darnley, in Holyrood Chapel according to Catholic rites. Lords of the Congregation rise in rebellion and are chased into England.

1566

9 March - Murder of Scottish Queen Mary's secretary, David Rizzio. Her son, Charles James Stuart, born June 19, christened with full Catholic rites at Stirling, 17 December 1566.

1567

9 February - Lord Darnley murdered. *24 April* - Bothwell carried off Queen Mary to Dunbar Castle. *15 May* - Mary marries Earl of Bothwell. *15 June* - + Carberry Hill. *24 July* - Mary forced to abdicate in favour of her infant son James VI. *29 July* - Coronation of James VI. *22 August* - Earl of Murray appointed Regent. Government by Regents until 1578. *20 December* - General Assembly determines Church independence and ratifies Confession of Faith.

1568

2 May - Queen Mary escapes from Lochleven. *13 May* - + Langside (Glasgow). Earl of Moray's army defeats the Queen's forces. *16 May* - Mary flees to England (exiled 1568-1587).

1569

23 January - Earl of Murray assassinated in Linlithgow.

1570-1573

Unrest and civil war in Scotland with plots to return Mary to the throne, and a Catholic revolution placing Mary on the throne of England conjoined with plot to assassinate Queen Elizabeth.

1571

24 August - St. Bartholomew's Day Massacre in Paris during the night, over two thousand Hugenots murdered by order of the French Court. *12 July* - Matthew, Earl of Lennox, appointed Regent; assassinated 4 September 1571. *5 September* - John, Earl of Mar elected Regent.

1572

2 July - Sixth Covenant in Leith for mutual protection and propagation of the gospel. Tulchan Bishops appointed. *29 October* - Regent, Earl of Mar dies 24 November 1572; Earl of Morton elected Regent. *24 November* - Knox dies at about 11 p.m., aged sixty-seven years. Plot of the Duke of

Norfolk to restore Mary and place on the throne of England, he is executed at Tower Hill on June 2.

1573

3 February - Articles of Pacification at Perth ends disputes between the nobles and the Catholic supporters. Mary Queen of Scots' cause is lost and Protestantism in Scotland assured.

1574

Leadership of the Kirk falls on Andrew Melville in July. He declines appointment at Court and becomes Principal at the University of Glasgow in November.

1578

4 March - James VI, age twelve, assumes government to his own hands. The Regent Morton is deprived of his post. *12 March* - James' personal rule proclaimed. *Second Book of Discipline* produced by Andrew Melville and adopted by the General Assembly.

1580

Protestant leaders pledge support for the Reformed faith and discipline in a National Covenant. Morton arrested and charged with complicity in the death of Lord Darnley.

1581

28 January - National Covenant, known as the King's Confession, signed by the King and others. Morton executed June 2. The Earl of Lennox (Esme Stewart) rewarded by Dukedom on August 8; he deals secretly with Spain and France inviting the Counter Reformation into Scotland.

1582

22 August - Ruthven Raid. James VI held virtual prisoner. His French favourite, the Duke of Lennox, forced to leave the country

1583

26 May - Duke of Lennox dies in Paris of dysentery and probably gonorrhoea. *August* - Arran returns to Court and reinstated in the Privy Council until his fall in November 1585. James VI wrote to the Guise family and accepted proposal to send troops to Scotland.

1584

February - James writes to the Pope and looks forward to "satisfying your Holiness in all other things." *11 February* - Andrew Melville called before the Secret Council and reproved for a sermon he had delivered., goes to

Berwick before he can be imprisoned in Blackness Castle. *14 May* - The exiled nobles in Berwick write to Elizabeth I explaining their position. *22 May* - Patrick Adamson, Archbishop of St. Andrews, leads the Lords of the Articles who are convened in secrecy to attend the Parliament in Edinburgh. *2 May* - Earl of Gowrie executed at 8.00 p.m. May 21. *2 November* – Proclamation: all ministers between Stirling and Berwick to compear before the Archbishop of St. Andrews in Edinburgh on November 16; called to Holyrood House and told by the King to conform or lose their stipend. Many subscribed but those who did not were deprived of benefices which were diverted to the King's use by an Order of November 23.

1585

2 January - Ecclesiastical Commissioners proclaimed to enforce the Black Acts and have ministers subscribe them. Dutch sailors discover papers on Scottish Jesuit Father Crichton disclosing papist plot involving Mary Queen of Scots and proposals to invade England. *2 November* - The exiled Lords appear before Stirling Castle and denounce Lennox, Arran, and his accomplices; James negotiates and accepts their demands. *December* - Commission of the Kirk makes representations to the Parliament at Linlithgow against the Black Acts and the annulment of the excommunication of Robert Montgomerie.

1586

Scottish Catholics continue to plot. Captain James Stewart, Earl of Arran, ordered to leave Scotland by April 6. *10 May* - General Assembly meets in Edinburgh. James again presses for bishops and his supremacy of the Kirk. Synod of Fife excommunicates Patrick Adamson; Andrew Melville warded to Angus. *5 July* - Treaty of Berwick, an offensive and defensive league between Scotland and England.

1587

8 February - Mary Queen of Scots beheaded at Fotheringay. *20 February* - General Assembly sends a Grievance about papistry to James VI. *20 June* - General Assembly at Edinburgh, Melville is Moderator. Five books of the Acts of the General Assembly returned but damaged and mutilated (apparently by Archbishop Adamson). *26 July* - Lords in Parliament pledge themselves to revenge Mary's death but nothing comes of it.

1588

6 February - General Assembly in Edinburgh urges action against papists, Jesuits. Spanish Armada defeated. Death knell of the Catholic Counter Reformation in Western Europe.

1589

January - Petition to James expressing concern at papistry rampant in Scotland. *February* - Treasonous letters found on servant Pringill, they are presented to James with a covering letter from Elizabeth I. James VI married fourteen-year-old Anne of Denmark by proxy August 28.

1590

James and his bride return May 1. Anne crowned Queen of Scotland at Holyrood, May 17. National Covenant of 1581 renewed.

1592

22 May - General Assembly establishes the Great Charter of Presbytery. Huntly, Erroll, Angus plot again with Spain; George Ker apprehended with the "Spanish Blanks."

1593

5 January - plot disclosed but the conspirators decline to compear and James VI does not pursue them. *17 November* - a Committee of Security required James to postpone the trial of the conspirators in Perth Estates propose a compromise; requires the conspirators to conform to the true religion by 1 February 1594.

1594

Catholic conspirators ignore the Estates and a subsequent order to go into ward. *3 April* - Raid at Leith. *3 October* - Argyll and clansmen defeated at Glenlivet. James advances from Dundee to Aberdeen but the Earls refuse to do battle.

1595

Huntly and Erroll abroad; Bothwell flees to the Orkneys and eventually exile, penury, and oblivion in Italy.

1596

Eight Commissioners appointed to supervise finances—termed the "Octavians;" regarded with suspicion. *21 February* - Proclamation warns of Spanish arms being sent to Scotland. *24 March* - General Assembly meets in Edinburgh. The National Covenant of 1581 is renewed. *Sep* - Estates summoned to Falkland Seton (Octavians) is moved to recall the exiled earls. Andrew Melville arrived unannounced and uninvited to vehemently oppose the proposal. *29 September* - recall of the Earls approved at Dunfermline. *October* - the power of the pulpit employed against papacy and the failure to pursue the Earls. David Black, minister of St. Andrews, preaches a sermon that condemns James VI as the "devil's bairn" and Queen Elizabeth I as an atheist. Black declines the king's authority when summoned, and is banished beyond the Tay. Edinburgh

Presbytery took up Black's cause; tumult ensued. *17 December* - the mob caused James to remove the Court and the Lords of Session to Linlithgow.

1597

1 March - General Assembly convened at Perth which is packed with northern ministers favourable to the king's proposals. *10 May* - General Assembly at Dundee approves Commissioners to advise the king, and opens the door to episcopacy. *December* - an act of the Estates approves that the king's appointees to bishop, abbot, or other prelatic dignity should be allowed to vote in Parliament.

1598

7 March - General Assembly at Dundee approves the king's appointees to have Parliamentary vote. *July* Convention at Falkland agrees the General Assembly may submit six nominees to the king, from whom he can appoint to a vacant Prelacy. James privately prints *Basilicon Doron* or *His majesties Instructions to His dearest Sonne, Henry the Prince.*

1600

Charles I born Dunfermline November 19. The Gowrie conspiracy takes place August 5. *October* - bishops, not in episcopal orders, appointed to Ross and Caithness.

1602

Robert Cecil, later Earl of Salisbury, begins correspondence with James VI in preparation for his (James's) succession to the throne of England.

1603

24 March - Queen Elizabeth I of England dies. James VI of Scotland becomes King James I of England. 3 May - James arrives for his coronation in London.

1604-1605

The Aberdeen General Assembly resists the king's attempt to break the calling of Assemblies and establish his supremacy. *20 October* - Proclamation declares James's title as King of Great Britain, which is the first use of the title, implying union of the three kingdoms.

1606

July - Parliament meeting in Perth enacted James' supremacy; restored the estates of Bishops and granted privileges to royal supporters. *10 December* Conference at Linlithgow discusses Constant Moderators; records are falsified or altered to show appointment of Bishops as Moderators in their Sees.

1607

Flight of the Earls from Ireland. Montgomery and Hamilton settlements in Co. Down and Co. Antrim; first Scottish settlers mainly from Ayrshire and the southwest. At the opening of the English Parliament James VI/I brags that he rules Scotland by a pen. Andrew Melville imprisoned in the Tower (for four years).

1610

8 June - General Assembly in Glasgow. Called the "Angelical Assembly"
21 October - The Scottish bishops desired consecrated. Court of High Commission established under the Royal Prerogative.

1610-1630

The Plantation of Ulster begins; thousands of Presbyterian Scots migrate to the Province of Ulster, followed by a gradual build up of ministers from Scotland.

1611

King James version of the Bible produced.

1612

Henry, eldest son of James VI, dies; second son Charles becomes heir.

1616

13 August - Assembly at Aberdeen. Montrose produces list of fourteen topics the King desires the Church to improve. James seeks inclusion of the Five Articles (of Perth) in the Canons.

1617

16 May - James pays his only visit to Scotland as King of Great Britain. William Laud, puts on a show of English High Church ceremony which fails to impress the Scots.

1618

25 August - The Articles of Perth try to make Scottish worship the same as in the Episcopalian Church of England. The people resent the introduction without consultation; attendance at Communions decline. James produces his *Book of Sports.*

1621

4 August - Black Saturday, Edinburgh. Parliament ratified Articles of Perth.

1623

Prince Charles goes to Spain on a secret mission to seek the hand of the Infanta. King James requires conformity to the Canons. In a letter of February 10, Archbishop Law writes that the articles for the marriage were signed, and that the Infanta and her household were to be allowed liberty of religion, and all Catholics freed from the penal laws. Prince Charles indicates his favour for Rome and James secretly avows to give Catholics toleration. Suspicion and nonconformity increase in the land.

1625 -1630

27 March - King James VI/I dies. Charles I succeeds to throne and continues the Episcopalian and Erastian policies of his father. Charles marries fifteen-year-old Catholic Henrietta Maria, daughter of Henri IV of France, by proxy 1 May 1625. Religious revivals gather strength in Ireland and Scotland.

1628

Petition of Rights (Bill of Rights) presented to Charles I by the English Parliament. Tension between Charles and the English Parliament who resent his autocratic ways and demands for money.

1629-1640

The Shotts revival on 20 June 1630 led by John under Livingston five hundred converts at the meeting. End of war with France (1629) and Spain (1630), enables King Charles I to implement his "Personal Rule."

1633

Charles visits Edinburgh June 15, with a retinue of 908 servants and 1179 horses. His coronation, a sumptuous affair tinged with popery, was clumsily organised by Laud. Over seven days the Lords of the Articles submit 168 bills; all are accepted. Charles wins vote on right to prescribe clerical dress. *6 August* - Laud made Archbishop of Canterbury. Charles reprints the *Book of Sports,* eight hundred ministers refuse to read it from the pulpit.

1634

Spottiswood made Chancellor in Scotland; bishops are appointed to the Privy Council and, in October, a Court of High Commission is set up. Episcopacy ruled. *13 May* - Charles gave orders for a Liturgy and Book of Canons to be drawn up.

1636

19 April - Prayer Book for Scotland signed by the King. *9 September* - The *Eaglewing* sets sail from Belfast Lough with 140 Presbyterian migrants on board. Book of Canons introduced.. Rutherford of Anwoth, summoned by Sydserf, Bishop of Galloway, for disregarding innovations and law of the Church, for which he was ordered transported to Aberdeen.

1637

23 July - New form of service (Laud's Liturgy) rejected. Jenny Geddes throws a stool at Dean Hannay in St. Gile's Church, Edinburgh. *November* - The Tables established. Second Reformation begins.

1638

18 February - Protestation at Stirling in response to the King's Proclamation. *22 February* - Protestation at Edinburgh. Henderson and Johnston enjoined to draft a Covenant. *28 February* - The National Covenant renewed at Greyfriars Kirk. Copies of the Covenant distributed around Scotland. *22 September* - Royal Proclamation ceding some points, but requiring subscription to the 1581 King's Confession met by a Protestation from the Church. King Charles forced to allow a General Assembly. 21 November - The Glasgow General Assembly passed seventy-two Acts; removed the bishops, Episcopacy, and autocracy; and re-asserted an independent Presbyterianism.

1639

+ Brodick, on Arran. *21 May* - Black Oath introduced in Ireland. Charles tells the shires that the Scots intended to invade England. The Covenanters issue a pamphlet February 4 rejecting the claim. *27 February* - Proclamation in England summoned northern lords and their vassals to assemble at York. *12 August* - General Assembly. Trap by King to establish principle of a "Constant Moderator" is foiled.

1639-1640

King Charles tries to seize control by force but is defeated in both of the Bishop's Wars (May-June 1639 and August-October 1640). *18 June 1639* - Treaty of Birks. *28 August 1640* - + Newburn. *30 August 1640* - + Newcastle. *26 October 1640* - Treaty of Ripon (and London). Long Parliament begins in England, royal prerogatives abolished. Montrose and other nobles sign "Cumbernauld Bond" resisting Argyll's ambitious manoeuvres.

1641

14 August - 17 November - Charles visits Scotland. Argyll made Marquis; Alexander Leslie made Earl of Leven. *22 October* - rebellion in Ireland by the native Irish; the Irish Killing Time begins and lasts well into 1642. Pym's party in English Parliament pass act depriving bishops of temporal power and their seats in the House of Lords. The Grand Remonstrance against Charles I. Twelve protesting bishops sent to the Tower by Pym.

Wars of the Three Kingdoms in which Charles uses forces from three independent countries of which he is king.

1642

Charles tries to arrest Five Members of the English Parliament (Pym, Hampden, Holles, Hazelrig and Strode), but forewarned they escape. The King retreats to Windsor and then to York. *22 August* - Civil War in England; Royal standard raised at Nottingham and war declared on Parliament. Queen goes abroad to raise help; Charles gathers money and support from Catholics. *23 April* - Charles demands surrender of Hull; Sir John Hotham denies access on orders of Parliament; Charles is effectively deposed. *23 October* - Battle of Edgehill, near Banbury, Oxfordshire,. Cromwell raises his "Ironsides." General Robert Munro goes to Ireland with 10,000 Scottish troops; skirmishes continue until 1647; civil war continues mainly in the south of Ireland, finally ended by Cromwell in 1652.

1643

1 July - Westminster Assembly of Divines meets; works until 1649. *15 September* - in Ireland, Charles negotiates a treaty ("The Cessation") that links with Catholic Federation and cedes lands to them; promises toleration. *25 September* - The Solemn League and Covenant. English Parliamentarians sign forming an alliance. Scots army supports the English Parliament.

1644

19 January - Leven and 21,000 troops cross the Tweed, marching to York and Marston Moor where Scots perform valiantly. *2 July* - + Marston Moor; King Charles I defeated and the north of England lost. *April* - in Scotland, Montrose took royalist side, occupied Dumfries; made Marquis in May. *1 September* - + Tippermuir, start of Montrose's campaign. *13 September* - sack of Aberdeen. *28 October* - + Fivy. *December 1644 - January 1645* - + Inveraray campaign. Wars of the Three Kingdoms at a peak: Scottish and Irish troops are in England; English and Scottish troops are in Ireland; and Irish troops are in Scotland.

1645

English Civil War. *2 February* - + Inverlochy. *March* - + Dundee. *9 May* - + Auldearn. *14 June* - Charles defeated at + Naseby. Papers discovered that show he was going to use foreign (Catholic) forces to save his cause. Disagreement about the treatment of the king breaks the alliance. Cromwell emerges as a leader of the Army. In Scotland, Montrose's campaign continues. *2 July* - + Alford. *15 August* - + Kilsyth. *13*

September - + Philiphaugh. Montrose defeated after a brilliant run of victories.

1646

8 January - Act of Classes, bans all Montrose followers from public office. Ten ministers in Aberdeen deposed, and many are suspended and others rebuked for co-operating with Montrose. *5 May* - King Charles surrenders to the Scots at Southwell. *June* - House of Commons establishes Presbyteryianism but subject to Parliamentary control. (Erastianism). Slow to set up "classes" (church courts); people object to discipline and excommunication. *16 July* - Montrose ordered to cease hostilities; surrenders at Rattray on July 30. *12 August* - Scots seek to get out of the alliance. *19 August* - Alexander Henderson, stalwart of the Covenants, dies in Edinburgh, aged sixty-three years.

1647

3 February - English remit £400,000 arrears of pay for the Scots army; Charles is handed over to them on at Newcastle. Massacre at + Dunaverty in May. *June* - the King is seized by Cornet Joyce at Holdenby and made the prisoner of the New Model Army who swear their own "Solemn Engagement." *November* - Charles escapes to Carisbrooke Castle on the Isle of Wight. Westminster Confession replaces Scots Confession of Faith of 1560. *26 December* - "The Engagement" between King Charles and Scottish nobles led by Duke of Hamilton.

1648

Second Civil War in England. *17 January* - Prides Purge of English "Long" Parliament, Army takes charge. *2 March* - Scots Estates support the Engagement, and Acts passed 10 June ordering all subjects to concur. *12 June* - + Mauchline Moo. *19 August* - + Preston. *September* - + Whiggamore Raid on Edinburgh - Covenanters set up the Second Reformation and a clerical government in Scotland. *29 August* - in England, ordinance appoints "triers" to validate fitness of clergy to minister. Toleration of sects incompatible with proposed uniformity.

1649

23 January - Act of Classes purges the army of malignants and Engagers. *4 January* - House of Commons convenes a High Court of Justice to try the king, issuing three resolutions: (1) the people under God are the original source of all just power, (2) the House of Commons exercise that power, and (3) the laws enacted by the Commons bind all citizens alike. *30 January* - Charles I executed. *15 February* - in Belfast, the Presbyterian ministers declare a Representation against the execution of Charles. The Duke of Hamilton executed on March 9 in London. Huntly executed in

Edinburgh, March 11. Anglo Scottish war; the Scots fight for their new King (Charles II) to regain the English throne. *5 February* - Scots resent the execution of Charles I, declaring his son the lawful heir Scottish Parliament passes Act requiring King and successors to subscribe to Covenants, and seeking uniformity of religion (Presbytery) in the three kingdoms. + Lochgoin. *15 August* - Cromwell lands at Dublin. *3 September* - + Drogheda slaughter. By end of the year, Cromwell's forces taken Youghal, Cork, Kinsale, and Bandon.

1650

February - Montrose surreptitiously appointed by the King to be Governor of Scotland. *March* - English decide to invade Scotland. Montrose defeated at + Carbisdale on April 27 and executed on May 21. *1 May* - Treaty at Breda between the Scots and Charles II. *21 June* - + Letterkenny; Coote's army destroys Catholic forces. *23 June* - Charles II lands at Speymouth. *24 June* - Cromwell appointed to command the English Parliamentary Army. *3 Sepember* - Cromwell defeats the Scots at + Dunbar. *22 October* - Western Association made their Remonstrance, Covenanting ministers walk out on November 28. Schism between the Resolutioners and the Protesters divides the Church. *1 December* - + Hamilton. Kilkenny and Clonmel taken in Ireland.

1651

1 January - Charles II crowned at Scone. *2 June* - Act of Classes 1646 repealed. General Lambert routes Scots at + Inverkeithing *July 20.* Cromwell crossed the Forth and marched on Perth notionally leaving a route into England open. *31 July* - Charles and Leslie with 20,000 men left Stirling for Carlisle. *14 August* - Monck takes Stirling and Dundee. *22 August* - Charles reaches Worcester with 16,000 followers. *27 August* - Cromwell marched cross country to Evesham. *1 September* - Major General Robert Lumsden refuses to surrender Dundee; the city is sacked and looted. *3 Sepember* - Cromwell the decisive victor at + Worcester; becomes master of the three kingdoms. *16 October* - Charles evades capture, goes to exile in France. Peaceful tolerance for all faiths allowed by Cromwell. *October* – "The Causes of the Lord's Wrath against Scotland" published. The Tender of Union made by Cromwell, an offer of integration into the Commonwealth – a republic is born.

1652

15 January - Commissioners met at Dalkeith and started work on the Tender. *4 February* - Act proclaimed abolishing the authority of Charles II. English judges appointed, Impartial justice dispensed, magistrates fair. Rebellion and civil war in Ireland finally ended.

1653

20 April - Cromwell ejects Members from House of Commons, locking the doors. The New Model Army takes power and Cromwell becomes Protector. *21 July* - General Assembly at Edinburgh instructed to dissolve and do not meet again for thirty seven years. "Engagement" in Ireland, rejecting claims of Charles Stuart and his line. *May* - proposed transportation of Ulster Presbyterians to Kilkenny and Tipperary revealed at Carrickfergus. Cromwell overrules proposal. Land confiscations and resettlements of soldiers in Ireland, 1653-1665.

1654

Resolutioners and Protesters continue bickering. New era of free trade, proportionate taxation, and prosperity welcomed by the people. *February* - Gen. Monck lays Highlands waste; by end of July rebellion at an end. *4 May* - Protectorate and Union declared in Edinburgh. *3 September* - Protectorate's first parliament met. An Ordinance for the settlement of religion in Scotland is made.

1655

The Major Generals appointed by Cromwell to supervise districts in England. The Ordinance of 1654 eventually accepted by the Resolutioners (moderate party). Protesters opposed to it.

1656

Cromwell's second and last parliament meets in September. Scotland sent all thirty members.

1658

Cromwell dies Sepember 3. His son, Richard, takes over as Protector but is not successful.

1659

General Monck marched from Scotland to take command of a quarrelling army; declares for a freely elected government and monarchy. *7 May* - Rump of the Long Parliament assembles. All legislation since 20 April 1653 regarded as invalid. Parliament dissolved Ocober 13.

1660

14 May - Restoration of Charles II; declared for the second time in Edinburgh. *26 May* - Charles arrives at Dover. Charles II rejects the former allegiance to the Presbyterians and the Covenant, assumes the role of head of the Church and reintroduces the Bishops. Oath of Supremacy introduced. "Paper of 23rd August 1660;" *6 September* - Royal Proclamation announces abolition of Presbytery, restores the bishops, forbids clerical courts, bans objectors, and orders magistrates to imprison nonconformists. Persecution of nonconformists in England begins.

1661

Over sixty Presbyterian ministers ejected from their churches in Ireland. Act Rescissory 1661. Oath of Allegiance acknowledges King as supreme in all things: civil and ecclesiastical. *11 May* - Montrose's remains and skull reburied in St. Giles by order of the King. *27 May* - Archibald Campbell, Marquis of Argyll, executed. *1 June* - Rev. James Guthrie executed. *14 November* - Sharp appointed Archbishop of St. Andrews; he is not "called" by the Church. *15 December* - Bishops called to London; consecrated.

1662

8 May - *9 September* - Second Parliament meets; enacts the restoration of Bishops to the Parliament, with the restoration of their government of the Church. The Great Charter of Presbytery 1592 annulled. "Act of Presentation and Collation" (also called the "Glasgow Act") and "Middleton's Act" sets a dead line of November 1 for compliance to episcopacy by all Scottish ministers appointed since 1649 *24 June* - Covenanting declared as treason. Glasgow Assembly of 1638 declared treasonable. Abjuration Act 1662. *24 August* - Black Bartholomew's Day, about two thousand English nonconformist ministers ejected from their churches in consequence of the Act of Uniformity (19 May 1662). About eight hundred Scottish dissidents fined. Parliament and the Lords of the Articles summon ministers to appear before them. Evictions enforced; over two hundred manses empty by the end of 1662. Charles II married Catherine de Braganza, Infanta of Portugal.

1663

King's Curates fill vacancies. Reprisals include free quartering troops on parishes; and imposition of bonds on the heritors. *22 May* - + Blood's Plot in Ireland fails. *June* - John Leslie, First Duke of Rothes, returns as Commissioner, with Lauderdale as Secretary of State, replacing Middleton. First act is to reinstate the Lords of the Articles which, with the bishops' votes, places control of legislation in the king's hands. *10 July* – "Bishops Dragnet" enacted; enforced collation of ministers. *22 July* - Archibald Johnston, Lord Warriston, executed. Sir James Turner appointed to quell the disturbances in the southwest. *13 August* - The Twenty Mile Act; restrictions on ejected ministers.

1664

January - Court of High Commission set up at Archbishop Sharp's request to enforce compliance by ministers.

1665

Sir James Turner with 140 soldiers sent to the south west to enforce collection of fines. *7 December* - Privy Council rules that attendance at conventicles is seditious. Act of Eviction forces the last of the dissenting ministers from their manses. Proclamation demands appearance of eleven leading conventicle ministers; none appear. Commission for Discipline set up, requires influential people to aid the curates in enforcing church discipline (attendance, etc.) on pain of fines and becoming outlawed. Great Plague of London - 70,000 dead.

1666

11 October - Proclamation for procuring obedience to ecclesiastical authority. The Pentland Rising by Presbyterians in Galloway and a march on Edinburgh. *26 November* - Covenant renewed at Lanark. *28 November* - Covenanters routed at + Rullion Green. First show of organised militancy by the Covenanters; excuse for greater persecution. *7 & 22 December* - twenty Covenanters executed in Edinburgh and at least another fifteen in the countryside, at Ayr and Glasgow. Great Fire of London.

1667

25 March - Proclamation non jurors, non churchgoers to surrender weapons and horses. *13 June* - Proclamation, heritors, and parishioners liable for penalties and are to pay compensation for affronts to well-effected clergy (includes curates). *15 August* - Pentland fugitives ordered to appear; none do. All condemned as traitors, forfeited, and sentenced to death in their absence.

1669

15 July - First Act of Indulgence offers some relief, but splits the Presbyterians into the "indulged" and the "not indulged" or "honest party." *16 November* - Assertory Act.

1670

28 July - Conventicles banned, fines and imprisonment on unlicensed preachers, the hearers, and the house owner in which a meeting held. Convening conventicles deemed treasonable, death penalty for unlicensed preachers. Five hundred merks reward for capture of unlicensed preachers and indemnity against killing in the course of arrest. Heavy fines for baptisms by unlicensed preachers. Absence from church punishable by fine. Neighbour required to inform on neighbour. Conventicles start to be armed.

1672

15 March - Declaration of Indulgence for all English nonconformists; sets precedent. *12 June - 11 September* - Parliament enacts more stringent legislation. *29 May* - Restoration Day, a festival day. Act against conventicle keepers, reduces to four the number of strangers who can be present at private family prayer. No outed minister can lead prayer except in a house beyond the parish to which his licence refers. *3 September* - The Second Indulgence. Privy Council appoint 120 ministers (curates) to vacancies in disaffected parts.

1674

Conventicles held by Blackadder, Welwood and Welch in Fife. Reward for Welch and Semple £400 sterling; others 1000 merks. *4 June* - Fifteen women declared seditious, for petitioning that faithful ministers be allowed to preach; some of the women thrown into prison; three banished from Edinburgh. *16 June* - Act for apprehending rebels (especially Welch, Semple, and Arnot); informants offered big rewards paid from fines on the seized conventiclers. *18 June* - Proclamation: Heritors responsible for deeds of their tenants; masters for servants; magistrates for burghs, and required to give a bond. Husbands liable for the acts of their wives (attending conventicles). *16 July* – Act: witnesses forced to give evidence on oath of conventiclers. Royal Commission appoints three special courts, mostly of nobles, to exterminate conventicles.

1675

13 July - Act establishes thirteen garrisons to deal with disorder. *6 August* - Letters of Intercommuning issued against one hundred ministers, heritors, ladies of title, and dames of influence.

1676

1 March - Proclamation against Conventicles starts renewed attacks on absentees from church. Prosecution of all Papists and schismatics who do not attend with families. Seizure of all preachers who do not attend with families. Fines on all magistrates and heritors for conventicles held on their property. Teachers and chaplains licensed. Rewards for informers; fines on magistrates who are remiss. Census on all who had taken oath of allegiance and supremacy. Special courts established to ensure laws executed in every shire. *20 July* - Committee of Public Affairs appointed; it is a Star Chamber court to engineer the persecution. *3 August* - Fifteen more ministers intercommuned. Estimate that 17,000 people subject of legal action of some kind at this time.

1677

Secret convention of Presbyterian ministers held in Edinburgh to try and resolve difference between indulged and non indulged. Renewal of requirement for land owners to give bond for their tenants' good behaviour. William of Orange marries Mary, daughter of James II. *23 August* - Sir George (Bluidy) Mackenzie appointed Lord Advocate. *11 December* - martial law declared in Scotland.

1678

3 January - royal warrant to prosecute murmurers against persons in authority. Persons aged sixteen to sixty required to have licence to leave Scotland. *February* - Highland Host in Ayrshire, Renfrewshire, and Lanarkshire. + Crookham. *26 March* - in a letter the King approves of the action taken. Welch and Blackwood held great conventicles at Meiklewood and Skeoch Hill. Another at Irongray where 14,000 people remained for three days with large numbers taking Communion. *23 September* - John Graham of Claverhouse given a commission to harrass the people.

1679

The Liturgy approved by the Privy Council for family worship. *27 February* - new sheriff deputes appointed including Claverhouse and Captain Andrew Bruce of Earlshall commissioned for Annandale, Dumfries, Kirkcudbrigh, and Wigtown. Robert Grierson of Lag was associated with them in Wigtown. In Fife and Kinross, the notorious William Carmichael of Easter Thurston was appointed. *3 May* - Archbishop Sharp murdered on Magus Moor. *4 May* - Hue and Cry declared with names of the assassins and 10,000 merks reward for their apprehension. Order to heritors and masters in Fife to assemble all inhabitants at four centres for examination; absentees reckoned to be assenters to the murder. Heritors and masters responsible for offences of the suspects not apprehended or evicted from their lands, or service. Forbidden to carry arms without a licence. *8 May* - + Fintry. *13 May* - Proclamation empowered all officers to proceed against traitors; enabled Claverhouse to begin his attack on the dissenters in the south west and feather his own nest. *29 May* - Declaration at Rutherglen. *11 June* - + Bewly. *13 June* - Declaration at Hamilton. *18 June* - Shawhead Muir meeting. "Causes of the Lord's Wrath against the Land" published. *26 June* - Proclamation against rebels, lists sixty-five people, some dead or abroad. A crime to have any dealings with them whatsoever. *29 June* - Third Indulgence. Another rising in Galloway results in minor battle on June 1 at Drumclog, with victory for the Covenanters. *22 June* - Bickering, disputes about indulgers and stubbornness by their leaders splits the forces, who lose the help of the "indulged," and are beaten at +

Bothwell Brig. *July* - Mackenzie responsible for dispossessing and seizure of the lands of thirty-five Dumfries and Galloway lairds. *1 November* - Lieut. General Thomas Dalziel of the Binns appointed Commander-in-Chief of the army and reported direct to the king. *13 November* - two proclamations; first, banned parishioners who had not taken the bond, from hearing licensed preachers; the second, offering peasantry another chance to take a bond. *18 November* - five innocent Covenanters executed at Magus Moor in retaliation for Sharp's murder. Seven district courts set up to enforce the law, lists of rebels drawn up; effigies of the five killed at Magus Moor ordered to be displayed to warn the public. *4 December* - Duke of York takes his seat in the Privy Council. Does not take the oath of allegiance and to religion; supremacy implicit in what he does despite debate raging in England about his succession as a Catholic. *10 December* - *Crown* sinks off Orkney. Of the total Covenanter prisoners on board, 211 drowned and only 49 survived; the latter were transported as slaves to the American Colonies.

1680

The Covenanters begin to believe that by breaking his oaths made at Scone in 1651, the king had forfeited all rights to civil obedience. Major change of direction led by Richard Cameron and Donald Cargill; armed resistance becomes a tactic. *4 June* - + Queensferry Paper discovered on body of Henry Hall. *22 June* - Declaration of Sanquhar by Cameron, effectively declares war on the government. *22 July* - + Airsmoss, Cameron and brother killed. *30 July* - David Hackston of Rathillet executed. *28 November* - Proclamation made to explain the need for use of force. James, Duke of York, is made the King's Commissioner in Scotland. Oppression tightens its grip.

1681

8 April - Proclamation: Heritors to provide lists of their tenants attending conventicles. *26 January* - Isobel Alison and Marion Harvey executed for their opinions. *5 May* - + Loudon Hill. Landowners required to inform about conventicles held on their land. *27 July* - Rev. Donald Cargill executed. *28 July - 17 September* - Parliament sits under James, Duke of York, and passes 193 acts. *13 August* - Act secures the Protestant religion and bans popery; second act asserts succession of the crown depends on lineage, not religion. Declared treason to assert otherwise. Act makes heritors liable for fines on conventiclers, which are doubled, and powers to evict dissenters. *31 August* - The Test Act. Parish ministers to forward to bishop signed list of persons withdrawn from worship. Bishop then signs and passes to the magistrates for prosecution. All officers and those in public trust to take an oath before 1 January 1682 or be attainted. Extended to include persons holding heritable offices of the King. *8*

October - Proclamation: Sheriffs empowered to eject any traitors from property and pursue to the death; list of rebels. Act of Succession makes it clear that the Catholic James, Duke of York, would succeed to the throne. *15 December* - society people form their Union or General Correspondence at Logan House.

1682

12 January - Declaration at Lanark. *15 March* - Priesthill meeting of the Societies. John Maitland, Duke of Lauderdale, replaced by Morton. *24 August* - Lauderdale dies in Tunbridge Wells. Project for a colony in Carolina (first mooted 1681) resurfaces. Thirty-six noblemen and gentlemen subscribe; brings them into contact with English interests including the plotters of the Rye House escapade; Baillie of Jerviswood and the two Campbells of Cessnock, charged with complicity. Use of the Porteous Rolls, the Test and the justiciary courts continued; more and more dissenters and fugitives are arrested, tried and hung in quick succession.

1683

13 April - Proclamation concluding Covenanters' "difference of religion and tenderness of conscience" was nought but a cover for disloyalty and disaffection. Laws about association with rebels to be strictly enforced, even conversing with relatives. Circuit justiciary courts at Stirling, Glasgow, Ayr, Dumfries, Jedburgh and Edinburgh to punish recusants. An indemnity to anyone taking the Test on his knees before 1 August 1683, later extended to 1 March 1684. *5 June* - Justiciary Courts begin in Stirling; prosecutors in attendance with their rolls, ledgers, and Porteous Rolls to prove charges. Wholesale taking of the Test. One Hundred eighty fail to appear and are added to the Fugitive Roll. *12 June* - Court moves to Glasgow. Some alarm expressed about Claverhouse and the Justice Clerk who are most assiduous in their prosecutions; Claverhouse a "mean informer" against his own class. *16 September* - Escape of twenty-five prisoners from the Cannongate Tolbooth, including James "Long Gun" Harkness of the Enterkin Pass rescue. September James Renwick arrived in Scotland from Holland. *October* - Edinburgh Synod, ordains ministers to stand throughout divine service; to pray for bishops and archbishops; to pray for the King as head of the Church in all causes; and orders the people to sing the doxology and stand for prayers. *3 October* - General Meeting of the Societies at Darmead, Lanarkshire. Renwick attends and presents his qualifications. Receives a call from the remnant, preaching his first sermon there on November 23. *8 November* - Duke of Hamilton prosecuted for not dispersing a conventicle at Shotts. He did not hear of the event until 14 days after it took place; he was assoilzied (acquitted). Rye House Plot, in England, attempt failed to assassinate the king and his brother.

1684

3 January - Justiciary Commission appointed with full powers to "pass sentence and see justice done accordingly, conform to law." Martial law brought to the doorstep. Attending Conventicles declared treason. Landowners in Ayr imprisoned in Tolbooth, required to take the Test and pay fines. *5 May* - Proclamation with List of Fugitives, 1956 named and enounced fugitives, including sixteen preachers and twelve women. *15 July* - Act for a Committee of Public Affairs sets up Committee to call to account magistrates for their dealings with fanatics, and to imprison or dismiss prisoners. *22 July* - Proclamation of Hue and Cry to seize followers of Cameron and Renwick. *29 July* - Enterkin Pass rescue. *1 August* - Order in Council for reports on prisoners in custody and recommendations to sentence to death immediately, with execution within six hours of sentence (three hours in Glasgow and Dumfries). Clear out of the prisons begins. *6 September* - Royal command to "extinguish disaffection." Four circuitry courts ordered; twenty-eight instructions issued. *8 November* - Renwick's "Admonitory Vindication against Intelligencers and Informers" declared. Threatens armed resistance and pursuit of their persecutors. *20 November* - soldiers Kennoway and Stewart, killed at Swynne Abbey. *25 November* - Abjuration Oath approved. Used against Renwick's followers, and others. *4 December* - Lieut. General Drummond ordered to take one thousand foot and horse, and "to take, try and kill rebels and their abettors" in the southern and western counties. *11 December* - Peter Pierson, Curate of Carsphairn murdered. *16 December* - Kirkcudbright Gaol raid, one hundred prisoners released. *18 December* - Skirmish at Auchencloy, five Covenanters killed, three taken prisoner. *30 December* - Proclamation denounced Renwick's Declaration and orders its upholders to be "executed to the death," all living south of the Tay to assemble and take the Abjuration Oath, and obtain a certificate for travellers aged over sixteen years. Inn keepers forbidden to shelter persons without certificates and empowered to examine suspicious passes. General reward of 500 merks for the discovery leading to conviction of a Society man. The Killing Time begins.

1685

9 January - Magistrates in burghs ordered to enforce the Abjuration Oath in every parish. *13 January* - Privy Council issues order about trials, especially ordering execution by drowning for women who have been active in their support of Cameron/Renwick. Commissions given for eleven Lowland counties to pursue "nonconformists in the least jot and tittle to be their prey." *6 February* - Friday, King Charles II died about noon succeeded by his Catholic brother, James. He died a Catholic. *21 April - 1 June* - Lieut. General Drummond given free rein to pursue whomsoever for any unlawful act. Regular militia and Highlanders to accompany him; any person with arms to be instantly shot. *23 April - 22 August* - Parliament called by James II amid great and vehement rhetoric against the Covenanters. A spineless Parliament submits to a despot's will. Act for confirming previous acts of Episcopalian Protestant church. Act to raise militia and to supply same. Treason to take or own the Covenants of 1638 and 1643. Husbands liable for fines of non-churchgoing wives. Death penalty and forfeiture for hearers and preachers at conventicles. Acts providing for taking of the Test, and empowering justices. Heritors obliged to keep tenants orderly. Acts for apprehending and forfeiting rebels, and resetters. Assaults on orthodox clergy punishable by death; re-establishes hierarchy in its dignities, possessions and immunities. Forfeited lands of Argyll, Baillie, Hamilton and others distributed to James' favourites. Thirty-one executions in Edinburgh and 113 executions in the countryside during the year. *17 April* - convention of exiled politicians meet in Amsterdam and support Argyll in a "Council for the Recovery of religion against the Duke of Albany and York." *11 May* - Solway Martyrs. Margaret Wilson and Margaret McLachlan executed by drowning at Wigtown. Raid at Little Blackwood, release of prisoners from the Ducat Tower. One hundred sity-seven Covenanters imprisoned in the Whigs Vault at Dunnottar Castle, for fear they might aid Argyll. *20 May* - The 9th Earl of Argyll lands at Campbelltown, Kintyre; rebellion fails and he is captured and executed June 30. *28 May 1685*. Renwick issued his Declaration at Sanquhar against the accession of the Catholic King James II. Thirteen prisoners escape from the Canongate Tolbooth. Rebellion by Duke of Monmouth in England fails; he is executed July 15. James Renwick continues holding conventicles. Prisoners, including some from Dunnottar, sent to colonies as slaves or voluntary exiles. *November* - + Midland. *7 November* - letter from King orders that the Duke of Gordon, the Earl of Seaforth, the Earl of Traquair, and twenty-three other nobles are not to be required to take the Test (because they are Catholics).

1686

7 April - General meeting of the Societies at Blackgannoch authorises Renwick, Boyd, Hill, Wilson, and Michael Shields to draft a Vindication of the Remnant; published in Holland. Two proclamations against Renwick and offers of rewards. *29 April* - Parliament sits with the Earl of Moray, a Papist, as Commissioner. Distribution of seized lands to Jacobite courtiers. Act giving Papists right to worship in private is objected to. Parliament is dissolved. *21 August* - James issues a royal fiat putting into force some easing of the Penal Statutes which authorises home worship for Catholics; assured them of protection from assailants and critics. Resistance from the prelates, although some accept it.

1687

12 February - First Indulgence of James II, mainly intended to help Catholics, sent by letter to the Scottish Council. Penal enactments against dissenters, except conventiclers, annulled. *31 March* - Second Indulgence. *5 July* - Third Indulgence freedom of worship in approved buildings. Some exiled Presbyterian ministers return. *21 July* - Request for Toleration by some ministers. (See Appendix 18.) *5 Oct* - Declaration of Toleration inflames Renwick who condemns both the giver and the takers of Toleration. Discontented churchmen now mainly the Episcopalians.

1688

Testimony against Toleration by Renwick and the Societies. *17 February* - James Renwick captured, tried, and executed in Edinburgh. *15 May* - Fourth Indulgence. *10 June* - a son, James Francis Edward, born to James II (also known as Old Pretender). *June* - George Wood, a sixteen-year-old lad from Sorn, the last Covenanter to be executed. *October* - William of Orange made a Declaration as to the reasons for his support for Protestantism and the freedom of Scotland. *24 October* - Societies meet at Wanlockhead; agree only to league themselves with unadulterated Covenanters, refusing amalgamation with the Dutch. *5 November* - William of Orange lands at Torbay with 14,000 troops; is in St. James' Palace on December 19. Curates in south west Scotland purged. Claverhouse with 6000 troops heads for London. Armies disbanded; Claverhouse now Viscount Dundee, returns north with a small troop. *2-3 December* - King James II escapes to France at second attempt (probably allowed to escape because of fear of Jacobite rising if he stayed.). Privy Council order martyrs' heads to be taken down, Papists placed in custody of the heritors; muster declared for "Protection of the Protestant Religion." *10 December* - Holyrood Palace rabbled by a mob, twelve killed.

Interregnum 11 December 1688 - 13 February 1689

1689

4 January - Declaration at the Cross of Douglas, by Societies, disassociating them from the rabbling. Meeting at Sanquhar January 23 resolves to renew the Covenants, list defections, and organise their supporters before the Estates next met. *22 January* - English convention in which House of Commons and then House of Lords resolve that James II, having violated the fundamental laws and withdrawn himself out of the kingdom, had abdicated the government, and that the throne had thereby become vacant. The two Houses offered the throne to William and Mary as joint sovereigns. Sovereignty established as result of Parliamentary vote and theory of divine right ejected. Bill of Rights in England bans Crown from suspending laws and no Catholic allowed to succeed to throne.

Glorious Revolution in England leads to Protestant William of Orange and Mary succeeding to the throne. *6 February* - William issues Proclamation for the Keeping of the Peace. Seeks tolerance of one another and not to accentuate the differences. *3 March* - Covenant renewed at Lesmahagow. *March* - + Siege of Londonderry. *29 April* - Societies General Meeting at Douglas; Cameronian Regiment formed. *14 March* - Convention of the Estates in Scotland; William Duke of Hamilton (anti-papist) took the chair; 189 members present. King William`s letter of October 1688 read, meeting convened as a free and lawful Parliament. Committee reports April 3 with proposals for settling the government; April 4 adopted, and resolution passed that James had forfeited the throne. *11 April* - William and Mary Declared in Scotland. Scottish Claim of Right presented to William and Mary May 11, and sworn to by the new sovereigns. Scotland becomes a legal, limited, monarchy. *14, 21 and 28 April* - Proclamations read, discharging obedience to James II and ordering public prayers for the new sovereigns. *30 March* - Claverhouse, now Viscount Dundee, rebels against King William. Declared a rebel by the Estates; shot dead at + Killiecrankie on July 27. His army wins the battle but the war loses momentum under new leadership. Some rabbling continues. *6 August* - Proclamation protects ejected ministers, provided for informing on disobedient clergy, and made rabbling a criminal offence. By November 182 pulpits vacant. *21 August* - Cameronian regiment earns its honours at + Dunkeld.

1690

15 April - Parliament reassembles, Melville as Commissioner. King's letter assures the Estates of his affection and care in relation to the establishment of Church Government "agreeable to the inclinations of the people." Melville instructed to adjust the religious settlement according to "that interest is strongest." *25 April* - Acts repeals Supremacy Act of 1669 and restores the ministers ejected since January 1661. Orders Episcopalian successors to vacate manses and glebes by Whitsunday. The Acts which condemned the National Covenant of 1638 and the Solemn League and Covenant of 1643 as unlawful oaths, and the Acts which declared the General Assembly of 1638 as unlawful and seditious, are left untouched to the great despair of the Covenanters. *1 May* - + Cromdale; James II military challenge in Scotland ended. *26 May* - Westminster Confession of Faith read and approved. *7 June* - Act Ratifying the Confession of Faith and Settling Presbyterian Church Government in Scotland; does not deliver all that the Covenanters had fought and died for. *1 July* - + Battle of the Boyne. James II flees to France. Protestant ascendancy established; but contentions between Episcopalians and Presbyterians continue in Ireland. *16 October* - General Assembly sits in Edinburgh with most major issues, such as the Confession, already decided by Parliament. Representations from the Societies rejected out of hand. Linning, Boyd and Shields leave the Societies without a minister until John MacMillan joins them in 1706. Presbyterianism and the Church of Scotland has its liberty and freedom restored, although not in the manner desired by the strict Cameronians or Society people who continue to go their own way until they are able to form the Reformed Presbytery on 1 August 1743 at Braehead.

1691

8 May - Sir George Mackenzie dies in London; buried in Greyfriars Kirk Yard, Edinburgh. *3 October* - Treaty of Limerick acknowledges William of Orange, King of Ireland.

1692

10 August - Declaration at Sanquhar. Societies continue independent of the Church of Scotland.

1694

Queen Mary dies.

1701

King James VII/II dies in exile.

1702

21 February - King William III died from pneumonia following a fall from his horse; Queen Anne succeeds to the throne.

1704

Test Act in Ireland forces Presbyterians out of public office.

1707

Act of Union with England. Resented by many English and Scots alike.

1708

British Parliament passes Treason Act and undermines Scottish legal independence.

1712

Toleration Act allowed episcopalian church in Scotland. Direct contravention of the Act of Union and seen as an attack on the Kirk.

Glossary

See also Part III, Topics and Events Concerning the Scottish Reformation.

Advocate - In Scotland equivalent to a barrister, takes cases in the superior courts.

Arian - A follower of Arius of Alexandria (280-366). He rejected Christ's divinity.

Arminianism - Arminus a Dutch theologian of the 16th century denied the Calvinistic doctrine of pre destination and asserted that the free will of man determined personal salvation. It emphasised the role of ceremony in the Church.

Bawbee - An old Scottish silver coin of six pence (equal to an half penny sterling).

Boll - A measure of volume, of grain especially, equal to 6 imperial bushels (or 48 gallons). Also weight of 140 lbs.

Boot - A metal case that wrapped round the leg into which wedges were driven by hammer blows, ultimately crushing the leg. Used, by law, in the presence of the Privy Council to torture many Covenanters.

Burgess - Freemen merchants and craftsmen usually belonging to a Guild. Only the burgesses had the power to vote, operate businesses, and to trade within the burghs, while only the burgesses of Royal Burghs could engage in overseas trade. Membership could be acquired through marriage.

Burgh - A town with certain privileges which are prescribed in a charter.

Burgh of Barony - A corporation of inhabitants on defined lands within a barony. Governed by an elected council or nominated by the baron of the district.

Burgh of Regality - A burgh of barony which has exclusive criminal jurisdiction within its boundaries.

Bushel - A measure of capacity, equal to four pecks or eight gallons.

Carrick - District of Ayrshire, south of the River Doon.

Cashielaws - Torture instrument; metal case fitted tightly round the leg and heated.

Chalder - A measure usually of grain, often quoted as part of a minister's stipend. It was equal to 16 bolls or 64 firlots of corn (768 gallons).

Not to be confused with a chaldron which was thirty-six bushels (288 gallons) of grain, and 25.1/2 cwts of coal.

Chapman - A travelling saleman; a pedlar.

Churchales - Festivities such as dancing, sports etc. held in churchyards – equivalent to church fetes; common in England.

Commission of the Church/Kirk - A standing Committee of the Presbyterian Church that deals with matters between General Assemblies.

Committee of Estates - Committee of the Scottish Parliament, usually 12 members from each estate and three Lords of Session. Effectively the government of Scotland.

Council of State - Committee of the English Parliament. The effective government after the English Civil War.

Compear - To make an appearance, usually in a court of law.

Court of Session - The supreme civil court in Scotland.

Depone - Scots Law, to give evidence on oath in a court of law. Also used as to depose.

Ell - A measure of length - English ell forty-five inches (1143 mm). Scots ell thirty-seven inches (939.8 mm)

Erastian - Follower of Erastus, a Swiss physician (d. 1583) who held that the church was subject to the state in matters of government and discipline.

Episcopacy - Government of the Church by Bishops.

Escheat - The reversion of rights, usually land, to the superior landlord. The land obtained by the Crown in Ulster when the Earls fled in 1607 was escheated land. This formed the basis for the Ulster Plantation and disposal of substantial plots to the Undertakers.

Evangel - Preaching the Gospel; the first four books of the New Testament—Matthew, Mark, Luke, and John.

Evangelism - The forms of Christianity which regard the atonement of Christ as the ground and central principle of the Christian faith.

Exercises—Discussion groups to discuss religion and educate lay persons.

Feu-ferme - The selling of property with hereditary rights (often church lands) with a large down payment, called the 'grassum,' and an annual 'feu duty' payable in perpetuity. The land was usually bought by nobles, lairds, rich urban dwellers and merchants creating or adding to family estates.

Fifth Monarchy Men - Flourished in 1650s among clothworkers in London and taken up by some senior officers in the Army. Believed especially Revelations and Book of Daniel prophecies that the four empires of Babylon, Persia, Greece and Rome would be followed by the Fifth Monarchy—King Jesus' reign (see Millenarian). The execution of Charles I was seen by these people as indicating the Fifth Monarchy was imminent and interim rule should be by godly men under the biblical laws of Moses (Mosaic law).

Firematches - Slow burning cord used to ignite the gunpowder in the priming pan that fired old rifles. Also used for torture by inserting between toes and fingers thereby burning the skin.

Firlot - An old Scottish dry measure of volume. Four firlots made one boll. A firlot was equivalent to 1.1/2 bushels or 12 gallons.

General Assembly - The highest church court of Presbyterianism, usually meeting annually. The Moderator, or chair, is elected at each meeting.

Glebe - Ecclesiastical lands in a parish from which the minister would derive an income, either victuals and or rents. But often in the control of the bishops; also leased or sold or gifted to nobles with consequent loss of income to the minister.

Hardheid - A coin valued at three halfpence, devalued in 1574 to one penny (Scots).

Heritor - A proprietor or landholder in a Parish.

Huguenots - The French Protestants. Given limited religious freedom by the Edict of Nantes in 1598. This was revoked by Louis XIV in 1685 and much slaughter took place. Widespread migration to Ulster, England, and the American Colonies.

Immanence - The essence of God, the Holy Spirit, indwelling in the universe. As opposed to transcendentalism, which holds that God has an existence apart from the material world.

Independent - Term for those not of the Church of England, who preferred a degree of religious toleration. Later synonomous with Congregationalism. Cromwell was an Independent.

Jouges - Metal collars on a short chain fixed to the wall of a building e.g. tollbooths, for holding prisoners.

Kyle - District of Ayrshire between the rivers Doon and the Irvine.

Ladder - Tipped off the ladder. A ladder propped on a scaffold which the prisoner climbed and sat on the top rung or a cross bar, from where the executioner "tipped him off."

Land tenure - Nobles, lairds and 'bonnet 'lairds were the only land owners who enjoyed heritable tenure and could pass on land title to others. Nobles and lairds were also called rentiers and did not actually farm the land personally. The bonnet laird was a smaller land owner who tilled the land himself and with servants. They were common in Ayrshire, Galloway and the region to the southwest of the river Clyde—the main Covenanter country.

Maiden - The guillotine of Scotland, used for executing criminals between 1564 -1710. Used to execute the Marquis of Argyll, and his son the 9th Earl. Now in the Museum of Scotland, Edinburgh.

Mercat Cross - The market or town cross, the traditional meeting place where proclamations were read by the Herald.

Merk - A small silver Scottish coin equal to thirteen shillings and four pence Scots (two thirds of a pound).

Mile - English mile 1760 yards; Scottish mile 1984 yards.

Millenarianism - The one thousand-year rule of Christ that will precede Judgment Day. Commences with the defeat of the forces of Antichrist (Armageddon). Antichrist frequently associated with Catholicism in the sixteenth and seventeenth centuries.

New English - Protestant settlers in Ulster and Munster in the sixteenth and early seventeenth centuries who dominated the Dublin administration. Reform and Laudinism struck them very hard.

Notary - A person, usually a solicitor, authorised to record statements, certify deeds, to take affidavits and statements on oath. Records, especially sasines (land transfers) used to be kept in Protocol Books until 1617 when the Register of Sasines was introduced.

Old English - Catholic descendants of English settlers in Ireland before the Reformation. Wentworth resisted their demands for relaxation of laws against Catholics (the Graces) He confiscated their lands and re-allotted to Protestants.

Papist - A supporter of the papal system; an adherent to the Pope; a Roman Catholic.

Pasquill/Pasquin - A satirical piece of writing, sometimes verse, a lampoon. Usually anonymous and posted on prominent buildings, etc.

Patrimony - Inheritance from the father. The estate and endowment of a church; thus the sources of its income, the benefices, and who receives it.

Patronage - The right to present a person to an ecclesiastical living or benefice. Advowson.

Peck - Unit of measure/volume used for grain. Equivalent of two gallons or twenty pounds of water. A peck of flour weighed fourteen pounds; a peck loaf of bread weighed seventeen pounds, six ounces.

Pilniewinks - Thumbscrews.

Plack - Coin valued at four pence, devalued in 1574 to two pence (Scots).

Plenishings - Furnishings of a house; movable goods.

Ploughgate - Land measure of 104 Scottish acres (120 acres English) For taxation valued at forty shillings hence forty-shilling land. Quarter of a ploughland was a husband-land (twenty-six acres) or ten-shilling land; and half of that an oxgang (thirteen acres) or five-shilling land.

Porteous Roll - A portable roll; record of defaulters, fugitives and fines. Used by the Justiciary Courts and by the militia to collect dues. Consolidated in the List of Fugitives of 5 May 1684 with authority to apprehend some 1956 persons unless taken a Bond or the Test by 1 August 1684.

Pound - Scottish pound worth one shilling and eight pence English (8.1/3rd pence modern currency). Twelve pounds Scots equalled one English pound sterling. The pound consisted of twenty shillings each of twelve pence, thus 240 pence equalled £1. Also a measure of weight made up of sixteen ounces.

Prelacy - The office or dignity of a bishop; government by bishops.

Prelate - Formerly an Abbott or prior. A bishop or other church dignitary of equal or higher rank, such as Archbishop.

Presbyter - A priest or elder in the early Christian Church; member of a presbytery.

Presbyterian - A person belonging to the Presbyterian Church, which is governed by ministers and elders all of equal rank.

Presbytery - A body of elders in the Christian Church; a court superior to the Kirk Session consisting of all the pastors in a district and a ruling elder from each church. In a cathedral the space between the altar and the choir; also a priest's residence.

Presbyterianism - The principles of the Presbyterian church; a system of vesting the government of a church in ministers and elders possessed of equal power.

Puritan - Members of the Church of England in the late sixteenth and early seventeenth century who sought further reformation in the church. They sought godliness and a high moral purpose in the people (Sabbatarianism and ban on churchales), and greater simplicity in the church and its practices; against the use of liturgy, ceremony, vestments, and any relics of Popery. Believed moral reformation essential to purging sins and thus necessary to achieve salvation. Very similar to Presbyterians at the time.

Sabbatarianism - Opposition to use of Sunday for relaxation or working on the Sabbath. The day to be spent solely on religious activities and exercises.

Sasines - Scottish law (transfer of heritable property) land, buildings, mineral rights, fishing rights, etc. that are geographically fixed. Not money, livestock, etc. that are moveable property. Until 1845 done by taking possession of a piece of land, such as a clod of earth. Sale of land or pledge for a loan was recorded in the Register of Sasines since 1617.

Session - A lower court of the Presbyterian Church in which the Minister and Elders confer on church business. The Session Clerk records the business. The Deacons' Court is usually considered the "lowest"court. Generally the Session is charged with the *spiritual* oversight of the local parish/church, while the Deacons' Court attends to the monetary, material, and building matters.

Simony - The offering or accepting money or other reward for nomination or appointment to an ecclesiastical office. In the sixteenth and seventeenth centuries, often associated with appointments of Bishops.

Stipend - Money paid for the services of a minister, a minister's salary. Derived from tiends, or tithes.

Synod - A convention or council. In the Presbyterian church government an assembly of ecclesiastics in a church court that is superior to Presbyteries but subordinate to the General Assembly.

Teinds - Tithes, the tenth part of income liable to assessment for paying the stipends of the ministers of the established church. The Court of Teinds is the inner House of the Court of Session responsible for dealing with teinds.

Thumbkins - A mechanical device that locks the thumbs together and prevents assault by the prisoner, also a screw device that tightens on the thumb and can crush it. Alleged to have been introduced by Bishop Paterson; also said to have been imported from Russia by Thomas Dalziel of the Binns.

Tollbooth - Originally a strong building at or near the gate into a town for collecting tolls on goods and merchandise, but also for locking up criminals pending trial by a local magistrate or transfer to a more secure prison or dungeon. Often contained Council offices and sometimes a market hall.

Transubstantiation - The belief that the Communion host, bread and wine, become the actual flesh and blood of Christ. A doctrine of the Roman Catholic Church that the "whole substance" is changed by the priest's consecration of the elements.

Unitarians - Denied the doctrine of the Trinity, thus denying the divinity of Jesus.

Wapinschaw – A review of men in a neighbourhood to ensure each individual was properly armed according to rank.

Whig - A name given the Covenanters who marched upon Edinburgh in the Whiggamore Raid, September 1648. Derived probably from the water and sour milk drink they consumed; or from the cries that drovers from the western shires used "whig, whig" meaning "get on, get on." Later used as a term of contempt in English politics.

Writer - A solicitor. A Writer to the Signet was a solicitor privileged to prepare Crown writs.

Bibliography and Sources

For those readers able to use the facilities, many of the resources are to be found in the National Archives, the Public Library and the National Library of Scotland, all in Edinburgh. The on-line catalogue of the National Library is especially helpful in identifying sources and may be accessed on the Internet at <www.nls.uk>. Major libraries are to be found in Glasgow, such as the Mitchell Library, and local libraries. Family History societies in the southwest of Scotland also hold publications of interest.

The bibliography below includes some small pamphlets as well as major scholarly works. It is in four broad categories and offered as a source of further reading. Many of the books are out of print but may be available from antiquarian booksellers and companies specialising in reprints. It is always worthwhile to enquire of your local library about a book which may be available through an inter-library loan service.

Presbyterian and Covenanter specific
Many will fall in the "difficult to obtain" category

Anderson, James. *The Ladies of the Covenant.* New York: Redfield, 1851.

Balmaghie Kirk Session. *The Kirk above Dee Water.* Balmaghie: Scotland, n.d.

Calderwood, David. *The History of the Kirk of Scotland.* (8 volumes) Ed. Thos. Thomson. Edinburgh: Wodrow Society, 1842.

Cameron, Thomas. *Peden the Prophet.* Edinburgh: Blue Banner Productions, 1998.

Campbell, Thorbjorn. *Standing Witnesses.* Edinburgh: Saltire Society, 1996.

A Cloud of Witnesses for the Royal Prerogative of Jesus Christ. Ed. John H. Thomson. Edinburgh: Hunter & Co., 1871; reprint Harrisonburg, Virginia: Sprinkle Publications, 1989.

Cook, Faith. *Samuel Rutherford and his Friends.* Edinburgh, Banner of Truth Trust, 1992.

Daviot, Gordon. *Claverhouse.* London: Collins, 1937.

Dodds, James. *The Fifty Year Struggle of the Scottish Covenanters.* London: Houlston & Sons, 1868.

General Assembly of the Church of Scotland. *A Solemn Testimony Against Toleration.* Edinburgh: A. Ker, Clerk to the General Assembly, 1649; reprint Edmonton: Still Waters Revival Books, 1996.

General Assembly of the Church of Scotland. *The Declinatour and Protestation of the some sometimes pretended Bishops.* Edinburgh: J. Bryson, 1639; reprint Edmonton: Still Waters Revival Books, 1996.

Guthrie, William. *The Christian's Great Interest.* Edinburgh: Guthrie, 1658; reprint Edinburgh: Banner of Truth Trust, 1969.

Furgol, Edward. *A Regimental History of the Covenanting Armies, 1639-1651.* Edinburgh: John Donald Publishers, Ltd., 1990.

Hetherington, W. M. *The Works of George Gillespie, The Presbyterian's Armoury.* Edinburgh: Ogle, Oliver & Boyd, 1846.

The History of Christianity. Ed. T. Dowley. Tring: Lion Publishing, Ltd., 1977.

Howie, John. *The Scots Worthies.* Revised. Ed. W. H. Carslaw. Edinburgh: Johnstone, Hunter & Co., 1870; reprint Edinburgh: Banner of Truth Trust, 1995.

Howie, John. *Biographica Scoticana.* Glasgow: John Bryce, 1781; reprint Edmonton: Still Waters Revival Books, 1996.

Johnston, John C. *Alexander Peden, The Prophet of the Covenant.* Glasgow: Johnston, 1902; reprint N. Ireland: Mourne Missionary Trust, 1988.

Johnston, John C. *Treasury of the Scottish Covenant.* Edinburgh: Andrew Elliott, 1887.

Knox, John. *The Works of John Knox.* (6 volumes) Ed. David Laing. Edinburgh: Bannantyne Club, 1846-1854; reprint Edmonton: Still Waters Revival Books, 1996.

M'Crie, Thomas. *Life of John Knox.* Edinburgh: William Blackwood & Sons, 1855; reprint Edmonton: Still Waters Revival Books, 1996.

M'Crie, Thomas. *Life of Andrew Melville.* (2 volumes) Edinburgh: William Blackwood, 1819; reprint Edmonton: Still Waters Revival Books, 1996.

M'Crie, Thomas. *The Lives of Alexander Henderson and James Guthrie.* Edinburgh: General Assembly of Scotland, 1856; reprint Edmonton: Still Waters Revival Books, 1996.

M'Crie, Thomas. *Memoirs of His Own Life and Times.* Edinburgh: Sir James Turner, 1829.

M'Crie, Thomas. *Sketches of Church History.* (2 volumes) Edinburgh: John Johnstone, 1846.

McGregor, A. A. *The Buried Barony.* London: Robert Hale, Ltd., 1949.

McWard, Robert. *A Collection of Tracts. Banders Disbanded, the poor man's Cup of Cold Water, A Testimony against the Cess, 1679.* Dalry: John Gemmill, 1805; reprint Edmonton: Still Waters Revival Books, 1996.

Moir, W. Bryce. *The Flodden Wall. The Covenanters Prison on Greyfriars Yard Edinburgh.* Edinburgh: T. & A. Constable, 1910.

Penninghame Kirk Session. *Extract from the Session Book of the Parish of Penninghame.* Dumfries: J. McDiarmid & Co., 1826; reprint Edmonton: Still Waters Revival Books, 1996.

Pollok, Robert. *Ralph Gemmell, A true story of the days of the Scottish Covenanters.* Kilmarnock: John Ritchie, n.d.

Renwick, James. *The Life and Letters of James Renwick the Last Scottish Martyr.* Ed. W. H. Carslaw. Helensburgh: Oliphant, Anderson & Ferrier, 1893.

Ritchie, George. *Stones of Destiny.* Scone: Kirk Session of Old Scone Parish Church, 1986.

Roy, David. *The Covenanters.* Airdrie, The Covenanter Theological Institute, 1997.

Rutherford, Samuel. *Lex, Rex or The Law and the Prince.* London: John Field, 1644; reprint Harrisonburg, Virginia: Sprinkle Publications, 1982.

Rutherford, Samuel. *Letters of Samuel Rutherford.* Holland: Robert McWard, 1664; reprint Edinburgh: Banner of Truth Trust, 1996.

Sawyer, Beatrice Mair. *Seven Men of the Kirk.* Edinburgh: Church of Scotland Youth Committee, 1959.

Simpson, Robert. *Traditions of the Covenanters.* Edinburgh: Gall & Inglis, 1867.

Smellie, Alexander. *Men of the Covenant.* London: A. Melrose, 1903.

Spottiswoode, John. *History of the Church of Scotland.* Edinburgh: Spottiswoode, 1655; reprint London: Mernston Scolar Press, 1972.

Stewart, J. and J. Sterling. *Napthali, or the Wrestlings of the Church of Scotland for the Kingdom of Christ.* Edinburgh: anon., 1693; reprint Edmonton: Still Waters Revival Books, 1996.

Stewartry District Council. *Covenanting Sites in the Stewartry of Kirkcudbright*. Dumfries: Stewartry Museum Service, 1995.

Testimony Bearing Exemplified, A Collection. Paisley: Neilson, 1791.

Thompson, J. H. *The Martyr Graves of Scotland.* Edinburgh: Johnstone, Hunter & Co., 1877.

Vos, Johnannes G. *The Scottish Covenanters*. Pittsburgh, Pennsylvania: Board of Education Reformed Presbyterian Church of North America, 1940; reprint Edinburgh: Blue Banner Productions, 1998.

Westminster Assembly. *The Westminster Confession of Faith*. Edinburgh: Andrew Anderson, 1679.

Wylie, James. A *Story of the Covenant.* Edinburgh: Blue Banner Productions, 1998.

Historical

Acts of Parliament, Chapter 8. Edinburgh: Estates of Parliament, 1592.

Beveridge Henry and Bonnet Jules. *Selected works of John Calvin*. [Edinburgh: ca 1850-1860]; reprint Edmonton: Still Waters Revival Books, 1996.

Calvin: Institutes of the Christian Religion. Ed. John T. McNeill. Louisville: Westminster John Knox Press, 1960.

Coward, Barry. *Stuart England, 1603-1714*. London: Longman, 1997.

Davies, Godfrey. *The Early Stuarts, 1603-1660*. Oxford: Clarendon Press, 1959.

Dick, C. H. *Highways & Byways in Galloway & Carrick*. London: MacMillan & Co., Ltd., 1927

Durisdeer, Ian. *More Stewartry Sketches. Scotland.* Castle Douglas: Glencairn Studio, n.d.

Fraser, Antonia. *King Charles II.* London: Weidenfield & Nicolson, 1979.

Fletcher, Anthony. *The Outbreak of the English Civil War.* London: Edward Arnold, 1981.

Grainger, John D. *Cromwell Against the Scots.* Midlothian: Tuckwell Press, Ltd., 1997.

Kenyon, John and Jane Ohlmeyer, ed. *The Civil Wars, A Military History of England, Scotland and Ireland, 1638-1660.* Oxford: University Press, 1998.

Lockyer, Roger. *Tudor and Stuart Britain, 1471-1714.* London: Longman, 1985.

Maclean, Colin. *Going to Church.* Edinburgh: National Museum of Scotland, 1997.

Magnusson, Magnus. *Scotland, The Story of a Nation.* London: Harper Collins, 2000.

Official Guide to the Ruthwell Cross. Edinburgh: Historical Scotland, 1998.

Oxford Book of Quotations. Ed. Angela Partington. London: Oxford University Press, 1941.

Prothero, G. W. *Select Statutes and Other Constitutional Documents of the Reign of Elizabeth I and James I.* London: Oxford University Press, 1946.

Robertson, Charles Grant. *Select Statutes, Cases, and Documents.* London: Methuen & Co., Ltd., 1904.

Shapiro, Hyman. *Scotland in the days of James VI.* London: Longman Group, Ltd., 1970.

Smout, T. C. *A History of the Scottish People 1560-1830.* London: Fontana Press, 1985.

Terry, C. Stanford. *A History of Scotland from the Roman Evacuation to the Disruption, 1843*. Cambridge: University Press, 1920.

Stroud, Angus. *Stuart England.* London: Routledge, 1999.

Wilkinson, John T. *1662 and After, Three Centuries of English Nonconformity.* London: Epworth Press, 1962.

Wilson, Derek. *The King and the Gentleman*. London: Hutchinson, 1999.

Ireland

Many churches in Ulster have produced publications about their history. A selection is included below.

Carson, John T. *Presbyterian and Proud of It.* Belfast: The Sabbath School Society for Ireland, 1948.

Cromie, Howard. *Ulster Settlers in America.* Belfast: T. H. Jordan, Ltd., 1976.

Curl, James S. *The Londonderry Plantation 1609-1914*. Chichester Phillimore & Co., Ltd., 1986.

Dickson, R. J. *Ulster Emigration to Colonial America, 1718-1775.* Belfast: Ulster Historical Foundation, 1966.

Hamilton, T. *History of the Irish Presbyterian Church*. Edinburgh: T. & T. Clark, 1887.

Hamilton, Thomas. *History of Presbyterianism in Ireland.* Belfast: Ambassador Productions, Ltd., 1992.

Herlihy, Kevin, ed. *The Religion of Irish Dissent, 1650-1800.* Dublin: Four Courts Press. (1996)

A History of Irish Catholicism. Ed. Patrick J. Corish. Dublin: Gill & MacMillan, 1971.

Houston, C. J. and W. J. Smyth. *Irish Emigration and Canadian Settlement.* Toronto: University of Toronto Press, 1991.

Latimer, W. T. A *History of the Irish Presbyterians.* Belfast: James Cleland, 1902.

Larne Kirk Session. *Historical Sketch of the First Presbyterian Congregation of Larne*. Belfast: M'Caw, Stevenson & Orr, Ltd., 1889.

Lecky, W. E. H. *A History of Ireland in the Eighteenth Century.* London: Longmans, Green & Co., 1913.

Lockington, John W. *Robert Blair of Bangor*. Belfast: Presbyterian Historical Society, 1996.

Long, S. E. *The Emergence of Presbyterianism in Post Plantation Ulster*. Belfast: Education Committee, Grand Orange Lodge of Ireland, n.d.

Loughridge, Adam. *The Covenanters in Ireland.* Belfast: Cameron Press, 1984.

Maitland, W. H. *History of Magherafelt*. Draperstown, Moyola Books, 1916, reprint 1988.

McCartney, D. J. *Nor Principalities Nor Powers, The First Presbyterian Church, Carrickfergus (1621-1991).* Belfast: McCartney, 1991.

Moore, Tom. *A History of the First Presbyterian Church, Belfast, 1644-1983.* Belfast: The Kirk Session, 1983.

Perceval-Maxwell, M. *The Scottish Migration to Ulster in the Reign of James I.* London: Routledge & Kegan Paul, 1973.

Reilly, Tom. *Oliver Cromwell, An Honourable Enemy.* Ireland: Brandon, 1999.

Robinson, Philip. *The Plantation of Ulster.* Belfast: Ulster Historical Foundation, 1984.

Stevenson, John. *Two Centuries of Life in Down 1600-1800.* Belfast: McCaw, Stevenson & Orr, Ltd., 1920.

Ulster 1641, Aspects of the Rising. Ed. Brian MacCuarta, Belfast: Queens University Institute of Irish Studies, 1993.

Wilson, William. *1623-1973, 350th Anniversary of First Bangor Presbyterian Church.* Bangor: Kirk Session, 1973.

Antiquarian sources - rare or difficult to obtain

The Acts and Monuments of John Foxe. (8 volumes) Ed. George Townsend. London: Seeley, Burnside & Seeley, 1846; reprint Edmonton: Still Waters Revival Books, 1996.

Acts of the General Assembly of the Church of Scotland, 1638-1649. Edinburgh: General Assembly of the Church Scotland, 1682; reprint Edmonton: Still Waters Revival Books, 1996.

The Booke of the Universall Kirk of Scotland. Ed. Alexander Peterkin. Edinburgh: Blackwood, 1838; reprint Edmonton: Still Waters Revival Books, 1996.

Eglesheime, George. *The Forerunner of Revenge upon the Duke of Buckinghame, for the poysoning of the Most Potent King, James, of happie memorie, King of Great Britaine, and the Lord Marqueis of Hammiltoun, and others of the Nobilitie; discovered by Mr George Eglesheme, one of King James his Physicians for his Majestie`s persoun above the space of ten yeeres.* N.p.: n.p., 1626.

The Hamilton Manuscripts. Ed. T. K. Lowry. Belfast: Archer & Sons, 1867.

Hewison, James King. *The Covenanters. A History of the Church in Scotland from the Reformation to the Revolution.* (2 volumes) Glasgow: John Smith & Son, 1908; reprint Edmonton: Still Waters Revival Books, 1996.

Hill, George. *The MacDonnells of Antrim.* Belfast: Archer & Sons, 1873.

Ireland under Elizabeth and James the First. Ed. Henry Morley. London: George Routledge & Sons, Ltd., 1890.

Mackenzie, William. *The History of Galloway from the Earliest Period to the Present Time.* Kirkcudbright: John Nicholson, 1841; reprint Bowie, Maryland: Heritage Books Inc., 2002.

Metcalfe, William M. *A History of the County of Renfrew.* Paisley: Alexander Gardner, 1905.

The Montgomery Manuscripts. Ed. George Hill. Belfast: James Cleland, 1869.

Old Belfast. Ed. R. Young. Belfast: Marcus Ward & Co., 1896.

Paterson, James. *History of the Counties of Ayr & Wigton.* (2 volumes) Edinburgh: James Stillie, 1863.

Records of the Kirk of Scotland. Ed. Alexander Peterkin. Edinburgh: John Sutherland, 1838; reprint Edmonton: Still Waters Revival Books, 1996.

Shepherd, Thomas. *Modern Athens, Edinburgh in the Eighteenth Century.* London: Jones & Co., 1829.

Shields, Alexander. *A Hind Let Loose.* Glasgow: John Kirk, 1797; reprint Edmonton: Still Waters Revival Books, 1996.

Walker, Patrick. *Six Saints of the Covenant.* Ed. Hay Fleming. London: Hodder & Stoughton, 1901.

Wodrow, Robert. *History of the Sufferings of the Church of Scotland.* (4 volumes) Glasgow: Blackie & Son, 1836.

Index

www.ingramcontent.com/pod-product-compliance
Lightning Source LLC
Chambersburg PA
CBHW060546280326
41932CB00011B/1413

* 9 7 8 0 7 8 8 4 3 1 8 8 3 *